AT WAR WITH MY
FATHER

SALLY MILNER PUBLISHING

First published in 2023 by
Sally Milner Publishing Pty Ltd
734 Woodville Rd
Binda NSW 2583 AUSTRALIA

©Lynette Ramsay Silver 2023

Design: Natalie Bowra
Editing: Kathryn Lamberton, Bridging the Gap
Printed in China

A catalogue record for this book is available from the National Library of Australia

ISBN: 9781863515016

All rights reserved. No part of this publication may be re produced, stored in a retrieval system, or transmitted in any form or by any means, electronic, mechanical, photocopying, recording or otherwise, without, prior permission of the copyright owners and publishers.

10 9 8 7 6 5 4 3 2 1

AT WAR WITH MY FATHER

Fred Howe:
Prisoner of War

By Lynette Ramsay Silver
Based on memoirs of Fred Howe and Dianne Elliott

SALLY MILNER PUBLISHING

Dedication

For Di and Fred,
and all those whose lives have been
blighted by war.

Contents

Acknowledgements vii
Prologue ix
Introduction xix

Chapter 1	The Early Years	1
Chapter 2	Prelude to War	5
Chapter 3	Following Fred's Footsteps: Singapore to Malacca	23
Chapter 4	Moving closer to War	29
Chapter 5	Into battle	45
Chapter 6	Following in Fred's Footsteps: Malacca to Mersing	61
Chapter 7	Baptism of Fire	65
Chapter 8	Cut off	81
Chapter 9	The Retreat	91
Chapter 10	The Bridge at Parit Sulong	107
Chapter 11	Every Man for Himself	119
Chapter 12	The Massacre	139
Chapter 13	Following in Fred's Footsteps: On the Road to Parit Sulong	153
Chapter 14	Back in Action	169
Chapter 15	Following in Fred's Footsteps: Singapore	197
Chapter 16	Into Captivity	211
Chapter 17	Following Fred's Footsteps: To Changi	223
Chapter 18	Into the unknown: April 1942 to December 1942	231
Chapter 19	Slaves of the Emperor: December 1942 to June 1943	259
Chapter 20	At what cost?: June 1943 to January 1944	277
Chapter 21	The Work Continues: January 1944 to August 1945	293

Chapter 22	In Fred's Footsteps: Following the railway	315
Chapter 23	Homeward Bound	333
Chapter 24	The Aftermath	345
Epilogue	Mysterious Love Affairs in the Jungle	352

Nominal Rolls — 359

    2/19 Nominal Roll: 395 killed/died while serving in Malaya and Singapore — 359

    2/19 Nominal Roll: 422 captured and killed or died while POW — 363

    2/19 Nominal Roll: 1073 survived (including those who escaped when Singapore fell) — 367

    2/19 Members of Ramsay Force who died and survived — 378

    Members of the AIF in Fred Howe's tunnel party — 379

Select Bibliography — 380

Index — 384

Acknowledgements

The author acknowledges the generous support given to this project by Paul Elliott, Dianne's husband, whose assistance in locating and retrieving material from her archives after her death was invaluable. Thank you also to Derek Lawson for providing information and statistics on the construction of the Burma-Thai Railway; to Charles Lewis, Ron Lovett and Loris Fletcher for their input into the Tavoy Melbourne Cup; and to Claire Jordan, of Poppy Research, for her additional research in the UK.

The author particularly acknowledges the outstanding contribution by Di Elliott to the nation's military history in the compilation of the first accurate nominal roll of 2/19 Battalion, from primary documents known as Routine Orders, and also researching the members of the Tunnel Party. The author also greatly appreciates the support and encouragement of Libby Renney and Ian Webster at Sally Milner Publishing and the unstinting practical and moral support of her husband, Neil Silver.

Fred in uniform

Prologue

It is June 2008, and I am on a hillside overlooking the NSW country town of Boorowa, sitting beside the graves of my parents, who lie side by side under identical slabs of rather forbidding dark grey granite. It is a long time since I felt any need to visit the cemetery, but today I have come to talk to my father.

Despite decades of weathering, the simple epitaph on his headstone, etched with the Rising Sun emblem of the Australian Army, and the words 'Lest We Forget', is still clearly legible.

Frederick Howe
A loving husband and father, departed this life 7 August 1975 aged 69 years.
Erected by his loving wife and family

The grave, a few sepia-coloured photographs, his old and yellowing dog-eared exercise book, some small keepsakes and copies of articles he wrote for a local newspaper, 60 years ago, are the only tangible reminders I have.

The photo that captivates me most is the one of him in his army uniform, taken on his arrival in Malaya in 1941, more than seven years before I was born. It was sent home to his family in the form of a postcard and became my mother's most precious possession; her only link to her husband, the father of her four surviving children and now a prisoner of the Japanese. It was a talisman almost, giving her the strength to keep going, especially through the dark and difficult years that Dad was 'missing, believed prisoner of war'. The photo must have been kept close at hand, as Mum wrote a shopping list on the back.

The image that stares back unblinkingly at me from its wooden frame is one of a man in the prime of his life – a kindly, friendly face with dancing eyes that promise more than a hint of mischief. This was my father before he went into battle. Before his life, and that of his family, changed forever.

I am visiting my parents' graves today to talk to Dad about my experiences, disappointments and frustrations during a recent two-month stay in Thailand, undertaking research on the notorious Burma–Thai railway, where he spent almost all of his time as a POW. For the past 13 years I have been attempting to follow my father's footsteps as a way of understanding him as a person and thereby, hopefully, to understand things about myself. So far it has been a long and eventful journey with many highs and a good number of lows.

As a young girl, I heard no discussion about his being in the war or any talk of the effect it had on his health. I didn't really know anything about the Japanese, so was never taught to hate them, for what I was later to learn they did to him. The only thing he ever told me was that, during the fighting, his mates either side of him were shot and killed. At the age I was then, this didn't mean much to me. I just didn't understand. I never asked any questions, so I received no answers – answers that I would come to crave.

No one talked about anything much in our house. Dad went to work and, when he came home, he went straight to the vegetable garden and worked there until 'teatime' – we didn't call it dinner in those days. Mum kept a spotless and comfortable family home; meals were always on the table at a precise time – always meat and the proverbial 'three veg', which sometimes stretched to five, depending on the garden. When Dad was called in for dinner, he would come in the back door, put his Akubra hat on the top of the dresser, wash his hands and sit.

If the resident boarder was not home for dinner, Mum knew how to get him to the tea table, quick smart. In those days the hotels had to cease trading at 6 o'clock in the evening; hence the '6 o'clock swill' when the pub patrons hurriedly gulped down their last schooners. Most households with a drinker knew that, soon after six, dinner would be served. Sometimes the pubs were a bit tardy at obeying the call of 'time, gentlemen, time', so Mum would make an anonymous call to the bar of the closest hotel and tell them that a police car was heading their way. The bar soon emptied. After dinner Dad read the newspaper, listened to the radio or, when we finally got one, watched television and went to bed.

I do not remember exactly when I discovered where Dad had been during the war, but I do know that it was many years after his death. However, it was not until 1995, the 50th anniversary of the end of WWII, that the government instituted a program called *Australia Remembers*, in which I became really interested and decided to learn all that I could about that part of his life.

As a child, I didn't know the difference between my father and anyone else's father. As far as I knew, all fathers were probably cranky old bastards. I knew that Dad had served in the war, as he marched on ANZAC Day and came home drunk afterwards. I also knew that there was a problem with the Japanese, because my mother would not allow anything marked 'Made in Japan' in the house. Perversely, Dad taught me to count to twenty in Japanese – ichi, ni, san, shi, go, roku, shichi, hachi, ku, ju, ju ichi, ju ni, ju san, ju yon, ju go, ju roku, ju nana, ju hachi, ju kyu, ni ju, but it was not until years later that I learned just what counting in that fashion meant to him. What I can't understand is why he wanted to be reminded.

My very early memories are of very loud, heated arguments between my parents that focused on Dad's drinking bouts, the primary cause of the bitter altercations. However, there were periods when he did not drink at all, and became very irate with anyone who did. This caused a great deal of friction with my brother, who was at that time a heavy drinker. Unlike Dad, he was violent, which increased my trauma. My father blamed himself for my brother's problems; because of the war, he was not there at a crucial time in his son's life. Tragically, my brother eventually committed suicide.

Dad rarely had a day off work, even when really sick, let alone took a 'sickie', but he was often ill and moody and locked himself in the bedroom. I was forbidden to go anywhere near him. We never knew from one day to the next how to approach him. What was said one day would be fine, but say it the next day and all hell would break loose. He never wanted us to have other people around the house when he was there. He wanted his home, and us, all to himself.

One visitor he certainly didn't like was Mum's elderly aunt, who lived a few blocks away. She had two Pomeranian dogs as companions and they always announced her visit by running ahead and arriving at the house before her – obviously they knew where she was heading. If Dad saw the dogs coming down the path, he shut the doors and we had to

Boorowa's ANZAC Day march.

stay as quiet as mice until we heard the front gate shut on her way out.

If anyone else called unexpectedly, Dad disappeared out the back door to either the garden or his shed, or took his fishing line and headed down the back paddock to the river. I always thought he went fishing to catch fish but I now think there was a lot more to it than that. It would have given him time to himself, time to think and maybe reflect on the things that still played heavily on his mind. Sometimes he went off for the whole weekend by himself to places like Taemas Bridge, Wee Jasper, Cavan and Childowla on the Murrumbidgee and Goodradigbee rivers.

As time passed, Dad's health deteriorated and the arguments with Mum mercifully ceased. He also stopped drinking and smoking, which was a great relief to Mum as Dad often spent most of the night puffing away, the glow of the cigarette waxing and waning in the dark. Their bedspread was fluffy pink chenille with a raised decorative pattern. Rather than use an ashtray, he simply brushed aside any ash that dropped, eventually wearing away all the pile on his side of the bed. For reasons I didn't know then, Dad obviously found it very hard to sleep.

My father also suffered from bouts of recurring malaria, which saw him confined to bed, but his health problems mostly seemed to be intestinal. He had a couple of operations, but his troubles persisted. I recall how ill he was about a year before he died and his look of embarrassment when my mother tried to care for him. He suffered from horrendous haemorrhoids, caused by the effects of severe dysentery, and the doctors didn't seem to be able to help him. Chronic diarrhoea plagued him, and on many occasions he couldn't make it out of his bed to the toilet. This was when Mum took over. I never once heard her complain. In fact, I can't recall her ever complaining, no matter what he did. I guess she understood.

This is where my pain comes in: if only I had understood. To me he was a cranky old bastard who was always sick and drank to excess. His heated arguments with Mum were accepted as a normal part of life. There was no physical violence, but the yelling and abuse was enough to scare a small girl and left an indelible mark. Our lives seemed to be disrupted so often because of him and I wondered why I had such a miserable old father.

However, he was certainly not a shirker. In recent years, the men who worked for him in civvy street told me that, on occasion, he would be so sick at work that he would have to spend some time lying down in the lunchroom. We knew nothing of this at home: Dad lived away from Boorowa for the last few years of his working life, only returning at the weekend. He wanted to retire on a higher superannuation so he and Mum could do a lot of the things they had not had the chance to do previously. Sadly, he was forced to retire early because of his ill health and his plans came to nought.

For the last three years that I lived at home I worked for our family doctor. I do not remember Dad coming to the surgery very often in those days – perhaps because he didn't want me knowing what his problems were. It is most likely that, eschewing our GP, he visited a doctor in Crookwell, almost 90 kilometres away. By necessity, the visits would have been sporadic.

Not having continuity with one medical practitioner may have had an effect on his not receiving a better pension or treatment from what was then the Repatriation Department. Suffering loss of vision, caused by vitamin A deficiency from a woefully inadequate diet as a POW, he fought for years with public servants, who declared that his eyesight must have been defective before he joined the army – despite the fact that on enlistment everyone had to undergo an eye test, and his proficiency with a rifle was legendary. His delight in finally receiving a pair of unflattering round-lensed, government-issue spectacles was pitiful.

Early in 1961, Dad was sent to Sydney for surgery on a duodenal ulcer. I had no idea that he had suffered from the same complaint in Malaya, but I do remember vividly the family being summoned to the lounge room of my Aunty Doris, a very religious lady, where we all went down on bended knees to pray for his recovery. No one had explained to me just how ill he was, so this terrified me. My mother was not there to console me as she was with Dad in Sydney. In those days, adults did not bother to explain things to children – we were to be seen and not heard, as the old saying goes. I later learned he had haemorrhaged so badly during the operation that the medical staff thought he would not pull through.

After I left Boorowa to live in Sydney in 1968, Dad's health deteriorated further. When I married two years later, Dad gave me away, although he was far from well on the day and was forced to retire from work in early 1971. It was good in a way for Mum – she was alone with only my dog for company after I left – as Dad spent the last three years of his working life at Crookwell as the Goulburn and District Line Inspector for the PMG. He would leave home early Monday morning, board in Crookwell through the week, and not arrive home until after dark on Friday.

Not long after his retirement, Dad received a telegram from Prime Minister John Gorton, informing him that '*the Queen has been pleased to bestow on you the Imperial Service Medal for long and valuable service to the Commonwealth. Warm congratulations and best wishes for your retirement.*'

Naturally we were all very proud of him and, in October that year, the whole family gathered at Government House in Sydney for his investiture by the NSW Governor, Sir Roden Cutler. When Dad moved forward to receive his medal, the first thing Sir Roden said to him was, 'You haven't paid your subs this year for your RSL membership'. Dad had paid them but had failed to put the new clip on the top of his badge.

In the later years of his life, Dad didn't go to the RSL's ANZAC Day march and service in

PROLOGUE

Fred, the father.

Boorowa, or attend the lunch. Maybe he just didn't want to think, or have anyone remind him, about that time in his life. Or maybe he was afraid he might start drinking again. He didn't. I don't know if he had sworn off it or just felt too ill to drink. He spent quite a lot of time in Boorowa Hospital and also at Young, where he was often visited by his wartime Commanding Officer and post-war friend Colonel Charles Anderson. His eyes lit up and a smile appeared on his time-worn face every time the Colonel entered his hospital room – always with some gift in hand, more often than not a bowl of fruit.

Despite not touching a drop of alcohol for years, in 1975 Dad dragged himself from his sick bed, went to the ANZAC Day march and lunch and got drunk. On his return home, he went straight to his bedroom and shut the door. We didn't see him until next morning. What was it about this particular ANZAC Day? Maybe he knew it was going to be his last time for remembrance – remembrance of his mates who died in battle and as prisoners of war. He died less than four months later, on 7 August, eight days shy of the commemorations to mark the 30th anniversary of the end of WW II. *The Boorowa News* reported:

> The funeral service was held at St John's C of E on Saturday August 9th where members RSL carried out the duties of pallbearers and formed a guard of honour outside the church, together with members of the Women's Auxiliary. At the cemetery, following the prayers led by Canon T Whiting, an RSL service was held during which Mr Ron Bryce carried out the duties of bugler. Fred's CO in the 2/19th Battalion, Lt Col Charles Anderson VC, gave the Valedictory and spoke feelingly of Fred, both as a man and a soldier.

Frustratingly, all I can remember of that day is Colonel Anderson's gentle voice; I can't recall anything he said. However, I do recall Ronnie Bryce playing the Last Post with tears running down his face.

Dear Mum, my poor dear Mum, left alone again with no-one but my dog for company, and

Di with her father on her wedding day, 1970.

he could be a cranky bugger at times too, just like Dad. She continued to honour her husband's memory and his service to the nation by never missing an ANZAC Day commemoration. As a Life Member of the Boorowa RSL Ladies' Auxiliary – usually as secretary or president – she considered it an honour and privilege to help cater for the lunch for returned servicemen and women. It was her special day of the year but, later in life, when younger members 'took over', Mum was relegated to sitting in the corner buttering the bread; something they obviously thought she was now only capable of doing. She felt very hurt, and I think it was the start of her downturn in health because after that she seemed to lose her spark. As time wore on, she developed dementia and then cancer. Just before Christmas of 1988, she died.

I put aside these thoughts and look again at the last three words on Dad's headstone – lest we forget. Lest we forget indeed. My life is now consumed with his memory and of his time away from home during the war, a period I knew very little about when he was alive. I didn't ask him, and he didn't tell me. If only I could turn back the clock.

As a child, I remember an old battered suitcase that sat on top of my parents' wardrobe. In it were a few pieces of paper, old telegrams, a couple of photos, a few badges and some coloured bits of felt that I later learnt were his army colour patches. There was also a bulging exercise book, each page filled with Dad's neat and fluent handwriting – the catalyst that sent me on my quest for knowledge of my father. When my sister took possession of the suitcase after Mum died, one of her grandchildren transcribed the contents. However, the story was hard to follow as some of the pages of the book had become detached from the spine and replaced randomly.

Another sister discovered that, from December 1948 to May 1949, the local Boorowa newspaper, in those days known as *The Burrowa News*, had published 27 weekly articles written by Dad, based on the notes in his old exercise book. At the time, the only copies were held at the State Library in Sydney but, thanks to modern digitisation, I now have a copy of the entire series and in correct chronological order. Two of the articles had been published earlier – one on 7 December 1945 and another on 18 January 1946, within months of Dad's return home and when his recollections were very fresh. Perhaps it was his way of trying to deal with what had happened to him.

However, as I had no idea of the historical context, his articles didn't really help me to comprehend in any way what it was all about, until I read my first book about the Burma–Thai railway, Hugh Clarke's *A Life For Every Sleeper*. From this book and Dad's articles I worked out that he must have been on a POW draft known as A Force. The book mentioned that a 'Tom' Morris, from Canberra, was also a member of this group. I found him listed in the telephone directory, under his real name, John Gilbert Morris, and he agreed to see me.

I arrived on Tom's doorstep with a bunch of flowers and a million questions. I was shaking so much it is a wonder the flowers had any heads left on them. Tom was very generous and actually loaned me a copy of his personal story about his time as a soldier and as a POW. He also suggested other books to read, and that was the beginning of my personal library, a library that would grow to more than 500 books about the war in the Pacific and, in particular, prisoners of war.

In the course of my search, I met dozens of former POWs, who related their experiences to me, both good and bad. Exploring the POW camp sites and walking along the trace of the railway with some of them has been a very emotional experience. I was in the company of men who were there and, as I listened to their recollections, I found myself imagining that my father was talking to me about his experiences.

These old soldiers had a quality not found in others. Having been to hell and back, they shared a special bond; a unique understanding of themselves, of life and of life's priorities. Thinking back, I realise that I should have recognised this quality in my father too, but I was too focused on his moods and illnesses. I now realise that at times there was an amazing gentleness and a far-away look in his pale blue eyes, the same look that I have seen in other ex-POWs.

How I envied those whose fathers were able to relate their experiences to family members. If only it could have been my father, telling me. I know now that I was not always the daughter he deserved. I could have been more patient with him. I could have even loved him more – if only I had understood.

Why is it that so many POW children were not told their fathers' stories? Did they want to protect us or was it their way of protecting themselves? What I also don't understand is why my brothers and sisters, all born before the war, didn't talk to me about what must have been a difficult time in their lives. I was not born until three years after Dad came home, so I was totally in the dark. Did my siblings not know much either or did they block out that part of their lives? In recent years, when I thought I had found out something about Dad and related it to my sister, I was told, 'Yes, I knew that'. Well, why didn't you tell me? The obvious answer is, I guess, I didn't ask.

My brother, who was only one year old when Dad went off to war, spoke to me of his memories when Dad returned home. Aged seven, he was terrified of this 'person' who was coming into his life, for what felt like the first time. When he saw his father alight from the train, he was most relieved to see he just looked like any other man.

However, when I talked about going to Thailand, my brother-in-law Hilton, a POW in Singapore and Japan, was most upset. In an abusive phone call, he accused me of only wanting to go to Thailand for a holiday, a holiday that would mean absolutely nothing to me. Furthermore, he ranted, I would come home in two weeks' time, forget what I had seen and not understand what it was all about anyway.

I was devastated. I seriously considered not going at all, mainly for the sake of peace in the family. Then I thought, 'No. I know why I am doing this, and he is quite wrong. Damn it, I am going even if it means he never speaks to me again'. Well, he almost didn't. The silent treatment continued until he learned that we were also going to Singapore to trace some more of the story. From that day on, every time I spoke to him, he told me more about his own wartime history, which also included stories about my father as, at times, they had been together during battle. He spoke about the effect that being a prisoner of war had on both of them. He especially felt sorry for Dad following their return to Australia. Hilton was based in Sydney where there was a facility where ex-POWs could meet and talk. Living in a small country town, Dad had no outlet like this to provide relief from his frustration and trauma and sought refuge in alcohol.

It has at times been a lonely search but, for the past ten years, I have had an ally, Lynette Silver, historian to the then 8th Australian Division Association, the division in which my father served. She had spent years researching the Malayan Campaign and the fate of thousands of prisoners of war. I first learned about her work in 1993, but it was not for another five years that we actually met, after I heard her speaking about POWs in a radio interview and gate-crashed the launch of her most recent book. Drawn together by a mutual love of wartime history, we clicked and became best friends, soul mates, as well as research colleagues. Apart from being completely in tune with my thinking and investigations, Lynette has 'sniffed the ground' with me on the battlefields of Malaya and Singapore.

Now, sitting alone by my father's grave, memories come flooding back. Some are good, others are disturbing, darker. Like many soldiers who had spent years as a prisoner of war, my father came back a totally changed man. The person with the laughing eyes, whom I never knew, was no more. In his place was a wrecked soul, prone to bouts of heavy drinking, unpredictable bursts of temper and erratic mood swings, who ran the house like an army camp. Every morsel of food on my plate had to be eaten; rules were made to be obeyed, no matter what. I lived in a state of anxiety at times, not knowing how he would behave from one day to the next. I dared not bring friends home from school for fear that he might be drunk, or in one of his moods. Preferring to spend time on his own, he was often taciturn and uncommunicative. I did not question his behaviour and thought that all fathers were like that.

In these enlightened times, I now know that he was suffering from post-traumatic stress disorder, as was almost every other ex-prisoner of war. Not being diagnosed, it went untreated, leaving sufferers and families to fend for themselves, abandoned by officials who simply advised, 'forget about the war and get on with your lives'. But how could they ever forget?

Men returning from the horrors of prisons camps were told by the medical fraternity that they might not live to a ripe old age and possibly never father children because of the years of near starvation and vitamin deficiencies. Some ex-POWs took the advice very seriously. I learnt of one man, who never married because he didn't want to leave a young wife a widow – a childless widow. He did not buy a home as he thought he would not be around to pay it off and enjoy it. Eventually he did become a homeowner, but never married. Like him, most returning POWs accepted the fact that they would probably be sterile. However, the number of babies born nine months after the prisoners returned home certainly put paid to that theory!

I was born in November 1948. By that time Dad had been home from the war for just on three years and had regained employment with the PMG Department. Prior to that he had been away from his family for five years and four months. Of the four years and eight months spent in Malaya, Singapore, Burma and Thailand, three and a half years were as a prisoner of war.

My arrival was one huge surprise to many, especially my parents. At the time Mum was 44 and Dad 42. Whilst they were not ancient, they weren't young either and had already had six children before Dad enlisted. By the time I made my appearance, the youngest child was aged 10, and the eldest 18. My grandmother told me that Mum was too embarrassed to do the shopping because she felt she was too old to be pregnant.

I don't know if her marital relations with my father ceased around the time of my birth, but I do know that, when I was about six, he made his way to my bed at night. At that time. I was suffering from the effects of rheumatic fever and was sleeping in my parents' bed. Shortly after tucking me in, he would return, and climb in beside me. The abuse never progressed beyond fondling, but he groomed me to reciprocate. It continued for many months, until I was moved into my own bed. Although at the time I was too young to realise the implications, later this nocturnal activity was something I tried to forget for decades. However, I was forced to confront my demons in the winter of 1972 when I visited a psychiatrist, after my doctor could not find any physiological reason for pains in my legs and thought it might be psychological.

It did not take long for the specialist to realise I had unresolved anger and was troubled. My trauma at having these memories resurface so vividly was not improved by the fact that my father had volunteered to drive me to my appointments. However, I didn't ever confront him. Perhaps I should have, but in those days child sexual abuse was not spoken about and, in any case, the memory of it was too painful. It is ironic that, having laid my soul bare to a complete stranger, the pain in my legs was finally diagnosed as being linked to the rheumatic fever.

Although I was never close to my father in the normal sense, we enjoyed some happy times together as a family. There was not a lot to do in Boorowa, a small farming community, but I spent carefree days playing with my cousins. The entire family also enjoyed fishing for trout in the nearby Boorowa River and sometimes we would venture further afield to the Burrinjuck Dam on the Murrumbidgee River, about 90 kilometres south of Boorowa. In those days, most families, unless very well-off, did not go on interstate or overseas holidays. Instead, we visited my eldest sister in Dubbo on the western plains and at least once a year packed up the car and drove to Tilba Tilba, a picturesque town in rich dairy country near Narooma on the NSW south coast, where my uncle had a farm. I loved it. It was always so lush and green there, unlike Boorowa, where the paddocks dried out in summer and the grass crackled under my feet.

Trips away from home were usually limited to visiting family but, on one occasion, we travelled to Bundanoon in the rugged Southern Highlands south of Sydney, where Dad showed me where he had lived for a period during his teenage years. We then ventured into the nearby national park and to Echo Point, where we let out a cooee that rattled around the sandstone gorges and returned to us, high up on the escarpment. The deep ravines, cliff faces and mountainous terrain, riddled with caves, are amazing, so it is no wonder the Aboriginal people of the Gandagara tribe called the area 'Bantanoon', now Bundanoon, meaning place of deep gullies.

As I look again at his headstone, I ask myself for the thousandth time: why did I leave it so long to learn about his time as a prisoner of war. I knew that he had been captured, but that was about it. I never asked, and he never volunteered anything. Although he was not the kind of father who invited cosy chats by the fire, I am so angry that I never raised the subject. He could have told me so much.

To date, it has taken me 13 years to reconstruct my father's life, in the hope that I might better understand his moods, his drinking binges, his unexplained flashes of temper, and his desire to spend so much time by himself. I also feel guilty that I never appreciated how tough life had been for my mother, who never complained, and just got on with it.

The abuse is something that can never be explained, as I was too young to be aware of the nuances of inter-family relationships. It is only years later, knowing of the torment my father went through, the indignities he suffered, and the physical and mental depravation he had to endure, that, like Mum, I feel that I may, in time, be able to forgive him.

I now realise why, for so much of my life, I have been at war with my father, literally and by following in his footsteps. I am also finally understanding the degree to which his experiences impacted our relationship.

Fred Howe was a prisoner of war for more than three years. I have been a virtual prisoner for sixty.

Introduction

Aungganaung, Burma
June 1943

Sergeant Fred Howe struggles to stay conscious. A hundred needles from the barbed wire securing him to the tree pierce his bony body; cigarette burns inflicted by his tormentors sting his bare skin; the hot tropical sun escalates his thirst and hunger tears at his gut. Just hours beforehand, he had sent one of the Japanese camp guards flying backwards with a well-aimed punch to the jaw. The guard, who had been amusing himself by spitting on Australian prisoners of war as their work party filed past, had pushed Fred to breaking point.

In his lucid moments, Fred ponders his decision to enlist. After all, he was 34 years of age at the time, a married man and father to four children, aged between one and eleven years, whom he dearly loved. Was it because of his sense of patriotic duty? The lure of adventure? Or was it something far more basic than that? Was it simply because, having struggled to survive the Great Depression of the 1930s, army pay was better than anything he could earn in civvie street.

As another guard walks past and stubs out his cigarette on Fred's arm, common sense tells him that, if he survives this – his first real taste of the sadistic treatment meted out to so many others – he should not test his captors again. He wonders how much longer he can last, both physically and mentally. Will the war soon be over and those who have made it thus far be on their way home, or will it drag on until not a single one of them survives?

It is 16 months since he was taken prisoner of war by the invading Japanese Army when Singapore fell and 15,000 men of the Australian 8 Division, Australian Imperial Force, were ordered to surrender. Would his rash action in thumping the guard now be the reason he might never see his wife and family again – he knows only too well that others have been executed for far less. Fred's last thought, as he slips into merciful insensibility, is that the Burmese jungle is a very long way from Boorowa.

POW Camp at Aungganaung.

CHAPTER 1
THE EARLY YEARS

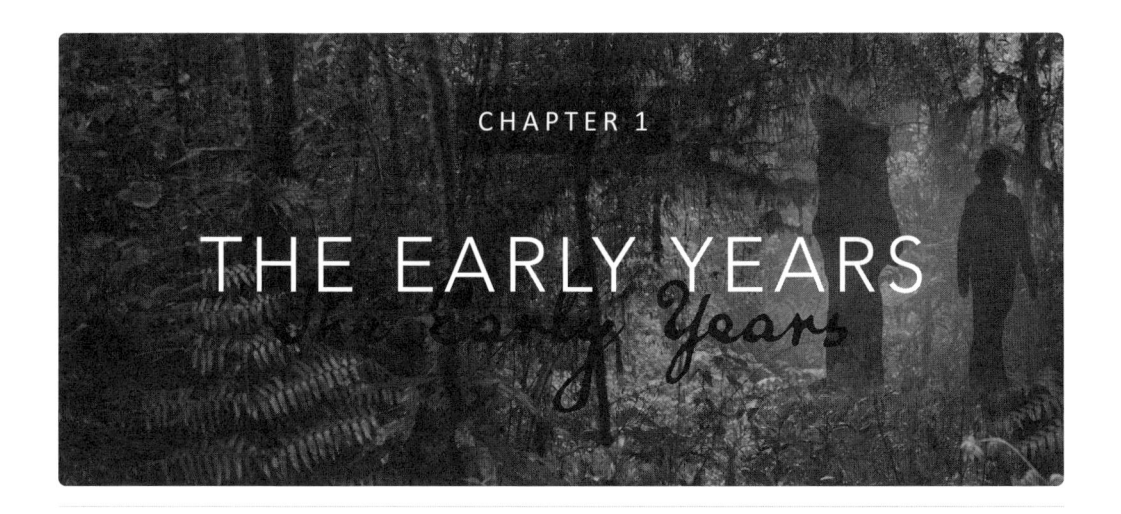

Fred's father, Frederick Washington Howe, like his father before him, Frederick Henry Howe, was a railway worker. In 1903, 12 months after transferring from Sydney to the NSW country town of Marulan, he met and married a local girl, Alice Bell. After a posting to Goulburn, where the couple's first child, Doris, was born, Frederick was transferred to Uralla, in the New England District. Here his son, the third generation to be named Frederick but always known as Fred, was born in March 1906. His marriage, however, was in trouble and ended the following year.

Alice and the two children moved back to Marulan where they lived in a quaint little cottage at the railway end of the main street. Fred and Doris attended the local public school and soon became involved in school, sport, church and community activities. Fred, who became a keen cricketer, played for Marulan Recreation Cricket Club when he was just 13 years old.

In May 1920, Doris moved to Sydney to begin teacher training at historic Hereford House in the inner suburb of Glebe. Formerly the home of prominent Sydney identity Thomas Woolley, it operated as an annexe to Sydney Teachers' College, offering a 12-month short course to students, prior to appointment to infant and primary schools.

Fred's schooling, however, was cut short when he went to work at around the age of 15 to support his mother and also to help financially with his sister's continuing education until she qualified as a teacher in 1921.

The following year, Fred and his mother moved a short distance from Marulan to the historic town of Bundanoon, where Alice helped the family finances by taking in two lady boarders. When she later took up a post as a live-in domestic at *Springfield*, one of more than sixty guesthouses in the area at the time, Fred went with her.

With the opening of the rail line from Sydney to Goulburn in the 1860s, towns like Bundanoon had sprung up on land previously devoted to farming and fruit growing. By the 1920s, Sydneysiders had discovered that Bundanoon was a great spot to spend a weekend or a holiday and flocked to the area, either by train or, for the more affluent, by motor vehicle. To accommodate the influx of visitors, boarding houses and guest houses proliferated.

The town was also a popular honeymoon destination and a summer retreat for those wanting to escape from the heat of Sydney. It certainly had a lot going for it and, in 1924, a local 'enthusiast' was inspired to extol its delights in verse, declaring that 'For happy moments morning, night and noon / There's nought surpasses glorious Bundanoon'.

While living at Bundanoon, Fred worked as a farm labourer for James Young on a nearby property. However, in 1924, at the age of just 18, he found himself in hot water, when he was charged with deliberately setting fire to the bunk of a fellow farm worker named Murphy. Fortunately, for his reputation in the small community, *The Scrutineer* and *Berrima District Press* published a report on what had actually happened.

> Frederick Howe was charged with maliciously setting fire to a hut, the property of James Wallace Young, at Bumballa, on 4th May.
>
> According to Young's evidence the defendant had been in his employ for the past ten months, which he left on 3rd May on his own account. On the following morning he and his wife inspected the hut and found there had been a fire, and that everything in the way of bedding, a spirit level, and several other articles had been burnt.

Fred admitted that:

> He lit a cigarette and got into bed. He later threw the butt of the cigarette onto Murphy's bunk and went to sleep. When he woke up sometime after, the hut was full of smoke and he was nearly suffocated. He left the hut for a while and then came back again and the blankets on the bed were burnt but the fire had gone out and he put the fire out on Murphy's bed.

Fortunately, the magistrate held that there was not sufficient evidence on the question of malice to send Fred to trial, and discharged him.

In the 1924–25 and 1925–26 cricket seasons, Fred was opening batsman for the Bundanoon side. The opening batsman for Bowral, one of the other teams in the competition, was a promising young cricketer named Donald Bradman. Fred considered that Bradman was a 'bit of a smart arse' and, despite his admiration for him as a cricketer, was not all that keen on the man himself. What he thought of Donald's war service is not known but, when his medals were on display in an exhibition at the Australian War Memorial in Canberra, Fred's family was surprised to learn that Bradman had attained the rank of lieutenant.

Bradman had joined the RAAF in June 1940 but, as the air force had too many aspiring recruits, he transferred to the AIF four months later and received a commission. In January the following year, he was called up for service and appointed to the post of physical training officer. However, despite his presumed fitness, the physical activity caused muscle problems, diagnosed by the army doctor as fibrosis. After a fortnight's sick leave, he 'ceased to be called up for service' and, on 16 April 1941, was placed on the retired list. He evidently overcame his physical ailments as, after the war was over, he was once more playing cricket for Australia.

In August 1926, at the relatively young age of 44, Fred's mother Alice died from 'dilation of the heart and endocarditis'. A short time after her death, Fred moved to Boorowa, a picturesque and historic country town on the western slopes of New South Wales, known for its fine merino sheep. Here he took up part-time employment as a telephone linesman with the Post Master General's Department, or PMG, which controlled all of Australia's communications. In 1975 the PMG was split into two to become Telecom, now known as Telstra, and Australia Post. On his transfer to Boorowa, Fred lived at the *Queen's Arms*, a boarding house in Brial Street, owned and run by Mary Weekes.

Mary's niece Elsie Clifford, aged 22, was employed in the daily running of the boarding house and it was not long before she attracted the attention of the new man in town. A

THE EARLY YEARS

Left: Fred the cricketer. Below: Fred and Elsie 1927. Below left: The family home at Boorowa

courtship ensued, and they were married in June 1928.

Fred continued to play cricket for the Boorowa Federal Cricket Team and, over a nine-year period from 1927 until 1936, regularly featured in the sporting pages of the local newspaper. He also played football and mini golf and discovered he had a talent for rifle shooting. In May 1935, during his eight-month stint with the local rifle club, the paper proudly reported that he had scored 18 consecutive bull's eyes.

He certainly did not waste any time in creating a family and, by the time he and Elsie celebrated their tenth anniversary, he had fathered six children – two girls and four boys. However, a son and a daughter died either at birth or shortly afterwards.

Life was tough during the early years of their marriage, which saw the world in the grip of the Great Depression. With money tight, and employment haphazard, the couple was very fortunate to be given a house by an aunt. During this period, Fred was able to supplement his part-time income at the PMG by trapping possums for their skins. It was a lucrative, but illegal, business and Elsie lived in fear of the 'possum inspector', who was likely to turn up in town unannounced and at any time. So fearful was she that she buried the skins in the backyard and there they stayed until the buyer's next visit.

Although possum trapping was against the law, it was also a lifesaver when the Depression started to really bite and Fred's part-time work ceased. His talent with the rifle now came in handy and a fair bit of rabbit found its way to the dining table at No 8 Court Street, Boorowa, along with honey robbed from hives in the bush.

During the Depression, an Unemployed Association, which worked in tandem with the Boorowa Shire Council, was formed, and in 1932 Fred was elected as a committee member. As those who had lost their jobs were too proud to simply sit back and wait for unemployment relief, the association obtained grants from the government to allow the unemployed to work in lieu of the dole. They busied themselves keeping the town area and parks clean, repairing footpaths, maintaining the cemetery, gathering wood for the hospital and banding together to fight bushfires.

It is not known if Fred was on relief work or if he had found a job, but in 1933 he was gainfully employed in the construction of a bridge at Coffey's Crossing on the Boorowa River, about nine kilometres north-east of the town. While he was working on the bridge, his daughter Pauline fell on the axe at the wood heap at home and cut her leg badly. She was playing merry hell and Elsie decided that the only way to calm her down was to fetch Fred. A message was sent that 'they couldn't do anything **with** her'. However, by the time it was passed from one person to another, like a game of Chinese whispers, the message had morphed into 'they couldn't do anything **for** her'. On receipt of this alarming missive, Fred set off on his bicycle, expecting to find his wife prostrate with grief. It was said that, in his efforts to reach home, he possibly broke some sort of world land speed record.

Things improved financially in early 1937 when Fred was re-employed by the PMG on a full-time basis. However, the good times did not last. In September 1939, Great Britain declared war on Germany. Prime Minister Robert Menzies solemnly announced that, as a consequence, Australia, loyal offspring of the Mother Country, was also at war.

The sounds of the broadcast had scarcely faded away when Boorowa's menfolk started enlisting – Fred Howe among them.

CHAPTER 2
PRELUDE TO WAR

By the time Fred enlisted on 1 June 1940, France had fallen, Italy had entered the war and the remnants of the British Expeditionary Force, after a disastrous campaign, had been evacuated from Dunkirk. More importantly, expansionist Japan, which had already invaded China, was increasingly perceived as a possible threat to British interests and her Dominions in the Far East.

Having earmarked all their trained troops for the war in the Middle East, Australia and New Zealand believed they were now vulnerable to attack, despite constant reassurances from British Prime Minister Winston Churchill that war with Japan was nigh on impossible. In 1939, to allay fears that the Japanese might have plans to expand even further, he reminded them that Singapore was an impregnable fortress, armed with five massive guns capable of firing at targets far out to sea, and garrisoned by almost 20,000 men. Furthermore, as the fortress could only be taken after a siege by at least 50,000 troops, he was certain that the Japanese would never embark upon 'such a mad enterprise'. In any case, should they show signs of aggression, Britain would come to the aid of her kith and kin by immediately dispatching her Far Eastern Fleet to Singapore's great naval base.

Known as the Singapore Strategy, it had been the accepted plan for years. However, as France was now out of the picture, Britain, fighting for her very existence, was faced with the task of containing both the German and Italian navies, and the much-vaunted Far Eastern Fleet was now nothing more than a pipe dream. If the Japanese were foolhardy enough to take on the might of the British Empire, a possibility still deemed to be highly unlikely, the whole of Malaya would have to be held by land and air forces. Fortress Singapore was inviolate from attack from the sea but, in order to ensure Malaya's security, more planes and troops were needed, far in excess of those already garrisoned there. But who would supply them? Although Fred didn't know it at the time, he would be one of those earmarked to shore-up Malaya. However, as that decision was still some months away, attention in Australia remained focused on the Middle East.

Processing soldiers who had volunteered to serve in the 2nd Australian Imperial Force (AIF) was a brisk business. Twenty days after enlisting at Boorowa, Private Fred Howe, now NX35481, was officially 'marched-in' at the Regional Recruitment Depot in Wagga Wagga, from where he was posted to 2/8 Battalion, 6 Australian Division, whose first contingent of troops had recently sailed for the Middle East. However, exactly five weeks later, Fred was 'marched out' to join 2/19 Battalion, in the fledgling Australian 8 Division, the nucleus of which had only been formed a fortnight earlier, in expectation that it too would be deployed in the Middle East. The following day, 29 July, having 'marched-in' to his new battalion at Wallgrove on the outskirts of western Sydney, Fred was 'taken on strength' and began training.

With the hutted accommodation occupied by Militia (Army Reserve) units undergoing a three-month training period, the newcomers were issued with tents and cooking and kitchen equipment left over from the Great War. Bedding consisted of a straw-filled palliasse, or mattress, and grey army blankets. As each new group lined up to receive its kit and equipment, the earlier arrivals bellowed their catch cry, 'You'll be sorry!'.

It was bitterly cold, being mid-winter and in an area exposed to biting westerly winds sweeping in from the nearby Blue Mountains. Early morning PT sessions were very unpopular, and it took all the persuasive powers of the non-commissioned officers (NCOs) – corporals and sergeants – along with more than a few threats, to clear the tents in time for the parade. To make matters worse, there was no hot water, and a particularly virulent virus, a mixture of influenza and laryngitis dubbed 'Wallgrove throat', spread quickly throughout the camp.

Almost every man in the 2/19th, like Fred, came from rural NSW. Born and bred in the country, with eyes puckered from years of squinting against the sun, they moved in long loping strides. Many were excellent bushmen and handled a rifle with ease. Apart from 16 recruits from New Guinea and 42 from the Sydney area, the entire battalion was drawn from volunteers from the Monaro and Riverina areas of the state, giving rise to the name The Riverina Regiment.

Pledged to uphold the traditions of their forebears, the 'Fighting Nineteenth' of the 1st AIF, 2/19 Battalion's colour patch reflected its antecedents, a brown over green diamond shape, set onto a grey oval signifying 8 Division. The Commanding Officer was Lieutenant Colonel Duncan Struan Maxwell, a medical practitioner from Cootamundra, a pretty

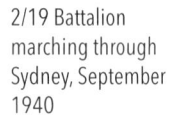

2/19 Battalion marching through Sydney, September 1940

country town not far from Boorowa. A distinguished veteran of the war of 1914–18, Maxwell had been awarded a Military Cross for his brave actions and direction of his troops at Mouquet Farm on the Western Front. The battalion's second-in-command, or 2IC, was Major Charles Groves Wright Anderson, a 44-year-old grazier from Crowther, near Young. Bespectacled, and with a quiet, unassuming manner, Anderson was born in Cape Town, South Africa, and had served with the South African Rifles in East Africa during the Great War.

Fred was only three weeks into his training when the battalion moved camp to Ingleburn, south-west of Sydney. Situated on a hillside dotted with eucalypts, this camp was hutted, and promised a higher degree of comfort than Wallgrove. Training was stepped up to include two days on assault boats; two nights in field training; four days' rifle range practice; the stripping and reassembly of rifles and Lewis machine-guns; squad drills, digging drills and bayonet drills; PT; assault courses and grenade courses; field craft and lectures in discipline and military law. Specialists like Fred who, with his PMG experience, had been posted to Headquarters Company as a signaller, spent time practising their respective skills which, in Fred's case, involved communicating via telephone, wireless and motor bike. There were also platoon, company and battalion route marches, with 'Piccolo Pete' out the front setting the pace on his penny whistle, the distance gradually increasing in length up to 20 miles (32 kilometres) a day. It was a gruelling program. The men were in the field four nights a week and there was no weekend leave.

In mid-September the troops' marching skills were deemed to be of a sufficiently high standard to allow them to parade through the streets of Sydney, led by the battalion's pipe band. In order to ensure they could stand up to the rigours of the march, on leaving the train at Central Railway Station each man was issued with an instant energy boost in the form of two lumps of sugar. Everyone loves a parade and, although the bulk of the men came from country areas, the streets were nevertheless lined with excited cheering crowds.

Two months later, in November, the battalion was transferred to a new training camp, recently vacated by 7 Division and situated outside Bathurst, on the western flanks of the Blue Mountains. When the battalion was joined by other troops from 22 Brigade, training increased considerably, with mock battles on the sun-scorched hills and the digging of an entire trench system, in anticipation of desert warfare.

In late December, scarcely six months since his enlistment, Fred was deemed to be ready for war and granted ten days' embarkation leave, allowing him to return to Boorowa to farewell the family before he left for 'somewhere overseas'. Little did any of them know what lay ahead or how long they would be separated, let alone Fred's destination.

With his leave over, it was back to Bathurst for Fred in the short term and the beginning

The camp at Bathurst

of a great and lonely struggle for Elsie. For her husband, however, it was quite the opposite. After a life spent in a quiet country town with just his family, he now had the company of hundreds of men who would, in time, come to rely upon each other for their very survival.

In mid-January 1941, Fred was appointed Acting Corporal. It had been an action-packed six months. Since his enlistment he had undergone rigorous basic and specialist training and moved camps three times, nearly freezing to death at Wallgrove – now, fortunately, a distant memory. He had also been inoculated against various diseases, receiving vaccines to which, under normal circumstances, he would never have been subjected and which could result in the most unpleasant reactions, or even death.

With training complete, on 2 February the battalion left Bathurst for Sydney by train, bedecked with signs that read 'Berlin or Bust' and 'Look out Adolf – here we come'. After detraining at Darling Harbour, the men boarded the ferry *Kulgoa* for transfer to their troopship, the 81,000-ton ocean liner *Queen Mary*, pride of Cunard Line. Now known simply as HT QX, the ship's distinctive livery had been completely obliterated by a coat of camouflaging grey paint. Although stripped of much of its peacetime grandeur to accommodate the large number now on board, there was no disguising the opulent interior decoration. As the vessel was moored in Sydney Harbour, just off Bradley's Head, the new arrivals amused themselves by looking through binoculars at the animals at nearby Taronga Zoo, the first time that most of them had ever seen exotic species.

Also on board, in a crate supposedly containing medical supplies and marked with a large red cross, was the 2/19th's mascot, a baby kangaroo called Joey. Brought in from Menindee, in the far west of the state, Joey had been smuggled aboard with the connivance of the battalion's medical officer, Captain Lloyd Cahill.

Right: 2/19th's CO, Lieutenant Colonel Duncan Maxwell and Major Charles Cousens

Below: Joey, the battalion's mascot

Opposite top: The battalion arrives at Darling Harbour

Opposite bottom: 2/19th troops on ferry *Kulgoa*

PRELUDE TO WAR

Queen Mary, before the war

The troops' destination was supposed to be a secret, but it was taken for granted that 22 Brigade was headed for the Middle East. However, when Fred saw cargo waiting to be loaded on the ship, clearly marked 'Elbow Force, Singapore', he realised the fallacy of that assumption. The departure was also supposed to be a low-key affair but, with *Mary*, as well as two other troop ships, about to depart for overseas duty and escorted by the Royal Australian Navy's light cruiser, HMAS *Hobart*, word soon circulated that this was an occasion not to be missed.

Also in the fleet were the 45,000-ton *Aquitania*, a former World War 1 troopship, and the much smaller *Nieuw Amsterdam*, a slightly smaller Dutch liner, carrying another 6000 troops. With 12,000 men leaving their homeland to go to war, thousands of sightseers lined every vantage point around the harbour foreshore, while, on the water, ferries and hundreds of small craft jostled for position, with well-wishers holding up placards in an effort to send one final 'hooroo'. Some troops tried to return greetings by tossing overboard bottles with messages inside, but circling patrol boats thwarted their efforts. On board a nearby vessel were the Governor General, Lord Gowrie, the nation's longest serving head of state, and the hugely popular Australian singer Gladys Moncrieff, fondly known as Our Glad, who serenaded the troops with *Harbour Lights* and the haunting *Maori Farewell*.

After a few last-minute adjustments to the battalion numbers, when newcomers arrived to replace those suffering from various ailments, ranging from tonsillitis to venereal disease, it was finally time to depart. With a blast from her huge bass foghorn, *Queen Mary* slipped her moorings and sailed out of Sydney Harbour on 4 February, a bright sunny Tuesday. According to Roly Dean, Fred's signaller mate, the last sound they heard was Our Glad's voice gradually fading in the distance.

After passing through the harbour entrance, flanked by the majestic sandstone cliffs of the North and South Heads, the great ship continued in an easterly direction before turning south. Fred's future son-in-law, Hilton Morgan, known to his army mates as 'Tod', after a famous American boxer who shared the same surname, was also on board. He recalled that 'after leaving Sydney I went below deck to sleep. When I woke up and went back on deck next morning I couldn't see land and I didn't like the idea very much.'

He and Fred had plenty of company though. Crammed onto the ship were almost 6000 troops: the 2/19th; two more infantry battalions, the 2/18th and 2/20th; engineers; mechanics; anti-tank gunners and artillerymen; medical personnel; signallers; transport drivers and other support troops, as well as administrative staff.

The Australian 8 Division, comprised of three brigades and nine battalions, had far more troops than the 6000 on board *Mary*. The division's original three brigades were 22, 23 and 24. However, 24 Brigade had been sent to Egypt in December 1940 to shore up the depleted troops in 9 Division. The 27th, which replaced it, and the 23rd were to follow the 22nd to Malaya but, although the 27th would be dispatched in July that year, the 23rd's three battalions were split. Designated as Lark, Sparrow and Gull Forces, they would be sent to the islands of Rabaul, Timor and Ambon, to Australia's north, in a futile effort to repel the Japanese.

Another ship, *Mauretania*, joined the convoy a few days later in Bass Strait. The small flotilla reached Fremantle on 10 February and set sail again two days later, with the cruiser HMAS *Canberra* replacing *Hobart* as escort. The following day, the troops on *Queen Mary* were officially informed they were going to Malaya – something that Fred and anyone else who had seen the Elbow Force crates and had attended lectures on malaria and tropical hygiene had already deduced, but fervently hoped was not true. Those who had clung to the belief that they were bound for the Middle East were bitterly disappointed. They had volunteered to fight for the Empire, not spend their days on garrison duty in an Asian backwater, where they expected to see no action. However, many were buoyed by the fact that, in due course, they would be relieved by Indian troops, allowing them to join their comrades in the Middle East.

With the destination no longer secret, lectures on life in Malaya began in earnest – conditions, climate, medical facilities, recreation, ethnic communities, currency and history. Other topics on the agenda included exotic flora and fauna, with emphasis on tigers, poisonous snakes, scorpions and killer wasps. However, while these creatures were best avoided, their potential to do harm faded into obscurity when compared with the greatest killer of all, the Anopheles mosquito, responsible for transmitting malaria. Another mosquito spread dengue fever, which caused high fever and intense pain in the joints, giving rise to the name 'broken bone' disease. The prospect of succumbing to either of these diseases was alarming enough, but there were plenty of other nasty complaints, including enteritis, yellow fever, cholera, dysentery, sandfly fever and hookworms. To prevent infestation by the latter, troops were advised not to go bare footed and, if they had to sit on the ground, to place a tin helmet between the earth and their nether regions.

Among lesser, but nevertheless worrying conditions, were numerous skin disorders, about which little was known, and common fungal infections, such as ringworm, tinea, Singapore ear and dhobi's itch, which affected the scrotal sac and was supposedly caused by the dhobi (laundry) boys not rinsing clothes sufficiently well. Although all were bothersome, and some life-threatening, the most common and debilitating illnesses were venereal disease and malaria, giving rise to an order to avoid contact with women and mosquitoes.

As the ship made its way further north, the conditions for Fred and the other ranks quartered below deck became almost unbearable. *Mary* had been built for the North Atlantic run and was not air-conditioned. The quality of the accommodation ranged from First Class cabins (officers only) to steerage, with an empty swimming pool lined with double-decker bunks also pressed into service. In the roomier cabins and suites, extra bunks had also been added. With such a diversity of sleeping accommodation, its allocation had been democratically decided by ballot, with those on an upper deck drawing the longest straws. In an effort to gain respite from the heat and the stale foetid air, many of the troops on the lower decks made their way topside at night, with a good number venturing onto the exclusive 'officers only' decks and resisting all efforts to eject them. However, their relief was not destined to last, ending abruptly when someone was caught smoking in defiance of the blackout.

It was not all bad though. There were three bands on board, with repertoires that included popular music and the latest hits. Various entertainments were organised, as well as sporting events, the most popular of which were boxing tournaments. The brigade had a number of amateur boxers, some of them very talented. The 2/18th's Jimmy Darlington, who was of Aboriginal descent, was a most accomplished fighter and won the ship's heavyweight championship. In Malaya he would go on to be crowned the Division's heavyweight champion.

Right: Jimmy Darlington, heavyweight champion

The vessel's crew numbered about 1000. Many were not happy, as they had been away from home for more than 12 months and had just learned they were not en route to England. The frustration boiled over, resulting in more than a few fist fights and a number of combatants ending up in the brig. The saving grace was that the food, prepared by experienced chefs, was of excellent quality and drew no complaints from the rank and file, who tucked into three meals a day in three sittings in their mess, formerly the grand ballroom. There was also a wet bar, with plenty of cheaply priced beer, which kept everyone happy.

The 'passengers' were invited to do a bridge to bilge inspection of the ship, which took around six hours to complete. To the great amusement of Roly Dean, on the main deck was a conspicuously displayed notice warning that 'THIS SHIP WILL NOT STOP TO PICK UP ANYONE WHO FALLS OVERBOARD' followed by 'A lifebuoy will not be thrown either'. As Roly remarked, 'Better to drown quickly than slowly, hanging onto a lifebuoy'.

On 16 February, as they neared the Cocos-Keeling Islands, the silence was shattered by five tremendous blasts from the ship's foghorn, heralding the approach of a vessel, the British cruiser HMS *Durban*, and bringing the men abruptly to their feet. The time had come for the ships in the convoy to go their separate ways – *Mary* and *Durban* north to Singapore, and the remainder in a westerly direction across the Indian Ocean to the Suez Canal and the Middle East. The Singapore-bound vessels circled the three other

Left: Lifeboat drill for the 2/19th.

Below: Major-General H Gordon Bennett

ships, which formed a line and dipped their flags in salute as *Mary* steamed past, less than 150 yards away, to the cheers of thousands of men. Adding to the sense of occasion, the unit bands played *Waltzing Matilda*, *Beer Barrel Polka* and, finally, when the time came to actually part, the *Maori Farewell*. For all those on board, including Hilton and Fred, it was an unforgettable and surprisingly emotional event.

Now free of the slower vessels, *Mary* made excellent time as she steamed north. However, German propaganda had reported that a German raider had sunk the ship, with all on board lost. While the troops, on arrival in Singapore, received the news with much mirth, it caused great concern to Elsie and thousands of others back home. To make matters even more confusing, *Moscow News* reported that the ship had arrived in Singapore on 11 February – a time frame that was clearly impossible. In actual fact, the vessel reached its destination without incident, exactly a fortnight after sailing from Sydney, on Tuesday, 18 February.

It was through a clearing rainstorm that those on the ship's port (left) side were treated to their first glimpse of Singapore. As the harbour facilities were far too small to cope with such a large vessel, *Queen Mary* headed for the eastern entrance of the Straits of Johor, the waterway leading to the Naval Base on the north-eastern side of the island. Near the entrance to the strait, guarded by three huge guns, they could see the distinctive 'black-and-white' officers' bungalows at Changi Military Camp, clearly discernible against lush tropical foliage. As the ship swung around Changi Point, with its white sandy beaches and attractive palm-fringed village, those on the starboard side could almost touch the thatched huts of local fishermen, jutting out from an island on spindly poles.

Nearing the naval base, the vessel was intercepted by a smart-looking, cream-coloured motor launch with blue trim, manned by members of the Malay police force. A Jacob's ladder was lowered and who should scramble up but the Division's commanding officer, Major General Henry Gordon Bennett, accompanied by Brigadier Harold Taylor, 22 Brigade's commander.

When the ship berthed at the Naval base at 1 pm, there were more VIPs at the dock – senior British military personnel in immaculate uniforms. The sight of so many dignitaries, far from intimidating the Australians, merely spurred them on. As the newspapers reported, the whole event took on a carnival atmosphere, with the newcomers waving and shouting from portholes and every conceivable vantage point. Some troops amused themselves by heating copper pennies with cigarette lighters and throwing them onto the docks, where those who raced to pick them up dropped them even faster. Others formed a choir, singing well-known Australian folk songs, described by their audience as 'strange', while their conductor kept time with a shirt on the end of a stick. The top brass, dignitaries and their wives, including Governor Sir Shenton Thomas, resplendent in a dazzling white suit and tropical headgear to match, were not amused. The media, however, had turned out in force and were intensely interested in the brash new arrivals.

Despite the secrecy and hoopla that had accompanied the brigade's departure from Australia, and the official army line that the men were now 'somewhere in Malaya', the AIF's presence and the reasons for it were no secret in Singapore. The publicity had begun days before they arrived, with the *Malay Tribune* declaring that 'the name "Anzac" first became a by-word for bravery in the last war … when you mix Australian brawn, courage and initiative in a fighting man, you get a potent cocktail. The mixture was one of Britain's prize recipes for victory a generation ago; it promises to be no less effective today'.

Consequently, by the time *Mary* reached her berth, the press was avid for more news. A welcome speech by the governor and a response by General Bennett were broadcast on the radio, providing an opportunity to debunk the story that *Mary* had been sunk and allowing Bennett to indulge in a little sabre rattling. The speeches, along with eyewitness accounts and messages from some of the troops, were also relayed to Australia, putting Elsie's mind at rest. Not to be outdone, the print media covered the arrival of the Australian troops in great detail, describing them as 'bronzed and lean and fighting fit'. Should the Japanese have the temerity to make a move, the *Malay Mail* had confidence that the Australians would 'get at the foe and stamp him out, as their kith and kin have stamped out Mussolini in North Africa'.

Disembarking took some time, with Fred and the bulk of 2/19 Battalion finally going ashore at 11.45 pm. To their disappointment, they were given no time to regain their land legs, let alone sample the delights of Singapore. Shouldering their kit, they marched immediately to a railway line about 1.5 kilometres away to board waiting trains.

Leaving the transport units and others to remain behind until the vehicles and heavy gear were unloaded, the trains crossed the one-kilometre causeway linking Singapore to Malaya and headed directly north. An all-night journey took them as far as Gemas, where members of 2 Gordon Highlanders, garrison troops usually stationed in Singapore, served cups of tea and sandwiches on the platform. The train then continued on its journey and, after several more hours, Fred and the 2/19th alighted at Seremban, approximately 330 kilometres from Singapore in the state of Negri Sembilan. Other 8 Division units were posted to Kuala Lumpur, Kampong Bahru, Malacca, Port Dickson and Kajang.

After detraining at an impressive colonial-style railway station, the weary travellers split into two separate groups. Fred's Battalion HQ, along with A Company, were marched a short distance to King George V School, a substantial white-painted, two-storey colonnaded building. Completed in 1928, it squatted on a hillside overlooking verdant sporting fields and boasted several wings, as well as a handsome clock tower. Opened on St George's Day that year, the school had adopted as its emblem St George slaying the dragon, with the Latin motto Veni, Vidi, Vinci: I came, I saw, I conquered – a quote popularly attributed to the great Roman general, Julius Caesar, and regarded by those who knew their Latin phrases as a good omen.

PRELUDE TO WAR

Left: Seremban railway station.
Below: King George V School, Seremban. Bottom: School's motto.

The battalion's remaining companies were billeted at St Paul's School, a rather grand and elaborate two-storey building, not unlike a European palace, with graceful arches and architectural flourishes. Situated behind the main business district, only a kilometre or so from King George V, it was founded in 1899 and was the first English school in the state.

The officers had excellent separate accommodation a short distance away but, like all those who had taken up residence at St Paul's, Fred and his mates were more than satisfied with their new digs at King George V, which were far superior to anything experienced in Australian camps. Each man had a bed and bedding, complete with sheets, pillow slips, a blanket and a mosquito net; a locker for his gear; a peg on the wall on which to hang his webbing; and racks where rifles could be stored tidily when not in use. A wet and dry canteen was being organised and there were even 'dhobi wallahs' (washermen) assigned to take care of all their personal and household laundry. The downside was that the latrines were rather primitive compared to those at home, but the showers were adequate, with the water heated by the tropical sun.

The Australians were in very unfamiliar territory, with scenes only depicted in travel books suddenly a reality. Everything in Seremban was so strange and new, and so very oriental. Apart from government and school buildings, built in the colonial style, and several Christian churches that looked as if they had been transported directly from the old country, the architecture was completely alien, with its exotic Indian and Chinese temples and streets lined with distinctive shophouses and colourful market stalls. Nothing was off limits in the shopping districts, apart from photographic agencies run by Japanese. As spies were everywhere, troops were ordered under no circumstances to use these establishments for the development and printing of their happy snaps.

With Australia suffering the worst drought since 1914, the lushness of the jungle and the startling green of the school's sporting ovals were in vast contrast to the parched land they had left behind, while the clothes the locals wore were far brighter than the subdued colours preferred back home. Not only were the sights different, so too were the smells. The aroma of exotic food and strange spices, cooked by the street vendors, bore no resemblance at all to the plain 'meat and three veg' they were so used to, while the stench from open drains, better described as sewers, could turn the most hardened stomach. However, despite the sometime poor sanitation, there was a complete absence of flies and mosquitoes, due entirely to strict health controls, which had eliminated both pests from the township.

Also noticeably absent were women and children. As the battalion's Gilbert Mant recorded:

> Thanks to Japanese radio propaganda about the 'terrible Australians', the local reception was somewhat chilly at first. Some of the Chinese shopkeepers boarded up their shops. Hardly a woman ventured into the street for at least a week. Rape, murder and looting were to be expected from these terrible Australians.
>
> These ugly stories were soon dispelled by the quiet behaviour of the AIF. Soon women came timidly into the open, their virtue inviolate. Soon 2/19 Battalion lines were swarming with cocoa-brown Malay youngsters with wide eyes and flashing white teeth.
>
> They bartered words in Malay for Australian postage stamps. The children spoke perfect English themselves, a tribute to the fine English schools in Malaya. They were jolly children, solemn one moment, then breaking into infectious merriment. Within a few weeks the Australians were firm friends with Malays, Chinese and Indians.

Left: The 2/19th marching through Seremban. Below: Local children.

Below: Fred's telegram to Elsie

ARRIVED DESTINATION WELL LOVE

FRED HOWE

The 2/19th came as strangers to a strange land, but any feelings of alienation were quickly dispelled by the friendliness of the locals, who invited the newcomers into their homes or to enjoy the hospitality of their own clubs. They were also most impressed by the brand new ANZAC Club, established by an Australian resident in Kuala Lumpur for troops on leave, which had opened on 25 February. The following day Fred dispatched a telegram to Elsie, letting her know that he had arrived at his 'destination'. There was no clue as to where this was, or the location of the post office that dispatched the telegram, which was simply marked 'sans origine' (without origin) by the Post Master General's Department, Fred's former employer.

However, reports in the Australian press that the new ANZAC club was in Kuala Lumpur revealed to the world where 22 Brigade was actually located, rather than 'somewhere in Malaya'. The club and its facilities had the enthusiastic support of General Bennett, a commander renowned for looking after the welfare of his men, and was kept well supplied with goods by the Australian Comforts Fund.

The Australians accepted all invitations with enthusiasm, irrespective of the race or cultural backgrounds of their hosts. Unused to white people behaving in this fashion, the local ethnic groups constantly extended the hand of friendship, with the Chinese community in Seremban opening an 'Oriental Garden', a very popular move, as its menu included steak and eggs, fresh fish and, most importantly, Australian beer.

Generous as well as gregarious, the troops handed out sweets and treats to the local children. Before long, the mere sight of an AIF convoy, with 8 Division's distinctive emu/boomerang logo displayed on the vehicles' mudguards, ensured that village streets and towns were lined with cheering youngsters. The well-paid Australian soldiers also outrageously overpaid the rickshaw coolies, much to the annoyance of the local Europeans.

The rapport between soldiers and local civilians was regarded as exceptional, so much so that a Tamil schoolteacher in Port Dickson wrote:

> Talk of the Australians and everyone has a good word to say about them. We meet them everywhere, happily engaged in studying the lives, customs, manners and occupations of the different races that they meet. The market, the stalls, the hawkers, the eating shops and the coffee shops have all roused their interest and they have tasted all the food and drinks sold in the town. In a word, they have adapted themselves to the country.
>
> These people are not tongue-tied, reserved or highbrowed. They are untarnished men of sterling qualities with whom we have communed freely and have been treated alike. An evening spent with them is worth one's while, for you will know more of their country, life, customs, manners, and a host of other things than one can ever get to read in any books.
>
> They love children and in return children have taken a great liking to these men in uniform. Wherever Australians are, we see schoolboys amongst them actively discussing topics of common interest. The behaviour of the children shows that their heart is good and young. It is indeed a blessing to have such men fight for the cause of justice and freedom. Further, we are convinced they will sell their blood dearly for our welfare.

This easy-going egalitarianism so admired by the schoolteacher and total disregard for the entrenched British class system would, in the coming months, create a lasting rift between the Australians and the British expatriates, especially the *tuan besars*, or 'big bosses'. At the top of the strict social pecking order, they enjoyed a despotic and arrogant lifestyle, paid no income tax and lived in comfortable bungalows with every convenience and legions of servants. The arrival, therefore, of the Australians really threw a spanner in the works and, although there were certainly instances of hospitality offered by Europeans, more often than not the hosts used the occasion to counsel their guests on maintaining the prestige of the white man. The Australians took absolutely no notice. They continued to treat everyone as equal and to gratefully accept lifts into town from 'inferior' citizens, especially when such invitations were not forthcoming from the supposedly 'superior' white community.

However, it was in Singapore that the AIF encountered the most overt hostility. Rumours that they would wreck the place when on leave did not help their image and neither did their tendency to indulge in practical jokes or to ridicule anything, or anybody, they considered remotely stuffy or pompous.

In a society that pandered to trivial social niceties, the presence of the brash Australians was, for many white civilians, an irritation to be endured. There was plenty to criticise. They started up conversations with complete strangers, called out 'g'day' to all and sundry and seemed to have no sense of propriety. For an ordinary soldier to address a European woman or girl or, in many cases, a man, anywhere in Singapore without an introduction was to invite a most calculated snub. A simple request for directions could result in not only being cut dead completely, but a loud remark to the effect that these 'dreadful soldiers', who actually fraternised with the 'natives', were everywhere.

Starved of female company, the troops spent much of their leave at amusement parks – the New, Great and Happy Worlds. Besides the usual sideshows, shooting galleries and refreshment stalls were dance halls, where, for the price of a ticket, soldiers could dance with beautiful Chinese and Eurasian girls. Known as 'taxi dancers', as they were hired, their English was limited and fraternisation definitely did not extend beyond the few minutes spent dancing. To make sure it did not, the girls were closely chaperoned by an army of formidable older female relatives and amahs. The dance lasted only as long as the song being performed, and cost about 30 cents. However, the taxi-dancers received just 8 cents.

Apart from the amusement parks, there were not many places that catered for the rank and file. The very swanky Raffles Hotel on Beach Road in Singapore was completely out-of-bounds, as were the European clubs and better restaurants. Barred from these establishments, soldiers on leave were forced to seek their amusement in the sleazier parts of town. Consequently, some Europeans, when countering criticism levelled at them for their ostracism, protested that they would have liked to be more hospitable to Australian troops but it was so damnably difficult to do so, as they were always hanging about the red-light district.

Not everyone in the white community held the AIF's rank and file in such low regard. Shortly after Fred arrived in Malaya, Singaporean resident Mr H Fogden donated a fair-sized plot of land on Bras Basah Road, in the heart of the city, for the erection of the Singapore ANZAC Club. A recreation and accommodation facility for Australian and New Zealand servicemen, it was built 'as a mark of an Englishman's appreciation of the Dominion troops'. Also financed by the Australian Comforts Fund, the club was officially opened in July by General Bennett, replacing a temporary club located on the first-floor verandah of the nearby Victoria Memorial Building. Established by Australian and New Zealand residents, this facility had been offering rest and reading rooms and light refreshments to troops for the past two months.

Ticket concessions were granted by the Malayan Railways so that those stationed up country could enjoy the amenities provided by the new club, which included well-priced meals, cooked and served on a voluntary basis by expatriate Australian and New Zealand women. Set in spacious surroundings, the club was a huge hit, a home away from home, and a magnet for troops on leave yearning for contact with females. As one patron pointed out, it was probably the sight of the smiling ladies that made the meals so enjoyable. There was also a comfortable, airy lounge fanned by sea breezes, where the men could enjoy a smoke or an afternoon siesta, or dip into the vast array of books on the library shelves.

Unflattering comparisons were also drawn between the Australians' laid-back style and the spit-and-polish, parade-ground image of the British troops. However, as the 2/18th's Brigadier Varley pointed out, the AIF's dislike of ceremonial drill did not mean they could not do it and, in order to prove his point, ordered his men to drill for an entire week. There was no appreciable difference, so he announced a drilling competition with a prize of four days' leave to the best platoon. It certainly did the trick, with only a single mark separating the first two teams. With both the men and Varley proving their point, life then returned to normal.

Meanwhile, back at home and hungry for good war news, the newspapers in Australia, following the *Malay Mail*'s lead, picked up the ball and ran with it. Their editions were filled with interviews and reports, along with images of the AIF at work and at leisure – going on route marches, eating in mess huts, doing various mundane chores and playing on the football field with Joey, who had survived the sea voyage in excellent shape. All fairly routine stuff, had it not been set against a backdrop completely foreign to Australian eyes. Unfortunately, all this press attention, generated locally and back home, aroused resentment among the British troops, who had been stationed in Malaya and Singapore for years and were miffed by the fuss being made over the newcomers.

Food at both King George V, where Fred was billeted, and nearby St Paul's School, was the usual staple army fare – plain, but plenty of it. At midday the troops, hungry from the morning exertions, tucked into bully beef and biscuits, supplemented by mountains of sausages. However, the evening meal was monotonous – tinned herrings in tomato sauce, night after night. After a while no one could face another herring and, after disposing of them in the garden, the hungry diners ate in town. An army marches on its stomach and, not surprisingly, complaints came thick and fast.

An enquiry established that the lack of variety in the menu was not due to lack of imagination by the much derided army cooks, but to a couple of enterprising blokes, one a warrant officer, who were trading the battalion's meat ration with the locals for tins of herrings and pocketing the profits. The unfortunate diners viewed this scam in a very poor light but, before any revenge could be exacted, the offending pair were shipped off elsewhere – one back to Australia as medically unfit and the other to another unit, where he was promoted! Years later, a relative of one of the offenders would become Australia's Governor General, the nation's highest office.

Unused to the heat and humidity, Fred was not the only one who found the tropical conditions debilitating, but they soon settled into a daily routine of warm-up training around Seremban, awaiting the unit's transport arrival on 22 February. Restored to normal strength, the battalion was now introduced to the rigours of jungle training, interrupted in early March to allow the troops to take part in a Far East Defence Exercise near Kluang – an event organised by Malaya Command.

The training schedule was gruelling. By day they sweated and toiled in the jungle; by night they sweated as they tossed and turned on their bedrolls, protected from insects by mosquito nets, but worried that they might roll over onto a king cobra during the night. To test how the battalion's fitness level was developing, a 12-hour, 50-kilometre march in fighting order was attempted with 30 chosen men. Only four finished. To underline how tough they were, as soon as they returned to barracks they showered, changed and went off to a dance.

During training, the troops were warned not to touch, scar, cut or interfere in any way with rubber trees growing on plantations where they conducted exercises or bivouacked. To do so would incur a fine of five Malay dollars as compensation to the plantation owner. In addition, any tree felled in Johor, to create transport harbours or a field of fire for the artillery, or to provide timber to 'corduroy' muddy roads or to construct bridges, attracted a royalty of five dollars per tree, payable to the Sultan, who owned the forests. The exchange rate at the time was 2/11 (30 cents) to the dollar. When the AIF racked up a bill for $105,000 (AUD 6300 – equivalent to AUD $117,558 in 2021) for the 21,000 trees it had chopped down, the Sultan promptly submitted his invoice, which was just as promptly paid.

After about three weeks, there was a change of scenery when orders were received to up sticks from Seremban and relocate to the Malay Barracks at Port Dickson, a picturesque town on the west coast, to the north of Malacca. The men were not keen on leaving Seremban, with its friendly townsfolk and good amenities, and entreaties to remain delayed the move for a fortnight. However, their new home proved popular – they were by the sea, their accommodation was comfortable, there was an excellent outdoor picture show screening a variety of films and, as a bonus, they were to split their time between Port Dickson and Seremban.

In May, while stationed at Port Dickson, Fred was diagnosed with a gastric ulcer and was admitted to 2/10 AGH at Malacca, where the Australian medical and nursing staff had taken over the Colonial Service Hospital. Built in 1934, it was a large, white, modern five-storey building with large airy wards and verandahs on all sides, set on a hill in almost 20 acres (8 hectares) of beautiful gardens and grounds. Originally a 400-bed hospital, it had recently been increased to take 600. The troops were impressed, but the locals dubbed it The White Elephant, due to its size, colour and, until the Australians arrived, lack of patients.

Although a purpose-built hospital, the standard of equipment supplied was much lower than the medical staff was accustomed to in Australia. However, it was a good deal

Above: Port Dickson Barracks, 1941.

Left: Fred treats his friends to ice cream at Port Dickson.

Malacca hospital, the 'white elephant'

better than a field hospital and very busy. With doctors removing tonsils and circumcising any soldier who was not, to forestall problems at a later date, there were hundreds of operations, resulting in hundreds of patients.

Lieutenant Colonel Albert Coates was the senior surgeon and skilled in gastro-intestinal surgery, so Fred was in good hands. After the best part of three weeks, he was discharged and sent to 2/2 Convalescent Depot, where he spent another five weeks recuperating at Tanjong Bruas, on the coast about 13 kilometres north of Malacca. Renowned for its sandy beaches, waving coconut palms and a Government Rest House with a swimming pool, the depot had accommodation for 600 men, as well as recreational and occupational facilities.

While Fred was enjoying his enforced 'holiday' by the sea, Japan was moving one step closer to war. On 2 July one million men were called up for military service, following an Imperial conference, at which it was decided to advance into Indo-China and Thailand, even at the risk of precipitating war with Britain and the United States.

Meantime, in Malaya and Singapore, life went on as usual, with no sense of urgency, at all.

CHAPTER 3

FOLLOWING FRED'S FOOTSTEPS: SINGAPORE TO MALACCA

In 2007, I finally knew enough about my father's war story to make a pilgrimage to Singapore and Malaya. Lynette Silver and her husband Neil accompanied us. First stop was the naval base which, being a restricted area, was not accessible to the public, but the terrace of the nearby Singapore Yacht Club was, providing an excellent vantage point and allowing us to see where Dad and the brigade had disembarked in 1941. The handsome pillars at the entrance to the base still stood and traces of the old rail line were also discernible, leading towards Woodlands and the one-kilometre-long causeway linking Singapore Island to Malaya.

However, before we crossed the straits and headed north, we took time to look around some of the places that Dad had visited when on leave in Singapore. As a mere corporal, the magnificent Raffles Hotel, situated at that time on the seafront, and accessible only by officers, was definitely out of bounds, but China Town, Change Alley, and the Indian and Arab quarters, with their exotic temples and shops filled with tantalising spices, were not. Neither was the Haw Par Villa in Pasir Panjang, which we visited.

The park was created by two brothers, Aw Boon Haw and Aw Boon Par, and was originally known as Tiger Balm Gardens, named after the medicinal ointment created by their father. The park reflects their passion for Chinese culture, although they were actually born in Burma, now known as Myanmar. When war broke out, the family fled to Rangoon (Yangon) and the park was then used as an observation point by the Japanese army. When the war was over, Aw Boon Haw returned to Singapore and rebuilt the park.

St Andrew's Cathedral and the vast town green, or padang, situated right in front of the nearby City Hall, were also open to the rank and file, but the fabled Singapore Cricket Club at the far end of the padang was definitely 'officers only', unless a member of one of the division's teams. Given his prowess at cricket, I am sure that Dad was among those allowed to enter the hallowed halls.

Ironically, 50 years on, while we were able to visit Raffles, the Cricket Club was restricted to members only. However, as is often the case, it was not what you know, but

Right: Singapore's colonial district, with which Fred would have been familiar.

Below: The Cricket Club, far left, Supreme Court and City Hall, fronting the padang where Fred played cricket.

Bottom: Raffles Hotel, out of bounds to Fred in 1941.

who. We dined at this very pukka establishment as guests of Professor Brian Farrell from the National University of Singapore. We had first met some years earlier at the Australian War Memorial when I recognised him from his appearance in a documentary on the Fall of Singapore, a very controversial subject. There is a tendency for Australians and British commentators to play the blame game regarding the loss of Singapore, so both Lynette and I were impressed by Brian's impartial analysis.

We also had a memorable and expensive time at Raffles Hotel, named after Sir Stamford Raffles, the father of modern-day Singapore. In the famous Long Bar, we enjoyed our Singapore Slings and upheld the tradition of throwing peanut shells onto the floor. I think we misbehaved and threw a few at each other also. A round of drinks for four cost close to 100 Singapore dollars, which at that time was at parity with the Australian dollar.

The Singapore defences were on my list of places to visit, before moving on to Malaya. Singapore had long been dubbed 'the impregnable fortress', so I was keen to see what was left of WWII's forts. They stretched from the western to the eastern entrances of the Straits of Johor, along the southern coast of the island, with a concentration around the harbour area. The fields of fire overlapped each other, making Singapore impregnable to any approach by sea. Three forts only remain today.

The first was at Pasir Panjang, now known as Labrador Battery, complete with cannons, bunkers and underground tunnels. Although originally constructed in the 1880s to help protect the entrance to Keppel Harbour, the gateway to the nearby Fortress HQ at Fort Canning, in 1938 two six-inch guns, with a range of about 10–14 kilometres, were installed and additional bunkers and tunnels added.

On 12 February, the Malay, Indian and British artillerymen stationed there, along with gunners from nearby Fort Siloso, sank a Japanese ammunition barge. The next day, during the fierce fighting by the heroic Malay Regiment on Pasir Panjang Ridge, now known as Kent Ridge, the guns were turned around to fire on the advancing Japanese. Sadly, the guns did not save the Malays, who were cut to ribbons by the enemy's vastly superior forces. After Singapore fell, the guns were destroyed to prevent them falling into enemy hands.

Labrador is now a beautiful nature reserve, covered in jungle, and the fortifications, rediscovered in 2001, are open to the public. The British also built a number of concrete machine-gun pillboxes to help defend the area. Three only have survived modern development – two at Labrador and another on a nearby roadway.

Nearby Fort Siloso was established on the heavily defended Blakang Mati Island, the 'island of the dead', renamed Sentosa. Back in WWII, it could be reached only by boat. Today there are two means of access – over a road bridge or by aerial cable car from Mt Faber. We chose the latter and I doubt I have ever been so scared in my life. After boarding the car on the sixth level of a tower, it moved off over the edge of the building, and there we were, suspended at a great height, heading out across Keppel Harbour. Huge ocean-going sea liners passed beneath us and I am sure we sat only inches from their huge blackened funnels.

Sentosa is now a popular tourist destination and the guns and defences at Fort Siloso are fascinating. They are far more extensive than those at Labrador, so we spent some time looking through the various exhibitions. We also saw the very large colonial-style buildings that had housed prisoners of war, including 'Australia House', where a good number of men from 2/18 Battalion spent their captivity in relative peace and comfort.

Seremban, in Malaya, was the next place on the list. After crossing the causeway by taxi to Johor Bahru, we headed off on foot up a back alley to collect our hire cars. The Silvers are old hands at driving in Malaysia, and thankfully we were not only following them, but had contact with them by two-way radio. Otherwise, we might still be going round in circles – and people reckon driving in Canberra is bad!

We headed north along a wide multi-laned expressway, which many of the locals regarded as a race track, especially the drivers of Singapore to Kuala Lumpur express buses. I am sure that Dad's train journey to Seremban was far less stressful than our drive and surely far more interesting. The jungle that once covered so much of the area along the roadway has gone, every last vestige of it, torn out and replaced by monotonous and environmentally disastrous palm oil plantations, as far as the eye can see. As we sped along, familiar place names appeared on road signs – Labis, Ayer Hitam and Yong Peng – names that I had only read about in books.

We soon arrived at Seremban where, after some difficulty negotiating one-way streets, we located the King George V School. It was instantly recognisable as it had changed very little from the wartime building in Dad's photographs. Security guards prevented us from entering the grounds, so we spent a considerable amount of time walking around the outer fence taking photos of the school, and also the sporting field across the road, on which the battalion's football and cricket teams had played. It was sobering to recall that, after the Japanese captured Malaya, the King George V School was used as the Military Police (kempei tai) Headquarters by the Miyazaki Butai Regiment, who converted the dressing room alongside the stage in the assembly hall into a torture chamber.

I had wondered why Dad was missing from a photo of the battalion's signallers, taken at a deserted guest house while on a training exercise in Seremban, until Jimmy Stewart, a fellow signaller, explained that the exercise was to test signalling equipment, and that Dad was among those who remained behind to receive the incoming signals. I also learned he had a soft spot for Jimmy. When he discovered that Jimmy was hardly out of short pants when he lined up in 1940 to serve his country, Dad took the youngster under his wing. Although Jimmy claimed on enlistment that he was born in 1919, his birth year was 1924, making him just 16. Dad, regarded as one of the 'old blokes', was 34, not only making him old enough to be Jimmy's father, but earning him the title of 'Dad'.

From Seremban we easily found the road leading to our next destination, Port Dickson

Above: Seremban Railway station.

Right: Oval on which the 2/19 football team played.

Left: Signallers minus Fred.

Below: Troops outside the swimming pool at the barracks, which fronted the sea.

on the west coast. Hundreds, if not thousands, of new houses seemed to spread forever as we drove west and, once they petered out, palm oil plantations again took over. Just outside the town was the army base, still in use, where dad and the 2/19th had stayed while on duty. The posting was a plum one, with excellent facilities for both rank and file and officers. I could see why Port Dickson, with its lovely historic precinct and beautiful coastline, was so popular with the Australian troops. As we wandered along the small beach area at the end of the street, where Dad and his mates had gone swimming, we could see the island of Sumatra in Indonesia, on the far side of the Malacca Straits.

Next stop was Malacca, now known as Melaka, an old pirate haunt and a favourite destination for Australians on leave. Some, including the artillerymen of 2/10 Field Regiment, medical staff serving with 2/10 Australian General Hospital and 2/3 Reserve Motor Transport personnel were actually stationed there. Malacca, first settled in the 10th century by Chinese, had been sequentially occupied by the Portuguese, Dutch and finally the British. Steeped in history, it was a fascinating mix of cultures and architectural styles, completely alien to Australian eyes.

The town takes its name from the Malacca tree and was so named in the early 1400s by a Sumatran prince who, attracted by what he considered to be a good area for a port, decided to settle there, becoming Malacca's first sultan. However, it didn't take long for Chinese sailors to also appreciate the location and for the settlement to become predominately Chinese. In the early 1500s, after an unsuccessful attempt by Siam (Thailand) to invade 60 years earlier, the Portuguese conquered the settlement and abolished the sultanate, only to be ousted, in turn, by the Dutch 120 years later.

Malacca town square 1941.

At the very end of the 18th century, the British took over, without a single drop of blood being shed. To prevent the town falling into the hands of the French, the Dutch handed Malacca to the British, who remained in control until the Japanese arrived. During their period of benign colonisation in Malaya, the British created an excellent network of roads, provided electricity and water to the towns, along with a fair justice system, a highly organised civil service, railways, hospitals, schools, better housing and food.

The numerous cultural influences are reflected in many of the buildings in the old area, notably the Cheng Toon temple, the oldest of its kind in Malaya; what is left of the Portuguese fort and St Paul's Church, constructed high on a hill; and the Dutch-built Stadhuys and Christ Church, painted a deep, distinctive red, along with the rest of the buildings flanking the town square.

The hospital where Dad was admitted for his operation is now the Meleka General Hospital. On his discharge paperwork there is a notation that he had a scar on his abdomen and groin. The abdominal one was obviously from the surgery on his ulcer, and it is a fair bet that the other was because the surgeon decided to take out his appendix at the same time, as a precautionary measure. If he did, it was a good move. Many POWs died from peritonitis, caused by a ruptured appendix.

Tanjung Bruas, where Dad enjoyed his convalescence by the beach, is no longer a quiet seaside village but a very busy container port. However, Malacca Hospital is still very much in evidence. It has been considerably expanded, with car parks and new buildings replacing a fair slice of the botanic like grounds, but the original structures and grand entrance gate are unchanged. The hospital now has more than 800 beds, plus a maternity unit, and is an important regional medical facility. I don't know how much of Malacca Dad saw while he was in hospital, which is about five kilometres from the old town, but it is a good chance that he spent time there on leave, while he was based at Port Dickson.

Photos held at the Australian War Memorial and in private collections attest to the large number of Australians who visited the town, including the noted photographer, George Aspinall, who continued to take photos in captivity. One of his images in the national collection shows members of 4 Anti-tank Regiment standing outside a building with very ornate veranda posts. After a short walk down Jonkers Street we found it, exactly as it was in 1941.

CHAPTER 4
MOVING CLOSER TO WAR

It was not until 17 July that Fred, now fully recovered from his surgery, was allowed to return to the unit to resume his training.

According to the Malay press, apart from being fine physical specimens, the Australians were 'equipped to the last button and trained in all arts of war'. Unfortunately, it was pure propaganda. They were certainly well trained, but not for jungle warfare. A few minutes in the rainforest that covered most of Malaya was enough to convince General Bennett that almost everything to do with desert fighting must be scrapped – tactics, equipment and clothing, along with now totally useless textbooks.

It was obvious that waging war in the jungle was a whole new ball game. Apart from Bennett, the only other commander to appreciate this fact was the Argylls' Lieutenant Colonel Ian Stewart, who had been in Malaya since the end of 1939. As those at Malaya Command had 'no clear idea how a jungle battle should be fought', Stewart and his Argylls, along with the two Indian battalions that formed 12 Indian Brigade, had undertaken training exercises near Mersing, on the eastern coast of Johor state.

However, no one at Malaya Command took any notice of Stewart, whose ideas were regarded by Britain's Brigadier Torrence as 'those of a crank'. Consequently, any information he passed on to his superiors was given short shrift. When a junior officer based in Singapore followed Stewart's lead and organised a jungle training exercise in Johor, his commanding officer did not bother to turn up and observe, much less take part. He was far too busy playing cricket.

While the garrison troops continued to enjoy the good life and indulge in such frivolity, the Japanese were moving closer to war. Extensive battle experience in China had been followed by months of intensive training and carrying out mock exercises that simulated conditions in Malaya. Years of planning and preparation ensured that all Japanese troops knew what to expect and, to make sure they did, each was given a jungle-fighting manual. Entitled *Read this Alone — And the War Can be Won*, the publication covered everything from the political situation and personal hygiene to care of weapons and movement through every kind of tropical vegetation.

With no guidelines to follow and no one else taking any interest, the Australian brigade was forced to develop its own jungle training program by trial and error, with clothing and equipment either modified or scrapped, and short-range weapons favoured over longer range.

As soon as the troops had settled into their bases, they were sent on daily route marches

Above: Jungle training. Below: The 2/19th on a route march.

to toughen them up, before jungle training began. Unused to the constant high humidity and heat, they suffered greatly from fatigue and cramp caused by salt depletion and experienced at first hand the skin diseases they had only heard about. Prickly itch was of particular concern until the battalion's Duncan Maxwell used his medical knowledge to find a cure. To the troops' disgust it involved liberal applications of sweet-smelling Johnson's Baby Powder.

While at sea, the Australians had attended lectures on what to expect in the jungle. However, when confronted with the real thing, they were not prepared for either the physical or the mental assault. Having trained for months for open desert warfare, they found the jungle a rather frightening experience, full of poisonous reptiles and spiders, along with myriads of stinging insects. Forced by necessity to ignore the discomfort of being constantly wet, they also had to cope with the energy-sapping tropical heat, wild animals, huge pythons and countless creepy-crawlies. However, the most important lesson they had to learn was to work with the jungle, not against it, and to adapt to conditions at a moment's notice.

A booklet issued by Australian army headquarters in Australia warned that the Japanese were experienced, ruthless, highly trained, had few physical requirements, could live off the land and, unencumbered by excess gear, could move across the country at great speed. They also had a well-organised fifth column among the Malay population as well as Japanese traders and shopkeepers.

This accurate analysis was completely contradicted at lectures by staff officers, who maintained the fiction that the Japanese were small and bandy-legged, had poor eyesight and, as a consequence, could not see in the dark. Furthermore, they were poorly equipped, with guns salvaged from the war with Russia in 1905 and obsolete rifles not much better than pea-shooters, while their inferior aeroplanes were made from recycled pots and pans. Some troops, aware of the fierce fighting that had been taking place in China for years, queried this assessment, only to have their questions brushed aside.

Far from being ill equipped for war, the Japanese were also in possession of top-secret intelligence. Back in August 1940, accepting that the Eastern Fleet was a pipe dream, defence chiefs in London had reappraised the situation in Malaya: if all the country were to be held, the defenders would need more troops and an extra 336 aircraft, none of which could be spared for the time being. At the end of September, this policy paper, along with other top-secret documents and assessments, was placed on the merchant ship SS *Automedon*, bound for Penang and Singapore.

At about 7 o'clock on the morning of 11 November, the German raider, Atlantis, disguised as a merchant vessel, intercepted *Automedon* about 450 kilometres north-west of Sumatra. It was not until Atlantis had reduced the range to less than 5000 metres that the raider revealed its identity by uncovering its guns and raising the German ensign. *Automedon*'s wireless officer attempted to send a distress signal but only managed to transmit the vessel's name, position and RRR, meaning under attack by an armed raider, before the Germans jammed the signal.

Closing in on the doomed merchantman, *Atlantis* opened fire with four salvos from a range of 2000 metres, hitting *Automedon* amidships. The first shells found their mark, destroying the bridge and killing the captain and everyone on it, apart from the helmsman. Another crewmember, who tried to reach a gun to return the fire, was also killed. The tally was five dead and 12 wounded.

A boarding party gave the crew of 31 British and 56 Chinese, along with three lone passengers, three hours in which to remove all their possessions, along with a cargo of frozen meat and other foodstuffs, as well as the ship's papers. However, it was not until a woman passenger asked for her tea set to be restored to her from the baggage room that the Germans discovered 125 mail bags, including 15 destined for Far East Command, containing decoding tables, intelligence reports and other classified documents. A small green bag was also retrieved from the chart room near the bridge. Marked 'highly confidential', it had been perforated with holes so that it would sink when thrown overboard – a plan that failed to eventuate with the death of the captain. Inside it was an envelope containing the defence chiefs' report, entitled *The Situation in the Far East in the Event of Japanese Intervention Against Us*, and a document headed *Assistance to the Dutch in the Event of Japanese Aggression in the Netherlands East Indies*, which admitted that British resistance in the event of a Japanese invasion would probably fail, because of Britain's huge commitment to the war against Germany. The enemy now had an evaluation of the strength of British naval forces in the Far East, a detailed report on Singapore's defences, and the roles expected to be played by the Dominions, should war eventuate.

Automedan, too badly damaged to salvage, was scuttled. The precious documents were transferred to another captured vessel and sent to the German Ambassador in Tokyo, who handed a copy to the Japanese government. The originals were carried by hand to Berlin via the Trans-Siberian Railway. The Japanese, who had long believed there was an integrated plan of defence for Malaya and Singapore, now knew that fortress Singapore was an illusion.

According to some historians, the contents of the green bag influenced Japan's decision to go to war. However, the captured report was compiled at the height of the Battle of Britain, when the United Kingdom was stretched to breaking point. In the few weeks that had passed, that crisis was over, but, whatever the situation, the Japanese were mighty pleased with their unexpected windfall, which they considered to be beyond price. As a reward, the Emperor presented an ornate Samurai sword, known as a katana, to the captain of *Atlantis*, one of only three foreigners to be so honoured, the other two being Nazi heavyweight Hermann Goring, head of the German Air Force, and the brilliant soldier, Field Marshal Erwin Rommel.

The Australian army booklet also emphasised the need for specialised jungle training, as the difference between trained and untrained troops in any theatre of war was 'immense'. As the jungle and densely planted rubber estates were unlike the battlefields in Europe or the Middle East, it was stressed that action should be offensive, not defensive. A new syllabus was implemented that included outflanking manoeuvres, movement along narrow jungle trails, ambushes and night attacks, house-to-house fighting in villages, and tactics suitable for a variety of vegetation, from thick jungle to padi fields and plantations. To further enhance the training, Saki tribesmen, who lived in the jungle, were employed to give survival demonstrations and advice on how to live off the land.

The equipment the local media had also boasted about was generally in short supply, non-existent or unsuited to jungle conditions. Conventional vehicles, including trailers used to tow the artillery, bogged down as soon as they left the sealed roads. When they did find a suitable position, the vegetation was so thick that there were no fields of fire. The anti-tank battery had no weapons, at all, until the arrival of a single anti-tank gun, an Italian Breda minus its gun sight, captured in the Middle East. The troops' heavy rifles were useless for close encounters in dense foliage and, while bayonets and Thompson sub-machine guns were ideal for the job, the sole Tommy gun issued to each platoon was zealously guarded by the platoon sergeant. Bren guns were due to arrive in June but, until they appeared on the scene, each battalion had to make do with Lewis machine guns from the Great War.

Personal equipment also failed to measure up. Supplies of a new style of shirt, designed to combat humidity and facilitate laundry care, arrived without any buttons. These, it was promised, would arrive in due course. Heavy leather boots, made even heavier when wet, hampered movement, as did gas masks, which caught on foliage. Steel helmets, which were mandatory during training, amplified the sound of anything striking them, even an object as small as a falling twig. However, apart from serving as handy hookworm barriers, they also doubled as a washing basin or a makeshift pillow.

Attempts to keep the malarial mosquito at bay were less than successful – the insect-repelling cream stung, the green netting veils attached to the helmets were too dark to see through and the fabric gloves proved stiff and cumbersome. The men gave all three up as a lost cause, but were still required to wear their very unflattering army-issue Bombay Bloomers – knee-length, baggy khaki pants that rolled up, converting them to shorts.

In May, the troops, much to their annoyance, had learned that the publicity surrounding their presence in Malaya did not stop with the hard-news media. A few weeks earlier, a female journalist, Adele Shelton Smith, had arrived to compile special reports for *The Australian Women's Weekly*. Feted by the officers who, after ensuring that the food would be of a higher standard than usual, invited her to dine with them in the Officers' Mess, Adele was given access to the troops, along with their training and facilities. Her articles, published throughout April, May, June and July, brought 'first-hand news of how our boys are faring in the tropics', under sensational headlines such as 'Sarong Siesta', 'Curry Tiffin with 400 of the AIF' and 'Sunday Swimming Party'.

'Their quarters are more comfortable than at home', she gushed, 'and there are no flies, mosquitoes, or dust. They are receiving marvellous hospitality from the local people. Mails are arriving regularly, the canteens are cheap, and they are getting plenty of leave'. The hard-working nursing sisters at 2/10 AGH in Malacca, who had looked after Fred, also came in for their share of publicity, with a provocative piece entitled 'They treat us like film stars'. To underline their supposedly Hollywood-like status, a photograph of white-suited staff, deferentially serving a sumptuous afternoon tea, accompanied the story.

Although Adele modified her report somewhat with the revelation that the nursing sisters had air-raid drills, and included photos of three nurses wearing tin hats and carrying gas marks, the troops' intensive jungle training received only a passing mention. The small snippets that were included were illustrated by photographs – not of men up to their armpits in murky, mosquito infested swamps, or fighting their way through the jungle with the aid of a compass, but of clean-looking soldiers in open country, picturesque villages or rubber plantations. After completing their exercises, Adele wrote, they indulged themselves with ice creams from the local vendors. In one issue, an entire page was devoted to pictures of the AIF 'keeping cool' – in a huge private swimming pool owned by a Chinese millionaire – and relaxing on Port Dickson's sandy beaches, which were favourably compared with Sydney's Palm Beach. Private Cecil Richardson of the Australian Army Service Corps, who came from the Sydney beachside suburb of Maroubra, was also featured, sitting in a giant Chinese ceramic pot and tipping a dipper of water over his body. The more conservative

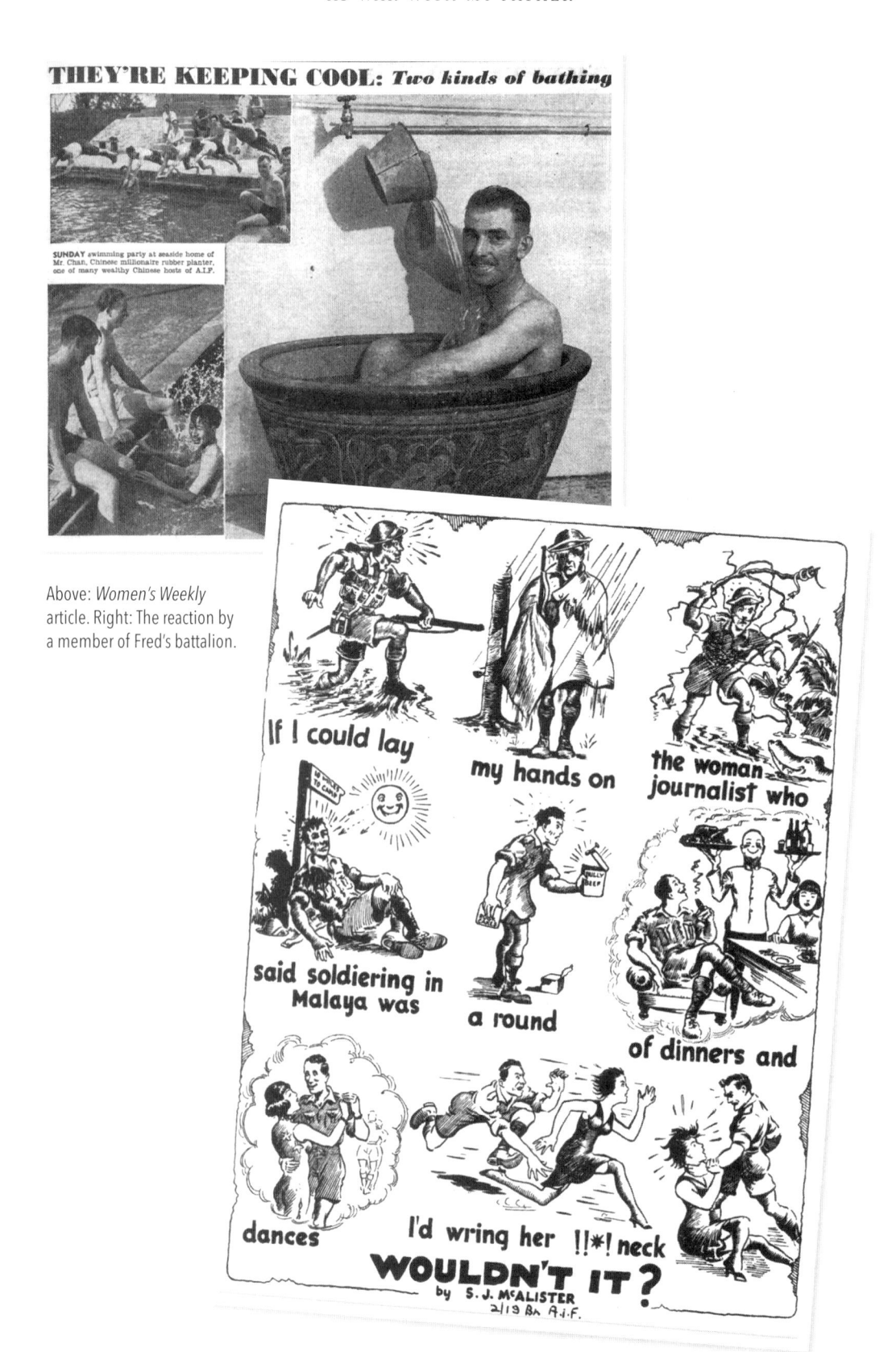

Above: *Women's Weekly* article. Right: The reaction by a member of Fred's battalion.

newspapers were also caught up in the hype, with *The Sydney Morning Herald* writing in a similar vein, illustrated with photographs of 'the boys' playing two-up, riding in rickshaws or 'on the job' with their rifles.

The exotic life being enjoyed by the AIF, dubbed the 'tid apa (no worries) boys' by their local friends, and 'Menzies' mannequins' by a tabloid newspaper in Australia, created a furore. Members of the public and families at home, especially wives and girlfriends, were most upset and wrote letters to their men protesting about the 'holiday posting'. Troops based in Darwin, at that time a frontier town with few amenities, were not happy either. When copies of the actual articles arrived in Malaya, neither were the subjects of Adele's stories.

They were incandescent with rage, not only with *The Weekly*'s journalist but also with the officers who had invited her into the fold. In a letter to his wife, the battalion's Captain, Rewi 'Ray' Snelling, described the articles 'the worst ever, unspeakable tripe' and wrote that 'if ever the lads lay their hands on that damned fool woman, they will tear her from limb to limb'. When girlfriends, made aware of the taxi dancers, wrote that they too knew how to have a good time, the situation became so volatile that senior officers were forced to issue statements refuting the articles. The general feeling was summed up by the battalion's Private Stanley McAlister who recorded 'if I could lay my hands on the woman journalist who said soldiering in Malaya was a round of dinners and dances I'd wring her !!*! neck.'

By the time the final stories were published, the men were not simply fed up with *The Weekly*'s articles, they were fed up with Malaya, with garrison duties, the heat, the humidity, the jungle, the gloomy, endless rubber plantations and, above all, the inability to come to grips with a real enemy. Aware of the situation, senior officers did everything in their power to combat the boredom and frustration. Weekend leave, with transport laid on, was granted in Singapore, Kuala Lumpur and other towns, much to the annoyance of British commanders, whose troops had to provide their own transport. Sporting competitions were held on a regular basis. Apart from the three football codes – Rugby, Australian Rules and the far less popular Soccer – there were tennis, swimming, water polo and athletic teams, and of course, rifle clubs. Concerts and other amusements were also organised, but these diversions did not resolve the underlying problem.

Morale had become even lower when word spread of the death in April of the battalion's much-loved mascot, Joey. Chased by some local boys, in his panic Joey had crashed into a concrete drain and injured his back. A local vet put him in a plaster cast but, when it became clear that the poor creature would never regain the use of his hind legs, the only option was to put him out of his misery and shoot him.

It did not take long, however, for the battalion to adopt another mascot – one far more suited to the jungle – a tiny spider monkey. In the care of one of the unit's truck drivers, he had grown from the size of a kitten to that of a small cat. Named Stanley after a politician whom he supposedly resembled, the little creature was devoted to his master, and enjoyed waking him from sleep by tugging at his hair.

In May, the British appointed a new General Officer Commanding (GOC) Malaya, who arrived to take up his post in mid-May. He was Lieutenant General Arthur Percival who, as a lieutenant colonel in 1937, had helped the then GOC, Major General William Dobbie, prepare an appreciation of Malaya's vulnerability. It had backed up a previous, and long-forgotten report, which, in 1924, concluded that north-east Malaya was a strategic location for attack during the monsoon season, between November and March, a time previously considered to be most unlikely. The War Office was unmoved, sticking to its policy that, in the event of war, a fleet would sail for Singapore, which had the capacity to withstand a siege for an extended period.

Dobbie, however, had not been put off, warning that an attack from the north during the monsoon was a potential and great danger and that the jungle was not, in most places, impassable to infantry. To this end, he managed to obtain funds for defensive works, and some work was carried out in Johor. However, when he was transferred to England, all work came to a standstill, with only one-third of the allocated £60,000 actually being spent.

Percival was an excellent staff officer and highly skilled, theoretically, in the science of war. However, he had virtually no battle experience as a commander and was described by some as being 'good on paper but no leader'. Tall and thin, with a pale complexion, receding chin, an indifferent and somewhat sparse moustache and rather prominent teeth, he did not impress the highly critical Bennett, who summed him up as 'more intellectual than dynamic'. To other detractors the new GOC was a former schoolmaster. who should have perhaps remained so – a 'nice, good man' who appeared to consider the current situation nothing more than a 'field day at Aldershot'.

The image of a rather mild, ineffectual commander is in sharp contrast to the reputation that Percival forged while serving in Northern Ireland during the turbulent pre-war period. According to historian Nigel Hamilton, who describes Percival as the 'most ruthless of the English intelligence officers in the Cork Brigade', he is still remembered as a 'vicious sadist, the man responsible for the Essex Battalion Torture Squad, a man who had personally taken a rifle with fixed bayonet from one of his troops and bayoneted one man ten times'.

While the new commander was not exhibiting any of this alleged aggression at his new posting in the Far East, and was dismissed as ineffectual, lacking charisma and natural leadership skills, he certainly had an impressive military record in the Great War as a battalion commander, receiving a Distinguished Service Order and Bar, Military Cross, and a French Croix de Guerre.

In June, shortly after his arrival, Percival embarked on an inspection tour of Malaya. As the army had no aircraft of its own and, as the RAF was reluctant to make its planes available except on 'special occasions', the GOC Malaya was compelled to resort to civilian airlines or a small De Havilland Moth aircraft, piloted by Volunteer Air Force pilots. The trip was certainly an eye opener. He discovered that northern airstrips had been constructed in positions impossible to defend and that they were standing idle, as the RAF did not have sufficient men or aircraft to operate them. Furthermore, work on defence installations was at a virtual standstill because the armed services were not permitted to entice coolie labour from the plantations and mines by offering higher rates of pay.

Orders were issued immediately to construct defences on the main road linking Malaya to Thailand and to add anti-boat, anti-tank and anti-personnel defences to the list of other defence works planned for beaches in the Mersing area and to the north. Owing to the labour shortage, the workforce was composed of mostly young, untrained and inexperienced Indian soldiers, who should have been devoting their entire time and energies to training. As the prime objective was to protect the naval base from attack, not hold Singapore Island, still regarded as impregnable, no consideration was given to the preparation of beach defences on Singapore's northern, western and eastern shores.

Meanwhile, in England, Prime Minister Winston Churchill was still sticking to his assertion that the likelihood of Japan entering the war was remote. Therefore, there was no need for any further arrangements for the defence of Singapore and Malaya, apart from 'the modest arrangements already in progress'. The Chief of his General Staff disagreed, stating that, while the threat from Japan was at this stage classified as only potential, it 'may bring even greater dangers than those we now face. Singapore is of course the key . . . It is vital to take, as soon as possible, the necessary measures to secure the defence of Singapore.'

Within days of this statement, the threat of war with Japan increased when Germany invaded Russia on 22 June. Although Japan did not join its Tripartite partner in this attack, it went ahead with a plan to gain military control over southern Indo-China – using force, if necessary. On 21 July, the pro-German, Vichy French Government in Saigon gave in to Japanese demands to occupy French Indo-China. Japan was now virtually on Malaya's doorstep, separated only by the Gulf of Siam.

Furthermore, while Germany's decision to open another front against Russia took some of the pressure off Britain, it had a most unfortunate effect on plans to strengthen security in the Far East. The British could not afford to allow their new ally, Russia, to be defeated. Although there were no troops to spare, a considerable quantity of weapons and equipment, which should have been earmarked for the Far East, was diverted to the Russian front.

The 676 aircraft and 446 tanks dispatched to Russia would have more than satisfied Malaya's requirements. However, Malaya was last on the list of British priorities. The defence of the United Kingdom, the destruction of the German U-boats creating havoc with shipping in the North Atlantic, the campaigns in the Middle East and Mediterranean, and the dispatch of war materiel and supplies to Russia were all of far greater importance.

Nevertheless, in May, in the hope of improving defences, Brigadier Ivan Simson had been dispatched to Percival's HQ as Chief Engineer, in order to 'install the most modern types of defences throughout Malaya, and to bring all existing defences up to date – specifically against beach landings and against air and tank attack'. On 1 June, he sailed for Singapore.

Ten days later, Australia, which had so far resisted Britain's suggestion to send 8 Division's two remaining infantry brigades to Malaya, agreed to a compromise. The three battalions of 23 Brigade would remain on standby to fulfil an undertaking to reinforce the Dutch Indonesian islands of Ambon and Timor, and to defend the New Guinea island of New Britain, should this become necessary. The other brigade, the 27th, which had just completed training in Bathurst, would immediately go to Malaya. With 27 Brigade due to arrive in August, Fred's CO, Lieutenant Colonel Maxwell, was promoted to Brigadier and placed in command. The 2/19th's 2IC, the mild-mannered grazier from Crowther, Charles Anderson, elevated to the rank of lieutenant colonel, became Fred's new senior officer.

The embarkation of 27 Brigade was a complicated affair. Unlike 22 Brigade, not all the men left from Sydney. Some joined the convoy in Melbourne, while others made the long overland journey by train from Bathurst to Fremantle, across the Nullabor Plain. On 29 July, those boarding in Sydney arrived by train from Bathurst, and were immediately shuttled by ferry from Darling Harbour to three troopships berthed in Woolloomooloo Bay – two Dutch liners, *Johann Van Olden-Barneveldt* and *Marnix Van Sint Aldegarde*, and an Australian vessel, SS *Katoomba*.

As was the case with 22 Brigade, the Sydney departure was supposed to be a secret but, even without the attention-grabbing *Queen Mary* in port, word quickly spread – fuelled, no doubt, by the knowledge that the convoy's escort was HMAS *Sydney*, a twin-funnelled light cruiser and dear to the heart of the city for which she was named. As the flotilla made its way down the harbour, hundreds of small pleasure craft followed, adorned with large signs wishing various units and men 'Bon Voyage' and 'Good Luck'.

In Melbourne, more troops embarked before the fleet headed west, keeping far to the south of the continent following reports of German raiders. It was hardly a pleasurable experience. The combination of the oily, spicy food served by the Dutch Javanese cooks and the continual heavy swells of the Antarctic seas convinced many voyagers, stricken with debilitating seasickness, that they would surely die. Indeed, many were so ill that they wished they would. Instead of death, however, came bright, sunny, hospitable Fremantle and the prospect of eight hours' shore leave. The convoy was expected, the people of Fremantle having been tipped off to the imminent arrival of troopships by the removal from the streets of all portable, and therefore souvenirable, traffic signs. There was no security clampdown, so phone and telegraph lines ran hot, relaying news of the convoy's progress to friends and families in the eastern states.

At Fremantle, *Katoomba* was replaced by another Dutch vessel, *Sibajak*, and HMAS *Sydney* by HMAS *Canberra*, a heavy cruiser and, at 10,000 tonnes, a third heavier than *Sydney*. With the troops who had travelled overland safely on board, the convoy sailed north the following morning. However, with 5000 men now crammed onto three small vessels, conditions for the rank and file, ordered to sleep below deck in hammocks strung from the roof, were far from comfortable. The overcrowding, combined with nauseating odours from the galleys, the overworked sanitation facilities and slimy bilges, forced many to seek refuge topside. They bunked down where they could, only to be awakened well before dawn by over-zealous crewmen hosing down the decks.

Again, there had been no official notification of the final destination. With no crates marked 'Singapore', and the vehicles in the ships' holds painted the colour of desert sand, the overwhelming consensus was that the ships were definitely headed for the Middle East. However, a day or two out of Fremantle came the announcement that they were to join 22 Brigade in Malaya. As if to underscore this news, lessons in the Malay language immediately commenced and winter clothing was exchanged for tropical kit. Regulation dress was now shorts and shirts by day and long trousers by night. The good news was that the much-derided Bombay Bloomers, dubbed 'goon pants', were, mercifully, to be kept for field exercises.

Early on the morning of 15 August the convoy reached Singapore. As the ships were much smaller than *Queen Mary*, they were able to berth in Keppel Harbour. Despite Malay Command's usual policy of publicising any new troop arrivals, it was a very low-key affair and barely rated a mention in government press handouts. Either through disinterest, or sloppy attention to detail, *The Straits Times* reported the arrival of 31 ships from Australia.

In complete contrast to the hoopla that had accompanied the disembarkation of 22 Brigade only six months before, there were no crowds of beribboned dignitaries to greet them, nor welcoming brass bands. There were, however, troops from each of 22 Brigade's battalions to help the newcomers settle in, as well as 'helpers' from British infantry units. The only top brass to be seen was the brigade's new CO, Duncan Maxwell.

As the Australians prepared to disembark the heavens opened up. Their natural exuberance somewhat dampened, they were then trucked to various camps and bases around the island. However, despite the supposed secrecy, their arrival did not go entirely

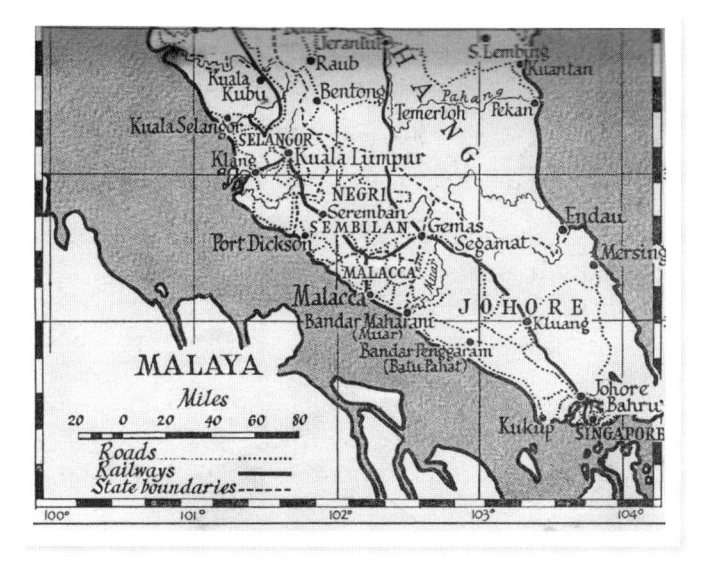

Above: More troops arrive in Singapore.

Left: Southern Malaya, where Australian troops were deployed.

unheralded. The girls in Lavender Street, a notorious red-light district, were ready and waiting for their patronage, with a huge, boldly lettered banner, WELCOME TO THE AIF, strung above the road. Once at their camps, which ranged from canvas tents to permanent barrack buildings, the men were addressed by senior officers with a list of dos and don'ts, the most alarming of which was to keep clear of young Chinese women, as 95 per cent had venereal disease, a figure that was almost immediately upped to an even more alarming 99.9 per cent. This high rate was not attributed to unbridled promiscuity, but to an old Chinese belief that sleeping with a young Chinese virgin was a cure for men suffering from gonorrhea.

    The newcomers hit the ground running and training began almost immediately. Within a week of arrival, they were undertaking 30-kilometre route marches all over the island, to the horror of the Gordon Highlanders' CO, who told one Australian senior officer that he would 'kill them all'. After a month or so of localised exercises in rubber estates and patches of jungle, the brigade moved to Malaya for more intensive training. The afternoon rest, an indulgence allowed during the 'acclimatisation' period, and one to which British troops continued to cling, was discontinued as training had now begun in earnest.

Meantime, there was no slacking at 22 Brigade. In August, Fred's battalion went on a five-day jungle trek, before practising river crossings at Sungei Linggi situated between Port Dickson and Malacca. On 29 August, Bennett took control of defences in Johor state, moving his divisional headquarters from Kuala Lumpur to Johor Bahru, at the northern end of the causeway.

Shortly afterwards, the Australians were placed on a war footing. As 27 Brigade was to support 22 Brigade, all were assigned strategic battle stations, to be taken up in the event of an attack – 22 Brigade to the east coast of Johor state and 27 Brigade to the west at Segamat, Tampin (near Malacca) and Bahu Pahat, as well as Jasin, just over the border in Negri Sembilan.

On 1 September, Fred's unit farewelled the west coast with its delightful beaches and towns and moved to Kluang, situated on the main railway line roughly 115 kilometres from Singapore and in the centre of Johor state. Apart from being on the rail line, it was of further strategic importance as the road linking Batu Pahat on the west coast, with Mersing on the east, passed directly through it. Kluang also had a newly completed airfield, which the 2/19th had been assigned to defend.

To this end, a camp under canvas was established in a gloomy rubber plantation but, as the area had been subjected to heavy monsoonal rain, it was soon reduced to a quagmire. Vehicles became hopelessly bogged, and the dirt track leading to the camp churned to a muddy morass. The troops struggled for days with stones, rocks and scrap timber to create a navigable roadway only to have it washed away. Fortunately, they were relieved from their purgatory with the announcement that they were moving to a new site on sunny grassy slopes near the airfield.

Kluang was not a large town, but it had a cinema and other places of entertainment. Unfortunately for Fred and his mates, in early October it was time to move again, eastwards to the Jemaluang-Mersing area to replace 12 Indian Brigade, now held in reserve. Infantrymen from Australia's 27 Brigade took over the 2/19th's defence duties at the airstrip.

At around the same time as the move, Fred was promoted from Corporal to Sergeant. After spending a week near Jemaluang, the Australians were ordered to 'stand to', with 2/18 and 2/20 Battalions moving north to occupy the coastal areas at Mersing and Endau, leaving the 2/19th in reserve at Jemaluang. Fred's HQ Company, along with A, B and D companies, camped around the village and the road linking Mersing in the north with Kota Tinggi to the south.

It was a strategically important area. Mersing was accessible by road from Johor Bahru and was the only place on Johor's east coast where heavy equipment could be brought ashore. Just south of Jemaluang, the Sedili Besar River was also navigable for a considerable distance inland. To prevent any possible incursion, C Company was dispatched to the river in the first week of September, to join 2/18th troops already stationed there.

The news that they were no longer reserve troops had come just in time for 22 Brigade, as morale was being maintained with difficulty, despite the organisation of many sporting

MOVING CLOSER TO WAR

Left: In the mud at Kluang.

Below: The aerodrome camp Kluang.

Left: Boom on the Sedili Besar River.

events and other entertainment. After months spent on garrison duties, and no sign of action, all but the most optimistic were convinced that the war would pass them by. Enemy propaganda, claiming that all they were doing was 'protecting rubber estates belonging to big British capitalists', had not helped, and neither had white feathers, posted from Australia in response to the much recycled accounts of their 'glamorous' lifestyle, which had, in turn, prompted a flurry of requests for transfers to the Middle East.

However, the change of scenery and a sense of purpose, generated by the need to set up new positions and build defences in response to the growing threat from Japan, did wonders for the brigade's flagging morale. The 2/19th's Captain Reg Newton, a rather assertive individual with a booming voice, known as Roaring Reggie, noted that 'the boys are now extraordinarily fit and entirely happy'. They were also certainly very energetic. In the following weeks the entire Mersing-Endau area was surveyed for artillery deployment and the beaches criss-crossed with 400 tonnes of barbed wire.

As any beach landings would have to take place on a full tide, machine-gun posts were constructed just above the high water mark. About four metres square and a metre in height, they were built in the shape of a four-sided fort, with outer and inner walls made of logs laid horizontally between stout posts, driven deep into the beach. The space between the walls was then filled with sand to provide extra protection. Sited at strategic points several hundred metres apart, they gave the gunners murderous intersecting lines of fire. More firing posts were constructed behind the machine-gun emplacements and the beach strung with three fences of conventional wire, with coils of high tensile, anti-tank Dannert wire stretched between them.

Still further back, between the beach and the road, the entire area was sown with anti-personnel mines and defensive positions were constructed astride the road. Anti-tank and anti-personnel minefields were laid in other strategic areas. Along one 13-kilometre beachfront were three 90-centimetre beach lights, 19 Bosch lights, 38 medium machine-guns, eight 75-millimetre guns and 7000 mines. The wire in the area occupied by 2/18 Battalion at Palm Beach, Mersing, extended 800 metres into the sea. Anti-tank ditches were dug, and trenches and floating booms made of logs were constructed at the entrance to the rivers. This included the Sedili Besar, patrolled by the 2/19th's C Company, whose area of responsibility extended to the village of Mawai, further upstream on the road to Kota Tinggi. The main road and the waterway itself boasted pillboxes made of reinforced concrete, erected in 1939 at strategic spots along the river banks, the legacy of Major General Dobbie. Fred saw the structures for himself when he went to check on the signallers. Dobbie's pillboxes and the defences erected by 22 Brigade were so formidable that one Japanese colonel later commented, 'It made me shudder just to look at it'.

Unfortunately, the situation was not the same elsewhere. Aircraft were in very short supply and those that were available were obsolete. Apart from the array of guns defending Singapore's southern shoreline, there were virtually no other defences constructed on the island, although Brigadier Ivan Simson, an engineer, had been sent from England specifically for that purpose.

His arrival in early August had not been received with enthusiasm by General Percival, who viewed him with some distrust, as his written authority had not yet arrived. Simson, however, was not to be deterred and embarked on a six-week tour of Malaya and Singapore, covering 10,000 kilometres along every major road and railway. He visited all formation commands at brigade level and above, and inspected every likely landing beach and every

Concrete pillbox near Jemaluang.

airfield in use or under construction. The only exception was to the north of Endau in the Kuantan area where, because of a lack of roads and railways, travel was difficult.

The Brigadier was appalled. Apart from a sickening lack of defences and equipment, the troops, with the notable exception of the Australians and Colonel Stewart's Argylls, had been softened by years of garrison living and were not in a state of readiness, let alone fit enough to engage in jungle warfare. Returning to Singapore, he reported that Malaya could not possibly fight off a full-scale attack from the air, on the land, or from the sea, and informed Percival, in detail, what needed to be done.

His carefully thought-out plans and recommendations cut no ice with his superior, who ignored Simson's persistent entreaties with a curt 'Defences are bad for morale – for both troops and civilians'. In addition, as Malaya Command considered the use of tanks in the jungle as simply not possible, they did not constitute a threat. Consequently, many Allied troops had never seen a tank, let alone had any idea of how to halt and destroy one as there had been no attempt to distribute thousands of unopened bundles of booklets on this topic issued by the War Office. Simson had found them in cupboards belonging to the General Staff, where they must have lain for months, if not years. Horrified, he distilled the most important elements of anti-tank warfare into a 40-page pamphlet, along with diagrams for anti-tank blocks. It was ready for issue on 6 December.

Simson had also informed Malay Command that the War Office had photographs of Japanese troops landing in China in 1938, in rough seas at the height of the monsoon. Yet, despite this information and the report Percival himself had prepared in 1937, the belief that invasion during the rainy season was impossible remained entrenched. Not even the news that there was a build-up of Japanese air, sea and land forces in southern Indo-China and the South China Sea caused any anxiety. In mid-November, General Archibald Wavell, Commander-in-Chief India, expressed doubt that the Japanese would ever attack Malaya.

If they did, he was sure they would 'get it in the neck'. Unlike General Wavell, Captain Anthony Hewitt, a British army officer based in Hong Kong, had observed the Japanese and could see that they posed a great threat. He reported that they were very advanced, with excellent weapons and highly trained, only to be told by his commanding officer that he was 'probably exaggerating the problem'.

The civilian population was equally apathetic. The war in far-away Europe had been in progress for over two years, but it had had very little impact in Singapore and Malaya. In any case, if the Japanese left their bases in Indo-China and came too close, heavily defended Singapore would be a safe haven, protected by the might of the Far Eastern Fleet, ably assisted by the air force – a totally indefensible line that the RAF's Air Vice-Marshal Pulford was still spinning as late as 27 October 1941.

In an article in *The Straits Times*, he declared 'I bring you good news – there is no need to worry about the strength of the Air Force that will oppose the Japanese should they send their army and navy southward … The Air Force is on the spot, and is waiting for the enemy – clouds of bombers and fighters are hidden in the jungle, and are ready to move out onto camouflaged tarmacs of our secret landing fields and roar into action at the first move of the Japanese towards this part of the world … The planes consist of the most modern planes Britain, Australia and America are producing.'

With reassurances like these, no one could see any need for air raid drills or air raid shelters. And, since it was a well-known fact that myopic Japanese pilots were unable to fly in the dark, neither was there any reason to invoke blackout regulations.

At Mersing, the Australians continued to maintain their defences, unaware that the rest of Malaya was ripe for the picking.

CHAPTER 5
INTO BATTLE

With the defence works completed, 22 Brigade was ready for whatever action came its way. There was good cause to be confident. Not only was the entire area fortified against sea and land attack, the men were now well trained in jungle warfare tactics. Following a huge combined-service exercise at Kluang at the end of October, they were elated when the judges announced that the enemy had been well and truly annihilated.

Although held in reserve, the battalion was kept busy conducting various patrols in a radius of 16 kilometres from Jemaluang as the crow flies, but the distance was more like 28 kilometres, via the myriad of footpaths and jungle trails that criss-crossed the area. All tracks had been explored and mapped, making them a valuable resource. Time was also spent trying to bring a batch of recently arrived reinforcements, poorly trained and badly disciplined, up to scratch.

As November neared its end, there was a feeling that something might happen before too long. It did. An order was issued on 27 November to take up full defensive positions, followed two days later by instructions to double the guard and not to leave camp unless on duty. In addition, officers were to move about in pairs, accompanied by an armed orderly. Forty-eight hours later, when reports were received that Japanese forces could be moving into southern Thailand, the brigade was placed on second degree of readiness, all leave cancelled, and any Japanese in the area rounded up. Orders were also issued to send all surplus gear, personal effects, papers, notebooks etc. to the General Base Depot in Johor Bahru. The same orders included a sobering warning to all troops: if captured give only name, rank and serial number. As if to underline the seriousness of the situation, on the evening of 3 December C Company at Sedili Besar was ordered to return to the battalion.

Despite the reports of Japanese intentions to move into Thailand, and troops being placed on a war footing, there seemed to be no sense of urgency among senior staff at Malaya Command, who were possibly lulled into a feeling of false security by the arrival in Singapore of the British battleship, *Prince of Wales*, and the battle cruiser, *Repulse*. Things were so relaxed that, on 3 December, a cable was sent to General Bennett in Cairo telling him not to hurry back as 'things are quiet and there is no prospect of hostilities'. Bennett, who was visiting Australian troops in the Western Desert, decided to return to Malaya as planned. He had a feeling that something might happen, and soon.

His instincts proved correct. Just after noon on 6 December, Australian pilot Flight Lieutenant John Ramshaw from Number 1 Squadron RAAF, based at Kota Bharu, was carrying out a reconnaissance in his Hudson aircraft. He had reached the extreme limit of its range when, through gaps in the cloud cover, he saw three Japanese vessels 185 nautical miles from Kota Bharu, heading north-west towards southern Thailand. Fifteen minutes later, the pilot of a second Hudson spotted an even larger convoy – one battleship, five cruisers, seven destroyers and 22 transports – 265 miles from Kota Bharu and heading due west. Within 15 minutes, Flight Lieutenant Emerton, piloting another Hudson, reported another large force on the same course.

Despite this, no move was made at Malaya Command to implement Operation Matador – a plan to forestall Japanese troops should they seek to enter northern Malaya from Thailand – as a cable from the British Minister in Bangkok had warned that to do so was an irrevocable act. 'For God's sake', the message read, 'do not allow British forces to occupy one inch of Thai territory unless, and until, Japan has struck the first blow in Thailand'.

Were the Japanese, as the intelligence reports indicated, bound for Malaya, or were they up to something else?

To preclude any possibility of breaching Thai neutrality, thereby creating an international incident, further evidence was required, so a Catalina flying boat was dispatched to shadow the approaching convoys during the night. When this aircraft failed to make contact, a second flew off on the morning of the 7th, only to be shot down at about noon in the Gulf of Siam by Japanese fighters, giving its unfortunate aircrew the dubious distinction of becoming the first casualties in the Pacific War. Despite poor weather, three Hudsons based at Kuantan then took to the air. At 3.45 pm a pilot reported a Japanese vessel with a large number of men on deck, dressed in khaki.

Just over two hours later, Australian pilot Johnny Lockwood spotted a cruiser and a merchant ship 112 nautical miles north of Kota Bharu, heading in the direction of Singora in southern Thailand. The cruiser's lookouts saw the plane and the gunners opened fire, forcing the Hudson to take evasive action. It was hit, although not seriously, making Lockwood's aircraft the first Australian plane attacked by the Japanese.

An hour later, there was a further report of four vessels, 60 nautical miles off Kota Bharu, steaming south. The commander of 8 Indian Brigade, tasked with defending Kota Bharu, also reported ships off the coastline, but no action was taken. According to the RAF, there were 'no hostile ships in the neighbourhood'.

There was no undue alarm either at Percival's GHQ, which held the view that the Japanese expedition was directed against Thailand and that the ships were bound for Bangkok. It was also evidently considered that the enemy's firing at Lockwood's plane, and hitting it, along with the shooting down of the Catalina, were not sufficiently aggressive acts to warrant offensive action. Whatever the reason, Operation Matador was not activated.

Governor Sir Shenton Thomas also appeared to be very relaxed. When informed that enemy ships were off the northern coast of Malaya, he allegedly said, 'Well, I suppose you'll shove the little men off'. This complacency was widespread. That same morning, Sunday, 7 December, *The Malay Tribune* reported that enemy ships were steaming towards Thailand or Malaya or both. Its attention-grabbing headline announced: 'Twenty-seven Japanese transports sighted off Cambodia Point'. As soon as the paper hit the stands, Malaya Command phoned the paper's editor reprimanding him on the impropriety of printing such alarmist views and protesting that 'the position isn't half so serious as *The Tribune* makes out'. When the editor arrived at Singapore's Seaview Hotel, a favourite meeting place with Europeans on a Sunday morning, there was indeed no hint that anything was amiss. The venue was filled to capacity, with the hotel's orchestra entertaining patrons with selections from the popular Walt Disney movie, *Snow White and the Seven Dwarfs*.

While the high command, ostrich-like, was ignoring these warning signals, Japan was poised to attack with an invasion force of 80,000 combat troops and 30,000 line-of-communication troops, supported by tanks and a modern navy and air force. The Allies, on the other hand, had few ships, mainly obsolete planes, and had managed to raise just over 90,000 men, of whom only the Australians and Stewart's Argylls were trained in jungle warfare.

British garrison troops earmarked for Singapore's defence numbered about 21,000. The Australians, responsible for Johor, accounted for more than 13,000, but less than 6000 were front-line soldiers. The rest were either support or administrative personnel, many of whom had been sent to Malaya in the belief that an entire division, not merely two-thirds of it, would be deployed there. There were also almost 17,000 Chinese, Indians and Malays in the various local volunteer forces, with 1300-odd British civilian volunteers. The remainder, a staggering 37,000, was composed entirely of Indian Army troops. While some units, such as the fabled Gurkha regiments, had an impressive list of battle honours and were renowned for their fighting prowess, others were composed of young, inexperienced soldiers. Recruited in a hurry from the streets of India's overpopulated cities, most had been only sketchily trained and were led, for the most part, by British officers whose main qualification, it was claimed, was an ability to converse with their men in their mother tongue.

If quality was in short supply, so was quantity. Seventeen more infantry battalions, four light anti-aircraft regiments and two tank regiments were still needed, as well as Hurricane aircraft, promised only if, and when, the Japanese attacked. There was not a single tank to be had. For poor neglected Malaya, the outpost too far, it was the beginning of the end.

At Kota Bharu, in Kelantan state on Malaya's far north-east coast, the Indian Army defenders were spread thinly along a 50-kilometre stretch of coconut-fringed shoreline. The beaches closest to town, including the exotically named Beach of Heavenly Passion, had been fortified with three belts of barbed wire and a line of concrete pillboxes, placed a kilometre or so apart. Further south, however, it was a different story. Here the coastal defences were much scantier, with nothing but dummy gun emplacements along an entire 16-kilometre stretch. As was the case at Sedili Besar, a boom had been constructed to the north of the town beaches, across the mouth of the Kelantan River, which extended a considerable distance inland. However, the area further to the north of the river was patrolled by just a handful of troops.

At 12.30 am on 8 December, without any declaration of war, the Japanese invaded southern Thailand and shelled the Malay coastline near Kota Bharu. Seventy-eight minutes later, at 1.48 am Malayan time (still 7 December in Hawaii), the United States Naval Fleet at Pearl Harbour was heavily attacked from the air. Also bombed in a multi-pronged assault were Manila in the Philippines, the island of Hong Kong and the Pacific islands of Midway, Guam and Wake. In Shanghai, China, the International Settlement was occupied.

As had long been predicted, but totally ignored, the Japanese 5 Division came ashore at Singora and Patani, in Thailand, virtually unopposed, and by 11 pm that night, 8 December, the commander of the Japanese 25 Army, General Yamashita, had 'persuaded' the Thai government to allow his troops to pass through Thailand. At the same time as the landings there, barges laden with battle-hardened assault troops from the Japanese 18

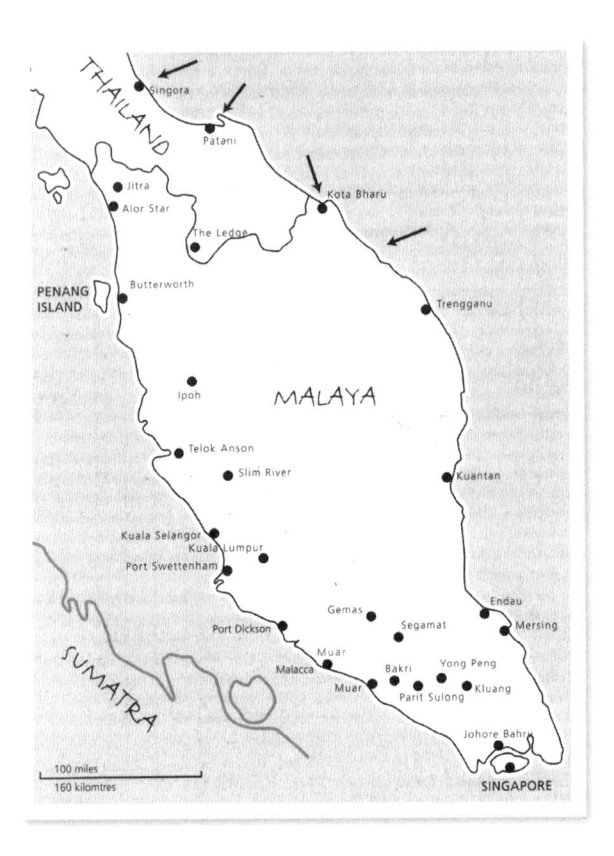

Japanese landings 8 December 1941

Division left three transport ships anchored about three kilometres out to sea and headed for the beaches near Kota Bharu. Guided by fifth columnists, known as the Tortoise Society, their objective was the airfield, less than four kilometres away. As the armour-plated barges neared the beach, the 18-pound guns of the defending artillerymen opened up, and machine gunners directed concentrated fire on the enemy troops pouring ashore. The first wave suffered heavy casualties trying to force a path through the wire, but some barges managed to reach an inlet to outflank the pillboxes either side of the creek, which fell into enemy hands. Before long, the invaders had complete control of a two-kilometre stretch of beach.

At 1.40 am, one hour and ten minutes after the shelling began, and 55 minutes after the enemy came ashore, Malaya Command dispatched an urgent message to all senior commanders: 'Cannamore. [the code word that an attack was taking place] Landing is being attempted at Kota Bharu.'

When news of the invasion force reached Air Force HQ at Kota Bharu, all available Hudson aircraft, manned by Australian crews, were ordered into the air. Dropping down to coconut-tree height, they attacked the invading troops and transports. All three ships were damaged, one permanently but, although the Australians played havoc with the enemy's second and third waves of assault, sinking many landing craft and damaging others, the Japanese pressed on, gaining a considerable foothold. The hopelessly outnumbered Indian troops continued to fight, and with great tenacity, until they were finally overrun.

At daylight, Hudsons from the Australian Number 8 Squadron at Kuantan were also brought into the fray. However, despite the efforts of the ground troops and the additional aircraft, it was a lost cause. Late that afternoon, permission was given to evacuate the Kota Bharu airstrip. With the aerodrome abandoned, there was little point in the infantrymen remaining, and they too withdrew to avoid annihilation.

Meanwhile, Japanese aircraft had also been bombing and strafing airfields in the north-west, destroying at least ten Brewster Buffalo fighters and Blenheim bombers on the ground. Two fighter pilots managed to take off from a water-logged grass strip as the bombs burst round them, only to discover that their guns were without any ammunition. Another attack followed, and by 10.45 am only four serviceable Buffaloes were left. All remaining aircraft were ordered to the safety of the Butterworth base, near Penang on the west coast.

By the end of that first day, half the 110 aircraft stationed in northern Malaya were out of action. Within 48 hours, the equivalent of three bomber squadrons and one fighter squadron were lost, either in the air or on the ground, forcing the evacuation of other airfields. Ground troops were rushed to the Thai border, but it was all too late. The Japanese had already crossed over.

At 4 o'clock on that first morning of the war, while the defence chiefs were still discussing the landings in Malaya, the Japanese air force turned its attention on Singapore. Although it was more than three hours since the attack on Kota Bharu, the entire city remained ablaze with lights. Unopposed, 17 enemy planes converged upon the island to unleash their deadly hardware. Most bombs dropped on Tengah and Seletar airfields, causing little damage, but others fell on the city itself, with Chinatown taking the brunt of the attack. European residents, woken by the sound of aircraft engines overhead, were unaware of the destruction taking place in the Chinese quarter and stood, transfixed, at their living room windows or in their gardens, enjoying what they assumed was a spectacular and very realistic air force exercise. It was not until those near enough heard the anti-aircraft guns, and the crump of exploding bombs, that they realised the city was under attack.

Although the aircraft responsible for the raid had been detected by radar when still 55 minutes away, everyone was taken by surprise as the Governor had not authorised activation of air raid alarms, for fear of frightening the population. By the time he decided it might be a good idea, another 35 minutes had passed. Harry Grumber, who had detected the unidentified aircraft on his radar screen, alleged that he had telephoned RAP Headquarters on his direct line, only to be told that the chief warden, who had the keys controlling the master switch to the city's lights, was at the late night cinema. While Grumber tried desperately and unsuccessfully to have the lights extinguished, another 25 minutes was wasted in a fruitless search for the air-raid warden and his keys. Even though there were three Australian Buffalo fighters on standby, their engines warmed in readiness, they remained on the ground. Despite perfect moonlit conditions, the Allied fighter planes were not permitted to take off and attack the raiders, as the air force chief was afraid that incompetent anti-aircraft gunners would accidentally shoot them down.

Apart from forcing the introduction of a total blackout between 6 pm and 6 am, effective immediately, the early morning raid made little impression on the population of Singapore. An official news bulletin simply added to the general air of complacency, stating that the Japanese had been repulsed at Kota Bharu, where only a few bombs had fallen harmlessly on the airfield, that the few hostile troops on the beach had been machine gunned and that all enemy surface craft were retiring at high speed. The commanders-in-chief also issued a joint statement in English, Chinese and Malay, which was posted up all over town. It assured the public that everything was under control, that the military was well prepared, that defences were strong and the Japanese would soon discover they had made a grievous mistake. Consequently, after curious sightseers had finished gawking at the damage to Robinson's department store and marvelled at the size of the bomb craters, life went back to normal. It remained that way until the next raid, a good three weeks later.

Although Malaya Command and the civil administration were promoting a most unrealistic view of the situation, the Commander-in-Chief Eastern Fleet, Admiral Tom Philips, had received reports that enemy transports were heading for Malaya, escorted by one battleship, five cruisers and twenty destroyers and was of a different mindset. Despite the size of this formidable opposition, Philips now decided that sea-borne landings could not go unchallenged and issued orders for the newly arrived *Prince of Wales* and *Repulse* to sail to the Gulf of Siam as a show of strength.

The elderly *Repulse*, launched in 1916, and the brand-new *Prince of Wales*, pride of the British Fleet, had attracted a great deal of attention in Singapore following their arrival. Their very presence indicated that 'Britain meant business' and, according to the excited crowds who flocked to see the vessels at the Naval Base, Japan had 'stuck her neck out too far and would now have to pull it in again'. Unfortunately, the rest of the 'fleet', on which Singapore's defence rested, consisted of three small and outdated cruisers, seven destroyers (of which four were small and obsolete), three gunboats and a collection of small craft, ranging from motor-launches to minesweepers.

Ignoring Admiralty advice that the ships would be 'more of a bait than a deterrent' and a 'major strategical blunder fraught with the gravest of risks', 14 hours after Kota Bharu was attacked the two warships, accompanied by four destroyers, including the Australian vessel *Vampire*, only in port for a refit, set off as ordered. As the British aircraft carrier *Indomitable*, which was to have accompanied the two capital ships, had run aground in Jamaica during an exercise, and the airfields in the north of Malaya had been abandoned, the small fleet, dubbed Force Z, had no air cover.

Aerial reconnaissance had been promised but, because of the limited range, the aircraft could only fly for 160 kilometres to the north-west of Force Z from 8 am the following day. It was a risky enterprise but Phillips, on board *Prince of Wales*, hoped that experienced handling of the ships and accurate anti-aircraft fire would not only be sufficient protection, but that the element of surprise would bring about a positive result.

At first, frequent rainstorms and low cloud provided perfect cover for the Allied fleet from the air and at sea but, on the afternoon of the 9th, enemy aircraft were sighted. Realising that any chance of catching the Japanese off-guard had been lost, the Admiral abandoned his plan to sail to Singora and turned for home. However, less than four hours later, he received a signal of a reported enemy landing at Kuantan, to the south of Kota Bharu. As it was not far off their intended course, Philips diverted the fleet, only to discover all was quiet. Before they headed south again, vessels thought to be enemy landing craft were spotted, and he altered course yet again to investigate.

At 10 am the following day, 10 December, the British destroyer *Tenedos*, on its way back to Singapore as fuel supplies were running low, reported that it was under attack from enemy aircraft 140 nautical miles to the south-east. Earlier that day, an enemy submarine had reported the fleet's presence to Saigon and a strike force of 34 high-level bombers and

51 torpedo bombers had responded. Having failed to find their quarry, the aircraft were returning to base when, at about 11 am, one of the reconnaissance planes spotted the ships.

The subsequent attack concentrated on the greatest prizes – *Repulse* and *Prince of Wales*. Five torpedoes struck the former, which sank just after 12.30 pm. *Prince of Wales* was hit by two torpedoes, reducing the engine speed to 15 knots and putting the steering gear out of action. Now a sitting duck, and hit repeatedly by further bombs and torpedoes, the great, grey goliath slid beneath the waves at 1.15 pm.

For some reason, neither ship had sent an emergency signal until some time after the attack began. Eleven Brewster Buffaloes were dispatched immediately from Sembawang field on Singapore Island, but they arrived just in time to see *Prince of Wales*, listing heavily to port, disappear beneath the water, taking Admiral Phillips and Captain Leach with it. A total of 845 sailors died but more than two thousand others, covered in oil and struggling to stay afloat, were picked up by the escorting destroyers, which had not been targeted.

With the loss of the ships and so many highly trained naval personnel, any hope of impeding or preventing sea-borne landings in Malaya was gone. So too was the value of the magnificent naval base, on which Singapore's security depended. Churchill was devastated. 'In all the war', he wrote, 'I never received a more direct shock ... As I turned over and twisted in bed, the full horror of the news sank in upon me. There were no British or American capital ships in the Indian Ocean or the Pacific except the American survivors of Pearl Harbour, who were hastening back to California. Over all this vast expanse of waters Japan was supreme, and we everywhere were weak and naked.'

While Churchill tossed and turned in bed in London, in Malaya life went on as normal. Over at Batu Pahat, on Johor's west coast, word arrived at 2/30 Battalion that Force Z had intercepted the Japanese convoy, which had turned tail and fled. On the strength of this excellent news, the unit's CO gave permission for a concert to be held, at which he made the announcement public. There was no panic either at 22 Brigade, not even when the true situation became known.

From his tent in a rubber plantation at C Company's position near Jemaluang, the 2/19th's Captain Ray Snelling was full of good cheer. In a letter to his wife on 13 December he reported that, although he had to send his portable wardrobe, chest of drawers and other items back to the base depot, he had his stretcher and was living in the lap of luxury. Meals were arriving regularly in hotboxes and Indian barbers continued to visit the various positions every day to cut hair and shave the men – at no cost. However, as war had been declared, the barbers were now allowed to dress in khaki, wear tin hats and carry respirators.

While Snelling was making light of the situation, Fred and the signallers at Battalion HQ were becoming increasingly concerned. Scores of signals were sent and received each day but, since the beginning of December, when the Brigade was based on a war footing, there had been a marked increase in traffic. Many dealt with normal domestic matters – administrative instructions, transfers, rations, clothing and equipment supplies, anti-malarial control measures and routine patrol reports. However, some were most disquieting. A message from Kelantan reported that the main feature of enemy infantry tactics was infiltration and the ability to push through country that the British had regarded as impassable. It also warned that defenders at widely separated posts could find themselves isolated.

Meanwhile, as the Japanese thrust their way into Malaya in a three-pronged attack from their beachheads, any hope of stopping them near the Thai border had been abandoned. It did not take long for the next line of defenders to realise that the enemy not only had tanks and infinitely superior aircraft, but employed tactics that they, having not received any jungle training, found difficult to counter. Rather than attempt an outright assault, small enemy parties infiltrated the Allied positions, threatening the flanks and rear and forcing them to withdraw. The only way for the defenders to deal with the incursions was to ensure that the rear and flanks were covered, and then counter attack.

However, for troops trained for conventional warfare, and for troops trained hardly at all, it was an impossible task, especially as the invaders were equipped with tanks. Out-manoeuvred and outclassed, the Allied soldiers were fighting a lightly clad enemy that lived off the land. Dog tired, and with no prospect of relief, no air cover and their own transport unable to use anything but sealed main roads, even the most tenacious and spirited units had no option but to withdraw.

It was not long before the whole of northern Malaya was in retreat. On 11 December, evidently in an attempt to shore up morale and strengthen the resolve of those not yet attacked, especially as there were considerable desertions among Indian troops, General Percival dispatched a signal to all Allied units. Fred and his 2/19th comrades received a special Order of the Day stating:

> *In this hour of trial, the General Officer Commanding calls on all ranks Malaya command for a determined and sustained effort to safeguard Malaya and the adjoining British territory.*
>
> *The eyes of the empire are upon us. Our whole position in the Far East is at stake. The struggle may be long and grim, but let us all resolve to stand fast come what may and prove ourselves worthy of the great task that has been placed in us.*
>
> *Commanders are to make sure that all ranks are informed.*

In what appears to be a barb directed directly at the AIF, he added:

> *It is needless to add that the Far East includes Australia.*

Despite this exhortation, in northern Malaya key Allied positions continued to fall like wheat before the scythe. Terrified citizens fled south, if they could, adding to the general chaos. Just two weeks after Kota Bharu was attacked, enemy troops were penetrating deep into Malaya's heart – on bicycles.

The invading troops had brought thousands of pushbikes with them and had no trouble finding replacements – they simply commandeered whatever was needed from villagers. Mounted on two wheels, the Japanese could not only pedal faster than the Allies could run, they made use of plantation tracks and, on main roads, were not hindered by roadblocks or stopped by streams whose bridges had been demolished as part of a scorched earth policy. Picking up their bikes, they simply waded across the river, crossed on logs supported on the shoulders of engineers standing in the stream, or rigged makeshift bridges using planks, stockpiled nearby by fifth columnists. Not even flat tyres stopped the remorseless advance, as the bikes ran perfectly well without any tyres at all – an unexpected bonus when the noise made by the metallic rims on the hard-paved roads tricked an Allied commander into ordering a retreat in the face of what he believed was a tank attack.

As one senior Japanese officer later crowed, 'Even the long-legged Englishmen could

Above: Signal received by Fred at Jemaluang. Below: Order of the day.

not escape our troops on bicycles. This was the reason why they were continually driven off the road into the jungle where, with their retreat cut off, they were forced to surrender. Thanks to Britain's dear money spent on the excellent paved roads, and to the cheap Japanese bicycles, the assault on Malaya was easy.'

As the Japanese continued to ride easily down the well-sealed trunk roads, their transports followed, gathering up 'Churchill supplies' – ammunition, weapons, vehicles, fuel and food, all abandoned by the retreating army. A British special forces' officer,

The Japanese invade Malaya on bicycles.

involved in inserting Chinese guerrillas behind enemy lines, watched with amazement from his hiding place in the jungle as hundreds and hundreds of Japanese rode by, 'pouring east towards the Perak River. The majority of them were on bicycles in parties of 40 or 50, riding three and four abreast ... travelling as lightly as they possibly could ... in marked contrast to our own front-line soldiers, who were at this time equipped like Christmas trees with heavy boots, web equipment, packs, haversacks, water bottles, blankets, ground sheets and even great coats and respirators, so they could hardly walk, much less fight.'

None of this, however, was reported in the press. The public in the south remained in the dark, along with the troops. Although the newspapers were delivered to the Australian positions each evening, along with tea and a plentiful supply of cigarettes, the defenders in Johor had no idea of the seriousness of the situation.

They were, however, in a state of readiness. At Jemaluang, in accordance with Percival's exhortation to stand fast, on 13 December the 2/19th evacuated the village and razed all buildings in order to provide fields of fire and plant minefields. They were also ordered by Malaya Command to shoot on sight any Japanese dressed in civilian clothing who was armed – an order evidently in response to infiltrating enemy troops passing themselves off as Chinese. As a consequence, all Chinese men in the 2/19th's area were stopped and searched.

However, the real action was a very long way away and on 22 December a rather bored Ray Snelling wrote 'still no war ... As far as the landing in Kelantan is concerned there is little cause for anxiety, as troops cannot move out of there, and the only object was the aerodrome at Kota Bharu'. The main thrust, he reported, appeared to be developing in the west and was 'rather more organised now, but there will still be some hard work ahead of us before the show is cleared up. Brother Jap has some bad shocks in store for him before long'.

The 2/19th on patrol, Jemaluang.

According to Snelling, he and the rest of the 2/19th were having 'the best rest we have had so far in Malaya', and were becoming 'fat, well-fed and lazy'. Indeed, the daily timetable at C Company could hardly be considered arduous: up at 5.30 am; breakfast, shave and bath in a nearby stream at 6.45; start the day's work at 9 am (washing clothes perhaps, or a little digging or wiring); lunch at 12.30 pm; sleep until about 5 pm; tea, then night routines, such as sentry duty.

On 22 December, while 2/19 Battalion was enjoying its 'best rest ever' and Snelling was relieving the tedium by writing to his wife, the largest air battle of the entire campaign was taking place. That day a dozen Brewster Buffaloes from the Australian 453 Squadron, the only fighter aircraft still based in Malaya, took off from Kuala Lumpur to intercept 20 enemy fighters, mainly the vastly superior Navy Zeros. By nightfall, only four Buffaloes were left. The next day, the air base was evacuated.

For the two Australian brigades, far removed from the scene of battle, Christmas Day passed with reassuring normality. For lunch there was turkey, ham, baked potatoes and peas, followed by fruit salad and ice cream, with a bottle of beer each to wash it all down. After a rest, it was time for tea – roast meat, roast fowl, plum pudding and cream.

Meanwhile, the Japanese were not taking time out. By Boxing Day, Ipoh had fallen, followed by Penang. Using vessels that the British had failed to destroy in their haste to flee Penang, they began landing small parties on the west coast. Telok Anson was lost on New Year's Day, followed a week later by Slim River, where 11 Indian Division, which had been fighting non-stop for an entire month, was savagely mauled, with the well-trained Argylls and Gurkhas losing many men as they tried to defend their positions against the devastating firepower of medium tanks. With the collapse of the line at Slim River, the Japanese steamrolled their way into Malaya's capital, Kuala Lumpur.

The exodus from the city began on the morning of 10 January. By the 11th, it was abandoned.

An interminable convoy, wrote war correspondent Ian Morrison, *composed of all manner of vehicles, began to roll south. Large lorries filled with British troops so dog-tired that they slept in spite of the bumps and jolts; civilian motor-cars commandeered by the military and hastily camouflaged by being spattered with mud; lorries bearing the names of half the rubber estates in Malaya; despatch riders darting in and out of the traffic on their motor-bicycles; eleven steam rollers belonging to the Public Works Department which had steamed all the way down from Kedah and Perak; two fire-engines also making their way south; enormous tin-dredgers towed by diesel tractors … so broad that they took up most of the road, and so heavy that their treads churned up the tarred surface; low trolleys towing sticks of heavy aerial bombs saved from the northern airfields for future use; private motor cars, from Austin-7s to Rolls Royces, carrying Local Defence Volunteers, ARP wardens, police officials; camouflaged staff cars through whose windows one caught a glimpse of red tabs and hat bands; Red Cross ambulances, ordnance vans, trucks fitted with cranes and lathes and all equipment needed for field repairs.*

English, Scottish, Australian, Indian, Malay and Chinese drivers were at the wheel. Soot-blackened Tamils were keeping the steam engines chugging along. In the villages and towns along the route, Malays and Chinese and Indians stood in silent little groups, watching the long processions wind their way south.

With Kuala Lumpur abandoned, the occupying forces were soon toasting their success with troops who had cut a swathe down the east coast. Far from being unable to move out of Kelantan state after taking Kota Bharu on 8 December, as Snelling had told his wife, within five days the Japanese, using water craft, jungle tracks and horse transport, had overcome the lack of roads to reach and overrun Trengganu, about 160 kilometres to the immediate south. They had then pushed on, arriving in Kuantan on the 31st. From there the invading force had split, some heading south-west to Kuala Lumpur, and the rest continuing southwards towards Endau, Mersing, and 22 Brigade. Meanwhile Japanese forces in the west had made rapid progress south from Kuala Lumpur, diverting some of their forces to Port Swettenham and Port Dickson. The main column, however, continued on the main trunk road towards Gemas.

While the hard-pressed Indian and British units had been striving, without success,

Japanese troops in action.

to hold back the remorseless advance of the enemy, and Ray Snelling and the rest of the well-prepared 22 Brigade were waiting for the war to reach them, over in the west General Bennett had been deploying the troops under his control for battle, mindful of Percival's warning that 'if this position is lost, the battle of Singapore is lost'.

The 45 Indian Division was detailed to cover the main coast road at Muar, south of the river, with detachments and patrols along the river to a point about 50 kilometres inland. These recently arrived troops, originally intended for Burma, were to be supported by the Australian artillerymen of 65 Battery, 2/15 Field Regiment, which, at long last, had received its eagerly awaited 25-pounder guns. The rest of Bennett's force was to defend the Segamat road, down which the Japanese Army's 5 Division was expected.

A fervent advocate for offensive action, Bennett was determined to lure the Japanese into a trap: a large-scale ambush along the Tampin-Gemas road. The 2/30 Battalion, a battery from 4 Anti-tank and another from Field Regiment 9 were to spearhead this defence. The centrepiece was the ambush, for which the infantrymen had been rehearsing along a nearby jungle-bordered road.

The two other battalions from 27 Brigade, the 2/26th and 2/29th, along with the remaining artillery, anti-tank and Indian units, were allotted various other responsibilities further to the rear. The role of 2/30 Battalion and the gun crews was that of a 'shock absorber', inflicting as many casualties on the enemy as possible and holding the line for at least 24 hours, before falling back to the main positions.

The site chosen for the ambush was ten kilometres west of Gemas – a 500-metre stretch of road that included a steeply sided cutting, about four metres high and 40 metres in length. The dense jungle growing along both sides of the road gave way, at the cutting's end, to low scrub offering little or no concealment. Sixty metres beyond the cutting was the Gemencheh River, spanned by the Tiga Besar bridge. On the far side of the bridge, the road ran in a straight line for about 250 metres, with open ground on either side.

The ambush plan was well thought out. The 11 Indian Division, now retreating from Kuala Lumpur, was to make a clean break from the enemy, who would then meet no resistance for the next 45 kilometres. Bridges were to be left intact for the last 32 kilometres, heightening the impression of a hurried retreat. It was hoped that the Japanese, cock-a-hoop with events to date, would be lulled into a feeling of false security, causing them to become overconfident and less cautious. Once their forward troops had been allowed to pass over the bridge and enter the cutting, the bridge would be blown up and those in and near the cutting mown down by concentrated fire. Troops on the far side, unable to cross the river and trapped in the open, would fall victim to grenade launchers and small-arms fire, as well as artillery, whose guns would open up from a road block at the rear, on receiving a signal that the trap had been sprung.

It was teeming with rain as the 2/30th took up its relevant positions and engineers mined the bridge. To communicate with the artillery and battalion HQ to the rear, signallers laid their cable in a gutter, running along the left-hand side of the road. During the night, the now very exhausted Indian Division completed its withdrawal, followed at around 10 am by about 40 transport vehicles. With everyone now safely through, all the attackers had to do was wait. Fortunately, the rain had stopped.

Despite having encountered no opposition for the last 45 kilometres, the Japanese were not taking any chances and sent two men dressed in native-style clothing to examine the bridge. Satisfied that it was not mined, they then disappeared back down the road. At about 3.30 pm a Japanese plane flew along the road but, despite its low altitude, it failed to detect the well-camouflaged troops hidden in the jungle.

Shortly afterwards, just before 4 o'clock, a few enemy troops mounted on bicycles rounded the bend on the far side of the bridge. Behind them came the chattering main column, cycling along without a care in the world, five or six abreast and with weapons and tin hats strapped to their bike frames. Some even had their arms draped around their companions, as if they were on a picnic outing, not going to war. The first two or three hundred cyclists were allowed to pass by. As soon as the next seven or eight hundred were packed inside the ambush position, the engineers blew the bridge.

As shattered timber, chunks of concrete, bodies and bicycles hurtled skywards, the Australians, from their well-concealed vantage points, hurled hand grenades and raked the entire area with fire from rifles, Bren and Tommy guns. The din was so great that, when it was time for the artillery to open up, the forward observation officer thought the 25-pounder guns were already firing. Unfortunately, they were not – the signal wire to the rear had been spotted and cut by enemy troops allowed to clear the ambush. With no other means of contacting the battery, the plan to shell the rest of the column, now backed up in confusion beyond the bridge, was no longer possible.

Nevertheless, the ambush was deemed a huge success. In 20 minutes it was over and the road, on both sides of the bridge, was littered with hundreds of dead and dying enemy soldiers. However, as the Australians withdrew, they were attacked by Japanese, who had passed through the ambush or escaped the carnage and were now lying 'doggo' among the bodies of their slain companions. It was only after engaging in fierce hand-to-hand combat that the majority of the ambush party eventually reached the Australian lines.

However, the enemy quickly regrouped and within six hours had repaired the bridge, using ready-sawn timber from a nearby mill. By the next morning they were in control of the area and ready to roll.

Shortly after 9 am, two Japanese tanks neared the 2/30th's roadblock, but withdrew immediately when anti-tank guns opened up. The gunners missed them, but made short work of the next three – setting the leading tank on fire with high-explosive shells and disabling the second, which had to be towed away by the third. A half-track troop carrier and three more tanks appeared, supported by mortars and machine-guns brought up by Japanese infantry. However, fire directed by the Australian mortar men and anti-tankers was so effective that all four were put out of action, the cutting erupting into 'a spectacular

The wrecked bridge at Gemas.

The ambush at Gemas (Murray Griffin).

mass of smoke and flame'. In the meantime, the artillery battery, positioned in front of the infantry, was firing over open sights at the advancing column. In 60 minutes, the attack was over.

With the enemy proving its ability to recover far more quickly than anticipated, the Australians became concerned that their position might be overrun and withdrew to the main Allied force waiting beyond the Gemas River. Unfortunately, three of the artillery's four precious, newly acquired 25-pounder guns became bogged in the soft ground and had to be left behind. Also lost were two anti-tank guns – one put out of action by tank fire and the other abandoned as the guns' trailers had been sent to the rear and there was no transport available to tow it back.

In 2/30 Battalion's two-day action, one officer and 16 men were killed, four officers and 51 men were wounded, and nine were missing. The Australians estimated that Japanese casualties ran into some hundreds at the ambush site and another hundred or so at the roadblock. The senior Japanese officer who had made the disparaging remarks about 'long-legged Englishmen' only a short time before, now conceded that the Australian 8 Division had 'fought with a bravery we had not previously seen'.

Since the landings at Kota Bharu on 8 December, 38 days before, the Imperial Japanese Army (IJA) had covered many hundreds of kilometres and, until now, had met with little real resistance. With four-fifths of Malaya conquered, they had no reason to suspect that the crack troops of the Imperial Guard, advancing along the west coast, would have any problem adding Muar, Bakri and the village of Parit Sulong to their long list of successes.

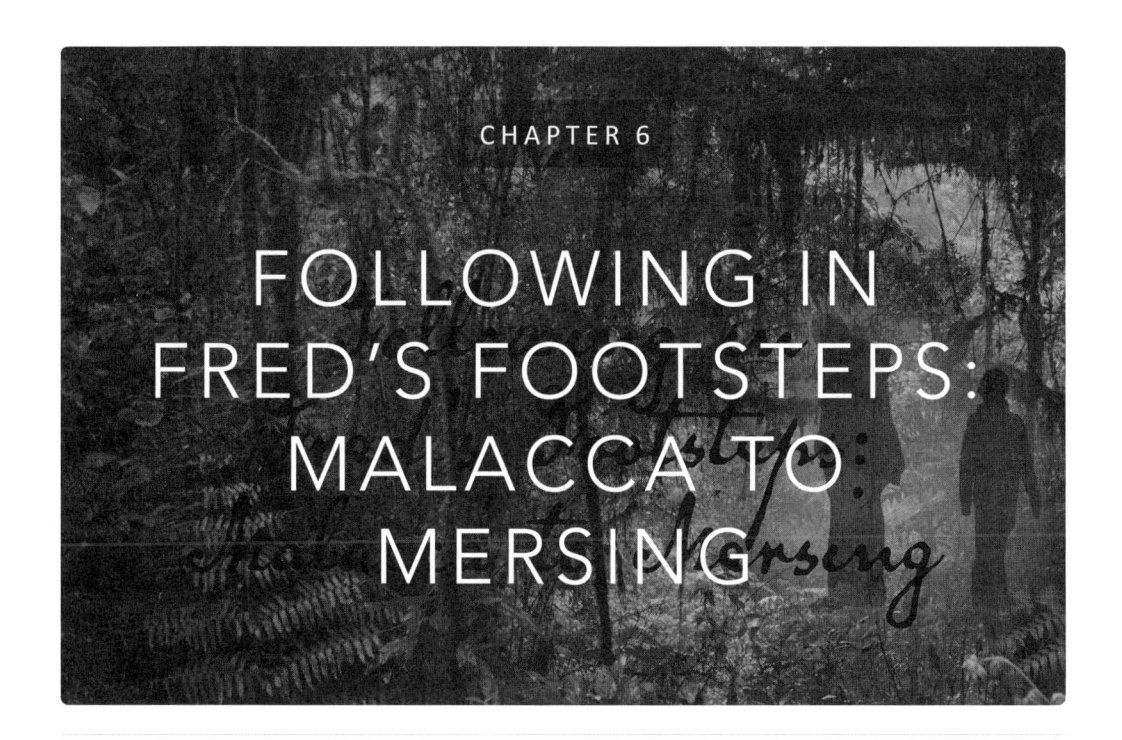

CHAPTER 6
FOLLOWING IN FRED'S FOOTSTEPS: MALACCA TO MERSING

After an exciting time exploring Malacca, we were on the road again, this time south to Ayer Hitam, before heading for the east coast, via Kluang, where some of the 2/19th were deployed to provide airfield defence. I recalled that one of the reinforcements, Private Thomas Summers, aged 25, had committed suicide here on 10 December 1941, two days after the landings at Kota Bharu and just weeks after being taken on strength. What drove him to kill himself was not disclosed. The newcomers, described by the old hands as 'untrained and poorly disciplined', had to be knocked into shape, so maybe the training had proved to be too hard. The official cause of death was 'died of injuries accidentally received'.

As we followed in Dad's footsteps further east, towards Jemaluang, there were yellow and black signs warning of elephants on the road, not unlike our signs in Australia alerting us to watch out for kangaroos and wombats. The 2/19th had often encountered monkeys and elephants while on patrol, as well as other exotic wild life. Some troops actually took part in an elephant hunt, driving away a herd that had emerged from the jungle-covered mountains to the east of Seremban and then rampaged through a village, destroying crops and buildings. However, we didn't encounter any elephants and this was probably just as well, given the size of our small sedan, but we saw plenty of monkeys scampering through the trees and along the sides of the road. Not surprisingly, quite a few had ended up as road kill, which was rather unnerving as their bodies looked like small humans.

On nearing Jemaluang, we reached a T-junction, strangely referred to in war diaries as the Jemaluang Crossroads. The road on the left led to Jemaluang and the seaside town of Mersing, where members of the brigade had spent much of their leisure time. With its colourful fishing fleet, olde worlde shophouses and attractive shoreline, Mersing is a lovely little coastal town and I could appreciate why it was a favourite with the troops.

Further to the north, across the river, was the far less appealing settlement of Endau, where D Company was involved in a short but fierce battle in January 1942. Two men,

Above: Elephant crossing on the way to Mersing.

Right: Mersing in 1941, a sleepy little town.

James Wasley and William Ferguson, were killed in action. Alan Oag and Thomas Verdon were captured and executed.

The Company's Charles Orme also saw action at Endau and it is erroneously recorded that he died there. It is also claimed that he fought at Parit Sulong in January 1942. Neither is true. After surviving the fighting at Endau, he made his way to the General Base Depot at Johor Bahru, where he rejoined his unit, only to die in battle on Singapore Island. Despite Endau's historical significance, we didn't find anything else of interest, and did not linger as the town held little attraction.

Mersing was of far more historic and personal interest, as Hilton, my brother-in-law, had been 'on a hill' there in December 1941, when he witnessed Japanese planes flying over on their way to conduct bombing raids on Singapore. It didn't take long to find the hill he had referred to: it is in the main part of the town and has a huge sign, 'M E R S I N G', spread across it in capital letters, very much like the Hollywood sign in California.

Strangely, Mersing does have a tenuous link to Hollywood. Thirty-two kilometres off the coast is the island of Timoan where the movie South Pacific was partly filmed. Australian soldiers also enjoyed spending leave there. More significantly, what is left of the wrecks of HMS *Repulse* and HMS *Prince of Wales*, ravaged in recent years by metal scavengers, are in nearby waters.

With the aid of wartime photos, we went in search of some landmarks. The beach, not surprisingly, is pretty much as it was in 1941, and the new bridge spanning the river was easy to find as we had already crossed it on our way to Endau. The old bridge was destroyed before our troops pulled out of the town and retreated south. With the help of a local we then found the retaining wall by the river, which we had assumed to be close to the river mouth, but was near the bridge.

Next morning, as we headed back towards Jemaluang, we passed through what had been the Nithsdale Rubber Estate where 2/18 Battalion had put up a strong fight against

Hilton's Hill

the Japanese on the night of 27 January 1942. The rubber has gone, but the area has changed very little, so it is easy to discern where the fighting took place, although the actual hill where more than 60 men lost their lives has been terraced and planted with oil palms. An Australian trench on top of the hill, located some years ago and still littered with bits of ordnance, was destroyed by the bulldozers creating the terraces.

Approaching Jemaluang, more than 60 years after Dad had moved into the area with his battalion, I tried to imagine what it must have been like for the villagers in December of 1941 when the 2/19 torched their homes to create a clear field of fire. During this operation, burns were sustained by the tall and dashing Major Charles 'Bill' Cousens, a well-known ladies' man as well as a popular announcer with Sydney's radio 2GB, resulting in his transfer to hospital in Johor Bahru. It was not all bad news for him though – Australian physiotherapist Edith Howgate, attached to 2/10 AGH, who had met him in Singapore while on leave and had engaged in a 'daring' affair with him in Malacca, had been posted to the hospital after all medical staff were evacuated to Johor Bahru from Malacca.

I wondered how I would feel if foreigners forced me out of my home and burnt it to the ground, so that they could get a good view to shoot at another lot of foreigners who might come along. The people of Jemaluang were innocent folk trying to go about their daily lives in their own country, so to be caught up in the horror of someone else's war must have been devastating and very frightening. Their little town, totally rebuilt after the tide of battle passed by, bore no resemblance to the one that was destroyed, and it is unlikely that the current inhabitants have any connection to those who lived there in 1941.

Using a wartime map, we drove south along the Kota Tinggi road for a short distance from the so-called Jemaluang Crossroads, before turning to the right onto a dirt track leading to the old 2/19th camp site – a large open area surrounded by low jungle growth and now used as a sand and gravel dump by the local Public Works Department, known as JKR.

Before heading west to follow the route taken by 2/19 Battalion in mid-January 1942, we decided to visit the site of the boom on the Sedili Besar River and also Mawai village, which Dad had visited in the course of his duties. Driving through endless groves of oil palms, we were surprised to discover the large reinforced concrete pillboxes that Dad had seen, guarding the road to Kota Tinggi. They were still pretty much intact, apart from the ironwork grills that had been scavenged, but were covered in graffiti.

Further south, we turned left towards the east coast, following a road that skirted the Sedili Basar. In place of the floating boom, erected to block enemy incursions from the river mouth, was a huge brand new bridge. From the river mouth, a series of stout pillboxes stretched at regular intervals to our next port of call, Mawai Lama (Old Mawai). According to local historians, it was originally called Mawas – the name given to the creature universally known as Bigfoot, which some villagers claim to have seen. It was a sleepy little place – just a string of old timber shophouses, set back from the river, and a sturdy concrete jetty.

There is a pillbox near the village, but about 12 kilometres downstream is a much larger structure, surrounded by jungle. The interior, which is well preserved, shows evidence of wartime occupation by Australian troops – in particular, members of 2/26 Battalion, which moved into the area when C Company was ordered to rejoin the rest of the 2/19th at Jemaluang in early December 1941. Like people everywhere, some of the soldiers who were manning the pillbox could not resist a few doodles here and there, and inscribed their names on the walls in pencil. Two of the inscriptions that are easily decipherable are those of two privates, William James Brosnan and Edward John Murphy.

Brosnan, a married man, aged 32, from the inner riverside Brisbane suburb of New Farm and a barman in civilian life, survived the horrors experienced by F Force on the Burma-Thai railway and returned home safely. There is a good chance that his slightly older co-scribbler, Edward Murphy, was a mate, as he also came from New Farm, where he lived with his mother. Murphy, an optical mechanic in peacetime, was fortunate to remain in Singapore throughout captivity, possibly because his optical skills could be put to good use in Changi Camp. He also survived the war and returned home, where he married.

After continuing on to take a brief look at Kota Tinggi, a sizeable town on the line of retreat to Johor Bahru, we retraced our steps to the Jemaluang Crossroads. Our next destination would be the west coast, where Dad and the men of the 2/19th took on the Japanese and wrote themselves into the history books.

The Sedili bridge

CHAPTER 7
BAPTISM OF FIRE

While the IJA's victorious 5th army was moving down the main road towards Segamat, on 10 January General Bennett had ordered his 45 Indian Brigade and the Australians from 65 Battery, 2/15 Field Artillery, to take up positions in the town of Muar, to prevent Japanese advancing down the west coast from crossing the river.

Holding the enemy at Muar was vital. It was a natural strongpoint as the river there was 400 metres wide and could only be crossed by ferry. Should hostile troops manage to cross the river, they would be able to access two major roads, both leading to Yong Peng – one inland via Simpang Jeram and Parit Sulong and the other along the coast via Parit Jawa and Batu Pahat. If allowed to reach Yong Peng, they would cut off the Allied line of retreat from Segamat.

The Indian Brigade's only supporting troops were the Australian gunners. After arriving at a nominated rendezvous and finding no sign of the Indians, the artillerymen continued along the Muar road, searching without success for a place to park their vehicles and guns. There were some scattered plantations providing good cover from the air, but the ground was so soft that the heavy guns and the tractors towing them quickly became bogged. At the first stopping place near a T-junction, known as Bakri Crossroads, it was only by laying corduroy tracks and much swearing and cursing that they managed to winch the guns and vehicles back onto the roadway.

The Australian gunners finally located the Indian brigade at Muar and took up their positions in and around the town. The infantry was dispersed along the river, covering a front that extended for almost 40 kilometres, with small fighting patrols north of the river and detachments stationed at the village of Simpang Jeram, to the east of Muar, and also at Parit Jawa, to guard the coastal road to Batu Pahat and another leading inland to the small village at Bakri Crossroads.

Bennett had made it quite clear that there could be no withdrawal, but the gunners were confident they would make short work of the advancing enemy. Prior to taking up battle stations, their morale had been boosted by a message from Divisional Headquarters, stating that the Japanese had been fortunate so far not to have encountered Australian troops, which now formed a solid line right across the Malay peninsula.

Their mood would not have been as buoyant had they known that the Japanese forces numbered not 200, as reported by British Intelligence, but 10,000: 5200 experienced and battle-hardened infantrymen from 4 and 5 Regiments of the crack Imperial Guards

Aerial view of Muar and the river crossing.

Division; a reconnaissance regiment; a heavy field artillery regiment of 48 guns; a medium tank regiment of 30 sixteen-ton tanks; a light tank regiment of 30 eight-ton tanks; one heavy five-inch mortar battalion consisting of 32 mortars; one field anti-aircraft battalion of 24 three-inch mortars, able to be converted to field artillery; an engineer regiment; a divisional signals regiment; a transport regiment; a medical unit; two field hospitals; an ordnance service regiment; one river-crossing material company and one bridging material company. The total number of troops was 10,049. No less than 914 vehicles were in support.

To make matters worse, most of the soldiers of 45 Indian Brigade who were about to face this formidable opposition were in no way prepared for jungle warfare or, indeed, warfare of any kind. Most were aged between 17 and 18 and had left their homeland only a few weeks before. The vast majority of the brigade lacked the most basic rifle skills, while many of the very junior British officers who led them were unable to speak their language. Since arriving in Malaya, only one unit had any practice in moving through the jungle and some troops, sent on a three-kilometre route march, had not even made it to the halfway point.

On 11 January, Muar was bombed, sparking a mass evacuation by the civilian population. The next day air activity increased, with dive bombers concentrating on the southern bank of the river. In response, the artillery's Lieutenant James Shearer and Gunner Max Fisher were sent across the river to establish a forward observation point, about 800 metres up the Malacca road.

On 14 January, the day on which the ambush party at Gemas sprang its trap, 4 and 5 Regiments of the Imperial Guards Division and their supporting units entered Malacca unopposed. The Guards' commanding officer, General Nishimura Takuma, had intended to rest his troops there but, flushed with the success of his rapid advance, and keen to out-

General Yamashita

triumph his rival, 5 Division's Lieutenant General Matsui Takuro, he decided to press on in the hope of cutting off the Allies' line of retreat at Yong Peng.

At Muar, the last of the civilians quit the town, leaving the defenders to endure their fourth day of aerial bombardment, which was now stepped up. Dive bombers homed in on a Chinese coastal-trader, sinking it mid-stream, while other aircraft dropped leaflets depicting a wrecked field-gun draped with bodies and with the message 'To All British Soldiers – this means nothing more than death to you'.

As it appeared that an attack was imminent, an Australian officer and signaller climbed to the top of a water tower where, with the aid of binoculars, they could keep an eye on the river mouth. For the next two days they maintained a round-the-clock watch, sustained by food delivered to them at intervals and the contents of a bottle of whisky, which the signaller had the foresight to bring with him.

The following morning, General Nishimura's men advanced further south. Two battalions of 4 Regiment headed towards the northern bank of the Muar River, while a third, using some of the boats not destroyed at Penang, bypassed Muar completely and made for Batu Pahat, hoping to outflank the Allies from the sea. In the meantime, three battalions of 5 Regiment struck inland to cross the Muar River further upstream and encircle the town from the rear.

Lieutenant Shearer, from his observation post on the northern side of the river, calmly announced over his field telephone that enemy soldiers were now moving towards the ferry. As the Japanese advanced towards him from all directions, he ordered Fisher to leave, covering his escape and continuing to direct artillery fire until contact was lost. Fortunately, after coming under fire, Fisher reached the ferry crossing where he dived into the water, hiding under the ferry ramp for the rest of the day. After dark he swam the river and made his way to Brigade headquarters, where he was able to give information on the enemy's strength and dispositions. Lieutenant Shearer, aged just 22, was never seen again.

While Fisher was lying doggo under the ferry ramp, enemy troops, using their usual infiltration tactics, overran the infantry deployed on the north side of the river, where they found dozens of small boats, abandoned by the fleeing Indians. Determined to stop the enemy advance, one of the Australian gun crews moved its 25-pounder gun to the southern end of the ferry ramp, to fire over open sights at the Japanese and army transports on the opposite shore. Another crew concentrated its attention on a fleet of small, non-motorised sampans, crammed with enemy troops trying to enter the river mouth. The boats were repulsed by the artillerymen, but that night, using a number of small skiffs taken from nearby padi fields, the invaders crossed the river further upstream. They then used larger craft, conveniently moored along the southern bank, to ferry their comrades across. Moving into a gap that had opened up between the town and the defenders on the river, the enemy troops then looped back towards Muar, taking a company of Indian soldiers by surprise.

Far from resembling the short, buck-toothed, myopic soldiers promoted by Allied propaganda and lampooned by cartoonists, the Imperial Guards did not resemble regular Japanese troops at all. For a start, they were generally much taller and far more robust. As an elite corps, they were well schooled in all facets of regular warfare and also proficient in martial arts. Unlike the khaki-clad regulars of 5 Division, who were engaging the Australians at Gemas, the Guards wore a drab darker olive uniform. Emblazoned on their caps in place of the usual five-pointed star was their distinctive and easily recognisable emblem – a star encircled by an oak-leaf cluster. However, in common with other troops, each member of the Guards carried a Meiji .38 long rifle, a bayonet, three ammunition pouches containing 120 rounds of ammunition, a small haversack and a water bottle. Slung across each back was a canvas bag holding basic rations, mess gear, a ground sheet and an entrenching tool.

Once across the river, one enemy detachment headed for Simpang Jeram and set up a roadblock, cutting off the Indians deployed there from the Muar town defenders. At the barricade, a small detachment of Australian gunners, which tried to reach the village, came under fire. With three men wounded, the party was forced to retreat. The Indians, who then came under attack, panicked and in the ensuing melee shot one of their own officers. The survivors then turned and fled towards Bakri Crossroads.

Back at Muar, other artillerymen were engaging a large number of enemy troops attempting to cross the river, and successfully repulsing about 40 motorised landing-barges brought overland from Singora, in Thailand, many hundreds of kilometres away.

By this time a number of raw, inexperienced Indian soldiers, terrified by the bombing – the 'daisy-cutter', anti-personnel variety in particular – had stripped off their uniforms, boots and rifles and fled into the safety of the jungle, barefoot and clad only in loin cloths. The Australians, always alert to an opportunity to scrounge, traded their antique .303 firearms for the Indians' abandoned, far more up-to-date weapons, and also souvenired quite a few spare pairs of boots.

With many of the Indian soldiers deserting the town, a handful of infantrymen deployed elsewhere was brought in to stiffen the resistance, but to no real avail. The rot had set in. Many of those who had not already decamped now abandoned their trucks, blocking entire convoys, while others ran hither and thither in their panic, lighting fires to cook their chapatis and shedding clothes everywhere.

One Indian battalion, better trained and disciplined than the rest, put up a spirited resistance against Japanese troops, who had infiltrated across the river in small groups and gradually encircled the town. Realising that their line of retreat to Parit Jawa was about to be cut, two of the battalion's three remaining officers led a scratch force of 30 men to mount an attack but, in the firefight that ensued, both officers were killed. The surviving officer ordered his 120 men – all that remained of the battalion – to pull back along the road to Parit Jawa, and then move inland to the Crossroads. Left without any riflemen to defend their guns, the Australian artillery had no option but to follow suit.

On the evening of the 16th, on hearing that resistance had collapsed, General Bennett decided to send his 2/29 Battalion from Segamat to reinforce the Muar front, instead of allowing it to relieve the 2/30th as planned. He did not envisage any problems in dealing with the enemy incursion in the west as British Intelligence was still reporting that Muar had been taken by an enemy force of only about 200 men.

The 2/29th, ordered to move out at 5.30 am the following day, 17 January, was under-strength. Some men had been detached in response to a report that paratroops were landing at Labis, north of Yong Peng on the Gemas road, while others had been ordered to guard a group of engineers blowing up a railway bridge at Gemas. There were no tanks, of course, but the 2/29th had a Bren-gun carrier platoon – armoured, all-terrain, tracked vehicles large enough for a crew of three and each equipped with a .303-calibre machine-gun. These utilitarian vehicles were like a tracked Jeep with light armour plating – a little too light. Depending on the angle of fire, the Japanese infantry's standard issue Arisaka rifle was capable of going right through them.

Unaware of the true size of the opposition, Bennett ordered the 2/29th to carry out a counter-attack and regain control of the area. A composite troop of gunners from 4 Anti-tank (some of whom had seen action at Gemas) and four armoured cars from a British unit were assigned as support. As soon as their 'immediate task' was completed, they were to return to their previous locations. However, should the Japanese be encountered in any strength, Bennett stressed that it was imperative to hold any further advance along the Muar–Yong Peng road for seven days to allow the main Allied force at Segamat to withdraw.

At a noon conference held on the 17th between senior Allied commanders, it was agreed that, as a withdrawal from Segamat would be very damaging to morale, an attempt should be made to hold both the Muar and Segamat fronts. To strengthen Muar, 2/19 Battalion was ordered to proceed from Jemaluang as soon as possible to join the 2/29th, leaving newly arrived British troops to cover the alternate route from Muar to Yong Peng, via Batu Pahat. The British were also responsible for holding the bridge across the Simpang Kiri River at Parit Sulong and a defile on the Parit Sulong–Yong Peng road, near the road junction leading to the coast and Batu Pahat. As there were long stretches of jungle-lined road between Batu Pahat and the defile, it was emphasised that constant patrolling was necessary to prevent enemy infiltration.

The British troops ordered to defend these areas had only just arrived after 11 weeks at sea and were not battle-ready. As one British major observed, 'the jungle was a completely strange and seemingly hostile environment to most officers and men, the majority of whom had never moved far from their homes. The enervating heat, the mosquitoes and strange jungle noises at night deprived them of sleep and aggravated the softening effects of their long sea journey.'

Having received its movement orders 24 hours ahead of the 2/19th, 2/29 Battalion arrived mid-afternoon on 17 January at 45 Indian Brigade HQ, located near Bakri Crossroads in a planter's commodious bungalow, set in a large grassy area on the northern side of the road. After receiving further orders, the Australians proceeded a little further west to the 101-mile peg on the Muar road. After resting a few hours, they were to mount the counter-attack to regain control of Simpang Jeram village, and then Muar.

The brigade's Indian troops, about to be withdrawn to the rear, were stationed along both sides of the road at mile 101 in a rubber plantation. As they had dug in, the newcomers were pleased to inherit a number of ready-made slit trenches, but on closer inspection discovered that, because of recent rain, they were full of water.

There were to be no creature comforts here. Now the Australians were at the front line, gear was kept to a minimum. There was a water truck but, until the ration trucks arrived from the rear with a hot meal, they were on hard tack.

Stripped of all but their combat and essential support troops, the four 2/29th companies were evenly distributed along both sides of the road. Beyond the Australian perimeter, to the right, was an extensive area of jungle and swamp. Battalion HQ was on the crest of a small rise in a patch of rubber only about 150 metres wide, with the Regimental Aid Post (RAP) nearby, about 50 metres in from the road. Approximately 80 metres to the rear was an open swamp, on the edge of which a mortar was set up. Further to the left, about 100 metres away, were padi fields and a deserted Malay house.

During the afternoon, a couple of ammunition trucks arrived and parked under the trees, away from the road. One of the drivers had given a lift to two Australian war correspondents – an official photographer with the Department of Information and a cinematographer. The pair, who had arrived at Brigade HQ a little earlier with another war correspondent, wanted to visit the front line. After explaining the various company positions, the 2/29th's CO, Colonel Robertson, told them to get busy and dig themselves a foxhole.

Although it was planned for the Australian gunners to provide harassing fire against any enemy advancing inland from Parit Jawa, four anti-tank gun crews had also been dispatched to the front line. However, Colonel Robertson, who did not believe the Japanese would use tanks, was not at all pleased to be saddled with the anti-tankers, or their guns, and told them in no uncertain terms that they were not wanted.

Robertson was a highly respected and much-loved officer, so this was not an auspicious start. It was, however, to become worse. The anti-tankers were barred from planning conferences, forcing their CO, Bill McCure, to glean information from other officers. After a quick reconnaissance, he stationed two guns, positioning the most forward gun behind a large earthen mound to cover a slight bend in the road, about 400 metres away. The second was situated further back in a cutting on the edge of the road. The two remaining guns and their crews were sent back to Brigade HQ.

It took them over an hour to reach the bungalow as many of the withdrawing Indians were in a complete rout. As darkness fell, they had taken to whatever vehicles they could find. The anti-tankers, driving three-ton trucks and towing their guns along the narrow roadway, were confronted by a scene of utter chaos and confusion. Indian drivers, racing their engines in low gear, headlights blazing, and blowing their horns furiously and shouting at each other, impeded the 2/29th infantrymen, who were doing their best to rush their troops and carriers to the front line.

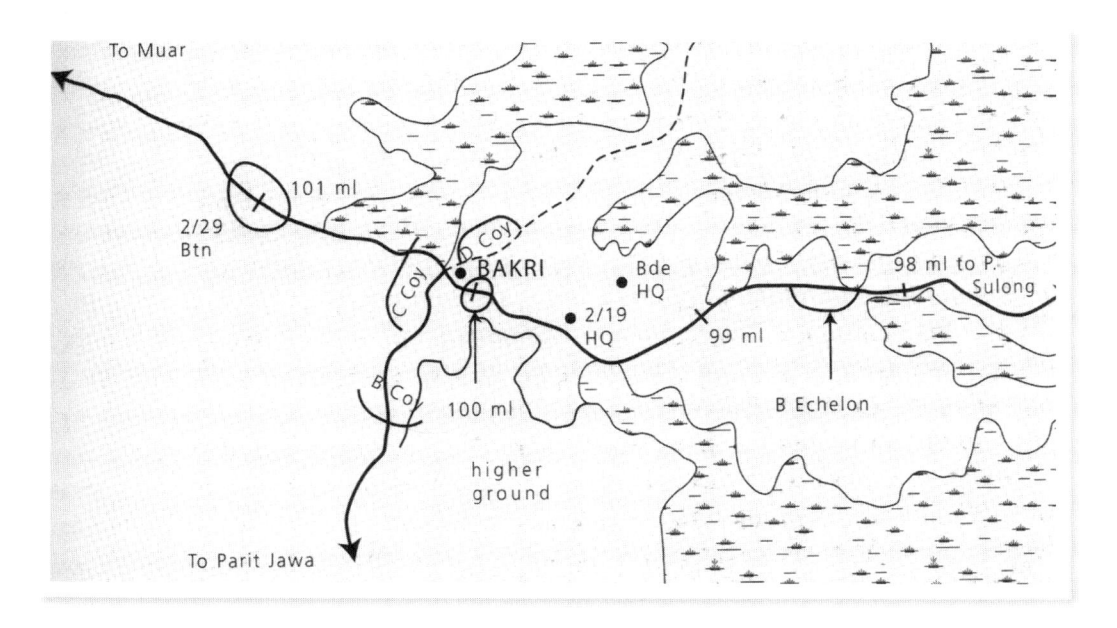

Map showing Australia positions around the Bakri Crossroads.

Despite their hopes, there was to be no rest for anyone at the 2/29th position that night, nor any chance that Simpang Jeram would be retaken. The first real inkling that the enemy was much nearer than had been supposed was when a despatch rider, sent to Bakri Crossroads to guide two ration trucks with the evening meal, overshot the battalion position on his return and disappeared. The 2/29th troops were so well concealed that he had roared straight past them, followed closely by the first truck. There was no chance of stopping them but, on hearing the second vehicle approaching, several of the infantrymen slid down the embankment and ran onto the road, waving their arms wildly and bringing it to a shuddering halt. In the distance came the sound of small-arms fire.

Moments later, an armoured car, about to leave on a forward reconnaissance when the motorcycle and first truck sped by, followed them up the road. In less than ten minutes it was back: the way ahead, near the 103-mile peg, was impassable owing to felled trees and fire from automatic weapons. The ration truck was lying in a ditch. There was no sign of the driver or the motorbike or its rider.

Shortly before dark, Australians in the left forward position exchanged shots with a Japanese patrol. Neither side suffered any casualties, but 30 minutes later the battalion came under heavy attack from mortars. The men were well dug-in and, as most of the shells fell off target, the casualties were light – one killed and several injured. However, under cover of the barrage a small enemy force had begun to close in and, almost immediately after the attack ceased, the Australians at the most forward positions heard a strange clicking sound. Peering through the trees they saw enemy troops, silhouetted against the last of the evening light. The figures charged, screaming and shouting and hurling grenades, with the apparent intention of frightening a company of Indian engineers, who had occupied the position previously. Several enemy officers and NCOs were waving their swords about and it was the rattle of the empty scabbards against their other equipment that had created the strange sound. Confused firing broke out, killing a number of Japanese and forcing the others back. When it was over, the 2/29th discovered that, of their eight men wounded, six had been shot by their own side. From then on, when engaging in combat at night, it would be strictly grenades and bayonets.

For their next attack, the Japanese charged through the trees, their soldiers with fixed bayonets and the officers swinging their swords. To the astonishment of the defenders, who had been assured that all Japanese soldiers were undersized and puny, the attacking troops were big men. Protected by their fixed defences, the Australians fired directly at the aggressors. Those who managed to penetrate the line were met with fierce hand-to-hand combat. Unable to make any headway, the Japanese withdrew, dragging with them their dead and wounded, estimated at between 70 and 80. The battalion's casualties were three men killed and 12 wounded.

The Australian mortars continued to exchange shots with the other side but, at around midnight, the barrage died down, allowing an Indian ambulance to evacuate the wounded. At about the same time, a proposed counter-attack was called off.

Just over five hours later, as dawn broke, Robertson's 'no tank theory' was shot to pieces, literally, when five tanks of the Gotanda Medium Tank Company were heard trundling towards the 2/29th lines from the direction of Muar. Waiting until the tanks were side-on to their position before they fired, the anti-tankers hit the first two, but the armour-piercing shells they were using passed right through and the vehicles kept on

Tank attacks at Bakri

going. Seemingly oblivious that advancing enemy infantry were a scant 60 metres away, the anti-tank crew dragged its gun out onto the road, swung it round a full 180 degrees and kept on firing.

By this time, the tanks, their speed reduced to a slow walk, were in the cutting, less than 40 metres from the rear gun, where the crew waited tensely for the order to attack. It was not until three tanks were in their sights that the gunners fired. The high-explosive shell tore through the leading tank, setting it ablaze and bringing the rest of the convoy to an abrupt halt. With a second tank hit and burning fiercely, a third, which had not been hit, tried to escape, but became jammed between the other two. A British officer from the Indian engineers immediately raced over and threw a hand grenade down the turret, blowing it up. Hearing a shout for high-explosive ammunition from the anti-tank gun, McCure and his batman raced across with the shells, which were used to devastating effect.

Mortar men firing at very close range also joined in, while enterprising infantrymen felled trees between each tank, preventing any possibility of escape. As the mortar shells burst in and around the immobilised tanks, turrets flew open, but the crews didn't stand a chance as they were mown down by the machine-gunners positioned at the top of the cutting. Those still inside were finished off when McCure joined the cool-headed engineer, still dropping explosive charges through the turrets. Over the din, the anti-tankers heard a rumbling and a clanking, indicating that more tanks were on their way.

The gunners waited as the first of three tanks appeared around the bend. It opened fire, aiming low, so that the shells would explode beneath the Australians' gun, wrecking it and the gunners as well. Fortunately, the defenders were one jump ahead. An anti-tanker, who had encountered this tactic at Gemas just the day before and had lost a man in the process, had passed on the benefit of his experience. Forewarned, the Australians had manhandled their gun back behind the earthen bank and the shell discharged harmlessly into the mound.

The anti-tankers then opened up. The leading tank stopped dead in its tracks, burning furiously. A second attempted to shelter behind the billowing smoke screen, while a third tried to seek refuge in the jungle. The gunners fired, damaging it. Enemy infantry, who emerged from the jungle and jumped into the tank, seeking protection from its armour, were subsequently annihilated.

Despite heavy fire from enemy snipers in trees and troops manning machine-guns, an Australian infantryman managed to get close enough to the rear tank to dispatch it with an anti-tank rifle. With its traction partially smashed, it tried to turn. Unable to withstand the onslaught, the hatch opened and two enemy soldiers emerged. One was shot as he left the turret. The other dived into a monsoon drain, but was killed by a well-aimed hand grenade. Two other tanks in the column that tried to turn and flee also had no chance. Hit by anti-tank shells, they caught fire, igniting the ammunition inside.

Enemy infantry, trying to follow up the determined attack by the tanks and machine-gunners, were held in check, but it took the efforts of three Australian carriers, their armour pierced by enemy bullets and almost every man in them wounded, before the snipers and machine guns were silenced. The battle, which had raged for 45 minutes, was over.

Once it was safe enough, the war correspondents ventured from the safety of their foxhole to record the scene for posterity. A magnificent spectacle greeted them, with burning Japanese tanks spread out in a row along the road. Even more impressive – the nearest tank had finally been stopped no more than 12 metres from the muzzle of the rear anti-tank gun.

A number of photographs were taken for posterity, but the one featuring the anti-tank gunners in their baggy Bombay Bloomers, staring over the sights of their guns at the wrecked and burning tanks in the cutting, was destined to become one of the most famous and enduring images of the Malayan Campaign. When the fires were out and the metal had cooled sufficiently, one of the anti-tankers returned for a closer look. A Japanese officer in the first tank had taken the full impact of a two-pound, high-explosive shell. Beside him, dressed in the uniform of a Japanese officer, was the body of a tall, fair-haired European, thought to be a German adviser. In another tank, a headless driver sat with his hands still clutching the controls, while others held only charred remains.

About an hour later, evidently oblivious of the carnage that had taken place, a squad of Japanese infantry, mounted on bicycles and estimated by Captain Charles Lovett to be in the vicinity of 100–150 in number, came into view and into the sights of one of the 2/29th's Bren guns, which made short work of them with the help of well-directed rifle fire.

No excuse was offered by the Japanese for what amounted to an ambush, but, according to a Japanese historian, the men of the Gotanda Tank Company had been 'careless and mistaken' in their attack as 'the British had dexterously camouflaged anti-tank weapons in the proper locations'. A Japanese artist went one better, transforming the rout into a victory, by depicting a burning tank as undamaged, removing another entirely and airbrushing away the bodies of the dead. The caption accompanying this miraculous transformation stated that 'our troops advanced rapidly. When our enemy fled they blocked the road with fallen trees. However, such tactics did not obstruct our advancing troops.'

Meanwhile, at the 2/29th's aid post, casualties were arriving in a steady stream, some of them shot by enemy snipers. A number, however, were victims of 'friendly fire' or, in some cases, bayonet thrusts – mostly Indian troops still retreating from Muar, who had rushed headlong into the Australian perimeter during the night.

Sometime before 11 am, two Japanese officers, waving a white cloth, emerged from the rubber trees. They wanted a short truce, to collect the remainder of their dead and attend to their wounded, numbering some 220 men. Looking at his watch, Robertson said, 'You can have half an hour. At 11.30 we will open fire.'

The truce had less than 30 minutes to go when Robertson learned that the line to Brigade Headquarters at Bakri was dead. A signals' truck was on its way with a wireless transmitter but, until it arrived, or the landline was repaired, there would be no further communication. As Robertson needed to confer with Brigade HQ, he hitched a ride on the back of a dispatch bike, unaware that, while the Australians were busily mopping up after the tank attack and Japanese stretcher bearers were collecting their dead, other enemy troops had taken advantage of the truce to encircle the 2/29th's position from the rear. They had not only located and cut the signal wire, they had set up a roadblock.

The motorbike carrying Robertson had only covered about a kilometre when, rounding a slight bend, the rider saw the road ahead was blocked by two felled trees. Slewing around, he sent his machine into a dangerous side-skid as the Japanese opened fire. By some miracle, he managed to keep the bike upright and was racing back towards the bend when a bullet struck Robertson in the thigh. Another tore through the rider's upper left arm and entered his chest. He managed to maintain control with his right hand, but he

Anti-tank gunners in their Bombay bloomers, in action.

could feel the Colonel's grip slipping. He slowed the bike but, about 200 metres short of the battalion's line, Robertson fell off, landing in a deep ditch. On the point of collapse himself, the rider kept going. Four men went at once to rescue their CO, but the head injuries from the fall proved fatal.

Also at around 11 am, while the Japanese were removing their dead and Robertson was preparing to ride to his death, advance elements of the 2/19th had begun arriving at Bakri. The 719-strong battalion was not up to its full strength either, as men from one company had been detached to the east coast on other duties.

Fred and the rest of the battalion had left Jemaluang at midnight on 17 January and driven west, passing through their old camp at Kluang before joining the main road at Ayer Hitam. A further 20 kilometres north, at Yong Peng, they took a minor road and headed north-west. Like all roads in Malaya, each mile was marked with posts to indicate the distance between Johor Bahru and major centres.

Just beyond mile 78 was the Bukit Pelandok-Bukit Belah defile, which the British had been ordered to defend. Since everyone was on a battle footing, the first elements of the 2/19th to pass through – a transport convoy carrying ammunition, rations, kitchen equipment, blankets, clothing, personal effects, motor transport stores, reserve petrol and water – were surprised to see that the British transports were parked head to tail along the road, in full view of reconnaissance planes, and that a carnival-like atmosphere prevailed.

Beyond the defile, at mile 79, a road on the left led to Batu Pahat. From this junction, for the next couple of miles, the Muar road extended along the foot of a 150-metre-high, jungle-clad ridge. At the 81-mile peg, swamps and jungle on the left gave way to the slopes of the 270-metre-high Bukit Payong. For the next mile, the road was hemmed in on both sides by high, jungle-covered ground. Perfect ambush territory.

From mile 82, the road continued to skirt the northern slopes of Bukit Payong for another two miles, where the thickly vegetated slopes gave way, once more, to rubber plantations extending all the way to the tiny village of Parit Sulong, just beyond mile 84.

As the transports continued towards Bakri, their CO, Captain Roaring Reggie Newton, kept an eye out for suitable sites for a transport harbour. After leaving Parit Sulong, where a distinctive five-span, concrete-arched bridge crossed the fast-flowing Simpang Kiri River, the road continued north through rubber plantations until, in the vicinity of the 87-mile peg, it turned in a more westerly direction. From near mile 88, where rubber gave way to jungle and then to much lower lying ground and extensive padi fields, the road was a virtual causeway, running straight as an arrow to beyond mile 94. Two miles beyond, it turned towards the south, the padi fields narrower now and bordered, for another mile or so, by tree-swamps up to three metres deep. From here the road headed west, passing through gently undulating land planted with rubber, interspersed with jungle and swamp. Near the 99-mile peg, the swamps disappeared, only to reappear again in the vicinity of the 101-mile mark, where 2/29 Battalion was deployed.

Roaring Reggie was not happy. As the artillerymen had discovered just a few days before, the terrain either side of the road was hostile to motor vehicles and, for most of the way from Parit Sulong, deep monsoon drains, or parits, well over two metres wide, ran along both sides of the road. He eventually found a side track leading into a patch of rubber at about mile 98.5, a mile east of Brigade HQ and a little under two miles from Bakri Crossroads. Situated on the left-hand side of the road, the entire area was less than 600 metres by 800 metres, with the higher ground at either end split by a small creek. On the far side of the road and, indeed, surrounding the entire position, were deep swamps. The site was much further forward than Newton would have liked but, if he moved further back, there was a risk that, with the road vulnerable in three key areas – the defile, the Parit Sulong bridge and the causeway – the supply line could be cut, should the Japanese employ their usual infiltration tactics. To defend the position, he had about 100 men, some carriers, a detachment of mortars and nine automatic weapons. As an added precaution, he intended to send a patrol back along the road to the Parit Sulong bridge at regular intervals.

Leaving his transport team to sort itself out, Newton reported to Brigade HQ at Bakri at about 9.30 on the morning of 18 January. At 10 am, during a planning conference attended by all senior commanders, Colonel Robertson reported that the enemy troops attacking his position were Imperial Guards – the first indication that these elite troops had joined the battle.

As there was still no sign of an Indian battalion, recalled from its position further up the Muar River, the 2/19th was ordered to join the artillerymen at Bakri Crossroads to add depth to the 2/29th's position. When the Indians arrived, the 2/19th could go on the offensive.

After leaving a detachment to guard the Parit Sulong bridge until the British arrived, the first of the 2/19th combat troops reached Bakri at around 11 am and went immediately to their action stations. B Company was about 1300 metres down the Parit Jawa road, with A Company to its rear. Supporting them were the remaining guns of the artillery, stationed at Brigade HQ. Captain Snelling's C Company was forward of Bakri, on the Muar road. D Company was deployed just to the north of the intersection, while the rest, including Fred's HQ company, were at Battalion HQ, about 800 metres east of Bakri village.

Also near Battalion HQ, with the unit's trucks, was the battalion mascot, Stanley, the spider monkey. He had made the journey from Jemaluang seated in the front cabin with his master, taking a great interest in everything going on around him.

At midday, an armoured car from the 2/19th, sent along the road towards the 2/29th, encountered the roadblock, on the other side of which Robertson had come to grief less than an hour previously. The vehicle was fired on from both sides of the road, but the driver managed to turn around and escape. A company of men from the 2/29th, caught on the Bakri side of the roadblock, were ordered to attempt to break through to their battalion with the aid of armoured carriers, an armoured car and mortars. The first attack at 1 o'clock failed. However, the engagement revealed that enemy firepower on each side of the road was estimated at 20 rifles and one automatic weapon. When a second attempt was made around 90 minutes later, with the aid of two platoons from the 2/19th, it was discovered that an abandoned 2/29th truck was blocking the road. Although under fire, an officer managed to fasten a tow rope to one of the 2/19th's carriers, which then broke through the tree barricade. The enemy was routed, leaving behind a number of dead and wounded. An infantryman with a minor neck wound was the only Australian casualty.

At 4 o'clock the carriers arrived back at Anderson's HQ, bringing news of Robertson's death and of the cut-off Indians, now only about 10 kilometres away. An hour later, Bakri was shelled.

Fred had already organised his team to connect the battalion's various positions by wire but, now that the Muar road was open, setting up wireless communication with the 2/29th was of top priority. After extending their aerial with bamboo poles that they had the foresight to bring with them, the signallers immediately began establishing contact. Shortly afterwards, a ration truck arrived with water and food, including a load of bread and golden syrup, left in heaps alongside the slit trenches so that the troops could help themselves whenever they felt hungry.

There was now no chance of bringing in the still missing Indians before dark, but it was hoped that, at 7.30 am the next day, troops from the 2/19th would be able to mount an attack along the Muar road, creating a diversion to allow the Indians to reach the main force. With darkness about to fall, other Indian troops who had retreated from Muar were brought in from their position, 3 kilometres away along the Parit Jawa road, as they were deemed to be unfit for further fighting and had only two junior British officers left. As the bedraggled troops, many without firearms and equipment, passed through the 2/19th lines, Fred saw that they were indeed a sorry sight, but it was not until later that he learned that many of them, being camp followers, dhobi boys, water carriers and barbers, were non-combatants. Having lost all their senior officers and most of the older senior NCOs, they had no idea of what was going on or what they should be doing, as no one could speak their language.

As the 2/29th began to withdraw to its night perimeter, enemy infantry again attacked the forward company, but were repulsed with bayonets and grenades. A number of wounded, packed into the now empty ration trucks, were still awaiting evacuation. However, when 2/19th patrols reported that there was enemy movement between the two battalion positions, this was deemed too risky, especially since, in their last two attacks, the Japanese had shed most of their uniforms and gear and looked more like coolies than soldiers.

Apart from intermittent shelling, the remainder of the night was relatively quiet in the 2/29th's sector, except for one incident in the early morning, when a Japanese soldier hiding in a slit trench attacked an Australian sergeant checking on the forward positions. Fortunately, just as the Japanese looked like gaining the upper hand, Sergeant Benedict, an Indian engineer, came to the rescue and shot the aggressor dead. Benedict was a well-trained and well-disciplined soldier who, after fixing explosive charges to the bridge at Parit Sulong, had spent the next two days improving defences for the 2/29th.

At the 2/19th's Battalion HQ it should also have been a relatively peaceful night. However, as Fred recorded:

> The Australian troops were situated with the 2/29th forward and contacting the enemy, with the 2/19th a mile further back and covering the Bakri crossroad. The 45th Indian Brigade HQ was a half-mile further back, with our transport another mile beyond them and hidden in rubber country.
>
> As the tropical darkness fell – a darkness accentuated by the thick foliage of the rubber trees, which reduced visibility to practically nil – the Australians and Indians formed a perimeter. Twice during the night the Indians opened fire on an imaginary enemy, using thousands of rounds of precious ammunition, only desisting when their magazines were empty.
>
> This procedure kept us all in a state of nervous tension, as we could not tell whether a real attack was developing or not.
>
> As the first silvery lights of dawn crept through the trees the Japs launched their real attack on our left flank. Shells and mortar bombs rained onto our positions in hundreds. We were lucky that the screening rubber trees caused most of them to explode before reaching the ground and they were not taking their full effect. The trees began to take on the appearance of a forest swept by a tornado, split and broken branches stripped of their leaves by the blast littering the ground. The trunks, splintered and torn by shell and bomb fragments, remained upright in defiance of the attack whilst, underneath, maimed and wounded men fought desperately to stem the attack, succeeding in driving the Japanese back.

Things were also certainly hotting up elsewhere. The British at the Bukit Pelandok defile had been attacked from the air and enemy forces had been encountered south-west of Batu Pahat. Allied troops had also run into trouble at Segamat and, as a result, a leap-frogging retreat had been ordered, making it vital that the Muar front be held for as long as possible.

At Bakri the 2/19th had also come under attack. Fred recalled:

> Heavy Japanese shelling continued throughout the night, forcing the withdrawal of our field artillery, whose positions became untenable owing to the accuracy of the Japanese gunners.

The barrage was only the beginning. At 8 am, one company was attacked by an estimated 300 Japanese and forced from its position on a ridge. As it was of vital importance, Anderson gave orders to retake it immediately. Using a combination of frontal attack and outflanking manoeuvres, the enemy was routed after a 90-minute battle, which saw some fierce hand-to-hand fighting. At the height of the engagement, one calm and fearless individual wiped out a number of the enemy when he stood up and announced in his distinctive drawl, 'Keep your heads down fellows. I'm going to throw some grenades.'

The Australians, however, did not have it all their own way. A counter-attack overran one section, forcing them to pull back. Another achieved more success after engaging in fierce fighting. One of the 2/19th's officers, trying to signal some of his men from among a heap of about 15 apparently dead Japanese, noticed a corpse had come to life, holding a grenade in his right hand and raising himself from the ground with his left. As the Australian fired, the grenade exploded, killing the enemy soldier and sending bits of shrapnel in all directions, one of which hit his attacker in the shoulder. By the end of the skirmish, 15 Japanese had been killed and a machine gun and a small mountain gun captured.

The 2/19th's total casualties were ten killed and 15 wounded, but the toll could have been far higher. An Australian sergeant, collecting weapons and searching the bodies of enemy dead for unit identification, was rolling over a seemingly lifeless corpse when it jumped up, a grenade in its right hand. Reacting instinctively, the sergeant grabbed the left hand, preventing the pin from being pulled. In the ensuing struggle, the sergeant lost his steel helmet and was hit on the temple by the grenade. Warding off further blows, he managed to land a few of his own before a comrade heard his bellows for help and rushed to his aid. While the sergeant pinned the arms of his assailant, his mate finished him with rifle and bayonet. When others reported similar close shaves, orders were issued to bayonet all enemy troops who appeared to be dead or wounded.

At 8.30 am, while the 2/19th was busily fighting off enemy attacks, a carrier driver from Newton's transport group arrived at Battalion HQ, seriously wounded. The troops at the transport harbour, including the group left at Parit Sulong bridge to wait for the British to take over, had come under attack from 400–500 Japanese troops who appeared to have come from Parit Jawa. Fighting was fierce, and a number of Australians had been killed or wounded.

As soon as the attack began, Newton had ordered a heavy water truck and a transport truck, with a carrier as escort, to go at once to HQ to warn Colonel Anderson that the Japanese had infiltrated the area and that the battalion was in grave danger of being cut off. As the vehicles approached mile 99, Japanese troops constructing a roadblock fired on the convoy. The carrier, whose driver was shot, ran off the road and into a ditch, while the water tender overturned and caught fire. The wounded carrier driver managed to free himself from the wreckage and, with the driver of the other truck, crawled into a swamp. Back at the transport harbour, an attempt was made to evacuate the remaining vehicles during a lull in the fighting. However, they came under heavy fire and only three utilities and a van escaped, as a water truck immediately behind them overturned and blocked the road.

As the attack at the transport harbour continued, casualties grew, forcing the defenders to tighten their perimeter. Newton, acutely aware that he had all the rations as well as the reserve ammunition, had no option but to stay put. However, from the sound of small arms fire in the distance, it was obvious that the battalion was also under attack. Worried that they might be running short of ammunition, a wounded driver volunteered to try to run the gauntlet in the company command truck which, being smaller and faster than a regular transport vehicle, might be able to get through. A carrier was assigned as escort.

It was a forlorn hope. At mile 99 the two vehicles ran headlong into the now completed roadblock. An anti-tank shell hit the truck, killing the driver and enveloping the vehicle in flames. The carrier turned tail and fled, but hit an anti-tank mine. It was a write off, but the crew managed to escape the wreckage and reach the safety of the jungle.

Now totally isolated, and under increasing attack from all sides by a vastly superior force, the surviving troops at the transport harbour had no option but to withdraw and seek refuge in the nearby swamps. Although seriously wounded, Captain Hamish Macdonald provided covering fire, remarking 'it's like shooting grouse on the moors', as the remainder crossed the road in small groups, taking the less seriously wounded with them. A total of 101 reached the safety of the swamps. The only casualty, the cook, was hit in the abdomen and fatally wounded. The other wounded, including the gallant Macdonald, were left to the mercy of the advancing Japanese.

CHAPTER 8

CUT OFF

Forward of Bakri, the situation at the 2/29th was deteriorating. The road had been cut again and a truck loaded with wounded strafed by an enemy plane, killing many of the occupants. The aircraft then dropped a bomb that exploded near the truck, killing troops who had taken cover in the nearby jungle and further injuring those still alive in the vehicle. Shortly afterwards, another bomber began circling. Its interest, however, lay elsewhere – the large, white and very conspicuous planter's bungalow, serving as Brigade HQ. There was a loud 'whumph' and the building disintegrated.

The wireless room took a direct hit, killing everyone inside and destroying the signals cyphers, vital for maintaining secure communications. All senior officers were either killed or badly wounded and the brigadier severely concussed. The carnage was hideous. The 2/29th's Lieutenant Ben Hackney, evacuated from the 2/29th's position with a bullet wound to his lower leg, was unfortunate enough to witness the aftermath.

> There were bodies lying about everywhere, many twisted in lifelessly grotesque positions, others as though comfortably asleep but dead also – parts of bodies strewn everywhere – portions of soldiers' stomachs hanging on limbs among the leaves of the trees – torn, bloodstained limbs scattered about with only a lump of bloody meat to indicate the body from which they were torn – just beside the road a naked waist with two twisted legs lay about two yards from a scarred bleeding head with a neck, half a chest and one arm – on the side of an ambulance the blood and pieces of flesh of a body that had been shattered to pieces – and the appalling sights were everywhere. There were some still alive but bent over, and others crawling, with every manner of injury.

The artillery's senior officer, Major William Julius, was in a critical condition and needed expert medical attention. To reach it, the Australians knew they must try to force the roadblock at their rear. However, two lorries crammed with wounded Indians, accompanied by a carrier, had already tried to break through and had come under heavy fire. The carrier had returned but the two trucks and their occupants were cut to ribbons by the heavy machine-guns. Nevertheless, one gunner willing to run the risk to help his CO was Max Fisher, who had evaded capture at Muar by hiding under the ferry ramp. Julius was placed on the back of a truck and, with a carrier escort, the little convoy set out on what was, literally, a do-or-die mission. Julius, Fisher and the carrier driver did not survive.

With Julius deceased and the Brigadier incapacitated by the bomb, the 2/19th's Charles Anderson assumed command of the brigade. His first task was to have his signal team transmit a report on the situation to General Bennett. Common sense dictated that the best option available would be to withdraw the 2/29th from its perilous position, but the lost Indians had not yet appeared and, unwilling to abandon them, Anderson decided to delay any withdrawal for the time being.

Despite mounting difficulties, Fred and his signallers were able to maintain communication within the battalion areas. When signal wires were cut, either by the enemy or by shells (fired by both sides), verbal orders were sent with runners and despatch riders. Communication with Bennett was possible only by wireless, and was the responsibility of six signallers operating in pairs from their Ford trucks – one each with 2/19 and 2/29 Battalions and the other with the artillery. Although the signal staff and their vehicles were under constant small-arms fire, they managed nevertheless to maintain contact through innovative repair work and replacing flat batteries with others salvaged from damaged motor vehicles.

While awaiting the arrival of the Indians, 2/19 Battalion had come under increasing pressure from the south and south-west. At 11 o'clock in the morning, B Company was heavily attacked by enemy troops advancing along the Parit Jawa road but they were driven off, suffering heavy losses. An hour later, the 2/29th reported it was under mortar and artillery fire and that the enemy had infiltrated with considerable strength between it and 2/19 Battalion.

At 3 pm, Japanese who had massed along the Parit Jawa road with heavy machine-guns attacked the 2/19th's B and A Companies. Despite several serious incursions, the Australians held them off, but they were kept under considerable pressure until nightfall, when the enemy withdrew. A determined attack on B Company's flank was also repulsed with the help of four carriers and 400 shells, fired from two three-inch mortars. A small battery of two-inch mortars, manned by a warrant officer, two pioneers and Padre Harold Wardale-Greenwood, who had removed his ecclesiastical insignia to 'praise the Lord and pass the ammunition', pumped out well-directed fire with devastating effect. It was estimated that over 300 Japanese were killed. The 2/19th's losses were 15 killed and 35 wounded.

Apart from a bomb dropped harmlessly from one of three planes constantly circling the area, it had been a reasonably quiet few hours at 2/29 Battalion, enabling the dead to be buried and slit trenches dug at the RAP as protection for 18 wounded men awaiting evacuation. At about 1.30 pm, the long-overdue Indian troops began emerging from the jungle on the battalion's right flank. Desperately thirsty, they stormed the water cart. Supplies were limited but some of the troops, because of religious dictates, insisted on drinking only from their hands, resulting in wastage and creating a near riot that was controlled only at pistol point by two senior officers and the 2/29th's doctor, Captain Victor Brand, who, on hearing the ruckus, had come from his nearby RAP.

By 2.15 pm the Indians, their thirst quenched and their hunger sated, were pronounced sufficiently fit to help the 2/29th break through to 2/19 Battalion. However, as the two forward companies moved along the road, shots rang out. Taking to the jungle and swamp on the northern side of the road, they managed to by-pass the Japanese and reached the 2/19th's perimeter at about 3 pm, with few casualties. As the 2/19th was under attack at the time, the new arrivals were sent back to Brigade HQ and ordered to form up for further

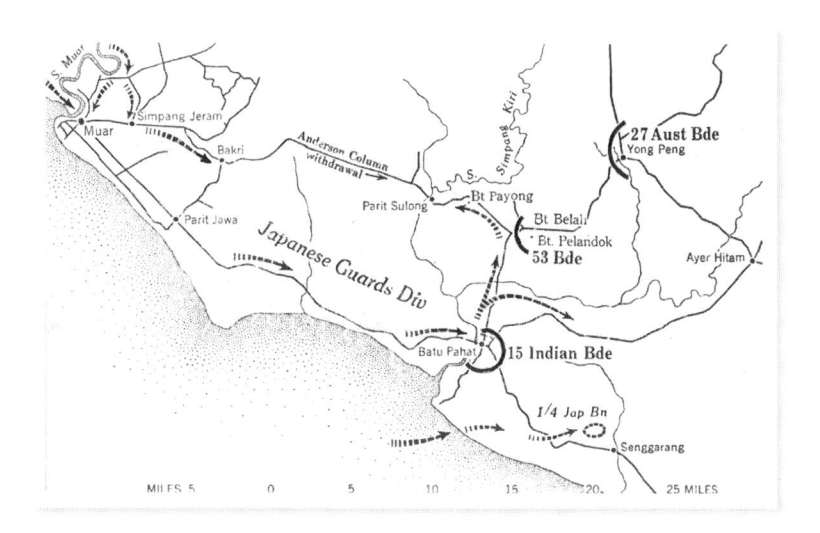

Japanese and Allied positions, Muar to Yong Peng.

action. As soon as their CO arrived with the remainder of their battalion, they would be sent to the aid of the beleaguered transport unit, from which mortar bombs could be heard exploding.

However, no more Indians appeared. On hearing the shots fired at the first two companies, their CO had gone forward to assess the situation. As he raised his head to peer over an earthen bank, a Japanese swordsman decapitated him. When another officer, who rushed to his aid, met a similar fate, the rest of the column turned tail and fled back towards the 2/29th position in a state of great disorder, only to be mown down by enemy machine-gunners and riflemen firing from the shelter of the rubber trees.

Not surprisingly, the survivors were severely rattled and in no way able to cope when, at 3.30 pm and after a concentrated aerial attack, two 5.9-inch howitzers suddenly opened up in an efficient and devastating 'box pattern' attack, their deadly accurate fire directed by spotter planes. As entire rows of rubber trees toppled, the Australian troops scrambled for the protection of their foxholes, but the Indians, who had not dug any, were panic stricken. Some piled in on top of the wounded, whom Brand and his team had placed in the newly dug trenches. Others ran around hysterically with chunks of flesh missing, or crouched behind rubber trees, only to have themselves and the tree explode to bits in a mass of liquid latex and body parts. In an effort to escape the terror, a number ran to the forward company area but it, too, came under methodical attack. Others found refuge under the RAP truck, where they clung, terrified, to the axles and chassis.

After an hour the shelling stopped, only to be replaced by concentrated mortar fire. Enemy machine-gunners, silly enough to try the old tactic of creeping up under cover of the barrage, were given a hot reception on the right flank. On the left, however, it took a determined counter-attack before the Japanese finally broke and ran.

As soon as the bombardment ceased, Brand's RAP was flooded with critically injured men requiring immediate evacuation. Several trucks, escorted by carriers, managed to reach Bakri but, when the carrier drivers arrived back at the RAP, their faces and necks peppered with steel splinters and torsos raked with metal fragments, it was obvious that any movement along the road was extremely hazardous. As RAP staff began loading the trucks with even more wounded, the vehicles were stormed by Indian troops frantic to get away, forcing Brand to once again produce his pistol. The situation at the aid post was now bordering on desperate, with wounded men lying all over the place and no hope, at least that Brand could see, of getting them out. Fearing that the Japanese might break though, he fixed a large Red Cross sign to a tree in the centre of the area where his wounded were concentrated, in the hope that they would not be attacked.

Although the situation was very grim, Anderson was left in no doubt that the 2/29th had no intention of giving up. Despite their truck coming under constant fire, the signallers had maintained the communication link with Fred at the 2/19th, operating by the light of a small torch throughout the previous night while the infantry repulsed enemy attacks and mortars exploded round them.

The 2/19th was also having problems of its own. Ray Snelling reported that, just after the Indians had arrived, the enemy had overrun one of his sections, leaving only one survivor. With no hope of reopening the road, and not enough men to shore up the forward positions, Anderson ordered all troops from the Parit Jawa and Muar roads to fall back to the east of the Bakri junction, thereby concentrating the battle to one narrow front. It was their only chance of delaying the Japanese and preventing them from reaching Yong Peng. If forced to make a further withdrawal, the Parit Sulong area, with its open swamplands along either side of the causeway, would be an excellent place to make a stand.

It was a decision Anderson had to make on his own. His report had been received at Bennett's HQ, but the answer, ordering him to destroy all non-essential equipment and

Colonel Anderson

pull back, was unintelligible and would remain so. The bomb that hit Brigade HQ had not only killed the intelligence officer, the signals officer and his staff, it had also destroyed all copies of the cipher used by 45 Brigade. Fred, at Anderson's HQ, was one of the few aware of the gravity of the situation.

With the signal wire to the 2/29th cut, Anderson had dispatched an armoured car with a message to Major Olliff, Robertson's replacement, to withdraw back to the 2/19th lines. Shortly afterwards the vehicle returned, reporting that the enemy had set up a machine-gun post on the south side of the road. However, the signallers somehow managed to restore communication, allowing Olliff to speak to Anderson. The conversation brought the stoic 2/29th officer no joy. As the 2/19th was under constant attack and could not get through to help them, the 2/29th must fight and cut its way back to Bakri. The only assistance Anderson could offer was covering fire from the artillery. Fred recorded:

> This was indeed a serious position, but as yet not irretrievable. But it meant that the 2/29th must withdraw into our perimeter. This they did, suffering severe losses, with only about one quarter of the battalion reaching our lines.

As Olliff was ordered to leave nothing behind that might be of use to the enemy, the mortar platoon fired off the remaining shells and smashed the sights on the mortars before dismantling and throwing away the various components. While other officers set fire to papers and maps, Brand and his RAP team removed bed rolls and other non-essential equipment from the three or four remaining trucks and utilities, and began loading the wounded on board. The Indians again tried to storm the vehicles, forcing Brand to once more draw his pistol.

Since the southern side of the road, now on the retreating battalion's right, was being raked constantly by machine-gun fire, the troops were forced to use a track running through the rubber plantation on the left (northern side) of the road and parallel to it. Being 1.5 metres below road level it offered good protection, apart from one section that passed through a patch of lalang grass, some 20 metres wide. As there was no cover, there was only one way to cross it – on the double. After waiting 15 minutes for the infantry to get clear, the transport was to follow, by which time the promised artillery barrage would have taken care of the roadblock.

With the wounded, numbering about 50, now on the trucks, the convoy moved onto the road, nose to tail. Olliff's truck was at the head of the column, with the signals' truck immediately behind. Behind the trucks carrying most of the wounded were the last three remaining carriers, whose crews had volunteered to form a rearguard, along with the anti-tankers and their guns. Also at the rear were Victor Brand and more wounded, packed into the RAP truck, its exterior protected by armoured steel plates scavenged from an anti-tank gun.

At Bakri, the gunners had put hundreds of trees to the axe to create a field of fire. The big guns were then dragged about 400 metres to the crest of a hill, in order for the shells to clear the ridge in front. At 6.20 pm the artillery began its barrage, the signal for the first of the 2/29th troops to start to move off, in single file and with fixed bayonets. In order to reach the track, some had had to walk over scores of dead and dying Indians.

All went well until the leading group reached the lalang patch. As the troops streaked across it, enemy machine-guns positioned either side of the road opened fire, killing two officers and several men. The next group, which was moving along the right-hand side of the road, waiting to cross, immediately took cover. Accompanied by an officer and four men, Olliff left his truck and crept forward, beyond a slight bend in the cutting, to assess the situation. They could see nothing – the machine guns were cunningly sited inside two abandoned brick houses and the tree snipers were well concealed. Olliff was deciding what to do next when the machine guns once again opened up, killing one of his men. The others hurled themselves into an overgrown drainage ditch, a few metres away to the right. They began crawling towards the bend but, before they could reach it, the entire trench was raked by a long burst of fire, killing three outright and mortally wounding another. Olliff, who had four fingers on his left hand shot off, was still looking at it in astonishment when another burst of fire ripped through his back, killing him.

Other brave souls, having identified the enemy machine-gun positions, tried to attack, but each attempt was met with even more intense fire, resulting in further casualties. A small group of men managed to reach a shed, about 50 metres from one of the houses, where they holed up, cursing the destruction of the battalion's mortars. An infantry major who was with them called for volunteers to mount a bayonet charge. Met with stunned silence at this suicidal proposal, he 'volunteered' a corporal and three other ranks (ORs) to carry it out. All went to their inevitable deaths in a hail of fire, accompanied by a burst of wild shouting from the Japanese.

Meanwhile, another group was still pinned down on the right side of the road, unsure of what to do next. Their battalion commander was dead, along with at least four other officers and a number of ORs, and there was no sign of the rest of the battalion, supposedly following behind. Unable to move forward, word was passed from man to man to move across the road and shelter in the surrounding jungle. As they moved off, a sergeant was shot and wounded. A second bullet finished him off. At least five others who sprinted from the shed were also cut down before they reached the safety of the jungle.

Back at Bakri, where the 2/19th's forward company had fought off a number of enemy probes, casualties were mounting. At 7.15 pm the immediate area had been reported free of enemy troops, but five minutes later two of the Indian troops at the rear began firing at nothing. Panic broke out as others ran around in the dark, shooting indiscriminately. In their confusion, they fired not only at each other but at trucks laden with the wounded, causing further injuries. Although Anderson and another officer shouted to them to stop firing and the infantrymen took more direct action by tackling the Indians and knocking them out, it took 20 minutes before order was restored. All hope of rescuing Newton's men had now been abandoned. The Indians who had arrived were far too jumpy, and all of 2/19 Battalion's reserves – the pioneer platoon and those at HQ, including Fred and his signallers – were already deployed.

Shortly afterwards, reports were received that the enemy had cut the road between the battalion's night perimeter and Snelling's forward company. To preclude any possibility of accidentally shooting the retreating 2/29th, a platoon was ordered to patrol down the road, using bayonets only.

At about 8 pm they came into contact with the first of 45 troops who had managed to cross the lalang patch. The patrol escorted them to Snelling, but abandoned a plan to return in search of others when intense firing came from the 2/29th's position. Although contact was lost, the remainder succeeded in reaching safety half an hour later. At about the same time, two other groups also turned up. Skirting the roadblock area, they had headed to Bakri by an alternate escape route – the track made by the Indians who had bypassed the road block position earlier in the day. Captain Maher, aged 31 and now the most senior of the 2/29th's officers, assumed command of what was left of the battalion – seven officers and 190 men. Although the 2/19th waited until midnight before pulling out, there was no sign of Brand, the wounded or others with him.

While the survivors from the 2/29th who had reached the 2/19th lines waited with growing anxiety for the rest of the battalion to appear, those who had not made it past the road block were engaging in a new struggle for survival.

Unaware that a good number of troops had taken to the jungle, the Australian artillerymen had opened up with their 25 pounders. Several 2/29th men were attempting to skirt the enemy machine guns when a shell exploded, hurling them to the ground. Two were killed outright and several others injured. Before the rest could get to their feet, another tremendous blast erupted, cutting an Indian soldier in half and lifting others bodily into the air in a shower of mud and grass. Staggering to their feet, the survivors stumbled towards the swamp where they joined a number of others. There were some very serious casualties, but fortunately the line of fire moved away and no further shells fell.

It was soon pitch dark. By now there were 150 Australians and about 50 Indians in the leech-infested swamp. As the only way out was through the swamp, the officers announced that anyone who could not walk would have to be left behind. Some of the seriously wounded, aware that they would be bayonetted by the Japanese, asked to be given a coup de grace and were shot through the heart with a pistol. Others committed suicide. Some, who begged not to be left, were helped along by their mates.

Moving deeper into the swamp, the troops formed a long line, each man clinging to the one in front. However, with so many hidden roots and overhanging branches it was hard to keep a footing. Hearing the inevitable splashes as one after another tumbled into the water, as well as the cries and moans of the wounded, the Japanese machine-guns fired from the edge of the swamp, the bullets tearing through the foliage just above the fugitives' heads. The wounded tried hard to stifle their cries, but for those who were badly wounded it was impossible. Guided by their groans, the enemy laid on a mortar barrage but fortunately their aim was off.

Shortly before midnight, the party reached a stream where an Australian corporal, suffering from a terrible wound to the abdomen, begged his mate to shoot him. There was the sound of a rifle bolt being drawn back, followed by a single shot and a slight ripple, as the body was lowered into the water.

After finding a place shallow enough to cross, the column moved into the stream, each man blindly following the fellow ahead. On the far side, the water gave way to mud and slush and then, finally, relatively dry ground and long lalang grass. Using a compass, they continued on, hoping to link up with the main force at Bakri. There was no doubt where the battle was concentrated. The light from parachute flares and the sound of heavy fighting revealed that the main thrust was ahead of them, and to the right.

In the early hours of the morning of 20 January, the officers called a halt in a rubber plantation. Everyone was sopping wet. They were also very cold, so all were ready to move off again by 5.30 am. Trudging in an easterly direction, the party encountered more jungle and swamp, some of it thigh deep in mud, before reaching a stream. They waded knee deep along it for the next three hours, moving under cover of the overhanging jungle whenever enemy planes, clearly searching for them, came into view. Finally, when the jungle gave way to rubber plantations, they left the river and moved between the lines of trees in single file, along the pads worn by the bare feet of the rubber-tappers.

Around mid-morning they were following one of the many plantation tracks when they spotted three khaki-clad figures just ahead of them. For a heart-stopping few seconds they thought it was the enemy, until someone recognised one of the men – the despatch rider who had mistakenly ridden his motor bike into the Japanese lines while escorting the ration truck from Bakri. Presumed to be dead, as he had not been seen since, he was obviously very much alive and was eager to tell the tale of his miraculous survival.

> Well, I'm burning down the road, you see, and I know the mess truck is right behind me, and I'm thinking about what's on the menu, what's for tea. I'm feeling pretty peckish, I suppose, and not concentrating too well. Then I come around this bend and I think, 'I don't remember this bit', but then, with all this rubber, the whole bloody place looks exactly the same from one end of the road to the next, so on I go. But then I suddenly see a bunch of blokes in khaki uniforms on the side of the road ahead of me. I thought, that's not our uniform, it's not the Brits or the bloody Indians. Shit! I thought, and I'm still riding along – it's the f...ing Japs!

> Anyway, I'm just hitting the flamin' brakes as hard as I can and they're starting to open up on me with everything they've got, when suddenly there's one of these side roads right beside me on the right. I swing the bike in and bore off up the road hell-for-leather. Not a scratch. Just as well they're bloody lousy shots.

> Well, I travelled for a while on the bike, but the road didn't lead anywhere. It was one of those roads that goes round and round in a big circle for the rubber tappers. I knew roughly the direction I should be going, but the road wouldn't take me there. I tried riding through the rubber for a while, but I kept getting stuck in the ditches and eventually had to leave the bike. Then I met a Chinese bloke who gave me a meal and put me up for the night. In the morning he gave me directions for getting back to our own lines, but I could hear all sorts of fighting going on in the distance so I tried to skirt around to come into the battalion from behind, but wherever I went there seemed to be Japanese. A couple of times I nearly got caught. Anyway, I just kept going towards where I thought I'd meet up with our own forces – and here I am.

The column continued along the track, as it appeared to be going more or less in the right direction. However, when six Chinese on bicycles spotted them and immediately pedalled off in the opposite direction, they re-entered the rubber and made towards a jungle-clad mountain ridge, slightly further to the north. At the edge of the jungle, they came across two abandoned Indian Army trucks, yielding rifles, Tommy guns and grenades, as well as flour and tinned pineapple which, when added to ration tins of bully beef, provided their first meal in two days. It wasn't much – one tin of bully beef between eight men and two biscuits, and a piece of pineapple each. The wounded were also allowed a swig of whisky, confiscated from a drunken rubber tapper earlier in the day. Somewhat refreshed, especially those who had had a chance to wash their feet and change their filthy socks, they continued for another half-hour or so, stopping for the night just inside the jungle's edge.

Although all were dog-tired, it was a miserable night. Drinking water was scarce and mosquitoes voracious. To make matters worse, there were tensions between the seven Australian officers; the officers and the rank and file; and the Australians and the Indians.

The AIF branded the latter as 'useless', while their three British officers, who lit fires after dark and had a most cavalier attitude towards the enemy, were pronounced 'most irresponsible'. After a fitful night, at six the next morning they were on the move again, travelling north-east towards Parit Sulong, all hope of reaching Bakri long since abandoned.

In spite of this, spirits were generally high, due in no small part to an old Chinese woodcutter, who assured them that the Japanese were far away, and then treated everyone to a meal of hot rice, flavoured with butter, sugar and chunks of left-over pineapple. From his hut, a rough track led cross-country to Parit Sulong, but, as it was impossible for four of the wounded to make such a journey, they were left behind in his care.

Meanwhile, Victor Brand and his party of wounded were also heading towards Parit Sulong. After Olliff and the infantry had moved forward to try to break through to the 2/19th, Brand and the remainder of the convoy had waited for word that the road was clear. However, as time went on and no-one appeared, not even the Japanese, Brand had sent the heavy water tanker ahead to assess the situation. Rounding the bend, it ran into a hail of automatic fire before careering into a deep monsoon drain.

By this time, it was getting dark, so dark that the Indian drivers had turned on their headlights. Refusing all requests, then direct orders, to turn them off, Brand and an anti-tanker resolved the impasse by walking along the column and smashing every light with their rifle butts. Believing that the Japanese might allow the severely wounded to be carried past the roadblock, Brand urged the Indian troops to pick up their wounded and follow him. They refused point blank. Realising that without their assistance he did not have

Above: Route taken by the 2/29th through the swamp.
Right: Victor Brand

enough fit men to do the job, he sent three carriers to try to force a way through, but only one managed to run the gauntlet of concentrated fire. With no carriers left and only about 25 exhausted riflemen to offer any kind of defence, Brand concluded that his party had no option but to await the arrival of the main Japanese force and surrender.

However, as he stood behind the rear truck, hoping that the Red Cross sign he held would protect his wounded, two of his men convinced him that the walking wounded should try to make a break through the jungle. As he assembled the few who could walk at the edge of the jungle-covered swamp, shots rang out from their rear, forcing them to scatter and take to the swamp. Reaching a patch of jungle, Brand came across two signallers with several of the wounded. Where the others were, no one had any idea.

One of the wounded volunteered to lead them around the roadblock, using the stars to steer in the right direction. They headed north first, then north-east through knee-deep water, but the foliage was so dense that, before long, the wounded man's strength gave out. Brand now took the lead, using the weight of his body to bulldoze a way through the growth and then trample it flat with his boots to make a track for the others. The screams and yells they could hear coming from the road behind them meant only one thing – the Japanese had reached the wounded in the trucks and were taking no prisoners.

After spending some hours forcing their way through the swamp, they stumbled, literally, onto an atap platform, constructed by a Malay family as a refuge. Nearby was a tiny hillock, with just enough room for the men to lie down out of the water. However, although they were all bone weary, hordes of mosquitoes made sleep impossible.

The next morning, 20 January, following directions supplied by the Malay family, they followed a nearby waterway, which they hoped would lead them to safety. About an hour after leaving the hillock, they met a party of Indian troops and four men from the 2/29th, led by a young English officer, who had a map.

The two groups travelled together to the edge of the jungle but, as the Indians ran around in the open every time a plane came over, Brand decided they were a liability and parted company. When they met up again some hours later, he discovered that all but one of the 20 men, who had fled into the swamp with him initially, had joined the other party. While trying to figure out the best way to go from the map, a Malay man showed them a floating path made of saplings that led through the swamp to the Parit Sulong road.

Ten kilometres and many tedious hours later they emerged from the mud and slush, just as night fell. A cautious reconnaissance revealed that there was no sign of the enemy, so they crossed the road to seek refuge for the night at the rear of an empty house. They had only just settled down to sleep when they were woken by the sound of heavy vehicles moving along the road towards them. While the others remained hidden, two of the able bodied, armed with hand grenades, waited tensely beside the road as the vehicles, accompanied by the sound of tramping feet, drew closer. They were fearing the worst when, to their utter astonishment, they heard a voice in an undeniably Australian accent proclaim, 'I'll have to drop out soon for a piss'.

He was a soldier from 2/19 Battalion. They had found Anderson and his men.

CHAPTER 9
THE RETREAT

While Brand and his party had been slogging their way through the swamps on the evening of 19 January, trying to outflank the Japanese, Colonel Anderson was finalising plans to pull his force back towards Parit Sulong. In the hope of opening up communications with Bennett, at 6 pm he signalled:

> Situation very grave. Will need maximum assistance to extricate force. Haxo [code name for the 2/29th] were mauled. Enemy road block valley 7 miles. Maximum air support throughout area essential.

Bennett received and understood the message but, as night fell, wireless transmission failed completely, putting an end to further communication. However, Bennett immediately contacted Malaya Command with a request for air support, confident that the aircraft would be provided. Although the infantry and ground troops had seen precious little of either the RAF or RAAF, the planes that were left were still taking to the skies, despite being few in number and vastly inferior to enemy aircraft.

That morning four Glen Martins and five Wirraways, crewed by Australians and New Zealanders, had attacked enemy headquarters, troop concentrations and motor transport at Muar. The eight obsolete RAAF Brewster Buffaloes escorting them were assailed by 15 Zeros. One of the Brewsters, all the Glen Martins and one Wirraway were shot down. Although outgunned, the Brewsters accounted for three enemy fighters.

Back at Anderson's HQ at Bakri, Fred was under no illusion about the seriousness of their situation.

> A heavy battle was in progress towards our B Echelon and we were aware that the Japanese had completely surrounded us, our only hope being that the force was not in sufficient numbers to stop our withdrawal to Parit Sulong, where British troops from the Norfolk Regiment held the bridge.

At midnight, with communications still cut to Bennett's HQ, and with the improbability of anymore 2/29th men breaking through, Anderson and his senior officers began making preparations to pull out at first light. The distance from Bakri Crossroads to the Parit Sulong bridge was about 15 miles (24 kilometres). Although the first three miles passed through jungle and rubber plantations and provided good cover, at mile 97 the terrain changed, revealing extensive rice fields backed by deep swampland. From mile 95, troops on the narrow causeway separating the rice fields would be at the complete mercy of enemy aircraft. The only hope of making it across this section was under cover of darkness, so it was imperative that they reached the 97-mile peg before nightfall. Once across the causeway it was only another four miles to the Norfolks guarding the Parit Sulong bridge and, from there, only a relatively short distance to Allied troops holding the Bukit Pelandok defile. Unbeknown to Anderson, his plan was fatally flawed. The Japanese were now in control of the road between Parit Sulong and Yong Peng, cutting off the Australians' only line of retreat.

The British had run into trouble on 19 January, when a company of Norfolks defending Bukit Pelandok was taken by surprise by Japanese advancing along the coast road from Muar. Although a second company managed to retain its position on a hill on the other side of the road, the Japanese occupied the lower slopes. Later that afternoon, British troops entered the jungle in an attempt to retake Pelandok, but found the going extremely tough and withdrew.

Only too aware that, if Anderson and his column were to survive, the road must be retaken, the British brigade commander ordered a counter-attack. At 4 o'clock in the morning of the 20th, two companies of Indian troops set off for Bukit Belah. At the same time, another company moved off to occupy a position about 500 metres further north. Once the Indian troops were in position, they were to provide covering fire to allow the Norfolks to recapture Bukit Pelandok and so regain control of the road.

Although the Indians sent to occupy the northerly position did so unopposed, disaster struck. The Norfolks atop Bukit Belah, believing they were enemy troops, opened fire. This appalling mistake had only just been realised when grenades burst further along the ridge. Assuming it was friendly fire, the Indians' CO called a halt. The enemy then attacked, killing him and a considerable number of others and prompting the rest to flee. With insufficient men left for a counterattack, any further action was postponed until the next day, pending the arrival of artillery support.

The situation further deteriorated when the Norfolks guarding the bridge at Parit Sulong, having received no rations for two days, concluded that they had been cut off. Abandoning their posts, they set off cross-country for Batu Pahat. As they moved out, the Japanese moved in.

Oblivious to the situation developing along the Yong Peng road, Anderson's troops at Bakri prepared to withdraw. All were suffering from severe sleep deprivation, as the enemy's artillery, which wiped out one 25-pounder and four gunners, had continued to fire throughout the night. As the shells rained down, mechanics worked non-stop, carrying out repairs to carriers and trucks and permanently disabling any beyond salvation. With artillery and mortar stocks running low, ordnance men distributed all available ammunition, taking particular care that the advance and rear guards had sufficient supplies for what was expected to be a difficult retreat.

At 4.30 am, the order came to destroy all captured enemy material and ditch all non-essential gear to make room in the trucks for the large number of casualties. With Victor Brand and his entire RAP missing, his counterpart at the 2/19th, Lloyd Cahill, assumed responsibility for organising the evacuation of all the wounded. He estimated that there were 50–60 trucks, with 6–10 wounded in each. He had only a few field dressings, so when they ran out of bandages, he tore up clothing, some of it taken from those killed in action. Morphine supplies were all but exhausted, but the wounded were comforted with the judicious administration of a nip or two of South African brandy from a supply of

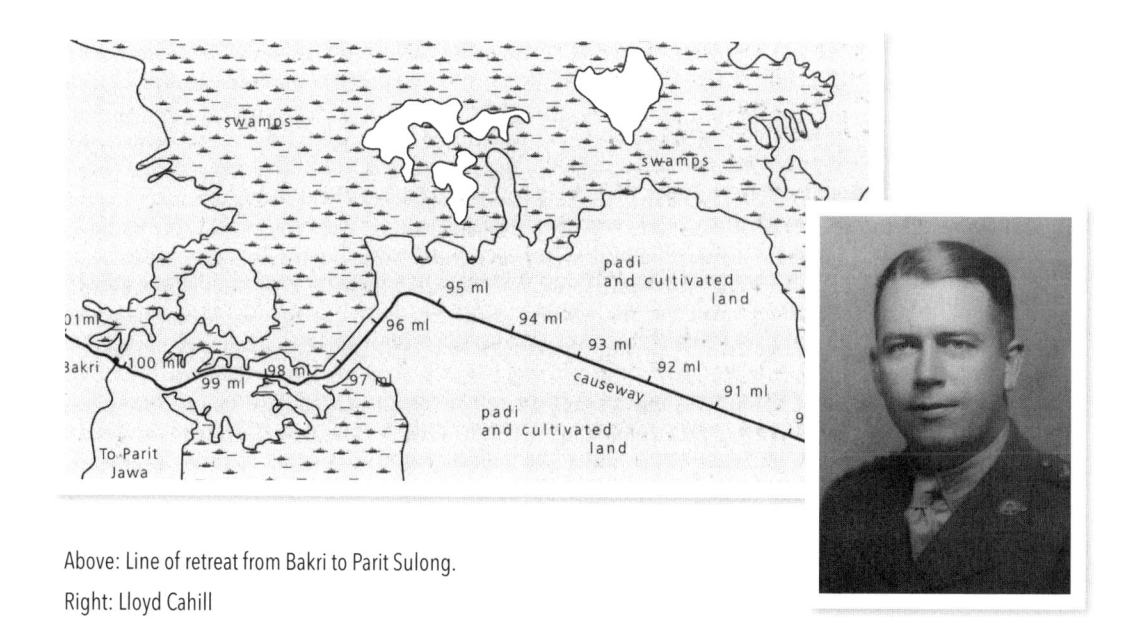

Above: Line of retreat from Bakri to Parit Sulong.
Right: Lloyd Cahill

144 bottles that one of Cahill's men had discovered, stacked in 12 cases in an abandoned building at Jemaluang. As dawn and the time of departure approached, the dead were hurriedly buried in graves dug during the night by the indefatigable Padre Wardale-Greenwood and the 2/19th's pioneer platoon.

With so many of the 2/29th and the Indian troops dead or missing, the force was rearranged into a scratch infantry battalion of five rifle companies, with two Indian attachments. At 7 am the 2/19th's B Company moved off with a section of carriers and two British anti-tank guns. The main body, headed by Fred's Battalion HQ, came next. Then followed a troop of artillerymen, the 2/19th's mortar and pioneer platoons, another section of carriers and the trucks carrying the seriously injured, with the walking wounded clinging to the tail-boards, running boards, cabin roofs and mudguards. Another section of carriers and the two armoured cars came next, with Snelling's men, held in reserve, following. The Indians were positioned on the transports' flanks. At the very end was the rear guard, composed of 2/19th troops, with a section of artillery and anti-tankers to act as 'stiffeners'.

Along each side of the column, the infantrymen fanned out through the rubber, rifles outstretched and bayonets pointing slightly downwards. One group moved in line with the main body to provide an outer flank on the right, with another on the left.

There was no opposition as the column moved off, past Brigade HQ where corpses still lay among the debris. Nearby, lying beneath a tree, was Stanley's master, but of the little monkey there was no sign. He had taken to the jungle in fright. However, when the column and the pursuing Japanese had moved on and all was quiet, he descended from his hiding place. Seeing his master lying asleep beneath the tree, he tugged his hair to wake him up, but there was no response. Chattering and bewildered, he circled the prone figure. He was reaching out to touch the battered face when a movement startled him and he scampered up the tree. Ten Japanese soldiers, leading an Australian prisoner, came into sight. With the battle now over, the Japanese were searching the bodies of the enemy dead.

As they began rifling through the pockets of the recumbent figure at the foot of the tree, a small tornado came at them, biting and scratching, defending to the last the man who had cared for him for so long. It only took one hefty swipe with a rifle butt and Stanley, too, lay dead.

Unaware that their beloved mascot was in the nearby jungle, keeping vigil over their dead comrade, Fred and the men of the 2/19th had moved on. At 8 am, shortly after leaving the Brigade HQ area, the advance troops of the Anderson column met a wounded carrier driver. While scouting the road ahead, he had been shot by Japanese dug in amongst the rubber at the 99-mile roadblock, where the shattered bodies of Julius and others were scattered among bullet-riddled vehicles.

Armed with machine guns and with swamps bordering both sides of the road, the enemy had complete command of the position. As the Australians approached, the Japanese opened up from the left, killing the two forward scouts and wounding an officer. The men on the right attacked vigorously but, although supported by the artillery, machine gunners and carriers, who poured fire into the Japanese position from 100 metres away, they were unable to penetrate any closer than 50 metres. One platoon, working its way round to the left, fixed bayonets and charged. Four attackers reached the Japanese trenches, but lost their lives in the attempt.

With both forward platoons pinned down, the column was bunched up along the road and extremely vulnerable to air attack. At 8.30, as communication had been restored, Anderson signalled Bennett that he was trying to force the roadblock. Fifteen minutes later, he ordered the battalion's A Company to create a diversion by moving through the swamp in an arc on the right and mounting a rapid attack on the Japanese flank. As the men were very tense, he urged them to sing 'Waltzing Matilda' – an esoteric bush ballad so quintessentially Australian that it would, in later years, be adopted as the nation's 'unofficial' National Anthem.

Never had words about a sheep-stealing, suicidal itinerant swagman been sung with more enthusiasm or patriotic fervour. Employed purely as a morale booster, it certainly impressed the Japanese who, although they were prone to scream and yell as they went into battle, had never before encountered troops who sang. Passing through the swamp,

Bayonet charge through the rubber (Murray Griffin)

the Australians penetrated the enemy's thinly held flank on the south side of the road to emerge onto the open ground at Newton's now abandoned harbourage. There, in fierce hand-to-hand combat, the choristers killed at least a dozen enemy soldiers and routed the rest. They then moved behind the Japanese strongpoint, preventing any withdrawal and enabling them to fire into the heart of the enemy ranks.

An answer from Bennett to Anderson's message about forcing the roadblock came at 9 am, but was again in cipher and unintelligible. By this time, Japanese artillery had opened up from the rear and two machine guns were again preventing any advance. At 9.30, Anderson signaled:

> Continuous air support required. Bomb Bakri. Recce road [from the air] east of MS [mile stone] 97 and submit report. Machine-gun both sides of the road.

In an effort to stall the enemy advancing from the rear, Anderson now ordered the artillery to shell Bakri village, composed largely of two-storey wooden shop-houses. It was hoped that the resulting conflagration would be of sufficient size to prevent tanks advancing and create a smoke screen, hindering further observation. The unfortunate locals, unaware of the reasons behind this desperate action, believed the Australians had deliberately destroyed their village.

Another hour passed. Unable, because of the proximity of his forward troops, to bring artillery fire to bear on the enemy's machine guns, Anderson concluded that a determined attack would have to be made on the two machine guns causing them trouble. While the men of A Company had been encircling the enemy, singing at the top of their voices, another group had crossed the road and attacked, only to run into another fusillade. The battalion's youngest soldier, Charles 'Chick' Warden, aged just 16, was about to jump over a rotten log when he saw a Japanese soldier hiding under a small camouflage net on the other side. Warden shot him, but another Japanese manning a light machine gun took out the man on Warden's right. Warden was next on the machine-gunner's list but, in his haste to turn the weapon, the tripod toppled, giving the Australian the split-second advantage he needed to fire first. Taking refuge behind the log, he took a quick look over the top. Less than two metres away were a pair of legs and a backside. After shooting the owner in the rear end, Warden came face to face with another Japanese, lying down beside a rubber tree about four metres away. Both fired simultaneously. As Warden pulled the trigger, a bullet passed through his left shoulder, knocking him off balance. Using his good arm, he tossed a grenade before going to ground, as grenades lobbed by another Australian, about three

The village at Bakri Crossroads, destroyed by the shelling.

metres to the rear, found their mark. As Warden lay hugging the earth unable to move, his dead and fatally wounded mates on either side of him, he realised that the entire action had taken all of two minutes. Looking up, he was startled to see Colonel Anderson, only a short distance away.

The CO had joined the most forward platoon to lead the main assault. He had always put great store in hand grenades, so much so that he was in the habit of ditching his binoculars and carrying three or four Mills bombs in the empty case. Creeping forward with Donnelly, his bodyguard, he tossed a couple at one of two machine-gun nests. At the sound of the explosions, a Japanese manning the other gun poked his head up from the butt of a nearby tree. Anderson, armed with a pistol, didn't miss. Yelling 'Mine, Donnelly', he shot a second machine-gunner through the head. With the CO leading, the rest of the platoon charged. At the same time B Company, which had wiped out the Japanese at the transport harbour, burst in from the left side of the road.

The Australians attacking the enemy machine guns had killed 30 of the enemy, with a loss of 15 men and 20 wounded. Some had fallen victim to tree snipers. However, there was no time for the teenage Warden to grieve for his mates. Once a field dressing had been slapped onto his wounded shoulder, he returned to his platoon.

The column moved off again at 11 am, with A Company taking over as the advance guard. In a desperate effort to make sense of Bennett's replies, Anderson ordered Fred's signallers to transmit, in clear language:

> Your signals indecipherable. Request use transposition cipher using Christian and Surnames of IO [Intelligence Officer, Stuart Burt]. Gymo [2/19 Battalion's code-word] as keyword.

Bennett refused. Anderson insisted and, at 12.30 pm, was at last able to decipher the reply, 'Withdraw on Yong Peng'.

Passing by the transport harbour, the column saw evidence of a grim and bloody battle, with wrecked and twisted vehicles lying in bomb craters and bloated corpses turning black under the fierce tropical sun. Most of the dead were Japanese. Fred and the others looked around and located a few of their comrades, but rapid decomposition had set in, making visual identification difficult. Fred hoped that the lack of bodies meant the others had made good their escape. In one of the trucks, they found one man still alive, along with an Indian army officer who had been cut off from his unit and had wandered into the position. Also, amazingly, there were some much-needed supplies in the ration and ammunition trucks.

There was no sign of Captain Macdonald. It would not be until after the war ended that his beheaded remains would be found, far away on the other side of the river at Muar, where he and others captured were executed.

Warden described the battleground simply as 'a mess'. However, Gunner Russell Braddon recorded it was

> a series of violent, desolate scenes – starred windscreens; the dead crews; the clenched fist which protruded through the glass of a driver's window; the sweet stench. In silence, we collected the few tins of food that the attacking Japanese had not carried off. I moved a leg off a case of bully beef and tried not to notice that it belonged to the most cheerful driver in the regiment. We broke open the cases and carted the contents out

to our faithful infantry. Ten minutes later the whole of our convoy had passed the scene, rolling quietly downhill so that even the harsh grinding of Marmon Harringtons in low gear was, for once, subdued. And as the first truck reached the bottom of the long slope, the fierce yammering of a machine-gun broke out.

The yammering Braddon heard came from a roadblock near the 98-mile peg. About 400 metres east of the transport harbourage, where the swamp again encroached upon the road, was some high ground. About 70 metres beyond, and just around a slight bend, A Company had encountered the first of two very substantial road blocks – a barrier of felled trees, interlaced with two of Newton's trucks and the water tender. Two heavy machine-guns guarded the approach, with at least another four further back on either side of the road. Defended by at least two companies of well-entrenched troops, the site was well chosen – only about 500 metres wide, with heavily-treed swamps on either flank, and a piece of low, swampy ground protecting the left approach.

Deployed on the right side of the road, there was no room for the 2/19th's forward platoon to manoeuvre, at all, and no cover. Its leading scout was killed and the rest were pinned down. The men fought grimly, but could make no progress.

A platoon from the 2/29th was despatched into the jungle on the left to test the enemy's strength, but went off course. A platoon from the 2/19th, sent in after them, reached the position and, as soon as they opened fire, another platoon from 2/29 Battalion moved through the swamp on the left. When they were about 60 metres short of the guns, they attacked, singing Waltzing Matilda as the enemy machine-gunners mowed them down. As the survivors pulled back, another platoon assaulted the enemy from the rear. Hopelessly outnumbered, this small force lost 23 of its 42 men. The remainder, unable to rejoin the main body, took to the jungle.

In the meantime, a company from the 2/19th that had moved up on the left could make no headway in the swampy conditions, while the rearguard reported that it, too, was being strongly harassed. There were just five hours of daylight left. With Anderson unwilling to commit his reserve troops and the rear under threat, the forward troops would have to stand fast without further reinforcement.

Fred recalled:

Long and bitter was the struggle. We were no longer a unit with different sections, each doing a special job; we were a unit with every man a fighter irrespective of his training. Signallers conducted bayonet charges or wielded axes to cut the obstructing trees the Japs had fallen to form the roadblocks, while stretcher bearers hurled hand grenades at the entrenched enemy.

At about 2 pm, enemy artillery began shelling the tightly bunched transports from the rear, causing further casualties and setting fire to several trucks, which the hard-pressed defenders had to extinguish. Cahill and the stretcher bearers moved constantly up and down the line, but had nothing to offer the wounded in the way of relief, other than the South African brandy, which Cahill also added to the water bottles of exhausted combat troops, to give them a lift.

For the wounded, helpless in the back of the trucks and fretting over their inability to assist in the fighting, the journey was nerve wracking. Onward for a minute; halt for 20; on again for another two minutes; halt once more for 30, and so on. Even when progress was made, it was excruciatingly slow – just crawling along, dodging abandoned vehicles and detouring around felled trees, used as temporary road blocks or tossed onto the road by bomb blasts. With the situation deteriorating, Anderson signalled Bennett 'Who holds Parit Sulong Batu Pahat Yong Peng'. There was no reply.

The 2/29th's Ben Hackney, propped up in the back of a utility truck with his wounded mate Hugh Tibbits, recorded:

> During each halt, more wounded fellows would be brought in and placed in the vehicles; sometimes lifeless looking bundles being carried by their mates, others being helped along. Each time a few words as to how it happened, and always whilst they were doing a job, somewhere, perhaps in front, or along the sides, or in the rear, as all the time the enemy surrounded this ferocious little force.
>
> As time went on, the trucks became closer and closer, with the Japs closing in in ever increasing numbers, and their fire becoming heavier and heavier; every little while a barrage of shells, some dropping along the sides of the road, very few on the road and many in the rubber nearby; bursts of machine gun fire which seemed to come from only a short distance away; overhead always circling were enemy aircraft which often added their lot, by either bombs or machine guns, to the efforts of their ground forces.
>
> Just after one particularly heavy attack, I produced a flask I had been carrying all the time. It had been given to me full before leaving Australia and had not been touched. I passed it to Hugh saying something about keeping some of it until things got hot again. Of all the things I had been given, I had only a few with me now – a wallet, a pen, two watches, a flask, a pair of binoculars and a pistol. God knows what had happened to the rest.
>
> Very often, a bullet or splinter would find its way to our truck, thudding often against some piece of metal, or tearing a hole in the sides or cabin. On one occasion, a burst of machine gun bullets tore a line of holes along the side of the vehicle. I heard a peculiar grunt beside me, and looking round saw that the poor fellow sitting there, already wounded badly, had been killed. His body slumped forward, revealing a fresh blood patch where the bullet had entered his back.
>
> After each halt, more vehicles would be passed, some perhaps previously abandoned, others shattered to pieces and rendered useless by a recent shell or bomb landing nearby; sometimes the remains of a road block, the branches of the trees scraping the side of the truck as it passed through; and often trees that had been blown down had to be removed to allow passage.
>
> One felt helpless and useless under those conditions and, knowing also that we were an impediment to the others, far from improved our feelings. Just lying there, unable to do anything, not even scramble out of the truck when the shells were coming over, to seek perhaps some shelter in a nearby drain; sometimes fellows bringing in wounded and telling of the tremendous odds against which they were relentlessly hitting back – the more Japs they killed, the more seemed to be coming in to take their place – and still one was unable to do anything to help them.

At 3.30 pm, when the Japanese stepped up their attack on the convoy's rear, some of the demoralised Indians, who had become difficult to control, disappeared into the undergrowth. Weakened by their loss, the rear guard fell back, abandoning the last four vehicles. However, the Brigadier, now recovered from his concussion, rallied the remainder of his men and led them in a coordinated attack. With members of the 2/29th and the help of the artillery, they drove the enemy back and recovered the vehicles, but the attack cost the Brigadier his life.

At the front of the column, where the forward troops had encountered yet another road block, mortars on either side of the road opened up in a ten-minute, rapid-fire barrage. As infantrymen pinned down near the enemy machine-guns yelled ranging instructions to the mortar men, four carriers provided support by firing from atop a small knoll over the heads of infantry, while artillerymen weighed in, armed with rifles, bayonets and axes.

In response to Anderson's request for air support, at around 4.30 pm RAF planes finally arrived, only to create further casualties by dropping bombs on the convoy. The excuse proffered later by Malaya Command for this appalling error was that, owing to the scarcity of information regarding the exact location, the pilots had difficulty in defining an accurate bombing line.

It was now only two hours until dark – two hours in which to push through to the all-important mile 97. The 2/19th's infantry was now ordered to make a determined attack on the enemy's left flank to test the efficacy of the mortar fire. However, as they waited to advance, they were shelled and several men were hit, so Anderson decided to bring his reserves into the attack – Ray Snelling's company, three of Fred's signallers and some Indians who had attached themselves to the unit. Anderson had entertained thoughts of leading the attack himself, but his 2IC's 'No bloody fear' persuaded him it was not a good idea. However, he was able to address the men, who moved off at 5.30, cheering and in excellent spirits. Taking advantage of the smoke-screen caused by the mortars, the infantrymen, led by Snelling, charged.

> We started off, recalled Signaller Roly Dean, at a gentle trot, and somebody started singing Waltzing Matilda. We all joined in. Our band of Indians who firmly joined in this charge were a motley crew, many without rifles, but as we picked up speed and started to yell they joined in the yelling. They had the most bloodthirsty yell I have ever heard; it was like all banshees out of hell had been let loose.
>
> Altogether we covered about 750 yards. At one stage I was running on the side of a ditch and it seemed a good idea to drop into the ditch, which I did, landing on my haunches. Just as I did there was a burst of machine-gun fire where I had been a second or so before. 'Missed, you bloody bastard', I said, as I continued to run. I was running flat out when there was a burst of machine-gun fire just in front of me. I could not stop. Fortunately, it was no more than knee high, so I leapt into the air as high as I could, and went over the top of it. Fortunately, neither of my two offsiders was hurt. Rocky Ned [the company sergeant major and a wheat lumper in civilian life] skewered one Jap on his bayonet, and tossed him over his shoulder like a sheaf of wheat … Old habits die hard.

Among the casualties was Lou, who had served in the Great War and was badly wounded in the upper arm. Finding there was no room on the truck, which was packed like sardines with wounded men, some moaning in pain from the wounds received that morning and the day before, he picked up his rifle and bayonet and walked back into the battle, saying that he'd 'get some more of the bastards'.

The 2/19th's battle diary recorded that 'every man was fighting mad'. Lou certainly was. On returning to the action, he bayoneted three Japanese, only to be assailed by five more a few minutes later. No one watching the encounter was able to fire as Lou was jumping about, fighting like a fiend as he dispatched three of them with his bayonet. The other two sensibly called it a day and decamped into the rubber.

Fred knew that to breach the roadblock was a do-or-die effort.

> Between us and our goal was the cream of the Japanese army, their backs to the wall, determined at all costs to stop this puny handful of Australians from reaching safety.
>
> Across the road they had drawn two old cars and surrounded them with rubber trees, forming a most effective block. But the Australians still had something in reserve, and they knew that here was the supreme test. Here they must go through, or die. Behind us the Japs were closing in eager for the kill, fully confident that here the small force of Australians, who had all day defied their efforts to stop them, would be trapped hopelessly and slaughtered.
>
> The Australian guns, those remarkable 25 pounders, were brought into action and, at point blank range, poured shell after shell into the road block, lifting the two cars completely off the road. Then, under a hail of lead the carriers roared up to the block. Their guns, coupled with the noise made by the defending Japs, made the closing day a hideous cacophony of sound. Crashing mortars, as many as sixteen bombs in the air at the one time, added their detonations to the overwhelming din. The battle area was a sight I never wish to see again. Mangled bodies lay in heaps along the roadway.

Leaving the infantry to clear away a small number of shrapnel-riddled iron sheets and chassis parts, the gunners moved on to a second barricade. It was constructed from felled trees, interlaced with coils of thin, black-enamelled wire that appeared to be attached to a large metal toolbox. Believing it could be a booby trap, the infantry sprayed the box with automatic fire from a range of 30 metres. Nothing happened. Realising it was a delaying tactic, the axe-wielding gunners moved in, chopping through the remaining tree trunks and also at the Japanese who lay behind them. As they came under heavy machine-gun fire, a youthful gunner, his chest torn with bullets, toppled backwards into the arms of an older comrade, who held him protectively until he died a few seconds later. Eyes glittering, the older gunner rushed back into the thick of it, his axe flailing.

The carriers, after adding their weight to the destruction, turned their attention to a house by the side of the road, which the enemy had turned into a machine-gun stronghold. From a range of less than 100 metres, two carriers opened fire, all but shredding the four-inch-thick concrete walls. The 35 or so Japanese who poured out were cut to ribbons. Noticing movement at the rear of the building, a group from 2/29 Battalion moved around the side wall and accounted for another twenty. With the machine-guns silenced and the axe-men attacking the barricade, infantrymen pushed along the left flank to clear out any tree snipers, while Roly Dean and his mates, cheering at the top of their voices and with bayonets at the ready, chased the fleeing Japanese down the road and into the jungle.

Suddenly, all went quiet, apart from the occasional desultory shot. For Fred, the silence after the clamour of the past few minutes was almost unnerving, with phosphorescence left on the trees and ground by high explosive shells adding to the sense of unreality. The road was open, but the cost of clearing it was high. Among the many wounded was Ray Snelling, his thigh being shattered while leading his company during the initial assault. At least 65 Australians lost their lives between the first road block near the 99-mile peg and the last at mile 97.5. The only consolation was that the Japanese had lost many more, as was evidenced by the piles of mangled corpses strewn along the road.

With the way ahead now clear, the convoy prepared to move forward, with troops from the 2/19th as the advance guard. Next came the carriers, then the vehicles with the wounded, protected by more armoured vehicles at the rear. As night fell, the grim cortege with its wounded and dying men was finally able to move. When the sun sank its fiery head beneath the horizon, Fred realised that at last they were in sight of their goal.

The infantrymen still on their feet trudged along at either side of the convoy. Braddon, perched on the tailboard of a truck, could barely see them in the gathering gloom, but he could hear them humming an occasional tune or uttering the odd swear word or two when someone tripped. How they kept going, he couldn't fathom, for there was very little water left and the only canned food was unsweetened condensed milk. Tired as they were, they were still able to offer a cheery greeting or a cigarette to their wounded and very grateful mates. For the next hour, as the trucks and gun tractors crawled along in low gear over undulating ground, those fortunate to have hitched a ride peered out into the darkness, well aware that they were still passing through country eminently suited to an attack. But no matter what happened, all were united in the one aim – to clear the eight-mile-long causeway before dawn.

At about 7 pm they were free of the rubber plantations, just past the 97-mile, when a shout went up from troops at the front. The way ahead, bombed or mined by the Japanese, was inundated with water from the padi fields and no longer visible. All vehicles ground to a halt.

Standing on the tailboard of the truck, Braddon leaned across the canvas canopy and clicked off his rifle's safety catch. A muffled metallic sound, echoing down the line, told him that scores of others were doing the same. Fireflies flitted about, crickets chirruped. The convoy held its breath and waited.

Suddenly, someone nudged Braddon in the ribs and pointed. Ahead he saw a red glow, then another and another. Convinced that the enemy was signalling to each other, the riflemen took aim. As they waited for the order to fire, a figure appeared beside Braddon's truck and whispered urgently to the driver 'See those lights? Drive between them. It's our blokes on either side of the roadway drawing on fags. It'll be as rough as guts, but it's the best we can do.' And, with that, he scurried off to the next vehicle.

Wading out into the water, the infantrymen had felt about with their feet until they found the edge of the road, where they now stood, drawing on cigarettes held in cupped palms. Braddon recalled:

> The leading truck needed no encouragement. There was a splash; for a moment it seemed to flounder, and then it could be heard wading steadily through the water. Another followed, and a third. And the next instant we, too, were slopping our way down that dimly indicated lane. As the truck slogged into each crater and the engine protested violently at its watery reception, we manhandled it out again, always led on by the friendly warmth of a fag that glowed for one quick draw in a closely cupped hand. For some distance this miracle of spontaneous organisation was maintained. Somehow the path ahead – apparently just a featureless expanse of water – was always indicated by those silent infantrymen with their cigarettes.

The column was at about the 95-mile peg, nearing the long, straight section of the causeway, when Brand heard the 2/19th soldier with the over-full bladder announce his intention to relieve himself. Loading his wounded onto the already overburdened trucks, Brand and the rest of his party joined the foot-sore soldiers marching along the road.

They had only just set off again when a group that had fled Newton's transport harbour also emerged unexpectedly from the darkness on the left side of the road. They were the infantrymen who had remained at Parit Sulong until relieved by the British. After losing contact with Newton and the others in the swamp, they had headed cross-country in the direction of Yong Peng. With the swamps mercifully behind them, they were in fairly open country when they learned from Malay villagers that Australian soldiers were to the south, on the Parit Sulong road. Striking out immediately, they caught up with the tail end of the column, where Anderson told them to remain, to reinforce the rear guard.

> Fred was among the many tired and weary Australians formed up at the causeway, for the time safe, as the Japanese, aware that their blockade had failed, broke off their contact in the rear and retired to consolidate the gains they had already made.
>
> And so the long ten-mile trek to Parit Sulong Bridge began. But every man was happy; knowing that at the other end was safety and friends. As the trucks and carriers slowly forged their way along the causeway, the troops marched in single file along each side, safe in the knowledge that the swamps prevented the Japs from making a flank attack.

However, even though the road was no longer flooded, it was hard going. One stretch was so badly cratered that it was only by a combined brute effort that the vehicles could be pushed around them, through ground so marshy that, had the momentum faltered, the rest of the convoy would have been stranded. At about 10 pm, they were near mile 94 when a carrier went off the edge of a narrow, rickety bridge, forcing an unexpected but very welcome rest. It was safe enough – with padi fields on either side for three miles to the rear and another five miles in front, there was no chance of a surprise attack.

At about midnight, the advance guard met an Indian soldier coming from the direction of Parit Sulong. He was lucky that the first person to spot him was a corporal observant enough to realise he was carrying a Lee Enfield rifle, which stopped him from being run through with a bayonet. His news was not good. After finding himself cut off at Bakri, he had headed for Parit Sulong, only to find that the bridge and the village were in enemy hands.

This was not what Anderson, or Fred, wanted to hear.

> Here we were again trapped, and with the column on a ten mile stretch of road with swamps feet deep in water on either side – with Japs behind and now Japs in front! What a target we would be for aircraft when daylight came if we could not reach the small patch of rubber trees, which marked the approach to the bridge. All our transport was on the road, with no chance of getting off.

Hoping that the news was not true, Anderson halted the convoy while the signallers again dispatched a message to Bennett, 'Who holds Parit Sulong'. There was no response, so two of Fred's signallers, despatch riders 'Ted' Levick and Ron White, went forward to investigate. Meanwhile, the convoy pushed on, its progress again slowed by bomb craters. The riders returned to report that they had passed through the looted and deserted village without any problem but, on reaching the bridge, had been challenged in a foreign language which definitely was not Malay. Switching off their headlights, they had slewed the bikes around and raced away.

A well-earned rest
(Murray Griffin)

At 2.30 am, convinced that the village and the bridge were in control of the Japanese, Anderson halted the convoy at mile 89 and ordered rations to be distributed – one tin of bully beef to eight men, and a biscuit each. At 4 o'clock an eight-man patrol left on foot to reconnoitre the village, a little over three miles distant. At around 7 am, just after sunrise, the convoy's forward companies reached a rubber plantation at mile 88.

Fifteen minutes later, the patrol leader returned with the news that, on approaching the bridge, they were challenged and attacked. One Australian was seriously wounded, but the rest had killed or wounded a number of enemy soldiers, some armed with swords. With the patrol were two English-speaking Malays, who insisted that members of the Royal Johor Military Forces, the Sultan's private army, were holding the bridge. Anderson didn't believe a word of it. Only too aware that, with a large enemy force to his rear, there was no time to waste on further reconnaissance, so Anderson ordered three of his very depleted companies to advance, leaving a fourth to provide cover for the main body, yet to arrive.

Since the Malays were so certain the bridge and village were in friendly hands, Anderson ordered them to accompany him with a small advance guard. The remainder spread out through the rubber on either side of the narrow asphalt road, bordered by wide and deep parits, filled with water to a depth of over one metre.

About 600 metres from the village, after allowing Anderson's small group to pass by, a well-concealed enemy force on the left-hand side of the road opened up on the advancing troops. As the firing began, the CO's party dropped to the ground and crawled into a nearby ditch, where Anderson yelled out loudly for all four companies to attack at once, fully aware that only the most forward group was able to do so. The bluff worked. The enemy, about ten per cent of whom understood English, began to pull out. With controlled and well-directed fire, the Australians repelled a bayonet charge of 120, leaving the attackers exposed on open ground and allowing one of Anderson's companies to swing around on the left and attack the right flank, pinning them down.

A despatch rider was sent back to call up two carriers. They moved down the right-hand side of the road where, with the infantry firing from the left, they brought enfilading fire on the Japanese forces, very few of whom escaped. There were also several hand-to-hand encounters. As Chick Warden moved through the battlefield collecting weapons, a Japanese soldier about four or five metres away got to his knees to throw a grenade. Warden fired, hitting him in the chest. As he pitched forward, the grenade, which he still held in his hand, exploded alongside his head.

He was dead but, even if he were not, there was no question of taking him prisoner. Unlike the Japanese, who had thousands of men and two fully equipped field hospitals in their column, the Australians were in retreat and fighting for their very existence. They had no medical facilities, no supplies, and no method of confining anyone taken captive. As was the case at Bakri, all those who moved, as well as those who did not, were bayonetted or shot. The number of enemy dead was estimated at 300, while the Australians had sustained only a few casualties. Meantime, taking advantage of the situation, the Malay hostages had scarpered. It was a sensible move. Another civilian, who tried to spin the same yarn to Anderson, was taken away and shot.

Multiple problems were also being encountered at the rear of the column, as the enemy had brought up tanks and motorised infantry and had over-run a portion of the rearguard. Two anti-tank guns had disabled two of the tanks, halting the advance, but had then been

Above: The gunners take on the enemy tanks outside Parit Sulong (Murray Griffin).

Right: Parit Sulong bridge, looking north from the Japanese position.

lost. The 25-pounder guns had fired over open sights at the tanks and infantry transports, stopping further movement but, in so doing, one of the guns became bogged and was abandoned. To make matters worse, the Australian transport and artillery that managed to reach the rubber plantation were unable to move under the cover of the trees, as the ground was too boggy and the vehicles were too heavy for the ramps over the parits.

It was now 8.30 am. While a company from the 2/19th and the two Indian companies remained in reserve to protect the convoy, and troops from the 2/29th engaged the enemy at the rear, 1500 metres away the forward troops resumed their advance towards the village. However, within the hour concentrated machine-gun fire from houses and buildings pinned them down, about 500 metres from the bridge, which was not visible owing to a slight bend in the road. Meanwhile enemy aircraft appeared, strafing everything within sight.

Although under attack, Fred's signallers worked tirelessly to maintain wireless communication with Bennett. The batteries were failing but, at 11 am, just as the enemy's heavy artillery opened up, a faint incoming signal revealed that help was on its way. An attack had been ordered at 2 pm to clear and retake the road to Yong Peng and a party of trained guerrillas was on its way to clear the bridge. Unaware that this assistance depended, in part, on the yet-to-be-realised attack to gain control of the defile, the spirits of the beleaguered column rose, especially when they heard the sound of distant firing from the Yong Peng side of the bridge. It was not, however, the relief column. It was the British artillery, registering its guns while awaiting orders for the infantry to retake the defile.

A series of miscommunications, logistical hiccups and wrong assumptions ensured that these orders were not issued. After putting the time of the attack back to 6 pm, it was then deferred a further 12 hours, until 6 am the following day.

Back at Parit Sulong, believing that help was coming, Anderson continued to deploy his forces as best he could. At the rear, where snipers were active, Chick Warden had been dispatched to be the 'eyes' of the artillerymen, allowing him to witness the 25-pounders in action, up close, for the first time.

> At about 10 am the gunners yelled at me to take cover, which I did without hesitation and jumped into the black mud swamp-drain alongside the road. Looking north along the road, I could see two tanks coming round the bend, guns blazing. The gunners stayed behind their gun and as cool as ever I had seen, lowered their elevation and fired two or three quick shots at the tanks over open sights. By this time the tanks were less than 50 yards away. Both tanks just seemed to open up and explode. There was no excitement amongst the gunners about their hits because they were too tired, the same as all of us, and we were now really too tired to get excited about anything. Actually, we knew we were fighting for our lives. The gunners re-elevated the gun and again continued to fire at the enemy.

The situation was equally desperate at the front of the column. With the remaining mortar ammunition committed to holding the enemy off at the rear, and the artillery unable to fire at the bridge because of the bend in the road, the short range and the rubber trees, all available personnel were now thrown into the attack. Every spare gunner, all transport drivers and the walking wounded were deployed along the flanks, leaving the column's main strength to concentrate on the head and the tail. The convoy's drivers, who had brought their vehicles as far as they could, grabbed their rifles and joined the infantrymen, returning only when it was time to move on. Some did not make it back.

At 11 am the reserve Indian troops, ordered to attack from the west (right-hand side) of the road, came under heavy fire. Swinging wide, they managed to by-pass the village to reach the river, where they exchanged fire with enemy troops on the other side. In the village, the 2/19th had suffered a number of casualties. Pinned down by enemy fire coming from the protection of houses, they were unable to gain any ground until two carriers arrived to pepper the buildings at point-blank range. As the Japanese poured out, the infantry's light automatics cut them down. The carriers then turned their attention to the machine-gun nests, but made no impression until the gunners realised the troops manning them were lying on the ground. Manoeuvring their vehicles so that they could fire at a height of 15 centimetres, they enfiladed the posts with deadly effect. After this tactic was repeated several times, the infantry was able to occupy the village – or what was left of it. Some of the buildings were on fire, others had been blown apart by grenades and mortars, and bodies of enemy dead lay everywhere. Chick Warden, now back at the head of the column, reckoned that at least 500 or 600 troops from the Imperial Guards Division had been killed.

Fred recorded:

> The western approaches to the bridge were now in Australian hands but attempts to cross were doomed to failure. A solid wall of lead met every attempt to storm it. Our transport could not leave the road because of the water-filled ditches on both sides. The Japanese again made contact with our rear and were closing in. Here we were again, trapped like rats. But still with plenty of fight left and that is about all we had. Our ammunition was almost exhausted, our trucks were full of wounded. All we could do was hang on and wait for help.

As the afternoon wore on and pressure on the rear increased, they did not have much firepower left, with the artillery down to just 100 rounds and an increase in attacks from the air. At about 4.30, there were cheers as a plane bearing the distinctive roundel of the RAF began circling, but the cheers were short lived. This pilot was just as inept as those of the previous day. A bomb dropped on 2/19 Battalion HQ, wrecking the signals truck. Fred was unhurt, but the arm and leg of the signals' officer George Gill were severed and a signalman, one of Fred's football mates, had his leg blown off. Brand, only about 40 metres from the blast, reported that another seven or so were injured, some fatally.

There was still no sign of the much-hoped-for relief column, but Fred's spirits rose when, at around 4 pm he heard the sound of heavy firing towards Yong Peng.

> Here at last was the long-awaited rescuing party! We renewed our efforts on the bridge, hoping to keep the Japs so busy that our friends could retake the lost bridge and we could cross to safety.

> The sounds of battle came nearer and nearer. How we prayed for them. Men's haggard faces lit up with a new hope. If only we had something to fight with, we could go to meet them or die trying. A sudden lull in the firing gave us more cheer. We thought the Japs had broken and our men were coming through. Then the firing broke out again and this time it was further away. Each new burst receded into the distance and then died away altogether.

> This was the end. Well, if we must die, it would be fighting!

CHAPTER 10

THE BRIDGE AT PARIT SULONG

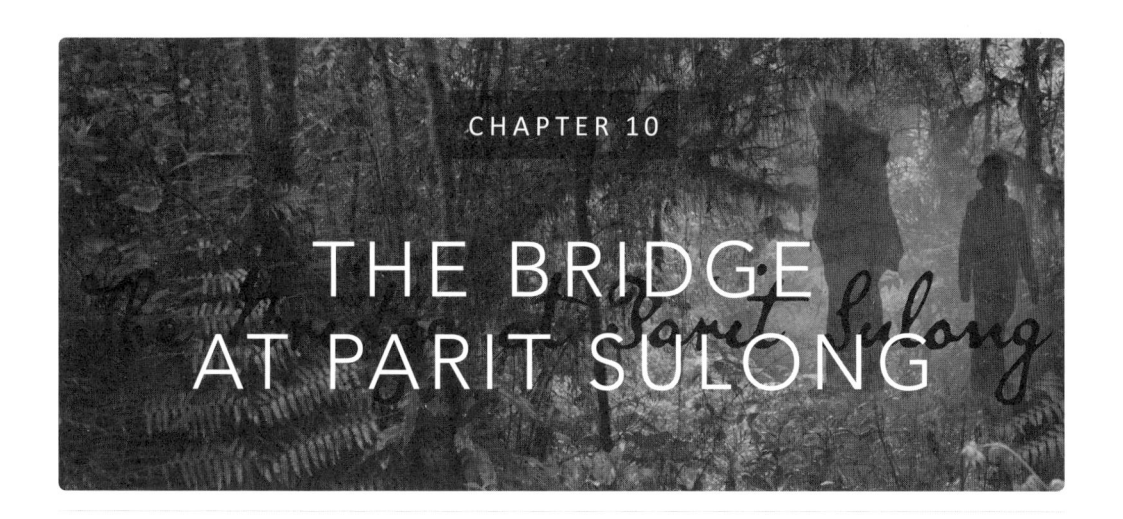

The situation was desperate. The Australians had formed a square perimeter with vehicles jammed head to tail on the road, unable to move because of the parits on either side. The trucks, filled with the wounded, some of them with injuries four days old, were now being hit again by the cross-fire, shelling and bombing. There was little that could be done to help them and, as there were no medical supplies other than the makeshift bandages and field dressings that every soldier carried, Brand and Cahill could not perform even the most minor surgery.

For half-an-hour after the attack on Battalion HQ, aerial bombing and strafing claimed more casualties, including seven mortar men. At the same time, shelling and small arms' fire from ground troops intensified. Snipers too were active. Heavy and accurate mortar fire burst on contact with the rubber trees, creating more deadly projectiles.

It was fortunate that Anderson was not among the casualties. 'I'd left the road', he recalled, 'crossed the parit and was sitting next to a rubber tree, looking at my map and wondering what I would do. I saw the bomb leaving the plane. I threw myself down behind the rubber tree, the bomb fell on the other side, and from where I was lying I could just touch the edge of the crater. Next war, I'm taking a rubber tree with me.'

Despite the seriousness of their situation, morale among the wounded remained high. However, their bravado did nothing to reduce Brand's anxiety. At 5 pm, in the hope that the Japanese would grant safe passage, he and Cahill obtained permission for an ambulance and a truck, carrying 15 of the most severely wounded, to drive slowly towards the bridge in the hope that the Japanese would allow safe passage.

A volunteer stretcher bearer went with them, along with Lieutenant Bunny Austin, wounded but still on his feet after a bullet passed through his neck and shoulder, to carry out any negotiations. Constantly harassed by enemy fire, it was almost dark before Brand and Cahill finished organising the transfers and the tiny convoy was able to crawl to the crest of the bridge, where it halted in front of a sandbag-and-oil-drum barricade. One of the drivers, acting as an envoy, walked forward alone, bearing a white flag.

Any hope of attacking the bridge had been abandoned for the time being. There was also no hope of holding the line, which extended as far as the river. As night fell, taking care not to be silhouetted by the fires still burning in the village, the forward troops began withdrawing to form a triangular-shaped perimeter, its apex at the bridge and expanding to a 300-metre-long baseline at the rear.

Everyone knew the situation was perilous. The troops, without proper sleep for days, were under constant attack; the injured, lying helpless in the backs of the trucks, were being wounded a second and third time, often fatally; mortar and artillery ammunition was almost exhausted; medical supplies were virtually non-existent; and food and water rations were all but spent. No one had eaten for almost 24 hours, and there was very little food to be found in the village.

Although most of the wireless equipment had been destroyed, two of Fred's signallers, one of whom was wounded, kept the wireless going with spare parts cannibalised from defunct sets. Their Morse key was burnt out, but they created enough spark to 'tap' out their messages by striking the two loose ends of the terminals together.

At four that afternoon, Anderson, who still hoped to be able to break the bridge defences the following day, had signalled Bennett's HQ requesting aircraft to bomb the southern approaches of the bridge at dawn, to machine-gun the road to the rear and to drop morphine and food. The answer, by necessity, was transmitted in plain language. Confident that no Japanese eavesdropper would be unable to make head nor tail of the reply, HQ signalled 'Look up at sparrow fart', confirming that planes would fly over at first light the next day.

Pressure had continued on the rear throughout the afternoon and, as night closed in, a number of Indian troops began to become demoralised. Others, completely broken, threw away their weapons. Deemed 'an absolute nuisance', some were such a hindrance that they were eventually sent outside the perimeter to become prisoners of war. The defections, voluntary or otherwise, now placed even more strain on the rapidly thinning line.

With bullets flying about everywhere, some of the walking wounded left the vehicles to find shelter away from the road. Hackney and two others sought refuge under the chassis of their ute. However, it was a poor substitute for a slit trench. Bullets ripped through the sides of the vehicle and pinged off the more substantial metal components, with some passing so close that the men constantly checked each other to ensure they were still all right. Discovering that they were, Hackney passed his hip flask around for a medicinal nip. There was no sign yet of any relief from the direction of Yong Peng but hopes were high, as Bennett had signalled that an 'independent company' of well-trained guerrillas was coming.

The 'independent company' was a platoon of Australian infantrymen recruited in December 1941 to form a small irregular unit. Dubbed Rose Force, it was composed of unmarried men, seven from each battalion, who had volunteered for hazardous duty, including commando-style operations. At noon that day, 21 January, Bennett had ordered the unit's CO to take all his available men along the Yong Peng road to Parit Sulong, hoping that, by attacking the enemy at the bridge from the rear, they would be able to gain control of it long enough to allow Anderson's men to escape.

Rose Force's total strength, including HQ staff, was 50. However, as a platoon of 15, commanded by the 2/19th's Lieutenant Sanderson, had been detached to the upper Muar River to gather intelligence on enemy movements, and a number of others had been transferred back to their regular units or were ill, the independent company now consisted of just 18 men. To let Anderson know in plain language that help was on its way, HQ signalled in plain language 'look out for Sandy'. Although Sanderson was not in the relief party, the message was clear enough, as Anderson knew him and was aware of his recruitment to Rose Force.

The much-depleted Rose Force party reached Yong Peng at seven o'clock that evening, after being held up for an hour by an air raid. Their CO was collecting information about the battle situation along the road to Parit Sulong when 20 AIF from the transport harbour and a considerable number of Indian troops arrived in a state of exhaustion. Whether the Indians were cut off at Bakri or defectors from Parit Sulong is not clear. However, both Rose Force and Bennett were under the impression that they (and others, the next day) had come from the latter, via the Simpang Kiri River and a road servicing a nearby iron mine that joined the Yong Peng-Parit Sulong road at mile 78, six miles from Yong Peng. Learning that the iron mine road was now impassable, owing to a large number of enemy troops, Rose Force headed out along a foot track, further to the east. They camped out that night unaware that, as the track led to a dead end, they would be too late.

They were also unaware that Sanderson's party, whose whereabouts were unknown and by this time had been reported overdue, was also heading for Parit Sulong, but from the opposite direction. Sanderson, two guides and his 15 ORs had left Bukit Siput, near Segamat, at 5 pm on 19 January to carry out a reconnaissance along the River Muar. Their instructions were to return, if possible, within 12 hours: after that time the main force would be withdrawn south to Labis and the bridge would be blown, cutting them off.

They reached Lenga, 50 kilometres upstream from Muar, at three o'clock the following afternoon, having obtained no information of any value, since the Japanese had not yet moved that far inland. Although the group had clearly missed the 12-hour deadline for Bukit Siput, one of the guides was a former government surveyor who knew the area well. He advised that they could do one of two things: attempt an overland trek and reach Labis through very thick jungle, or head south to Parit Sulong, via the Pagoh-Kangkar track, to link up with Anderson's men moving along the Muar-Yong Peng road.

As the second option held more appeal than the first, the party pushed on towards Pagoh, stopping for the night about 10 kilometres from the village. Although they saw no sign of the Japanese, the sound of gunfire and shelling on the Bakri-Parit Sulong road, about 16 kilometres away, was clearly audible. The next morning, they arrived at Pagoh in good time, having firstly piled into an ancient Austin 10 car, 'acquired' by a resourceful corporal. However, it had lasted only long enough to take them down the first six kilometres of the track before giving up the ghost – from lack of petrol or water they were not sure. They had then transferred to purloined bicycles before finally hitching a ride in a bullock cart.

The remainder of the track beyond Pagoh passed through some very wild country but, as woodcutters had been busy, large areas had been cleared. Even so, it was becoming dark by the time they reached the outskirts of Kangkar, a rather squalid, dilapidated village, split in two by a river that was spanned by a decrepit, wooden semi-circular bridge. For some time, they had been able to hear the continuous sound of concentrated rifle, mortar and automatic fire, coming from the direction of Parit Sulong, now only eight kilometres away.

At about 8 pm, having organised transport in a lorry driven by the Kangkar village headman, they set off down the tarred road towards Parit Sulong, with the intention of joining Anderson's Force, when mortar and automatic gunfire erupted from both sides of the road. Abandoning the truck, the Australians and their driver took refuge in a parit on the left side of the road. When the firing petered out, they heard footsteps but, for some reason, Sanderson did not investigate to determine if they belonged to friend or foe.

The troops, firing at them with weapons identified as Bren guns, were almost certainly picquets posted by 2/29 Battalion. Since Rose Force had been raised specifically to carry

The 'Fighting Padre', Harold Wardale-Greenwood

out missions behind enemy lines, Sanderson's failure to identify their attackers or, at the very least, infiltrate the area to gain intelligence, is inexplicable. Instead, he ordered his men to return to Kangkar, where they camped out in the jungle for the night. The following morning, swinging in a wide arc to the east, they by-passed Parit Sulong and emerged onto the Yong Peng road, about three kilometres south of the bridge. From there they eventually made their way to Batu Pahat, where they linked up with British forces.

Meanwhile, throughout the night their countrymen were locked in a bitter battle of survival. Anyone who could crawl and carry a rifle manned the perimeter, one rank deep and thinly spaced, protecting the vehicles and the wounded men. At each attack Padre Wardale-Greenwood, who had done such sterling work at Bakri, left off tending the wounded to join his batman at a two-inch mortar at the foremost position.

Just inside the rear sector, positioned near one of the four remaining 25-pounders, Braddon, his mate Hugh Moore and another gunner scratched out shallow foxholes and waited to see what the enemy would do next.

They didn't have long to wait. Previous bayonet charges having failed, the Japanese began to drop their mortars along the line of parked vehicles, hitting one of the trucks. One of the artillery's ammunition limbers also erupted into flames, bathing the area in light and silhouetting the troops in front of it. Shouting triumphantly, the Japanese opened up, creating a fusillade of such intensity that the gunners, hugging the ground behind their pathetically inadequate earth mounds, were spattered with a mixture of pulverised earth and latex, dripping from the shattered rubber trees above them.

At around 8 o'clock, after another bayonet charge had been repelled, Braddon's group decided to take it in turns to sleep. The first shift had only just dropped off when the ominous rumbling of approaching tanks was heard. Realising they had broken through the perimeter, Braddon, Moore and two other gunners sprinted to their gun, set up on the road. A two-pound anti-tank shell, fired by one of the captured guns, whistled past. It was evidently focusing on the 25-pounder, but its aim was way off, missing its target by metres and slamming into a tree on the edge of the road. The four Australian gunners, arming themselves with grenades, left their gun and jumped into the parits on either side of the road.

The leading tank stopped, the turret opened and a head popped out. No one moved. With a shout of 'let 'em have it', two of the gunners lobbed their grenades into the turret, disabling the tank. Suddenly there was another shout, this time from the rear. 'Clear line: down in front'.

Braddon turned his head and looked. Standing behind the gun, illuminated by the glare of the still-burning ammunition limber was a lone artilleryman. With great deliberation, he lined up the barrel and, in the absence of any sights, looked along it. Taking his time, he checked again before fetching a second shell, in case the first missed the target. There was nothing wrong with his aim. As the high-explosive shell slammed into the leading tank, it staggered and burst into flames, creating a most effective road block and turning night into day. With the aid of the rest of his crew, the artilleryman fired again, shattering the next tank, which was blown a metre into the air before catching fire and disintegrating. The infantry wiped out two more. The rest turned and fled. Returning to his fox-scrape, Braddon volunteered to keep vigil for an hour while the others, including two suitably admiring infantrymen, slept.

His watch, however, was far from peaceful.

Three trucks of wounded were set alight by mortar fire and the men in them incinerated before anyone could lift them out. This was followed, a few yards to Braddon's right, with a frontal attack by infantry, which was repulsed. Then, as Braddon watched, a shadowy figure began moving towards him, flitting from tree to tree.

> At first I thought it was merely a product of my imagination (which I knew to be fruitful). When it was only three rubber trees away, I realised uneasily that it was, in fact, a Japanese soldier. Terrified because of my inefficiency with the bayonet (not to mention a natural tendency to terror anyway), I shook the two infantrymen and Hugh. But I might as well have shaken the tree behind me – one does not awaken, after four days and nights without sleep, at the mere shake of a hand. So, in desperation, I moved alone to the tree in front of me and, as the Jap ran crouching towards it, stepped out with my bayonet from behind it and presented him with a firmly held rifle and bayonet. Upon this he promptly impaled himself. At the moment of impact, as I tucked my right elbow securely against my hip and moved my left foot slightly forward, I found myself thinking 'just like a stop volley at tennis'.

Foiled by the gunners from using the road, at about 2 am other tanks tried an outflanking movement through the rubber, but were repelled with grenades and anti-tank rifles, with one company from the 2/19th destroying five. Unable to break through, the tanks moved around to the western side of the road. The line was penetrated, but tank-hunting parties, who slipped grenades into the tracks and bogeys, and covered gun openings and driving slits with mud, destroyed them all. The occupants, unable to see where they were going, opened the hatches, at which point the hunter popped in a grenade. A member of the 2/19th's pioneer platoon accounted for another four tanks by shoving bottles of kerosene up the exhausts. Wounded several times by cross-fire, he died when a machine-gunner caught him in the glaring light of a burning tank, as he tried to blow up a fifth.

Meanwhile, there had been movement from the two-vehicle convoy back at the bridge. At about 9 pm the envoy had arrived back at the Australian perimeter. He reported that, on reaching enemy lines, he had been interviewed by a Japanese officer who spoke English. The Japanese commander had agreed to allow the wounded safe passage, but only if the entire force surrendered. If it did not, the vehicles would remain on the bridge, as a roadblock. Furthermore, if any attempt were made to move them, they would be machine-gunned. Anderson's response was firm, brief and unequivocal. 'We will fight to the last man, rather than surrender.' Fred recorded that 'every man there agreed with him to the utmost. Even the wounded men were against it'.

As the envoy did not return to the bridge, Anderson's reply was not relayed to the Japanese. However, the lack of response sparked no reaction and neither was there any attempt to guard the two vehicles. There was also no interference about an hour later, when Bunny Austin and another wounded officer released the hand brakes on both vehicles, allowing them to roll back down the incline. Covered by the noise of battle along the flanks and to the rear, the two men then started the engines and reversed along the road into the safety of the Australian perimeter.

> Fred expected that the Japs would now close in, realising our plight by the small return we were giving to his fire. But for some reason he failed to hammer home his advantage, apart from desultory tank forays, which met with little success as the darkness allowed us to reach them with grenades and Molotov bombs.

The return of the desperately wounded was the only good news in what was later described as a 'nasty' night. It was also very long. Even when the firing stopped, the Japanese maintained a constant racket – banging gongs, blowing bugles and yelling – with bayonet charges, shelling and mortar attacks thrown in for good measure. Enemy troops tried to force their way through one side of the triangle, then the other and then both simultaneously. Time and again they were repelled. Patrols who called out in English 'Hello Joe', 'Where are you Joe?' and 'How would you like to be back in Sydney?', as they tried to probe each sector, were sent packing with hand grenades.

But for the Australians, to move within their perimeter was just as suicidal. The cracking of a stick, a ragged breath, a moving shadow. Best to take no chances. Shoot first. It might be Japs. Just before dawn there was an unearthly scream from the 2/19th's sector. Daybreak revealed that the unfortunate victim was an Indian soldier, bayonetted by mistake.

Australians were also killed by nervous, overwrought comrades. Twenty-four-year-old Private Len Wood, a bandsman and stretcher bearer from 2/19 Battalion, known for his gentleness and quiet ways, was shot and badly wounded as he moved about in the dark tending the injured.

Leonard Bronte Wood hailed from Gunnedah in NSW, where he taught manual arts at the local high school. He was also a renowned artist, with many of his works appearing in various battalion magazines throughout 1941. He was a finalist in the prestigious Wynne Prize for Australian landscape painting, held in conjunction with the Archibald Prize for Portraiture, in both 1940 and 1941, with paintings entitled *Gunnedah Landmark*, *The Reclusery*, *Fantasy*, and *Bush Track, Sirius Cove*. By the time his mate, the poet Private George Harding, found him, it was too late. Len had died from shock and loss of blood. Official reports attributed cause of death to bayonet wounds.

As the night shadows faded, the pre-dawn light revealed a scene of utter desolation – wrecked and smouldering tanks; shattered remnants of rubber trees; bodies and bits of bodies – the all-pervading, sickly stench of death hanging heavily in the hot, moisture-laden air. Hackney, crawling out from under the ute's chassis, saw that those in the convoy had suffered horribly during the night. Many of the trucks had been reduced to twisted shells, some burnt beyond all recognition. Practically all the glass on every other vehicle was shattered; tyres were flattened and petrol tanks ruptured. A large number of the wounded had died from old or recently inflicted wounds, direct hits or exposure. All trucks still laden with ammunition or equipment, and still relatively intact, were unloaded and the wounded transferred to them.

The first sight that greeted Braddon that morning was the victim of his involuntary stop-volley, lying on his back with his mouth wide open and displaying a set of remarkably good teeth. As the gunner surveyed the burnt-out tanks squatting grotesquely on the roadside, one of his mates, Johnny Ison, let out a yell. A bullet fired by a sniper had slammed into the right-hand side of his steel helmet, leaving a dent. Ten minutes later, a bullet from the same marksman creased the left, while a third pulped the wood on the barrel of Braddon's rifle. Thirty minutes later, mortars opened up, killing the infantryman on Braddon's right.

Fred recorded:

> Daylight found the enemy attacking strongly from the rear and right flank and a strong mortar barrage on the left. The tanks were now closing in on the rear and, with the transport unable to leave the road, were subjected to an intense fire, many of them catching alight and endangering the others nearby. Moving the wounded from the trucks to the comparative safety of the rubber trees was a nightmare job, as the Jap planes were now spraying the roads with machine-gun fire.

Those at the rear were certainly taking a pasting. When Braddon crawled back to his truck to fetch a map, he found the vehicle riddled with bullet holes and all nine men inside dead. As he made his way back to the perimeter, he was startled to see one of the gunners standing in the open, a heavy anti-tank rifle at his shoulder. His target was a treetop, concealing a sniper. Aiming the rifle high he fired, only to be flung backwards by the recoil.

The sniper was using the trunk as a shield, but the gunner figured that, with Braddon's help, he could gain enough elevation to enable the shell to penetrate the trunk, and so bring about the sniper's demise. Seemingly oblivious of the bullets that were flying about, the gunner rested the barrel on Braddon's shoulder. Holding the butt against his own, he took aim and fired. The result was instantaneous. Braddon crashed to the ground, his companion was flung against a tree, and the sniper toppled from his perch to fall to earth with a resounding thud.

Returning to his fox scrape, Braddon passed around a tin of condensed milk he had found in the truck, their first nourishment in over 24 hours. Shortly afterwards, the young soldier who had spent the night on Braddon's left was hit in the right thigh. The path of the projectile could be clearly seen and the wound oozed blackish blood, but the infantryman said nothing and kept on firing.

It was now well and truly sparrow fart. At 6.50 am, two obsolete RAF Albacores, escorted by three RAAF Brewster Buffaloes, emerged in the early morning light, their flight from Singapore made under cover of darkness. Guided by a flare, the pilots of the Albacores made their run over the Australian perimeter, dropping eight canisters packed with food and medical supplies. At the sight of the containers, drifting to earth on their parachutes, one man panicked and ran, yelling 'Look out. They're land mines'.

The Albacores banked and turned for a second pass, this time letting loose a stick of bombs. Most fell on the Japanese positioned on the south side of the bridge, but one fell at the side of the road inside the Australian perimeter, killing a group of signallers trying to rig up a field radio. Braddon and Moore saw the explosion and ran towards three rubber trees, now lying uprooted beside a huge crater. All that remained of the men who had stood there seconds before was a boot, a shoulder blade and a tin hat – a tin hat with a dent on the right-hand side and another on the left.

On their return to base, the Albacore pilots reported that three containers had landed on the road, north of the bridge, but

> NO movement to collect them seen. 6 to 10 lorries seen stationery NE side of road between bridge 676915 [map reference] and Parit Sulong facing south. Firing taking place SW from bridge. Area surrounding bridge devastated.

The four canisters the troops were able to retrieve – two containing water (which had not been requested), one with food and the fourth packed with morphine and shell dressings – were a godsend but, unfortunately, the bombs dropped on the enemy troops did not do enough damage to allow the Australians to storm the bridge. Grabbing the medical supplies, the two doctors went to work. Armed with a supply of morphine, Cahill, helped by his batman Wally Hammond and stretcher bearer Chris Guerin, and Brand, accompanied by the RAP's Val Lynch, climbed into truck after truck, giving scores of injections, through clothing and sometimes even through waterproof capes. Some men asked for a shot to ease their pain, but others insisted they could do without it and to give it to their mates. Brand recalled:

> During this time there was no particular RAP site – the whole area was littered with dead and wounded. Stretcher bearers took Captain Cahill and myself to various places in the perimeter where we were needed, but no attempt was made to carry the wounded anywhere, apart from a tendency to concentrate them in my trucks, for no one position was less dangerous than another. I helped to remove the body of one man from the ambulance. He had died there 24 hours previously ...
>
> Lynch and I had given up all hope of getting out alive and I think most of the others felt the same. We had kept jokes going, but now when our eyes met we would shake our heads grimly. I wondered how my wife would take it and felt sad and desperate.

Profoundly shocked by the death of Johnny Ison, Braddon and Moore collected a field dressing from Brand and returned to the wounded infantryman. They had barely enough time to secure the bandage in place when mortars began to fall with increasing intensity. Braddon took a few seconds to look at his companions.

> Beards were noticeably longer; faces noticeably leaner and eyes more sunken. Every man's back and legs were splattered with black spots of congealed latex, which had spurted from the bullet-torn trees under which we lay. I looked along the line. Every man was the same. A detonation jolted me. Just across the road a bakelite grenade

had exploded under the chin of one of the reinforcements with whom Hugh and I had returned to Bakri days before. As blood gushed out of a torn throat, he said to his companion: 'I'm done for, Reg', and prepared stoically to die – whereupon Reg said, 'Like hell you are', and, binding up the throat so tightly that it could no longer bleed and its owner scarcely breathe, he presented the patient with his rifle and said; 'Now get cracking'. Looking chalk-coloured but determined, the wounded man did what he was told. The next second he brandished his smoking rifle in the direction of the now defunct grenade thrower and announced, in a most un-Christian croak of triumph: 'Got the little bastard' – which he indubitably had.

The canisters containing the food supplies were opened and the contents – bully beef, biscuits, tea and, rather incongruously, tins of beetroot – distributed. The meal, such as it was, had barely been consumed when the enemy's light bombers made their first run of the day, machine gunning the road and dropping bombs near the bridge. One large truck piled with stretcher cases was heavily strafed, resulting in more injury and death. Hackney, now back on the front seat of the ute, could do nothing but pray as the bullets thudded into the load of respirators piled in the back and tore holes in the cabin roof.

For Victor Brand, the attacks on his wounded were almost too much.

> The transport was crammed along the road, nose to tail and two abreast. There was one ambulance, and most of the trucks contained wounded. Mortar bombs were coming down along the road, and the trucks were occasionally machine-gunned by planes.
>
> Fighting was heavy; automatic fire seemed to come from all directions. Mortaring was constant and an artillery barrage began to open up. The area became a frightful shambles. Wounded and killed were lying everywhere. Wounded were being twice and thrice wounded in the trucks. It was like a heavily overdone battle scene in the movies. There were fearful sights. I can never forget one of our men, who was wounded in the neck. I found him pacing aimlessly along the road, his swollen tongue protruding from his mouth. I could do nothing but give him some morphia and beg him to sit down and rest. During this time, messages were coming through encouraging us with news that relief was coming. But as time went on, we lost hope.
>
> Passing by the ambulance, Private Browning pointed to his foot with a wry smile and said 'They got me again, Doc'. I had to hurry away to restrain my emotion, but when I saw Lieutenant Hackney, I broke down. I remember crying bitterly and repeating, 'They're machine-gunning the wounded in the trucks', while Hackney stroked my hand and muttered 'Don't worry, there's help coming soon'.

It wasn't. The much anticipated, much delayed 6 am counter-attack at Bukit Pelandok had failed.

The infantrymen had moved into position before light, and the carriers were standing by, ready to move up the road once the defile had been taken but, before any orders could be given, further tests on the range of the artillery revealed that the shells were falling short. With the ammunition, evidently hindered by faulty fuses and the climate, unable to reach the target, the attack was put back until 9 am. Nearby, the infantrymen lay in the open, waiting to advance. It did not take long for enemy aircraft to spot them. At 7.40 dive-bombers attacked, resulting in 30 casualties.

Mid-morning, with the element of surprise lost, the infantry, unable to advance without artillery support, and 11 kilometres of jungle-lined road separating the defile from Parit Sulong, the attack was finally cancelled. It was claimed that the plan was doomed from the start as there were insufficient troops on the spot to carry it out. However, following their withdrawal from Segamat, the retreating Australian battalions had spent the past 24 hours resting at Yong Peng, only eight kilometres away. Why they were not mobilised is a question that remains unanswered.

Back at Parit Sulong, unaware of the rapidly deteriorating situation at the defile, the bleary-eyed troops of Anderson Force were hanging on grimly. At 8 am the shelling increased. Brand reported:

> The Japanese hit us with everything they had. The area received such a battering that the rubber trees began to fall, one landing right across a poor fellow's back. Casualties were numerous. I saw one section of which almost every man had been killed or wounded in their shallow firing positions by shell splinters, but the unwounded lay grimly in their scooped out holes and faced their front. The stretcher bearers were doing a magnificent job, carrying on with their work up and down the road without troubling to take cover from the intense fire, which was being poured on us. I was so fatigued by this time that whenever I went to ground I immediately dropped off to sleep, in spite of bursting shells and mortars, until Lynch would shake me.
>
> Lieutenant Colonel Anderson read out a message received from the wireless truck – 'Australia is proud of you – HQ 8 Australian Division'. After this message we gave up all hope of relief. I saw Lieutenant Colonel Anderson quite a lot and admired his coolness … He seemed to be quite unworried in spite of the appalling position we were in.

Trying to expand the perimeter, 2/19th's B Company had met very stiff opposition, and now, as the shelling increased, their losses were even heavier. The only troops not wounded were a major and ten men. Another company at the rear had also suffered heavily. One platoon, caught in cross fire while successfully repelling an attack, was all but wiped out, with every single member killed or wounded.

Inevitably, some deaths were caused by friendly fire, with one dreadful mix-up costing the 2/19th's Private Faulkner his life. An order had been issued for every second man on the eastern side of the road to move forward five metres. Some did and some didn't. Faulkner did and one of his own men threw a grenade at him. Mortally wounded, he begged in vain for an officer to shoot him.

Reports now reached Anderson that enemy tanks, supported by infantry, were working their way round the western flank. They were held in check by the tank-hunting parties and the artillery, firing again over open sights, but some reached to within 50 metres of the perimeter, stopping hull down, with only their turrets visible, so that the anti-tank weapons could not fire at them. Realising that the position was hopeless and that they could no longer expect any outside help, Anderson, in a desperate bid to break out, ordered his forward company to test the enemy's strength at the bridge.

The access to the bridge was limited. It was hemmed in on both sides by substantial concrete parapets and three half-metre-high barricades – two constructed from sandbags and oil drums, with a third of sawn timber in between – placed across the road just beyond the crest on the far approach. Using cover provided by buildings in the village, the men moved up to the northern end of the bridge.

Because of the confined space, only one or two sections could attack at the one time.

The first two successfully negotiated three trip-wires, which the Japanese, fearing a night attack, had set up three metres apart on the northern approach. However, as they reached the crest, machine guns positioned behind stout concrete pillars at the southern end opened fire, along with others on the river banks to the left and right and also on high ground to the rear. Although supporting fire neutralised the machine guns on the flanks and beyond the bridge, the guns behind the pillars caught the attackers in murderous crossfire as they tried to clamber over the barricades. All were killed.

Yelling 'I will give it a go', another infantryman led his men onto the bridge. Rushing forward, they tried to rip the obstacles apart, at the same time lobbing grenades at the machine guns. Two men almost made it, but were cut down on top of the third barrier. Mick Curnow, aged 22, later wrote:

> Our A Company made a dash for the bridge but five machine guns in enfilade were too much for us. I was lying exposed on an embankment, waiting to go up, and the whole of the first burst went into the bank a foot over my head. The second got the three immediately behind me. Twenty of my nine lives have been used.

Of those who took part in this frontal assault, only five survived.

Carriers were called up but, owing to the position of the obstacles and the width of the bridge, only one could be used. As it advanced, heavy machine-gun fire spewed from behind a rubber-tree roadblock, about 100 metres from the bridge. Although the carrier crew managed to push through the first lot of sand bags and oil drums and silenced the two machine guns at the foot of the bridge, they were unable to broach the second barricade and were forced to withdraw. Anderson called off the attack. In the withdrawal, one man was killed and two badly wounded.

Throughout the morning, the convoy had been creeping closer to the bridge as the Japanese increased their stranglehold from the rear. At each move, especially when the shelling was heavy, Ben Hackney took refuge under the ute, the wisdom of his decision vindicated when he emerged each time to find the cabin increasingly perforated by bomb splinters and bullets. It was some time since he had seen the driver. Assuming he had been wounded or killed, Hackney managed to work out a way to move the vehicle himself, using one foot, the hand throttle and the hand brake.

As word had passed along the line that yet another move was imminent, Hackney dragged himself from under the chassis. Standing on his good leg, with one hand resting on the open window and the other on the seat, he was about to heave himself into the cab when a shell exploded behind him, the concussion knocking the breath from his lungs and flying shrapnel seriously wounding him. One piece entered his back, below his left shoulder blade. Another tore a chunk of muscle from his right calf, while a third lodged in his leg, behind his right knee. Another far larger piece passed between his arm and body, tearing a large hole in the door.

After some time, his clothes now soaked in blood, he managed to drag himself onto the front seat. He still had no driver and, as the ute was holding up the convoy, had no option but to try to drive it himself. His left leg was still useless and the right one was numb from the shrapnel wounds, but somehow he managed to get the vehicle moving, using only his hands.

Wounded men unable to reach the trucks had begun assembling at a small, white-painted wooden bungalow, about 500 metres from the bridge. Brand and Lynch were making their way towards it when a shell screamed overhead. It burst nearby, slicing open Lynch's right ankle. Brand placed him in the parit, waist deep in water, in the hope that it might afford some protection from further shelling, before continuing to the house, under which the wounded were now sheltering. While attending to them, he heard the convoy start up and saw the ambulance moving at some speed along the road.

This time the convoy did not stop after a few metres but kept on going. Leading the charge, the ambulance made a desperate dash onto the bridge, but was met with such a heavy burst of fire that it went over the eastern parapet, clearing the river but landing in swampy ground near the southern approach. The remainder of the convoy came to an abrupt stop, just short of the northern approach.

Anderson faced the inevitable. His men had done all they could, and could do no more. They had achieved the aim of holding up the enemy forces long enough to allow the main allied column to retreat to Yong Peng. There was no point in fighting any longer. There was no possibility of relief; the troops, weary to the point of exhaustion after days of non-stop fighting, were hopelessly outnumbered; the arms were in short supply and the ammunition was all but spent. However, the most compelling reason to call it a day was the desperate condition of the wounded. There was no way Anderson was going to surrender but, if he withdrew the rest of his force towards Yong Peng, leaving the wounded in the trucks under the protection of a Red Cross flag, the Japanese would surely abide by international convention and give them aid.

The decision made, the order was passed along. It was now every man for himself.

Above: House used by Brand and Cahill as an aid post.

Right: The Parit Sulong Bridge, post-war, with remains of wrecked vehicles

CHAPTER 11
EVERY MAN FOR HIMSELF

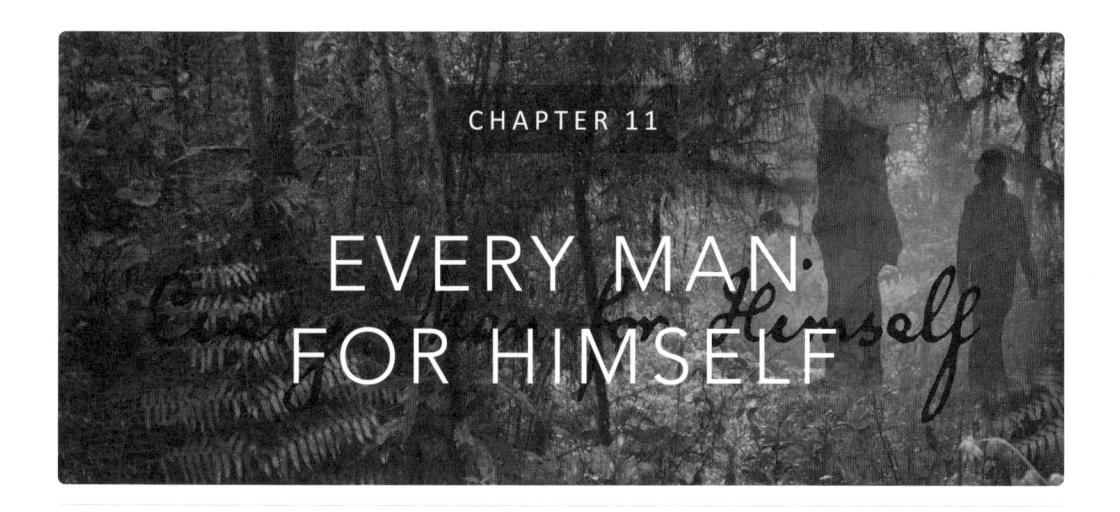

Orders for the withdrawal were issued to all company commanders at 9 am. After destroying any equipment that could not be carried, each company, and the Indian troops assigned to them, were to move off at ten-minute intervals towards the east, where there had been no recent contact with the enemy. Once across the Kangkar Senanggar River, a tributary of the Simpang Kiri, they were to head more or less north on a compass bearing of 340 degrees for a distance of three kilometres, to a track at the foot of the 330-metre-high Bukit Inas.

Personnel from the Intelligence Section were to coordinate the river crossing and provide guides to the track, which, after skirting the hill, led south, back to the Simpang Kiri, but well up-stream from Parit Sulong. After crossing the river, they were to make their way south-east through jungle and swamps to Yong Peng. Although Yong Peng was 25 kilometres from Parit Sulong as the crow flies, the distance to be covered on foot was closer to 50. Anderson warned it was imperative to reach Yong Peng no later than 6 pm the following day, 23 January, when the retreating Allied forces were to blow up the bridge, cutting off their escape.

Cahill and Brand placed all those who could not walk in the trucks, bar one. He was Major Anderson, 45 Indian Brigade's major. Badly wounded, he turned himself into a booby trap by placing a hand grenade under the base of his skull. He told Cahill, 'Do not move me. Do not touch my head. I will rest, and die, here and if any Nips move me I will take them with me'.

Anyone in the convoy who was at all mobile was encouraged to leave, on the pretext that it was to make more room for the badly wounded. It was not until the walking wounded were out of earshot that they learned that all those left behind would be at the mercy of the Japanese. Snelling, the most senior officer, was given a white flag, while Hackney and two other lieutenants were entrusted with the task of negotiating with the Japanese and appealing to them for proper care and attention.

Before the more able-bodied slipped away, guns were rendered inoperable, and carriers and trucks destroyed by filling the sumps and oil filters with laterite and leaving the engines running. Excess gear was dumped in the parits, along with any surplus ammunition, apart from hand grenades, which were left lying about with the pins pulled, some of them under enemy dead. Checkpoints were set up on the eastern side and, at 9.30, the troops began moving out. Although still under fire, many worked their way along the convoy at the bridge to farewell their badly wounded mates and reassure them that all would be well.

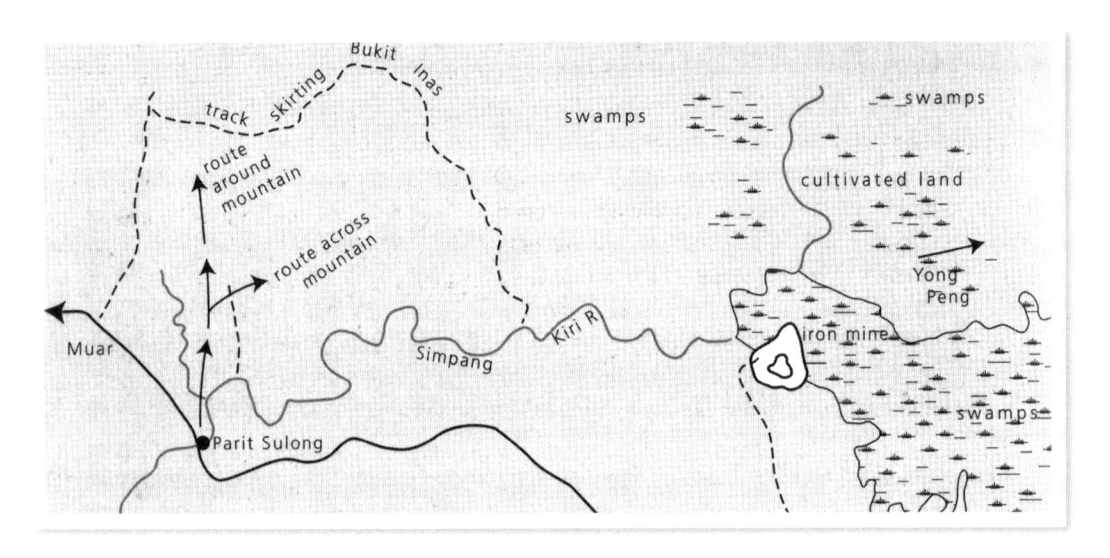

Escape route from Parit Sulong.

Ray Snelling, propped against the wheel of a truck, his shattered legs extending out onto the road, quietly smoked a cigarette from a rather elegant holder as he waited for whatever fate had in store.

The evacuation passed without incident and by 10 am all units were clear, apart from the rearguard and a handful of officers and several others. As the rearguard began its final covering manoeuvre, Anderson, three other officers and Padre Wardale-Greenwood moved off, taking with them about 20 or so shell-shocked and less seriously wounded men.

Although those forming the rearguard disengaged the Japanese by 10.45, it was not until noon that they finally passed through the outer perimeter, ensuring that their comrades had time to put as much distance between themselves and the enemy as possible.

The Japanese saw them leaving but made no attempt to pursue. The reason, Anderson concluded, was that the enemy was 'badly rattled and had no desire to follow up'. He was right. As a senior Japanese officer later disclosed, his men knew they were up against a highly trained force. In fact, some troops had been so reluctant to engage the Australians in battle that their officers had shot a number to force the rest to move into assault positions. However, while the fierce reputation of Anderson's troops may have been the primary reason for the lack of pursuit, the fact that Hackney and some of the other wounded were still taking potshots at the enemy probably had something to do with it.

Back at his HQ, 15 minutes after the rear guard left, Bennett ordered the despatch of a final message to Anderson and his men. He had no illusions about their chances: an officer sent forward to observe the situation at the defile had reported the position there was hopeless. There had been no wireless contact with Parit Sulong for an hour, but Bennett hoped that Anderson would receive his signal. The message, 'authorising' the agonising decision already taken, was sent in clear language, with instructions to repeat it at half-hourly intervals.

> Regret that there is little prospect any success [of] attacks 78-80 m [mile] to help you. Lloyd's party if successful should have appeared before this. 20 of your men and many Indians already returned via river to mine, then track to road which is at present [in]

our possession [at] 78 m. You may at your discretion leave wounded with volunteers, destroy heavy equipment and escape. Sorry unable to help after your heroic effort. Good luck. Gordon Bennett.

Although the rearguard had gone, not everyone had left. Fred had been informed of the intention to withdraw, but concluded that

> it was a blind on the part of Anderson to bolster morale, and to take the final battle as far away as possible from the wounded men, thereby giving them a chance of survival when the Japanese realised they were not in the position to resist capture.
>
> We were doomed to be annihilated. I did not care. All I wanted was to take as many Japs with me as I could when the time came. And I still believe that every man there, including Colonel Anderson, knew how very small were our chances of getting out alive and were reconciled to the same idea.
>
> When the order to break out was given, I and three other signallers were attempting to run a line forward to the bridge, where a section of mortars was operating. We were not having much success as enemy mortar fire was constantly sweeping the area, cutting the wire to pieces. When we eventually succeeded in reaching our objective, with the intention of giving the time for the withdrawal, we discovered that the mortar section had been wiped out by machine-gun fire. Their mortar and unfired shells were still in position and a stretcher bearer, Chris Guerin, was recovering the identification discs from the dead men. We could see the enemy massing on the opposite bank of the river attempting to launch a boat, and decided to try our luck firing the remaining bombs.
>
> Great was our joy when the first bomb landed fair and square in their midst, sinking the boat and killing all the Japs who were in it. We quickly fired two more shells, which landed amongst the Japs on the bank with varying results. We only had two left when the Japanese managed to land a shell right under our mortar, which, must to our surprise hurtled off into space leaving us dumbfounded but unhurt. The sharp staccato bark of a Jap machine gun and the whistle of bullets soon brought us to our senses. Deciding it was not our job to fight the Japs single handed, we left in a hurry, racing for cover among the rubber, with explosive bullets clipping the leaves from the trees around us. How we escaped being hit is still a mystery to both of us!
>
> When we returned to the battalion headquarters we were surprised to find that they had already moved out. Seeing movement at the truck convey we made our way there, to learn that we were to gather any wounded who thought they could walk, and try to make our escape. Going along the trucks we found a couple of wounded men who were awaiting an escort to help them make the break. Saying goodbye to the others we left, believing that the Japanese would treat them fairly. I think we must have been the last to leave the area.

One of the badly injured men left in the convoy was one of Fred's mates from Boorowa, Harry Grosvenor, aged 34, who had been wounded in both buttocks. A few other soldiers who had not yet left also moved along the trucks with no regard for their personal safety, doing what they could for the wounded and reassuring them that all would be well. Whatever the reason, to expose oneself for too long was fatal. Among those picked off by snipers was Lloyd Cahill's batman, Wally Hammond, one of the convoy's two remaining medics, who was shot in the head. Facing the prospect of either death or capture himself,

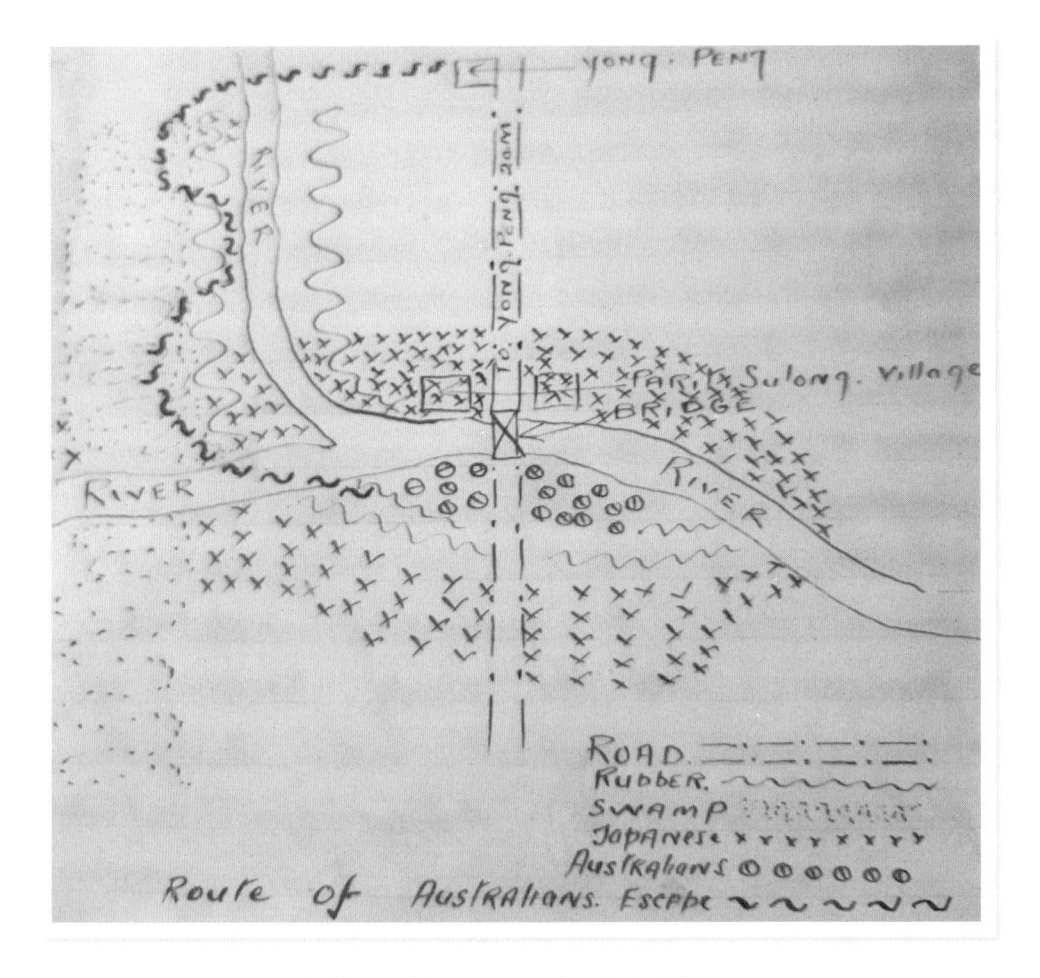

Fred's map of the escape route from the battlefield.

Guerin, the surviving stretcher bearer, told Hackney it was now time for him and the other four to leave.

By this time the majority of the force was already well on its way. Those on the eastern side of the road had a far easier time than those on the west. Not only were the latter compelled to run the gauntlet of two enemy aircraft strafing the roadway, they also had to take a flying leap to cross the western and then the eastern parit. As young Chick Warden dashed across the road between the strafing, he took a quick look northwards. The entire area was a mess – wrecked trucks and carriers and the remains of Braddon's 25-pounder gun, spiked by the artillerymen.

Leaving the cover of the rubber unchallenged, the various groups assembled on the banks of the Kangkar Senanggar. Further upstream it was only about 11 metres wide, but closer to the bridge it was nearer to fifty. Apart from the middle section, the river was fordable, but the current, on an outgoing tide, was very swift. Divesting himself of his rifle, tin hat and equipment, Mick Curnow swam across the river with some of his gear but, on returning to the river bank for the rest, discovered that someone had helped themselves to his belongings, the most important of which was his tin hat.

Since a number of Australians and almost all of the Indians could not swim, ropes

Roadway littered with wreckage (post-war photograph).

were fashioned by tying unravelled turbans together and anchoring them to trees either side of the river. Unfortunately, the strain on one of these makeshift lines proved too great and it broke, washing away a number of men who were swept downstream and drowned. Fallen trees were then dragged into the water, enabling the rest to get across. Other groups further upstream had more success, using a combination of bamboo poles and turbans. One, who thought he could not swim, simply stripped to the skin and dog-paddled across. Others removed their socks and boots and slung them around their necks, only to have the current carry them away, forcing them to make the long trek to Yong Peng bare-footed. The men in Roly Dean's party took turns to carry an apparently comatose patient on a makeshift litter, made from a ground sheet and two bush poles. Somehow, they managed to get both stretcher and patient across the river.

One of the last groups to reach the far side brought the devastating news that Anderson had been killed. There were no other details. Assuming command on the strength of this information, Major Dick Keegan ordered the troops to split into fighting patrols of 30 or 40 men and make for Yong Peng in company formation, as planned.

Much of the area was under cultivation, but there was also a great deal of swamp and jungle so, to ensure they did not become lost, a member of the intelligence section was attached to each group. To avoid leaving defined tracks the men split into small parties whenever they entered the jungle, re-forming again as soon as they were under the cover of the trees.

On leaving the rendezvous point, some decided that to climb Bukit Inas would be too energy sapping and elected to go round it. One group that opted for the hill was headed by Lloyd Cahill, who had been tending the wounded for several days and nights without rest. When he collapsed from exhaustion the men placed him on an improvised stretcher, made from bush poles and a couple of shirts, and carried him over the hill, by which time he pronounced himself rested enough to walk. Another group, whose wounded had injuries five days old that were giving off a nauseating stench, chose the longer, less taxing route. Their pace was slow, but when they reached the other side of the hill, they received additional help from others who had climbed over the top.

Jungle now gave way to swamp, waist-deep at times but, as they were unsure if the enemy were in pursuit, the fugitives could not stop to rest. As they pushed on towards an area of high ground, the rapidly fading light forced them to hang onto the bayonet scabbard of the man in front, lest they become separated and lost. At around midnight, one party, having covered a mere 300 metres through the muck in three hours and with no hope of reaching the knoll, called a halt. They laid branches across tree roots in an effort to get out of the bog, but sleep was virtually impossible. Not only was everyone cold and wet through, but the sandflies and mosquitoes descended in droves.

For Fred's party, trailing after the main group, it was a near thing.

> The Japs were closing in all round on the five of us and we could hear them on both sides and behind us, calling to one another. Then a small party of Indians broke across the road and ran for dear life along the river. We followed them, keeping far enough in the rear to allow them to run into any ambush, if one existed. We reached a spot where, judging by the tracks on the riverbank, the rest of the escaping party had crossed. We decided to follow, but were foiled by enemy fire. The Indians were trapped and were all killed. The Japs were too much occupied with them to notice us and we got away and crossed about a mile further on.
>
> I was the only one who could swim and had to make four trips to bring the others across. The last trip was only just completed when the enemy again opened fire, but we crept into the swamp and out of sight. The impossible had been accomplished but we were still a long way from safety.
>
> We stole silently into the swampy jungle, our only thought to put as much distance between us and the Japanese, in the shortest possible time. Progress was slow, and sunset saw us hopelessly lost but no sign of the enemy, although we could still hear their heavy machine-guns firing, back near the convoy.
>
> However, traces of the main party could be seen where the mud was still stirred up. It seemed an impossible task to reach Yong Peng if we had to keep to the swamps all the way. Late in the evening we found where the main party had left the swamps and taken to the mountains. We caught up with them resting in a patch of jungle just as darkness fell.
>
> Before our small group continued on, we took stock of our belongings. One of the men had a compass. After consultation we decided to move by compass bearing through the night, in the hope that we could outdistance any Japanese effort to head us off. The darkness was so intense that we could only move in single file, keeping in touch with the man immediately in front to avert the possibility of becoming isolated in groups. Till the early hours of the morning we stumbled along and climbed over fallen trees, when sheer exhaustion made us call a halt. We slept where we lay.

It was only with extreme difficulty that the able-bodied, walking with the bulk of the force, managed to get the wounded moving at first light the next day. Thorns ripped clothing and skin and vines entangled limbs as the men hacked their way through the stinking swamp water, varying in depth from ankle to waist deep. After finally reaching

Retreat from Parit Sulong (Murray Griffin).

the knoll, their next obstacle was the fast-flowing Simpang Kiri River. One of the privates swam across to a kampong on the far bank, where he persuaded the Malay villagers to ferry them, and any groups following, in their canoes. Once over the river, the party regrouped and, since the going was now much easier, split into three parallel columns to speed things up. Fortunately, the pro-British Chinese, who occupied most of the isolated farms and houses scattered between the rubber plantations, gave whatever cooked rice and fruit they had, along with water and tea, and also acted as guides. It was due largely to their assistance that an advance party of ten reached Yong Peng the next morning. On learning that other groups were following, the sappers held off blowing the bridge until midnight, thereby giving the rest a further six hours' grace.

Roly Dean and another seven men, who were carrying the comatose stretcher patient in relays, four men at a time, certainly needed the extra leeway. Unable to keep up, they were soon left behind. Fortunately, they met a young British officer, who had a map and a compass and assured them he could get them to Yong Peng. He seemed confident, so the

Australians were happy to follow his lead.

They were crossing some open flooded padi fields on a narrow, elevated pathway when they heard the sound of an approaching plane. Leaving their patient on the track, the rest took to the water, submerging their entire bodies as the aircraft passed overhead. They were not spotted, but were forced to dive under several times to evade further detection before they reached the safety of some thick scrub. After crossing the river, they reached a house owned by a friendly Chinese, who gave them a meal and assured them he would keep watch while they slept.

When Dean went to check on their patient's bandages the next morning, he found he was not wounded at all. He had simply wanted a free ride. Infuriated, the others left him behind, so the malingerer had no hope of pulling his scam a second time. The next group to arrive at the house was under the command of Anderson who, contrary to the previous report, was very much alive and well. Discovering that the white man, now dressed in civilian clothing and enjoying the hospitality of the Chinese farmer, was one of his own troops, the CO ordered him to get back into uniform and start moving.

No longer burdened by the stretcher 'patient', Dean's little band soon caught up to the leading troops and, just as the sun began to set, reached the Yong Peng bridge. Here the wounded were whisked away to hospital, where mud-encrusted wounds were cleaned and dressed, and gangrenous limbs amputated. When Dean was finally able to remove his swollen feet from his boots, he had to cut his socks off. He was luckier than most, as his putties had kept his feet fairly dry. Those with waterlogged boots discovered that, when they removed their socks, the soles of their feet came off too.

Anderson's party, which had swelled to 80, also made it to Yong Peng. They were finally picked up north of the Yong Peng crossroads, sometime after 9 pm. Stopping neither to wash nor to eat, within the hour the Colonel was at Bennett's headquarters, in a tent in a rubber plantation, delivering his report. The General later recorded that 'he was cool and calm and talked as if the whole battle was merely a training exercise. From this I understood why he was able to keep his men in hand. With such coolness, self-control, strength of character, and with such kindly affection and consideration for his men, he could overcome all difficulties.'

The wounded in Cahill's group made the last part of the journey in comfort. On reaching a village about 16 kilometres east of Yong Peng, Cahill pedalled into town on a bicycle belonging to a young Chinese boy. Although, on the way, he fell into a swamp from exhaustion, Cahill reached Yong Peng where he was able to arrange for an ambulance to transfer the wounded.

One of the last groups to arrive was Warden's, which emerged from the jungle onto the main road north of Yong Peng at 10 pm, a scant two hours before the bridge was blown. Another party of 33, most of whom were wounded, also made it in time.

Fred's group was lucky to meet the deadline.

> When daylight came we found we had travelled almost in a circle and, as for actual distance, had not travelled five miles. The man with the compass had confused his directions and had lost his bearings completely. Handing it to me, he said, 'You've got us this far. I think you're the one to get us out, if anyone does'.
>
> We could now hear the sounds of battle along the road towards Yong Peng and, taking our bearings from this, we again set out, with another signaller and me acting as forward

scouts. Moving forward we scouted out the area and then, if all was clear, we awaited the arrival of the rest.

Yong Peng was about 20 miles away. My geographical knowledge was all right but I knew little of the jungles and swamps we would have to pass through, to keep to the course that I set. It took us over jungle-clad mountains and down gullies, but no deviation was made.

At three in the afternoon we came across a path leading along the edge of a patch of rubber. Listening intently, we could hear voices ahead of us. I told my mate Chris to wait, while I went on ahead. If I fired a shot he would know I had contacted Japs, and was to rush back to the others and they could disperse into the shelter of the jungle-covered swamps. It was useless for us to attempt to fight, as we could not have mustered 50 rounds of ammunition between the lot of us.

Keeping on the edge of the swamp, I moved forward until my progress was blocked by an impenetrable mass of vines and jungle growth. It meant taking to the higher ground to find out what lay ahead. Taking advantage of what cover was available I crept forward and there, plainly in view at a native hut, was a large party of Japanese. I debated the question with myself. What could I do? The Japanese decided it for me. As they made preparations for resting, I retired back the way I had come and headed my mates back into the swamps and as far away from the Japanese as we could, before moving ahead again.

After travelling for two hours another scouting party went out, while the rest of us took our ease and awaited their report. At last they came back and told us that no Japanese were in sight. We heaved a sigh of relief and moved on, until we reached a rubber plantation. Skirting the edges we came in sight of a river. Telling my companions to remain concealed, I moved forward to reconnoitre and reached the river about 100 yards from a small native hut. Carefully making my way towards it, I spotted an old Chinese man fishing from the nearby river bank.

He didn't see me until I was almost upon him. Drawing my revolver, I marched right up to him, but he didn't so much as flinch or even remove his fishing line from the water. Instead he patted the ground next to him, and bade me in English to sit down. I asked him which way to Yong Peng. He pointed and said, 'Six miles'. I asked him if there were any Japanese about.

'No. Australians here yesterday. I take across river. Go Yong Peng. You go Youg Peng?'

'Yes', I said.

'I take you to road across river. You do as I say you get Yong Peng. You no do as I say you get Japanese.'

I asked if he had any food. He said, 'How many?' I held up five fingers. He smiled. Rolling up his fishing line he told me to bring the rest of the party to the hut.

We had only covered about half the distance when the old man met us, gesticulating wildly for us to take cover. As we did so he began to gather sticks from beneath the trees.

There were sounds of movement in the jungle, heralding the arrival of ten Japanese soldiers, who asked the man numerous questions that we could not understand. However, by his actions, it appeared he was directing them back along the river.

As soon as they had gone from sight he had us running for the river bank near his hut. Cutting away a portion of the bank he hauled out a long narrow boat, into which we quickly tumbled. Keeping to the shelter of the bank, he allowed the current to take us swiftly downstream.

After travelling for about a mile, he edged across to the opposite bank to a small hut. Alighting, we went inside and to our delight found freshly cooked rice, meat and biscuits, which he gave us to understand we were to take with us and eat as we travelled. Tired and weary, dirty and unshaven as we were, it was the greatest thing that had happened to us since our first day of battle.

He also gave me a packet of Chinese cigarettes and instructions on how to reach Yong Peng. Following his directions to the letter, we struggled into Yong Peng just at sundown, footsore and weary, but happy to know that we were behind the British front line, which was about four miles out along the Muar road. The main Allied force was slowly retreating to Yong Peng, where the 2/30th Battalion was covering the retreat. Once everyone was across the bridge, it would be blown.

We were surprised to find that some of the members of B Echelon had escaped and were already on their way back to base at Johor Bahru. The rest of the force had given us up for lost and were amazed to think that any of us had survived. From the reports they had heard it was impossible for us to get out.

There were more than 200 survivors who came through to Yong Peng; many more turned up later, some even reaching Java and Sumatra. One party, cut off from the rest of us, marched right across the Malay peninsular and arrived in Singapore a fortnight later.

But the relief of our escape more than compensated for what we had endured. I remember asking a 2/30th soldier for a cigarette: He said, 'Did you just come out of Muar'. When I answered in the affirmative he gave me six packets of cigarettes and a bottle of whisky. And that was the only time I ever enjoyed a nip of it! It seemed to banish all fatigue and gave me the feeling of being able to do as much again.
But could I?

After a rest in the shelter of the rubber, followed by a bath, change of clothes and a good night's sleep, we were loaded onto trucks and rushed down to base at Johor Bahru where, with the aid of reinforcements, we reformed the 2/19th Battalion.

For Mick Curnow and his party, Yong Peng was not the sanctuary they had envisaged. 'After reaching Yong Peng, where we were fed, we slept the whole night. The next morning I felt more scared than during the whole show – everyone was the same, probably the reaction. What caused our scare was a Jap plane, the only breed we seemed to see, bombing the road 100 yards behind us, and then machine-gunning the rubber plantation in which we were, and me with no tin hat.'

One group of 18 arrived after the bridge was blown. However, the following morning they managed to cross the river under their own steam and moved cross-country to the rear of the town. By the time they regained the Allied lines, they had covered the best part of 80 kilometres.

Although Anderson had despatched Fred to alert the mortar platoon at the Parit Sulong bridge that a withdrawal was imminent, other troops nearby had not received the order.

Private Charles Edwards, one of those who did not receive the order to escape.

Among them was the 2/19th's Private Charles Edwards who, with nine others, had been sent to plug a 100-metre gap in the perimeter near the river the previous day. That night they had blown up two tanks attempting to break through. The men survived the early morning aerial and mortar attacks, but a tank, advancing from the west, broke through their perimeter, raking the area with light machine-gun fire and killing the two forward troops. Edwards was sure he would be next but, instead of coming back for a second sweep, the tank turned towards the road.

After some time, Edwards and those who had survived the attack realised that things had become very quiet. A private, dispatched to cross the road to see what was going on, reported that there was no-one about, other than the wounded in the trucks. No-one believed him, so he was sent back. When he finally convinced the others that everyone else had left, they checked those lying about for signs of life. They located five who were still alive before they decided that it was high time to go, and headed west.

By some mischance, an entire platoon from the 2/19th also failed to receive the withdrawal order. Forced to fight their way out, they eventually reached Yong Peng and rejoined their unit, but another section, also fighting on the western side of the road, was unable to disengage. Only one man survived.

A number of others arrived safely at Yong Peng on 23 January, among them Lynch and Brand. After settling the seriously wounded into the trucks at Parit Sulong, Brand had gathered the walking wounded from beneath his RAP and retrieved Lynch from the drain. With a soldier, wounded in one arm, supporting Lynch on one side, and with Brand on the other, the three men had made their way through the rubber to the river crossing. Lynch could not swim, so he clung to the backs of the other two and they plunged in, without losing their stride or waiting to discard any gear. On the other side was a party of Indian soldiers who almost immediately vanished into the jungle, leaving behind their English officer, a very youthful-looking captain. He had a serious shrapnel wound in his thigh and told the Australians to leave him, but they refused.

Reaching a small kampong at the foot of Bukit Inas, Brand found about 30 stragglers. Six were wounded, one of them quite seriously. After dressing the English officer's injury and attending to other wounded, Brand led the party up the hill. There was no track, so a path had to be cut. For the fit, it was a gruelling climb; for the wounded, nigh to impossible. They had to be hauled, literally, up the slope and over rocky outcrops by the able-bodied. The Englishman asked repeatedly to be left behind but his entreaties fell on deaf ears.

About halfway up, everyone stopped for a breather. While they were resting, the English captain moved out of their line of sight, behind some bushes. Without warning, a shot rang out. Rather than hold them up, he had put his pistol to his head. He had left a note, explaining he was 'all in' and wishing them luck, along with a compass and a hand-drawn map, showing them how to reach Yong Peng.

Later that afternoon, they stopped in a rocky defile by a mountain stream where they bathed their feet and rested. It was agreed that one of the men, who knew far more about map reading than Brand, should lead the group, allowing him to take care of the wounded.

The following morning, they reached a road leading to Pasir, a small fishing village on the Simpang Kiri. They were about to follow it, when a Malay rushed up and begged them to go in the other direction, pointing towards the kampong and repeating 'Nippon. Nippon'. They could see he was telling the truth: fluttering from one of the buildings was the distinctive red and white Japanese flag. The Malay guided them to the village where the other groups had crossed. Before they boarded two sampans waiting to ferry them over, a meal was eked out from the remaining rations – one-fifth of a biscuit and one thirtieth of a tin of bully beef per person.

A little further on they met a group of 30 or so and the combined party, now swelled to more than 65, pushed on. Lynch was by this time becoming very weak and many of the others were on their last legs. Fortunately, late in the afternoon, they reached the outskirts of Yong Peng where the field ambulance took over the care of the injured. For his tireless efforts with the wounded, whom he shepherded to safety from behind enemy lines, not once, but twice, Victor Brand, aged just 26, was awarded a Military Cross.

Bert Mettam and a group of 2/29th men and anti-tankers, who had taken to the swamps at Bakri, also reached Yong Peng, after a valiant but unsuccessful effort to link up with Anderson at Parit Sulong. After leaving the four most seriously wounded men at the woodcutter's hut, they had set off for Parit Sulong on the morning of 21 January with high hopes of rejoining the main force. However, as they had been warned, the jungle trail was very hard going. There were constant delays trying to negotiate narrow rotten bridges and the entire afternoon was spent wading through a swamp. To keep themselves from dehydrating, they were forced to rely on rainwater that had collected in swamp bell flowers.

By about 4 pm they had only covered about 25 kilometres. They stopped for the night at a small kampong, where the friendly Chinese gave them a drink of hot chocolate and a meal of pork and rice. The following day, they set off at six, confident of reaching Parit Sulong, which, according to the locals, was still in Allied hands. However, they had not gone far when they encountered civilians from Kampong Kangkar hurrying past – in the opposite direction. That very morning, Japanese troops had arrived at the village and confiscated all the bicycles.

They pressed on, nevertheless, and were about five kilometres from the village when they met a schoolteacher who told them Parit Sulong was in enemy hands. The senior officers decided that, as it was impossible for such a large force to slip through enemy lines undetected, it must be 'every man for himself'. The men were ordered to subdivide into small groups and make their own way back to Singapore. Some of the officers intended to strike out for the coast and try to reach Sumatra, but others planned to head north and rest for a few days. When the enemy forces had gone past, they, too, would head for Singapore.

Mettam, believing that a party of 200 fit and well-armed men should not be disbanded, was angry and disappointed by the decision to split up. He requested a map and a compass for his group, but was told there were none to spare. He was, however, given a lecture on how to find north with his wrist watch, using the old Boy Scout trick of pointing the hour-hand to the sun and then bisecting the angle between it and the figure twelve. Returning to the platoon, he informed his companions of the officers' decision and ordered them to split into two groups of 16.

Mettam's band soon discovered that bayonets were not designed for slashing a path through thick jungle. If they wanted to reach Singapore, they would have to use jungle paths, drainage ditches, creeks, and anything else heading in a generally southerly direction. Late that afternoon, while making their way through a rubber plantation, they met an Indian civilian. After taking them through the estate's coolie lines, he led them down a jungle path to a spot where they could spend the night, promising to return the next morning and guide them to the river, where they could obtain a boat.

Concerned that he might betray them to the Japanese, the men took no chances, moving off the track into deeper cover. They had just settled down when they were awakened by the sound of voices and marching feet. Recognising the language as English and the accents Australian, they scrambled onto the track to find a group of men last seen at the Bakri roadblock.

The following morning the Indian returned. Even with his expert guidance, negotiating the swamps and jungle with the wounded took them quite a while to reach the river. They were then ferried, three at a time, to a small landing on the other side, their Malay boatmen keeping a sharp lookout for reconnaissance planes circling overhead. Reaching the jetty, they immediately headed along a dirt road leading to the main Yong Peng-Bakri road, expecting, in a very short time, to meet up with the Allied forces.

They were too late. The bridge had been blown.

As they neared it, a squad of enemy soldiers, mounted on bicycles, appeared around a bend in the road. The party scattered and ran in all directions. Some were later captured and sent to Pudu Gaol in Kuala Lumpur. As Mettam and some of his mates fled into a nearby rubber plantation, the Japanese opened fire, but fortunately were poor shots and did not bother to pursue them.

That night they slept in a drainage ditch running through a rubber plantation, where they could hear the sound of motor vehicles moving in a continuous stream along the main road. The following day they continued south. After passing nervously through a grassy area smelling strongly of tiger, they reached a deserted kampong where they found a container of cooked rice. Emptying it into a haversack, they retreated to a nearby rubber plantation where they waited until dark before bedding down under some bushes, a kilometre or so along the track.

The next morning, after reaching the Ayer Hitam road, they followed it east until they reached a causeway running through low-lying, marshy ground. As there appeared to be a roadblock at the far end, Mettam and a companion went ahead to investigate while the others waited in some nearby houses. The pair had covered about three-quarters of the distance, unchallenged, when Mettam's instincts warned him to go no further. Dropping over the edge of the road, the two men doubled back and joined the others. They were debating what to do next when they were startled by the sound of tramping feet. It was a company of British troops, marching in two columns, one on either side of the road, with a number of Indians straggling along at the rear. In the lead, mounted on a bicycle, was a forward scout.

Mettam voiced his doubts about the roadblock, but the British CO was unconvinced. He insisted that the Australian 2/26 Battalion had set it up and, to prove it, he and the scout marched up the centre of the causeway, only to return almost immediately, running for their lives. As shots rang out, the two men disappeared over the side of the road. Mettam and his party didn't hang about. Crossing the causeway, they headed south, followed by about 25 Indians. The British troops remained where they were.

By this time, the Australians were very hungry. The rice they had tipped into the haversack was now rancid and the houses they searched in abandoned villages yielded nothing, apart from a lone pineapple. They did, however, find a bicycle chained to a post. As one of the party with injured feet was slowing them down, the others snapped the chain with their bayonets and put him on the bike, enabling them to make much better time.

Spending the night in a deserted house, they set off next day through country that seemed to have been abandoned completely. Early that afternoon they reached a river where a Malay took them by canoe to a fairly large kampong. After a slight altercation between its Malay and Chinese communities over who had the right to offer hospitality to the visitors, they followed a Chinese man, who not only provided sweet biscuits and coffee, but also a guide. After leading them across a maze of padi fields and swamps, he left them at a well-worn track saying 'Singapore road, that way'.

Although it was late afternoon, the Australians pressed on until they reached a bitumen road. Greatly encouraged by the sight of bridges and culverts standing intact, they flew caution to the wind, certain that they were now ahead of the Japanese forces. Entering a cutting, they were suddenly challenged by several soldiers, with shaved heads and brown faces, staring at them across their rifle sights. The Australians did not understand the language, but one of the Indians at the rear of the column immediately answered the challenge. The troops were not Japanese, but Gurkhas, the prompt response from the Indian soldier probably saving all their lives. A couple of 2/19th men, challenged by Gurkhas while paddling a canoe down a river, had not understood the lingo and, consequently, had not replied. Both had been shot.

The Gurkhas were about to blow the bridge but, on learning that British troops were at Ayer Hitam and that other groups were working their way south, they held off. The British never arrived. After the Japanese had opened fire at the roadblock, the entire group was captured and taken to Pudu.

Now they were safely behind Allied lines, the Australians were driven to a police station north of Johor Bahru. It was 27 January. After eight days on the run, they were safe.

Mettam's group fared much better than many of the others who had split from the 'swamp' party. Some reached Yong Peng to find it in enemy hands. They then retreated back the way they had come, only to be captured or killed. Another party of ten, which reached a track about six or seven kilometres from Yong Peng, learned that they were too late. Turning south, they crossed a crocodile-infested river in a leaky sampan – a hair-raising experience that saw two of the party scrambling ashore when the boat sank, chased by a very irate crocodile. Three days later, wracked with fever and mentally and physically spent, they were heading east towards Ayer Hitam, when they walked into an ambush and were taken prisoner. Shortly afterwards, they too were on their way to Pudu Gaol. Another nine, who were also captured, were taken to the north of Muar and executed.

A few men reached Sumatra's west coast. One party from the swamp group, after obtaining a junk at Batu Pahat, sailed across the Straits of Malacca to Sumatra. They then proceeded south to the mouth of the Indragiri River where they joined an escape route, set up by the British special force, SOE Far East, which took them across the mountains to the west coast. From there a British cruiser evacuated them to Java, where they talked their way on board a merchant vessel bound for Australia.

Arriving home, they were shocked to discover that their escape was regarded almost as desertion. Unable to prove that the order 'every man for himself' had been issued by their officers, who then abandoned them, most were posted to mundane jobs for the rest of the war. Unlike many who had escaped from Singapore in similar circumstances, these men, dubbed the 'Malayan harriers', were viewed with suspicion for much of their lives, not only by the general public but also by returned prisoners-of-war.

Tired, and more than a little nervous on being told they were on their own, another party from the swamp group had set off on foot towards the south. However, believing that it would be easier to try to reach Singapore by boat, rather than battling through jungle and swamp, they split into two smaller groups and headed for the west coast.

Although they were spotted and strafed by an enemy plane as they took cover in a banana plantation, one of the parties reached a fishing village on a tidal creek. Ten dollars secured a small canoe and they paddled out to some large fish traps, just off the beach. After resting on one of the elevated platforms for 36 hours, they paddled closer in-shore to make a less conspicuous approach to a lighthouse on an island, about eight kilometres away. Crossing the mouth of a large river, they passed through scores of Japanese bodies, now in a state of advanced decomposition.

On reaching the island, they gorged themselves on bananas growing in a grove near the beach before settling down for the night. The following morning, they went up to the lighthouse which, judging from the number of tins of meat and fish pierced open with the point of a bayonet, had only just been vacated. Although all the canned food was spoiled, there was plenty of dried beans, rice, sago and cooking oil in the lighthouse keeper's bungalow, plus a vegetable garden, a water buffalo and chickens. They also found a boat tied up on the leeward side of the island, but it was holed and a complete wreck.

They stayed on Pisang (Banana) Island for about three weeks. When food stocks started to run down, and with the very crafty chickens impossible to catch, they slaughtered the water buffalo. There were no refrigeration facilities but, in the two days before the meat went 'off', they managed to cook and eat both hindquarters and one of the front legs. They also managed to caulk the boat but, although they made a tall mast and a huge sail, all attempts to get the craft out to sea failed.

Despair was just setting in when a small boat arrived. On board were planters, a party of guerrillas and a few 2/19th soldiers, all carpenters from one of the pioneer platoons. The newcomers had plenty of food to share but, even better, the carpenter sergeant cast a critical and experienced eye over the patched-up boat, which he pronounced seaworthy. Two nights later the 2/29th men were on their way.

It was after dark when they reached Sumatra where they swapped their sailing boat for a lift to the Indragiri River in a flat-bottomed riverboat. Joining the well-established escape route, they reached Padang on the west coast, where they waited in vain for a week for an evacuation vessel. On 17 March the Japanese occupied the town and took everyone prisoner.

Although many failed in their attempt to reach the Allied lines, Russell Braddon and Hugh Moore almost succeeded. At Parit Sulong, carrying the infantryman wounded in the thigh between them, they had stuffed their shirts with grenades, grabbed two rifles each, and run, crouching low and in short bursts, towards the rubber. Wriggling on their stomachs, and dragging the infantryman, rifles and machine gun behind them, it took an hour before they were outside the perimeter.

By midnight, when they stopped to rest, they had covered only about 16 kilometres. Their party had by this time swelled to about 40, as others, on discovering the trio had a map and a compass, joined them. When they awoke around 3 am, their muscles were aching agonisingly from cramp and the torrential rain had saturated their clothing and gear. After negotiating Bukit Inas, they entered the swamps where, finding it impossible to carry both the wounded man and the weapons, they dumped the latter in the water. However, as a precaution, Braddon kept four grenades stuffed down his shirt. The party now numbered about 140 – 100 of them infantry, under the command of a sole officer.

On reaching more open country, the infantry officer clashed with Braddon's party on the best way to go. He decided against continuing with his men to Yong Peng, which, he believed, would have already fallen to the Japanese. Braddon's group, which had not agreed with any of his decisions to date, kept going, and was joined by one of their artillery officers.

Nearing Yong Peng, they reached some mangroves where, with the assistance of Moore's rifle and one of Braddon's grenades, they persuaded Malay villagers to take them to Yong Peng in their sampans. After negotiating a series of oily waterways, the boatmen guided the small craft onto a broad river and then for some distance upstream. Turning into a small canal, the boatman pointed to his left and announced, 'Yong Peng'.

They had only covered about two kilometres of the 12-kilometre hike when they met an Allied officer. When he told them that the town would be held for another day or so, the artillery officer suggested that someone should go back for the infantrymen. Assured that guides would be awaiting their return, Braddon and Moore volunteered. Retracing their route up the river and through the mangroves, they located the party, only to discover their mission was futile. Calling them 'bloody fools' for returning, when he had already made his position clear, the infantry officer refused to go with them. Neither he nor his men were ever seen again.

The two gunners, by now thoroughly exhausted, made their way back to the swamp where, with some more verbal persuasion, backed up by a couple of hand grenades, they induced the boatman to take them back to the canal. They reached the rendezvous point, but found no guides waiting, as promised. They did, however, find seven other Australians, including an officer. The party of nine finally reached the outskirts of Yong Peng at dawn on 24 January to find the bridge blown and thousands of the enemy milling about. Beating a retreat into a nearby rubber plantation, they agreed their only option was to head for Singapore.

The ORs organised themselves into pairs and moved south, only to be ambushed. One was shot. The rest fled. Braddon and Moore, who were fleet of foot, would probably have escaped into the jungle on the other side of the path had the officer not shouted to all of them to stop and surrender. Although their instincts told them to keep going, their training automatically kicked in. The pair faltered and, having done so, lost their momentum. A Japanese soldier armed with a sub-machine gun cut them off. They were taken prisoner and transported to Pudu Gaol.

Another group of gunners, who came face to face with the Japanese, had better luck. They were heading south near a patch of jungle when they came upon a party of enemy soldiers. Nine were able to take cover in the dense foliage and later regroup, but one was captured. Although tied to a tree, his life was spared, and before long he too was on his way to Pudu Gaol. The others joined about 20 British soldiers and headed in the direction of Ayer Hitam where, after successfully negotiating a minefield, they met up with the Australian forces, which were due to pull out within the hour.

Many soldiers from 2/29 Battalion involved in the main retreat from Parit Sulong also ran into trouble. Some reached Yong Peng, only to be captured. Others who made it to the town simply disappeared – forever. Several more who reached Parit Jawa, Batu Pahat and Ayer Hitam were captured and killed.

While most of these deaths occurred in the days immediately after the initial retreat, the killings went on for some weeks. On 12 March, the 2/29th's Lieutenant Ron Cootes and Private Arthur Nicholls, whose platoon had taken to the jungle during the attack on the roadblock near the 98-mile peg, were captured by Malays. The men, who had been on the run for the best part of two months, were covered with jungle sores. With them were two corporals from their battalion. All four were handed over to Japanese troops, who tied them up and slashed them with bayonets. The senior Japanese officer – a tall, slim young man who spoke English – then ordered the execution of Cootes and Nicholls with a light-machine gun. The reason? They had jungle sores. The other two, whose physical appearance evidently did not offend the officer's sensibilities, were sent to Changi Camp in Singapore.

A large number of the men in Roaring Reg Newton's transport group tried unsuccessfully to reach the Allied lines. After taking to the swamp on 19 January, they had begun hacking a path through the swampy jungle, parallel to the road leading to Parit Sulong. The going was extremely tough, so tough that they ditched all surplus gear. Although the men were often up to their armpits in water, thirst was a constant problem as the only water safe to drink was rainwater that had collected in the bulbous flowers of a carnivorous plant known as 'Dutchman's Pipe'. Without food to keep them going, the fugitives' strength ebbed away, and on 20 and 21 January three of the wounded died.

The remainder emerged from the swamps somewhere between the 94 and 89 mile pegs on the night of the 21st, their skin soggy and wrinkled like prunes, and with inflamed minor wounds and scratches angry. The following morning, evidently unable to hear the sound of gunfire from Parit Sulong only a few kilometres away, Newton crossed the road and headed for a village about 11 kilometres from Parit Sulong.

On 23 January, having spent the previous day either slogging across swampy ground or cutting a trail through thick jungle, they met a small group of English soldiers. Learning that Parit Sulong was in enemy hands, Newton decided to head for the coast south of Batu Pahat and try to work his way down to Singapore.

However, by the end of the following day, although good progress had been made, the general situation was grim. The condition of the wounded, whose injuries were turning gangrenous, was deteriorating; the 'fit' men carrying them were close to exhaustion; and the party was desperately in need of protein, as the only provisions they had been able to purchase were fruit and a small pig, spit-roasted and shared among them all. That night, several men removed their boots to find that their feet had swelled so much they could not get them back on. Others, when they peeled off their socks, stiff with sweat and grime, had also lost the skin from their soles. If this were not bad enough, a head man told them that the Japanese had commandeered all fishing craft and rice stocks from kampongs along the Simpang Kiri.

The next day, Newton and a small advance party successfully crossed the river in a leaky boat, only to find that a large number of Japanese were on the other side. Fortunately, the boat remained afloat long enough to ferry them back to the village, where it promptly sank. The situation, in regard to food and the wounded, was now so critical that the group split into small parties of four to six men and proceeded independently in various directions.

Newton, with a party of sick and wounded, headed for the coast. It took them five days, despite the distance being only eight kilometres, and two men died en route. They remained hidden throughout the day, venturing out only after dark to look for a boat and forage for food. The Japanese had confiscated most of the rice and all of the livestock and poultry, but there was plenty of fruit, as the whole area was dotted with farms growing bananas, coconuts, pineapples and root crops.

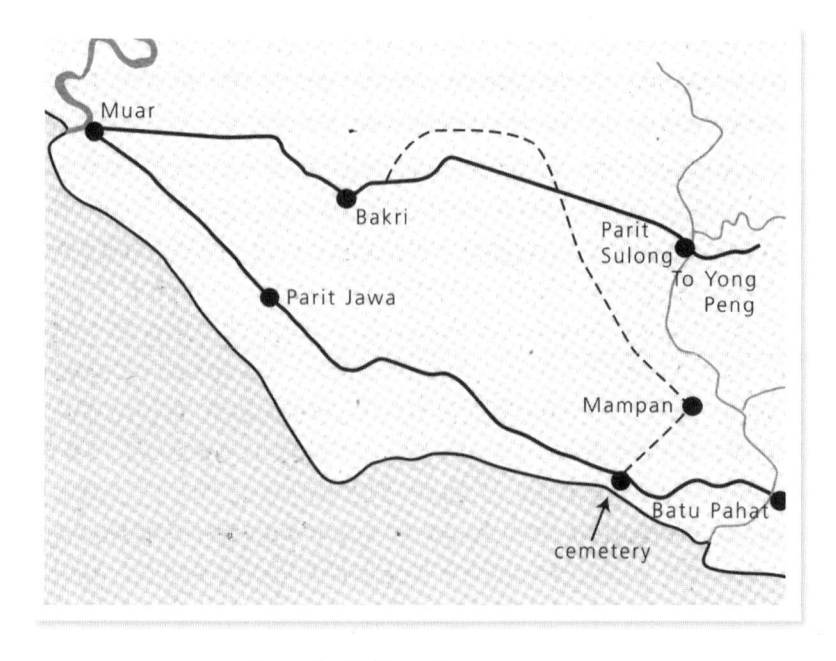

Route taken by Newton's transport party.

For nine days they searched up and down the coast, but found no trace of a boat. Coupled with the constant effort of having to dodge Japanese and Malay search parties, the expeditions were hindered by leg injuries sustained by Newton and two others. Of even greater concern was the condition of another three, whose wounds were turning gangrenous. However, on the tenth day their fate was taken out of Newton's capable hands. The Malays, in response to a cash reward offered by the Japanese, betrayed them. Before long, they were on their way to Pudu.

Of the remaining ten parties, two were captured after travelling only about eight kilometres. Three reached Sumatra; of these, two made it to Java and, ultimately, Australia. Three groups managed to work their way down the west coast to Singapore. The remaining two parties were never heard of again.

One of the two groups captured had reached the coast near Batu Pahat and managed to find a couple of boats. The first boat, aided by a fast-running tide, made it across the sandbars, but the second boat, which had no paddles, was just a few minutes too late. The water suddenly disappeared and they were left stranded.

Abandoning the boat, the occupants spent the next four hours struggling back to the shore through black oozing mud. They were still on the mud flats when the tide began to turn, bringing with it hordes of crocodiles that had been scavenging out to sea. They escaped the crocs and reached the shore, only to discover that they were unable to move any further: a party of Japanese had chosen that particular spot to set up camp. After a miserable night, eaten alive by sandflies, they had to wait until the enemy troops moved on, before turning inland to try and pick up the railway line leading south to Singapore.

Barefoot and ragged, their mosquito bites swollen and infected, they wandered about for some days, aware from notices offering increasingly larger rewards for their capture that the net was inexorably closing around them. Finally, as their resilience was nearing its limit, a posse of Japanese soldiers found them, just as dawn was breaking at the end of a 20-kilometre night trek. Too exhausted to run, they were surrounded and transported to Muar – a scene of utter desolation, with its blackened shells of buildings, burnt-out army vehicles and the corpses of hundreds of Indian soldiers, bloated and stinking, lying unburied in every street.

The prisoners were taken to the Official Residency, commandeered as Japanese Military Headquarters, where they were interviewed by a huge black-jowled Japanese major, accompanied by a turbanned Sikh captain. The Sikh did not care for Australians and tried to intimidate them by inviting them to view the backyard, strewn with the bodies of all those who had been captured. When it became obvious that the latest captives were not prepared to divulge any information, irrespective of how many dead were lying in the garden, the pair departed. They were replaced by another officer, obviously of much higher rank, who spoke perfect English. He looked at Lloyd Johnson, and smiled. He then informed the prisoners that their lack of cooperation was of no consequence as it was known who they were and, to prove his point, rattled off Johnson's details.

Certain that they were to join the corpses in the back yard, the Australians were astounded when, instead of being led away to face a firing squad or, even worse, a beheading, they were ordered into the officer's car. Taking the wheel, he ordered Johnson to sit beside him. It was not until he revealed his identity that the reason for the Australians' lives being spared became obvious: before the war, the officer, an executive with a Sydney wool-broking firm, had lived in the upper-crust harbourside suburb of Cremorne, near Johnson's family.

Johnson looked carefully, but the man who sat beside him, with his closely shaved hair and notched sword handle bearing grim testimony to the use to which the weapon had been put, did not remotely resemble the man he remembered. Even more astonishing to the Australian, with his ragged clothes, mud-encrusted beard, sunken cheeks and hollow eyes, was that the officer had recognised him. But recognise him he had, and he wasted no time in informing his 'guests' that he was now the Colonel-in-Charge, Advance Divisional Intelligence. Furthermore, they were to be the first prisoners to be allowed the privilege of living. The reason? When he had lived in Sydney, Johnson had often taken his children, Koko and Kasawa, swimming.

As he had other matters that required his attention, he was unable to keep the prisoners in his custody, so he drove them to a nearby base, where they joined a convoy of trucks bound for Kluang. After a most unpleasant stay at the gaol there, they were put on a train for Kuala Lumpur and then transferred to Pudu.

Another party of six was recaptured after leaving Newton. Subsisting on fruit and dry rations, they reached a kampong where the villagers gave them shelter and a meal of boiled tapioca root. The following morning, 1 February, they awoke to find that they had been betrayed and that the village was surrounded by enemy troops. They too were loaded into a truck bound for Pudu.

Unaware of the fate of all of those who had failed to reach Yong Peng, the remnants of Anderson Force, such as they were, were trucked to the base depot at Johor Bahru.

Within 24 hours, the story had hit the newstands around the world. Under the headline, BATTLE OF MUAR, *The Straits Times* wrote a lengthy account of the 'Greatest of the Campaigns in Malaya, gallantry, heroism, sacrifice' and 'Graphic story of trapped men, do or die dash through Japanese lines'.

Apart from the failure to mention any of the 'friendly fire' incidents, it was a surprisingly accurate and graphic account of the battle; a battle which, in a few days, would see a Victoria Cross, the British Empire's supreme award for gallantry, bestowed upon its commanding officer, Lieutenant Colonel Charles Anderson – the only VC awarded to any soldier in the Malayan campaign.

However, detailed and stirring as this report was, it was only one-half of the story. While the men of Anderson Force had been making their do-or-die dash through Japanese lines, their wounded, left at the bridge at Parit Sulong, had come face to face with the enemy.

CHAPTER 12
THE MASSACRE

Anderson had left his wounded behind under the protection of a Red Cross flag, confident that the Japanese, honourable allies in the Great War, would abide by the rules of the Geneva Convention pertaining to the treatment of prisoners of war. It never entered his head that it could possibly be otherwise.

At the bridge on the morning of 22 January, Hackney once more sought refuge beneath the ute, as enemy small-arms fire came closer and closer, and mortar and artillery shells fell sporadically. After a while, he noticed that the fire being returned from within the Australian perimeter was slackening. It was not long before they discovered why. Anderson Force was about to withdraw – without them.

Lying beneath the utility, Hackney knew it was now only a matter of time. Hoping that they might be able to hold out a little longer, his friend Hugh Tibbitts retrieved an abandoned Bren gun, lying only a few metres away. There was very little ammunition, so

Lieutenant Ben Hackney

he limped off in search of more, while Hackney, from his position beneath the vehicle's running board, fired bursts at random, as much to vent his fury and frustration as to try and dupe the Japanese into thinking that the Australians were still occupying their positions. The Japanese returned the fire, evidently unaware that most of Anderson Force had long since slipped away.

With Fred and stretcher bearer Chris Guerin gone, along with the rearguard, the wounded, numbering 110 Australians and 35 Indians, were now on their own. Hackney and Tibbitts kept firing but, at about 2.30 pm, they ran out of ammunition. The Japanese, more emboldened, but still cautious, crept closer to the trucks. By 3 o'clock there was only an occasional rifle shot and the odd burst from a machine gun, followed by an unnerving, unnatural silence. Ray Snelling, still propped against the truck wheel, evidently waved his makeshift white flag. Chattering figures came into view – chattering that gave way to shouting and yelling as the enemy, now emerging in increasing numbers from the western side of the road, closed in on the bridge and the vehicles with their dead, dying and wounded men.

With a great deal of unintelligible yelling, vigorous arm waving and forceful, painful persuasion, they made it clear that all those still in the trucks, as well as those lying on the ground, were to assemble in front of a single-storey building, set on metre-high concrete stumps on the western side of the road.

Now empty of the Indian labourers who used it as accommodation, the complex, consisting of living quarters, a one-car garage and a two-storey administration block, belonged to the Public Works Department (PWD). The single-storey living quarters, approximately 30 metres long and seven metres wide, were closest to the bridge. This structure had been split into a number of two-roomed units – a main living and sleeping area, with a narrow kitchen and cooking alcove at the rear. A metal door and three multi-paned, metal-framed casement-style windows, set side by side, opened onto a narrow verandah accessed by seven concrete steps. At the back, another set of steps led to the rear yard and a small ablution block, set immediately behind the first unit.

About three metres to the north of the accommodation block was a single-vehicle garage. Spanning the parit in front of it was a wooden ramp, just wide enough for one vehicle. Between the accommodation block and the Simpang Kiri River was a fair-sized plot of open ground, through which the western parit took a double, right-angled turn before widening into a small inlet and emptying into the river.

Although it was only a short distance from the trucks to the designated assembly area in front of the accommodation block, the transfer of the wounded was a long and difficult process. Only a handful could be classified as 'walking'. The remainder, some of whom were very seriously injured, were incapable of moving without assistance. Most were still in the trucks, but quite a number lay scattered about the convoy. Some had been too badly wounded to reach the shelter of the vehicles, while others had been shot trying to get away from them. Many incapable of movement or waiting for assistance were targeted by the Japanese who, infuriated by their lack of response despite much yelling and gesticulating, began kicking and bashing them with rifle butts. When this did not evoke the desired response, hapless victims were run through with a bayonet several times or shot at point-blank range through the head.

Those trying to hobble or crawl to the assembly point were subjected to kicks and blows, sometimes to the body, but mostly to the head. One soldier, badly wounded in the

Parit Sulong bridge, parit and PWD buildings (1996).

chest and thigh and trying to drag himself along, was hit several times before one of his tormentors put an end to his suffering by knocking him flat and bayonetting him. He and others, either dead or dying, were left lying where they fell, strewn like unwanted baggage along the edge of the road.

In due course, an enemy soldier reached Hackney and Tibbitts, still lying beneath the utility. Whether it was because of the Bren gun lying close by, or because the pair had not yet begun moving, he began to yell at them. Tibbitts stood up but was pushed away by the Japanese, who indicated that both Australians must get to their feet.

Try as he might, Hackney could not stand. He was struck several times and prodded with a bayonet until finally his tormentor allowed Tibbitts to assist. He managed to get Hackney upright, but the pain in his left leg, where the bullet had punctured the bone, was unendurable. With the other leg still completely numb from the bomb splinters, walking was impossible, even with support. The Japanese, screaming with rage, hit them repeatedly with his rifle butt until another Australian came to the rescue. Hackney managed to swing his body between their shoulders and move towards the building.

Before crossing the parit, all prisoners were forced to remove their steel helmets and drop them by the roadside, along with all equipment and personal items. For some inexplicable reason, the sight of the helmets provoked the Japanese, who scattered them with well-aimed kicks or threw them with force into the parit or onto the ground. After herding their prisoners across the ramp with more blows, the soldiers ordered them to strip down to their boots and socks and throw their discarded clothing into a heap. Naked and feeling very vulnerable, they were then made to sit in a tightly packed circle.

With the area secure, a large number of Japanese troops were now moving along the road from Bakri on foot, on bicycles and in vehicles. Occasionally, owing to the congestion of the abandoned Allied trucks near the bridge, the passing traffic halted, allowing the curious to come closer for a better view.

For some, the spectacle of enemy soldiers reduced to such a piteous state provoked great mirth. For others, it was an open invitation to release pent-up aggressions on the nearest victims, hitting and kicking them, prodding them with bayonets or beating them with rifle butts.

One Japanese officer, armed with a bloodied sword, amused himself and his companions by repeatedly dipping the blade into the water-filled parit and wiping it across the throat of one of his captive officers until the metal was clean. With the weapon now free of bloodstains, he then singled out various prisoners on whom he could demonstrate his swordsmanship. Measuring the distance between himself and his victim, he drew back his sword as if to run it through the prisoner, only to stop short. By way of variation, he forced others to throw their heads back, swinging their blades with a great swish so as to pass within a hair's breadth of their exposed throats. Other Japanese focused their attention on the prisoners' genitals – pulling and plucking, kicking and hitting.

While these recreational activities were taking place, an English-speaking Caucasian, most likely a German adviser, systematically and thoroughly searched the pile of clothing with Teutonic-like precision. Pay books in one heap; papers and wallets in another; pens, pencils, penknives, money and miscellaneous items in a third. After the search was complete, the clothes were flung at the prisoners, still seated in the circle, with an instruction to grab something and put it on.

While this was taking place, the Japanese officer in charge of proceedings examined the papers, seeming to pay particular attention to written material but then generally tossing the item aside after reading a few lines. His examination complete, he issued orders for the prisoners to move into the garage, only a few metres away.

Yelling and screaming, kicking, bashing and prodding, his troops took to the task with zeal, until most of the captives were crammed inside. Screams of pain, mixed with the groans and shrieks of the delirious, the volume increasing as those on the bottom of the heap, already crushed beneath two or three bodies, began to suffocate from the pressure of yet another body on top of them.

Determined to force everyone into the building, the guards began hitting and kicking those nearest the doors. They tried to scrabble away but time and again were forced back. When it became evident that no more prisoners could be added to the crush, those still outside, including Hackney and Tibbitts, were allowed to remain at the doorway, provided they packed together tightly.

The groans and screams from inside the shed died down, only to be replaced by pleas for water from those who had not drunk anything for a day or more and were now delirious. Hackney's request for medical assistance and water evoked no response.

New orders, however, were issued. The prisoners were to move from the garage to the two end units of the living quarters. Although they were only a few metres away, it was too far for many to make it unaided, especially with stairs and a narrow verandah to negotiate. Those unable to crawl or drag themselves along had to be carried, along with the dead. The guards did their sadistic best to hasten proceedings, lashing out with boots, bayonets and rifle butts, but it was a long and painfully drawn-out process. Some prisoners, incapable of moving, were run through with bayonets or battered to death with rifle butts.

With the transfer of the prisoners to the PWD building finally complete, the doors to the rooms were locked. A young Malay boy who had been with the convoy for days was allowed to remain outside, along with Hackney, Tibbits, Snelling and three other officers, who were ordered to sit on the steps of the end unit. The guards circled the building to make sure no one escaped. All requests for water were ignored.

However, the prisoners were certainly attracting the attention of passing enemy soldiers, who left their convoys to find out what was going on. One discovered a dead Australian, left lying on a table in one of the office trucks. Rigor mortis had set in and his body was as stiff as a board. The table was dragged from the truck and the rigid corpse propped against it – greatly amusing the Japanese soldier concerned and creating an object of ridicule for troops who followed.

Soldiers ransacking the vehicles discovered a wounded Indian hiding in one of the trucks. The top of one hand had been blown away and blood from an injury to his thigh had saturated his trouser leg. Dragged to the front of the PWD building, he was knocked unconscious and his pockets ratted. When he started to come to and tried to sit up, the Japanese officer now in charge moved in, kicking him viciously time and again, before bayoneting him with a rifle grabbed from one of the patrolling guards. As the blade thrust deep into his body, the Indian writhed and heaved, with one thrust sending him perilously close to the deep, water-filled parit. Another deep jab and he was in it. He went under, but the survival instinct was strong. As his bloodied, battered face surfaced, the officer levelled the rifle and fired. A jerk, another shot, and the head disappeared.

With the entire area now under Japanese control, a large number of Japanese staff cars was moving along the road from Bakri, bound for Batu Pahat. Seven cars containing an assortment of officers from Divisional Headquarters, along with three or four trucks, plus a tank and a motorcycle escort, pulled up. From the amount of shouting, bowing and saluting, Hackney deduced that the visitors, and one in particular, must be very senior indeed.

He was right. The officer who created the most fuss was also the most senior – Lieutenant General Nishimura Takuma, General Officer Commanding, Imperial Guards Division. Surrounded by a posse of fawning staff and aides, he approached the PWD steps, scowling at the Australian officers who were made to move aside. After peering through the window at the seething mass of pitiful humanity crammed inside the end room, he told the guard commander to 'dispose of the prisoners of war'. There was no doubt as to what he meant, especially when another senior officer added 'the bodies of the prisoners are to be cremated on completion of the execution'. The VIP party then left.

However, the prisoners were not earmarked for death just yet. Before the 'disposal', some were hunted onto the verandah, where guards held out cigarettes and cups of water, just out of reach, for the benefit of cameras from a media unit. With the photo opportunity over, the guards pocketed the cigarettes and tossed the water away before herding the captives back inside the building.

A request for medical help and water was again denied, along with the return of personal papers, still scattered on the grass beside the parit. Hackney could see his wallet lying open with the photograph of his cherished sweetheart, Helen St Vincent Welch, clearly visible, but tantalisingly out of reach.

Hackney had observed the relay of orders down the chain of command but, as neither he nor his fellow officers understood Japanese, he was unaware of what had been said.

Hackney's sweetheart, Helen St Vincent Welch.

However, believing that the visits by the media and the god-like senior officer would ensure better treatment, he hoped they would soon be transferred to the rear echelons, where they could get water and medical attention.

His hopes were dashed when his captors began to move about the area, setting up machine guns and making sure all the guard detail had rifles. This task complete, two guards walked towards the officers and ordered them to stand. Despite the severe wounds to their legs, Hackney and Snelling managed to get upright with assistance and remained so by leaning on the men next to them. After each officer's wrists were bound behind his back, they were forced towards his shoulder blades, and the rope passed around his throat before being secured to his wrists. The guards then tied each trussed prisoner to the next.

The guards responsible for securing the officers were not content to merely tie them up. They tormented them unmercifully throughout the entire procedure, jerking the ropes this way and that, and using the loose ends to belt them across the face and body. Anyone who stumbled out of line, or moved in the wrong direction, received a hefty kick. Hackney and Snelling, unable to stand unaided, were particularly targeted for 'hindering' the process.

With their officers now securely tied, the other ranks were ordered from the rooms. As they descended the stairs, their hands were bound behind their backs before the rope was passed to the next, linking them together. The first in line was then tied to the closest officer. Almost everyone was bashed or kicked. The worst of the wounded, who were classified as uncooperative, received special attention. Protests were made to the officer in charge, who took absolutely no notice.

Before long, in an effort to relieve the congestion on the verandah, those already tied up and waiting at the bottom of the stairs were forced to move towards the garage. The officers, being at the head of the line, went first. Snelling fell immediately and was attacked with boots and rifle butts. When he showed no sign of life, his body was cut free and left lying where it had fallen, near the bottom of the steps.

Although Tibbitts was doing his best to support Hackney, he too could not stay upright. Annoyed, the Japanese assailed him with even greater ferocity, kicking and striking him repeatedly on the body and head with rifle butts, with one blow splitting his right eyebrow so badly that the flesh hung down over his eye. Hackney struggled to his knees, blood cascading down his face. After a few more hits, the Japanese moved the others along, but Hackney fell again. More blows rained down. Although he tried to drag himself along with his 'good' leg, the guards continued to bash him before cutting him free of the others and leaving him for dead.

However, despite his injuries, he did not lose consciousness or his powers of observation. The enemy soldiers were well drilled and he could see, from the few instructions given and the way the guards knew exactly what to do, that the procedure was well rehearsed.

It most certainly was.

Three days before, on 19 January, between 200 and 300 Australian and Indian prisoners had been captured while trying to break through the roadblock from the 2/29th's position at mile 101. Among them was John Benedict, the Indian Army engineer who had saved the life of the Australian sergeant that morning. Later that day, Benedict was shot in the leg. He reported to Brand at his platoon commander's insistence but, after being patched up, rejoined his men, only to be taken prisoner.

The next day, 20 January, after Anderson Force had retreated, the Japanese occupied Bakri, where they concentrated the prisoners at the PWD bungalows near the crossroads. That evening they were taken at rifle point, two or three at a time, to three separate locations on the bank of a stream about 150 metres away. All, apart from Benedict and three Indian engineers, were beheaded.

Benedict was taken to the killing ground but, as he reached the bank, he knocked the rifle from the hands of one of the guards, took a deep breath and dived into the stream. The Japanese fired at him, but missed. Once out of immediate range, Benedict surfaced and hid among some fallen trees, watching the massacre continue until it was too dark to see. Hearing a cry for help, he swam to the opposite bank where he found two young soldiers, one with a tremendous sword cut to his neck. Benedict managed to get both men back across the stream and care for them until 2 February, when they were all recaptured near Muar, and taken into custody.

Unaware of the fate that had befallen the prisoners at Bakri, or the ruthless efficiency with which they had been dispatched, Hackney continued to watch the guards who, having run out of rope, were now using lengths of signal wire to tether the prisoners. Unfortunately, as the more able-bodied had been let out of the room first, those bearing the brunt of the guards' increasingly bad temper were the severely wounded who, being helpless, were more difficult to tie up.

Either because the supply of rope and wire dried up, or the Japanese simply tired of tying up the prisoners, they left the last 20 or so unbound. The rest were linked in groups of about 20 or 25. The dead, for the time being, were left lying in and around the building, while the severely wounded had been dragged outside and now lay scattered around the steps, most unconscious from pain and exhaustion. Some of those unable to stand had been clubbed to death with rifle butts.

With the building now cleared of the living, the prisoners were kicked and beaten until as many as possible were standing. As the lines moved off along the parit towards the end of the accommodation block, some of those being dragged along managed to get to their knees, but lost their balance and fell repeatedly. Near the end of the building, they were cut free, only to be dragged feet first by the guards or killed with repeated bayonet thrusts.

Among the rank and file were seven men from Hackney's battalion, including a young private, Reg Wharton, aged only 18, and Sergeant Ron Croft, who had taken shelter with him and Tibbitts under the ute during the height of the battle. Somehow, Croft and Wharton were among the last to leave the building and, consequently, had not been tied up.

View from the bridge, showing the PWD building and the killing field near the large tree, far left.

Once around the end of the building, the prisoners were prodded and bullied into one group. By the time the last were in position, many had collapsed from exhaustion. All were suffering from battle wounds, as well as cuts, bruises, lacerations and broken bones inflicted by their captors over the past few hours. The Japanese, armed with rifles and machine-guns, lined up in front of them. The Australians, aware of what was about to happen, had no intention of submitting quietly. As the bullets spewed forth, they went to their deaths shouting and cursing.

Although the majority fell in the first volley, death was not necessarily instantaneous. Many who fell were only wounded. A few, killed with the first shots, pulled others down with them. Some, unscathed by the initial volleys, remained upright, until cut down with further bursts of fire. Those merely wounded, but unable to stifle their groans, were soon silenced. Although Croft fell with the first round of firing, he was not hit. Neither were Wharton and several others. They lay perfectly still, hoping and praying that the Japanese, satisfied with the afternoon's work, would go away.

It seemed at first as if their prayers would be answered. Leaving a handful of guards to finish off any who still cried out or moved, the remaining Japanese returned to the labourers' quarters. Hackney, lying in deep shadows near the garage, had not been able to see the killing but, being only about 40 or so metres away, he had certainly been able to hear it. He now watched as the Japanese troops began dragging off anyone cut loose on the way to the killing field, mostly from the far end of the building. Once they had been removed, the soldiers turned their attention to the corpses strewn about. Snelling, sprawled in the space between the main building and the garage, was left until last. When they did not return for Hackney, he realised that he had either been forgotten or simply not noticed in the gathering darkness. He also realised that his only chance of survival was to feign death in the hope that the corpse-collecting detail would not bother with him.

He certainly looked dead. His head, neck and shirt were covered in blood, and the meaty flap of his eyebrow dangled over his right eye. His shirt was saturated below his shrapnel wound, which had bled so profusely after his beating that he was now lying in a pool of blood. The various bayonet jabs had also bled, and his lower right leg was scarlet. The kicks had opened up the wound behind his knee and the more substantial injury to his calf, the flow of blood soaking his sock and boot. The left leg below the knee also looked a mess: the dressing on the bullet wound was filthy and discoloured; one bayonet thrust had gone through the bandage and entered his calf above the bullet's exit hole; and near his ankle was another bayonet gash, which had also bled heavily.

Knowing that his life depended on it, Hackney lay absolutely still, although the ropes around his wrists and neck were painfully tight. He was left alone for some time, but finally became aware that he had company when a group of passing Japanese wandered over. They looked at him for several seconds before one pushed the seemingly lifeless body with his boot. Hackney allowed himself to go limp. Satisfied that it was indeed a corpse, the Japanese kicked him several times before departing.

Meanwhile, the murder squad had been busy. After collecting the dead, they fetched four-gallon cans of petrol from the Australian trucks and splashed the contents at random over the prisoners. Some, still alive and aware of what was about to happen, began to yell and curse. Others, already on the borderline of insanity from their ordeal, let out frightful, inhuman shrieks. Then, with one loud whoomph, the Japanese set them on fire. A man

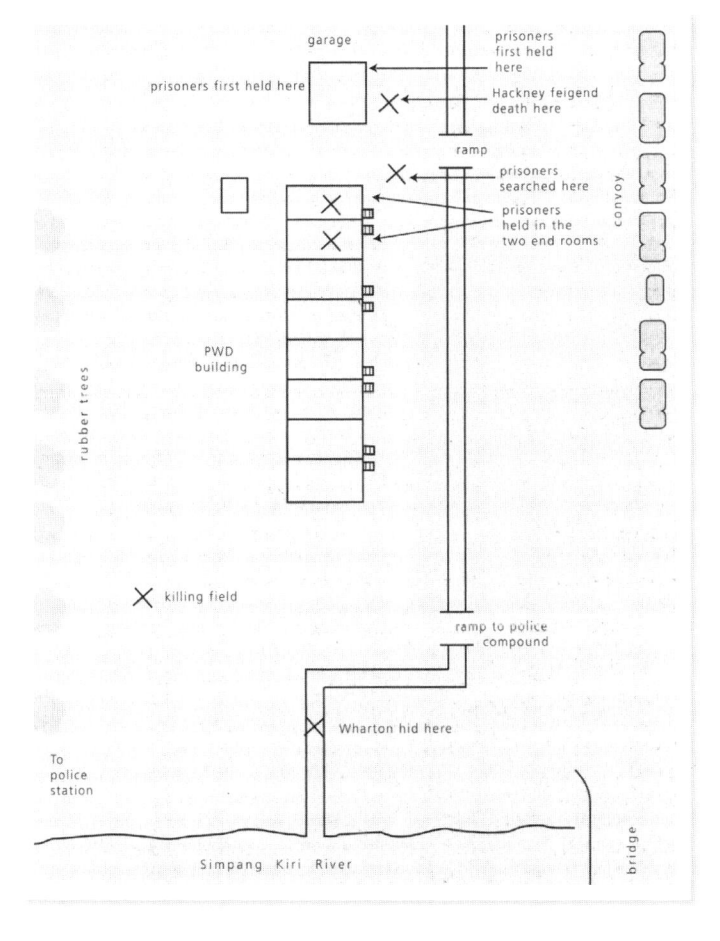

Movements of prisoners, from capture to massacre.

lying next to Croft screamed as the flames reached him and was immediately shot dead. Others, unable to move because of their bonds or the weight of other bodies, cried out in agony, but had to wait until one of the officers, running around with a pistol, put them out of their misery. Miraculously, Croft and a mate managed to escape the conflagration. Although they were soaked in petrol, they rolled clear of the flames and into the shadows, where they lay perfectly still, scarcely daring to breathe.

Wharton, who suffered only a couple of superficial burns under his left arm, also managed to get clear, only to be rounded up with a number of others in the nearby rubber trees. All were lined up and shot but, by some miracle, the bullets missed Wharton. He escaped further attention by feigning death, until one of the Japanese came over for a closer look. Not convinced he was dead, the enemy soldier bayonetted him twice, one thrust puncturing a lung and the other wounding him in the abdomen. The Australian was then flung into the inlet leading to the parit, along with the others. One, still alive, groaned. The Japanese fired four shots. Three hit him in the head. The fourth parted Wharton's hair. Although bleeding profusely from his bayonet wounds, Wharton remained among the reeds until it was safe to move. As he lay there, he saw that not all the dead had been collected and added to the funeral pyre. The bodies of those who had died on the bridge were being used to fill bomb craters, levelled by vehicles driving back and forth over them.

Hackney, who could see the flicker of the flames and hear the tortured cries of his comrades, knew what was happening on the open ground beyond the end of the building. The acrid smell of charred clothing and the sickly sweet aroma of burning flesh strengthened his resolve. He must continue to play dead, until he was certain the Japanese had gone.

They took their time. While Hackney lay there, several passing troops came down from the road to see what was happening. Some paid him no attention, others gave him a push or a prod, while yet others, filled with hatred for the enemy in general, took great delight in kicking and beating the lifeless 'corpse'. On several occasions he was used for bayonet practice, sustaining more than 20 wounds. Some were only pricks, but two were full-bodied thrusts. One passed through his ribs. It missed his heart, but he realised it must have penetrated his lung – every time he breathed, aerated bubbles of blood came out through the hole in his chest. The other pierced his right elbow, rendering it useless for many days. Through it all, he stoically maintained the pretence of death, his body now injured in so many places that it was impossible to distinguish one pain from another. Hideous though the bayonetting had been, perhaps the worst ordeal was when a Japanese, eyeing off the 'dead' man's boots, decided he must have them, twisting Hackney's feet until the boots came off and causing excruciating pain to his broken left leg.

As the hours passed, activity in the area became less and less. There was now no sign of any Japanese guards, but Hackney waited a considerable time before he was certain that none were still patrolling. Although still trussed like a chicken ready for the spit, the psychological sense of freedom was immense; the mixture of emotions almost overwhelming. He later recalled the relief he had felt from the eternal strain of waiting, watching and listening; of not having to maintain any longer a complete stillness and dead-like appearance that, until then, had been vital to his survival; of not having to suffer further ill treatment; of no longer wondering if what he had endured would all be for nothing, because of what might happen next or, if at any minute, he would experience what could be the beginning of the end. However, his most predominant thought was that, from now on, his survival would depend entirely on himself.

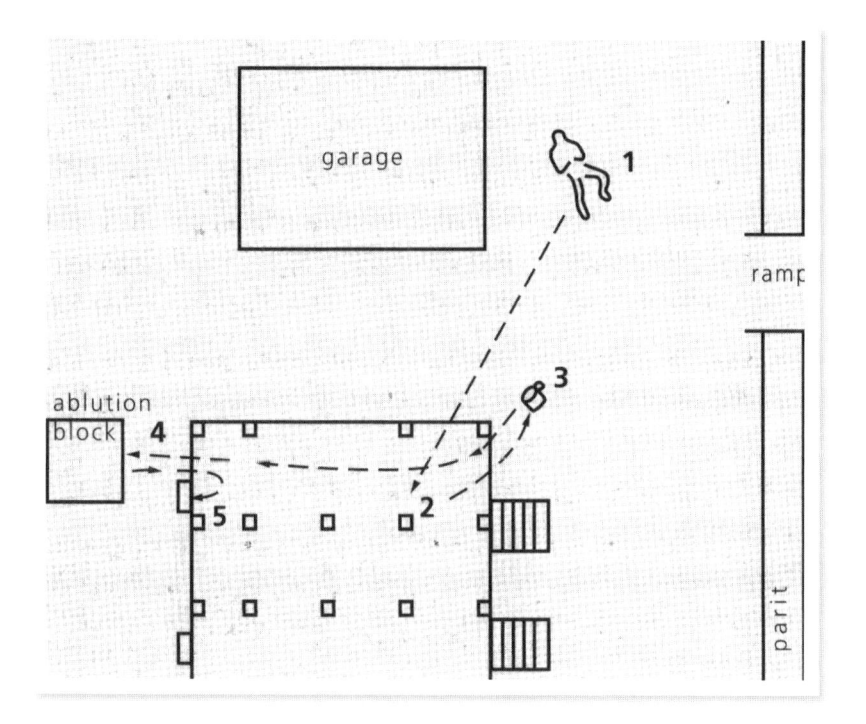

Hackney's movements at the PWD building.

Firstly, he must take cover under the building and try to free himself from his bonds. The distance was not great, only about seven metres to the edge of the foundations but, with his injuries and his arms secured so tightly, it was a Herculean task. He tried to roll, but the pain from his injuries and the physical effort required to create momentum were too great. Instead, he flattened himself on the ground and then, using his right leg to give him some purchase, hoisted his body in the middle before flattening out again, just like an inchworm. He was forced to stop from time to time when vehicles, their headlights blazing, passed along the roadway. Worried that they might pick up his silhouette, he lay perfectly still whenever he heard the sound of a motor. Able to move only a few centimetres each time, it took him well over an hour to reach the end of the building. Realising he must seek deeper cover, he kept on going, until he was well under it.

The exertion all but drained him, but he must now find a way to be freed of his ropes. After dragging himself to one of the concrete foundation supports, shielded from the road by the solid flight of steps, he propped his back against the corner of the block and began to rub. It was tedious and very, very tiring. His arms and shoulders ached, forcing him to stop frequently and rest. Every now and again, sure that by now he had done enough to snap the bonds, he strained for all his worth, only to have his wrists swell from the effort and the rope hold firm. He was almost at the end of his endurance, his wrists rubbed raw and the skin on his throat painfully abraded when, at long last, one of the strands finally broke. It was not long before he was completely free.

His next priority was water. Whilst doing his inchworm impersonation, he had spotted an aluminium mug, discarded on the grass outside after the photo opportunity. Crawling to the edge of the foundations, he retrieved it and, after a rest, made his way to the ablution block, about two metres from the rear of the building. There he drank until he was satiated.

Suddenly, he heard someone approaching. Startled, he crawled back to the sub-floor area where he climbed into a rectangular concrete bin, used to collect ash falling from the fireplace of the kitchen area above. Open on one side, it was not overly large and he was able to get only partly inside it, but it was better than being caught in the open. Looking beyond the sub-floor piers, he saw two men advancing from the direction of the river. As they came nearer, one of them spoke. Hackney recognised the voice immediately. It was Sergeant Ron Croft.

Croft and his companion had not spotted Hackney. When he called to them softly, they immediately froze, and it was not until he identified himself that they moved forward. Croft, physically unhurt but very nervous, was supporting his mate, who had been wounded in the stomach by a burst of machine-gun fire and was clearly in a bad way. Both smelled very strongly of petrol.

Deciding to put as much distance as possible between themselves and the pile of roasted corpses, Croft carried his mate to a clump of thick vegetation beside the river before returning for Hackney. Croft not only weighed a good deal less than Hackney, he was also much shorter, had been without food for days and had suffered terrible physical and mental privations. Yet, somehow, he managed to get Hackney, who tipped the scales at 90 kilograms, across his shoulders.

As dawn broke the next morning, they saw that there was a track close by – far too close for comfort – so they moved to deeper cover on the other side. Shortly afterwards, the badly injured man died. The others did not have the means, or the energy, to bury him, so they laid him with his arms across his chest and covered him with foliage. They then concealed themselves under branches and leaves, to wait until dark. They could not see any Japanese, but they could certainly hear them. Vehicles were moving in both directions along the road and there was some kind of commotion between their hiding place and the PWD buildings. However, apart from the thump of shells or bombs exploding a long way off, there was no sound of any fighting.

The activity they could hear, but not see, was taking place at the massacre site. While killing the prisoners had been relatively simple, disposing of the bodies was not nearly as straightforward. Evidently unaware that to reduce even one corpse to ash took hours and required an immense amount of heat and fuel, the Japanese had no idea that, once the petrol they had poured upon the bodies had burned off, the fire would go out. Instead of a heap of anonymous ash, they were left with a mass of charred and semi-roasted flesh. As the orders were to 'not leave any trace' of the prisoners, another method of disposal would have to be found.

The area was criss-crossed with small parits, providing ready-made graves, so burial was the obvious solution. Since the Japanese had no intention of expending any energy in this direction, and as the villagers had fled when the fighting began, word was spread that it was safe to return to the village, and that all who did so would receive free rice. One of the first to arrive was a local school teacher, who soon discovered that he had been duped when he and a handful of equally gullible villagers were escorted to the killing ground, ordered to undo the signal wire and ropes linking the corpses together, and drag them to a nearby pit to bury them. The teacher, who had no stomach for the task, managed to avoid handling the bodies, but he did look into the makeshift grave. It was a sight that would haunt him for the rest of his life.

Back at the hiding place, Hackney and his companions continued to lie low, unaware of the nature of the gruesome activity taking place such a short distance away. That evening, just after sunset, they decided to move further away from the road bearing its dangerous convoys of troops. They eventually reached a house, where they were given food and shelter, and the next morning decided that they should split up. Although Hackney doubted he could survive on his own and did not have much confidence that his hosts would remain hospitable, he persuaded Croft to go to the river, find a boat and make for the sea.

Shortly afterwards Hackney was also on the move. The occupants of the house refused to allow him to remain anywhere near their dwelling, but offered to carry him to a new hiding place and to keep him supplied with food. Placing him on a sack, they carried him about 500 metres to a rubber plantation where they dumped him near a mosquito-infested drain.

Despite their assurances, they did not come back. For the next five weeks Hackney crawled slowly from one hiding place to the next, at the mercy of the elements, drinking from rain puddles and relying on occasional handouts of food from local farmers and compassionate passers-by. Sometimes, alarmed that he was hiding too close to their homes, householders placed him on the sack and dumped him in a new place.

In an attempt to discover what was happening on the battlefront, Hackney elicited the help of cooperative locals who, in response to towns he nominated, replied either 'English' or 'Jar-pun'. Although the response was generally the latter, he was not disheartened, continuing to focus instead on the best way to reach the Allied lines.

Throughout his wanderings he begged time and again for refuge in the kampongs but, although the villagers might bring him some food, they were always too frightened to allow him to stay in, or anywhere near, their homes. Entirely dependent on their charity, he had to be content with concealing himself beside a track, close enough to call to passers-by but far enough away to remain hidden, if need be. The Malays gave him a wide berth, but occasionally the Chinese would take pity on him.

After staying in one place for a couple of days, sometimes less, he moved on again, still on his hands and knees but, with each day that passed making better progress. Every morning he crawled to a tree and, with his arms around the trunk, tried to haul himself to his feet. Time and again his legs refused to support him and he slumped to the ground, defeated and dispirited. However, after persistent effort, he eventually managed to stand on his right leg, which, although very weak and wobbly, was able to take his weight. Being upright improved his morale immensely, especially as each day he gained a little more strength.

At around midday one day, he was some distance from his shelter, practising his standing with a rubber tree for support, when he heard someone coming. Thinking the sound heralded the arrival of food from a nearby Chinese house, he was startled to see a small boy running through the rubber tree seedlings towards him. Holding up three fingers, he warned that the 'Jar-pun' were on their way. Two local men suddenly appeared, demolished his shelter and took off.

Crawling to the fork of a fallen rubber tree about 30 metres away, Hackney covered himself with branches and leaves as best he could and waited. It was quite a long time before the searchers, a Malay police sergeant and three constables, arrived. There was no chance of their missing the abandoned campsite – the flattened grass and crushed foliage showed only too clearly the signs of recent occupation. It was only a matter of time. While one policeman covered him with a rifle, the police sergeant advanced towards the tree and ordered the fugitive to come out.

Realising the game was well and truly up, Hackney removed the branches and sat up. When he indicated that he could not walk, his captors provided support for the short distance to a river, where he was transported by boat upstream. He had no idea where he was going but, after some time, a distinctively arched concrete bridge came into view. Hackney recognised it at once. After five weeks on the run, he was right back where he had started.

Aware that he must not allow the Japanese to suspect that he had been among the Australians fighting there, he said he had been cut off from the main force and had been wandering aimlessly ever since. After questioning at the police station, he was taken to a collection depot further along the road, beyond the PWD building, for transfer to Pudu Gaol.

He passed by the killing field, but there was no trace, at all, of the massacre that had taken place.

CHAPTER 13

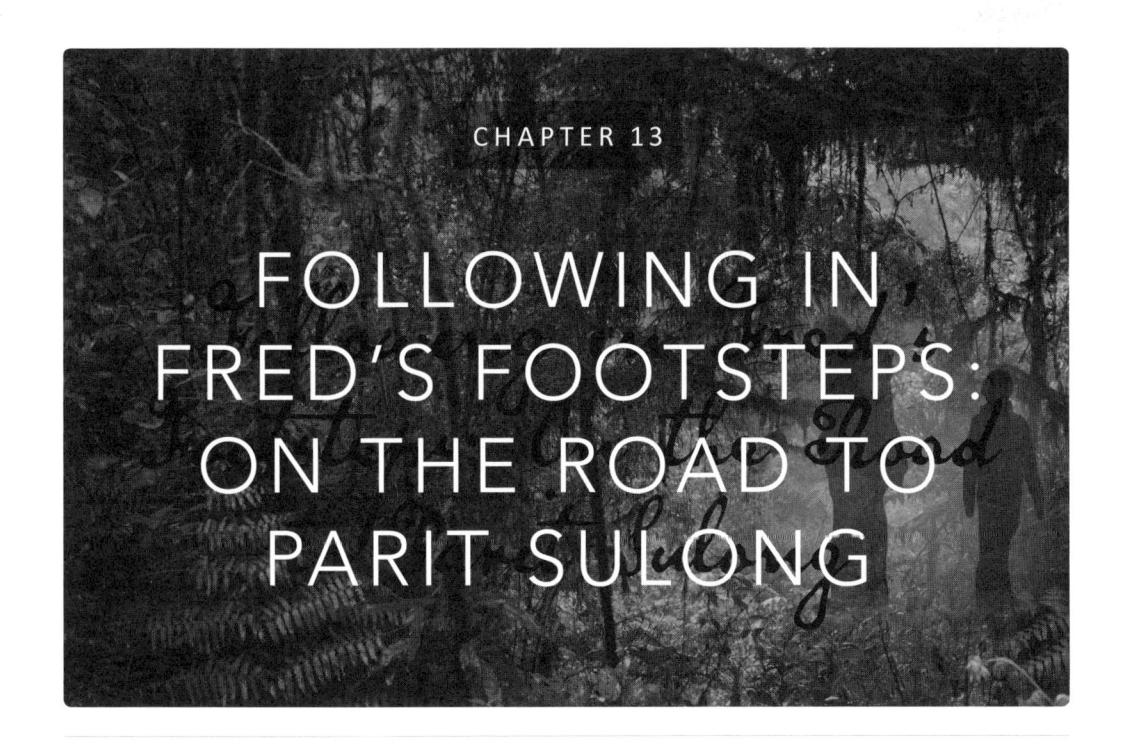

FOLLOWING IN FRED'S FOOTSTEPS: ON THE ROAD TO PARIT SULONG

Leaving Jemaluang, we returned to the west coast, following the route taken by Dad and his battalion to Bakri, only as far as Yong Peng. From there we drove cross-country to the northern bank of the river Muar to follow the path of the Imperial Guards as they closed in on the town, and then to trace the Australians' line of retreat.

The ferry used to cross the wide and muddy Muar was long gone, and with it the ramp that Gunner Max Fisher had hidden beneath as the enemy advanced. A large and impressive bridge now leads into the town, a bustling metropolis. We headed off along the road to Simpang Jeram, where the Indians managed to accidentally shoot their officer, and then passed through the town of Bakri which, confusingly, is a long way from Bakri Crossroads.

Lynette had brought a copy of an original wartime map, showing the contours, parits, side roads and mile pegs, so we had no trouble identifying the spot where the anti-tankers had set their ambush for the enemy tanks. We also had the photos taken by the war correspondents – the road had not changed and there were still rubber trees about, but the thick jungle was no longer.

On the left-hand side of the road, we spotted a two-storey Chinese house in ruins. Once a very grand place, it was constructed of concrete and had the date 1934 proudly inscribed over the entrance porch. I wondered how it had survived the artillery shells, hand grenades and bombs, and also what had happened to its occupants during the battle. I assumed that, if they had any sense, they had scarpered, quick smart. From here, a short drive through the 2/29th's area brought us to the 'crossroads' where Dad had been deployed and where his battalion fought hand-to-hand to hold off the Japanese advancing inland from the coast road.

From the crossroads, the road passed the site of Brigade HQ and the white bungalow where so many had lost their lives, before winding through the roadblock area where Major Julius and many others had come to grief while trying to force their way through. I

Above: Chinese house.

Right: Malay house at 101 mile peg.

could almost hear the men of Anderson Force singing *Waltzing Matilda* at the top of their voices as they charged the barricades. It was easy to relive this part of the retreat, with the jungle closing in on both sides of the road and no sign of any habitation.

The warriors who sang had also fired the imagination of Private George Harding, a prolific poet, known as the Bard of the 2/19th. George composed this poem, immortalising the fighting spirit of his fellow comrades in what was arguably the greatest fighting retreat by Australians in World War II.

Incident in Heaven

Saint Peter paused in musing
And listened, eyes a closed
As a strange new thing came drifting
Into heaven's sweet repose.
It was the lusty chorus of a Digger's marching song
About a ragged rascal sitting by a billabong.

The song drew slowly nearer,
Peter peered with age-old eyes
As a band of men came marching,
From earthwards through the skies,
A band of weary soldiers whose voices raised a song
About a merry rascal sitting by a billabong.

Then Peter's hand made motion
And Gabriel came forth
He listened to the singing
And made to judge its worth.
It isn't very musical, was Gabriel's comment,
But it bears some strange heroic in its innermost content.

The marching men drew nearer
And halted in their stride
'We've come from Parit Sulong'
Said the first man, full of pride.
St Peter looked at Gabriel, and this was his oration,
'These men have come by Heroes' Lane', then made an invitation.

The portals swung wide open
And the weary men marched through
And angels gathered round them
With pots of boiling stew;
And from the lips of soldiers came a story for the Gods
Of the battle for the causeway against enormous odds.

They don't sing 'Alleluias'
Where the haloed harpists play
Since the Diggers made their entry
On that wild immortal day.
They sing the vulgar chorus of a wild Australian song
About the merry rascal sitting by a billabong.

At the end of the roadblock area, the causeway was readily identifiable, stretching seemingly forever in a dead straight line. The padi fields alongside it had long gone, but the numerous small houses, constructed below road level, still looked very vulnerable to flooding. It was clearly evident why Colonel Anderson had been so anxious to cross the causeway in the dark. To have come under air attack, out in the open and with no way of leaving the road to seek cover, would have been the end of all of them.

At the end of the causeway, a road entered from the left, formerly the track to Kangkar, which Sanderson's men had used to try and link up with Anderson, only to run into mortar and gun fire. Assuming it was the enemy, despite identifying the weapons as Bren guns, they had retreated and continued to Yong Peng, by-passing Parit Sulong. It served no purpose to wonder what might have happened had they lent their weight to the battle, but I couldn't help myself.

The main road had turned towards the south and the bridge over the Simpang Kiri River. As we drew nearer, I could barely contain my excitement. After years of reading about it, hearing about it and wondering about it, I was almost there. When we reached the sign, Parit Sulong, and could see the road rising up and over the bridge in the distance, I could hardly breathe. This was where my Dad was; this was where the most unimaginable horrors had taken place, taking the lives of so many young Australians, some of them only boys.

Lynette pointed out a wooden house on the western side of the road, used by Victor Brand and Lloyd Cahill as their aid post in the last hours of the battle. She had identified it on her first visit, years before, from a photo taken in late 1945. When it appeared in the Official History, *The Japanese Thrust*, someone wrongly identified it as the place where the prisoners were held, prior to the massacre.

Right: The sign post.

Below: The weatherworn house used by Brand and Cahill for the aid post, minus most of its paint.

Amazingly, it was still standing. Reduced by weathering to a somewhat bleached greybrown, I could still see remains of the white paint that had coated it in 1942. A nearby rubber warehouse, identifiable by its distinctive roof and also in the photograph, had somehow survived modern-day development. As I looked at the aid post, I thought about the wounded sheltering under it, and of Len Wood, the stretcher bearer, killed by friendly fire. His mate George Harding was so affected by his death that he wrote this poem in his honour.

Len Wood - Stretcher Bearer

He wasn't like the soldiers that you read about in books.
He didn't have the manner and he didn't have the looks.
He was tall, some say ascetic, but me, I call him lean.
I used to watch him workin' on the painting of a scene
That caught his eye. That's like he was an artist sort of bloke
With a bit of education showin' in the way he spoke.

E wasn't one for soldierin', his hands were lady-wise,
An' he had a dreamy sort of look about his greyish eyes.
Like a man what sees another world what men don't understand,
Like a man what sees the better things of life as God 'as planned.
'E wasn't any planter but 'e knew a lot of things
An' scorned a lot a' ways to which a human being clings.

The night at Parit Sulong when the Japs had us hard pressed,
Was a night of hidden fear I had never known or guessed
And a lot of men were lost that night by nervous comrades' shots
As they crept about the jungle like an undistinguished blot!
The crackling of a stick and breath was stifled in the breast!
Take no chances! Might be Japs: a bullet did the rest.

An' Len was tendin' wounded with 'is soft white hands,
Giving ease an' comfort like a man who understands
The pain of others' sufferin' _ and some time in the night
'E was stricken while 'e tended to a dyin' soldier's plight.
I found 'im in the morning _ but I found him just too late
'E was dyin' then from shock and blood _ and Lennie was my mate.

Way back at Parit Sulong, where the rivers wide and deep,
The body of my hero mate is takin' its last sleep.
An' I'm thinkin' of a thousand men (pr'aps there's even more)
Whose spirit means so much to Man but blotted out by war.
The world has lost the gift of light they carried in their hands,
Snuffed by human ignorance. Perhaps God understands.

As we drove on towards the bridge, bedecked in flags, the long, low-set PWD accommodation block came into view on the right. On the left, in a riverside park, were more flags and a brand-new memorial, hidden beneath a tarpaulin. It was to be dedicated the following day, and all of Parit Sulong was celebrating. Lynette had suggested the establishment of a memorial in 1997, and it had taken her 10 years, three months and four days to bring her idea to fruition. In the meantime, she had spent six years researching and writing *The Bridge at Parit Sulong*, an epic book that pieced together, for the first time, the entire battle, the massacre and the aftermath, as well as documenting the long chase by investigators to bring to justice General Nishimura, who had ordered the massacre. He was hanged at Manus Island in June 1951.

Lynette had also traced the fate of every single Australian across a huge battlefield, extending from Muar to Yong Peng, and was able to determine what had happened to Dad's mate, Harry Grosvenor. Dad must have been too distressed by the story of the massacre to tell the family that Harry had been badly wounded and left at the bridge, because his son, Harry junior, knew only that his father had been 'killed in action'. With the publication of Lynette's book in 2004, we now knew the names of the 107 Australians left at the bridge, along with Hackney, Croft and Wharton, the sole survivors. However, it would not be for another six years, in 2010, that she would finally determine what had happened to the bodies of the massacre victims.

No trace of any of those killed had ever been found, not even immediately post-war. In fact, nothing at all had been found – no discarded water bottles, webbing, sundry equipment, clothing or personal effects. Just a heap of rusty, twisted and wrecked vehicles on the north side of the bridge and the ambulance, still sitting in the mud on the far side of the river.

According to the Japanese, the bodies of those massacred were cremated to ash. According to the schoolteacher ordered to untie them, they were placed in some kind of mass grave close to the end of the PWD building. And, according to other locals, they had been disposed of in the river.

Lynette had already proved that, although covered in petrol and set alight, there was no cremation as such. Apart from Hackney being close by, to reduce so many well-fleshed men to ash, as the Japanese officer in charge of the disposal had reported, would have taken multiple truckloads of wood and hours of constant stoking. Thinking that the building was made of timber, as wooden planks, used as formwork for the concrete, had left a pattern resembling weatherboards, which had then been painted, the Japanese officer claimed that they had demolished the building to provide the necessary fuel.

With cremation clearly impossible, this left the mass grave described by the schoolteacher and the river as options for disposal. However, as Lynette had established that British soldiers captured at Bukit Pelandok, as well as local Chinese, had been bayoneted on the bridge and toppled into the river some days after the massacre, it seemed likely that these were the corpses seen drifting back and forth on the tide by villagers, when they returned to their homes.

Following a vigorous review of Lynette's evidence and the discovery of human bones on the river bank, Australia's Unrecovered War Casualties Unit initiated a joint archaeological survey of the site with Malaysian authorities. In March 2010, Lynette was invited to join the search team, comprising more than thirty archaeologists, anthropologists, surveyors, geologists, researchers, labourers and a forensic dentist.

The entire area was heavily overgrown. Following a ground survey, several 'hot spots' were identified. The most significant was the old main parit behind the PWD building. Filled in long ago, when a new parit was constructed to get rid of the dogleg, in 1942 it had widened out to form an inlet, large enough to accommodate a small boat, before emptying into the river.

The excavation extended to the virgin clay, to a depth of two metres or more. As the mechanical excavators took out each bucket load, the archaeologists and geologists, aided by other members of the party, examined the exposed ground and the spoil for any signs of a mass grave.

While the excavations continued at a slow and steady pace, Lynette interviewed several local people. Although there were many reports of bayoneted Chinese civilians and British troops floating in the water, moving back and forth on the tide, no-one had ever reported

The search for remains.

seeing, or ever hearing of, any burnt bodies among them. More significantly, no-one had seen any sign of a cremation fire or piles of bones.

As the village was 'out of bounds' for three weeks after the battle, no-one Lynette interviewed had any information about the massacre, although some had seen the bodies of soldiers killed in action lying in parits further up the road. She also learned that, about a month after the fighting, the river, swollen by monsoonal rains, had broken its banks to the east of the village and swept these corpses away.

One day, while going back and forth across the plank spanning the PWD parit to interview villagers, Lynette noticed there had been a significant change in the water level. Further observation revealed that, at each low tide, the parit near the PWD, which now discharges into the river via a large underground pipe, was completely drained of water, leaving a layer of sludge and mud exposed. At high tide, the water was about one metre deep.

The river is tidal, filling and emptying the parits every six hours. As Hackney had reported that, on the afternoon of 22 January, the Japanese had drowned the Indian soldier in this parit, Lynette concluded that it must have been close to high tide at that time, as the body had disappeared completely beneath the surface. Therefore, with the six-hour tidal change, low tide the next day would have been late that morning, the time when the schoolteacher was ordered to participate in the burial. Also, at around that time, Hackney had reported hearing a disturbance at the killing field from his hiding place in the nearby jungle.

AT WAR WITH MY FATHER

Right: Neil Silver with his metal detector.

Below: Lynette with the schoolteacher's daughter.

The archaeological search was extremely thorough, extending far beyond the actual massacre site. However, despite sifting through tonnes of earth, the searchers found nothing, apart from bits of rubbish and odd artifacts, none of which was considered to be war-related. And, although Lynette's husband Neil spent many hours running a metal detector over heaps of excavated material and archaeological assistants manually and diligently searched every pile, not a single solitary bullet was found, despite the fact that hundreds of rounds had been expended during the massacre.

Indeed, the most remarkable feature of the excavation was that there was nothing at all to indicate that the area had been subjected to fierce fighting, or that a substantial number of Allied troops and civilians had been killed there.

With no grave found, despite an exhaustive search, Lynette re-examined the previously known facts, along with the new information about the tidal difference in the parit that had just come to light. She then realised that there was an element of truth in each of the methods of disposal claimed over the years – cremation, burial, and in the river.

There was no doubt that the bodies were doused in fuel and set on fire. However, once the fuel burnt off, the flames went out. With cremation very incomplete, the following morning local people were forced to untie the corpses and drag them to a nearby 'burial pit'. Lynette knew that the Japanese, who rarely dug graves to bury their victims, made use of shell holes, slit trenches, wells, ditches and monsoon drains. At Parit Sulong, on the morning of 23 January, the section of the parit behind the building was completely drained of water at low tide – a most convenient method of disposal.

Lynette also discovered that the Japanese officer in charge of the massacre did not arrive at Divisional Headquarters at nearby Batu Pahat until 7 pm on the night of 23 January, the day of the 'burial'.

It is now believed that, late that afternoon, when the burial pit filled with water from the incoming tide, the corpses were floated into the inlet and then to the river as the tide receded, possibly with the help of bamboo poles. This would account for the length of time that the Japanese officer remained at the site. Any bodies that remained would have been flushed out over the next few days by either monsoonal rains or subsequent tides. By the time the local people returned to the village, three weeks later, there was no trace of the massacre victims.

Any residual remains still lying in the mud, along with any gear and equipment, would have been swept away by storm water and/or the subsequent floodwaters that inundated the area. This scouring accounts for the total lack of any visible equipment when the Australian army's investigating team arrived at the village at the end of the war, and explains why Ben Hackney, after his recapture, saw no sign of the massacre as he passed by the killing field.

During the excavation, the schoolteacher's daughter had sat for two days at the site of the old parit, the place where her father had said the corpses were buried, convinced that the searchers would uncover a mass of bones. She could not understand it when the digging revealed nothing.

As Lynette remarked, 'Mother Nature had done her job well'.

Of course, this research had not been completed in 2007, but I had followed Lynette's progress carefully as she pieced together the rest of the story. I had also read her book from cover to cover, reliving the battle with my father. It didn't take long for realisation of where I was to set in, and that was when what had happened here hit me like a bomb blast. I could see it all unfolding before my very eyes – the wounded crammed into the garage, then into the end units of the PWD building, the brutal treatment as they were tied together for what would be their last walk, and then the hideous massacre that followed. I had read Lynette's gruelling and detailed account several times, but being there, where it all happened, was harrowing.

I thought of young Tom Jiggins, who died in the massacre. He had joined the AIF under his father's name and lied about his age. Born on 1 February 1925, not 1 May 1920, as he claimed, he was only 15 when he enlisted in June 1940 and died a week before his 17th birthday. He has been immortalised in his hometown of Griffith, in NSW's Riverina district, the heart of 2/19th country, with the establishment of Jiggins Park and a plaque in his honour.

After looking through the accommodation block, I crawled underneath to see the indent worn into the pillar where Hackney had managed to free himself from his binds. I could now appreciate fully why he had chosen it – he was hidden from view behind the stairs, but he had a clear line of sight to the garage and the only access ramp over the parit.

To the right of the PWD building were the ruins of the police station, where Lynette discovered Hackney had been held for a short time after his recapture. The inlet to the parit, where the small boat that transferred him up the river had moored, had been reclaimed to create a forecourt to the police station and was now open space. The jungle, where Hackney, Ron Croft and the badly wounded soldier hid immediately after the massacre, had given way to farmland. I pondered on how lucky young Reg Wharton was to escape what should have been certain death and to make his way to Singapore.

After walking to the rear of the building to what had been the killing field, I continued to the river and looked across to the southern bank.

It was here that my Dad had fired off the mortars, sinking the boat on the other side along with its Japanese occupants. I was standing where Dad would have been when the Japanese on the opposite shore fired back. I then walked up the bank, across the road and along the river a fair distance, just as Dad had done when he made his escape. I couldn't imagine what it must have been like back then, when fleeing for their lives. Although Dad and Chris Guerin didn't realise it, they had seen their mates for the last time. As Dad had never spoken about the war, let alone Parit Sulong, I had no idea how he felt about leaving Harry Grosvenor behind, or when he learned that Harry was among the 107 slaughtered at the bridge. Not surprisingly, by this time my emotions got the better of me and I broke down but, being surrounded by people who understood, managed to regain my composure.

We spent the night in Batu Pahat, the closest town with any kind of reasonable accommodation. It was much bigger and noisier than the pleasant seaside settlement where the members of 2/30 Battalion, posted there in August 1941, had enjoyed the same kind of local hospitality extended to Dad and his 22 Brigade comrades. The Chinese community was very welcoming to the 2/30th, inviting officers and NCOs to a dinner at their ornate and very grand Chamber of Commerce. As a group photo was definitely in order, the local Chinese photographer, known as Mah Lee, did the honours.

However, he was not Chinese at all. He was Japanese and a member of the huge spy network operating all over Malaya and Singapore, which Dad's battalion had been warned about at Serembang. Oblivious to Mah Lee's actual identity, members of 2/30 Battalion had flocked to his shop in town to have their photos taken and the brass had welcomed

Above: Hackney's line of sight while cutting through his bonds. He is sheltered from view by the steps, but can see anyone approaching across the ramp spanning the parit. Below: The spot where Fred sank the Japanese boat.

The photo that resulted in death for the Chinese hosts.

him to the camp, where he took photographs of the various companies and platoons. It seems certain that the enemy used this intelligence to bomb the camp at Batu Pahat but, by this time, the British had taken over the Australian position. The happy snap taken as a memento of the dinner was used by the Japanese to execute a large number of Chinese businessmen.

Batu Pahat is not classified as a tourist town, so the only decent hotel was packed with veterans and their families, plus staff from the Australian High Commission in Kuala Lumpur and the Office of Australian War Graves in Canberra, which had overseen the construction of the memorial for the Department of Veterans' Affairs.

Arriving at the memorial site the next morning, we discovered that the official Mission Party, easily recognisable from their specially designed outfits, was a mixed bag of veterans and officials. However, the Department certainly had not done its homework properly. People who had no connection to the Muar battle had somehow managed to secure a place, travelling in style at the expense of the government, while others, including Lynette, who had worked on the project for ten years in an honorary capacity, paid their own way – as I and many other families had done.

I later drew this to the attention of the Minister, pointing out that people who did not qualify had denied a place on the party to those who did. He agreed wholeheartedly that more stringent measures would be put in place in future. I had actually discovered when the Mission list was published that there were some ring-ins. However, as it would have been a major embarrassment had I made this known at the time, I bit my tongue. In hindsight, I wish that I had spoken up as my annoyance detracted from the day's events.

Lynette was regarded as the expert on the historical side, so she was entrusted with the task of overseeing the wording used on the information panels at the memorial and suggesting suitable images. Apart from being irked over the composition of the Mission, I was also upset that the photo of Ben Hackney that Lynette had obtained from his family had been replaced by 'neutral' artwork, after a member of the public, whose father died at the bridge, had objected to Hackney's image being featured. The bureaucrats, wanting to keep the peace, rolled over. Never mind the fact that without Hackney we would not have known anything!

Although Colonel Anderson was featured on the panels, the presence of his family at the event was unacknowledged. Typical! Once politicians get involved it is all about them. Although Lynette was finally successful in her push for the memorial, others attempted to claim the kudos. She had worked on the project for many years, long before the latter-day glory seekers even knew what Parit Sulong was. This included the Minister for Veterans' Affairs, a couple of times removed by the time of the dedication, who tried to claim credit for the memorial, when all the department had done was to apply for the funding. However, I was pleased that the Australian High Commission, who had worked closely with Lynette to push the memorial through, made special reference to her work at the service, declaring that without her it would not have been possible. To recognise her input, she was invited to lay a wreath on behalf of the people of Australia, during the well-run but rather predictable service, attended by dozens of Australians, numerous dignitaries, various politicians and Parit Sulong villagers, including some who had been there as children during the war years and could remember the events that had taken place.

Above: The display of Hackney's photograph creates media attention.

Left: Di and the story boards at the memorial.

Although I was upset that Ben Hackney's photo was not on the information panels, he won out in the end as Lynette had brought along his framed photo, which sat alongside her on a spare seat in the VIP tent. After the service, she placed it on the memorial, provoking a lot of questions from the media, who then featured Ben in their stories.

Later that afternoon, we drove back along the causeway to beyond the Bakri Crossroads. At the ruined Chinese house, we came upon a busload of 2/29th family members conducting a private remembrance service. We were invited to join them, standing in silence for the roll call of the men from the battalion who had died or simply disappeared. This little private service was far more meaningful and emotional for me than the one held that morning at the bridge. There were no flowers, or music, or speeches by important people; it was all about the men and their families, and the heartfelt sadness at their loss. And, as an added bonus, there was not a single politician, official or coat-tail rider in sight.

The service had just concluded when, much to our surprise, out of nowhere appeared a Malaysian man, mounted on a motorbike with a cooler box full of ice-creams. I don't know if he was just enterprising, or had come to see what we were up to. Apparently, the authorities use itinerant pedlars to keep an eye on foreigners. Whatever the reason for his unexpected arrival, he was not short of customers as it was a very hot day.

We dropped by to see the memorial at Parit Sulong for one last time before following the line of retreat through Bukit Pelandok and Yong Peng, and on to Johor Bahru. At the memorial we discovered that the locals had helped themselves to most of the flowers, especially the artificial ones. I hope they adorn their homes for years to come and give them some comfort, as no doubt they too lost many relatives during the war.

The memorial helped put Parit Sulong on the tourist map and inspired the local authorities to restore the accommodation block. Although Lynette had approached the Department of Veterans' Affairs about restoring the buildings in 1997, she was unsuccessful. As a matter of policy, the Australian government does not supply funds for building restoration. At the time Lynette presented her pitch, the accommodation block was in fairly good condition – it had a watertight terracotta-tiled roof, undamaged multi-paned, metal-framed windows and strong doors securely fastened. The adjoining garage, made entirely of concrete, including the pitched roof, was completely intact. The vestiges of the wooden ramp over the parit were also evident, although the ramp itself had long since rotted away.

Over the years, the building slowly deteriorated as the locals scavenged materials for their own use. The roof tiles at the rear were the first to go, then the metal windows and doors for their recycling value. The wooden doors and single metal-framed window of the garage went next. Rain penetrated the accommodation block, rusting the steel reinforcing. As the building became more downtrodden, scavengers became increasingly emboldened, blatantly removing tiles from the front. Plants took up residence on the tops of exposed walls and in nooks and crannies, and a huge strangler fig enveloped the two units closest to the river. The building was looking very derelict by 2010, when the search for remains took place, and by 2015, what was left was ripe for demolition.

At this juncture, Malaysian history lovers stepped in, convincing the local authorities of the importance of the site. The building is now completely restored: it has a new roof, windows and doors, and the exterior has been re-rendered and painted. It looks better than brand new.

When Lynette showed me the photographs sent to her, I was astonished. To cap it off,

FOLLOWING IN FRED'S FOOTSTEPS: ON THE ROAD TO PARIT SULONG

Top: The ice cream man who appeared from nowhere.

Above: The PWD building in 2010.

Left: The PWD building in 2013. The parit was realigned and is much closer to the building than in 1942.

local artists had painted an entire blank wall of a nearby shop house with a giant mural, depicting the battle and featuring Colonel Anderson and Ben Hackney. Ben's image is enormous – vindication perhaps for the fact that our government saw fit to exclude him from appearing on the information panels. This huge upgrade is part of an ambitious proposed historic precinct.

It is a fitting memorial to our men and the local people who lost their lives in January 1942.

Right: The restored PWD building.
Below: The mural.

CHAPTER 14

BACK IN ACTION

All those who managed to reach Yong Peng before the bridge was blown were trucked to the General Base Depot (known as the GBD), just outside the village of Tampoi and about 6.5 kilometres north of Johor Bahru. However, it was not until the men assembled in their individual units that the true extent of the loss was realised.

The 45 Indian Brigade, which had lost all its battalion commanders and 2ICs, was left with one adjutant, two British officers and about 400 men. The leaderless 2/29 Battalion, with its two COs killed and almost all its officers and NCOs dead or missing, could account for only 130. It still had its undeployed company intact but would need 500 ORs and 19 officers to bring the unit up to strength.

The gunners had taken a mauling too, with just 98 artillerymen answering the roll, 24 of them wounded. Of their eight officers who had gone into battle, only two had reached safety. All the 25-pounders, which had fired a total of 6519 shells, had been lost, along with the anti-tank guns, all transport, the carriers and almost every other weapon.

After his 52 wounded comrades had been whisked off to hospital, Fred was one of just 174 in his battalion still standing. They were filthy, their uniforms in tatters, and most had to have their boots and socks cut from their feet. The badly mauled 2/19th needed a whopping 650 reinforcements, and the bulk of them were very green indeed. Of the 550 marched in from the GBD, just 100, who had been in Malaya since August, had any training. The rest, who had just arrived, were mainly from NSW and had been raised in a hurry. The plan was to put them through basic and jungle training in Malaya, but the speed of the Japanese advance had put paid to that idea.

Like most of the division's reinforcements, they had been in the army a bare fortnight, just long enough to have a medical, collect their kit, take pre-embarkation leave and board the troop ship. Almost all had no experience of life outside their own communities, had never seen a Bren gun, a machine gun or an anti-tank rifle, had no concept of bayonet fighting and most had not even held a .22 rifle, let alone fired one. According to an incredulous General Bennett, they were recruited in Martin Place in Sydney on a Friday and sent to Singapore the following Monday. As soon as their ships berthed in Singapore on 24 January, the bulk of them were transported to Johor Bahru and posted to their units just in time to join the retreat back across the causeway.

With the reforming of the battalion, Fred remained with HQ Company as Signals' Sergeant. On 30 January,

> after a week's reorganisation we again marched out to a position to cover the withdrawal of the whole of the British forces onto Singapore Island.
>
> An all-night vigil failed to make any contact with the enemy, and at daylight we received the order to cross the causeway. We were followed by a Scottish Regiment of Argylls, whose pipe band played a stirring march as this gallant force, now only about 200 strong in comparison with the original strength of 1,000, crossed the causeway. Having fought the Japs all down the Malay Peninsula from the Thai border, they marched as if they were on the parade ground. They were the last to cross.

As the 30,000 battle-weary Allied troops, accompanied by thousands of frightened refugees, trudged onto the island, the army engineers, waiting to blow the causeway in the hope of delaying the Japanese advance, heard the sound of bagpipes. Along the road, with heads held high and backs erect and looking anything but defeated, came the Australians, followed by a company of Gordon Highlanders, and then, finally, the Argylls, marching defiantly to the stirring strains of 'Heilan' Laddie' and 'A Hundred Pipers'.

At the very end of the column was Drummer Hardy, Brigadier Stewart's batman. Noticing that Hardy, who had never been known to run, was moving with absolutely no sense of urgency, the CO exhorted him to step on it. However, Stewart's psychological pep talks, that there was nothing exceptional about the Japanese, had been heeded by the bandsman, who had not run from the enemy to date and could see no valid reason why he should do so now. Despite Stewart's bellowed admonishments, 'For God's sake, Hardy, hurry up and get a move on', Hardy stubbornly maintained his carefully measured pace. With the rearguard watching his every step and the engineers waiting, hands poised over their demolition plungers, the lone figure of Drummer Hardy finally crossed the causeway. In so doing, this lowly ranked soldier earned for himself an undying place in history, not simply for being the last man to leave Malaya, but also its most unlikely hero, who dismissed protests over his lack of haste with a laconic: 'Japs are only Japs, and it is undignified for an Argyll to take any notice of them'.

Fred, who was watching this drama unfold, recorded that

> hardly had they cleared the end of the causeway before a terrific explosion rent the air, hurling great lumps of jagged concrete into the sky. A hole appeared in the centre of the causeway. Now we could really give the Japs something to think about!
>
> Singapore Island was the scene of feverish activity. The retreat across the causeway now completed, the Japanese were in undisputed possession of the Malayan mainland.

It was pure fantasy to imagine they might stay there. Although Bennett had urged the entire causeway be blown, Percival had disagreed and sanctioned the destruction of just 70 feet (about 21 metres). The breach was only a short distance from the northern shore and presented no barrier to the Japanese, as the water was not much more than a metre deep at low tide, allowing them to wade across. Not surprisingly, they would waste no time restoring the causeway, allowing their tanks to cross.

There were now 85,000 Allied troops crammed onto Singapore Island. Of those classified as combat troops, many, because of their lack of training, were completely useless as a fighting force, while the battle-hardened, after weeks of constant combat,

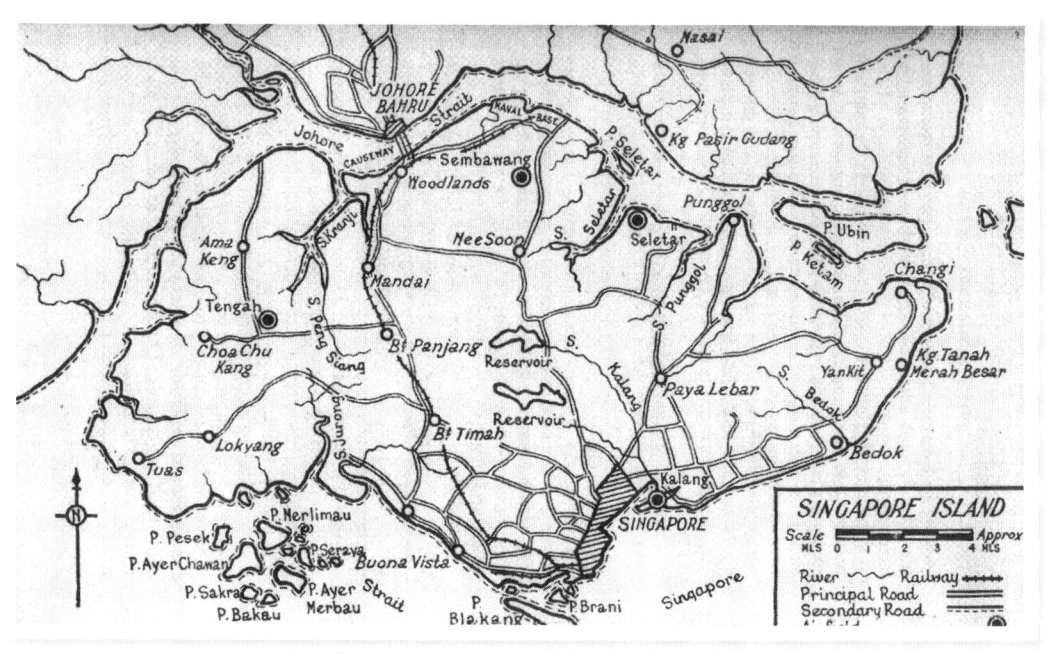

Top: The breach in the causeway, viewed from Johor Bahru. Above: Wartime map of Singapore Island

Above: Bomb damage. Below: Grief-stricken Chinese women mourning for their dead child.

were suffering from fatigue and needed to be relieved. With this largely inexperienced and battle-weary force, Percival expected to hold the island.

Contrary to the opinion of General Archibald Wavell, the Far East's Commander-in-Chief, that the main Japanese thrust would be to the west of the causeway, Percival believed it would be to the east. However, instead of concentrating his troops at this point, he elected to form an outer perimeter 115 kilometres long. The accepted strategy at that time was one battalion for every 455 metres of front line. In Singapore it was one battalion for every 4800 metres, along a perimeter whose only section considered to be well fortified was the area around the big guns, on the other side of the island.

Although the larger guns, which could traverse through 360 degrees, had a rather flat trajectory, they could have been put to good use against Japanese troops amassing in Malaya on the other side of the causeway, had someone thought to obtain high explosive ammunition. The stocks of armour-piercing shells, while devastating against warships, were entirely ineffective against troops, artillery or land targets. They certainly had more than enough range but, with no armour to pierce, the warheads simply buried themselves in the soft earth without detonating. There were actually about 30 rounds of high-explosive ammunition for each of the 9.2 inch (23 centimetre) guns but, if Singapore were to hold out for six months, as the British High Command expected, only one round per week could be fired. With the big guns virtually useless, Singapore's existence, as was the case at the legendary Rorke's Drift during the Zulu wars of 1879, depended on an extremely 'thin red line'.

While Fred and all those who had been in action in Malaya were well aware of the imminent danger they all faced, the civilians and the local authorities were still living in a fool's paradise. On the grounds that the public would become demoralised, Governor Sir Shenton Thomas had placed a complete censorship on all war news, unless it was given a positive spin, hence the extensive coverage of the heroic Muar battle. As he also refused to allow publication of alarming casualty statistics, the bodies of hundreds of civilians killed in daily air raids were quickly gathered up and buried, many of them unidentified. While this was a sensible move, given Singapore's tropical climate, it served to hide the truth about the gravity of the situation.

People were allowed to insert notices in the newspaper regarding the whereabouts of missing persons, but death notices were not permitted as the long lists would make depressing reading. Consequently, with the Governor doing his best to be upbeat and suppress anything of a worrying nature, the pubic regarded the war with Japan as merely an inconvenient skirmish. The propaganda was so effective that citizens believed the withdrawal over the causeway was a plot to lure the Japanese onto the island to allow the Allies to fight on their own patch. The Governor did not help matters by urging citizens with green thumbs to plant vegetables, should supplies from traditional market gardens dry up. Anyone wanting to give it a try was supplied with fertiliser, free of charge.

Not even the bombing was taken seriously for a long time. Although air raids had increased markedly during January, the locals exhibited a rather cavalier attitude to the entire proceedings, standing in the open to watch aerial dogfights and swarming in considerable numbers to view damage caused by bombing raids. They might as well watch, as scarcely any public air-raid shelters had been constructed, apart from a few in the gardens of the more affluent, mainly for their novelty value. While the solidly built brick European bungalows provided some shelter for their occupants, the flimsy, often makeshift houses of the Malay and Chinese population were no protection from the bombs, which fell with impunity, killing thousands and burying their bodies in the rubble.

Many of the shops and factories were closed, but milk was still delivered and, as soon as the all-clear siren sounded, larger stores reopened, inviting female shoppers into their brilliantly lit interiors to indulge in the purchase of 'snappy American frocks for day and afternoon wear'. At palatial Government House, Sir Shenton Thomas, who was nearing retirement and was more socially than militarily inclined, was insisting that his dinner guests wear collar and tie and observe all the niceties of gracious living.

Military chiefs, however, had become concerned about the number of women and children still on the island. They had by this time overcome their initial disbelief that the Japanese had dared take on the mighty British Empire and, with enemy troops now just 800 metres away on the other side of the causeway, were urging the immediate evacuation of all 'useless mouths'.

Evacuation instructions had been issued for weeks but, ostrich-like, Sir Shenton had repeatedly refused to pass them on. He not only neglected to inform the civilians that evacuation had been recommended, but also that all evacuees would be transported to a safe port, free of charge. Consequently, throughout December and January, ships ferrying troops and materials to Singapore had been returning to their home ports virtually empty.

Unaware of the free passage being offered, those who had sensibly decided to evacuate had paid large amounts to the enterprising shipping companies still issuing tickets. The Australian shipping line, Burns Philp and Company, confidently advertised that their first-class tickets to Melbourne, carrying a price tag of £1000, were interchangeable for the return voyage. Other would-be evacuees, who had heard about the free passages, turned them down on the grounds that they wanted to go to England, not Australia or India or New Zealand. Consequently, as the Japanese counted down the days until their inevitable invasion of the island, Singapore was still full of defenceless women and children.

While the public carried on as if no state of war existed, the AIF regrouped to take up defensive positions. In spite of intelligence reports to the contrary, Percival was sticking to his theory that the Japanese would attack to the east of the causeway and had ordered huge supplies of ordnance to be placed there for use by his freshest troops – the recently arrived British 18 Division.

The Australians were relegated to the western side of the causeway, with the strongest units of 27 Brigade, the 2/30 and 2/26 Battalions, closest to it and the heavily reinforced 2/29th in reserve. Much further west, on the other side of the Kranji River, was 22 Brigade's 2/20 Battalion, which had seen little action to date. They occupied the north-west tip of the island, with the 2/18th, which had sustained losses in battle near Jemaluang, on their left flank. The 2/19th, reinforced but by far the weakest in terms of experience, was further to the south.

On the western side of the Kranji River, between 22 and 27 Brigades, was a newly formed company of 2000 Chinese irregulars, under the command of Englishman Colonel John Dalley. After years of trying to break down racial prejudice and opposition to form such a group, Dalley had finally been given the go-ahead. However, his men were scarcely a fortnight out of training camp and, as the weapons intended for their use were on the bombed-out *Empress of Asia*, attacked just off Singapore, they were armed with antique Martini Henry rifles, some of which had been converted to shotguns, evidently unearthed from some forgotten corner. Ammunition for these single-shot weapons, which

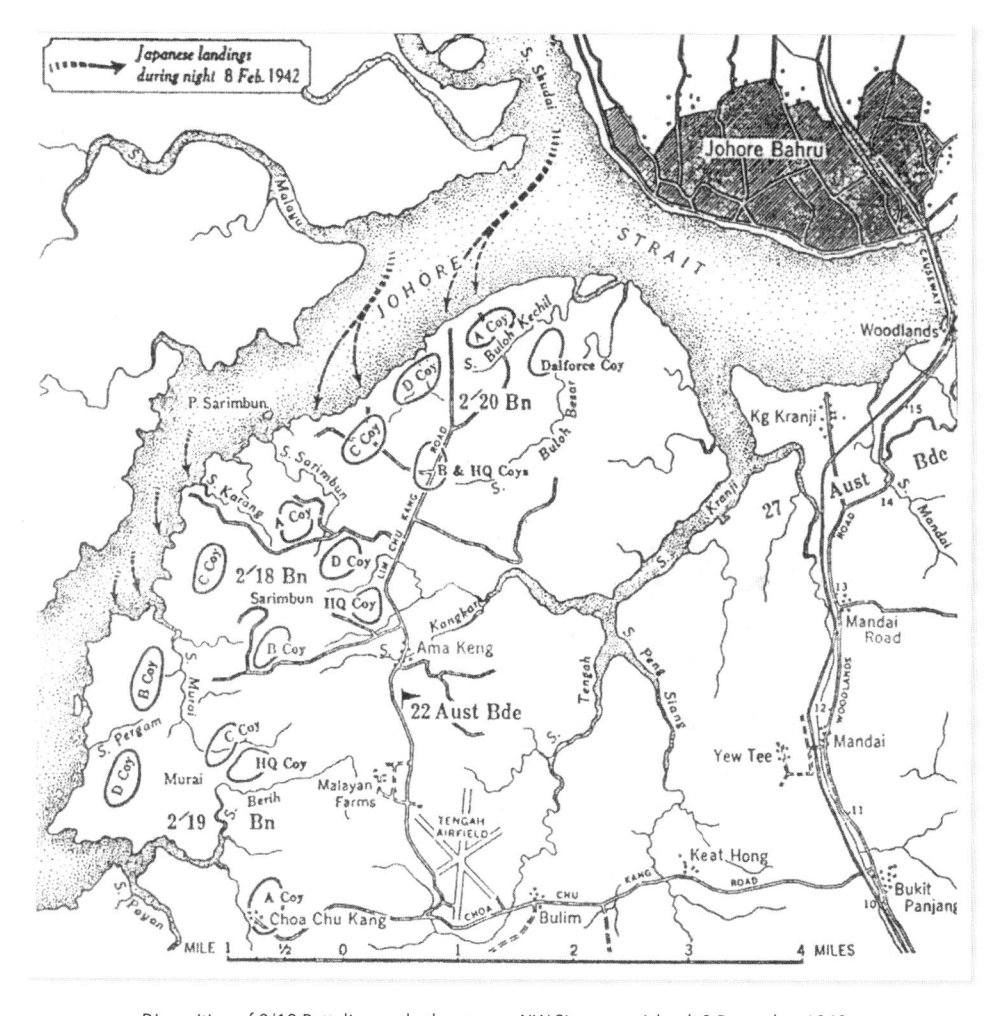

Disposition of 2/19 Battalion and other troops NW Singapore Island, 8 December 1942.

had not been used by the British army since the 19th century, amounted to exactly five rounds apiece.

The recently arrived Australian 2/4 Machine-gun Battalion was divided among the infantry, with gunners from 2/15 Field Regiment supporting 22 Brigade, and the 2/10th supporting 27 Brigade. As the 2/10th Field Regiment had been working with 22 Brigade and the 2/15th with the 27th for months, neither the gunners nor the infantry were happy with the switch. Apparently, the rearrangement was due simply to the order in which the artillery units had crossed the causeway.

Realising that he did not have the manpower to adequately defend such a large and difficult area, Bennett gave orders for all surplus support troops from the Army Service Corps and various Ordnance units, as well as reinforcements for the machine-gun battalion, to form a 'special' battalion.

Tasked with the defence of the entire north-west of the island, Fred and other battle-hardened Australians were under no misapprehension about the job that faced them. Apart from not having enough troops, trained or otherwise, on reaching their assigned zones, they had looked about in vain for the fortifications and defences that they had heard about for so long. Fred, who was expecting defence works along the lines of those erected at Mersing was appalled.

> A survey of our defences showed that the preparations were totally inadequate to meet an enemy coming in the back door. For 12 months we had firmly believed Singapore to be impregnable and for years had been led to think that no enemy could possibly conquer the fortress. But the enemy was not going to attempt the impossible by storming the island from the sea, when an almost open door awaited them across the narrow causeway. There was not so much as even one strand of barbed wire. No prepared positions - in fact, nothing that could be used effectively as a barrier to stop the invaders. As well, our air support had met its doom or had withdrawn to safer areas.
>
> We now realised that Singapore was NOT the impregnable fortress we had been led to believe. Hurriedly we endeavoured to prepare our positions, knowing full well that the Japs would not allow us much time.
>
> So we worked at top speed to make the most of what was available, almost an impossible task, because their planes had full control of the air and our efforts to defend our area were blasted, almost as soon as they were made. In the hours of darkness we erected gun emplacements only to see them blown to pieces in the first few hours of daylight.

A British engineer who had been blowing up bridges in Malaya also noticed the lack of barbed wire. Hurrying off to Singapore's depot to collect some of the tonnes of ordnance stored there, he came back empty handed. The depot was locked and deserted – he had arrived on a half-holiday.

When Percival discovered that the ever-resourceful Ivan Simson had installed defensive devices, including petrol barrels that could be set alight with tracer bullets to flood the waterway with blazing fuel, underwater obstacles, floating logs festooned with loops of barbed wire, and car lamps to illuminate the shoreline, he ordered their immediate removal to the east.

The area to be defended by the Australian 22 Brigade was immense, with each battalion assigned a frontage extending for approximately nine kilometres. Fringed by muddy tidal flats edged with mangroves, and fragmented by a myriad of tidal streams, the entire expanse was covered in stunted rubber and tangled undergrowth, interspersed with swamps. There was no field of fire and, once the infantry troops were deployed, they were at least 100 metres apart. Movement was only possible along infrequent native tracks, winding in out of rotting vegetation. Ticks and mosquitoes added to the misery. Mick Curnow, positioned 'on the edge of a mangrove swamp, full of sandflies and mosquitoes' lamented that 'one of these days I'll get a bath and some clean clothes.'

The sector assigned to Fred's battalion lay between two rivers, with a company posted at the entrance to each. As the most southern river, Sungei Berith, had quite a large estuary, another company was placed upstream where the river narrowed. The fourth company and Fred's HQ company were inland, between the two beach companies, with Indian units responsible for the defence of the entire area to the south. As the Kranji River estuary blocked access from the causeway zone, the only way in or out of 22 Brigade's area was via Lim Chu Kang Road, a dirt track that passed through the village of Ama Keng, linking Tengah Airfield with the north-west tip of the island.

Fred realised that maintaining communication between Battalion HQ and the various companies across such a fragmented battle zone would be of vital importance. However, he also knew it would not be easy. All the battalion's signal equipment had been lost at Muar and Parit Sulong, and many key personnel killed. New equipment had been issued at Johor Bahru but it was of World War I vintage. Discovering that all they had were several field telephone handsets and only a few miles of cable, the signallers went off to scrounge whatever possible from any available source.

A search of the barracks at Johor Bahru had yielded reels of cable and portable telephone sets, with even more equipment at the Postal Department. A trip to Nee Soon Camp, on the island, resulted in more gear, including four heliograph mirrors for visual signalling, and a book of blank indent vouchers and army stamps that allowed them to obtain 'possession' of the items. As a bonus, they also came across an abandoned Indian Army signals' truck, which had eight Lucas lamps – portable Morse lamps for use in daylight – and also batteries in good condition.

The battalion's signal platoon was now up to full strength but, like the rest of the battalion, had been heavily reinforced with raw recruits. As an incentive to undergo signal training, in addition to learning infantry basics, the newcomers were offered an extra shilling a day. As an extra seven bob a week was not to be sneezed at, they burnt the midnight oil.

However, Fred's signals' officer, Lieutenant Minto, was far from happy. Not only were his signallers working across an extended front to a depth of four kilometres, with one infantry company out on a limb, almost nine kilometres away, but the terrain was the worst headache: the swampy ground did not permit cables to be buried, so lines had to be strung through the ever-present mangroves in the forward areas. In the rear areas, they were able to bury and duplicate the coverage using different routings, but the big worry was the forward locations, as many of the routes and tracks going in and out were under water at high tide.

With the Australian sector constantly subjected to enemy aerial and artillery attack, the cables were constantly cut, forcing the signallers to try to find more cable and then restring it or bury it more deeply. The few wireless sets issued were virtually useless, as their range did not extend beyond 150 metres. The Lucas lamps were of value but, as only a few old blokes, like Fred, could read and transmit Morse code, and lines of sight were very limited, reliable communication was once again in the hands of runners.

While Percival was deploying his forces, the Japanese began an elaborate feint. Once Johor Bahru was cleared of all non-military personnel within a radius of 20 kilometres, army vehicles began moving after dark along the eastern shoreline of the strait, headlights blazing, to give the impression that any attack on the island would be east of the causeway. Once at their destination, the vehicles returned, headlamps extinguished, before repeating the process. On 7 February, as a further deception, they landed troops on Pulau Ubin, an island just off the tip of Changi peninsula, in the Johor Straits. In the meantime, thousands of enemy assault troops and their equipment massed west of the causeway, directly opposite the Australian positions.

The Japanese knew exactly where the Allied troops were. They had not only made use of their extensive spy network, but had also cultivated a handy fifth column, composed of disaffected civilians chaffing at colonial rule. As had been the case at Bakri, where fifth columnists had indicated the precise location of the Brigade HQ's bungalow, key positions

Top: Johor Bahru Administration Building. Above: Singapore oil tanks ablaze

within the Australian sectors were identified by arrows created from branches or palm fronds on the ground, or flour or paint on rooftops.

As if this were not enough, the Japanese had secured an excellent vantage point from a glassed-in room atop the Johor Administration Building, directly opposite 27 and 22 Brigades. From here, they had a fine view of everything going on. When Australian gunners finally detected that the tall, square-shaped tower was being used as a command post, it took 24 hours and a violent argument from Bennett to obtain permission to fire on it: Percival was concerned that the Sultan might be upset. Eviction from their prime position worried the Japanese not one skerrick. They simply took to the skies in a hot air balloon, floating frustratingly out of the reach of small arms fire, while continuing to see everything they wished.

Meanwhile, enemy planes swarmed overhead, some bound for Singapore city and others concentrating on bombing and strafing the northern shoreline of the island. In the boggy Australian forward positions, surrounded by jungle and mangroves, the troops had no alternative but to seek refuge in water-filled foxholes.

On 6 February, columns of black smoke towered into the sky from the direction of the naval base, as huge oil tanks were set on fire. However, the Japanese had not caused the destruction, as Fred and his battalion first assumed. It was the British, who had abandoned the base and were implementing a scorched-earth policy. The knowledge that the oil supplies, machinery, stockpiles of valuable equipment and the superb floating dry dock, the envy of the Far East, were being deliberately destroyed did little for the moral of troops ordered to defend the magnificent base to the last man. They hoped that the top brass knew more than they, and got on with the job of preparing for battle as best they could.

With the naval base no longer defensible, the big naval guns facing seaward now swung round to the north and fired their armour-piercing shells. There was no mistaking what they were. The burst of fire from these great weapons created a tremendous rumble and shook the very earth, as the massive projectiles whistled overhead. Unfortunately, none hit anything hard enough to explode. However, Fred heard later that, as it fell to earth, one had landed on the roof of the Johor Bahru railway station, causing damage to the structure but reportedly leaving a Japanese troop train unscathed.

That evening a call went out to all members of the 2/19th to write letters home: the few planes still airworthy were to be flown to Java with RAF and RAAF personnel the next day. The deadline to hand in the mail was 6.30 the next morning, 7 February. Everyone scrambled to get a few words out to loved ones, but the mail would not be delivered until mid-March. One letter from a member of the 2/19th shows that, despite war being imminent, morale was still high. In fact, the letter writer seemed more concerned with lost incoming mail than the looming battle. On the evening of 6 February, he wrote:

> So far it has been a peaceful day and the Japanese have not started any attack, which we are glad about, for every day gained will allow us to improve our defensive positions. No doubt, when he does come, the fighting will be hard and heavy. At the moment the only activity is some bombing and a few artillery shells in our area, fortunately none in our immediate vicinity. I hope that these conditions will continue for some time to come.
>
> Living conditions are fairly good and the meals, whilst simply a lot of meaty stews, are filling at least. Noticed in the local papers that the Japs shot down a plane of ours containing mail, so it is possible that our mail has gone west.

On 7 February, to the dismay of the 2/19th, Colonel Anderson was admitted to hospital with dysentery, and would remain there for the next seven days. Colonel Robertson, 2/20 Battalion, took over temporary command.

The day after Anderson's hospitalisation, the Japanese were finally ready to mount their attack. Fred wrote that the

> Japanese brought all their guns to bear across the straits and pounded us night and day. Sunday the 8th commenced with the heaviest barrage we had encountered.

The 'softening up' barrage began at 10 am, with the roar of artillery and the crash of shells reaching a level of such intensity that older soldiers, who had served in the Great War, likened it to the bombardments on the Western Front. The racket was clearly audible at Government House, on the other side of the island, where Sir Shenton complained that it disturbed his bath.

The constant shelling and mortar fire took their toll on the 2/19th area. C Company, positioned inland alongside Fred's HQ Company, was hit, sustaining a number of casualties and cutting the communication wire linking it to Battalion HQ in 28 places. A good number of casualties were reported from forward companies but, with the soft ground absorbing the impact of the shells, they were mainly light. However, as the battalion's strength would be reduced by 25 per cent if the wounded were withdrawn, there was no question of evacuating anyone other than those who were badly injured. The remainder were patched up at the RAP and sent back to their posts.

With Fred's signallers working flat out to repair damaged wires, they welcomed the arrival of wireless sets sent away for repair on 31 January. These were quickly distributed, but hopes that the constant need for repairs to the landlines had come to an end were dashed by an order to maintain radio silence.

Worried about the continual breakdown in communications, Harold Taylor, the Brigade commander, issued instructions on what to do if a strong enemy force overwhelmed any of the positions: troops must fight their way back to their next HQ, in most instances company level, and, as a final resort, form a perimeter around their battalion headquarters. If they had to fall back, all knew the routes to take and had practised movement along the various paths in daylight and at night.

The enemy assault continued throughout the day with little let up. Over at 2/18 Battalion, 80 shells a minute fell on one company, but 65 a minute was the average. It was estimated that 25,000 rounds, all told, landed in the 2/19th area during the 15-hour barrage. Seasoned veterans of the last war assured the younger men that it would eventually stop and, at around 10.45 pm, it did. However, the ear-shattering noise of artillery and mortars was now replaced by something far more unnerving. Total silence.

Fred and the Australians waited. It had been raining pretty much all day but, although the downpour had finally stopped, Fred recorded Mother Nature was not on their side, but on that of the enemy.

> That night, with fog enveloping the whole of the Straits, he made his landing. Our searchlights were useless as they failed to pierce the fog and were only a target for the enemy.

Straining to see through the gloom, the infantrymen and machine gunners at the forward posts focused their entire energies on the narrow black strip of water in front of them. Scarcely 800 metres wide, it was all that separated them from the invaders who had 300 water craft at their disposal. The Australians were hopelessly outnumbered. Nine Japanese battalions were pitted against 2/20 Battalion, tasked with defending the extreme north-west coast, with another seven battalions ready to storm the thinly dispersed 2/18th and 2/19th, further to the south.

As they watched, eyes watering from the strain, they became aware of a shifting of the shadows as dark, indefinable shapes detached themselves from the inky black shoreline opposite. As the shadows drew nearer, the faint splash of oars could be heard and suddenly the shadows were shadows no longer, but hundreds of barges and boats, filled with thousands of fanatical enemy troops. The 2/19th's most forward company broke wireless silence to report that at least fifty barges or boats were heading towards it.

Covered by a mortar barrage, fired from the barges, the first line of Japanese infantry reached the shore as the Australian machine gunners opened up. Thousands of rounds spewed forth in murderous cross-fire, killing hundreds of the enemy, but still they came. The Australian infantry now joined the attack, their grenades and rifle and Bren fire adding to the slaughter.

The forward companies also sent up coloured Verey lights, expecting the artillerymen of the 2/15th Regiment, positioned well back, to pour concentrated fire on the enemy troops and boats. However, with wireless transmission failing and signal wires cut by the shelling, the artillerymen waited in vain for orders from their forward officer to open fire, not daring to do so for fear of hitting their own side. Finally, on being told to 'bring fire down everywhere' the gunners went into immediate action, firing a total of 4,800 shells. The 2/10th Field Regiment, supporting 27 Brigade and yet to be attacked, fired another 400 shells onto the opposite side of the Straits, where more Japanese were reported to be amassing.

Despite their efforts and the massive bombardment, it was too late. The Japanese were unstoppable. Scrambling over the bodies of the dead, they poured ashore, infiltrating between the widely spaced defenders. While the battle-experienced held their ground,

The mangroves and jungle of the Australian positions

many of the reinforcements, rattled by the mortar barrage, pulled back, creating even bigger gaps in the line. It was not long before the forward Australian positions were overrun, leaving those still alive with no option but to withdraw. Some of the defenders were able to make their way along the jungle tracks to previously arranged positions, but many, cut off in the dark and isolated, were forced to fight their way out, metre by bloody metre.

Some members of the 2/19th, surrounded by the enemy and with no hope of getting out, owed their lives to selfless machine gunners who continued to man their weapons, keeping the enemy at bay to allow them to escape. Their ammunition spent, they then wrapped the red-hot barrels around the nearest tree and, fixing bayonets, joined the infantry, now fighting hand-to-hand.

Further back, Padre Harold Wardale-Greenwood exhibited the same cool resolve that had sustained him at Bakri and Parit Sulong. With no regard for his personal safety, he moved amongst the wounded, applying field dressings wherever possible and keeping up spirits.

The company of Dalforce Chinese, positioned in the creeks and mudflats on the Australians' right flank, found itself up against a Japanese machine-gun battalion. When their five bullets had been fired from their shotguns and rifles, the Chinese fought hand-to-hand. The wounded, propped up with their rifles, fought until they died. Not one of these gallant warriors survived. It was left to a British officer to report the fearless courage of the Chinese soldiers, so long rejected by the British army.

Meanwhile, back in Fred's sector:

> The machine gunners took toll of many thousands of Japs but their resistance only drove the enemy to greater efforts in other sectors. And the weakest link gave way. The Indians on the left flank of the 2/19th broke and retreated. The Japanese poured through the gap infiltrating and completely surrounding the battalion which, when daylight came, found itself again cut off from all support, and fighting desperately to regain contact with the rest of the AIF.
>
> Colonel Robertson gave an order to attack with bayonets up a hill. It was carried out with grievous loss and, just when success seemed assured, the order was countermanded and the order to retreat was given.
>
> Under the circumstances there was only one place to retreat and that was into the mangrove swamps. Once again the 2/19th had become a chopping block for the Japanese.
>
> It was a sorry plight. The men trying to cross the mangrove swamps found themselves in positions exposed to enemy fire from the high ground and also from the ever-present aircraft. Hundreds of them fell in the swamps badly wounded, and were sucked down into the treacherous mud.
>
> The survivors who reached the shelter of the screening rubber on the other side had been through the gauntlet. Many of the wounded urged their mates to give them a mercy bullet and make good their own escape, but that was never the attitude of the 2/19th. If it were possible to bring them through, they did.

As the 2/19th's positions were overrun, some survivors made it back through the dark to Company HQ, only to find it abandoned. Undaunted, they fell back to Battalion HQ, but at dawn the aerial onslaught started again, with planes strafing anything that moved

Tengah, where what was left of 2/19 Battalion regrouped (Murray Griffin)

within the perimeter. Realising that they were virtually surrounded, their attempt to get the seriously wounded out in trucks ended in disaster when the vehicles were remorselessly attacked. Once again, it was every man for himself. With no other option available, the able-bodied and walking wounded moved out on foot, hoping to reach Brigade HQ near Tengah airfield. Those too badly wounded to evacuate were left behind, under the protection of a Red Cross flag.

Others got out the best way they could. Some, unable to swim, tried to cross rivers and were drowned, others fell victim to strafing and shellfire. A party that included the indefatigable Padre Wardale-Greenwood and about 40 others, many of them wounded, managed to reach Jurong Road through the swamps. Once they made contact with Indian forces, the Padre was able to get his wounded to hospital.

After withdrawing from Tengah airfield, the survivors of the badly mauled Australian units reformed. It was a pitifully small force. For the second time in a month, the 2/19th had ceased to exist as a fighting force, the majority of its men killed, cut off or wandering around in the rear areas completely disoriented. The 2/18th and 2/20th had suffered similar casualties.

Fred and other members of the 2/19th made their way from Bulim village to Woodlands Road, and then to the intersection of Jurong Road, where the Padre had found transportation for his wounded. From here, Woodlands Road became Bukit Timah Road, which led directly to the Botanical Gardens, directly opposite the Australian GBD at Tanglin Barracks.

The withdrawal through the rubber took us to a company from a service corps, who were acting as infantry and awaiting their turn to face the Japs. The 2/19th at this time seemed to be a leaderless legion. Major Vincent, our 2IC, had been killed. Major Hughes (the Adjutant) also lay on the battlefield with an anti-tank shell through his chest, and Colonel Robertson was missing.

So, with no one in control, I and the other NCOs held a conference and decided to go to the General Base Depot near the Botanic Gardens, and await instructions.

The remnants of the once proud and famous 22 Brigade were marshalled together and men of 18, 19 and 20 Battalions formed into one battalion to fight together for the first time. Previously our battles had been fought individually, much to our disappointment and the disappointment of our leaders. Each unit had suffered terrific casualties in the initial onslaught of the enemy landing and each had been in a different sector. Had we been kept together from the outset at Muar, Jemaluang, Mersing and on the island when, time and again, supporting troops fell back, leaving the Australians to bear the brunt of the enemy's fiercest attack, we would not have sustained such a terrific list of casualties. Too late, we were banded together, a mere handful from each battalion, but still with our fighting spirit unquenched. Veterans of Muar, Parit Sulong, Endau and Mersing marched side by side with the newest recruits, content that we were together again.

We formed what was known as X Battalion. All that day we marched in single file along the road towards Bukit Timah, to retake an area that the Japanese had captured from the Indians. It was planned that a simultaneous attack from all points would be made at dawn the following day.

Meanwhile, throughout the night of 8 February and the following day, it had been relatively quiet in the 27 Brigade sector. However, that evening, the Japanese, having completely routed 22 Brigade, crossed the Straits of Johor and attacked the shoreline

Australian gunners at the causeway.

immediately west of the causeway. Although there were some incursions along the left flank, the tenacious Australians, supported by the artillery, managed to hold their own.

Unfortunately, Duncan Maxwell, the brigade commander, believing his men to be in danger of being cut off and not wanting a repeat of what had happened at Bakri and Parit Sulong, ordered them to withdraw to a new position about five kilometres back. Before leaving, they were instructed to destroy all oil and fuel stocks by opening the cocks of nearby storage tanks. As thousands of litres of highly volatile aviation spirit flowed down the nearby waterways, the defenders set it alight, incinerating a battalion of enemy troops attempting an outflanking manoeuvre.

General Nishimura was seeking permission for his Imperial Guards to call off the assault when, by the light of the burning fuel, he saw that the Australians were leaving. Scarcely able to believe his good luck, he seized the initiative and pressed home his attack. Once the territory had been lost, it proved impossible to regain. Despite a planned counter-attack, the Australians were once more in retreat.

Galling as this was, Fred and the 200 other soldiers of X Battalion had been having an even worse time.

Towards dusk on the afternoon of 10 February, their commanding officer, Colonel Boyes, received an order to advance to high ground between Jurong and Reformatory Roads, near Bukit Timah, an area that none of them knew, but soon to be in darkness. As they passed through Bukit Timah village, now a mass of flames, they learned that the enemy was just ahead. Having had no sleep for the past three days, they were extremely tired. After making their way through terrain littered with the bodies of hundreds of dead Indians, they headed towards their designated position, a trig station known as Jurong I. However, they were unaware that the Indians on their right had not arrived and that another scratch battalion, Merritt Force, pushing its way through swamp and jungle, had holed up for the night to their rear, making X Battalion the most forward of the units supposed to take part in the attack.

> Our destination was near Bukit Timah, where heavy fighting was in progress. Darkness found us some five or six miles from the start point for the attack. A meal was taken and our leaders, after consultation, decided to move on to our rendezvous point in easy stages. Contact with the other troops involved in the attack was maintained by wireless up until midnight when, for some unaccountable reason, contact was lost. X Battalion, still moving forward, was not aware that there had been a change of plans by Malaya command, and that the objective was not to be attacked.
>
> Who was to blame for this loss of contact is hard to say. It was certainly not X Battalion signallers, because we were able to contact every other station in the area, apart from the one issuing the change in orders, which was unaccountably silent.
>
> We were to go in at daylight the next morning and, after a forced march until about 1 am, we reached our position. We were given instructions to sleep until called. As the Indians were between us and the Japs, and the fighting had died down, it was considered quite safe to do so. Having marched all night we were glad of the chance and were soon stretched out and fast asleep.
>
> The first intimation we had that everything was not as it should be was the terrific din made by bursting grenades as the Japs charged in a couple of hours later. Taken completely by surprise, it was no wonder many panicked and raced right into

devastating fire, which the Japanese now poured in from all points. A lot of the men were raw recruits and this was their first experience of Japs' night methods.

The knowledge we veterans of the Muar campaign had gained now stood us in good stead. Realising the Japanese could not see us, instead of moving we stayed put and therefore had the advantage. Unless we went over the skyline, as the rest had done, we could outwit them.

There were four of us left in the bivouac area, so we lay quiet and spoke in whispers to take stock of the situation. A Jap racing with a fixed bayonet tripped when I put my leg out. He fell never to rise again - the thud of something striking flesh told me my mates had seized the advantage I gave them. After a whispered conversation we decided that to follow our mates over the hill would be suicidal, as the Japs had three machine guns pouring a continuous stream of bullets at anything that moved across the skyline.

Our best chance to get away lay in taking the offensive with hand grenades against the machine guns on our left and by keeping in the shadows. Hurling a grenade each, we waited for the effect. They were perfect shots. We crawled on hands and knees across the spot where the gun, only a minute before, was spewing forth death.

Believing that the attack was still going ahead, the surviving members regrouped and made the assault, little knowing that we were single handed against an enemy that outnumbered us at least 50 to 1. For four hours our handful of men fought and held the enemy until entirely surrounded. After some of the fiercest fighting seen on Singapore, we fought our way out with Mills bombs to safety. We then split into small parties of ten or a dozen and hours of dodging patrolling Japs followed. Weary and dispirited we reached the outskirts of the city proper, where we made contact with divisional headquarters. No one seemed to know just how the mistake had occurred, leaving us to carry out the attack single-handed. We soon came in contact with a few of the other survivors of the action, who also had stories to relate of thrilling escapes – and of hours dodging the Japs in the darkness, never knowing whether movement was of friend or foe.

There were many tales of individual heroism. One tall, bespectacled signaller from Cootamundra crawled on his hands and knees through a cordon of Japanese to get water for a wounded comrade, only to find on his return that the Japs had found his mate and bayonetted him to death. Another, a former schoolteacher from Maitland, trying to clear a track for an ambulance full of wounded, drove his motor bike into a bunch of Japs, losing his own life in the process.

The action by a dozen men in wiping out three Japanese machine gun nests was worthy of the strategy of the greatest general. One man sacrificed his life in providing a target and a distraction, while his mates crept up unnoticed to the rear of the enemy and drove them out with hand grenades. An officer, who sacrificed his life to draw off a Jap patrol to allow his wounded men a chance to survive, is typical of the attitude of all ranks who took part. The officer was not seen again.

The two signallers whose actions were so admired by Fred were both from 2/19 Battalion, Corporal Stan Cox and Private Stuart 'Ted' Levick. Cox, aged 40, a former railway train controller, was married. Levick, aged 34, the dispatch rider who had ridden into Parit Sulong to check if the British were still holding the bridge, loved motorbikes. He

Top: Hero Stan Cox.

Left: Alfie Flint, who survived a beheading.

had found himself on the wrong side of the law in 1925 when, as a 17-year-old schoolboy, he was arrested for riding at excessive speed down the main street in the NSW country town of Taree. As there had been previous complaints about his daredevil behaviour, he lost his licence for three months, a penalty that could have been much more severe were it not for his youth. Too young to enlist in World War I with his three older brothers, he had joined the AIF in June 1940. Much admired for his skill as a despatch rider, the story of his death so moved George Harding, the Battalion's Bard, that he wrote a poem about him. Like many of Harding's poems, it was written down by others and passed from hand to hand, a practice that led to his poetry being attributed to others. In 1946 the poem about the despatch rider was published in the newspaper as a memorial to Levick and as a tribute to Harding, who did not survive the war.

Fred and his surviving mates in X Battalion were lucky to escape annihilation, on the battlefield and afterwards. About 20 men who were captured were trussed and made to kneel beside a monsoon drain on nearby Jurong Road. Before long, most were sprawled in pools of blood at the bottom of the ditch, either beheaded or bayonetted by officers and men of the advancing Japanese 18 Division. One who survived the carnage was Alfie Flint, from the 2/19th, who crawled from the drain and managed to reach a casualty clearing station, holding his badly cut neck together with his hands.

Some time later, after the enemy had passed by, a private from 2/18 Battalion, 'Titch' H. Burgess, regained consciousness and realised that one of the bayonet thrusts meant to kill him had severed his bonds. Although severely wounded, he managed to free three others, all from his battalion and the only men still alive. Suffering from multiple stab wounds and deep sword cuts to the neck, they managed to drag themselves out of the ditch to the safety of a house, where a Chinese family took them in. Despite their horrific injuries, the three rescued men lived. Their saviour, Burgess, who had lost far too much blood, did not.

Members of the 2/19th, who had gathered near the racecourse off Bukit Timah Road with remnants of Fred's HQ Company, first became aware that a terrible calamity had overtaken X Battalion when a few terrified survivors arrived at 22 Brigade headquarters. In the wake of the ambush, fierce fighting had broken out along the Reformatory Road ridge, where the much-depleted 22 Brigade was battling to contain the Japanese advance. Flushed with success, the enemy began to drive home their attack from a nearby ridge. As they increased the pressure on Brigade HQ, all able-bodied men – staff and attached officers, signallers, machine gunners, support troops and infantry – were ordered to counter-attack across Reformatory Road and push the enemy back. Although under attack from mortars, the Australians managed to repel the Japanese with grenade and bayonet, at a cost of one officer killed and two officers and two men wounded.

> We reached Singapore where transports took us to the Golf Links, where we again formed some sort of fighting unit. For the next two days we guarded the pipeline bringing the water supply into the city, driving off numerous Jap patrols until the Jap bombers wrecked the storage reservoir and made the pipeline a useless asset.

By the time General Wavell arrived that morning for a conference with senior commanders, it was obvious that Singapore would not be able to hold out. After ordering the air force to plough up the airfields, destroy all bombs and petrol supplies, and leave immediately for the Dutch East Indies, Wavell informed Churchill that the battle was 'not going well'. Unable to comprehend the gravity of the situation, the Prime Minister replied, in his inimitable Churchillian style.

> Defenders must outnumber Japanese forces, who have crossed the Straits and, in a well-contested contest, they should destroy them. There now must be at this stage no thought of saving the troops or sparing the population. The battle must be fought to the bitter end at all costs. The 18th Division must make its name in history. Commanders and senior officers should die with their troops. The honour of the British Empire and the British Army is at stake. I will rely on you to show no mercy to weakness in any form. With the Russians fighting as they are and the Americans so stubborn in Luzon, the whole reputation of our country and our race is involved.

After paraphrasing Churchill's message into an equally wounding exhortation for Percival to distribute to the battle-weary Allied forces, Wavell ate his dinner and flew to the safety of Java. The AIF's Colonel Kent Hughes, instructed to deliver the message to the

Fighting the fires, Singapore city

Australians, refused to pass on what he regarded as 'a slur on the troops in Malaya' and threw it away.

Meanwhile the battle raged on. The Allies, forced back into an ever-diminishing circle, were now fighting on the outskirts of the city itself. Owing to the soaring number of casualties in the infantry units, 22 Brigade could scarcely find enough men to form a battalion, some battalions being down to company strength. As survivors regrouped and stragglers found their way back to their own lines, more composite 'battalions', numbering only 200 or 300, were formed from a handful of frontline troops, greatly reinforced by non-combatant transport, supply and service personnel. Realising that there was no hope of regaining control of the island, Malaya Command ordered all Allied troops to fall back and form a tight perimeter around the city.

On Thursday, 12 February, small wooden boxes had been dropped by Japanese planes, urging surrender. The following day, Bennett and other senior commanders held a conference at Fort Canning where those in attendance agreed that further resistance was hopeless. The troops were exhausted and even the newly arrived British 18 Division was 'done in'. Ammunition stores were dwindling, troops were constantly falling back and the Indians, in particular, were demoralised. Sooner or later the Japanese would reach the city streets, filled with army stragglers and terrified civilians, who were being killed and maimed in their thousands from the constant bombing and shelling. As the situation was hopeless, the commanders sent a message to General Wavell, urging him to agree to immediate capitulation. Meantime, plans were to be set in train at once to evacuate 1800 army personnel, whose contribution to the war effort was considered vital. The AIF was allotted 100 places. As Air Vice Marshal Pulford, one of the British evacuees, farewelled Percival, he remarked, 'I suppose you and I will be held responsible for this, but god knows we did our best with the little we had been given'.

As Bennett made his way to his headquarters at Tanglin Barracks on Holland Road, he saw that

> there was devastation everywhere. There were holes in the road, churned-up rubble lying in great clods all round, tangled masses of telephone, telegraph and electric cables strewn across the streets, here and there smashed cars, trucks, electric trams and buses that once carried loads of passengers to and from their peaceful daily toil. The shops were shuttered and deserted. There were hundreds of Chinese who refused to leave their homes. Bombs were falling on a nearby street. On reaching the spot one saw that the side of a building had fallen on an air raid shelter, the bomb penetrating deep in the ground, the explosion forcing in the sides of the shelter. A group of Chinese, Malays, Europeans and Australian soldiers were already at work, shovelling and dragging the debris away. Soon there emerged from a shelter a Chinese boy, scratched and bleeding, who immediately turned to help in the rescue work. He said 'My sister is under there.'
>
> The rescuers dug furiously among the fallen masonry, one little wiry Chinese man doing twice as much as the others, sweat streaming from his body. At last the top of the shelter was uncovered. Beneath was a crushed mess of old men, women young and old, and young children, some living - the rest dead. The little Oriental never stopped with his work, his sallow face showing the strain of his anguish. His wife and four children were there. Gradually he unearthed them - dead. He was later seen holding his only surviving daughter, aged ten, by the hand, watching them move away his family and

other unfortunates. This was going on hour after hour, day after day, and the same stolidity and steadfastness among the civilians was evident in every quarter of the city.

When Bennett arrived back at AIF HQ, Wavell's reply, forwarded by Percival, was waiting. There would be no surrender. All troops would fight to the end. However, the message distributed by Percival was considerably shorter than the one he had received. He had omitted to include Wavell's final instruction that 'when everything humanly possible has been done, some bold and determined personnel may be able to escape by small craft and find their way to Sumatra through the islands'.

That same day, Colonel Anderson was discharged from hospital. He had been admitted to 2/13 AGH, which had relocated to St Patrick's Boys' College on the beach at Katong, east of Singapore city, well outside the new perimeter. As Japanese troops had crossed the eastern end of the Straits of Johor and were advancing towards the hospital, anyone fit enough to be discharged was permitted to either attempt to escape, or go back to his unit. All who remained at the hospital, including the battalion's medical officer, Lloyd Cahill, and a number of other 2/19th men, would become prisoners of war.

Quite a number chose to go, using boats drawn up along the beach or moored nearby. Some made it to Sumatra, where those lucky enough to avoid the Japanese joined the escape route across the mountains. Others elected to go to the much closer Dutch Indonesian island of Bintan, where they were eventually captured and executed.

Later that day, when an advance party of Japanese soldiers arrived at St Patrick's, they beheaded the five Australian soldiers guarding the entrance to the hospital, before going on their way. Rushing out, the medical staff saved the life of one of the victims, who had been only partially decapitated. Fortunately, when occupying troops arrived, they made no attempt to molest any of the patients or doctors, unlike the situation on the other side of the city where, the next day, 14 February, Japanese troops unable to break though the Australian sector made an assault on Alexandra Hospital.

For some time, the defending Indian troops, armed with machine guns mounted within the hospital grounds, resisted fiercely, inflicting casualties on the attacking force before they were forced to pull back. Using the excuse that the Indians had breached the neutrality of the Red Cross, the Japanese entered the hospital, massacring soldiers and medical staff alike. A padre, who managed to escape, watched in horror as Dr Griffith, an English ear nose and throat specialist, was bayoneted to death in the operating theatre, along with his patient.

With St Patrick's College in enemy hands, makeshift hospitals were established at St Andrew's Cathedral and on the ground floor of the Cathay Building, Singapore's tallest and most prominent structure. With enemy artillery homing in on such an obvious target, neither the building nor the convalescent depot, set up in the adjacent Cathay Theatre, provided a secure refuge. It was not long before shells hit both the building and the theatre, killing a number of the wounded.

The effect of intense shelling on the civilian population, now jammed into a very small area, was horrific. On the 13th, a day that would become known as Black Friday, the attack on the city centre increased, with an estimated 70,000 civilians killed in a two-day period. Private Tom Burns, a wounded Australian soldier taken to the Cathay Building for treatment, was sickened by the carnage. Bodies, or rather parts of bodies, were everywhere. They lay on pockmarked streets, in the bottom of monsoon drains, on shattered sidewalks and the front lawns of what were once immaculately tended gardens. Here and there, pools of rapidly congealing blood oozed from beneath piles of rubble, all that remained of a row of shops or houses, while elsewhere severed limbs were draped like bits of flotsam among the ruins.

In some places where the shelling was particularly intense, the ground was so slick with blood and remains it was difficult to keep a footing. Although in the sauna-like heat the sickly stench of blood and rapidly decomposing corpses was stomach churning, there was no hope of burying the dead. The able-bodied were too busy looking after the wounded, and each other, to do anything about those who were now beyond all earthly help. Fred watched the destruction of the city from the relative safety of the GBD.

> Singapore was now properly besieged, with enemy guns able to shell the city from all angles, and bombers adding to the destruction at will, bombing large oil tanks built alongside the railway line linking Singapore with the mainland. The spectacle was awesome, with huge black clouds of smoke rising into the air like an Australian bushfire, but with a more intense blackness. The Japanese planes took advantage of the smoke screen to fly in low over their targets. However, they did not attack the large number of Australians assembling near Tanglin Barracks.

With the situation dire, General Bennett had ordered the AIF to 'come home', to make their last stand, centred on the Tanglin Barracks area. He then cabled the Australian Prime Minister, John Curtin, to inform him that the AIF had formed a perimeter and would hold to the last. However, should others fall back and allow the enemy to enter the city to the Australian rear, he also advised it was his intention to surrender, to avoid any further loss of life. Malaya Command overruled him. If the enemy penetrated the city and captured the command centre at Fort Canning, troops would fight to the last man.

In spite of what was a rapidly deteriorating situation, Percival had received further orders 'to continue to inflict maximum damage on the enemy for as long as possible. By house to house fighting if necessary', a viewpoint obviously supported by Governor Shenton Thomas who, that very morning, in the single sheet edition of The Straits Times, had declared 'Singapore Must Stand; It SHALL stand. H.E. The Governor.' It was a headline that was to be repeated on the following two days.

In the midst of what was an increasingly desperate situation, there was one bright and glorious piece of news. On 14 February it was announced that Colonel Anderson had been awarded a Victoria Cross, the Empire's highest award for gallantry. While the announcement didn't make the papers in Singapore, it was big news on the radio and in newspapers all over Australia and also in the UK. Anderson's bravery and leadership had already been recognised by a Mention in Despatches (MID), but a Victoria Cross took his gallantry to the supreme level. His citation read:

> During operations in Malaya from January 18 to January 22, 1942 Lieutenant-Colonel Anderson, in command of a small force, was sent to restore a vital position and to assist a brigade. His force destroyed ten enemy tanks.
>
> When later cut off he defeated persistent attacks on his position from air and ground forces and forced his way through the enemy lines to a depth of 15 miles. He was again surrounded and subjected to very heavy and frequent attacks, resulting in severe casualties to his force.

He personally led an attack with great gallantry on the enemy, who were holding a bridge, and succeeded in destroying four guns.

Lieut-Colonel Anderson throughout all this fighting protected his wounded and refused to leave them. He obtained news by wireless, of the enemy position and attempted to fight his way back through eight miles of enemy-occupied country.

This proved impossible and the enemy was holding too strong a position for any attempt to be made to relieve him. On January 19 Lieutenant-Colonel Anderson was ordered to destroy his equipment and make his way back as best he could round the enemy position.

Throughout the fighting, which lasted for four days, he set a magnificent example of brave leadership determination and outstanding courage.

He not only showed fighting qualities of a very high order but through-out exposed himself to danger without any regard for his own personal safety.

There was no doubt among Anderson's men that the award was most certainly deserved. As Mick Curnow put it, in a very detailed account of the action to a mate in Australia, 'one thing was outstanding, the coolness and bravery of our CO, whom we have to thank for being here at all.'

The 2/19th couldn't wait to be reunited with Anderson. Obeying Bennett's order to 'come home', Fred had

> moved to the Botanical Gardens, where we again came under the command of Colonel Anderson. There was not one man who did not feel a new lease of life just to hear his voice. On Saturday, the 14th, we moved into Tanglin Barracks across the road where, because of the grueling time we had had over the last week, we were held in reserve at the Engineers' Barracks and rested.
>
> Stragglers who had been cut off from their units were still coming into the area with stories of narrow escapes. Some had avoided capture by wading up to their necks across swamps, coated in semi-burnt oil, making it impossible to distinguish them from the natives.
>
> From our area on the higher ground we could see the Japs through our field glasses, massing their forces about four miles away. They seemed to be in their thousands along Cemetery Hill, one of the strategic points overlooking the city, from which the Indians had withdrawn the previous night. To our rear, the 2/10th Field Artillery men had taken up position and were getting ready for action. We passed the word to them about the Japs and, while awaiting results, noticed that about 100 had entered a house on the extreme end of Cemetery Hill. After passing on the map references, we sat back and awaited the first shot. As a shell whistled over our heads we kept our eyes glued on the target and were rewarded when the shell landed right inside the back door of the building. Japs came hurtling out in all directions, only to run into a second and third shell, which landed either side of the building. The Japs had their revenge, however, when the planes searching for the guns overshot their targets and dropped their bombs right amongst us, fortunately causing only slight damage. The artillery kept up the barrage, driving the Japs from the hill but, under cover of darkness, they came back and dug in.

All the AIF on Singapore was now concentrated in the Tanglin area and was putting up strong resistance against the Jap forces. Rumour had it that Tanglin was to be another Tobruk – and we were doing our best to make it so!

Sunday, the 15th dawned to the sight of huge clouds of black smoke belching skyward from burning oil tanks. The Japs commenced their attack on the Australian positions only to be thrown back again and again as our entrenched men fought desperately. All day long this battle lasted and still we were not forced to give one inch of ground. At last the Japs gave up and confined their assault to a terrific bombardment, with shells and mortars, till late afternoon, when they bypassed us and headed for Singapore city, where the opposition was much weaker.

Over in the distance, near the causeway, we could see their observation balloon floating in the sky. What we would have given to be able to plant just one well-directed shot into it, but we were too far away and all our planes had long since been shot down or departed for Java.

Darkness fell – or at least what should have been darkness – were it not for the burning oil. The fires had now reached their greatest height and the whole sky was a rosy-coloured hue from the reflection cast by the flames rising and falling, as fresh drums bursting from the tremendous heat added more fuel to the conflagration. It was an awe-inspiring sight. Vivid enough by day, but by night it had the appearance of the supernatural. We could see men silhouetted against the glare, alert for any move the Japs might make, as we could see them as readily as they could see us.

The bombardment stopped. The sudden quiet was almost as hard to bear as the incessant noise of explosions. The silence at Battalion Headquarters was broken by the buzz of the telephone, which sounded loud and demanding. It was a message from Malaya Command. We were to lay down our arms. The sudden cessation of noise now had a dreadful significance.

The ceasefire was an actual fact. How different from what we had pictured ever since our arrival twelve months before. Surrender? Much better to die fighting than to suffer this! We wouldn't surrender. 'Make them drive us out' was the cry of nearly all those present.

More phone messages arrived. The Australians must cease fighting or the whole of Singapore would be bombed to the ground when the Japanese turned their planes loose on the city the next day. We all realised what this meant: the previous Friday, Black Friday, a four-hour bombing raid left the streets of Singapore littered with tens of thousands of dead bodies.

Well over a million civilians were in Singapore. It is one thing to be a soldier and take what is coming. One expects it when he joins up. But to see defenceless women and children, huddled together in thousands with no protection, receive the full force of the Japs' bestiality was more than we were worth. Singapore was doomed in any case and our holding out would only subject them to more untold horror.

The time for bravado was over. After consultation with his most senior Allied officers, Britain's General Percival had unconditionally surrendered all British, Australian and Indian troops to the Imperial Japanese Army, an action finally sanctioned by Wavell, who had sent Percival a message:

British troops surrender

So long as you are in a position to inflict losses to the enemy and your troops are physically capable of doing so, you must fight on.

Time gained and damage to enemy vital importance at this crisis. When you are fully satisfied that this is no longer possible, I give you discretion to cease resistance. Before doing so, all arms, equipment and transport of value to the enemy must of course be rendered useless.

He continued:

Also, just before final cessation of fighting, opportunity should be given to any determined bodies of men or individuals to try and effect and escape by any means possible. They must be armed. Inform me of intentions. Whatever happens I thank you and all troops for your gallant efforts of the last few days.

Percival had read the message and then censored it, again removing all references to Wavell's order to escape. He told no one, not even his Generals Bennett and Heath, and most certainly none of the tens of thousands of troops under his command, who would soon become prisoners of war.

Bennett, however, had no intention of spending the rest of the war in captivity, especially as he was one of the few combat commanders who had come up against the Japanese and who knew anything about jungle fighting. He waited for two hours after the ceasefire took effect, unaware that his escape had been urged by his supreme commander.

At 8.30 pm on 15 February 1942, the guns stopped and all hostilities ceased. As the eerie silence, punctuated only by the occasional cries of the wounded, descended over the smouldering ruins of the city, the soldiers and civilians were confronted by the reality of what had occurred. To the consternation of all those for whom the very thought of either defeat or surrender was an absolute anathema, the unthinkable had happened.

Singapore, the impregnable fortress, had fallen.

Fred Howe was now a prisoner of war.

CHAPTER 15

FOLLOWING IN FRED'S FOOTSTEPS: SINGAPORE

Now back in Johor Bahru, after following Dad's retreat from Parit Sulong, we explored several streets along the waterfront near the Administration Building, which, in 1942, was the tallest building in the town. It was instantly recognisable from historic photos, and some of the damage inflicted by the Australian artillery, when they were finally allowed to fire on it, was still visible. It is now called the Sultan Ibrahim Building, after the Sultan who officially opened it in 1940.

Many people think that the Administration Building is part of the Sultan's Istana, or palace, which also had an excellent view across the straits to the Australian positions. Although the beautiful Istana, set in spacious grounds, is not far away, it is a completely different building. However, it was used by the Japanese, with the Sultan's permission, to spy on the Australian troops once they had retreated to the island.

Although the Sultan was a friend of General Bennett and liked Australians, he was also friendly with Tokugawa Yoshichika, whose ancestors were military leaders in Japan for centuries. Through Tokugawa, Lieutenant General Yamashita Tomoyuki, commanding officer of the invading Japanese 25 Army, was welcomed into the Istana at the end of January 1942. I admired the survival skills of the Sultan, who certainly knew which way to jump.

Probably the only attractive building in the town, apart from the Istana, was the railway station. To our disappointment, there was no trace of any of the damage sustained when the armour-piercing shell fell on it. Although historians have spent decades trying to dispel the myth that Singapore was lost because the guns were facing the wrong way, it is a widely-held belief, and one that war hero and former Governor of NSW Sir Rodin Cutler, VC, repeated at a function in Sydney to mark the 50th anniversary of the fall of Singapore.

After exiting passport control at Johor Bahru, we began the one-kilometre walk across the causeway, to follow in Dad's exact footsteps. As we left the shoreline, I thought of the Argylls, with their bagpipes and drums, putting on such a brave face, and the defiant Drummer Hardy, who came to a terrible end in the Indian Ocean. Lynette had researched the rest of his story and discovered that he had managed to escape from Singapore after the surrender to make his way to Sumatra, where he joined the Allied escape route and boarded an evacuation ship, *Rooseboom*.

The vessel was only three days out from Sumatra's west coast when it was torpedoed. Only two Javanese sailors, picked up by another ship, and 135 others, either in or clinging to a lifeboat, survived the actual sinking. As the boat drifted aimlessly in the scorching tropical sun, the more fortunate died from thirst and exposure. Apart from four, the rest were murdered by a group of British Army deserters from Liverpool. Before they themselves died, they killed their fellow castaways and indulged in unspeakable acts of cannibalism before throwing the bodies overboard. Among their victims was Drummer Hardy.

After drifting for four weeks, the last four left alive – two mad Javanese crewmen, a British-Chinese secret agent named Doris Lim, and Sergeant Walter Gibson, the last of the Argylls – staggered ashore on an island off the Sumatran coast, where they were captured. Only Gibson made it to the end of the war. Doris Lim, who survived forced labour in a cement factory, married a local man, who murdered her in March 1945.

The causeway seemed to be a bit of a no-man's-land and I wondered how many of the retreating soldiers had any idea they were going from the frying pan into the fire. Probably none. At that stage they still believed that Singapore was an impregnable fortress.

Although we knew where to look, there was no visible sign of the paltry 21-metre gap in the causeway. Ironically, while the breach did nothing to slow the Japanese advance, it did have serious repercussions for our side.

When the causeway blew up, the engineers also destroyed the huge pipeline carrying the water supply from Malaya to the island's water storage facilities, including the reservoir at Fort Canning, just a block from St Andrew's Cathedral and right alongside the massive underground Command Centre, built at the same time as the naval base. Now known as the Battle Box, General Percival had moved there from his quarters at Sime Road when things became really grim.

Causeway, with the Administration Building visible on the skyline (2nd from left) and water pipe from Johor Bahru

Although the main water pipe was destroyed, there was an excellent supply available in three large dams. But having plenty of water was one thing; distributing it was quite another matter. With the Woodleigh Pumping Station, as well as the dams, in Japanese hands, fires raging, water mains and pipes shattered and just a trickle of water coming through some of the taps, lack of water was one of the major considerations in the decision to surrender. Troops could fight on reduced rations but, in Singapore's heat, they could not last long without water.

On reaching the other side of the causeway, we could not believe the difference a walk of one kilometre could make. In Johor Bahru everything seemed so grubby, with rubbish everywhere, men spitting in the streets, and open drains that doubled as sewers. The traffic was also heavy, as well as chaotic, making crossing the road extremely hazardous. The Singapore side, however, was the complete opposite – well-behaved traffic and people, immaculately clean pavements and nary a whiff of anything remotely resembling sewage.

From the causeway we headed to the nearby Commonwealth War Graves Cemetery at Kranji. It is on one of the few hills in the area and has a fine view of the Johor Straits, where the Japanese stormed ashore on the night of 8 February 1942. The distinctive Johor Bahru Administration Building, which once dominated the skyline opposite, has been all but lost among multi-storey towers.

The cemetery, accessed through a gracious sandstone archway, is beautifully tended by dedicated staff, who care for almost five and a half thousand white marble grave markers, marching up the hill in precise rows like soldiers on parade. The magnitude of this immense

Top: Entrance to Kranji War cemetery. Many of the Muar battle victims are buried just to the right.

Left: Grave of Major Tom Vincent, killed on 9 February 1942, during the initial Japanese assault.

loss of life, represented by so many headstones, left me with a feeling of despair: so many Australians, many of them Dad's mates, never saw their homeland or their families again.

We wandered among the graves of many of the 480 Australians who died at Muar, Bakri and on the retreat from Parit Sulong. The bodies of the 107 massacred at the bridge, along with most of those who lost their lives in battle in the village, were of course never found. However, Lynette told me that a local man gathered up the remains of many others, including George Gill, who lost an arm and a leg when the bomb dropped on the signallers at Parit Sulong. Removing one set of dog tags, he placed the bodies near the 101-mile peg. At war's end they were recovered, along with the dog tags, but those left on the bodies, made of a type of composite cardboard, had rotted away. It was impossible to identify who was who, so their headstones were erected left to right alphabetically. Until Lynette explained the system, I had thought that the burial teams had gone to the trouble of sorting everyone into alphabetical order.

All who died at Bakri and on the retreat lie near each other, united in death as they were in life. The names of those with no identifiable grave are inscribed on the massive marble walls in the colonnaded memorial at the top of the hill, on which 24,346 Allied names are recorded. Of the 1437 missing Australians, 2/19 Battalion has the dubious honour of heading the list with 246, and almost the most killed – 467.

Seeing the names of men from Dad's battalion and my hometown upset me greatly – particularly those inscribed on the panels. We left tributes there to four Boorowa boys: Harry Grosvenor and Frederick Kelly, who were left in the convoy; Darcy Percival, who died fighting with the Chinese guerrillas; and George Bradshaw, killed on the first day of the battle for Singapore Island. We also paid a special visit to George Gill's headstone. As we left the cemetery, I wrote a message in the register at the gate, but no words can ever convey what I felt.

A road now links the cemetery with the far north-west of the island, via a dam wall that has closed off the Kranji River to the sea and converted it into a reservoir. After crossing what was the river mouth, we passed the place where the gallant Dalforce Chinese had fought to the last man, before joining Chu Kang Road, linking Tengah Airfield to the north-western shores of the strait.

Unlike much of Singapore, the area is isolated and undeveloped. The entire western side of the road, right out to the water's edge, is under the control of the Ministry of Defence and entry is prohibited. To dissuade anyone from venturing into the area, signs depicting an armed soldier shooting at an intruder are prominently displayed at regular intervals. While this warning ensured that we could not enter the heart of the Australian positions, it has also ensured that the vegetation is very much as it was in 1942. No wonder the Australian line was infiltrated so easily – the foliage is so dense that someone could be standing a metre away and would not be visible.

The road ended at the edge of the mangrove flats. Jutting out a fair way into the straits was a rather rickety jetty, providing an excellent vantage point. I had no idea until then that the mangroves just opposite from where the Japanese launched their attack were so close to the area the Australians had to defend. It came as a shock and really brought home to me what an impossible task Dad and his comrades faced. I could visualise the machine gunners and the forward troops waiting in the dark, their tired eyes trying to penetrate the darkness and the fog, as hordes of Japanese, screaming and yelling, launched themselves at the thinly dispersed infantry.

The area allotted to the Australians on the Straits of Johor.

We drove back down the entire length of Chu Kang Road following Dad's retreat to Tengah Airfield, and then through Bulim village to Jurong Road, where his captured comrades from X Battalion came to an awful end beside the monsoon drain. Although it is no longer open space, with the aid of Lynette's maps we located the place where Dad and X Battalion were taken by surprise, and also where some of the members of Dad's HQ company routed the enemy in the desperate bayonet charge up the hill at Reformatory Road. The Boys' Reformatory School, which gave its name to the road, known as Clementi Road since 1947, existed until quite recently.

Before returning to the Jurong Road–Bukit Timah Road junction, we drove along Clementi to the top of a ridge. A wartime sandy track that petered out after a couple of hundred metres is now a proper thoroughfare, named Dover Road. About 100 metres along the road, on the right-hand side, was a killing field, where the Japanese beheaded scores of Chinese and also ten Australian commandos from Operation Rimau, captured after raiding enemy shipping off Singapore in October 1944. Lynette was successful in having the execution site recognised as a site of special significance by the Singapore government, which has erected an historic marker and placed the site on an official wartime trail.

We headed back down Clementi Road, as we had a special task: to find a duck pond that my brother-in-law Hilton said was somewhere in the area. I had promised to do my best, but deep down, realising how much of the area had been developed, I didn't like my chances.

The area nominated for the search was a far cry from the days when Hilton was there. Multi-storied buildings have sprung up everywhere, many of them owned by Japanese companies. However, I had a good description of the road as it was in 1942 and located the large, crescent-shaped bend that Hilton had mentioned, just north of Ulu Pandan Road.

After Hilton's party had retreated to this area, they settled in for the night and readied themselves for the next onslaught. All was reasonably quiet except for the sound of battle further to the north and the occasional contented quacking of ducks on a nearby pond. In the early hours of the morning, the ducks started quacking madly and took flight, alerting the Australians that the Japanese were close at hand.

Under the cover of darkness, enemy troops had set up a machine-gun post not far away and then began firing into the 22 Brigade HQ area. Hilton and other signallers went into action and, aided by men from the HQ, destroyed the machine gun and, no doubt, a few Japanese with it. However, the signallers did not escape unscathed. Geoff Bingham and Bobby Hook were badly wounded. Both were lying in the open without any cover and, although under fire, Hilton went to their rescue, brought them to safety, loaded them onto a truck and sent them to hospital.

I don't know who wrote the citation in regard to the rescue, but Bingham received a Military Medal. Hilton received nothing for his heroic action – not even a mention in his unit history. Many years later, just prior to Hilton's death, Bingham sought him out and thanked him. Rather belatedly, the story of the rescue now forms part of the display at the Australian War Memorial, along with Bobby Hook's medals but, unfortunately, Hilton didn't live long enough to see it.

The badly wounded Hook was taken to Alexandra Hospital where, on the afternoon of 14 February, the Japanese entered the grounds, killing about 50 staff and patients. The slaughter lasted for about half an hour.

Later that afternoon, another 200 patients and staff, including Hook, were rounded up. With their hands tied, they were marched a short distance to an old building where they were crammed, 70 at a time, into three small rooms. Wounded who fell on the way were bayoneted. Pleas for water were ignored and the doors were slammed shut. Moans and screams penetrated the night as patients became delirious and several, including Hook, died.

Later the next morning, the day of the surrender, the doors were opened and the occupants taken away in groups of two or three and bayoneted. Before the executions were complete, a shell hit the corner of the building creating a hole and allowing a number to escape. Five made it to the safety of British troops nearby, but the rest were shot.

While I was thinking about all this, I looked to the left of Clementi Road, where the duck pond was supposed to be, and spotted a large garden area and a sign, Clementi

Alexandra Hospital in 1945, scene of the massacre of patients and medical staff.

Neighbourhood Park. Crossing the lawns, I made my way down an embankment where I found an expanse of shallow water filled with reeds – the duck pond! I listened for the sound of quacking, but was disappointed. Progress had taken its toll and there was not a duck in sight. Nevertheless, I chalked it up as mission accomplished.

Ulu Pandan Road conveniently morphed into Holland Road, which led directly to the Botanic Gardens and Tanglin Barracks. However, we diverted onto Bukit Timah Road, Dad's line of retreat, to visit the historic Ford Motor Factory at Bukit Batok, where General Percival unconditionally surrendered to General Yamashita. We wanted to see the company's boardroom, where the surrender document was signed at a large teak table.

No one took any interest in the factory or its historical significance until mid-1961, when an Australian warrant officer, Andrew John 'Jack' Balsillie, visited Singapore during his posting to Malaya as part of Australia's commitment to the 12-year-long Malayan Emergency. His interest in old battlefield sites and war relics had been piqued some months before when he discovered .303 ammunition, an enamel plate and a fuse cap from a grenade at the site of the Gemas ambush.

On his trip to Singapore, Jack visited the Ford Factory where he met a member of staff who had been there since the war. He took Jack to the boardroom with its original teak table and linoleum covered floor, on which the Japanese had marked the positions of those present at the surrender.

Jack asked his guide if the company might consider selling or donating the table to the Australian War Memorial. The staff member couldn't see why not – after all it had been sitting there, unloved and neglected, for almost 20 years – and asked Jack to leave his contact details. Three years later, in 1964, Ford Malaysia informed Jack that the company had agreed to donate the historic table, along with the lino flooring, to the War Memorial. What an amazing coup! A perfect case of, if you don't ask, you don't get.

Much later, when the factory closed down, the facade and front section was retained and has since been converted into a museum aptly named 'The Old Ford Factory'. As Australia has the precious table, the one in the boardroom is a replica, as is another in a museum on Sentosa Island. I heard that, when the real table was loaned for an exhibition held in Singapore, the Australian custodians supposedly took a small sliver of wood from it, to ensure that the one that was loaned was the one that came back.

The surrender room is now preserved as a time warp, with continuous newsreel footage of the meeting between Percival and Yamashita on 15 February 1942. It is mesmerising to watch. Percival blinks nervously as Yamashita takes centre stage, thumping on the table and making it abundantly clear that it is unconditional surrender, or else. Sadly, it was a fantastic bluff. Malaya Command had no idea the Japanese advance was so rapid that their supply lines were overstretched and, had the Allies kept fighting and not surrendered for another 24 hours, the Japanese would have had to withdraw.

Old footage also shows the surrender party making its way to the factory entrance along a wide driveway, which has not changed. Captain Cyril Wild, who spoke fluent Japanese, was given the task of carrying the white surrender flag. Disgusted, he tossed it aside as he rounded the bend of the drive, only to have a Japanese soldier retrieve it. It was very sobering to walk the walk, and I understood exactly how Cyril Wild felt.

A very short distance from the factory gates is a road through jungle-covered Bukit Batok, leading to the site of a Japanese war memorial, built entirely with POW labour. Dad did not work on this project, but thousands of other Australians did. The memorial itself

The surrender party walking up the driveway at the Ford Factory.

was a massive timber pole, perched on the summit of the hill, accessed by a roadway, and then up a flight of 120 very wide steps, all constructed by hand.

The POWs assigned to this task were kept busy for months. They were not happy to be building a memorial to Japanese war dead, but were mollified somewhat when permission was granted to erect a much smaller wooden cross on a mound behind the main obelisk, to commemorate Allied troops killed in battle. This was not as compassionate as it sounds. The Japanese were motivated by propaganda value.

The Australian workers thought they had got their own back on their Japanese masters when they placed white ants at the base of the wooden pole unaware that, for a termite colony to survive, they needed a most important element – the queen. Consequently, the Japanese memorial and the cross survived the war – but not for long. As soon as hostilities ceased, the British destroyed both, along with an elaborate Shinto shrine erected with POW labour on the summit of nearby Bukit Timah.

Bukit Batok was soon forgotten and the road and steps, covered in jungle, were 'lost' until someone wandering around the jungle discovered them in the 1980s. Nearby, another site of significance that survived was a row of one-storey shop houses on Bukit Timah Road, used as accommodation by Australians working on the memorial site.

The next morning, we headed to Fort Canning Park and The Battle Box which, in the dying days of the Singapore Campaign, had been used by Percival to direct the battle. The park was originally known as Bukit Larangan, or Forbidden Hill, and Stamford Raffles, the founder of Singapore, built a house there in 1823. When Singapore became a Crown Colony of Britain, a fort was constructed on the summit of the hill to protect the settlement, but by 1900 it was made obsolete by more modern defences. In 1936, Fort Canning had a new

Official opening of the Bukit Batok Memorial.

lease of life with the construction of the underground bunker and beautiful administration and accommodation blocks, set into the side of the hill.

The bunker, built ten metres below ground level, with walls made of one-metre-thick reinforced concrete and a roof constructed of heavy steel and reinforced concrete, was capable of withstanding direct hits from bombs and shells. Completed in 1941, the 22-room complex included a telephone exchange connected to all military and most civilian switchboards in Malaya, various signal and operation rooms, a cipher room, sleeping quarters, mess rooms and toilet facilities. It was completely self-contained, with its own generator and air circulation system, and was protected with blast doors at the main entrances.

However, at the end of its five-year construction, when the bunker was declared too small for its intended use as a command centre, General Percival authorised the construction of a new Combined Operations HQ at the RAF Headquarters on Sime Road. It was finished in December 1941, coinciding with the commencement of hostilities with Japan. The bunker then became the headquarters of the Fortress Commander Singapore, Major General Frank Simmons, who was responsible for the defence of the island.

However, as the invading Japanese drew nearer to the city, Sime Road was abandoned and, on 11 February, Percival shifted his Combined Operations Headquarters to Fort Canning, taking up residence in a building adjacent to the bunker's northern entrance. When the city, including Fort Canning, came under increasing artillery attack, military personnel took refuge in the bunker which, at one stage, held around 500 officers and men.

On the day of surrender, Percival made his way from his quarters, up several flights of stone steps, and entered the bunker where, in a small room, he and the senior Allied

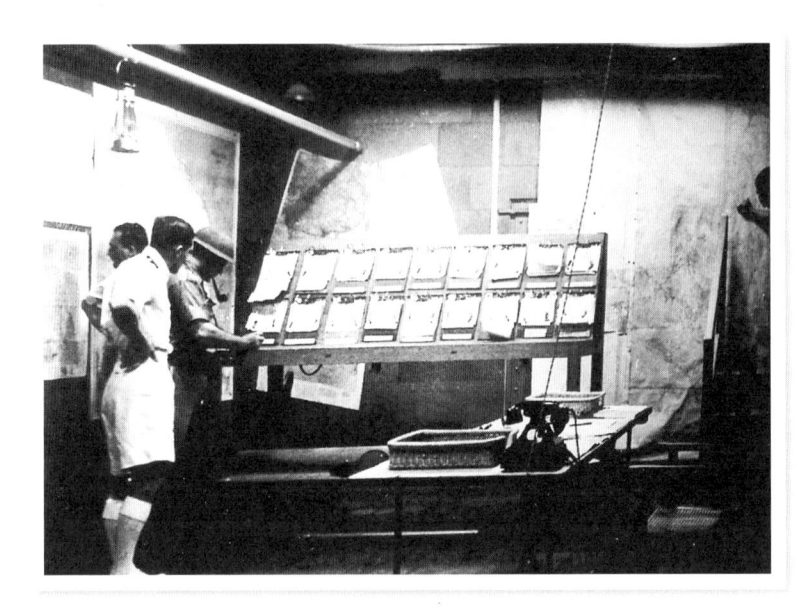

Inside the Battle Box, 1941.

commanders met to decide on the best course of action. Percival had hoped they could fight on but, with more than a million civilians crowded into the city, food stocks and ammunition low and the water supply virtually non-existent, the majority held the view that surrender was inevitable. The decision made, Percival went to a nearby basin, which had its own water supply, and washed his hands. He and a small party then drove through the devastated city to the Ford Factory to meet General Yamashita.

Once the Japanese had control of Singapore, they moved into the bunker, which served as their communications centre until hostilities ceased in 1945. Post-war, the buildings at Fort Canning were used as the Singapore Base District Headquarters, then as a Command and Staff College. The bunker, however, now stripped of most of its equipment, remained empty and in 1960 was sealed off due to safety concerns. As the years passed, its existence was forgotten until it was 'discovered' in 1988 by a journalist who had heard stories of the existence of a wartime underground bunker. A search revealed that the entrances had been sealed and were concealed by thick vines.

Once unsealed, the bunker's potential as a tourist attraction was realised and, in 1993, four years before the public was allowed to enter, Lynette was fortunate to be introduced to the curator, Ms Teng Teng, who took her through the labyrinth of rooms and tunnels, using temporary lights to guide the way. Lynette's father, a World War II wireless and communications expert, was able to determine, from the outlines of equipment on the walls, what some of the rooms had been used for, and the type of installations. There was also pencilled graffiti on the walls, written by British and Japanese occupants, but the most chilling message was one in chalk, scrawled in obvious haste on the heavy bomb-blast door of the telephone exchange room – 'LAST DAY 15 FEB 42'.

Under Teng Teng's administration, the Fort Canning bunker, renamed the Battle Box, was developed over the next few years into a museum recreating the final days of the battle of Singapore. However, during a trip to the island in 1995, two years before the Battle Box was opened, Paul and I had had a brief and unscheduled sneak preview of the bunker's

The telephone exchange, inside the Battle Box, present day.

interior. On the day of our visit, we saw a sign advising that 'restoration of this complex is in progress – please bear with us' but, as the door was open, in we went.

There seemed to be a smoky mist drifting about the rooms and tunnels, possibly haze or dust. However, the bunker appeared to be in pretty much the same condition it would have been in, in wartime, and we were enjoying our self-guided tour when we were accosted by an officious looking Chinese gentleman who ordered us out. The place was being fumigated and, in any case, we should not have been there as it was not yet open to the public. However, when I remarked that my Dad had been in Singapore in World War 11, when the bunker was operational, he gave us a very quick tour.

It was not until our current visit that we saw the completed project. Formally opened on 15 February 1997, the 55th anniversary of the fall of Singapore, the Battle Box featured life-like moving figures, with audio, installed in various rooms to add an air of reality. One room, in particular, was very interesting. It depicts that final conference, when the Allied commanders made the decision to capitulate. It is not a very large room, and in 1993 Teng Teng expressed her surprise to Lynette at the choice, as it was alongside a noisy air-blowing machine. However, Lynette realised that, as the acoustics in the bunker were excellent – people talking in quite low voices could be easily heard for some distance – the room selection was deliberate. All good spies know that the best way not to be overheard is to choose a noisy venue. As the conference was top secret, the thrum of the air blower masked any discussion.

After inspecting the sink in a corner of the room where Percival did his Pontius Pilate impersonation by washing his hands, Lynette had noticed that the original flooring, brown 20-centimetre-square rubber tiles, had been taken up and stacked in a pile near the door. Discovering that they were to be dumped, she asked if she could have one, realising that all the commanders on that final day had walked on them. She was given two, and they are evidently the only tiles to survive. Again, a case of if you don't ask, you don't get!

While wandering around the gardens at Fort Canning, we spotted the Cathay Theatre, just off Bras Basah Road, which served as a casualty clearing station immediately before Singapore's fall. It was originally part of the Cathay Building, 11 storeys high and the only 'skyscraper' in Singapore pre-war. Opened in 1939, the building housed the headquarters of the British Malayan Broadcasting Corporation, as well as police security services and SOE-Far East, the organisation that set up the escape route through Sumatra. The complex consisted of a residential and office tower, with a cinema, a dance hall and a restaurant

The Cathay Building, where the Japanese flag was flown as part of the surrender terms.

on the ground floor. Because of its height, pilots used it as a landmark when approaching Kallang Airport, now long gone except for the control tower, which was preserved.

When the Japanese took over the Cathay building, it housed their broadcasting and propaganda department and served as a broadcast centre for the Indian National Army (Indian Army personnel who changed sides), during the occupation period. When the war ended, it became the headquarters of Lord Louis Mountbatten, Supreme Allied Commander South-east Asia Command.

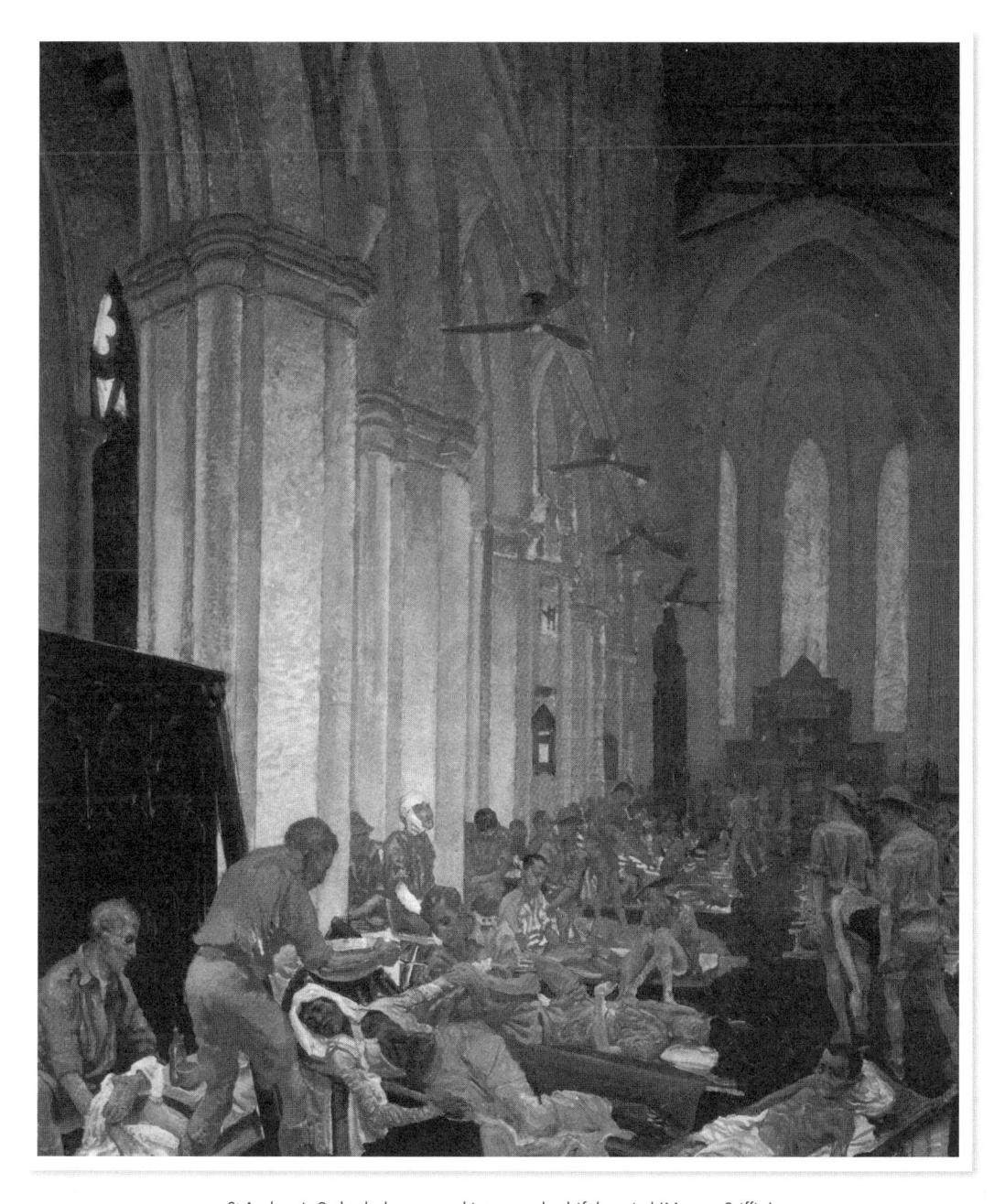

St Andrew's Cathedral converted into a makeshift hospital (Murray Griffin)

From the Cathay Theatre we took a taxi to the west of Fort Canning to look at the site of the New World Amusement Park, one of the few places where ordinary soldiers could relax. I recalled the furore created by Adele Shelton Smith when she wrote about the taxi-dancers, and the retaliation threatened by outraged wives and mothers. From here we drove south, along Outram Road, to the site of a notorious prison. Run by the Japanese kempeitai, the equivalent of the German gestapo, it was used as a punishment gaol for Japanese soldiers and Allied POWs charged with breaking military orders. The gaol was demolished some years ago, but its reputation as a place of unmitigated horror lingers on. It was so bad that inmates, facing death, were saved only by a transfer to the hospital at Changi Camp, a camp described by prisoners as 'like heaven'. Immediate post-war photos taken at Changi Camp, showing prisoners emaciated to the point of skin and bone, are not images of Changi inmates, but of recently liberated Outram Road inmates and POWs who had just arrived back from the Burma-Thai railway. The display of these photographs has resulted in Changi, the best-run POW camp under Japanese administration, being described as a hellhole. As the relatively few Australians, fortunate enough not to be shipped off to an overseas camp, later attested, Changi was about as close to heaven as was possible for a prisoner of war.

Circling back through China town, we crossed the Anderson Bridge, spanning the Singapore River, once covered in hundreds of sampans but now an upmarket tourist precinct. However, our focus was not on the river but the bridge where, in the early days of occupation, the Japanese had exhibited the heads of Chinese, executed for looting – a grim reminder to Dad and other Australians passing by on work parties that the new masters meant business. Our last stop for the day was St Andrew's Anglican Cathedral, traditional in design but clad in startlingly white paint and set in park-like grounds. A little bit of England in an exotic, tropical setting. Somehow it survived the shelling and was used as a hospital, with doctors performing operations in the nave, while the injured lined up on stretchers among the pews.

Our next stop would be the Botanical Gardens, and Tanglin Barracks to follow Dad into captivity.

CHAPTER 16
INTO CAPTIVITY

The ceasefire order was met with a mixture of disbelief, outrage and shock. Some of the Australians simply refused to believe it. The reality did not really hit home until they saw the white flag of surrender, and the red and white 'poached egg' of the Japanese ensign, hoisted aloft by an Allied flag party and now flying on the roof of the Cathay Building. This humiliating display was a condition of the surrender, as the Cathay could be seen from many places in the city, and most certainly by General Yamashita at Bukit Timah, the highest point on the island. At the sight, some Australians seethed with shame and frustration. Others wept openly, while yet others fumed at the injustice of it all. However, most simply felt cheated. As Fred put it:

> We all had the same feeling of frustration – as if we had left a job half-done and were powerless to do anything about it. Coupled with an intense feeling of homesickness was the terrible fear that the onslaught of the Japs could not be stemmed before they reached Australia.
>
> Monday morning dawned with an unusual feeling. Something bewildering had happened to us, leaving us with a sense that somehow we had been betrayed. Thousands of young men who arrived on Singapore island only a few short days before were now in captivity. Why had they been allowed to come? Surely the authorities must have known that Singapore could not be held, and that a few thousand young Australians would not make any difference to the final outcome.
>
> We veterans of the campaign considered the newcomers a useless sacrifice. Six of these new recruits had been drafted into my platoon, in time for the Japanese attack, just seven days before. During the fighting, one of my men had been wounded and was lying exposed to enemy fire about 100 yards in front of our position. I decided to bring him in if possible and detailed three of the new recruits to give my corporal and myself covering fire. It was so weak that the Japs took no notice and we were driven back, unable to reach the wounded man.
>
> Only one of these young chaps had fired more than one shot. The other two could not reload their rifles because they had inadvertently slipped on the safety catch. I asked them how long they had been in the army and was astounded to learn that they had enlisted just one week before sailing for Singapore.

The humiliation was absolute. Under the terms of the surrender signed by General Percival, all must lay down their weapons. The collection points for the Australians were

Tanglin Barracks

the Botanical Gardens and Tanglin Barracks, from where General Bennett had directed their last and futile stand. For those who had fought so hard, it was almost too much to bear. They knew that the battle was lost, but up until this point the capitulation had been beyond the control of the ordinary digger. Their laying down of arms not only stripped away the last vestiges of pride, it was so intensely personal, the ultimate act of surrender.

Although ordered to stand fast, some, like Bennett, chose to make the perilous journey across the sea to Sumatra, the only way of escape, rather than face the prospect of spending the rest of the war in prison. Senior officers, battle-hardened troops, civilians, and deserters intent on leaving at any price fled south in anything that floated. Some, attacked by surface vessels and aircraft, would come to grief, or fall into enemy hands. Others would make their way to the SOE escape route in Sumatra and live to fight another day.

However, few Australians attempted to leave. They waited, as ordered, at Tanglin where, now unarmed and vulnerable, their disbelief gave way to apprehension. Word had spread of the massacre at the Alexandra Hospital the day before. With a track record like that there was no telling what the Japanese might do next.

However, the fears of imminent mass murder and mayhem, at least for the military captives, were unwarranted. Few Japanese were seen at first and those encountered within the Australian perimeter seemed friendly enough, with many offering cigarettes and striking up a conversation in surprisingly good English. It was galling to witness triumphant enemy troops parading down the streets and to step aside for convoys of vehicles, their horns tooting madly and the odious Japanese flag fluttering on the bonnets. However, unlike the unfortunate Chinese, the only thing hurt was the Australians' sense of pride.

As was the case in the Chinese city of Nanking, the victorious Imperial Japanese Army gave no quarter to their long-time and bitter enemies. Tom Burns, still at the Cathay Building with the wounded, watched in horror as enemy troops moved into his area, torturing Chinese citizens and rounding up the weak, the frail and the elderly, along with women, babies and children. Delighting in their misery, soldiers with fixed bayonets hunted their victims, many of whom would meet their death within a day or two, from the ruins of their homes.

However, it was not just the Chinese who learned just how ruthless the occupying

Severed heads of Chinese civilians on display.

forces could be. To ensure that the Australians entered captivity with some degree of comfort, officers encouraged the rank and file to scout about for provisions and anything else that might come in handy. With bombed-out shops and warehouses overflowing with commodities, and the homes abandoned by the affluent stocked with expensive imported delicacies, there was plenty of choice.

Unwilling to leave supplies for the enemy to enjoy, the Australians, who regarded their activities as simply 'scrounging', had no qualms about appropriating items that did not belong to them. Local Indians and Malays, adopting the same logic, joined in with gusto. However, the IJA deemed it to be looting, a capital offence and, before long, some English soldiers and one Australian were strung up. The unfortunate Australian is believed to be 36-year-old Sapper Norman Stewart Wilson, the only member of the AIF unaccounted for on the two days following the surrender. Wilson, from Western Australia, was a member of 86 Light Aid Detachment, Australian Army Ordnance Corps, and had most likely been dispatched in a unit truck to scrounge what he could. Described officially as 'a non battle casualty', he and the truck were last seen in Singapore on the 17th.

A number of local people were also shot dead but, when shooting proved to be no deterrent, all citizens caught looting were decapitated. While such drastic punishment made no difference to the Australians, who continued to scrounge wherever and whenever possible, the sight of severed heads on display at street corners made even the most daring proceed with caution.

After standing-to in their appointed areas, and staying under cover, on 16 February the AIF was ordered to be ready to move east to the Changi area the following day. To add salt to the wound, those coming in from areas to the west of Tanglin were confronted by the sight of the Japanese flag now flying victoriously aloft the flagpole at nearby Fort Canning.

The troops were ordered to take enough rations to last ten days. Water carts, filled with water from the swimming pool, would be interspersed along the column. Fortunately, as all their personal kit was in storage, the Australian combat troops, who had only the clothes they stood up in, were able to access a stockpile of clothing at the barracks, which they crammed onto the few trucks provided as transport, along with their scrounged items.

After an all-day wait in the hot sun, it was late afternoon by the time the bulk of the AIF joined the long procession of Allied prisoners on the 27-kilometre march to Changi. Determined to put on a brave face to enemy troops scattered along the route, as well as local residents, the Australians marched with a carefree swagger, cracking jokes and calling out rude remarks to red-tabbed staff officers riding by in the comfort of a motor car.

Despite their apparent cheerfulness, on closer inspection they were a rather motley looking bunch. The majority, especially those who had raided clothing stores, were well-turned out, but others were arrayed in an assortment of battle-stained and tattered garments as well as some rather startling headwear, including rakish pork-pie hats, tropical sun helmets and an odd turban or two. Those fortunate enough to have retrieved personal possessions carried them in some kind of pack, but one very enterprising individual, determined to begin prison life with maximum comforts, had scrounged a high-wheeled baby carriage. Packed with all his worldly goods, he wheeled it merrily along the roadway. However, rank always has its privileges. Army Service Corps' Captain Jim Millner, who had access to one of his unit's motor lorries, loaded it with food and added his suitcase, full of personal possessions, including a good supply of clothes and 4000 cigarettes, which were better than cash when it came to trading.

The route of this march of humiliation was deliberately chosen by the victors to pass through Singapore's most populated areas: Napier, Tanglin and Scott Roads to Newton's Circus, and then Kampong Java, Norfolk and Serangoon Roads, East Coast Road to Changi Road. As the Australian prisoners tramped along, they could see, from the number of Japanese flags, some of them home made, displayed on shops and houses, that many of the Indians and Malays, in particular, had decided which horse to back. The Chinese, however, made it perfectly clear where their loyalties lay, risking punishment to press small gifts of food and cigarettes onto the troops and offering them water at every opportunity.

It was a long, slow, tiring and dispiriting march, made even more so by the sight of wrecked British guns and unburied military and civilian corpses. Even those who had started out chipper enough began to flag as daylight gave way to dusk. Apart from time out for a meal, there was no time to rest until, in the early hours of the morning, dog tired, hungry and footsore, the head of the column halted at Selarang Barracks on the Changi peninsula, pre-war home of the Gordon Highlanders. Normally, the new billets would have been something to write home about. Surrounded by the sea on three sides, the entire area pre-war was a showplace, consisting of four separate barracks areas, surrounded by hectares of lushly green, manicured parkland, dotted with tropical trees and brilliantly coloured ornamental shrubs.

The 14,860 Australians were to occupy Selarang, while the British, numbering around 37,000, along with Indian army officers and some Dutch prisoners, were billeted further down the road at Roberts, India and Kitchener Barracks, the latter on the most easterly end of the peninsula and not far from Changi village. The bulk of the Indians, at least those who had not changed sides, were in separate barracks in the centre of the island. Closer to the city, on the other side of the road from Selarang, was the recently completed high-security Changi Gaol, where British civilians would soon be interned.

The next day, feeling a little better after a couple of hours sleep, Fred and his fellow Australians took stock of their new home. For those who had seen Selarang in peacetime it was a bit of a shock. The battle-scarred walls of the main buildings, once painted in cream and yellow, had been coated with black camouflage paint, while the formerly immaculate parade ground was pock-marked with huge shell craters. Seven three-storey barrack buildings surrounded it, arranged in a U-shaped formation. While structurally intact, they had been completely stripped of furnishings, and all power, water and sewerage services wrecked.

The six infantry battalions, along with the medical units and field artillery regiments (temporarily housed across the road with 4 Anti-tank at the old Birdwood Camp site)

INTO CAPTIVITY

Above: Selarang Barracks, covered in black camouflage paint.
Below: Makeshift kitchen alongside a barracks building (Murray Griffin).

were allocated these buildings. Fred and the 2/19th were assigned a block on the barrack square, at the base of the U-shape. Selarang covered a large area and could have housed 5000–6000 troops comfortably but, when those captured in Malaya arrived, the Australians would eventually total more than 15,000. The main barracks were especially crowded but, as each of the buildings had a flat roof, as well as wide covered verandahs on every floor, the overflow constructed makeshift humpies from whatever materials were available. The rest of the AIF was spread among the numerous administrative buildings, several blocks of NCOs' flats, and spacious, mostly two-storey houses, normally assigned to married officers. There was also a 1000-bed hospital.

As the Japanese had done nothing about providing food and water, equipment or facilities, the Australians' first task was to make their camp more habitable by setting up cook houses, converting scrap metal into kitchen equipment, digging and constructing latrines, restoring basic services and scrounging whatever came to hand for bedding, since the alternative was the cold concrete floor.

The prisoners had been in camp scarcely three days when about 100 men from Selarang and Roberts Camps were marched off to Changi Beach. As they passed through the pleasant village and onto the white sandy shoreline with its coconut palms and fine views across the water, they were not prepared for the sight that confronted them – the bloodied remains of 66 Chinese men, massacred by the victorious IJA.

As soon as Singapore had surrendered, the Japanese had begun implementing a plan known as Sook Ching, or 'purge through cleansing'. The aim was to rid the island of all Chinese who were members of a volunteer force communists, looters, anyone who possessed arms, appeared in a list of anti-Japanese suspects collected by Japanese intelligence over many preceding months, or simply deemed to be an 'anti-Japanese element'. The latter category included members of secret societies, people sporting tattoos and anyone suspected of having western sympathies or leanings, including those who spoke English, adopted western clothing, were educated or wore glasses. The intelligentsia, such as teachers and university students, were especially targeted; in short, anyone capable of presenting the slightest threat to the new regime.

Notices and posters were displayed informing all Chinese males aged between 18 and 50 to report to designated screening areas. Loudspeakers were also used to spread the news. The actual screening was carried out by the kempeitai in urban areas, and elsewhere by members of Nishimura's Imperial Guards Division, the same troops responsible for the massacre at Parit Sulong. It was envisioned that the cleansing would be concluded by the end of February but, as there were so many Chinese who needed to be 'disposed of', the end date was extended to 4 March.

As no guidelines had been issued, the screening process was unsystematic and disorganised, with decisions made on the whims and prejudices of the screener. Some victims were selected because of their occupations, how they responded to questions or if they had tattoos, a sure sign, according to the Japanese, that they belonged to 'tong', or secret society. In some places, hooded informants, some of whom were intent on settling old scores, pointed out those who were allegedly criminals or thought to harbour anti-Japanese sentiments. All those lucky enough to pass the screening process were given a stamp to show they had been examined – on a piece of paper, imprinted on their skin or on their clothing – and allowed to leave.

Thousands, however, were not as fortunate. Loaded onto lorries, they were transported to remote areas and machine gunned. The bodies of those killed on the beaches were left on the sand or tossed into the water. Others, tied together in groups, were taken on boats out to sea, shot and dumped overboard. By the time the Japanese had finished their work, an estimated 50,000 Chinese lost their lives.

The killing had begun on 18 February. Two days later, the 66 Chinese males were taken to Changi Beach, tied up in groups of 8 to 12, forced to walk towards the sea and shot. As the ropes binding them loosened in the water a few tried to swim away or seek temporary refuge underwater, but were bayoneted or drowned. The POW work party was ordered to gather them all up and bury them on the beach.

Back at Selarang, once the camp had been organised, there was little to do and morale among the Australians, listless from the shock of their defeat and the subsequent surrender,

Changi beach

plummeted. Discipline in the AIF, which, compared to their British counterparts, had always been relaxed, fell to a low level. The consensus among the rank-and-file was that those at the top of the pecking order, officers in particular, were responsible for their current predicament, and the general feeling was one of barely concealed resentment. As all were now prisoners of war, the ordinary soldier could see no reason why he should behave as if he were on a parade ground 24 hours a day, let alone continue to obey orders without question.

The situation was exacerbated by a small, very poorly disciplined minority, described by General Bennett as 'black sheep', who should never have left Australia. Normally, they would never have set foot overseas, for the policy of the AIF was not to allow either the untrained or the poorly disciplined to engage in battle. Nor were they to be led by substandard or indifferent officers. To ensure that neither of these things occurred, in the early days all troops dispatched to Malaya had been put through a rigorous training program. While the odd few had slipped though the screening net, the system had worked fairly well until December 1941, when the urgent call came for reinforcements.

While most of the raw recruits who had arrived at Johor Bahru in the dying days of the Malayan Campaign simply lacked proper training, others had no concept of discipline, or any inclination to accept it at any level. Consequently, with no time to engender any sense of responsibility in the new arrivals before the battle for Singapore began, 8 Division found itself lumbered with a much higher percentage of sub-standard officers and men, including those described as 'lacking moral fibre', the army's euphemism for describing anyone who was not up to scratch when under fire, whom the diggers simply referred to as 'gutless'.

Determined that law and order must prevail, the AIF's senior officers instituted an immediate crackdown. Sloppiness in any form was not to be tolerated, attendance at early morning parade ground drills was compulsory, as was fastidious attention to personal grooming. Furthermore, recognising and maintaining differences in rank was rigidly enforced. To make sure everyone was kept busy, repetitious fatigue duties were also introduced. The punishment for infringing these regulations was to be placed under guard on reduced rations.

Not surprisingly, the overzealous enforcement of this code, especially by young and inexperienced lieutenants, did not go down well with most of the rank-and-file. As everyone was now in the same boat, they particularly objected to saluting officers and the creation of strictly separate officers' messes, complete with superior facilities. The allocation of large, roomy houses to officers and the appointment of a batman to even the most junior lieutenant certainly did not help matters.

It was not just the naturally rebellious or the green, untrained reinforcements who had trouble accepting the tightening up of discipline. Experienced soldiers, who appreciated the importance of unquestioning obedience and the need to improve morale, found the petty drills, the constant orders, endless saluting and pointless, time-filling tasks both irksome and unnecessary. However, as the Japanese had given the responsibility for the internal running of the camp to the Australian commanders, the men had no option but to obey orders, or face inevitable consequences.

Many did so with very bad grace. Covert as well as overt insubordination and rumblings of discontent were rife, resulting in punishments that fuelled further resentment, widening the gulf between the officers and the men. It was a rift that would continue with some groups throughout the war, particularly in some labour camps where officer privilege was abused.

However, it was not all plain sailing among Changi's upper ranks. Despite the united front in regard to camp discipline, petty jealousies flourished between individuals at all levels of seniority. Bitterness and recrimination over the handling of the campaign and the subsequent capitulation festered, with junior officers blaming senior officers, combat commanders blaming staff officers, junior staff officers blaming senior staff officers and senior staff blaming Malaya Command, General Percival in particular. The only thing on which the AIF community agreed was that Malaya Command and the local British administration had a great deal to answer.

The resentment intensified when General Yamashita and his counterparts in the navy and air force decided to lord it over their captives by conducting triumphal tours of inspection. On three separate occasions, prisoners from the various camps were ordered to line the roadways, three-deep, and dressed in their most presentable clothing, as the VIPs and their entourage swept past in captured limousines. The upside was that the VIPs, apart from an occasional staff car arriving with orders for guards stationed outside the camp, were the only Japanese Fred saw for three months.

Within a few days of the able-bodied settling in at Selarang, the wounded began to trickle in from the various hospitals and convalescent depots. Some were fortunate enough to make the trip in vehicles. Others, including amputees on crutches from the Cathay Theatre, walked all the way under their own steam. Fred's comrades from X Battalion, who had survived the beheadings along Jurong Road, also arrived, after managing to infiltrate themselves into the camp, their telltale wounds covered by neck scarves.

The feeling of lassitude and ennui pervading Selarang came to an end before the end of February when the Japanese decided to make use of their unexpectedly large and potential labour force. The first party of Australians, 750 in all, began work on 22 February, five days after they arrived, to start clearing up the city. However, the tasks assigned to

Fred, much closer to the camp, were certainly not what he had envisaged.

> Up till now we had not seen a great deal of the Jap soldiers. That was altered when they decided we would have to work – many different parties were taken out, some for road work, some to the wharves and some were taken to bury Chinese whom the Japs had tied together in lots of ten or twelve, taken out to sea, machine gunned and tossed overboard. The current had brought the bodies back onto the coast of Singapore. My lot fell to be in charge of this party. You can imagine our feelings when, on a couple of occasions, we found some of the poor wretches were still alive, and the Japanese guards forced us to bury them with the rest.
>
> We found a Chinese boy of about eleven years still alive. As the guards were occupied elsewhere we smuggled him into the shelter of the rubber trees and covered him with banana leaves. That night two of us sneaked out of our compound, over a mile away, and returned to get the child, who had a bullet wound in the chest. Another bullet had broken one arm. He was unconscious but still alive. Moving as carefully as we could we reached the village of Changi and, on the outskirts of the town, persuaded an old Chinese woman to care for him until he recovered or died, whichever it was to be.
>
> Many of the other bodies we buried were of Chinese women, mutilated beyond recognition, a sight too horrible for me to even attempt to describe.

In early March, shortly after Fred and his party completed these grisly tasks, the Japanese issued orders for the AIF hospital to move to Roberts Barracks and for the various areas at Changi to isolate themselves from their neighbours with a double row of barbed wire.

The delivery of hundreds of coils of barbed wire to enclose the various areas was of ultimate irony to the Australians, whose pleas to Malaya Command, prior to the Japanese attack, had fallen on deaf ears. To their disgust, they discovered that, now they were in captivity, they were to imprison themselves with the very same wire. Movement would be limited so, if anyone had ideas of escaping to Malaya, just across the straits, now was the time to go: the Japanese had made it clear that, once the wire was in place, anyone found outside it would be shot. Fred was one of those who considered escape, but fortunately rejected it as a bad idea.

> Numerous plans for making an escape were thought out and discussed, only to be discarded as impossibilities. On one or two occasions attempts were made, only to fail with a tragic ending, the escapees being captured, tortured and finally shot. Sane reasoning showed us the hopelessness of such attempts. We became apathetic as to our fate and took grave risks of being shot in attempts to supplement our diet, which consisted mainly of rice. How we hated it! Little did we think then that we would be compelled to live on it for just on three and a half years!

In common with his fellow Australians, Fred's experience with rice, regarded as food suitable for invalids, had been limited to baked rice puddings. The sudden switch from meat and vegetables to the gluggy mess produced by the cooks played havoc with digestion, and it was not uncommon for the prisoners to be constipated for up to a fortnight. The lack of vitamins and nutrition saw a surge in the number of patients admitted to hospital but, by April, things began to improve when all prisoners, whether working outside the camp or in it, received pay. As a sergeant, Fred was entitled to 25 cents a day. Corporals received 15 and privates, 10. The cash enabled the workers to purchase goods from enterprising locals, or from the canteen, to supplement the measly rations, and to buy and sell items at night at the flourishing 'Paddy's Market', until the camp administration realised that it was an outlet for Selarang's black marketeers and put a stop to trade.

Moving the sick to Roberts Barracks had taken the best part of a week and created a problem for anyone wanting to visit ill mates. With Selarang now a fair distance from the hospital, Australian visitors could not simply come and go as they pleased. After applying for permission, they had to line up and move, en masse, escorted by a Japanese guard holding a flag.

Unless there was a search of some kind, or an arrest to be made, the guards did not set foot inside the POW camps, which was a blessing. However, having to salute Indian guards, who had defected and were now working for the Japanese. was particularly galling. The incentive for Indian troops to switch sides was considerable. Many who resisted the invitation to join the IJA were tied up, blindfolded and used for bayonet or rifle practice.

However, outside the perimeter, all POWs were required to salute or bow to their captors, irrespective of rank, or risk a good clout over the head with a rifle butt. Civilians were subjected to the same rules. Breaking them, including failing to acknowledge a guard, whether by design or otherwise, could, and did, result in death.

AIF working parties sent into the city became used to the sight of severed Chinese and Malay heads, their hair parted neatly to one side, lined up on tables, tied to lamp posts or spiked onto bamboo stakes, for display at street corners. At first the Australians were horrified but, as far as the locals were concerned, the grisly displays seemed to be part and parcel of everyday life. However, while the POWs became inured to such sights to some degree, they could not come to terms with the way in which the Japanese casually snuffed out a life.

The 2/29th's Private Billy Young, a very much under-age soldier, was an eyewitness to their cold-blooded ruthlessness when sent on a working party to the wharves.

> One day, while loading rice, we were perched on top of a stack of bagged rice, idly watching a Jap sentry check papers and direct traffic while we ate our lunch when, from the far side of an idling truck, a rickshaw appeared. The Chinese coolie, oblivious to any danger and obviously not noticing the sentry, passed through the checkpoint on the blind side of the truck. With a cry of 'KORA!' (Hey!), the guard rushed forward, his rifle butt swinging. The first blow, delivered fair and square to the coolie's face, felled him, stone dead, but the sentry didn't let up. Like a madman he then attacked the rickshaw, smashing it to bits. In what seemed a matter of seconds, the rickshaw lay in pieces on the roadside, a crumpled mess, while beside it sprawled the broken body of an inoffensive Chinese workman: a fellow human being, who had been destroyed, cut down, right before our eyes; killed, not in the frenzied blood-letting of battle, nor while committing some wanton criminal act. He had been slaughtered simply to demonstrate who the masters were, an act so devastating in its message, so cruelly simple, and so simply cruel.
>
> Shouldering his rifle, the sentry returned to the truck, finished inspecting the papers and waved the driver on, as if nothing had happened. The poor, inoffensive coolie lay dead and forgotten in the burning sun. His remains were still there when we left the wharf at the end of the day's work.

At Selarang there were now many ways for the men to fill their spare time constructively. A well-stocked library was established, along with a 'university', offering a wide range of courses from basic primary education to legal studies, foreign languages, art classes and even cordon bleu cookery. Concerts were organised and the food situation also improved as the cooks, after an abysmal start, replaced their previously glutinously inedible messes with reasonably tasty, if somewhat repetitious, rice-based meals.

In response to an order from the Japanese that the camp must be self-sufficient in all but rice by the end of April, vegetable gardens had been planted and were now thriving. The plots covered 35 acres, and many of the 1000 gardeners so enjoyed the work that they enrolled in the university's agricultural course, with an eye to take up farming after the war. To obtain more vitamins for the sick, a fishing party had been formed, and there were plans for a poultry farm in May.

Thanks to an enthusiastic construction team, Anglican and Catholic chapels were now close to completion and, for those looking for an outlet for their creative talents, there was an Arts and Crafts Show. Held at the Education Centre on 19 April, art patrons were treated to works of high quality and innovation, including black and white sketches, topical cartoons, clay sculptures and woodcarvings. In the craft display were exquisitely carved chess sets, ornate walking sticks, elegant smokers' stands, ashtrays carved from polished coconut shells, woven rugs, bamboo artifacts and, for the purely practical, brooms.

More and more POWs were now working outside the camp – on the wharves, stacking and storing food and merchandise, gathering up scrap iron and furniture from homes and government buildings and loading them onto ships to be sent to Japan. Anything that appeared to be of the slightest use to the Japanese was removed from houses, shops and offices, including entire shop windows. The upside was that this officially sanctioned looting provided plenty of scope for scrounging.

Australians being Australians there were also the usual rorts, with one POW, assigned to drive a steamroller, drawing a daily petrol ration, which he then sold on the black market. One enterprising pair hit on an idea that kept them out of work parties but busy for many months and, if the story can be believed, the entire war. Somehow, one of them obtained a chain measure, a chain being an Imperial measurement of 66 feet or 22 yards, the length of a cricket pitch. Eighty chains made one mile. Armed with their tape measure, which was wound by hand into a flat circular case, they told the guards at the camp gate that they had been instructed to measure the road distance between Selarang and Singapore city, about 15 miles (or 1360 chains). According to the story, they made their way slowly, chain by chain, into Singapore and back, and then repeated the process. If asked what they were doing, they displayed their tape and their notebook, in which they recorded the distance, and continued on their way without being further challenged.

By mid-April, 6000 Australians were employed outside Changi, and enjoying it. Although initially there had been resistance to working for the Japanese, this had melted when it was realised that the opportunities for scrounging were endless, and there was now no limit to willing volunteers. Food was smuggled back into the camp by the day parties, the most favoured hiding place being on the scrounger's head, under his slouch hat. The Japanese looked in hands, under armpits, even in mouths, but never under hats and never in the prisoners' crotches. The amount of contraband smuggled in the latter was extraordinary, with the prize for the biggest item 'crotched' going to a pineapple.

However, the best item scrounged was a piano. The Australians had only been in Selarang for one day when a concert party began rehearsals. Initially, performances comprised individual acts, but a group of about 30 performers was soon formed. Appropriating an open-sided, steel-framed garage, they gradually transformed it into a theatre, complete with backdrops, curtains and lighting, using items brought into the camp by working parties or brave souls who ventured under the wire at night.

However, what they didn't have, and needed, was a piano. One night, 12 members of the concert party raided the mess of a nearby establishment, from which they liberated a Robinson upright piano and hauled it the 1.5 kilometres back to Selarang. With its original green paint now cream, the piano, under the skilled fingers of pianist Oswald 'Jack' Boardman, became the centrepiece of the concert party. After the war, the performers refused to be repatriated without their piano, which was lashed to SS *Largs Bay* as deck cargo. It is now part of the collection at the Australian War Memorial.

Smugglers often had to think quickly. A surprise search as they neared the gate saw one prisoner with a small three-legged stool in his hand. With no way to hide or dispose of it, he put it on the ground and stood on it. Others stood on tins of food. The guards looked in all the usual places, then passed on.

As the numbers inside Selarang dwindled, it became increasingly difficult to find enough man-power to take care of the day-to-day running of the camp, particularly the humdrum, menial and energy-sapping tasks, for which there were few volunteers. However, the problem was solved in typical army fashion – the less tractable, either at Selarang or on one of the outside working parties, found themselves hauling heavy carts or digging six-metre deep latrines, the latter requiring a labour force of 200 men, working in shifts.

In June there would be an even bigger exodus from the camp when the Japanese recruited a labour force to build their Memorial at Bukit Batok and the Shinto Shrine on Bukit Timah. However, Fred would not be a candidate for either of these projects. In May the Japanese called for a labour force of 3000 to 'go overseas'.

CHAPTER 17

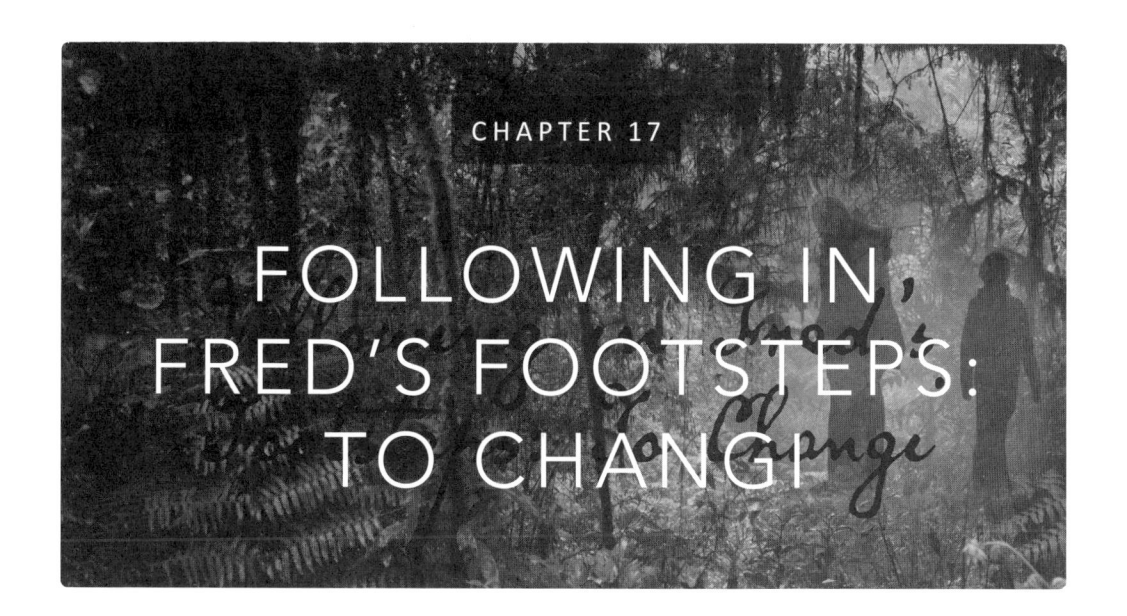

FOLLOWING IN FRED'S FOOTSTEPS: TO CHANGI

Like the rest of the AIF, Dad began his journey into captivity at Tanglin Barracks, opposite the Botanic Gardens. Knowing their significance, we went first to the gardens, an initial rallying point for X Battalion and for the 2/19th as a whole, when General Bennett told his troops to 'come home'. Ironically, the sight of hundreds of troops massing near the gardens, reported by a British woman on her way to an evacuation ship, would result 50 years later in accusations by the British press that, instead of being at the front line, the Australians had deserted.

The gardens are magnificent and, for the duration of the war, were cared for by British botanist Eldred Corner. Before hostilities began, he had intended joining a volunteer force in Singapore but was attacked by one of his 'workmen', a monkey trained to collect specimens from the tops of the trees. After the surrender, instead of being interned with the other civilians, the Japanese put him in charge of protecting and preserving the area. As an enemy alien, Corner was required to wear a red star, which allowed him to do his job in the gardens, but also gave him freedom of movement, enabling him to smuggle food and other items to prisoners of war.

Moving on, we crossed the road to enter the vast area occupied by Tanglin Barracks, where many of the buildings are still standing. Built in 1860–62 on the site of a former nutmeg plantation, the large and airy timber barracks were each capable of housing 50 men. There were also service facilities, officers' quarters, hospital wards, a school and a reading room. The main accommodation buildings, set on stumps above the ground, had wide verandahs and high ventilated roofs to draw out the hot air. In time, the complex was expanded to include more accommodation blocks, an officers' mess, a garrison church, gymnasium, swimming pool and a cricket oval, all set amidst beautiful lawns and gardens. The barracks remained under the control of Singapore's Ministry of Defence until 1989. In 2006, the main buildings were developed into a lifestyle, art and education precinct, with retail food and beverage outlets. St George's Anglican Church, which replaced the original garrison church in the 1920s, is still in use as a place of worship, but the much smaller and plainer original church, used by various denominations over the years, has been turned into a pre-school.

Wandering around the beautifully preserved buildings, it was easy to imagine the

Tanglin Barracks, now preserved for community use.

thousands of khaki-clad Australians milling about as they prepared to lay down their arms. Many ex-POWs have spoken to me about the sense of desolation they felt, of their disbelief that Singapore had fallen, and their worry that Australia might be next on the list. People at home were also shocked to the core, and wracked with anxiety about the fate of their loved ones. Mum did not receive confirmation that Dad was alive until 1943. By the time the Japanese issued postcards at Changi in June 1942, for Australian POWs to complete and send home, Dad had left Singapore.

Although Singapore has changed greatly, with motorways criss-crossing the island and what were small villages now thriving busy suburbs, we were able to follow Dad's route to Changi. Turning right from the barracks, we headed down Napier Road, past the massive Fort-Knox-style blockhouse that serves as the US Embassy, the more aesthetic and understated British High Commission and the Australian High Commission, its nine-hole golf course in the front lawn possibly giving a hint as to where Australians' priorities lay.

Leaving Tanglin 'village', with its row of picturesque Tudor-style shops, we headed down bustling Orchard Road, a massive retail shopping area where orchards once flourished, before turning left into Scotts Road, with its fine colonial style 'black and white bungalows' and the ornate, turreted Goodwood Park Hotel. Built in 1900 as the Teutonia Club, an exclusive enclave for expatriate Germans, it became a hotel pre-war before being 'acquired' by the Japanese as accommodation for high-ranking officers. At the cessation of hostilities, it served as the HQ of Number 1 Australian War Crimes Section, the unit tasked with tracking down war criminals, many of them high-ranking officers. It finally reverted back to its owner in 1947, after the Singapore trials ended.

At Newton's Circus, a complex intersection of several roads and famous for its hawker food, we followed Bukit Timah Road through what was Kampong Java, then into Serangoon Road and Little India, before working our way to Lavender Street, the former red-light district where the ladies of the night had hung out their banner to welcome 27 Brigade. Kallang Road led us past the control tower of the old airport, one of its runways now a major

Goodwood Park Hotel on Scotts Road.

thoroughfare, and then onto East Coast Road. Amber Road, on the right, led to the famous Sea View Hotel, where the orchestra played on and the laid-back European community met for lunch, despite the fact that Singapore had been bombed and Malaya invaded. The Seaview Hotel of 1942 no longer exists, neither does the waterfront. Something like 14 per cent of Singapore is now on reclaimed land, and the palatial beachside bungalows, although still palatial, are no longer beachside.

The next place of interest was St Patrick's Boys School at Katong, taken over by 2/13 AGH before the battle for the island began. Dad's medical officer, Lloyd Cahill, was there, as patient and doctor, and most of the 2/19th wounded were mercifully taken to St Pat's instead of Alexandra Hospital. One was Private Keith Botterill who, at war's end, would be one of just six survivors out of almost 2500 POWs sent to a labour camp at Sandakan, in Borneo.

Apart from being greatly extended, the college is much the same as it was in 1942, apart from the fact that it is now some distance from the sea. The wing facing east, and therefore the water, was the original building, and it was from the sandy beach in front of the school that patients, considered well enough to flee, left in small boats for Bintan Island, only to come to grief several days later. The gates where advancing enemy troops slaughtered the Australians guarding the entrance are still there.

Moving on to Upper Changi Road, I kept a good lookout for what was left of the gaol, all but demolished in 2004. Used to intern British civilians after Singapore's fall, it became part of a large POW camp in mid-1944, when the civilians were moved to another camp. Once on the seashore, this site is now a good distance inland. As we drove up a small rise, there it was – the tall concrete wall, grey and forbidding, the watchtower and the main entrance.

Above: Changi Gaol before demolition in 2004. Below: British gunners seated on one of the big guns, Johor battery

Selarang Barracks, where the Australians were imprisoned immediately after the surrender, was a little further on, on the left side of the road. Occupied by the military, it was classified as high security following the terrorist attacks in the USA in 2001, so we could not go in. The barracks around the square where Dad was billeted have been demolished, but Lynette, who was fortunate to enter the grounds before the security clampdown, told me that the rest was pretty much unchanged.

Directly opposite Selarang is a road leading to the Johor Battery. In 1941 it consisted of three massive 15-inch (38 cm) naval guns, placed 500 metres apart, which the Australians on *Queen Mary* saw as they sailed past on the way to the eastern entrance of the Straits of Johor. With two similarly sized guns at Buona Vista, guarding the coast to the south-west of the city centre, these 'monster guns' were the backbone of Singapore's seaward defences. The battery, completed in 1939, was named after the Sultan of Johor, the canny Malay ruler who managed to maintain cordial relations with both the British and the Japanese. To mark the year of King George V's Silver Jubilee in 1935, the Sultan had given him half a million pounds (about 35 million in 2020), of which the British government had used

£400,000 to instal the three great guns. Ironically, it was one of the 194 shells fired by two of the Sultan's guns, swung around to face Malaya, which had landed on his railway station at Johor Bahru.

Running beneath the gun emplacements was a labyrinth of tunnels and underground rooms, including powder magazines to store the massive shells. Weighing 800 kilograms, each shell was hoisted into position by a hydraulic lift. On 12 February 1942, when it became clear that Singapore would fall to the Japanese, the tunnels and rooms were sealed and the gun barrels and mountings blown up. The wreckage, which collapsed into the gun pit, was sold post-war for scrap, while most of the ammunition was removed from the magazines and dumped out to sea. One magazine, however, containing shells that were primed ready for use, was found to be flooded. Five years later, worried that this ammunition could explode, the British Army pumped out the water, recovered the unstable shells and disposed of them at sea. Once this task was complete, everyone forgot about the now defunct Johor Battery.

In 1991, quite by chance, the Singapore Prisons Department discovered the underground network. A replica of a 15-inch gun, with its 16.5- metre-long barrel, was installed, along with a dummy shell on a chain, to allow visitors to test the weight by trying to hoist it from the ground. However, it was not until the 60th anniversary of the fall of Singapore in 2002 that the battery was open to visitors. One special guest among the 200 veterans invited to attend was Stan Bryant-Smith, a sergeant with 2/29th's intelligence section, who recalled seeing the huge shells passing over his head from his battle station near the causeway.

Further along the road leading to Changi Beach, having obtained a special permit from the military, we detoured into Roberts Barracks to see the famous Changi murals. During the occupation, Block 151 of the barracks was used as a POW dysentery wing. At one end, on the ground floor of this very graceful colonial building, was a small room, which the POWs converted into a chapel. Aptly named for St Luke, the physician, it was a place of refuge and worship where patients and staff could seek spiritual comfort.

Bombardier Stanley Warren, an extremely ill British soldier lying in a ward above the chapel, was inspired by the sound of hymn singing floating up the stairs. As a thanksgiving for his partial recovery, he decided to paint a series of religious murals on the chapel walls. It was not his first attempt at POW religious art. While working on the Bukit Batok memorial, he was asked by a chaplain to decorate some fibro sheeting in the altar area of a small makeshift chapel, built by prisoners constructing the roadway. Using charcoal scrounged by the workers, he created two murals – The Nativity, featuring a Malay Madonna, and Descent from the Cross, depicting his fellow soldiers in uniform.

Shortly afterwards, he was transferred to Roberts Hospital in a comatose state, suffering from amoebic dysentery, complicated by a renal disorder. When he recovered sufficiently, his first task for his new 'commission' was to find brushes and paint. Fellow POWs managed to scrounge a tin of white paint and some blue billiard-cue chalk from the pre-war officers' mess, along with terracotta and grey paint from a naval storeroom. Domestic brushes were used in lieu of artists' brushes, supplemented by others made from human hair.

Stanley Warren had barely begun work in September 1942 when he was placed on a draft to the Burma-Thai railway but, fortunately, because of his illness, he was allowed to remain in Changi, which probably saved his life. As he was still very weak, he could only work for periods of 10 to 15 minutes, before being forced to lie on the floor behind the altar to rest. He planned to paint five murals in all but, worried that he might not survive,

Changi Murals, Roberts Barracks

concentrated on the two that were most important to the Christian faith. By Christmas he had finished The Nativity. This was followed by The Ascension. Finding himself still very much alive, he then painted The Crucifixion, the Last Supper and, very appropriately, St Luke in prison.

In mid-1944, following the completion of the nearby airfield, the Japanese moved the POWs out of Block 151 and converted it to an administration building. The murals in the chapel, which became a storeroom, were coated with whitewash and part of one wall was demolished to provide access to the adjoining room, destroying the lower half of the St Luke panel.

Fourteen years later, the then occupants of Block 151, the RAF, discovered traces of colour on the walls while cleaning out the storeroom. The paint was scraped away, revealing the murals, three of which (Ascension, Crucifixion and Last Supper) were fairly intact. After a 12-month international search, Stanley Warren was located, working as an art master in a London school. Like Dad, Warren had been greatly traumatised by his experiences as a POW but, after much persuasion, he eventually agreed to return to Singapore to assist in the restoration of his wartime artwork. He made three trips in all, firstly in 1963 and then again in 1982 and 1988, for more advanced restoration work. He died in 1992, aged 75.

Grateful to be permitted to see these very moving murals, we set off for Changi Museum, not far from the old gaol, where there are replicas of Stanley Warren's masterpieces on display. In 2003, when most of the buildings around Block 151 at Roberts Barracks were demolished, a plan was put forward to remove the murals from the walls and place them in Changi Museum. However, when it was discovered that any attempt to relocate the precious works of art would result in their destruction, replica murals were painted at the museum, in a mock-up of the chapel. We were indeed fortunate to be allowed to view the originals, as the replicas cannot compare with Warren's masterpieces, painted by a man of great faith as his 'gift to God'.

Also at Changi Museum is another replica chapel, St George's, which once formed part of an ad hoc museum outside the old gaol, where items donated by ex-POWs were exhibited. When the gaol was demolished, the museum was resurrected on a far grander scale in the brand new building further down the road, where the replica chapel is displayed in a courtyard.

Also on display is a model of Our Lady Help of Christians Chapel, erected by POWs of the Roman Catholic faith in 1944, when the prisoners moved to the gaol. At war's end it was saved from destruction, a fate that befell other places of worship when Corporal Max Lee of an Australian War Graves Unit arranged for it to be dismantled and packed into ammunition boxes lined with grass. In 1947, the chapel was freighted to Australia, with the intention of reconstructing it as a fitting memorial for 'Prisoners of War who had little recognition for the extreme adversity under which many had lived and died'. Nothing happened. The ammunition boxes remained untouched for the next 40 years. In 1966, a very disappointed Max Lee visited Canberra, to discover there was no sign of the chapel anywhere in the War Memorial or its grounds.

Years passed. Sometime in the mid-1980s, after the War Memorial told a group of veterans that Max's name was on the crates, they contacted him to enquire about the non-existent chapel. Fortunately, before dismantling it in Singapore, Max had made detailed drawings and taken numerous photographs of it, which he still had. However, in 1987 the War Memorial decided that the building was surplus to its requirements. It was then offered to the Department of Defence, whose Royal Australian Engineer Corps erected it in the grounds of the prestigious Royal Military College, Duntroon.

On 15 August 1988, the anniversary of the end of WWII, the POW Chapel, as it is popularly known, was dedicated as a National Memorial to the more than 35,000 Australians taken prisoner in the Boer War, both world wars and the Korean War. Max was present, along with several hundred ex-POWs, including a famous survivor of the Burma-Thai Railway, Sir Edward 'Weary' Dunlop, who unveiled it, and Vivian Bullwinkel, a former army nursing sister and the sole survivor of a massacre on Bangka Island, near Sumatra. Although there is a large memorial to POWs at Ballarat in Victoria, the chapel at Duntroon, in the nation's capital, is recognised as the National Memorial, as Max had intended.

It was now time to leave for Changi itself, a picturesque village set amid tropical trees, with a fine view across the entrance to the straits. After passing the photography shop where images, taken in great secrecy by POW George Aspinall, had been developed in even greater secrecy, we strolled onto a small arched bridge spanning a small boat harbour.

A short distance away is Pulau Ubin, an island in the middle of the Johor Strait where Japanese troops landed on 7 February 1942, as part of the feint to convince General Percival that the attack would come from the east. The island's original name was Pulau Batu Jubin, meaning island of granite rock. Granite from the quarries there was used to build the causeway.

Left: Changi chapel, Canberra

Below: Changi Beach

Some POWs who tried to escape from Changi Camp used Pulau Ubin as a 'stepping stone' to reach the Malayan side of the strait. The invading Japanese coming from the opposite direction shortly before the surrender also landed there before they continued marching towards the city, stopping off en route at St Patrick's College.

When *Queen Mary* sailed up the strait to the naval base, the ship passed so close to the island that the soldiers could almost reach out and touch the houses built out over the water. Most have now gone, but the remainder form Singapore's last remaining traditional water village. For how long, who knows?

The path across the bridge led us down to Changi Beach. It is a beautiful spot. With warm tropical water gently lapping the white sand, and local people picnicking in the shade of the trees, I found it difficult to reconcile such serenity with the appalling carnage that had taken place here during Sook Ching, and the horrible task given to Dad and his team to bury the bodies.

No one said a word. Leaving the beach with its many ghosts, we departed in silence to follow Dad on the next part of his journey into the unknown.

CHAPTER 18

INTO THE UNKNOWN

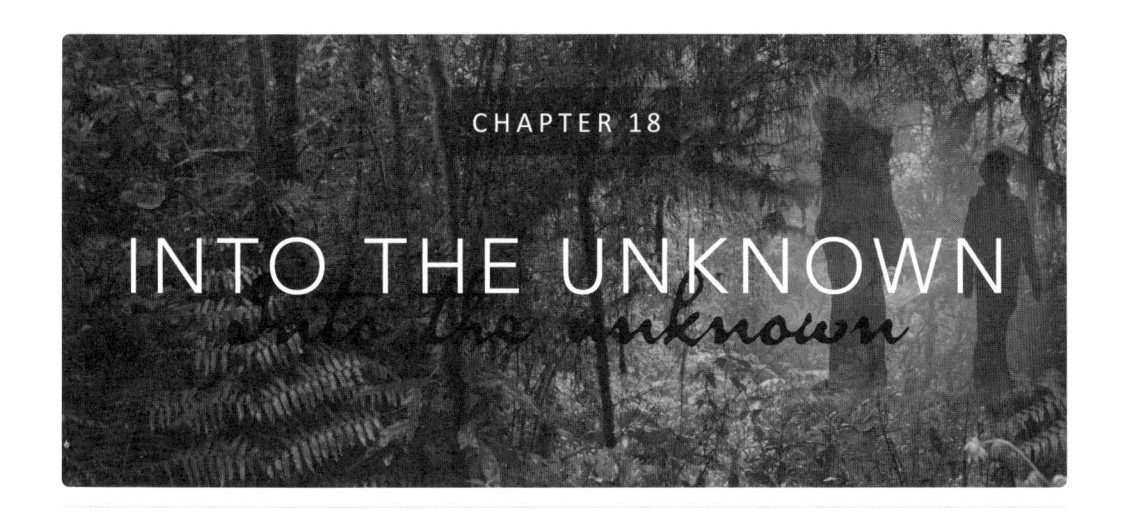

April 1942 to December 1942

At the end of April, the Japanese ordered Major General Cecil 'Boots' Callaghan, now the AIF's senior commander following General Bennett's escape, to supply 3000 men for an overseas working party. They were to be transferred somewhere up north, where there were better facilities, abundant food supplies and no one was required to work. Although Callaghan was suspicious of the rosy picture painted by the Japanese, many of those fed up with working on the wharves, or the monotonous, rice-based diet at Selarang, took it at face value.

The working party, known as A Force, was drawn mainly from 22 Brigade's infantry units, supplemented by artillery and 2/4 machine-gunners. Fred was one of a number of combat-experienced 2/19th men to have their names on the list. Mindful that a time might come when it could be possible to stage a revolt, the senior officers compiled the draft carefully. By ensuring that there was adequate representation of various combat units and a balanced command structure, they were able to form a mini 'brigade', composed of three 'battalions' (A, B and C), each comprising four companies (A, B, C, D and so on), and a headquarters, under the command of the 2/18th's Arthur Varley, now a brigadier. His 2IC was Fred's CO, Charles Anderson. It was hoped that, if the opportunity presented itself, this group would be able to function as a composite fighting unit.

> Rumours began to spread round the camp that we were to move in the near future, so it was no shock when some 3,000 of us were selected to move out of Changi. We were taken to Singapore wharves and placed onboard ships lying in the harbour.

A Force's three 1000-strong 'battalions' were designated as Ramsay Force, under the command of Lieutenant Colonel George Ramsay, Green Force, commanded by Major Chris Green and Kerr Force under Major Don Kerr. Each battalion consisted of medical staff, engineers, administrative staff and about 850 combat troops – infantry, machine-gunners and artillerymen.

The Japanese insisted that, as there would be no work at the new camp and good facilities, it was not necessary to take any medical supplies or equipment. Everything would be provided. A great deal of the division's medical supplies and equipment had been moved or smuggled to Changi after capitulation, but the Japanese allowed the medical staff to take only one emergency surgical kit, along with a microscope, and a small supply of drugs, including atebrin, quinine and sulphapyridine, plus compressed yeast for any 'temporary' illness that arose.

One of the doctors with 2/4 Casualty Clearing Station, in defiance of the orders, brought along some supplies in a pannier, but these were looted before he put foot in the new camp. Consequently, A Force was the only overseas working party to leave Singapore without proper hospital and medical equipment. Depending on the size of the group, other parties took with them a good supply of drugs and sufficient equipment for hospitals of up to 250 beds. As it turned out, conditions and the length of time at the new destinations would be such that the drug supply, rarely supplemented by the Japanese, would prove to be woefully inadequate.

On 14 May, Fred and the rest of A Force were transferred in trucks to Keppel Harbour, where they waited in the hot sun all day for their transport to arrive, only to discover it was already there – two rusty tramp steamers moored alongside the wharf. However, the upside was that the prisoners were ordered to load supplies of canned meat, condensed milk and tobacco from the dockside warehouses, a task that gave them the opportunity for a fair degree of pilfering. With the work completed at around midnight, they were mustered and counted, several times, and instructed to board. The 1028-strong Ramsay Force, including Fred, Chris Guerin and Jack O'Malley, another 2/19 mate from Boorowa, was assigned the first vessel, the 5800-tonne *Celebes Maru*.

One of the POWs, an ex-wharfie from Fremantle, immediately recognised the ship as a livestock carrier that had plied its trade between Australia and Japan pre-war. The two-legged 'passengers' were to be accommodated in sheep pens, 360 in the forward hold and the remainder in the aft. Although he didn't know it at the time, one POW was fortunate to fall into the hold from the ship's deck, breaking his leg and necessitating transfer back to Changi. Green and Kerr Forces, along with HQ staff, were assigned the larger *Toyohashi Maru*, a 7200-tonne cargo ship built in 1915, also converted to carry livestock.

After climbing with difficulty from the wharf on rope ladders, encumbered by their gear, the troops on *Celebes Maru* were herded into the pens, three at a time, backs to the hull and feet facing inwards. Fred barely had room to move and the heat was terrific. Being designed for sheep, not humans, there was no head room and only those less than 170 centimetres tall could actually sit up. If one prisoner moved, so did his neighbour, and so on down the line.

There was no form of ventilation below deck, apart from a kind of canvas funnel that only worked if the ship was moving along at a reasonable pace. It did not take long for the air to become foul, the stench left by the livestock exacerbated by dysentery sufferers, whose requests to use the topside latrines were refused. It was not until Colonel Ramsay made strong representations that the use of two three-hole toilets – one aft and one amidships – was allowed. The relief was short lived. The latrines were inadequate and were soon overflowing, fouling the feet of those returning below.

It was not until noon on the 15th that the ships left the dock, only to drop anchor three kilometres away, and it was not for another two hours that they finally set sail. With water severely restricted, the washing of bodies, let alone anything else, was impossible until, eventually, the Japanese allowed the decks to be sluiced with a saltwater hose. Finally, worn down by Ramsay's protests, the guards agreed to allow 50 men at a time on to the deck for 20 minutes' respite, where they were able to breathe in fresh air and enjoy a hose down before descending into what they described as the Black Hole of Calcutta – a notorious dungeon in Calcutta, India, in which 43 of the 65 British, imprisoned there overnight by Bengali soldiers, died from suffocation and heat in June 1756. Conditions on the ship were better for the senior officers, who camped out on deck under a tent that leaked like a sieve whenever it rained, which was every day and night, forcing them to sit under their rain capes to keep dry. Also topside was a small hospital into which Japanese troops suffering from syphilis retreated to get out of the wet weather.

Food was abysmal – a kind of watery stew made from soya beans and seaweed, plus the inevitable rice, lowered in buckets into the hold. Seasickness now added to the misery and all on board were relieved when they reached their first port of call at Belawan, the port serving Medan in north-eastern Sumatra. The vessels anchored off shore all day while more unloading and loading took place, including the embarkation of 350 Japanese troops, pushing the POWs even further into the bowels of the ship to make room for them. However, despite the abject conditions, Fred's mates still retained a streak of larrikinism.

> At Medan we were spoken to by a Japanese sergeant who wanted to know how far along the coast was Sydney. I firmly believe he really thought he was in Australia. One of our chaps told him it was only four hours' sailing. He seemed quite satisfied and asked us were there any messages we would like to send to our people in Australia. Someone remarked that it would be wasting his time, because we would beat the messages home!

> We stayed at Medan until the next day and then once more steamed off on our torturous journey. Thrills were many, as planes could be heard passing overhead and we never knew when we would be the target for bombs from our own planes. After about a week, we finally disembarked at Mergui, in Lower Burma. Dysentery had broken out and we were in a sorry plight.

Shortly after leaving Belawan on the evening of 17 May, two ships carrying Dutch and British prisoners, escorted by a Japanese sloop, joined the convoy. On reaching Victoria Point in Lower Burma, Green Force disembarked from *Toyohashi Maru*. The remainder sailed further north along the west coast and, on 24 May, nine days after departing from Singapore, they reached Mergui, situated at the entrance to a large river and dominated by a huge golden pagoda and Buddhist monastery, perched on the 60-metre-high cliffs of a nearby island. After admiring the pagoda, radiant in the tropical sun, Ramsay Force disembarked. Varley and the remainder of the troops continued to Tavoy, where Anderson replaced Kerr as commander, resulting in a name change to Anderson Force.

At Mergui, an Australian brass band, which had miraculously materialised, led Ramsay Force through the town, along with Dutch prisoners and 500 British from the other three vessels. The newcomers were under the command of Australian surgeon Lieutenant Colonel Albert Coates, whose team had looked after Fred when he was admitted to hospital at Malacca for the operation on his gastric ulcer. He must have been surprised to see Coates who, two days before Singapore fell, had left for Batavia in Java on HMS *Shu Kwang*, a former coastal steamer turned patrol boat.

However, the evacuation order had been made far too late. While trying to negotiate 'bomb alley', off the Sumatran coast, *Shu Kwang*, with 300 passengers on board, was one of dozens of craft sunk by enemy action. By great good fortune, Coates was among the more than 270 people rescued and taken to Sumatra. He was picked up by *Tenggaroh*, a luxury yacht belonging to the Sultan of Johor that was evacuating a number of senior Allied personnel.

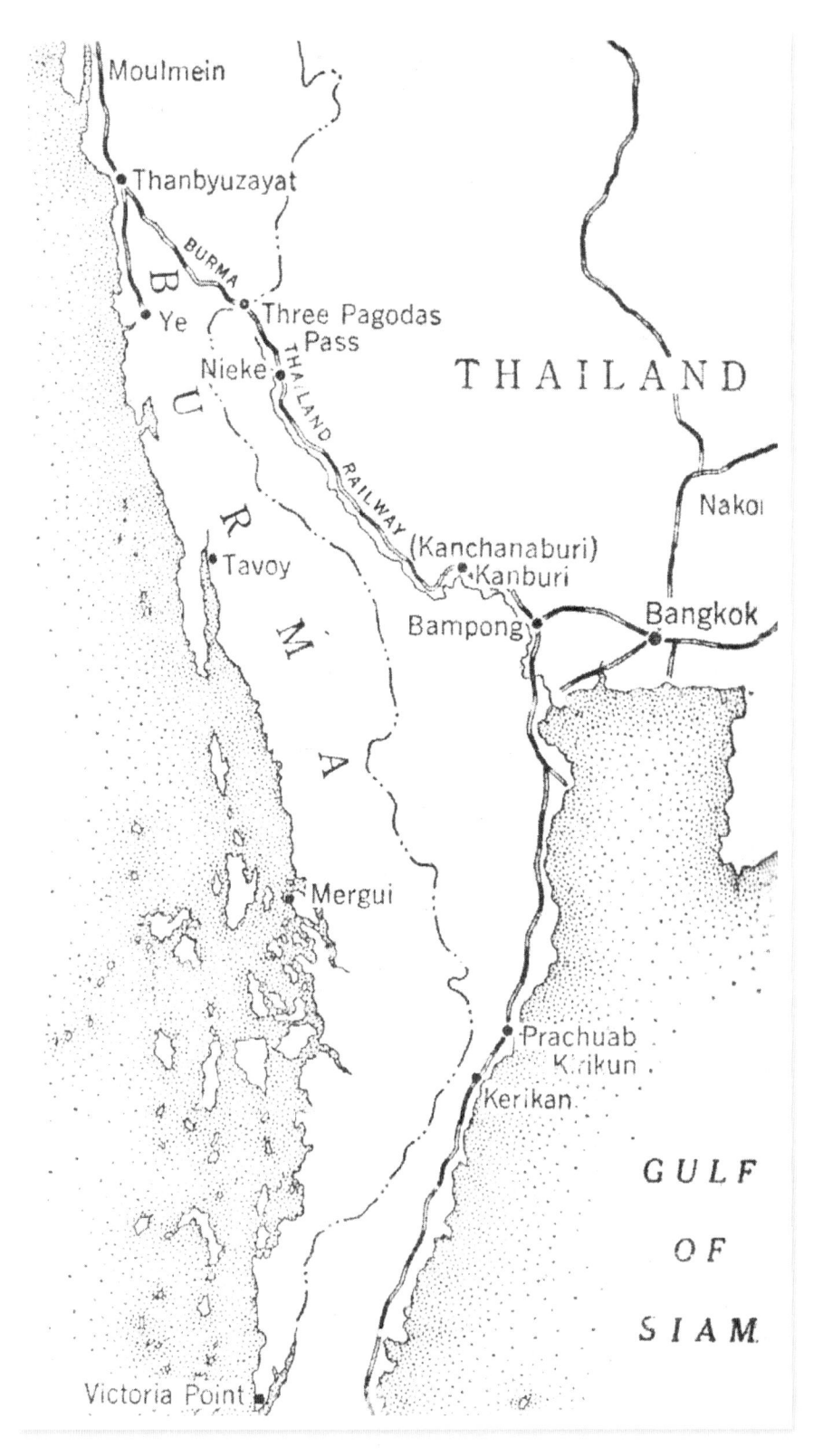

Map of Burma

When the wounded survivors were put ashore at Tambilahan, a small village on the Indragiri River, Coates had remained with them, taking over a small dispensary and aid post and rejecting all suggestions that he should flee to safety along the escape route while there was still time. He stayed there attending to his patients, who continued to arrive in a steady stream, performing seven major operations with the most basic of instruments, including a chopper donated by one of the locals. Eventually, when Coates ran out of patients towards the end of February, he headed west along the escape route to Padang, hoping to board an evacuation vessel. He was too late. He remained in Padang looking after the sick until the Japanese arrived three weeks later, when he too became a prisoner of war.

Like Green and Kerr/Anderson Forces, Fred and the now 1500-strong Ramsay Force had been sent to Burma to repair airfields, damaged by the British as they retreated into India, and to repair or construct service roads. However, although debilitated by the

Lt Colonel Albert Coates

nightmare voyage from Sumatra, Fred's first task was to unload supplies, including bags of rice, 'one bag, one man', weighing more than 100 kilograms – clearly mission impossible. After much discussion, in the form of rifle butts and bashings, the Japanese agreed on 'one bag, four mans'. Chris Guerin, tasked with unloading bags of cement, came in for a hefty bashing when the Japanese realised he was deliberately dropping the bags in such a way that they split open. However, as Fred soon found out, the brutality of the guards was tempered by small acts of kindness from the locals.

> The natives made numerous attempts to bestow little gifts of cigars and such things upon us, but were driven off by the Jap guards at the point of a bayonet. Nevertheless, they were so persistent that we did get some of them. Our living quarters here were an old native school. The attached grounds covered about two acres.

The Japanese at Mergui were not expecting them, so accommodation at the school, built for 200 children and occupying a space only 100 metres by 75 metres, was severely overcrowded, with 50 men packed into each 4 x 5 metre classroom. Washing facilities consisted of an empty milk tin on a string lowered into the school's nine-metre-deep well. After hauling it up, the men tipped the water over each other, providing endless amusement for the locals who gathered on a nearby hillside to watch. One onlooker was a woman with a small boy in her arms, who alternated between puffing on a cigar and suckling his mother's breast.

The latrine facilities, most of which were child-sized, were rudimentary at best and the so-called hospital ward was severely under-equipped as well as under-stocked. The dysentery that had plagued the Australians all the way from Singapore flared up, exacerbated by POWs from Sumatra who were badly stricken. Within three weeks of arrival, two men from Fred's battalion, Charles Overs, aged 22, who came from Leeton, and 37-year-old Stan Ledwidge of Wagga Wagga, died within ten days of each other.

As had been the case in Singapore, the local time had been changed to 'Tokyo Time', which was two hours ahead of Burma time. This meant that reveille at 6.30 am was actually 4.30 am, and lights out at 9.30 pm was really 7.30 pm. Normally, in the tropics, day and night are roughly of 12 hours' duration, 6 am to 6 pm. By advancing the clock, the prisoners began work in the dark, while the longer hours of daylight in the evening extended the working day well beyond the norm, should the Japanese feel so inclined.

Five days after arriving at Mergui, Fred was marched to the site of an airfield where the guards handed out picks, shovels and a native-style hoe, known as a cangkul (pronounced chungkool), along with open-ended rice bags and poles. It soon became obvious that, with no machinery available, the airfield runway was to be widened and reconstructed entirely by hand. On realising they were to be used as coolie labour, the Australians threatened to revolt, and it was only due to the diplomacy of Charles Cousens, now completely recovered from his burns, that the men accepted their lot and, despite their weakened state, got on with it. They formed groups of four – one to chip off the grass and surface earth, one to shovel it onto the rice bags and two to pick up the poles and carry the spoil away. There was no respite, apart from visits to the toilet, which the Japanese called benjo, until the order came to down tools, nine long hours later. Fred recorded that

> after spending two weeks in such appalling conditions most of the men were ill and the burden of looking after them was a terrific strain on the rest, who also had to work on the aerodrome for the Japanese.

After the grass had been chipped away, the prisoners were put to work resurfacing the runway with gravel, a task made almost impossible by heavy rain. Food was poor and there was never enough of it to go round, with meals consisting of a bucket of rice and half a bucket of seaweed to be shared among 70 workers. However, despite dire warnings, the local people continued to press dried fish, boiled eggs, fruit and money into the prisoners' hands as they marched by on their way to the airstrip or, if unobserved, at the fringes of the runway. Discovery of food inevitably resulted in a bashing. However, when the POWs began to receive 'wages' for their labour, a canteen was established, from which they were able to purchase eggs, bread and bananas to supplement their diet. Fred and the other NCOs received 15 cents a day (ten cents less than in Singapore), the privates 10 cents. Later this would rise to 30 and 25 cents respectively.

Officers were also paid, although they were not required to work. Theoretically, they were supposed to receive the Japanese equivalent of their army pay, but a good proportion was 'banked' by the Japanese on their behalf, and money for board and lodgings, such as they were, deducted. The bottom line was that their payout was about a quarter of their entitlement. Nevertheless, it was far more than the paltry wages the men received and did not vary according to the number of days worked – no work, no pay. If sick, no pay either. It is perhaps indicative of the difference in income between men and officers that Varley and Anderson, at Tavoy Camp, had an extravagant wager of one pound (about $35 in 2021) that the war with Germany would end by November that year.

It was inevitable that thoughts would turn to escape, with one group of hopefuls concocting a plan to somehow gain entry to the Japanese signals' room and transmit a message to the Allied air force or navy, calling for help. Fortunately, this rash and ambitious proposal fell by the wayside as the Japanese, who had previously shown a lenient attitude to prisoners leaving the compound to forage for food, had decreed that anyone found outside the wire would be punished, possibly executed. All POWs had been informed and a notice to this effect posted in both English and Japanese. The Japanese regarded prisoners as members of the IJA. The penalty for desertion in the Japanese Army was death. If a prisoner escaped, he was deemed to have deserted.

In the early hours of 30 May, Fred and the other prisoners were hunted from their bunks and ordered onto the parade ground, where they were forced to remain for three hours. The reason for this unexpected roll call soon became clear. The Japanese had apprehended two men, now tethered to a tree near the guardroom. It was dark and the Australians, unable to identify the culprits, hoped that they might be locals. However, a headcount showed that the Japanese were not bluffing. Two prisoners were indeed missing from the parade. The unfortunate pair were Privates Frank Davey and Joseph Bell (also known as Ernest James Bell), both of 2/29 Battalion. Slipping away at around midnight, they had managed to cover nine kilometres before Burmese police arrested them and handed them over to the Japanese. The escapees were in deep trouble as, during interrogation, they had allegedly stated that life in the camp was unbearable; that they were hungry and were looking for food; and they wanted to return home.

With the culprits having already spilled the beans, an excuse offered by their sergeant that they had gone to the latrine was not accepted by the Japanese camp commandant, Lieutenant Tokoro Kinichi, who warned Ramsay that the escapees could be shot. He pleaded for clemency, protesting that the men were of a low mental standard, which had deteriorated under POW conditions, and that to execute them would be a violation of international law. Tokoro replied that he would need to refer the matter to his commander, Captain Itsui Hiroshi, who was based at Tavoy. However, he did not do so until 10 June. In the meantime, the arrested men remained in confinement. On 16 June Ramsay was summoned to Tokoro's office. Itsui's decision, which had been received four days previously, was read out. The two Australians were to be executed by firing squad. Precisely when, was not disclosed.

Two days later, at 4 am on 18 June, the condemned men were woken and informed of their fate, before being driven to a rifle range on the western side of the nearby airfield. After digging their own graves, their hands and feet were bound, their eyes blindfolded. A firing squad, under the command of Lieutenant Goto, then executed them, without trial. Tokoro, who had failed to inform Ramsay of the impending executions, paid tribute to their bravery and, sensing that such wanton killing would raise the ire of the prisoners, doubled the guard.

The incident did, however, result in an improvement in conditions. Itsui issued orders for the POWs to move to a new camp, about 2.5 kilometres from the aerodrome, previously used by occupation troops as barracks. Constructed from timber and atap, the two-storey buildings were airy and roomy and would prove to be far superior to any camp accommodation the Australians were to encounter during their captivity. The rice ration was also increased considerably, allowing a good portion to be ground into flour.

> As the accommodation and food were much better and work on the 'drome was not so hard, we were now able to recover some of our lost health. From Monday to Friday we worked at the 'drome and on Saturday were allowed to go onto a padang for recreation – under guard, of course. On a hill overlooking the padang was a Buddhist temple where, on numerous occasions, we had seen the yellow-robed priests looking down curiously at us. One morning, while the Jap guard was on the opposite side to where we were sitting, I noticed the priests beckoning to me from the side of the temple. I acknowledged the signal and he threw three articles, which rolled down the hill almost to us. We walked across and picked them up. They were tins of 50 Gold Flake cigarettes, a gift fit for a king. For quite a few days we were prosperous indeed.
>
> We were forced to go to the beach to get salt water in which to cook our rice. On each of these trips, on our homeward journey, the side of the road would be lined with dried fish, eggs, fruit and cigars, donors making signs to show we were to take them. The locals charged the Japanese 5 annas for one egg, but we were able to sneak out after dark and purchase 20 eggs for 16 annas (one rupee). All this went on under the noses of the Jap guards who, if catching any Burmese openly giving, would punish him severely.
>
> The Japanese had also forced into work some thousands of the native population and, as we were all working together and some of them could speak English, they gave us some idea how the war was going. Also, they gave us numerous gifts of smokes and food, fruit and some vegetables. We had to smuggle them into camp past the Japs, but were seldom caught.

If they were, and admitted to trading, they were fined three days' Japanese pay. The unpredictable Japanese then handed the forfeited money to the men's units to purchase extra rations.

Internal discipline was at times difficult as some prisoners still resented being under the control of their officers. They considered that the Japanese were more than sufficient. Not everyone behaved and instances such as theft were reported and punished by the AIF administration.

In July, Bill Cousens was unexpectedly transferred to Tokyo. Discovering that he was a radio announcer pre-war, the Japanese decided they could make far better use of his talents by making him broadcast propaganda. Cousins argued the toss, and refused to obey, but was told that he would lose his life if he failed to toe the line. It wasn't until there was a show of hands from his comrades that he was finally persuaded to comply. They hoped that he could somehow get messages through to Australia, so that families back home would know where they were.

Before leaving, Cousens handed over his wristwatch with instructions to sell it and purchase food or medicine. He travelled to Tavoy by truck where he was to board a plane to Tokyo. However, plans were revised when the plane crash-landed at Tavoy, necessitating his transfer by sea to Japan, where he had no option but to broadcast with the infamous Tokyo Rose. Rose, an American-born Japanese woman named Iva Toguri, had been visiting Tokyo when Pearl Harbour was attacked, leaving her stranded in Japan. Compelled to renounce her American citizenship, she found work at a radio station where she was forced to broadcast Japanese propaganda.

Post-war, Iva Toguri and Charles Cousens were both charged with treason when they returned home. Iva was found guilty and served 10 years in a US prison, but in 1976 President Gerald Ford granted her an executive pardon. The charges against Cousens were eventually dropped, but he was decommissioned and refused permission by the Returned Services League to join the traditional parade on ANZAC Day. However, Fred and the men of the 2/19th would have none of it. Cousins not only marched on ANZAC Day, but led the battalion.

Above: Charles Cousens.
Right: Iva Tohguri, 'Tokyo Rose'

Fred and the other workers at Mergui had looked forward to the onset of the rainy season, assuming that there would be no airfield construction in wet weather. They were therefore astounded when Tokoro issued the order 'All mans will work in the rain'.

The work of shovelling and transporting the soil was monotonous enough in dry weather. In the torrential rain it was purgatory, as the workers struggled to lift the rice sacks, now piled with heavy mud. Very few of the prisoners had ground sheets, which in any case, provided only a modicum of protection. Within seconds, most were soaked to the skin. The cold, wet conditions inevitably took their toll, with more and more prisoners reporting sick each day. Under the rationale 'sick mans don't eat', Tokoro cut back the rations. During this time at least 17 prisoners (three British and 14 Australians) died, and Doctor Coates became critically ill. According to the men, he was pulled back from the brink of death purely by his own willpower and determination, attributes that would stand him in good stead in the days to come.

Towards the end of July, the gnawing hunger pains proved too great for the 2/30th's Private Bill Schuberth who, despite the deaths of Bell and Davey, decided to go outside the wire in search of food. The few friends in whom he confided warned him he could easily end up with a bullet instead, but he would not be dissuaded, adding that he intended to obtain eggs and bananas for the sick. After surveying the entire length of the fence, and watching the movement of the guards over several days, he found a spot to slither under the wire into the jungle and, after dark, headed for the village.

He was not at large for long. He was back by 9 pm, bashed and bloodied, escorted by Burmese police. Tokoro, who was at his headquarters in town, was informed of this latest escape by telephone. When interrogation revealed that Schuberth had left the camp to obtain food, Tokoro decided not to report the incident to Itsui and instead confined him to the guardhouse as punishment. However, Schuberth was warned that any further attempt to escape would result in death by firing squad.

It was advice that the Australian chose to ignore and, in the early hours of the morning, he escaped out the guardhouse window and decamped to the POW barracks. His startled mates cleaned the blood from him as best they could and told him to lie on his bed space and feign sleep. However, the alarm had been raised and the camp was already being searched. Unfortunately, Schuberth was extremely easy to identify, not from his cuts and bruises, but from his extremely hairy chest, so hairy that the guards would often pull hairs out, just in spite.

As he had no chance of hiding, and his very presence in the hut placed everyone in danger, Schuberth had decided to give himself up when he heard a huge commotion from the adjoining hut. The guards, seeking someone with a hairy chest, had picked the wrong man.

Schuberth ran to the source of the commotion, was immediately arrested and taken to Tokoro, who regarded his absconding from custody inside the camp as an escape. Displaying what the Japanese lieutenant regarded as a defiant attitude, Schuberth showed no remorse, simply stating that it was the duty of every prisoner to try to escape. Given the precedent already set regarding the escape of Bell and Davey, Tokoro announced that the only possible sentence was death. However, after listening to pleadings for clemency by Ramsay and his adjutant, he referred his decision and the request for commutation of the sentence to Itsui. There was no reply.

At 4 am on 30 July, Tokoro visited Schuberth in his cell and told him that he would be shot that morning. The prisoner showed no fear and maintained his defiant attitude. He was then heavily bound and bundled into a truck. A group of Australians working around the camp shortly before dawn saw the vehicle as it passed by and heard Shuberth yell 'Tell the colonel they are going to shoot me. God bless you.'

The execution shook Fred and the others to the core. In an effort to appease them, Tokoro called them back from work early and announced that there would be an improvement in rations, making it unnecessary for POWs to go outside the wire. It never happened. The work on the airstrip was complete and Ramsay Force received orders to make ready for a transfer to Tavoy, 240 kilometres distant, where conditions were better and the inmates fitter.

> Before we left a Burmese baker, who had supplied coffins and a means of transporting the bodies of two Australians who died to the cemetery, gave each man a loaf of bread that he had baked.

However, before anyone had a chance to take even one bite, the Japanese confiscated every loaf.

A couple of days later the order came to move. The group was split into two, with the majority of the fit prisoners in one, and the sick, along with medical staff and the remainder of the fit, in the other. Packed onto the deck and in the bowels of a type of barge, with a huge open hold and a small deck across one end, the trip was far worse than the voyage from Singapore. The vessel was smaller than Sydney's famed Manly ferry and the space so confined that the fit POWs were forced to either stand, or sit with knees tucked under their chins. Until a makeshift latrine was devised, using a plank suspended over the water, with a rope handrail to cling to, the dysentery sufferers had no option but to foul themselves, and those around them. Relief only came when those fortunate enough to be topside were rotated with those in the hold.

The 95 seriously ill cases, lying on stretchers made from rice bags and poles, or even old wire bed frames, were loaded with difficulty onto a small steamer of about 500 tonnes. On board, the stretchers were placed on the hatch covers, a tarpaulin the only protection from the sun and rain. Fortunately, permission had been granted to bring commodes from the hospital for those stricken with severe dysentery. Although all were aboard by 6 pm, the vessel did not leave until almost 6 am the following day. To sustain everyone on the journey, the Japanese issued a loaf of bread to each man, the same bread that had been confiscated a couple of days before, but now green with mould.

Two days later Ramsey Force finally reached Tavoy River, but the misery did not end there. They were transferred to the holds of smaller, more decrepit barges for the wearisome five-hour journey upstream, where the fit were required to march a short distance to their camp in the boarding quarters of the American Baptist School. Generally referred to as Tavoy High School, the conditions there were far better than expected.

After arriving at 2.30 am, each prisoner received a pannikin of hot meat and bean stew. The next morning, they moved to the main section of the school, a two-storey structure with a large assembly hall on the first floor, and with electricity in each room. There was also an excellent canteen providing plenty of sweet potatoes, onions, pumpkin and other items. Surreptitious trading with local people also added to the food store, with the result that the meals were the best they had experienced since becoming POWs. Fred was among the many who counted their blessings.

When the Japanese began to pay us for working for them at Tavoy, the Camp Commander gave us permission to open a canteen and allowed a native tribesman to come into camp and bring supplies. This native, whom the boys christened Ali Baba, was always willing to give us credit for any goods we needed, and never once did any man fail to meet his obligations on pay day.

The local people in this area were very pro-British, unlike the Malays, who were very similar to the Japanese in their ways and habits and could not be trusted to be good Allies to the white man. Many stories could be told of their treachery while we were fighting in Malaya. The Burmese were completely different. When, as often happened, we were taken in small parties to work in the town, they would take all kinds of risks to help us. One such incident occurred when we were demolishing a brick house and carrying the bricks from the building, along the main street to a place used by the Japs as their headquarters. At the rear of the building we were demolishing there was an old overgrown garden covering about an acre. Noticing a little dark-haired, dark-skinned Burmese girl of about seven years beckoning to me from the undergrowth, I strolled across in a leisurely fashion, taking care to keep out of sight of the guard, to see what she wanted. Taking me by the hand and speaking in almost perfect English she said, 'Come with me! My Daddy wants you!'

Once in the shelter of the old garden there was not much chance of the guard seeing us, so I followed her. She led me along an old path and into the shelter of an overhanging tree, and there, seated on the ground, were her mother and father. At our approach they both jumped to their feet and came forward with hands outstretched to welcome me. On a spotlessly white tablecloth spread on the ground was a collection of various foods – enough I should say, to satisfy at least ten hungry men.

When they saw my amazed expression the woman explained, 'We would so much like to help you and show how loyal we are; and this is the only way we can find to do it. My husband has watched from here now for two days and this is the first time we have been able to attract your attention. My husband was in the employ of the British Government – and still is – but I know you will say nothing. We have planned this so that, while you are working here, each man in turn can come and have something to eat. When you go back you will tell your friends quietly and one at a time, they can come.'

For transport, the upper class Burmese used a gharry, a small horse-drawn buggy that carried up to five passengers. Whenever one passed by while we were working in town, we would be showered with coins. One Burmese woman drove back and forth many times a day to scatter her gifts.

Anderson Force was in a hangar near the aerodrome, so it was not until a group from Ramsay Force was detailed to augment the workforce there that Fred learned that eight prisoners at Tavoy had attempted to escape. They hoped to reach India, which was in British hands.

All were anti-tankers from Victoria, led by Warrant Officer Matthew Quittendon: Tom Cumming, Clifford Danaher, Aubrey Emmett, Alan Glover, Arthur Jones, Arthur Reeve and James Wilson. At 36 years of age. Quittendon was by far the oldest in the party, with the majority in their 20s. The youngest was Arthur Reeve, who had just turned 21. Two were English by birth, with the remainder born in Melbourne or country Victoria. Aubrey

Emmett, aged just 23, who came from Ouyen in the far north-west of the state, had lost two uncles on the western front in World War 1. His elder brother, who also enlisted with 4 Anti-tank, was still in Changi Camp, but would later be sent to Thailand. Like Aubrey, most of the other members of the group were single, and their occupations ranged from railwayman to lorry driver to estate agent to fireman to grocer. In all, a very diverse bunch. Despite the warning issued by camp commandant Lieutenant Chiina that, 'If you want to go free Japan soldier shoot you dead', all were united by the compulsion to escape.

They had slipped away on the night of 1 June and, despite a search, eluded their pursuers until the 4th when, while trying to obtain food and water at a village ten kilometres from the camp, they were forcibly restrained by Burmese until the Japanese arrived. The POWs, who had believed that the locals were anti-Japanese, were unaware that each village had its informants, who reported any stranger seen in the vicinity. All the escapees were brought back to Tavoy, where they were imprisoned in the civil gaol. One, who had tried to evade recapture, had been shot in the lower leg.

Varley was summoned the next day and told by Lieutenant Chiina that the men would be executed. His pleas for mercy were useless, as was his petition advising that the killing was unlawful. The men had disobeyed military orders and would be executed, in accordance with Japanese army regulations. Varley and two padres were equally unsuccessful in their attempts to speak to or visit the condemned men. They were told that Japanese soldiers awaiting execution were allowed no visitors and that they 'could see after death'. However, spotting the eight men in the distance, Varley shouted 'You are for it, lads'.

As was usual in the Japanese military justice system, the accused did not go to trial unless a guilty verdict, already decided in advance, was assured. There was no provision for any defence. The trial was simply to formally pronounce a guilty verdict and hand down the punishment, also decided in advance. On 5 June, Quittendon's 36th birthday, the escapees were paraded before the 'court' and were sentenced to death.

The next day, 6 June, Fred's signaller colleague, Sergeant Ron Gaul, and 39 fellow POWs from Anderson Force, under the command of Captain Hennessey of 2/10 Field Regiment, were dispatched to the eastern end of the civil cemetery, just to the north-east of the airfield. After being forced to dig eight graves, facing east, and to drive in a stake at the foot of each, they were ordered to wait in the shade of a tree until their further services were required.

At 3.30 pm the condemned men were transferred by truck from the gaol to the execution site. Accompanying them in a car with Lieutenant Chiina were Varley and Anderson, who had been ordered to attend. At Varley's request, permission had been granted for Anglican Padre Fred Bashford to be present. Padre Henry Smith, of the Roman Catholic faith, was also at hand, but was not permitted to join the others. Entreaties to be allowed to speak with the condemned men, to receive last messages for their families and to provide spiritual comfort were turned down by Itsui with a terse, 'talk after death'.

At ten minutes to four on 6 June, a firing squad of 16 Japanese soldiers arrived to take up position. Knowing full well that they had only minutes to live, the Australians showed no signs of apprehension for the fate that awaited them. Far from being cowed, they betrayed not the slightest fear, as they said cheerio and wished each other luck, adding that they would 'see each other on the other side'. Blindfolded and with hands bound behind their backs, they were then led to the execution site, where they were instructed to sit, legs apart, leaning against the stakes, to which their hands were then tied. At 4 pm the marksmen, two assigned to each prisoner, took aim from five paces away and, on the order 'Ute', shot them in the foreheads. All eight heads flopped to one side. A second shot was fired, to ensure that all were dead.

With the proceedings at an end, as far as the Japanese were concerned, all Japanese present saluted and the firing squad, which had treated the whole affair as some kind of joke, presented arms.

Chiina, who had a grin on his face throughout the entire procedure, now permitted Varley and the two padres to approach, accompanied by two Japanese soldiers. After Captain Hennessey untied the hands of each of the victims, Bashford removed any personal items from their bodies and one of their two identity discs. As the chaplains were not aware of the religions of the deceased, they took four men each, saying individual prayers, before the burial detail filled in the graves. As all four bullets had hit each victim in the head, the deceased were unrecognisable, but fortunately one of their anti-tanker mates, Bombadier 'Titch' Jelly, who knew them all well, was able to identify them by other means, allowing crosses with their names to be erected on the correct graves.

The members of Green Force, who had reached Tavoy by barge on 9 August after an appalling three-day voyage on two small, filthy vessels, *Tatu Maru*, and an unidentifiable craft known simply as No 593, also brought the story of another disastrous escape attempt.

On arrival at Victoria Point, the group had been split into two groups. The largest, 600 men, was sent to work repairing the airfield, about 12 kilometres from town. The other 400 or so prisoners, tasked with unloading aviation fuel drums and bags of rice from ships, occupied houses along the waterfront.

The construction and repair group was accommodated in huts on the lower slopes of hilly terrain to the east of the airstrip, about 1000 metres north of the Japanese barracks. Towards the end of May, work began on repairing the airstrip, which had craters ranging from a metre in diameter to eight metres, some of them up to nine metres deep.

At 10.30 am on 8 July, Private Bob Goulden, one of the cooks working in the camp kitchen, was reported missing. According to his mates, he had last been seen at 10 o'clock the night before. By 11.30 am, finding no sign of him and discovering that his kit was also missing, the Allied camp administration had no option but to report his absence to the Japanese, who immediately dispatched three search teams, four soldiers in each, accompanied by local guides. They fanned out to the north of the camp, targeting one village about 20 kilometres away and two others, both more than 30 kilometres distant. The Japanese informed the Australian officers that when, and if, Goulden was found, he would be shot. Major Green's protests cut no ice with the Japanese, who placed him and two other officers in solitary confinement as punishment for the escape.

At 8.30 on the night of 11 July, after 70 hours on the run, Goulden arrived back in camp in a truck. He had been spotted by locals, perched in a tree in a coconut plantation on the coast, about 25 kilometres from the camp. When arrested, he was still in the tree, and made no attempt to resist. Major Green, who was allowed to see him the following morning, learned that Goulden had been worried about his wife, who was pregnant and was ill, and decided to escape. He had no idea that she had given birth to a healthy son on 6 March.

Green pleaded that Goulden had suffered temporary derangement due to the worry about his wife, but the Japanese would not be swayed. He knew the rules. He had been caught outside the wire, a capital offence. In any case, a grave digging detail of ten POWs had already left the camp in a truck, and a wreath and stretcher ordered. The Japanese, who had not ill-treated Goulden at any stage, asked if he wished to see any of his friends or write letters to his wife and family. He declined the offer of a visit, apart from Padre Armstrong who prayed with him, but penned two short letters.

After being paraded under guard before the POW assembly, a Japanese officer read out the charge and the sentence. Goulden, followed by Green, a junior Australian officer and the padre, was marched off to a gully about 500 metres from the camp, where he was lashed to a post and blindfolded. Three Japanese guards shot him at a distance of five paces. They were poor shots. Goulden slumped and cried out. Alerted by the two Australians that the victim was still alive, the Japanese in charge administered the coup de grace with a pistol shot to the head.

After the firing squad presented arms, the interpreter announced that the Australian administration could make arrangements for his burial. When the medical officer pronounced that life was extinct, Goulden's body was sewn into a blanket and carried back to the camp where he was paraded through the ranks with full military honours. He was then transported by truck to the Christian cemetery for burial by the padre, attended by Australian and Japanese military personnel.

With a total of 12 Australians from A Force executed for escaping, there were no further attempts made at Tavoy, where conditions were bordering on good. With the airfield nearing completion, the hours of work eased, along with the workload, which now consisted of tasks such as tidying up around the barracks and husking rice. The POWs were also ordered to build a cinema and, to their surprise, the Japanese made them go to the pictures. In addition, every ten days they had a day off, allowing them to play inter-company football matches and other sports, and to indulge in an impromptu concert at night. About three evenings a week, officers gave talks on a variety of subjects and a weekly debate was organised.

Only those who worked received pay, so, as there was so little work to do, most of it being small jobs around the Japanese quarters, a roster was organised to ensure that everyone had a chance to earn some extra money.

The prisoners saw little of the compound's Japanese commander, Sergeant (Gunso) Anshinn Kumada, who hardly bothered them and only held roll call once a week, on Sunday mornings. The guards, mostly veterans of the Sino-Chinese war, were quite decent and allowed the prisoners to do what they liked, within reason.

By 16 September, A Force had completed work on the airfield. However, POWs harbouring thoughts about a return to Changi were to be greatly disappointed. At the end of the month, the Japanese moved Green and Anderson Forces further north, to begin construction on a rail line into Thailand. They went by sea to Moulemein, a journey of about 30 hours, followed by a two-hour rail trip to Thanbyuzayat, about 56 kilometres to the south. On arrival, Lieutenant Colonel Nagatomo read out a 'manifesto', better described as a riot act. He left the prisoners in no doubt whatsoever that escape attempts, disobedience or disregard for any one of 87 regulations would not be tolerated and would be enforced by the guards.

The latter now included a good number of Koreans. Like Formosans recruited to guard POWs in other parts of the Japanese Empire, the Koreans had long been subjugated to Japanese rule, following annexation of their homeland in 1910. Regarded as second-rate citizens, they had jumped at the chance to join the IJA only to discover they did not qualify as combat or even administrative troops. Their task was to guard prisoners of war, who should have had the decency to kill themselves instead of surrendering. Having been at the bottom of the social pecking order all their lives, they now had someone even more lowly to torment, and they reacted accordingly. Almost without exception, the most brutal treatment meted out to POWs was perpetrated by guards from Korea and Formosa, a Japanese colony since 1895. However, their senior Japanese officers were complicit and, more often than not, did nothing to curb their excesses.

In October, the number of Australian prisoners at Thanbyuzayat was bolstered when two more forces arrived from Java via Singapore: Williams and Black Forces, composed of British, American and Australian personnel, including sailors from USS *Houston* and HMAS *Perth*, sunk in the Sunda Straits off Sumatra's southern tip in the early hours of 1 March. The troops from Java also included a large number of drivers from the AIF's 2/3 Reserve Motor Transport (2/3 RMT) who, besides being older than the combat troops, were below the normal physical standard required on enlistment.

Williams Force was under the command of Lieutenant Colonel Jack Williams of 2/2 Pioneer Battalion. His unit, along with men from 2/3 Machine Gun Battalion, had been on their way home from the Middle East with other members of 7 Division, when they were offloaded from their transport ship HMT *Orcades* in Java, which subsequently fell to the Japanese. The same fate also befell Major Leslie Robertson, Commander of Robertson Force, and his 2/6 Field Company, which would also transfer to Burma the following January.

Lieutenant Colonel Chris Black, CO of 2/3 RMT, was in charge of Black Force. His unit had served in Malaya, and held the distinction of being the first Australians to go into battle against the Japanese, a claim often made by both 2/19 and 2/30 Battalions. However, 2/3 RMT beat them to it when, at dawn on 12 December 1941, just four days after the Japanese landings at Kota Bharu, their spare drivers fought as infantry when Indians from 3/16 Punjabi Regiment were attacked at Kroh, in northern Malaya.

Once the Allies had all withdrawn to Singapore Island, 2/3 RMT was deemed to be surplus to requirements and the majority of the force was ordered to return to Australia. However, they too, like Williams' men, had been caught in Java to become prisoners of war. Williams, Robertson and Black forces also included a number of men from 8 Division who had escaped from Singapore to Java, where they too were captured.

It would be a while before Fred knew anything about the various Java forces as Ramsay Force remained at Tavoy engaged in a variety of tasks, nothing particularly onerous, until December. Consequently, the Australians were there on the first Tuesday in November, Melbourne Cup Day, possibly the second most important day in Australia after ANZAC Day. Realising that Cup Day was not too far off, a delegation of Victorians, led by Bakri veteran Captain Charles Lovett, approached George Ramsay to ask if the prisoners could celebrate the occasion, and he, in turn, sought permission from the affable Sergeant Anshinn. He consulted his senior officer, who not only granted the request, but declared that everyone should have a yasumi, or holiday. It was not as magnanimous as it appeared: the date fortuitously coincided with Meiji Day, a public holiday in Japan to honour the birthday of the Emperor Meiji, who died in 1912, but whose special day was revived in 1927. On receipt of this welcome, and rather unexpected news, the Tovoy POW Turf Club was up and running.

Secret radios operated by Green and Anderson Forces, along with an Australian radio

Lt Colonel George Ramsay

technician, who repaired wireless sets looted by the Japanese from the homes of British expatriates, had departed to Thanbyuzayat, so Ramsay Force had no contact with the outside world. Unaware that, back home, Australian Prime Minister John Curtin had banned mid-week races as part of an austerity campaign to conserve resources for war purposes, and that the race, known as the Austerity Melbourne Cup, would be held on Saturday, 21 November, the POWs' plans at Tavoy forged ahead for Tuesday the 3rd.

As the horses were actually the prisoners of war, their jockeys had to be light enough to ride on the backs of their mates, piggyback style. Form was taken into consideration and handicaps applied. Training soon began for the big day – 'silks' were made from coloured scarves and an official race caller appointed, dubbed 'Lachie Melville', after the one back home. Despite this, some of the skeptics didn't believe the race would eventuate. However, they changed their tune when the school's soccer field was turned into a race track with the addition of a starting barrier and white posts and railings, and Sergeant Anshinn was reported to have donated a trophy – a small two-handled brass cup mounted on a highly polished coconut shell.

Cup Fever took hold, with fees collected for entries and bookies taking bets, in occupation currency for the affluent and locally made cheroots for the less so, on a field of 38 starters for the main event. However, due to illness of some of the horses and jockeys, and the obvious fitness and superiority of one of the front runners, Sweet Potato (Private Wilfred 'Wiff' Muir, an outstanding Australian Rules football player), there were quite a few scratchings, reducing the field to 21, and the distance to about 70 metres.

Corporal Vincent McColl recorded the names of the 21 starters, and their pedigrees, in his notebook.

Geni by Woodcutter out of Bottle
Samuel Sue by Runner at Night out of Over the Fence
Sweet Potato by Ali Baba out of Canteen
Brown Bomber by Straight Stick out of Hollow Log
Irish Boy by Spud out of Goolah
Chapatti King by Rice Flour out of Spuds and Onions
Furphy by Xmas out of Tavoy
Tinea by Longwater out of Tong
Once Bitten Twice Shy by Mosquito out of Net
Coffee by Quartermaster out of Quick money
Eiffel tower by So High out of Top Flight
Streak by Quick Return out of Hoper
The Dreamer by The 15 out of Tavoy
Optimism by Easter out of Captivity
Portuguese Timor by Neutral Ship out of Singapore
Batman's Pay – by Hard to Get out of Officers
Tummy by Sour Rice out of Order
AIF by Xmas out of Tavoy
Sawdust by Crosscut out of Miss Rubber
Music by Piano out of Tune
All Truth by Missing Goat out of Tellamalie

Other colourfully named race day entrants included:

Cold Bottom by Arse out of Pants
Dysentery by Fly out of Latrine
Happy Days – by Release out of Burma
Concert Party – by Big Noise out of Drum
Eaten – by Bug out of Bed
Troops Starved – by Cooks out of Kitchen
Evacuation – by Rice out of Belly
Miraculous Escape – by Gordon Bennett out of Singapore
Basher Boy – by Wild Swing out of Bully
Music – by Piano out of Tune
Troop Starver by Cooks out of Kitchen
Spinebasher by Last out of Bed
Surplus by Profit out of Canteen

Back home in Melbourne, it poured with rain on Austerity Cup Day, reducing the crowd to a mere 35,000 punters, but in Tavoy the weather could not have been better for the running of their Melbourne Cup – brilliant sunshine with a slight breeze. Everyone, including the Japanese, entered into the spirit of the event. Sergeant Anshinn donated some pomelos and Ali Baba gave five shillings. Keeping with the tradition of 'fashions on the field', the 'ladies' were dressed in an array of finery they had scrounged from goodness knows where. As some of the racegoers were 'female', latrines with toilet paper supplied by the generous Anshinn were marked accordingly. Another latrine was converted into a judge's box. The trophies for all the races were displayed on a table and stalls were set up, with 'native women' selling chapatis and coffee made from ground, scorched rice. With such a large crowd, the course constabulary was kept occupied preventing any nobbling. There were seven races on the card so it was also a busy day for the bookmakers. There were several, including 'Joe' Wilson and Privates Laurence Goggin and Alfred Murrell of 2/29 Battalion, who traded under the name 'Ye Old Firm', with the motto 'We Pay. Others May'.

When 3 pm approached, the band, under the baton of conductor Norm Whittaker, struck up *God Save the King* and the POWs joined in lustily, finishing their rendition with a huge roar of approval. Escorted by a posse of 'mounted police', the 'Governor General', His Excellency George Ramsay, accompanied by his 'wife', entered the field on a brightly decorated bullock cart, pulled by six brawny human horses, to take their places in the Royal Box. Joining them was the 'patron', Sergeant Anshinn, who also arrived in a 'horse'-drawn cart, with a lieutenant from Japanese HQ and a suitable 'escort'. As the band members didn't know the Japanese anthem, they played *Auld Lang Syne* instead.

As the Grand Parade of 21 horses and jockeys passed the Royal Box prior to the big race, there was a commotion when Private Wally MacQueen shot from the crowd and stole the Melbourne Cup. Tackled by the constabulary, he broke free but was soon recaptured and arrested.

With final bets taken, including those from very enthusiastic Japanese punters, who were encouraged to back horses that had little chance of winning, the starter, Ron Wells, ordered the entrants to line up and they were off. 'Lachie Melville' had the crowd on its toes with his superb description of the race. First across the line, and ahead by two metres, was the favourite, Sweet Potato. This 'five year old gelding' was owned by Captain Charles Lovett, trained by Private Ron Wells and ridden by Private Alex 'Bluey' Campbell, all from 2/29 Battalion.

His Excellency presented the cup to the owner of the winning horse and a bamboo-and-coconut shell whip to the jockey. The officers' race, with 12 starters, was won by Hanging Rocks (Captain Lovett), ridden by Lieutenant Cyril 'Buster' Badger, who had assumed the name of a well-known jockey, Harold Badger. Lovett's second trophy of the day was a local scene painted by Private Wilson Mills. The race meeting ended with a mock trial of another owner, trainer and jockey for failing to allow their well-favoured horse to run on its merits.

The day didn't end there. That night, in the school hall, there was a Cup Ball. After the 'Matron' had presented her 'debutantes' to 'Her Excellency', the vice-regal couple led the opening waltz as the band played *Blue Danube*. Sergeant Anshinn was unable to attend but two young Japanese wireless operators, aged about 18, came along. One, after some persuasion, overcame his embarrassment to dance with one of the fifteen 'ladies'

Above: The running of the Tavoy Melbourne Cup. Below: The Tavoy Melbourne Cup trophy.

present. Private Roger Pietri, dressed as film actress Greta Garbo, was declared Bell of the Ball. After the Governor General delivered a witty speech and donated the proceeds of race day to the hospital fund, the evening ended with 1000 voices singing *Auld Lang Syne* with tremendous enthusiasm. Then, led by the band, everyone stood and sang *God Save the King*.

The actual cup, standing about ten centimetres tall, was created from scrap brass by a Dutch jeweller and prisoner of war, who had inscribed one side with TAVOY POW R C. MELBOURNE CUP 1942. PRESENTED BY ANSHINN GUNSO. The names of the winner, owner, jockey and trainer were added later to the other side. However, to prevent its confiscation by Japanese guards, before Ramsay Force left Tavoy the cup was buried in a grave at the aerodrome cemetery. It was quite common for POWs to bury items in graves. At Thanubayazat in May 1943, reports and documents that were too risky to keep in the camp were placed in the grave of Private Douglas Eyles. Which grave held the cup in Tavoy Cemetery is not known, but there were only three deaths at the camp between 3 November and 16 December, when Ramsay Force left – POWs Shepherd, Cooling and Busby on 4, 8 and 25 November. Unfortunately, the notes made by the war graves recovery team who exhumed the gravesites were destroyed.

However, the cup was recovered from the grave in 1945-46 and returned to Australia, where it was given to Wilfred Muir (Sweet Potato). It is believed that deterioration of the coconut shell during the three years it was buried was the reason why, post-war, a polished ball-shaped wooden base was added. The cup is now at Wangaratta in country Victoria where it is treasured by Muir's family.

The pencilled list of the original 38 cup entrants, recorded with age, sex, barrier draw and odds, made by Ye Old Firm's bookies' clerk, Warren Lewis, was hidden in the back of his steel shaving mirror throughout his captivity. Charles Lovett, who survived the war, returned home to Bendigo where he became president of the local race club, an appointment befitting a former 'Melbourne Cup winner'.

The Sandakan Melbourne Cup

Contrary to popular belief, the Tavoy event was not the only Melbourne Cup race held anywhere in the world on the first Tuesday in November in 1942. Another was organised thousands of kilometres away, at Sandakan POW Camp in British North Borneo, where the jockey-less horses advanced in lanes along a series of squares, using playing cards to determine each horse's progress. However, it was a very lame affair compared to Tavoy and, since the rank and file were out toiling on airfield construction, it was strictly an 'officers only' event, held in secret between two of the officers' huts. The improvised trophy was fashioned from an empty bully-beef tin, secured by nails to a wooden stem set into a roughly hewn octagonal base, with two galvanised handles joining the 'cup' to the plinth. When the officers were moved from Sandakan to another camp in Kuching, the cup went with them. Conditions there were such that they held follow-up races in 1943 and 1944. The trophy now forms part of the collection at the Australian War Memorial.

On 16 December, six weeks after Cup Day, Ramsay Force received instructions to move. Conditions at Tavoy had been good, so it was with some regret that Fred recorded:

> All good things must end. We moved again. This time we travelled by truck (40 to a truck and standing room only) to a place called Ye, about 160 kilometres away and the terminus of a railroad which, starting at Rangoon, runs southward through Moulmein and along the west coast of Lower Burma.
>
> From Ye we set off on foot, carrying all our belongings, walking from sleeper to sleeper along the railway line towards Moulmein. It was stiflingly hot and not a breath of air moved as, mile after mile, we trudged.
>
> Water bottles were soon exhausted. Both lips and tongue became swollen and painful but it was risking death to drink from any of the pools of stagnant water we passed. Men, who had set out carrying packs, which, with every mile, became more of a burden, began to discard articles they had treasured for months. Nobody else bothered to pick them up, as each man was carrying all he could. Nightfall found us, footsore and exhausted, blindly following the leaders away from the railway line until, at last, we halted in the grounds of a temple.
>
> This was like an oasis in the desert – a cool, clear well of water, which the locals declared was pure to drink and was the centre of attention until far into the night. The supply of water was inexhaustible and the bathing of sore and weary feet was a delicious sensation. Our bed in the open was like a glorious feather bed for the few short hours we were allowed to sleep.
>
> As the sun slowly poked its head above the surrounding hills we were again on our way. The muscles of our legs were like tight, corded ropes and, until the exercise warmed and loosened them, walking was torture. The soles of my feet, because of the pounding my only pair of boots had taken on the gravel-packed rail tracks, reducing the leather to paper-thin thickness, felt as if I were walking on coals of fire. Our progress was slowed somewhat by men whose blistered feet made walking absolute torture.
>
> Late in the afternoon of the second day we stopped at the banks of a turgid, muddy stream, across which the spans of a partly demolished bridge still stood. On the opposite shore was a line of railway trucks. With the heat of the sun beating down upon them all day they were like red hot ovens inside. After hours spent ferrying the party across the stream and placing them in the trucks, an engine arrived and, after much

bumping, shunting and whistle blowing, we began to move off, just as darkness fell. It was certainly a relief for our feet, but not our bodies. The unventilated steel trucks, which had stood in the blazing tropical sun all day long, had previously carried cargo of the most filthy nature. With 35 men crammed into each truck, the steel doors had to be kept closed to prevent anyone from falling out, as the train jolted and swayed its way along one of the worst railway lines it has been my lot to travel on. Our stomachs were rebelling when, after four hours, we at last reached the end of our journey.

Thanbyuzayat was to be the start of a railroad the Japanese proposed to build from Burma, through the Three Pagoda Pass and into Thailand, using us as slave labourers. Towering away in the distance were the mountains that formed the start of Hellfire Pass, through which the railroad was built. Stacks upon stacks of wooden sleepers lay everywhere, along with multiple heaps of steel girders. Thank goodness we did not know of the trials and tragedies we would have to face before the line was completed, or I am sure more of us would have suffered the same fate as the eight who had attempted to escape into India.

After the terrific heat we had experienced until now, the bitterly cold early morning air was like a breath of Australian winter. However, in our weakened condition we certainly felt its effect and we lost three men to pneumonia. With no medical supplies available, they did not stand a chance.

The accommodation at Thanbyuzayat consisted of old half-walled atap and bamboo huts, roofed with decaying thatch that let in the sun and the rain, and the usual bamboo-slatted sleeping platforms that were home to millions of bed bugs. Signs around the place stated that Australians were to be treated harshly to keep them under control. Consequently, bashings were handed out for the most trivial offences.

A POW hut, to house 90 men, similar to those at Thanbyuzayat.

With the arrival of Ramsay Force and the Java groups, the number of POWs under Varley's command, including 4600 Dutchmen, was more than 9500. Although actually in Burma, the A Force POWs were designated as 'No 3 Branch Thai Prisoner of War Camp', as they came under Japan's Thai administration. A second group, 'No 5 Branch', was created when around 2000 Australian, American and Dutch POWs were transferred from Java in January 1943, bringing the total labour force to 11,537, split into sub-camps dotted along the route of the railway from Thanbyuzayat to Kilo 108, near the Thai border. Once their allotted sections of the line were complete, the prisoners moved further east.

At Thanbyuzayat, as part of a dehumanisation process, each member of Ramsay Force was issued with a small wooden block on which a number was inscribed, along with the Japanese symbol for No 3 Branch POW Camp. The prisoners, now regarded as expendable commodities, were compelled to number off in Japanese at roll call and had to wear their tags at all times. Fred was POW 5551.

> After three days at Thanbyuzayt, the work party to which I had been assigned was ordered onto some trucks. We were driven for 26 kilometres along a dusty winding road, where we were off-loaded and told that this was the section of the railroad on which we were to work.

Black Force, which had been in Thanbyuzayat for some weeks and had gone on ahead, was also assigned to the camp at Kilo 26, known as Kunhnitkway (pronounced 'kun-nit-kway') Camp. The Japanese, in what was becoming a monotonous litany, had promised 'all mans' plenty of good food and medical supplies and very little work. However, the welcoming speech from the guard commander, Lieutenant Naito, at the direction of his superior officer, Lieutenant Colonel Nagatomo, set the tone for what the Australians could expect.

It was a tirade similar to that already delivered to Anderson and Green Forces: they were to consider themselves honoured that Nippon had given them the opportunity to help build a railway to Bangkok as they were remnants of a rabble army, who didn't even know how to dress properly. The latter assertion conveniently ignored the fact that what clothes the POWs still wore were the remnants of uniforms issued in 1941. The suppressed laughter of Naito's audience was misconstrued as beaming smiles and taken as a friendly greeting. However, any amusement derived from the speech was wiped out with his chilling closing remarks. 'You will be kept here to work for Nippon. We intend to build this railway, even if it has to go over your dead bodies'.

It was no idle threat. Sending desperately ill men out to work long hours of hard labour and the lack of food, shelter, medical supplies and equipment, would soon take their toll, despite the efforts of numerous dedicated doctors and surgeon Bertie Coates who, the night before he left Thanbyuzayat, performed an appendectomy on a patient, using a razor blade.

The route of the proposed railway more or less followed a British line, originally surveyed along the course of the Khwae Noi River by colonial authorities in 1885, to link northern Thailand with Burma. However, because of the hilly terrain, cut by a multitude of rivers, and a lack of financial backers, the idea was shelved. More than 50 years later, the Japanese, having seized control of Burma and facing a long and hazardous sea route to supply their troops, saw a rail line linking the existing railway systems of Indo-China, Thailand and Burma as a feasible alternative. Ships from Japan could offload troops and supplies in Saigon, and then use the narrow-gauge rail systems to transfer them to the front line, ready to mount an attack on India, the jewel in the British Empire's crown.

Their original intention was to use Asian coolie workers from Burma, Java and Malaya, an estimated 240,000 all told. However, with the fall of the Netherlands East Indies, Malaya and Singapore, the Japanese administration unexpectedly found itself with a large number of prisoners of war – a skilled, educated and disciplined workforce that could be put to good use to further the war effort.

Many of the Asian workers assigned to the Thailand side of the border were Tamils. Originally exported from India by the British to work on rubber plantations in Malaya, they had been well looked after, with housing, schooling and medical facilities provided by a benign colonial administration. Told by their new Japanese masters that they would receive good food and pay in return for light work, they arrived in their thousands, bringing their wives and children with them. By the northern summer of 1943, there would be up to 200,000 Asian labourers working on the line, plus another 60,000 Caucasian POWs. The Japanese regarded the Asian workers as totally expendable commodities. At one camp of 3000 Indian Tamils, the sole medical officer was an Australian doctor, Major Howard Andrews, of 2/10 AGH, who volunteered to provide what assistance he could. However, by the time the line was finished, many of his patients, along with tens of thousands of other Asian workers, would be dead.

The plan was to construct a line from Thanbyuzayat to Nong Pladuc in Thailand, connecting the capital cities of Rangoon, Bangkok and Saigon. Construction of the 111-kilometre Burma section, to the Thai border at Three Pagodas Pass, had begun on 15 September 1942, and the 304-kilometre stretch from Nong Pladuc in August. Japanese planning was initiated as far back as 1939, with officers in the Railway Corps aware that such a project was in the pipeline. However, construction was not actually considered until October 1941, when the corps' Commander in Chief, Lieutenant General Hattori Taro, discussed details of five alternate routes with his Chief of Staff Hiroike Toshio. Despite the talks, nothing further happened. Imperial HQ was not interested, as the Japanese navy was at that time in control of the oceans.

However, with the war now underway, in January 1942 Hiroike went to Bampong to begin surveying the route, and the Imperial order to begin preparations was signed on 12 March. Aerial photography commenced on 20 April and, on 5 June, the Japanese hammered a zero distance marker into the ground at Nong Pladuc and began organising the construction of a staging camp at Bampong, 5 kilometres to the west.

The project was ambitious, to say the least. The first 57 kilometres at the Thai end, from Nong Pladuc to Kanchanaburi, ran across open, flat terrain to the Mae Khlong River, a major obstacle which, when in flood, was up to 300 metres wide. From the river, the route proceeded in a fairly direct line for five kilometres to Chungkai on the Khwae Noi River, where the next challenge had to be overcome: the removal of 10,000 cubic metres of rock by hand to create two cuttings linked by a small bridge, 100 metres long and excavated to a depth of 15 metres. About 50 kilometres further on at Wampo (Wang Po), where sheer cliffs touched the river's edge, the design called for three separate viaducts, linking narrow ledges blasted from the rock face, 30 metres above the water. This 300-metre section, which snaked around the cliffs, would take a labour force of 2000 men six months to build. From here, the route proceeded through mountainous and less inhabited territory to Konyu, Hintok and Konkoita, and on to Songkurai, in remote country near Three Pagodas Pass. The project called for 688 bridges, some small, some substantial. Seven were to be constructed from steel, one at the Mae Khlong River and the other six in Burma.

Right: Map of the route of the railway in Burma.

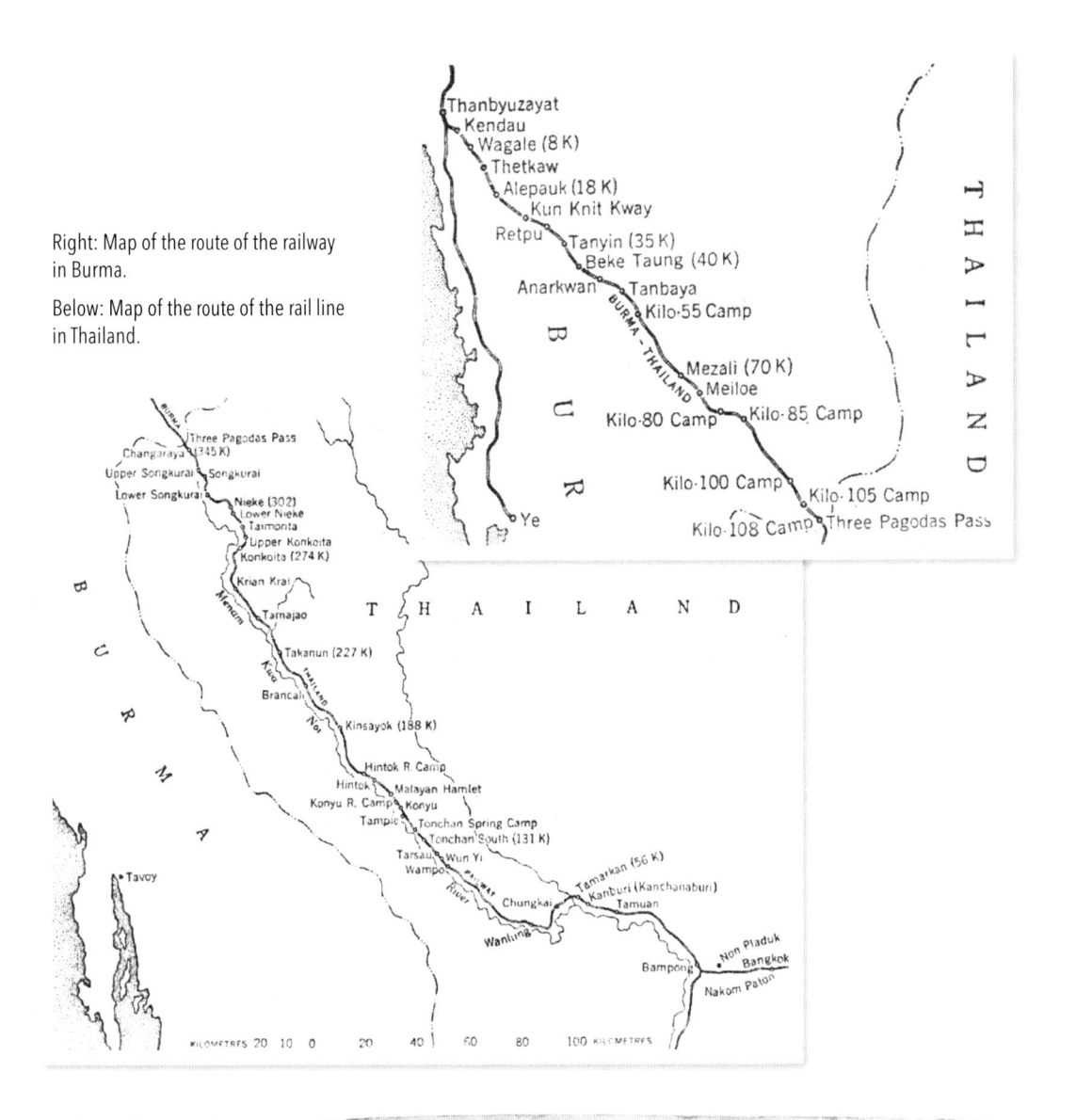

Below: Map of the route of the rail line in Thailand.

Right: Fred's postcard to Elsie

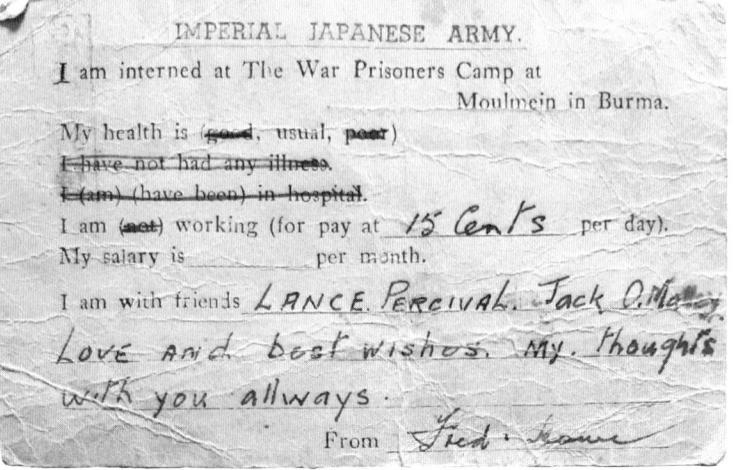

> IMPERIAL JAPANESE ARMY.
>
> I am interned at The War Prisoners Camp at Moulmein in Burma.
> My health is (good, usual, poor)
> I have not had any illness.
> I (am) (have been) in hospital.
> I am (not) working (for pay at 15 Cents per day).
> My salary is _____ per month.
> I am with friends LANCE PERCIVAL, Jack O.M...
> Love and best wishes, my thoughts with you allways.
> From Fred

Most of the construction material for the line was brought from rail networks in Malaya, the Dutch East Indies and Burma. Excluding sidings and passing loops, to build the single-track line would require 580,000 sleepers (locally sourced), 83,000 steel rails and all the necessary ironmongery to fix them in place, including 2.2 million spikes. Eleven steel spans for the bridge over the Mae Khlong at Tamarkan, near Kanchanaburi, came from Madioen in Java. The amount of rolling stock was considerable, with a total of 113 locomotives – 53 plundered from Malaya, one from Burma and seven from Java. The rest were manufactured in Japan and assembled in Bangkok, from as early as December 1941. The British estimate to build the 415-kilometre line was at least three years. The Japanese, with their enormous slave-labour force, were determined to complete it in just 13 months.

Already at Kilo 26, camped on the other side of the creek from Ramsay Force, were two of Fred's and Jack O'Malley's 2/19th mates, Lance Perceval and Roy Constance, who also came from Boorowa. On reaching Java after Singapore's fall, they had been taken prisoner to become part of Black Force. The unexpected meeting was a catalyst for both Fred and Lance to mention, in pro-forma postcards to their families, that they were all together, were well and, in Fred's case, that he was working for 15 cents a day.

Sent via the International Red Cross in Tokyo and then Geneva, it took ten months for the cards to reach Elsie and the Perceval family at their farm at Rugby, just outside Boorowa. The news that their sons and their friends were alive was of such moment that Elsie and the Percevals alerted the local press. Until the card arrived, Elsie had no idea if her husband, classified as 'missing' for 15 months after Singapore's fall, then as 'missing believed prisoner of war' in May 1943, were dead or alive. That he was a prisoner of war was confirmed when his name appeared on the casualty lists, a week or so after the card was delivered, but it took another six weeks for the army to note on his service record that he was 'in Thailand'.

At first sight, the camp at Kilo 26 had looked very promising. However, the former occupants, Burmese labourers, had no concept of hygiene. The kitchen area was filthy and the rickety huts were infested with bed bugs, rats, lice and all manner of creepy crawlies. Moreover, the previous occupants had not built latrines and had defecated where they wished. The only saving grace was a small nearby creek, with just enough water for the POWs to keep themselves clean. Fred, ever the optimist, downplayed the lack of basic hygiene.

> Our camp at Kilo 26 was composed of roomy atap and bamboo huts. Situated on the banks of a small stream, it only needed a tidy up to make it habitable. However, as a foretaste of what was yet to come, when we inspected the creek we found the bodies of three dead Burmese lying in the water. How they had met their death we did not know, but we suspected cholera. However, as the stream was our only source of water, we boiled it, and hoped for the best.
>
> With Christmas in just a few days, we hoped to make our Christmas dinner somewhat different from the usual day-to-day, humdrum rice meals. However, the prospects certainly did not look too bright and our ration of rice and chili water did not give us much encouragement.
>
> Overhearing a conversation on how the Japs were hauling timber out of the jungle, I had what people call a light-bulb moment. However, the feasibility of my idea had yet

to be determined. Confiding my plan to two of my mates, we discussed the scheme and decided that, with a little luck, Christmas Day might not be so bad after all.

From my inadvertent eavesdropping, I had learned that the Japanese were using bullocks to haul timber from the jungle for bridge construction and that each night the animals were yarded in a corral, about a mile from our camp. All we had to do was to steal one. Since two guards were stationed there to look after them, when we set out at midnight on Christmas Eve we had not the slightest idea how this might be achieved. Avoiding the guards patrolling our camp, we reached the edge of the jungle and crept past the Japanese guardhouse on hands and knees, undetected. Once out on the road, taking advantage of all the cover available, it did not take us long to locate the track leading to the corral.

We now had to plan some course of action. After deciding that an approach from the jungle would give us a better chance of a getaway if discovered, we reached the fence just as the guard on duty was being relieved. Lying in the long grass, we awaited our opportunity.

Most of the bullocks were lying down, but a few were wandering around trying to reach the grass just outside the fence. Slipping back into the long grass, I gathered a large armful and threw it over the bamboo fence. There was almost a stampede as the hungry animals surged towards it.

The guards were not interested in what was happening inside the yard as they were more concerned in watching the track down to the road. Posting one man to keep an eye on the guards, two of us began to undo the ropes holding the bamboo fence poles together. Luck seemed to be with us all the way and in no time we had a hole large enough for a bullock to walk through. Noticing that one seemed anxious to make a break, we slipped back into the long grass and waited. Sure enough, out came the hungry animal, right to where we were hiding. As the bullocks were very quiet and could be caught and led anywhere, we had no trouble leading it into the jungle, where we made short work of slaughtering it. That was the easy part. Getting the meat back into the camp under the noses of the guards was quite a different matter.

The bullock must have weighed well over 200 kilograms and, as there were only three of us, we cut it into smaller portions and carried it back to camp in six separate trips. Luck again was with us, and we finished the job just a short half-hour before daybreak.

Our Christmas dinner was now in the hands of the cooks – and what a job they made of it. As the Japs weren't interested in whether we had anything to eat or not, there was no risk that they might just drop by.

After dinner, the whole camp was ordered to search for the missing bullocks. All were recovered but one. Where it had gone everyone knew but the Japanese!

CHAPTER 19

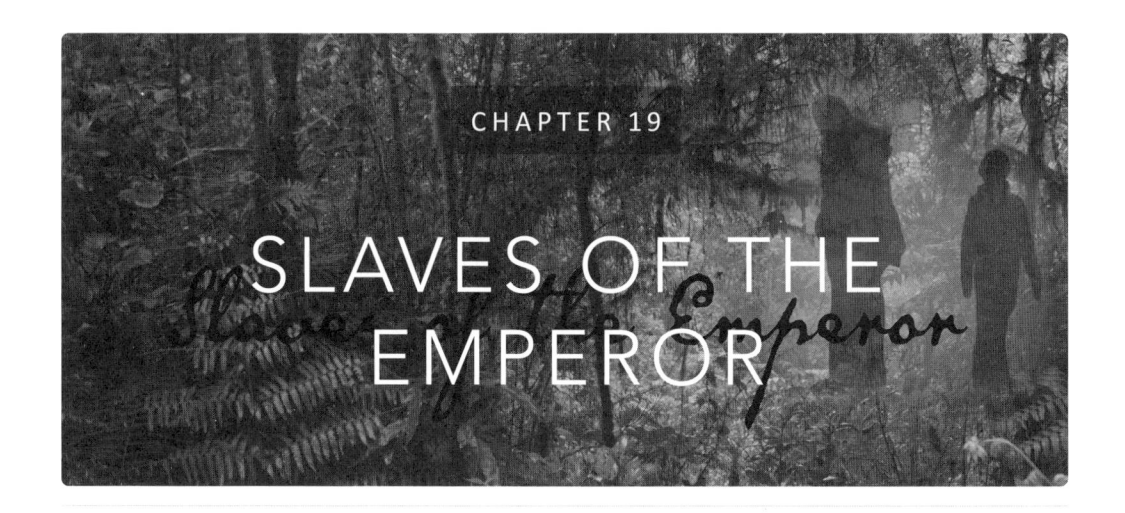

SLAVES OF THE EMPEROR

December 1942 to June 1943

Fred's rude introduction to railway construction had begun on 22 December when the prisoners were issued with picks, shovels and hoes to dig a 100-metre cutting through a hill, which had to be excavated to a depth of more than 10 metres at the centre. The work quota was set at one cubic metre of earth per day per man, working in gangs of ten. However, before they could begin, the entire area had to be cleared of thick scrub.

The prisoners were told that, as soon as the required amount of earth had been removed, work would be over for the day. Not yet a wake up to the wily tactics of the Japanese engineers, the men set to work with a will and were rewarded with most of the afternoon off. They kept up the pace. On Boxing Day, the engineer raised the quota, as they were such good workers.

> Our first task was to dig cuttings through the hills, by hand – picks and shovels to excavate the dirt and rock, and baskets with which to carry it away. Scorching hot days, with perspiration just pouring off our bodies when working, followed at night by bitter cold, was our lot for the next few months. Blankets had by now become the worse for wear, and many were without any.

The day after work began, word filtered through that an Australian at the Kilo 18 camp had been shot dead. The day before, a party of about 40 men had returned to camp minus a guard and Sergeant Ronald O'Donnell, a gunner from Queensland. Just before knock-off time he had gone into the bush about 6 or 7 metres from where he was working in order to defecate. Co-workers noticed that one of the guards, a Korean named Teimoto, was also absent, but thought nothing of it. When it came time to return to the camp, O'Donnell and the guard were still missing. Just after the workers arrived back at the camp, three shots rang out. Shortly afterwards, Teimoto ran into the camp perspiring profusely and in a state of agitation. A search party, which included Colonel Anderson, found O'Donnell's body about 200 metres from the camp. He had been shot three times.

The Japanese commandant claimed Teimoto, known to the prisoners as Peanut, had shot O'Donnell as he was trying to escape and had failed to obey three separate commands to stop. However, Anderson and a medical orderly, who had seen O'Donnell's body, disagreed. O'Donnell had been shot in the chest, not the back, and at quite close range. After he hit the ground, two other bullets had been fired at point blank range into his jaw

A POWs gang digging through a hill.

and chin, shattering the back of his skull. Furthermore, Anderson argued that O'Donnell could not possibly have been attempting to escape as he had left a tin of bully beef and a tin of milk in his hut, along with boots and spare clothing.

At a post-war trial the reason for the killing was not established. However, Teimoto had a known preference for young boys and had tried to befriend some of the younger prisoners by handing out delicacies and showing favouritism. The Australians believed that Teimoto had propositioned O'Donnell and, when he refused, had shot him.

Shockwaves reverberated through the Australian ranks and, with passions running high, Teimoto, now dubbed 'Dillinger', was spirited away to Thanbyuzayat for his own safety. It did no good. Although the Australians were thwarted from any retaliation, a group of Japanese engineers beat him almost to a pulp, more than likely because he was a paedophile, not because he had wilfully murdered a prisoner of war. As the war drew to a close, the Korean, fearful of what might come, tried to ingratiate himself with Australian POWs by claiming that it was his twin brother who had killed O'Donnell.

In Kilo 26 camp, where the prisoners, in common with other Japanese labour camps, had been forced to sign a 'no escape' declaration, the poor rations and overwork were taking effect. By the end of December, four days after O'Donnell's death, the medical officer declared that, of the 1550 men in the camp, 513 were unfit for work. The majority were laid low with dysentery, followed by beriberi, joint and bone injuries, and chest infections.

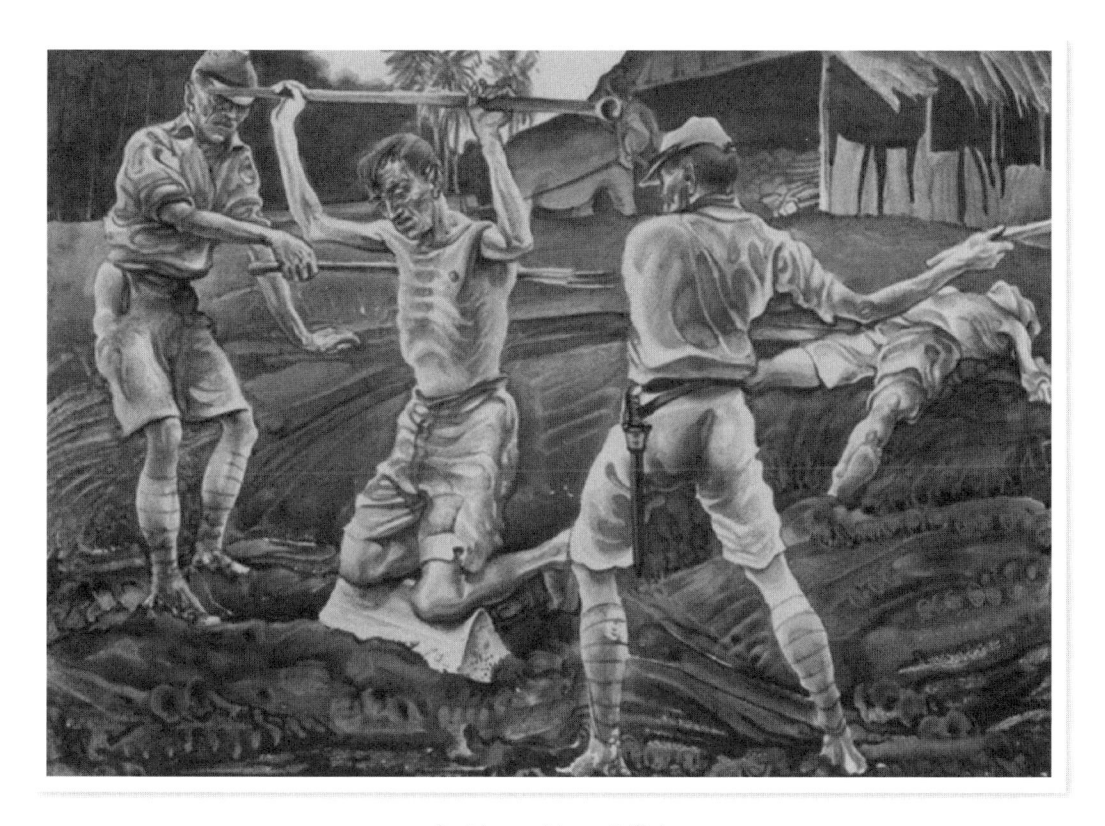

Punishment (Murray Griffin)

Despite this, the Japanese stepped up their demands and the soil quota was raised yet again until it reached 2 cubic metres a day. By mid-January the pace quickened even more, with constant shouts of 'kurrah, kurrah' and 'speedo' from stick-wielding guards, who beat the prisoners unmercifully, often to the point of unconsciousness. Any attempt at interference by Allied NCOs or officers resulted in a severe bashing. The Koreans, glorying in their newly found superiority, used their unaccustomed power to the limit.

The worst of these was Pak Jon Jo, aged 26, a peasant farmer in civilian life, who had previously been at Kilo 14. He had adopted a Japanese name, Arai Koei, but was known to the prisoners as The Boy Bastard. Quite good looking, with remarkably pale skin, and always turned out neatly, he was stocky in stature, powerfully built. and used his physical superiority to brutally beat any prisoner unlucky enough to catch his attention. A sadist, he also delighted in inflicting torture, placing lighted bamboo slivers under fingernails, and forcing POWs to kneel on sharp stones, before jumping on their thighs.

He was aided and abetted by a younger accomplice, Private Kanero, known as The Boy Bastard's Cobber. Always trying to outdo Arai, Kanero had no qualms in joining him at sick parade, removing bandages from ulcerated legs and giving the wounds a hefty kick. The guard commander, Lieutenant Naito, who was in an almost perpetually drunken state, did nothing to curb their excesses. Not content with simply exerting physical punishment, The Boy Bastard repeatedly taunted anyone who dared lift his head from the task at hand with 'You will never see your homeland again. You will work for the Nipponese until you die. This is a one hundred years' war.'

As the cutting grew deeper, it became much more difficult to remove the spoil, despite repeated bashings from the guards. Inevitably, the day came when the demands became too great. The Boy Bastard's wrath notwithstanding, the Australians went on strike.

They had reached the required level for the day when one of the engineers demanded that they continue working and remove another 5 centimetres. Exhausted by the day's exertions, the working party refused. The engineer, who became very agitated, began abusing the 2/18th's Lieutenant Ian McDonald, the officer in charge of the workers that day. Rallying to his aid, the strikers encircled McDonald and the engineer. Sensing trouble, the latter called for the guards, who arrived with fixed bayonets.

McDonald, who narrowly escaped being run through by one over-enthusiastic guard, was escorted back to camp where he was ordered to march into the scrub, turn to face the guard and close his eyes. Expecting the worst, he was relieved when the guard lowered his rifle and ordered him to return to camp, where he was put in the guardhouse and given a hiding. However, McDonald had the last laugh. When Ramsay complained to the Japanese warrant officer in charge, he released McDonald and gave the guard a good hiding.

When they reached a new section to be excavated, the prisoners were sometimes able to cut down on their workload by moving the pegs placed in the ground by the engineers to delineate the area allotted for the day's task. They then began digging at a much slower rate, to ensure that they did not finish too early. They managed to move the pegs for a period of six weeks. When the engineers realised that they had been duped, it resulted in the inevitable bashing for the ringleader. The others, forced out to work in the dark to make up for lost time, went cheerfully to their labour, singing at the tops of their voices.

The basic ration at this time consisted of 350 grams of rice per man per day, split into three meals: one flavoured with a thin, soup-like yak stew and the other two with an almost tasteless winter melon soup. The yaks (one small, emaciated beast per 600 men) were often in such a poor state that they had virtually no meat on them. However, despite their hunger pangs, the Australians did not follow the lead of equally ravenous Dutch prisoners, who eagerly snapped up the entrails, for which they were derogatorily referred to as 'Offal Eaters'. Before long, the lack of protein and vitamins, combined with hard manual labour, added malnutrition and tropical ulcers to the growing list of complaints.

> Footwear could not stand up to the rough usage and each day saw a new recruit in the barefooted brigade. The loss of boots and the failure to replace them was the cause of hundreds of tropical ulcers forming on the feet and legs of the prisoners.
>
> Never have I seen anything in Australia, which could be compared to a tropical ulcer. The beginning is a small festering sore, which rapidly spreads and deepens if not given the proper treatment, until the muscle is eaten away, exposing tendons and the bones, and causing the victim untold agony.
>
> Our medical supplies were practically non-existent – the Japs would not, or could not, give us any. The only treatment available for treating ulcers was known as gouging, followed by a saline dressing. The gouging was done with a small spoon, cutting away all the dead flesh and removing any accumulation of pus. The pain was agonising.
>
> One case left an indelible mark on my memory. The patient was only a boy, no more than 18 and who, up till now, had led a reasonably sheltered existence. He had a very bad ulcer behind his knee and was admitted to hospital. On his first morning he witnessed the gouging operation carried out on patients near him. Having recovered

from a slight attack of malaria, I was helping to feed the sick. With a look of horror in his eyes, he turned to me and said, 'I could never stand that!' I assured him that he would and could and he implored me to stay with him, when his turn came. He was a shivering wreck by the time the doctor reached him. Great beads of perspiration stood out on his forehead and the look in his eyes was that of a frightened child.

Taking his hands in mine, I held him. Great shuddering ripples coursed through his body, his teeth were clenched tight, and his eyes tightly shut as the doctor commenced the operation. But not a sound escaped his lips till the doctor told him the operation was finished. Even then it was only a great sigh of relief and a relaxing of his taut muscles as his grip on my hands slowly lessened. He opened his eyes. Gone was the haunted look – only a look of relief – and then a fervent, 'Thank God!'.

He then confided that at school the other children had always treated him as a coward, and in time he began to think that he really was. He thought that when he had to undergo any pain he would show his yellow streak, as he called it. His loss of faith in himself made him fearful of being seen as a coward. He had now proved he wasn't and, in so doing, had regained his self-respect, and that of others.

I saw hardened men yell for mercy when undergoing the same treatment, or during roll call, when the guards deliberately aimed their blows or kicks at a bandage, knowing it to cover some hideous sore. When the poor tortured wretch screamed in agony they shouted with laughter, at the same time training their machine guns on the rest of us, daring us to do anything about it. We were helpless to take any action but lived in hope that one day the tables would be turned.

Malaria was now making an appearance, adding to our many discomforts. Quinine was available, but later even this was denied us and cerebral malaria took its toll of lives, together with the other diseases we encountered.

By the end of January, many prisoners were so ill that the work parties did not have enough fit men to fill the demand each day. The medical officers did their best but, without medicine of any kind, the only thing they had to help counter dysentery and diarrhoea was charcoal. This and Condey's crystals were all they had in the way of medical supplies.

Those too sick to work were transferred to the POW hospital at Thanbyuzayat. Chris Guerin, suffering from beriberi, dysentery and 'happy feet' (an ailment caused by vitamin deficiency), arrived there in early March to discover that there had been an air raid by Allied planes on 1 March, the anniversary of the sinking of USS *Houston* and HMAS *Perth*. A pathfinder plane preceded the attack, dropping flares at various intervals and turning day into night. The Japanese, severely rattled, took to the trenches, warning that any POW who left the huts would be shot. One stick of bombs landed about 1.5 kilometres from the hospital, but no prisoners were injured, apart from a gunner who was pricked in the buttocks by a fear-crazed guard. While Chris was hospitalised, six Dutch prisoners attempted to escape with the inevitable results.

Back at Kilo 26, the good news was that Ramsay Force now had a radio. Black Force, whose members had managed to spirit radio parts into Burma from Java, had constructed a receiver. However, shortly after Ramsay Force had joined them, a search by the Japanese, convinced that news from the outside world was being received, found it hidden in the seat of a stool on which the guards often sat.

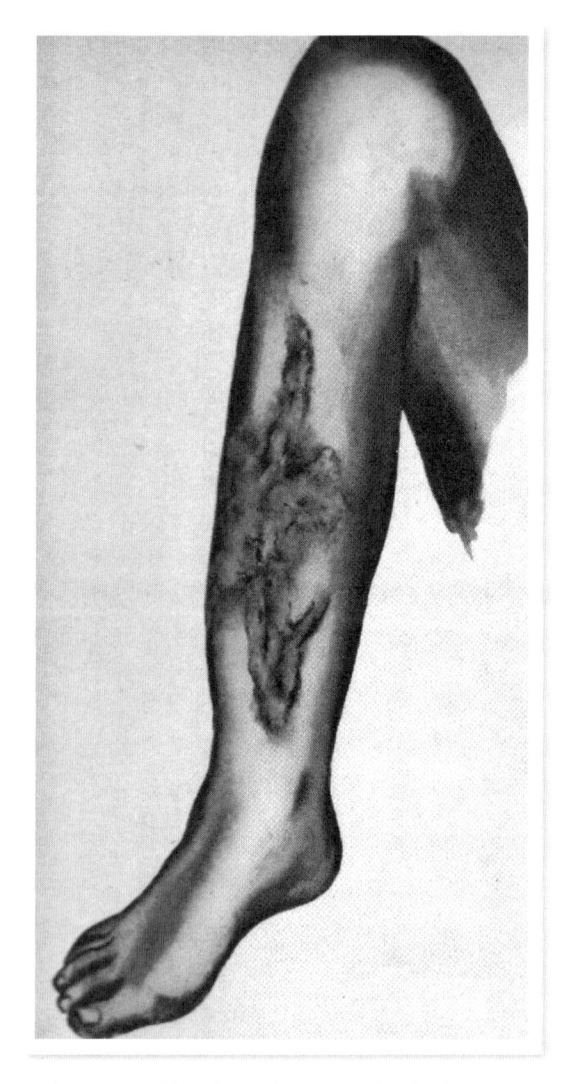

Above: A typical leg ulcer. Below: Hospital at Thanbyuzayat.

The new set was built by one of Fred's contemporaries, Signal Sergeant Les Hall, of 2/30 Battalion. Mindful that discovery could be given away by the slip of a tongue, Colonel Ramsay had given an address to the men on Christmas Eve in which he referred to a little bird that had visited the camp but could no longer be heard singing. The bird, a nightingale, was very timid and any attempt by anyone to locate its new nest might result in it ceasing to sing completely. They should also remember that there was another bird whose song could be confused with the nightingale, a lyrebird, who could mimic anything, and if anyone was in any doubt about which call was which, he should ask his senior officer, who would put him right. He also alluded to another tune that might be heard should anyone fail to heed his words: the Last Post.

Japanese engineers supervising the construction of one of the one of the hundreds of small bridges.

Construction of a larger bridge.

On March 18, with the cutting completed, Fred and the rest of the labour force left Kilo 26 Camp and proceeded south to the 75 Kilo mark at Meiloe. Twelve days after they left Kilo 26, members of Anderson and Williams' Forces, known as 1 Mobile Labour Force, moved in to begin laying the rails. Meanwhile, Fred's group was put to work at the new camp constructing bridges.

Although there were decomposed bodies of Asian cholera victims lying about, the accommodation was a pleasant surprise after Kilo 26, with sleeping platforms made from more comfortable flattened giant bamboo, instead of thin bamboo rods that bit into the skin. However, as Green Force had now joined them, it was very crowded, necessitating the construction of double tiered bunks in each hut. Nevertheless, the POWs were pleased to see that there was a good-sized river nearby, approximately 17 metres wide, in which they could swim but, as the camp was much further into the interior, canteen supplies were poor and prices had gone up.

The camp itself may have been better, but the work was gruelling. Before bridge construction could commence, the prisoners had to cut the timber and haul the logs to the site, where they were hand-trimmed in preparation for pile driving. This was accomplished by the erection of a huge bamboo frame around pre-dug holes, into which the log was tipped upright and then hit with a manually driven pile driver. The work of hauling on the multiple ropes by teams of POWs until the driver was about 3 metres above the head of the log, and then dropping it, was both hard and monotonous work. However, instead of chanting one, two, three, four in Japanese, as ordered, the workers created their own colourful chant, in the distinctly Australian idiom.

Bridge construction (Murray Griffin)

Above: Pile driving 1943 (sketch by Major Robertson).
Below: Rickety bamboo scaffolding.

About 24 piles were driven by the end of each shift, leaving those assigned to this task sapped of energy. Many, in their weakened state, fell from the rickety platform, resulting in numerous injuries. Meanwhile, the earthmoving teams were now shifting 1.7 metres per man per day but, after a visit from a Japanese general, the workload was increased to 2 metres with the promise that, if the railway was not finished on time, 'all mans' would have a very long rest.

Undeterred by this threat, the Australians staged a go-slow, beginning with a sit-down strike. Consequently, at knock-off time, only half the day's quota had been met. Demanding an explanation, the engineers were informed that the men were too weakened by lack of food, hard work and long hours to keep up the pace. However, the demand to allow them to return to camp was dismissed out of hand with a 'Many mans will collect bamboo, light fires and work until they have finished their 2 metres of earth removal'.

In what was amounting to a battle of wits, the Australians typically took advantage of the situation, using the darkness to down tools when they could and committing acts of sabotage. Many workers also snuck off into the jungle to rest while a skeleton crew toiled away to keep up the pretence. The punishments for loafing invariably involved a hiding with a bamboo stick but, with the hours of work extending from 8.30 am until 3 or 4 am the next day, the beatings were considered a reasonable price to pay for the luxury of a short rest.

The go-slow went on for two weeks. At the end of a fortnight, the Japanese could not understand why less work had been completed per shift, against the former 1.7 metre quota.

It was not just the earthmovers who were now working by night. The bridge building continued after dark with the aid of a power plant and hand-cranked generator, but the light it created was far too bright to allow anyone to sneak into the jungle for respite. However, if the POWs thought things were bad, Fred recorded that they were about to become a good deal worse.

> In April, increasing showers indicated that our first wet season was about to commence. We were now through Death Valley and working up towards the Three Pagodas Pass.
>
> The Japanese had instituted day and night shifts – the night shift extending well into the day and the day shift well into the night. This was known along the line as the Speedo. It seemed the Japs were determined to finish the line as per schedule, oblivious to the fact that the poor food and lack of sleep was slowly and surely killing the workers.
>
> By this time our clothes had ceased to be serviceable, and we were forced to improvise with whatever material we could find. No clothing at all was forthcoming from the Japs.
>
> Our wardrobe consisted of a very abbreviated G-string. We did not worry, as there was no one to see us but ourselves – and it did solve the problem of washing day! One could wash it at night, hang it up to dry, and have clean clothes to start the next day. Some of the models were certainly a work of art, although the wearers would undoubtedly have found themselves confined to barracks under any other circumstances.

With the Japanese determined to complete the railway on schedule, The Boy Bastard and his equally sadistic mate, The Boy Bastard's Cobber, did not let up on their brutal treatment. They were allowed to do whatever was necessary to get the work done, without any interference from the camp commandant, Lieutenant Hoshi Aiki, aged 48, a rather plump former schoolteacher. Showing total indifference to the welfare of the prisoners supposedly in his care, he permitted unfit men to be sent out to work and also sanctioned Naito's ruling that 'your sick shall starve until they die or go back to work. Any sick prisoner who can make it to work shall not die in vain, even if he has laid only one sleeper. No work, no food'.

As a result of the unrelenting workload and paucity of rations, the illness rate soared. Throughout April, camp commanders and medical officers did their best to transfer the sick to the hospital camp at Thanbyuzayat, where medical treatment was far better than at the work camps, before the monsoon rains made the tracks impassable. The hospital became so overcrowded that a new one, known as Reptu, with the drunken Lieutenant Naito in charge, was opened at Kilo 30, but by the beginning of May it too was filled to overflowing. With the size of the labour force steadily dropping, the Japanese began exerting pressure to discharge the patients and get them back to work, with often fatal results. There was no compassion for those who fell ill: sickness was no excuse for not working and those too ill to do hard labour were required to undertake other chores.

Food, as usual, was a problem, made even more so by the fact that Lieutenant Hoshi and his men took far more than their fair share. Hoshi also appropriated rations intended for the prisoners and sold them on the black market. However, as Fred noted, enterprising POWs found ways and means to supplement their diet, and to get their own back on the hated commandant.

> The Nip officer-in-charge of prisoners at 75 Kilo camp had a private fowl yard. When we first went there it contained about 50 fowls. These started to disappear in ones and twos until only 30 remained.
>
> The Nip decided to set a trap to catch the thief. Loading a rifle, he tied a string from the trigger to the door of the fowl yard in such a way that anyone opening the door would discharge the rifle and would be lucky to escape the bullet. Everything worked perfectly, but the Nip did not allow for one Korean guard who, when anything of this nature was to happen, always came to us and warned us.
>
> The gun was discharged all right! The Japs hurried out to hear someone rushing into the jungle. They immediately gave chase but were not successful in overtaking their quarry. But, when they arrived back and took stock, four more hens were missing.
>
> They also had a number of young pigs, over which a guard was placed day and night. One of the guards was a most timid type. In the early hours one morning, when the most unearthly noise began to sound in the jungle, he immediately took to his heels and fled, leaving his charges to the mercy of an Australian prisoner who, having created a noise like a screeching violin with a jam tin and string covered in resin, now took full advantage of the unprotected pigs. We who heard the noise were no less startled than the unfortunate Jap. The pig, along with the story, turned up in the kitchen next morning.

On 25 April, ANZAC Day, the Australians were permitted to hold a Dawn Service. Just before daybreak, they assembled on the roadway and marched a short distance to a large wooden cross, erected for the occasion. As the first light of the day began to streak the sky in the east, they laid a small wreath of jungle flowers and ferns, not to simply remember

POWs on the move (Murray Griffin)

the dead of the Great War, but to honour their mates, who lay buried under crude little crosses all along the line.

Towards the end of April, Fred's mate Chris Guerin made an unexpected reappearance. After spending six weeks in hospital, he was pronounced fit enough to return to work but, on reaching Kilo 26 by truck, found the camp deserted. Undeterred, he marched to Kilo 28 camp, where he worked for a few days, disowned by everybody, before moving on. Passing through 35, 38, 40 and 60 Kilo camps, he kept going through the night to Kilo 75, where he finally found Fred, and Ramsay Force.

In late April, Burmese labourers and their families also arrived at Kilo 75 to supplement the labour force. They too were weak and thin and suffering from various illnesses but, as they had no doctor with them, they either recovered or died. More often than not they did not pull through and it was not uncommon to find seven or eight bodies a day lying between the huts. As a precaution, the Japanese inoculated all POWs against cholera.

On around 6 May the work pace was again stepped up. The POWs, after marching 6–7 kilometres to the work site, slaved from 9 am one day until 4 am the next. The 'light duty' POWs, previously working for 3–4 hours a day, now toiled from 9 am to 8 pm. This punishing schedule lasted for a week, until 13 May, when the monsoon broke and orders were issued to relocate.

At about 9 pm that evening, Fred and about 1300 men were on the move again, this time on foot, to Aungganaung Camp at the 105 kilo mark, 30 kilometres away along the proposed rail line However, by road, the route taken by the prisoners, it was 42 kilometres. All gear had to be carried, as transport was available for only the seriously ill. With an occasional fleeting moon to light the way, it was a nightmare journey. Few prisoners had footwear of any kind, resulting in frequent falls on the treacherously slippery track and rocks. Some, losing their balance, slithered down embankments, resulting in an exhausting climb back to the track, grabbing onto thorny bushes and sharp rocks, to rejoin the column.

Bringing up the rear was The Boy Bastard who, when not using his bamboo stick to hurry things along, amused himself by firing repeatedly over the prisoners' heads. At Kilo 90 they were allowed to stop to rest, and slept where they fell. One POW, tired beyond belief but unable to sleep, heard a noise and looked up to see a herd of elephants emerging from the jungle. Before he could shout a warning, the lead elephant lifted her trunk and, followed by the rest of the herd, picked her way carefully through the prostrate bodies.

The respite, however, was brief: decomposing corpses of Burmese workers were found in a hut. To the shouts of 'cholera camp', the men were forced to their feet and ordered to keep going, but not before a few had drunk from the contaminated stream. Almost all were now on their last legs, and some began discarding their gear to lighten the load.

There was no let up by The Boy Bastard and, as a result, an estimated 20 to 30 prisoners died along the way. Sapper Rawlinson, suffering from severe dysentery, was forced to walk and, although he was carried a considerable distance, died about six weeks later. It was estimated that about 30 per cent of the prisoners who reached 105 Camp perished over the next six months.

> Our move to 105 Kilo took us further into the jungle, where we encountered cholera for the first time. The first to go was Private Fred Washington, who became ill on 25 May and died on the 27th, just five days after our arrival. This disease is just about

the quickest killer there is. Strong healthy men succumb in a few hours after the first symptoms appear. When this disease broke out, the terror-struck natives left everything they possessed behind and fled.

This course of action was not open to us, no matter how much we wished it to be so. We could wake up in the morning to find that the man sleeping alongside had died during the night from this dread disease. I always credit my escaping it to the fact that at all times I drank nothing but boiled water, which was still reasonably hot, and that I always sterilised my eating utensils before use.

The huts at 105 Kilo were made from the usual bamboo and atap, with two-tier bunks. The Asian workers who had occupied the site had moved out some weeks before, allowing the jungle to invade the camp and creep into the buildings. Gaping holes in the thatched roofs allowed rainwater to enter at will. However, once repairs were effected, the situation improved considerably, although the men on the upper bunks were not quite as comfortable as those on the lower.

Ironically, although it poured with rain, the camp had no permanent water supply – it was a case of water, water everywhere but not a drop to drink. POWs were detailed to go to a depot at Kilo 98, where they filled 44-gallon drums with water from the river and then transported the load by lorry to Kilo 105, where 'light sick' prisoners transferred it to the camp by passing buckets from hand to hand in a continuous chain. As the rain continued, the water detail spent a great deal of time trying to extricate the vehicle from the morass that was the road.

Over the next few days, Fred's group was joined by a number of the sick, also force marched from Kilo 75 Camp, bringing the total number of POWs at Kilo 105 to 1930. With Lieutenant Hoshi still in charge, there was no let-up in the beatings, and ill prisoners

A typical hut in disrepair.

were made to stand at attention in front of the guardhouse for up to 72 hours for the most minor of offences. If they fainted, they were revived with a bucket of water, the ordeal continuing until they finally collapsed, totally unconscious.

> It was at this camp that I had my first personal experience of Japanese torture. I had been subjected to numerous kicks, smacks and such like before, but this was my first real encounter with their fiendish cruelty. I suppose I was partially to blame.
>
> We were going out on a working party and, as we passed the Japanese guardhouse, a guard amused himself by spitting on as many prisoners as possible as we went by. He certainly did not suffer from parched throat. My turn came and when I received his charge fair in my face, something seemed to snap in my brain and, before I realised what I was doing, the guard was out cold, lying yards away, where my punch had lifted him. As punishment, I was tied with barbed wire to a tree in front of their guardhouse. As each of the 20 guards walked by, they ground their lighted cigarettes into my bare arms and back as additional punishment. However, the physical pain was nothing compared to the mental agony, especially as the contempt I felt had no outlet.
>
> When I was finally released after three days, my legs failed to support my body. I wanted revenge but the saner reasoning of my comrades convinced me that retaliation was useless and would and could only end in more torture and perhaps death. To add insult to injury, my tormentors sent me food and cigarettes, undoubtedly stolen from our own store. The reason why they did this, only they knew.

With the onset of the monsoon on 22 May, the day Fred arrived at 105 Camp, torrential, non-stop rain had put a temporary end to night-time construction, but not to work. The prisoners, clad in G-strings, their skin stung by driving rain, worked a 12-hour shift for ten days, and then had a day off. Tasks included cutting timber for railway sleepers and firewood, clearing the jungle to build a six-kilometre road and quarrying rock for ballast for the railway. As the quarrymen gouged out the rock face with picks, sharp fragments peppered their legs, creating small wounds that soon became ulcerated. Within a few days, the daily quota for earth removal increased from 2 cubic metres to 2.8, not of earth but of mud. With the constant wet weather, and the relentless workload, some prisoners, along with the earthworks, collapsed under the strain, only to be kicked to their feet again, if at all.

The work was backbreaking, food was scarcer than ever and disease was rife. As the rain converted tiny watercourses into raging torrents, the men struggled to keep a footing as they dug into the hillsides to meet a quota that had been raised, yet again, to 3.2 cubic metres. The relentless rain had made the road to their worksite impassable, resulting in no rations, so, aided by elephants, the 'unfit' were compelled to corduroy the roadway with logs cut from the jungle, the fit being required for railway duty. When the engineer realised that the elephants were doing all the heavy lifting, orders were given for the POWs to do their share – three men to each log.

On the last day of May, a large number of front-line Japanese troops passed through Kilo 105. They had no motor transport, which would have become bogged in any case, and were loaded down with gear, apart from the officers, who had piled theirs in handcarts pushed by their underlings. Some of the rank and file were also hauling what appeared to be a heavy, old-style mountain gun. Straining under the load, one of the soldiers

Elephant at work

collapsed. An officer approached, not to assist him, as the watching POWs anticipated, but to grind his head into the mud with a boot, followed by a hefty kick to the ribs to force him to his feet.

By the end of that week, rations had dropped to their lowest level, and the death toll began to rise, with hundreds of POWs, suffering from malnutrition or illness, lying on their bed spaces, unable to move or fend for themselves. Those unable to work were on half rations, which was a moot point for, as one POW quipped, 'What is half of nothing?' Desperate to find some sustenance for their ill mates, some of the fitter men went on foraging expeditions seeking frogs and, if lucky, snakes. They also gathered grass and bamboo shoots, which they boiled – anything that might provide bulk, if not nourishment. However, as the days passed the Last Post sounded with more frequency and the cemetery grew in size.

On 11 June, the 500 fittest were sent back to the dump at Kilo 98 to collect 38 bags of rice, a march by road of some 18 kilometres. On the return journey, pushing through the slush with the weight of the bags increasing by the hour from the rain, each kilometre felt like ten. Fortunately, they did not have to contend with air raids, which, at Thanbyuzayat, killed two British and four Dutch prisoners and injured 30 more, including Brigadier Varley.

At the height of the crisis at Kilo 105, a large group of Australian and British POWs from Singapore transited through the camp on their way further north. They were from F and H Forces, a combined labour force of 10,000, which, in April and May, had been sent to complete sections of the line that had been left until last because of the difficulty of construction. After an appalling 1700-kilometre rail journey from Singapore, crammed into steel rice trucks, they alighted at Bampong to discover that their first destination was up near the Burmese border at Konkoita, 280 kilometres away. As there was no transport, they had to make the journey on foot, carrying their gear with them. Cholera, malaria, starvation and disease ravaged the workforce as they moved further and further north. Conditions were such that even the most deprived of the prisoners sent to Burma and Thailand conceded that the experiences of F and H Forces were by far the worst.

At Kilo 105, the rain continued to sheet down throughout the month of June, streaming through the sleeping and hospital huts and churning the bare earth floor to a quagmire. With the roofs leaking like sieves, it was impossible to find a dry spot for the night. Despite their ill health, work parties toiled in the rain from dawn until dusk. The primary task now was to make ballast for the rail bed, which was no longer a pick and shovel task, but necessitated the use of heavy sledgehammers. While quarrying the rock was bad enough, hauling it to the site was even worse. The only way to move the ballast was coolie-style, piled on rice bags threaded on two poles. Once the sacks were sufficiently loaded, they had to be carried through knee-deep mud for about a kilometre. With a minimum quota set per day, the workers covered more than 20 kilometres in a single shift. Slacking was not tolerated and, to make sure no one tried anything on, a new punishment was introduced, should any prisoner incur the wrath of a guard – standing on a round stone holding a heavy rock over his head. Driver Donald Stuart was subjected to this punishment for two days and two nights.

CHAPTER 20
AT WHAT COST?

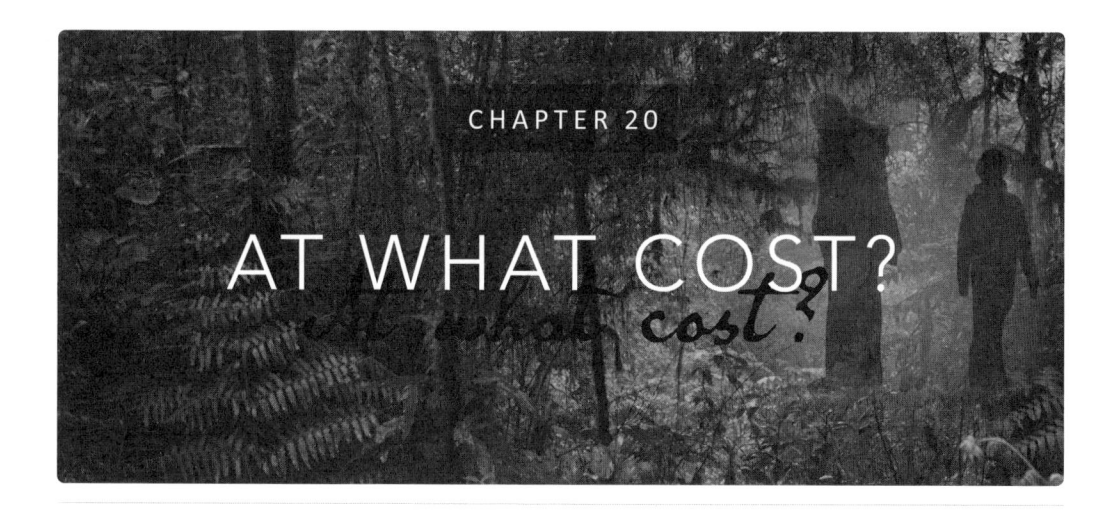

June 1943 to January 1944

By the end of June, there was scarcely a man in the camp who did not have an ulcer, described by POW Tom Fagan as 'horrible, messy-looking things, alive with maggots and yellow, smelly pus leaking away from them. Very few have any kind of bandage. Some gather leaves and pack them in. They don't help much but at least the ulcers are covered a bit. The pain is maddening. It rips the strength from one's body and you feel wrung out.'

Hoshi did nothing to alleviate the situation. In fact, he made it worse. He continued to keep the best rations for himself and his men, including palm oil for cooking, sugar and salt, and refused to obtain supplies to stock a canteen. He had light duty prisoners sign for a full day's pay and gave them half, pocketing the remainder. On one occasion, he sold Colonel Ramsay a bag of salt for 200 rupees, salt that the cooks were certain was the POWs' entitlement as they had not had any for weeks. Hoshi also continued to withhold clothing and footwear and sold medical supplies intended for the sick. By the time he had finished taking what he wanted, a month's medical supplies for 2000 men were reduced to two small bandages plus some Epsom salts, Condy's crystals and iodine.

At the camp, ulcers were treated with hot water packs, Condy's crystals and a knife. One Australian prisoner, suffering with a bad ulcer, agreed to trade his valuable wristwatch in return for a jar of sulphanilamide. The acquisitive Hoshi got his watch. The POW, having handed over his most valuable asset, received just half a jar of ointment. Ignoring their pitiful plight, Hoshi told the prisoners that the railway work must continue unabated 'even over their dead bodies'.

The situation had now reached a critical stage and, with so few men able to work, Colonel Nagatomo was called in by Brigadier Varley to assess the situation, but only in relation to the 'alleged' injured. He was not concerned with 'sick mans' who could be carried to the quarry to break up rocks, the only concession being the issue of light hammers.

The Colonel approached the long line of walking ulcer patients, with their suppurating flesh eaten away to expose their bones, then entered a hut to see the bedridden dysentery and ulcer patients. The stench was overpowering. After a cursory look, a very green-looking Nagatomo announced that all dysentery and ulcer patients, numbering 800, would be transferred to the 'new, well supplied' Kohn Kahn POW hospital at Kilo 55. Accompanied by Brigadier Varley, he then paid a visit to Bertie Coates, who was at Kilo 75 attending the sick. Coates himself was ill, struck down with a severe case of scrub typhus. After agreeing to be the Chief Medical Officer at the new hospital, he was transferred there some days later on a stretcher, as he was still too weak to get about himself.

Coates' 'hospital' was a series of bamboo and atap huts with bamboo sleeping platforms, formerly used to accommodate railway construction workers. It was in stark contrast to the fully equipped and well-supplied Japanese hospital nearby. A small lean-to hut, with an atap roof, dirt floor and bamboo table, attached to the end of the ulcer ward, served as his operating theatre. Here Coates would perform 110 amputations on his ulcer patients, of whom approximately 40 would survive. The remainder died from gangrene, loss of blood or the added complications of dysentery or malaria.

There were no bathing facilities for dysentery patients and no bedpans. The orderlies scrounged old tin cans, mess cans, half coconut shells and pieces of bamboo for the latter, and made do with large leaves for toilet paper, but there was nothing they could do about the lack of bathing facilities. There was no medical equipment and, as the emergency surgical kit was at Thanbyuzayat with Dr Hamilton, A Force's most senior doctor, Coates' instruments consisted of a scalpel and artery forceps he had brought with him from Sumatra; sharpened kitchen knives; a wood saw that Chris Guerin appropriated from a work party for amputations; bent forks to serve as retractors; a few darning needles, and a curette. Provided as a joke by the Japanese, Coates used it to scrape out ulcers.

There was also a spinal needle to administer local anaesthetic, reserved for cases where general anaesthesia was usually the norm. Using cocaine tablets given to Coates in Tavoy by Australian dentist Captain Stewart Simpson, Captain Von Boxtel, a Dutch chemist, had perfected a dilute solution that could be injected into the spine as an anaesthetic. He was also able to make use of novocaine, later supplied by the Japanese. For minor cases, such as amputation of a gangrenous toe or scraping out an ulcer, the patient was held down by three strong men.

Coates' share of the quinine brought from Changi had long since gone. Apart from

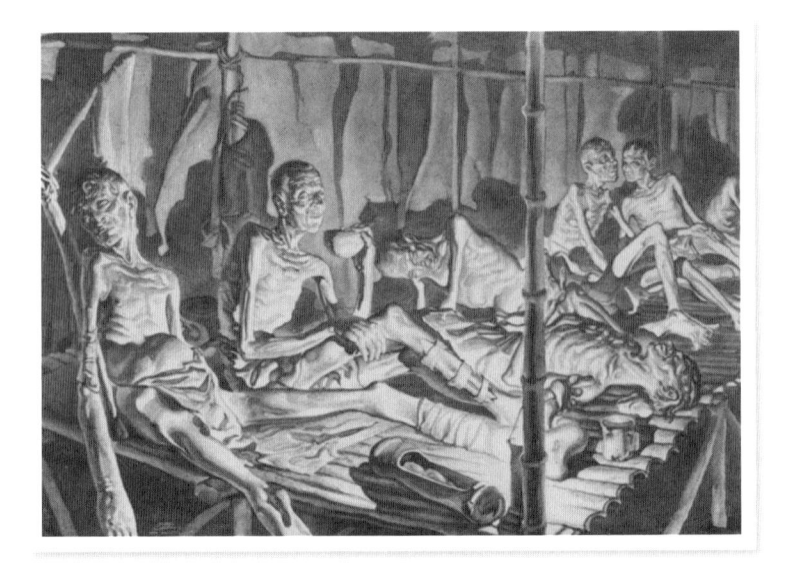

Typical hospital ward (Murray Griffin)

a small quantity of supplies provided by individual POWs, some iodine, and six two-inch bandages supplied on one occasion by the Japanese, everything else was scrounged. Bandages, recycled time and time again, were made from rags and strips torn from the bottom of mosquito nets. Dried gut, from the yaks killed to make stew, was soaked in iodine and used for sutures. To help counter fatal dehydration in cholera cases, a saline drip, using a water bottle filled with distilled water to which bicarbonate of soda had been added, was intravenously administered.

Of the 2400 hospital patients finally admitted to Kilo 55, 800 were suffering from ulcers and were packed three deep in the ulcer ward. As the only proper treatment was iodoform, which the Japanese did not provide for weeks, and then only in a quantity so small to be virtually useless, many substitutes were tried – Condy's crystals, eusol and lysol (disinfectants), saline solution, raw salt, hot poultices, an axle-grease-based ointment, and maggots. When one horrified patient looked with revulsion at his fly-blown wound, Coates assured him that the maggots only ate diseased flesh. When all else failed, offending limbs were amputated. Those with strong stomachs were welcome to watch, with Coates providing a running commentary.

As the new hospital camp was comprised of non-workers, everyone admitted was on half-rations. To make sure that prisoners received no more food than necessary, the Japanese weighed everyone each week and then issued rations in proportion to the combined weight. It was a vicious cycle. The less the patients weighed, the less food they received; the less they ate, the lighter they became.

Back at Kilo 105, the ration was 300–500 grams of rice a day, supplemented by a meagre amount of unidentifiable green stuff, euphemistically referred to as vegetables. As the POWs had not been paid for two months, no extra food could be purchased and the effect of the lack of vitamins had become evident.

> The rains had now set in properly and the camp area and the roads were soon feet deep in mud. Through this we had to trudge up to 10 kilometres to get our food supplies. Our days and nights were occupied pulling out the bogged and helpless trucks, repairing the roads and procuring timber to use to corduroy them. We were lucky to get four hours sleep in 24. Many men became so exhausted from overwork and lack of food they did not recover. Others literally starved to death, when they found it impossible to force any food down their pellagra-swollen throats. Not the quick, merciful death of cholera, but the slow, horrible death of starvation.
>
> We suffered greatly with beriberi. Swollen ankles and feet were the first symptoms. A finger pressed into the affected flesh left a depression that lasted for some time and stiffened muscles made walking difficult. As the disease took hold, different parts of the body swelled to four times the normal size and death was the inevitable result. Men suffering from beriberi were forced out to work, to save those who were weaker than they from the excesses of the guards.

Pellagra was due to a lack of niacin, or vitamin B3, in the diet. Untreated, it resulted in vomiting and nausea, pus-filled sores, crusty itchy skin and an inability to eat or drink. It usually went hand in hand with beriberi, caused by thiamin or vitamin B1 deficiency. Just one teaspoon of Marmite or Vegemite, the yeast extract so loved by Australians and rich in vitamin B1, B2, B3 and B9, would have been sufficient to keep both pellagra and beriberi at bay. Red Cross parcels sent from Australia contained more than enough Vegemite to counter the debilitating effects of the totally inadequate rice-based diet, but tragically few parcels ever reached the prisoners of war.

All along the line, men were suffering, but the most feared disease of all was still cholera. At the first sign of it, the trade-plying Burmese, who followed the POWs from camp to camp, disappeared at the speed of light. In their haste they left behind their yaks and their carts. The Australians could not possibly allow such a golden opportunity to pass them by and soon a black market flourished on two fronts – meat, and wood from the dismantled carts.

The Japanese, terrified of cholera, administered a second injection to the workforce, not for the prisoners' benefit but to protect themselves. Four of the eight Australians in Fred's camp who contracted cholera died but, amazingly, most of the 126 deaths between 8 July and 13 September were from dysentery or amputations of limbs to prevent the spread of tropical ulcers. At the Kilo 55 hospital, using his scalpel and borrowed wood saw, Coates carried out four or five amputations a day, although still recovering from his own illness, which had left him so weak that, for the first two weeks of his appointment, he had been carried from one patient to the next on a stretcher. Fred was among the many who regarded Coates with awe.

> How Colonel Coates did the job with the equipment available is a story in itself. As many as 17 operations in one day – how this man worked! His devotion to duty is worthy of the highest recognition. It was inevitable that the shock was too great for many men in their weakened condition, but it gave them a chance to beat the spreading gangrene that was slowly eating away their lives and they would certainly have died in the end, anyhow. Many of these men operated upon returned home, minus a limb certainly, but still able to enjoy life.

It was during this period that Fred was admitted to hospital, suffering from severe debility. While he was recovering, he witnessed at first hand the work of the much admired Bertie Coates. Chris Guerin had also been hospitalised, so, on 12 September, the pair decided to find out how long it took for Coates to perform an amputation on fellow 2/19th member Donny Reay, admitted with a tropical ulcer that had eaten away the lower part of his left leg. It took just seven minutes. Coates then removed Donny's foreskin, which he declared was 'a bonus'.

Bertie Coates had also saved the lives of many men suffering with amoebic dysentery, which, if unable to be treated with a drug known as emetine, resulted in ulceration and perforation of the large bowel or colon, which in turn resulted in peritonitis. Death was inevitable, unless a surgeon could perform an ileostomy to divert the contents of the lower ileum, the small bowel, to the outside of the body, allowing the colon to repair itself. That surgeon was Coates, who had pioneered the procedure in Melbourne in 1938. However, it had never been used on patients stricken with amoebic dysentery. His first case was at Tavoy, where Dutch doctors asked him to perform an operation on a prisoner, who would die of peritonitis without surgical intervention.

If the Japanese were to grant permission for Coates to use the Tavoy town hospital, five kilometres away over rough tracks, the patient must return to the compound immediately after surgery. As two other patients had not survived the transfer, Coates decided to operate at the camp, and in secret. Using the anaesthetic solution pioneered by Boxtel for the occasion, he successfully carried out the operation. To collect the diverted contents of the

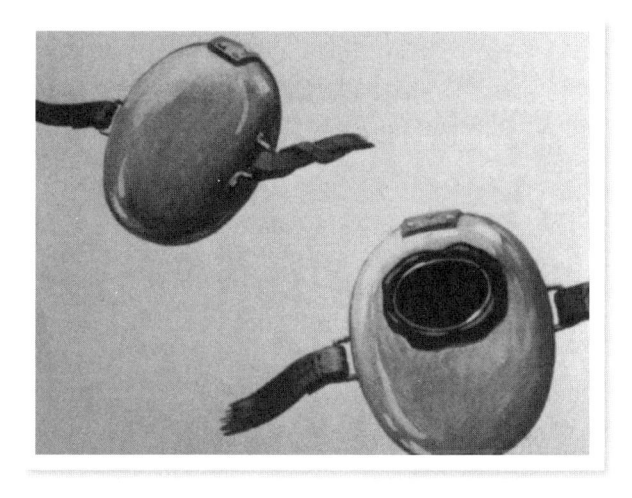

Modified Dutch water bottles, Coates' life saving innovation for amoebic dysentery patients.

patient's small bowel, a hole was made in the side of a flattened, oval-shaped aluminium Dutch water bottle, which was strapped over the stoma with a webbing belt. The patient then went back to work. His colon healed and, some months later, Coates was able to remove the bottle and stitch the stoma closed.

Back at Kilo 105 Camp, the rations had declined even more, the yak stew, such as it was, now a distant memory. With the watery melon stew now a staple in their diet, only one-third of the workforce was anywhere near fit, forcing malaria sufferers with temperatures of 40 degrees Celsius to go out to work. By mid-July the labour force had dwindled from 800 to 200, due to deaths or hospitalisation.

With the road construction finished, the men were assigned to railroad building, which was considerably worse. The work parties had a ten-kilometre walk to reach the site at Kilo 97 before they could begin the day's work. The initial earthworks did not take long, so the men moved onto the next task – grubbing out bamboo and jungle with nothing but crude axes and crosscut saws.

The 'speedo' continued in full swing. The Japanese were determined that the rail bed would be ready for the rail laying by the Mobile Forces in September, now weeks, not months, away. With the area cleared, it was back to earth moving once more, the quota now increased to four cubic metres per man per day.

How those still on their feet kept up the gruelling schedule is unfathomable, but finally, on 26 September, the rail workers on the Burma side linked up with their counterparts in Thailand. Although the Thai section was much longer, the rate of construction had been faster as the labour force was larger and the first section of the line passed through relatively flat land. All that was left to do was to fettle the lines into position on the sleepers and maintain the newly completed link. The weary workers at Kilo 105, pushed almost to the limits of their endurance, were finally allowed to down tools, with the promise that there would be 'plenty of rest from now on'.

Cock-a-hoop with success, the Japanese decided it was time for some propaganda. A couple of days previously, a film crew had forced prisoners to conduct a mock funeral so that their Japanese audiences could see how Christian burials were conducted. The cinematographers were now back to film 'happy prisoners' working on the railway. With

Japanese propaganda film crew.

the least fit placed at the rear, the Australians, shouldering picks, shovels and hoes, were lined up and ordered to sing 'Pack Up Your Troubles' as they marched off. They readily agreed and, as they reached the sound recordists, launched into an unprintable version of 'Bless 'Em All', which definitely did not portray their captors in a favourable light. Delighted by this display of such obvious enthusiasm, the elderly sound recordists were all smiles. It was not until later that the Japanese discovered this act of defiance and, when they did, there was hell to pay.

Ironically, it was the IJA's propaganda department that, for some months, had provided Fred and his fellow prisoners with something to laugh about, amid all the death and suffering.

> *While we were in Burma, no event was more looked forward to than the arrival of the newspaper, The Greater Asia. Printed in English in Rangoon and sponsored by the Japanese Propaganda Minister, it was circulated quite freely throughout the prison camps.* The Greater Asia *meant as much to Australian prisoners of war as comics meant to kiddies in Australia and produced just as much merriment.*

In Japanese reports of air battles, not once did one of their planes suffer the disgrace of being shot down – it was always 'crash-dived into enemy objective'.

A Japanese truck loaded with troops and travelling far too fast came to grief in front of our camp, when the driver failed to take a bend and ploughed into a big stump just outside the gate. The vehicle was hopelessly wrecked and some of the occupants injured. During the night someone risked life and limb to adorn the wreckage, not 50 metres from the guardhouse, with a sign painted in huge capital letters CRASH DIVED INTO ENEMY OBJECTIVE.

When the pilots were not crashdiving into enemy objectives, they were performing amazing feats of airmanship. The pilot of one Japanese plane, having used all his ammunition, flew close to an enemy Super Fortress and, standing up in the cockpit, threw two rice cakes at it. Taking evasive measures to avoid being hit, the pilot crashed into the side of a mountain.

Another Japanese pilot, a lieutenant, whose plane was absolutely riddled by gunfire, landed his plane on his home base and made his report to his superior officer. It was only when the report was finished that it was found that the lieutenant was dead and had been so for some hours as rigor mortis had already set in.

Stories involving the sea were just as unbelievable and just as colourful, with *The Greater Asia* reporting the sinking of an Allied convoy of 30 ships at Alice Springs, and that the water supply mains between Tasmania and New South Wales had been cut and the resultant water shortage was causing great hardship to the people of Sydney.

However, possibly the most imaginative article was one that made the headlines on the newspaper's front page, reporting an attack made by Australia's most savage and dangerous animal – a koala bear – on a Jap internment camp in New South Wales. It read: 'Typical Japanese Bravery. On Australian soldiers becoming panic stricken, when a camp they were guarding was attacked by Koala bears, the courage of the Japanese prisoners who showed the utmost disregard for their own safety in grabbing up the rifles, which were thrown away by the guards, calmly faced the bears till the animals were almost upon them and, shooting them dead, saved the camp from complete destruction. The Australian Government, in recognition of the brave deed, has ordered that the heroes be given extra cigarettes for the duration of their captivity.'

There were many other incidents of derring-do. A Japanese pilot saw a British destroyer and decided to attack, only to realise he was out of ammunition as he made his final approach. Undaunted, he flipped his plane over, swooped down and decapitated the admiral standing on the bridge with his sword. Another pilot, preparing to land, found that his undercarriage had been shot away. Kicking his feet through the fuselage, he landed safely by running along the airstrip. A story that the Japanese Air Force had bombed and machine-gunned India, wiping out thousands, and that the cowardly British had run, might have been believed, at least in part, had the 'nightingale' not continued to sing, undetected.

It appears that, as part of their overall propaganda exercise, the Japanese distributed postcards for prisoners to send home. Unlike the first lot, sent around Christmas 1942 and printed with various sentences for the sender to choose before adding personal details, this card had a lengthy pre-printed message. The only contribution the POW was allowed to make was to fill in the address and sign his name.

The message was reassuring, but not overly so, making it believable. Elsie must have been very relieved to read:

> **IMPERIAL JAPANESE ARMY.**
> I am still in a P. O. W. Camp near Moulmein, Burma. There are 20,000 Prisoners, being Australian, Dutch, English, and American. There are several camps of 2/3000 prisoners who work at settled labour daily.
> We are quartered in very plain huts. The climate is good. Our life is now easier with regard to food, medicine and clothes. The Japanese Commander sincerely endeavours to treat prisoners kindly.
> Officers' salary is based on salary of Japanese Officers of the same rank and every prisoner who performs labour or duty is given daily wages from 25 cents (minimum) to 45 cents, according to rank and work.
> Canteens are established where we can buy some extra foods and smokes. By courtesy of the Japanese Commander we conduct concerts in the camps, and a limited number go to a picture show about once per month.
>
> *F. Howe*

Fred's postcard to Elsie.

While Elsie may have had nagging doubts about the accuracy of the message, it would have certainly raised her spirits, if only for a short while. With four children to raise, the going was tough, and the family simply had to make do with what they had. In the depths of winter, her youngest son, who normally ran about barefooted, walked to school through thick frost in shoes so old and battered that he was unable to keep his feet dry.

A friendly neighbour had loaned the family a cow, so they were never short of milk. She was a placid old Jersey and Elsie had no trouble milking her. However, she had to be up early each morning as an old man, a bit of a tramp who lived down by the river, thought he should help out by milking the cow. As he had an aversion to soap and water, and was prone to dribbling, it was a bit of a race to see who got to the cowshed first. To keep the animal supplied with food during the drought, the older children cut branches from the willows growing along the river bank. However, through it all, Elsie remained cheerful, putting on a brave face for her offspring despite the difficulties.

Fred returned from hospital to Kilo 105 Camp on 17 October 1943, a red-letter day in the life of the railway. With the fettling finally finished, the last spike was hammered into place at 11.30 pm on 17 October on the Thai side of the border, at Kilo 153, Konkoita, 263 kilometres from Thanbyuzayat and 18 kilometres south of Three Pagoda Pass.

The Japanese, jubilant that the line had been completed, held an official opening ceremony on 24 October. Accompanied by a full brass band, the Japanese dignitaries and other invited guests stood proudly as the cameras rolled to record this momentous event for posterity and home consumption. The emaciated prisoners responsible for the railway's construction were kept out of sight. To add extra colour and drama for the cameras, smiling Japanese 'labourers', doused with water to simulate perspiration, drove in the 'final

AT WHAT COST?

Above: Decorated station at Konkoita for the official opening.

Left: One of the souvenir 'golden' brass spikes.

Below: A railway burial, one of many along the line.

spikes', around a length of 'golden' (copper) rail line, later replaced with conventional steel rails and spikes. As far as Japanese audiences were concerned, this remarkable feat of engineering was a source of national pride.

There is a long-held belief that the line was joined with a solid gold spike. This myth evidently had its origins in the widely reported fact that Japanese officers attending the ceremony were each presented with a 'golden' spike, made of brass to mark the occasion. It was certainly an amazing accomplishment: a 415-kilometre rail line, passing through difficult mountainous and jungle-clad terrain; the construction of 688 bridges and the removal of four million cubic metres of earth; little transportation for materials; the most basic of tools; virtually no medication; very little food, and all completed despite extremely difficult conditions in just over twelve months, at the rate of half a mile a day.

The line was joined but, as Fred remarked, 'what a cost!'

The cost was indeed sobering. A total of 3149 British Commonwealth servicemen, 1335 of them Australian, and 622 Dutch died while constructing the Burma end of the railway. Overall, of the estimated 200,000 Asian labourers working on the line, it is calculated that up to 100,000 died, while the POWs lost just over 12,000 of their almost 62,000 strong workforce, more than 2600 of them Australian: a combined death toll of well over 100,000. Of the 117 members of Fred's 2/19 Battalion who were with Ramsay Force, 12 died building the Burma end – eight in hospital, three at Kilo 105 Camp and one at Kilo 79 – a remarkably low death rate of 10.25 per cent, considering the conditions.

> Colonel Nagatomo, Japanese Commander of the group to which we were attached, had stated earlier that the railroad would be built even if it was over the dead bodies of every prisoner working on it. How near this came to being true only those who were there know. It is said that, for every sleeper laid on that 415 kilometres of line, there was a dead man.

This long-standing myth, repeated by Fred, that the construction of the railway cost a 'life for every sleeper' is also the title of a book by Australian Hugh Clarke, published in 1986, and a 'statistic' that has been repeated by other authors. However, Clarke was not the person who coined the phrase. The first use, in connection to the Burma-Thai railway, was in March 1945 when four British POWs, whose prison ship was sunk by US planes, were rescued from the sea off Luzon, in the Philippines. They told the press of the horrors they had endured while working in Thailand and stated that the rail construction had **probably** cost 'a life for every sleeper'. The same phrase was used by POWs liberated from Thailand in September 1945, but by this time the statistic had become actual fact.

However, these emotive words go back to 1882, the genesis of which was in Australia, when a newspaper described the considerable loss of life during the construction of a short tramway line linking Mourilyan Harbour with South Johnstone River at Innisfail (at that time known as Geraldton), in far north Queensland. Three years later, when a large number of Negro, Hindu and Chinese labourers perished while building the Panama Railway, in Central America, it popped up again. It next surfaced in a report on the Beira and Mashonaland Railway in Africa, begun in 1885, linking the Pungwee River in Portuguese Mozambique to Salisbury, in what was then Rhodesia.

So, by the time the Burma-Thai railway came into being, the catchy 'a life for every sleeper' had become rather hackneyed. It was also totally untrue. According to railway research analyst Derek Lawson, with the average width of each sleeper and the space between measuring about 71.5 centimetres, the number of sleepers required for the 415-kilometre-long railway was about 580,000, more than five times the number who died. If the sidings and loop lines are taken into consideration, the total distance is 650 kilometres, using 130,000 lengths of rail, 3.5 million spikes and more than 908,000 sleepers, equating to a life for every nine sleepers.

Clarke justified his title by stating that 'the cost was a life for every sleeper laid over its most difficult sections'. Just what these were is not stated. However, the death toll for the 4.5 kilometre Konyu section, which, from an engineering point of view was one of the most difficult, was 499, a life for every 12 sleepers.

In her book, *The Colonel of Tamarkan*, published in 2005, Julie Summers states that an Allied POW died for every sleeper laid, which equals one death for every 48 sleepers, or one for every 75 sleepers, including loop lines and sidings. To put it another way, if a life were lost for every Allied POW, the sleepers would be 33 metres apart.

With the line finally joined, Fred breathed a sigh of relief.

> How thankful we were the job was completed. We were informed that we were to be evacuated out of the jungle and into Thailand, where there would be good food and rest. This, however, could not be accomplished at once, and we were left cooling our heels awaiting our turn to move.
>
> It was at this period that the survivors of F Force were brought back from Burma where they had a hospital camp at the 50 kilometre area. Cholera had broken out in their ranks and the task of cremating the bodies – as many as twenty a day – was more than the weakened men could do. Large fires were kept going day and night to dispose of them.
>
> Our own hospital camp at the 55 kilometre was little better, although only about two deaths occurred from cholera. Dysentery, starvation and ulcers were responsible for the average of six deaths each day for some weeks.

As October merged into November, the dry season arrived with a vengeance. Instead of cursing the constant wet weather, the POWs were now scanning the heavens for clouds that looked as if they might bring some relief from the dry, scorching days. The vermin infestation in the overcrowded huts was at its height, but there was little that could be done, bar burning down the camp, to get rid of the millions of rats, fleas, gnats and bugs. Boredom set in, with the few books available in the camp the only diversion, apart from an occasional surprise search, which saw the confiscation of many precious 'treasures' not hidden in time.

Fortunately, the Japanese did not find 'the nightingale', which had just sung its heart out on 4 November with the news that Allied troops had half of Italy under their control. Nor did they find the two pistols, maps, compass and four diaries, buried by orderlies in the earth below Tom Fagan's bed space, a discovery that would have resulted in his name being added to that day's death toll. Although not confiscated, the mind-diverting books had no guarantee of survival if tobacco became available. Many bibles, prized for their thin rice-paper pages, had already gone up in smoke.

A fortnight or so later, the Japanese announced a two-day holiday, with the promise of additional rations, to celebrate the first anniversary of the formation of Number 3 Thailand POW Branch. As the commanding officer, Nagatomo issued speeches to be read out at the ceremony. On day one of the commemoration, 20 November, 2000 POWs assembled at the cemetery for a memorial service, attended by Nagatomo, who took no active part. However, in what appeared to be a sincere attempt to recognise the loss of life, he deputised Hoshi to read out his letter of condolence for 'the souls of all those who have died in war, even though they may be enemies'. Ramsay's carefully worded memorial address was a masterpiece of diplomacy, at the same time making it clear to everyone fluent in English that those responsible for the tragedy would be made accountable. He finished his moving oration with the immortal words of Lawrence Binyon's 'Ode to the Fallen'. The ceremony went off unexpectedly well and the prisoners were impressed.

Day two saw the camp population parade at a ceremony at which two speeches, one by Ramsay and one by Nagatomo, were read. After Nagatomo delivered his anniversary address, Ramsay took the podium. To make sure that he did not say anything contentious, he was required to submit it 48 hours in advance. Nagatomo was evidently satisfied, as no amendments were made.

Fred was still at Kilo 105 as his second Christmas in captivity approached. With the line finished, the Japanese allowed the POWs to hold a sports day and concert. One of the Japanese guards, on discovering a two-up game in progress, joined in. When he lost all his money, he became so annoyed that he grabbed the kitty, belted up the spinner, and left.

It was not until the end of the month that the bulk of prisoners in Burma who were well enough to move finally began to leave for the base camps in Thailand. However, some members of Anderson and Williams Forces remained behind, as the Mobile Force, and did not move south until 23 March 1944, their departure marking the final dissolution of A Force. By this time, about 10,000 POWs who had worked on the Thai section of the line were en route to Japan, or ready for transfer, to make use of their labour.

Fred's transport to Thailand.

AT WHAT COST?

The train Fred boarded was composed of steel boxes, with a sliding door on each side. Each wagon held up to 20 men, which was fortunate as other trains crammed in 37. The ration per wagon was a bucket of turnips and a bucket of water, most of which sloshed onto the floor as the train rocked back and forth on the uneven narrow gauge line. There was no ventilation and the doors were only opened when the train made comfort stops, usually at campsites, where the lonely cemeteries with their little stick crosses reminded everyone of the terrible human cost of building the railway. Surrounding one small cemetery was a bamboo fence with a sign attached – not the usual 'Lest We Forget' but 'We Won't Forget'.

Train on curved trestle bridge near Hellfire Pass.

For Fred and his fellow passengers, the entire journey was an unnerving experience, especially when the train jolted precariously over flimsy bridges in the mountainous area south of Neike. They would have been even more unnerved if they had been able to see the wrecked rolling stock lying at the bottom of steep embankments, 30 metres or more below the track. At every clickety-clack of the rails, at every rickety viaduct built high above the river, they wondered if their co-workers in Thailand had also indulged in little acts of sabotage that might see a bridge collapse or the train derail at any moment. There were no creature comforts in the bare steel wagons, so it was an agonising journey for the so-called fit and sheer torture for the ill, especially those who had undergone recent amputations at the Khon Khan hospital. According to Fred, by the end of the journey, 14 of the sickest prisoners were dead.

On New Year's Day 1944, Fred's train passed through the now infamous Hellfire Pass, stopping a little further south at Tampii where Fred and other members of the 2/19th met up with old mates, sent to Thailand with Roaring Reggie Newton's D Force. It was a time of great celebration, with members of the 2/30th's band, who had somehow retained their instruments, belting out many old favourites. As the train travellers virtually had nothing to eat for two days, the lunchtime meal provided by D Force was very welcome.

It was amazing what a good feed and a yarn with old mates could do to restore the spirits, and it was a far happier bunch of prisoners that continued on the journey south, fortunately without incident. In the early hours of the morning, two days into the new year of 1944, they reached the now famous 'River Kwai'. As the bridge had been bombed, they made the crossing in boats, marching the last couple of hundred metres to Tamarkan Camp, or Tha Maa Kham in Thai, meaning the place where horses crossed the river.

Surrounded by jungle, this large base camp was encircled by a tall bamboo fence, more as a demarcation line than a barrier. It was established in October 1942 when British troops arrived from Changi to construct two bridges, one of wood, the other of steel and concrete, over the Mae Khlong River, now known as the Khwae Yai. As the already substantial river swelled to a width of 300 metres during the monsoon, the bridges were a major engineering project. However, before the POWs could commence construction of the bridges or the 200 metres of railway embankments either side of the river, they first had to build enough 90-metre-long, bamboo-framed atap-clad huts, to house 1650 prisoners. In February 1943 the camp had been further expanded with the arrival of 1000 Dutch POWs.

The commanding officer was Lieutenant Colonel Philip Toosey who, without endangering the lives of his men, had done everything possible to delay and sabotage the construction. Termites were collected in large numbers to eat the wooden beams and the concrete was poorly mixed. Toosey also helped two officers and four men organise a daring escape, giving them rations to last a month and covering their absence for 48 hours, for which he was punished. However, after ten days the four soldiers were recaptured, made to dig their own graves and shot. The officers remained at large for another fortnight, when they were betrayed by local people. Both were bayonetted.

Construction of the wooden bridge, closest to the camp, was almost complete in December 1942, a scant two months after Toosey arrived, only to be partially washed away following a tremendous storm. The POWs' delight was short-lived. They were ordered to repair it, pronto. It was finished in January and the steel one, 100 metres upstream, in April. By February, trains loaded with Japanese troops were crossing the wooden bridge

The bombed steel bridge at Tamarkan.

which, to the prisoners' amazement, did not fall down. However, the bridge was a tried and tested design, developed during World War I by two American engineers who had published a handbook, complete with illustrations.

Over the coming months, the Japanese would move an average of 1000 tons of stores each month along the rail line. This was well short of the 3000 tons they had hoped to transport, but it was still sufficient to keep their troops in Burma supplied, as well as helping them organise an orderly withdrawal. Depending on derailments, repair work and bombing attacks, the travel time between Nong Pluduc and Moulemein was about 50 hours.

Both bridges, which remained in use for more than two years, were the target for no fewer than eight Allied bombing raids. To keep the line open when the steel bridge was out of action, the trains were diverted onto the wooden one. The bridges were repaired time and again until the steel one was eventually destroyed in June 1945.

Once the bridges were complete, Tamarkan was expanded to become a large hospital camp. In December 1943, with fewer and fewer patients arriving as the railway work wound down, it was designated as an Australian rest camp. Toosey was transferred further down the line to a large base camp at Nong Pladuc, 55 kilometres away.

The prisoners already at Tamarkan were shocked by the state of the new arrivals, with their washboard ribs and wasted, emaciated limbs. Willing hands gently lifted the stretchers from the wagons and took the sick to hospital, a hospital that had drugs, equipment and supplies thanks to a local underground network, supplied with funds by ex-patriates living in Bangkok. Although the doctors were always requesting more of everything, their hospital was light years away from the one at Kilo 55.

Entering the camp proper, Fred and his companions were greeted with an unbelievable sight – a cookhouse with plates piled high with a type of spinach the prisoners had dubbed 'Popeye'. It was all they could do not to grab the food there and then, and some actually did. After the usual roll call, and a most welcome wash, they sat down to a delicious meal. Tamarkan was a place that Fred had only dreamed about, a place of refuge, with a food supply that far exceeded anything the POWs had seen at their jungle camps.

> It was a vastly different place from the camps where we had spent the last 12 months. Eggs and vegetables were in abundance and within a month or two it was hard to realise that we were the same men who had come through the Valley of Death and the Pagoda Pass.
>
> However it was like fattening the calf for the kill. The condition in which we came out of the jungle was such that the Japs realised it was only a matter of time for death to claim us all. However, there was still work to do. The solution? Nurse us back to some semblance of health so that we could finish the job.

CHAPTER 21
THE WORK CONTINUES

January 1944 to August 1945

The first task Fred's group was assigned on arrival at Tamarkan was to join a labour force of hundreds to help repair the wooden bridge. With the Japanese deliberately locating the camp close to the bridge, to deter Allied planes from attacking it – a forlorn hope – it was inevitable that some bombs dropped overshot their target.

> We had not been at Tamarkan for long when Allied planes began to come over in greater numbers, pamphlets were dropped and, on a few occasions, found their way into our hands. One particular pamphlet was a map of Europe, showing areas blacked out where our troops were in occupation. On the other side was a map showing the Pacific area, treated in the same way. Printed underneath, in big letters, were the words 'Keep your chins up, boys; it's in the bag.' That day the Japs carried out a search of our belongings. Naturally we thought they were searching for the pamphlets. Eventually they lined us up on the parade ground and ordered 'the bag' to be produced. The laughter that followed did not make us too popular.
>
> However, our planes did more than drop pamphlets and I'm sure there is no worse sensation than being bombed and machine-gunned by your own countrymen! We did not blame them. They could not know we were scattered from one end of the railroad to the other. We were open to attack at all times, as the Japanese insisted in placing our camps alongside military targets, despite numerous protests from our senior officers. It was pure luck that, apart from about five instances, there were no casualties at the camps further up the line.
>
> However, our camp at Tamarkan was situated only about 200 yards from the rail bridge. As it was a prime target for Allied planes, there was a battery of anti-aircraft guns stationed just off the approaches, which seldom failed to open fire on reconnaissance planes, searching for such a target. Daily we lived in fear of retaliation and it came when we least expected it. I do not think that any of the bombs dropped by the 20-odd Liberators that attacked the bridge were meant to drop in the camp, but the position we were in almost made a miss impossible and, each time the bridge was attacked, the camp suffered casualties. It was the same situation at the POW camp at Nong Pladuc, where the heaviest casualties of all were sustained, the numbers running into the hundreds. The bombing of trains along the railway line accounted for many more, as

POWs were forced to travel on almost every train. Towards the end, the trains travelled only at night, because of the toll on engines and rolling stock.

The Australians in Tamarkan were later moved to other camps further down the line, and the officers' camp was relocated to another site in nearby Kanchanaburi, using building materials recycled from the old camp. During a high-level bombing raid at Tamarkan on 29 November 1944, which damaged three piers of the steel bridge, three bombs overshot the target and landed in the camp, killing 17 and leaving several dozen others injured. On 5 February 1945, a raid partially destroyed the wooden bridge and another on the 13th damaged both bridges, but they were repaired within days. The prisoners had been allowed to dig slit trenches in the officers' camp, which kept the death toll down to five, with several injured.

This was not the case at Nong Pluduc. A heavy night-time raid on 7 September 1944 on the Hashimoto railway sidings, marshalling yards and workshops, situated less than a kilometre from the camp, resulted in 360 casualties, 20 of them fatal, with 76 killed outright.

> After the completion of the railway, the Japs at Tamarkan, using prisoner of war labour, erected a large concrete shrine as a memorial to all who had lost their lives while the line was under construction. It was certainly an impressive structure, but we knew that the sentiment with which the unveiling ceremony was carried out did not mean a thing and was only another example of the Japs' hypocrisy.

The memorial was opened with much pomp and ceremony on 21 March 1944, shortly after Fred arrived, with 1123 POWs attending. Constructed from concrete, the four-sided tapered obelisk was set on a large concrete base, accessed by two sets of stairs, one on either side. Eight plaques for the various nations were inscribed in English, Dutch, Malay, Tamil, Chinese, Thai, Indian and Japanese. During the ceremony there was a roll call of the Allied prisoners who had died at Tamarkan to date. The British headed the list with 129, followed by 57 Dutch, 15 Australians and one American, a total of 202. The memorial was in a direct line with the bridge and, during an air raid, a 1000-pound bomb was dropped close to the obelisk, wrecking some of the POW huts and giving rise to the belief, and hope, that it had been destroyed. However, the memorial survived, undamaged, apart from a few pockmarks made by flying shrapnel.

At about the same time as the memorial was opened, a large number of the fittest POWs left for Japan via Saigon. Many were pleased about the move, thinking that Japan might offer more, as life at Tamarkan had become quite boring. However, as US submarines were active in the South China Sea, most of the prisoners were eventually transferred to Singapore, where they joined other Japan Parties from the railway, working locally until further transportation was arranged. By mid-1944, the majority of POWs, apart from F and H Forces, and maintenance parties, had left Thailand, either for Japan or to join working parties in Singapore.

In about May 1944, Fred was stricken with malaria and was admitted to Nakhon Pathom Camp hospital, approximately 75 kilometres to the east of Tamarkan. He was still there in June when American planes flew overhead on their way to Bangkok on a bombing raid. The camp was situated near the Phra Pathom Chedi, a huge Buddhist stupa, reputedly the tallest in the world. Covered in tiles imported from China that reflected the

The memorial at Tamarkan.

light of the full moon like a beacon, the stupa was a perfect landmark for bomber pilots as they set a course for their target area.

> I had thought when Allied fighter planes began to appear over our camps that it would not be long before something big happened. I considered that our forces would soon be close enough that escape to their lines would be possible.
>
> You can imagine how excited I was when, at 4 o'clock one afternoon in June 1944, 12 single-engine American fighters roared over the hospital camp at Nakhon Pathom, 65 kilometres from Bangkok. The planes were so low that the markings were plainly visible. After passing the camp, they broke formation and machine-gunned a 'drome about a mile away from our camp. And did they have fun!

When the raid first started we took to the drains alongside our huts, thinking we may come in for some strafing too. But it was very noticeable that each plane made its run on the target so that there would be no possibility of any stray bullets over-carrying into our camp. How I envied them. So near, and yet so far away.

After finishing their task they flew off, rocking from side to side as they passed over the camp – plainly a signal to us that they knew we were there. How happy everyone was. One would have thought we were being liberated next day, instead of having to wait another long, dreary, 12 months. The next day the Japs told us the planes were carrier-based and had destroyed ten of their planes on the ground before they had a chance to retaliate.

The following day, one of the biggest raids we had experienced took place. At 2 am the first plane droned overhead, followed five minutes later by a second and a third. Then the whole sky seemed to be filled with aircraft flying towards Bangkok. It was a perfect night – the moon being directly overhead and almost full. The roar of engines seemed to come from all points of the compass. Sleep was impossible. It was a spectacle I had dreamed of. None of the planes were more than 1,000 feet above us, giant four-engine bombers, carrying tons of explosives. There were many conjectures about their destination. Then we heard the bombs exploding, away in the distance like far-off thunder. The first planes had reached their target!

Bangkok we said! God help them! It certainly sounded as if they needed help. The detonations had developed into a continuous roar as plane after plane unloaded its deadly cargo. Anti-aircraft guns went into action, each shot appearing as a ball of red-hot iron soaring skyward. Brilliant flashes, like flickering lightning, marked the explosion of bombs and the flashes of nearer guns almost dazzled us with their brilliance.

The whole spectacle, coupled with the terrific noise of explosions, the roar of engines, as wave after wave of planes soared onwards, was amazing. More than 200 aircraft were counted passing over the camp. How anyone could survive seemed an utter impossibility. What a bombing! A year later I had the good fortune to see the results: Bangkok railway marshaling yards, some two square miles in area, had been completely annihilated, together with all the buildings the Japanese were using to keep the railway in operation. Not one bomb fell outside the target area!

I take my hat off to the Allied airmen.

Discharged from hospital, Fred was not destined to join the thousands of POWs being returned to Changi Camp. Instead, he was assigned to a new working party. The destination was Kui Yae, between Prang Kasi and Tarsao, 186 kilometres from Nong Pladuc, the southern starting point of the rail line.

There were 100 Dutchmen and 100 Australians in the party, and we were put to work enlarging cuttings. The Japanese engineers had no idea what constituted a day's work and we Australians were taking advantage of this and taking things very easy. The Dutch were learning to follow our example when one of their countrymen, an interpreter, came on the scene. We had met Dutchmen who were the salt of the earth, and then again we met many who were not. The interpreter, so the boys declared, was married to a Japanese prostitute in Java and flaunted his pro-Japanese connections. On many occasions, when a word from him would have alleviated a lot of suffering and turned

Phra Pathon Chedi, a huge Buddhist stupa near Nakhon Pathon, served as a beacon for Allied bombers.

things around, he steered the issue in the other direction. He could see we were not taking the job seriously and lost no time in telling the Japanese the Australians were no good and could be made do four times as much work as we were doing.

The following week, when a party of English and American prisoners joined us, we told them what had happened. One American said he would 'do' for the Dutchman, if it were his last act. The interpreter heard of this threat and lost no time in asking the Japs to send him somewhere else. Such was his influence that he left the camp that night and I did not set eyes on him again.

However, word reached us of another of his exploits at Kinsaiyok Camp, about 15 kilometres from Kui Yae. The Japanese storehouse there was near a road and, when he discovered that rice was stolen by the locals, he took it upon himself to catch the thief. It turned out to be a Burmese girl, aged about 18. He handed her over to the Jap guards, who tortured her in the most inhuman fashion with burning bamboo sticks until she lost consciousness, and then threw her out on to the road, where she died. The Dutchman said she deserved all she got. Not surprisingly, he was also transferred from that camp, as he was in fear of his life.

The Japanese took a great delight in giving the Americans the hardest and dirtiest jobs and took every opportunity to humiliate them. One Yank, too sick to walk down to the railway from the camp, was placed on a rough stretcher to be carried to the train for his return to hospital. The train was late in arriving, so he remained on the stretcher at the foot of an earthen bank until the train came. A Japanese guard made it his business to walk along the top of the bank as many times as possible, each time kicking a quantity of dirt onto the helpless man beneath. He suffered in silence till the Jap decided to urinate on him. Then he abused the Jap, calling him everything. Satisfied, the guard walked away and left him alone.

The Jap officer in charge of the Kui Yae camp was a sneaking cur. Waiting until all able-bodied men were out on working parties, he then mistreated those too sick to go to work. Believe me, you had to be sick in those days to stay in the camp. He ordered them out of bed and forced them to parade in front of their huts for hours in the burning sun. When the working parties returned, he was all apologies, saying it was all a mistake and he was very sorry.

He was also particularly hard on the Americans and those suffering from malaria received the full force of his spite. To help counter the attacks, the Yanks bought all the Aussie hats they could get hold of and, from that time, on passed themselves off as Australians whenever they could. When an English Colonel, whom we called 'Peanut', fell foul of him one day and was severely battered with his sword scabbard, he reported the matter to a more senior Jap officer and the cur was removed to another camp.

The English, who were mostly regular soldiers, took their captivity as a matter of course and were responsible for much of the better treatment we received due to the fights they put up for their rights.

We were still at Kui Yae on 8 December when two Liberators attacked a train carrying 300 Dutch prisoners, about 200 yards from our camp. At first the Japanese allowed the prisoners to leave the train and take shelter in the jungle, but then ordered them back and moved the train away from the siding. The prisoners, seeing the planes circling around, were not alarmed and began to attract the attention of the pilots by vigorously waving their arms. The planes, coming in lower to make certain, were met with burst after burst of machine-gun fire from the Japanese in charge of the train.

I suppose the pilots thought that a trap had been set for them and that the occupants of the train were Japanese. The leading plane dived and released eight bombs, which exploded only a few feet from the side of the wagons.

Trucks were hurled completely off the line by the blast and the prisoners, trapped inside them, suffered terrific casualties. The second plane, following the same line of attack taken by the first, caught the survivors in their panic stricken rush to reach the shelter of the jungle, killing and wounding many more.

When the first plane returned to strafe the surrounding jungle, the Jap guards in our camp opened fire and we came in for our share of bullets as well. Fortunately only one man was hit, as the majority of us had taken shelter in trenches, dug for just such an eventuality. The Japanese, however, lost 20 men.

The Japs ceased firing and the raid ended, as the planes were apparently running out of ammunition.

The pilots were not out of ammunition. Evidently satisfied that they had done enough damage at Kui Kae, where 30–40 Dutchmen lost their lives, they headed north to Prang Kasi, 22 kilometres away, where a work party led by Major Long was toiling in the railway yards. At 6 pm, as the planes roared overhead, some of the men raced for shelter on a river bank, about 200 metres south-west of the railway station.

As the bombs exploded, Private George Tatt, aged 24, who had previously been in Burma with Fred, was blown into the water and disappeared. Leading Stoker Ronald Grieve, a member of Williams Force, who had survived the sinking of HMAS *Perth*, was killed, along with several British and Dutch prisoners.

> We assumed that the Japanese would attend to the wounded on the train, but orders were that no man was to leave the camp. At midnight, five hours after the raid, the British officer in charge of the camp called for volunteers to sneak out and see what could be done. Five Australians volunteered – and, although I hate to say it, not one Dutchman, although there were 100 in the camp. However, the attempt was useless as the Japs had thrown a cordon around the train. The volunteers only succeeded in getting close enough to hear the moans and cries of the wounded.

> It was daylight before we were allowed out, and then only to help move the more seriously wounded to another camp across the railway line. The carnage along the rail track was the most sickening spectacle it has been my misfortune to see. Severed legs and arms lay strewn about the area. The heads of two men had landed yards away from their bodies, their sightless eyes staring towards the sky. Tangled and knotted entrails were scattered everywhere in a gory mess. The Dutch were given the job of burying their countrymen, if you could call it a burial.

> After spending a week building a by-pass around the wrecked train, when we were sent to clear the hopelessly smashed trucks we were confronted by the most hideous scene. The Dutch had simply laid their dead along a bank and pulled some dirt over them. The jungle animals had found the remains and we had to almost get down on our knees to the Japs to get permission to give what was left a proper burial. The stench was sickening. Although we were hardened prisoners, who had seen death in many forms, our stomachs were unequal to the task.

By this time, people in Australia had learned that thousands of their POWs were toiling under horrendous conditions, building a railway linking Burma to Thailand. The news had broken on 18 November 1944 when POWs, rescued by American submarines after their unmarked prison ship had been torpedoed en route to Japan, reached Australia.

One of those picked up was the 2/19th's Roydon (Roy) Cornford, of Williams Force. Cut off during the fighting on Singapore Island on 9 February 1942, he and a small group had made their way south through the sector abandoned by the Indian Army. The Australians had no idea of the situation elsewhere but, to the north-east, they could see the belching clouds of black smoke where AIF troops near in the causeway had set fire to the oil reserves. On 12 February they reached the southern shoreline, west of the now burning city, where they met a couple of British sailors, who had survived the sinking of *Prince of Wales* and had somehow acquired a sampan. Clambering aboard, the infantrymen used lengths of timber as paddles to coax the small craft towards a large ship, lying at anchor off Singapore Harbour

It was *Empire Star* and on board was a large number of RAF personnel, Australian army nurses, civilians, and members of the Australian Army Service Corps, all being evacuated to Java. Spotting the slouch hats lining the rails, Cornford and his companions managed to

Survivors from *Rakuyu Maru*, bring news of the death railway to the outside world, September 1944.

reach the side of the vessel and climb scrambling nets, lowered by willing hands.

However, their relief was short lived. As the ship joined a convoy and made its way south the next day, it was spotted by enemy planes and came under constant attack. Damaged, but miraculously still afloat, *Empire Star* reached Tanjong Priok, the port for Batavia, where the military evacuees went ashore to join the defenders there, only to become prisoners of war when Java, too, inevitably fell.

After being rescued from the South China Sea by a submarine, Roy and his fellow castaways spent the best part of two months in hospital before being pronounced fit enough to return home, where they were interviewed by the press. Until then, the outside world knew only that a substantial number of POWs were engaged in construction work on a railway in Burma and Thailand. The castaways' first-hand story of depravation and suffering shocked not only Australia but the world, causing great anxiety for Elsie and the other wives, who knew only that their men were in Burma or Thailand.

On 4 January 1945, Fred and his work party, unaware that their plight was now known to millions of people, left Kui Yae on the four-day return journey to Nakhon Pathom Camp. Two days later, Fred was admitted to hospital with malaria, his 20th attack. He was so debilitated that he remained in hospital until mid-1945. During this period, he suffered a burst gastric ulcer, resulting in severe haemorrhage. Albert Coates performed a life-saving blood transfusion, directly from the arm of Chris Geurin, who was recovering in hospital after a bout of dysentery.

While news was disseminated via the camp radios, *The Greater Asia* newspaper, formerly

A patient receives a blood transfusion at the camp hospital. Fred, however, was transfused directly from the arm of his mate, Chris Guerin

the source of much amusement, was no longer issued. In fact, access to newspapers of any kind was now strictly prohibited.

> After we moved from Burma into Thailand we were not allowed access to any newspapers. Occasionally, however, *The Bangkok Times* found its way into camp through sources that the American prisoners kept a closely guarded secret. Unfortunately, the Japanese were too smart for them and, in early 1945, Captain Ike Parker and another American were caught and severely punished. They did not, however, divulge the source of supply, withstanding the most devilish torture.

William 'Ike' Parker's accomplice was Melfred Laverne Forsman, known as 'Gus', a sailor who had survived the sinking of USS *Houston*. The pair had met in a prison camp in Java, where Parker served with an artillery regiment before capture. Forsman, after his stint on the railway, was working as the camp's goat herder at Tamarkan when a Portuguese doctor with the French-Indochina underground made contact, seeking information about the camp. After Forsman was granted permission to respond, by Parker and another senior officer, Major Rogers, he became the conduit not only for intelligence leaving the camp, but for information coming back in. Via his contact, he was able to smuggle in newspapers with war news, along with medicines, in a hollowed-out bamboo pole, until the kempeitai discovered his extracurricular activities. Parker, Rogers and Forsman were arrested, tortured and taken to Bangkok for trial, where all were sentenced to six months' solitary confinement. After two weeks spent sitting or standing to attention in a small cell at the

Japanese HQ in Bangkok, Forsman was transferred to Outram Road Gaol in Singapore, the kempeitai's notorious punishment prison.

Discharged from Nakhom Pathom hospital in June, when Dr Fisher was instructed to select 162 Australians fit enough to return to the base camp, Fred, Chris and eight other members of their battalion – Wally Banks, Joe Bennett, John Carson, Kevin Griffin, Bert Hopkins, Lloyd Lewis, John Mulcahy and Jack Phillip – left for Tamarkan by train on 24 June. However, they were forced to stay at Nong Pladuc for a few days as Allied planes were active along the line. Finally arriving at Tamarkan, they were given cholera shots and assigned the task of ferrying sick Japanese across the river, as both bridges were out of commission, following another bombing raid. The wooden bridge was repaired, yet again, but the steel and concrete bridge was beyond salvation. It was rebuilt after the war and remains in service today.

Due to its proximity to the bridge, the camp continued to come under frequent attack, before being closed down. However, the circumstances of an earlier raid were so extraordinary that Fred recorded the details.

He and the other POWs were unaware that, for many months before the war ended, the United States and SOE's Force 136, an offshoot of Britain's MI6, were infiltrating small parties behind enemy lines by parachute to train local guerrilla forces and to collect intelligence from a well-organised underground movement operating throughout Thailand. Arms and supplies from Force 136 HQ in India were dropped by aircraft in the jungle into demilitarised 'no go' zones, delineated by the Thai government, which the Japanese had agreed not to enter. The Thais enforced their agreement with the occupying power, shooting dead several Japanese who had the temerity to try to enter one zone, whose boundary was only one kilometre from the Kanchanaburi Camp.

Intelligence regarding bombing targets was transmitted by wireless by a member of Force 136, based near Kanchanaburi with a Thai radio operator. This story, recorded by Fred, involves one of the local British agents.

> Two Australian POWs were in the habit of sneaking out of the compound at night to make contact with a Chinese man, who supplied them with food and other commodities. He was working with the British Secret Service.
>
> One night the pair followed their usual procedure, to find that the Chinese man was not there to meet them at the appointed place. Eventually tiring of waiting, they decided to make their way back to camp. As they rose to their feet, they heard a noise in the undergrowth behind them. Thinking the Japanese may have set a trap, they crouched down and were amazed to see a small white dog trot into the open, running in circles to pick up their scent. He came over to the two men, wagging his tail and watching their every move.
>
> When the Chinese man failed to appear, and satisfied that there was no one else around, the Australians decided to call it a day. However, the dog, by his actions, seemed to want them to follow him, trotting ahead and then waiting until they caught up. After covering a considerable distance, they reached the bank of the river, where a small houseboat was moored. The dog then disappeared into the river.
>
> They heard moans coming from the boat and, after a whispered consultation, decided to investigate. The Chinese man was lying on the deck, unable to move. He was very surprised to see them and explained that he had intended to meet them as planned

but had slipped and broken his ankle. He had wanted to warn them that the British were making a big air raid that night, and that the prisoners should make sure they were under cover.

The Australians told him that they would never have found him, or the boat, had it not been for his dog. 'What dog?' he asked. When they explained how the small white dog had led them to him, he did not speak for some time. He then said 'Yes. That was my dog, but he drowned in the river two months ago. He is buried over there on the river bank'.

At this juncture, the first wave of aircraft passed overhead and the Australians returned immediately to the camp. The area was a mess, and they entered their compound with dread, expecting to find all their comrades killed or injured. However, to their surprise, almost everyone was inside a hut that had not been hit.

Just before the raid, a small white dog had appeared, running up and down the huts barking like mad. The prisoners, alerted by the noise, had given chase and followed him into the hut, just as the raid began.

After ferrying the Japanese over the river, Fred and his group boarded a train and headed back up the railway. A long and tiring stop-start journey, lasting several days, took them to Three Pagodas Pass. Disembarking, they then marched back along the line for about 12 kilometres to Songkurai, where they joined a party of 500 English and Dutch prisoners. Renamed Okawa Camp after the Japanese sergeant in charge, Songkurai was situated between Kami (Upper) and Shimo (Lower) Songkurai Camps. As the Japanese believed Field Marshal Slim intended to bring an invasion force of British troops into Thailand from Burma, via the pass, the prisoners were to construct defensive works.

Three Pagodas in the jungle at the Burma-Thai border.

In 1943 Songkurai Camp had housed parties from F Force. The atap huts they had used, roughly 40 metres long and five metres wide, were still standing but were very dilapidated, with holes in the roofs and partially collapsed bamboo frameworks. The earth floors were covered in bamboo slats, which did absolutely nothing at all to prevent the area underfoot turning into a quagmire in the rain. Two bamboo platforms either side of a central aisle provided sleeping space just 75 centimetres wide for each prisoner. As the Japanese Officer in charge of the labour force was Colonel Komazawa, they were known as Komazawa Battalion.

The workforce was divided into three work parties. Private Gerald Trewin was placed in charge of the AIF component of the smallest one, designated as Totai, which had fewer than 100 POWs. Staff Sergeant Ian Rennie was given responsibility for the Australians in one of the larger groups, known as Rotai, while Warrant Officer Hamilton Duprez, formerly of Ramsay Force, was assigned to Fred's group, Hatai. Hatai and Rotai remained for the time being in Songkurai, but Totai was moved back to a camp about three kilometres from Neike.

> We spent the final months of our captivity, up in the mountains of the Three Pagodas Pass, hemmed in on all sides by almost impenetrable jungle. With our wireless having become too dangerous to operate, we were shut off entirely from the outside world. We became known as 'The Legion of the Lost', and believe me, we certainly felt like it.
>
> Thinking back, I often wonder why more prisoners of war did not suffer from the dreaded disease, 'Jungle Mania', so common among the natives. Those affected go mad and become a menace to friend and foe alike. Shut up in that humid, suffocating atmosphere of rotting vegetation and jungle swamps, never being able to see more than a few yards, was a greater strain on our mental state than anything we experienced during our captivity.
>
> We began to realise why the natives would not stay in this locality. Night brought no relief from the heat. It seemed to accentuate the humidity, the mist that rose from the

The mountainous area near Three Pagodas Pass.

swamps bringing myriads of mosquitoes and adding to the discomfort. We could have obtained some relief by using smoke to drive them off, but this was not permitted as our planes were continually patrolling the area and the slightest sign of smoke would be an invitation for them to investigate.

To make our misery complete, the monsoon season had really set in. Rain, rain and more rain. Sweeping down from the mountains of upper Burma, it flooded the entire countryside. The average monsoonal rainfall was in the vicinity of 400 inches [about 33 feet or 10 metres].

Our living conditions were disgusting. The camp was just an area cut out of the jungle, with structures loosely described as huts. The sleeping platforms were not sufficiently high to escape the water that constantly poured through. However, we were so dog-tired that we hardly noticed. Rising at 3.30 am each day, we arrived back at camp at about 11 pm, when the second meal of the day would be served – that is, if we could keep our eyes open long enough to eat it!

The Japanese officer in charge of us was Lieutenant Naito. I had heard many stories about this inhumane monster but had not encountered him personally. If there was anyone worse, I am thankful I did not come across him.

The camp was a sea of mud – soft, slimy, smelly stuff that permeated everything, even the food we ate. The track out to the road, about 800 yards away, was a quagmire at least 18 inches [45 centimetres] deep, a struggle at any time but especially so when we returned in pitch darkness, weary to the point of collapse. We were not allowed out of our huts again, not even to wash, till the bugle sounded the next morning, calling us to duty.

Those who had boots soon began to suffer with trench feet. Those without boots, though better off in some respects, found the going pretty difficult when they reached the rough, metalled road. It was a nine-kilometre walk to our work site [at Kami Songkurai and Changaraya] and, with the weather being constantly wet, our feet had no opportunity to harden. With or without boots, everyone became footsore. It was sheer torture each morning to plough barefooted through the soft mud and then, unable to see where to place our feet, to walk miles along a loose metal road. After a few days of this we resembled old men hobbling along. Some even had to use sticks, although carrying a stick was a bad policy, as it was too handy a weapon when the carrier lagged behind and the guards wanted to hurry him along.

Our work involved climbing precipices on which crude stairways had to be built [to access defence positions]. Logs weighing up to three or four hundred pounds had to be hauled up and, as it was impossible for more than two men to handle the log, the work was particularly arduous. Many men collapsed through sheer exhaustion, but they received no sympathy from the Japs, who drove them on with blows and kicks. Other tasks involved tunnelling into the sides of the mountains, to create defensive positions, food and ammunition dumps – dangerous work, as dynamite was used and the tunnels were apt to cave in at any time.

In one tunnel the Jap engineer did not know how to place the detonators and fuses in the charge and ordered one of our men do the job. However, when the shot was set, he gloried in lighting the fuse and setting it off. One day the fuse went out and the Jap, after waiting a time that we considered was not safe, relit it. The Australian setting the charges prepared a trap for him on the next shot, cutting the fuse about two feet longer than needed and hiding the surplus in the drill hole. The end was left out, in the usual manner.

The Jap lit the fuse and we awaited results. The charge seemed to be taking too long to go off and he became impatient. Remembering that the previous fuse had failed to burn, he went into the tunnel to relight it, or so he thought. Result, one dead Jap engineer – and purely an accident!

From then on the Japs would not enter the tunnels at all and left the work of timbering to us. We took advantage of the lack of supervision to place the props in such a way that it would not take a great deal of concussion to collapse the whole structure. I would not have cared to be in one when our bombers came over. However the positions were never used and our efforts at sabotage went for nothing.

The long hours, strenuous work, lack of sleep and insufficient food were beginning to have their effect on all of us – not only physically, but also mentally. Tempers became frayed and little incidents, which, in normal times would not have been noticed, were used as excuses for quarrelling. My own nervous system was in such a state that, even when asleep, I would be still carrying logs up the mountain, using the pick or shovel, or cat-stepping barefooted over the metal road, awaking more tired than if I had been really working. When I was not dreaming in this fashion, I would be seeing plates upon plates of the most delicious food, always disappearing when I was about to eat it. So real were my dreams, the thought of eating the filthy rice so nauseated me that I would forego my meal and go off to work without any food. But to continue in that way meant total collapse and, as I had sworn to myself to see it through, come what may, I forced myself to eat.

The desire to sleep was so great that we were working in a daze. Every movement was automatic and will power alone kept us on our feet. One of our party, [John Durkin] became so exhausted that he wandered off into the jungle, his mind a complete blank.

From the time Fred and his party arrived at Songkurai, Durkin, a member of 2/2 Pioneer Battalion, had been suffering from malaria and dysentery. In July his condition became worse, and he frequently appeared to be delirious. Although in a pitiful state of health and weighing no more than 44 kilograms, he was forced to continue work and was constantly tortured and brutally treated by a young and vicious Korean guard, Lance Corporal Kitabata Shinichi. Dubbed 'The Screaming Corporal' or 'The Screamer' by the British and Australians and known as 'Bellamon' to the Dutch, because of his high-pitched voice when agitated or excited, Kitabata was of average height, with bandy legs and a baby face that belied his sadistic streak.

He was aided and abetted by his immediate superior, Sergeant Major Ishida Yoshio, also known as 'Wire Whiskers', who encouraged his subordinates to mete out harsh treatment. Kitabata, who had terrorised prisoners working on the railway cutting at Hellfire Pass, beating some into insensibility, had a track record for unprecedented violence. At Wan Yai camp, a British POW, whom he tortured beyond the point of endurance, threw himself under a train. At Prang Kasi, Kitabata had refused to allow the POWs to take cover during the air raid, resulting in six deaths and the bashing of a Dutch officer who had the temerity to protest. He also had no qualms in declaring that, if prisoners did not move fast enough, he would use an iron bar instead of his bamboo stick, boasting 'Me Number 1 bamboo presento honcho' (I am the best bamboo beater).

Fred could thank his lucky stars that, due to his prolonged hospitalisation, he had not been assigned to Kitabata's work party at Tha Kilen, about 98 kilometres from Nong Pladuc. In March and April, the Wampo bridge, just ten kilometres from the camp, had become a prime target for American B24 aircraft. When the planes first appeared, the prisoners loading trains at Tha Kilen siding were forbidden to take cover. Eight Dutch prisoners who disobeyed and ran for their lives were severely beaten by Kitabata.

After the final raid on the bridge on 1 April, one plane began circling over the siding where the work party was loading a train. No-one was allowed to stop work and, on the third pass, the aircraft dropped five anti-personnel bombs. Circling again, it dropped six more, killing two English and four Dutch prisoners, and mortally wounding another. Three men, including Australians Joe Collins and William Little, suffered serious leg injuries, while several others also required hospitalisation.

However, the ordeal was not yet over. On the 20th, Allied aircraft returned to strafe the area, sending the terrified POWs running in all directions. When they returned, they were paraded and informed that, if there was any reoccurrence, the offenders would be shot.

Now at Songkurai, and on the lookout for new victims, Kitabata took particular delight in targeting Durkin, often burning his buttocks with a lighted cigarette. By the third week of July, he was in a pitiful condition, with the soles of his bruised and swollen feet lacerated from walking bare-footed over the sharp stones and thorny bushes. Had it not been for the assistance of his fellow POWs, he would not have made it back to camp.

On the morning of 18 July, Durkin was in such an exhausted state and his feet so sore that he could not stand up. He lay on the floor of the hut, sobbing bitterly, unable to attend the morning parade. Fellow Australian, Sergeant Major Hamilton Duprez, who went to his assistance, tried unsuccessfully to prevent The Screaming Corporal from kicking and prodding him with a rifle butt. Hounded from the hut, Durkin eventually crawled on his hands and knees to the parade ground.

After being counted, the work party was marched off to work on some tunnels, about six kilometres away. Anyone too sick to work had to be carried on stretchers. Durkin, deemed fit enough to work, staggered along with the rest of the party until he saw his chance to move off into the jungle, unnoticed by Kitabata. Durkin had told Duprez before leaving the camp that it was impossible for him to carry on any longer, and that there was no point in the others trying to assist him, as he knew that he could not survive.

On arrival at the tunnels, Kitabata realised that Durkin was missing, but a search party of 40 POWs failed to find any trace of him. Prisoners not engaged in the search, which included Fred, were punished for the escape.

> The Japanese, who accused the rest of us in aiding and abetting his escape, employed various methods of third degree to make us confess. To find out how he had got away, they marched us down to a swampy area at nightfall, denuded us of all clothing, and informed us that, when we had told them all we knew, they would allow us to return to camp. In this part of the country were the most vicious type of mosquitoes I have ever encountered, along with a species of sand fly that we call gnats, which attacked at night in their millions, biting us unmercifully and even infesting our hair and beards. We knew no more about the prisoner's disappearance than our tormentors did, so we could tell them nothing.

I thought I knew all the bad language that existed, but I am only a novice compared with some of the chaps in the swamp that night. They cursed the mosquitoes, the sand flies and the Japs all in turn, but never a murmur condemning our unfortunate comrade who had caused it to happen. Daylight brought relief, however, when the nocturnal pests retired to sleep off the effects of their all-night feast.

The missing man's closest friends were put through an inquisition so severe that one, unable to stand it any longer, ran amok, killing one guard and, in an attempt to strangle a second, was clubbed to death by a third. Another, making a wild guess as to the escapee's hiding place, must have been guided by Divine inspiration, because he was found only 100 yards from the nominated spot which, as far as the Japs were concerned, closed the incident.

It was not Divine inspiration that led the Japanese to Durkin, but a local man, who betrayed him for a $500 reward. After wandering in a daze, Durkin had fallen asleep in a native hut near the work party site at Changaraya, where he was arrested on 21 July, three or four days after his disappearance. Taken back to Songkurai, his wrists bound together, he was interrogated, and then tied to a post outside the guardroom, in such a way that if he dropped from fatigue the rope around his neck would strangle him. On 27 July, Fred's party was moved to Konkoita Camp, about 20 kilometres to the south. However, 14 members were transferred to Rotai group and remained at Songkurai, where they witnessed the events that unfolded.

For the three weeks that Durkin was tied to the post he seldom had any protection from the sun or the cold nightly rain and very little food. He was given none at all for the first four days. One of his comrades managed to slip him a small amount of rice but Kitabata, in response to Durkin's pleas for water, slammed him across the head with a rifle butt. If he tried to sleep or recognised in some way a member of the working party passing by on the way to the tunnels, the corporal weighed in again, striking him about the face with a bamboo stick.

On 14 August, Durkin, his body and face a mass of bruises, carrying a hoe over one shoulder, was escorted to the rear of the camp by four guards. Several Australians, led by Private Les Hosier, furtively followed them. They spied Durkin in a small clearing, standing near some freshly dug earth, his hands tied behind his back. One guard held a rope, tied to Durkin's wrists, while the other three stood with bayonets fixed. At this critical point, one of the POWs tripped over a jungle vine, attracting the attention of the guards and forcing them to beat a hasty retreat. Shortly afterwards, the guard detail returned without the prisoner. Dutch POWs, who had also secretly witnessed the incident, reported that Durkin, who had been made to dig his own grave, had been bayoneted. Less than 24 hours later, Emperor Hirohito announced over Japanese radio that Japan had surrendered.

Durkin was not the only Australian to die at the hands of The Screaming Corporal. The day after Fred left for Konkoita, Kitabata zeroed in on a new victim, Private Keith Moss. Suffering from dysentery and cerebral malaria, he had become delirious and, when Kitabata stormed into the hut before daybreak to wake the prisoners, Moss slumped to the floor. Infuriated, Kitabata slapped and kicked him, before calling for reinforcements. Before any other 'help' arrived, Les Hosier and Sergeant Major Duprez managed to get Moss to his feet, supporting him on the parade ground while the head count took place. Noticing that the prisoner was swaying and mumbling, Kitabata rushed over and delivered several slaps to Moss's face. He fell to the ground, unable to move. He was still there when the work party returned that night – stone dead.

Another Australian POW also targeted by The Screaming Corporal was anti-tanker Allan Porter, from Victoria. At the end of July, at around the same time that Moss and Durkin were being subjected to brutal treatment, Kitabata was in charge of a 'light duty' group of sick POWs, tasked with transporting rations along a jungle track from the rail siding, about three kilometres from the camp. The corporal beat anyone unfortunate enough to fall behind with a heavy bamboo stick, carried specifically for that purpose.

Porter, suffering from recurring dysentery, was tackling the return journey, burdened with a bag of rice, when he slipped in the mud and broke his arm. When he was unable to continue to carry his load, Kitabata accused him of malingering and beat him mercilessly. On arrival at Songkurai, he was placed in the 'hospital' hut, where he received no medical treatment. He died on 27 August, while being transferred by train with Fred's group to Kanchanaburi, 12 days after the war ended.

Fred, who kept track of those who had died, recorded:

In the last three months of our captivity, 43 of our party of 250 lost their lives in the jungle camp, two on the train on the way back to freedom and five in hospital after we had been released. My own weight had gone down to six stone [38 kilograms]. My normal weight was 11½ stone [73 kilograms]. Every man was in the same condition and we all had beards that had not seen a razor for months.

It was a great relief when we moved down the line to Konkoita. This time our camp was only about 200 yards from our worksite. The guards, away from the influence of their superior officer, seemed quite reasonable and allowed us much more freedom of movement than at Songkurai. We did not have to leave the camp before 7 am, were given a section of tank trap to dig as that day's work and, when that was completed, we were allowed to go back to camp and then to the river, about 300 yards away, to bathe and bring back a supply of water.

The Koreans too had improved. When we first became prisoners, they were worse than the real Japs in the way they treated us but, when they learned that everything was not going so well, they went to the other extreme to try and curry favour. They even kept 'nit' for us when we were outside our compounds and would faithfully carry out their task, even to the extent of leading any suspicious Jap away from the place where we were likely to re-enter the camp. In fact, much of our trading with local civilians was done through, or with the assistance of, the Korean guards.

It was here at Konkoita that a Korean, who had been at all times one of the most helpful of the guards on the line, told us that we were all to be massacred as soon as the Allies made any attempt to invade Thailand. The next day he told us that, on 27 August, the Japanese would have no further use for the prisoners and would machine-gun all camps and throw the bodies into the rivers.

The date on which all surviving POWs were to be annihilated, 27 August, appears to have been a general order issued to commanders of all labour camps under Japanese control. However, the order was only carried out in British North Borneo, where five officers and ten ORs were shot in cold blood in the mountainous interior and another 55, carrying supplies for the Japanese, were shot on what became known as the death march track.

He then told us that the Japanese knew the Thais were getting ready to revolt against Japanese rule, and that would be the signal for the great massacre.

Our time seemed very short indeed. Even the Chinese, whom we contacted outside the camp every night, knew of the impending event and offered to help us escape into the jungle some days before the appointed date. They declared that the surrounding hills were sheltering thousands of Thai guerrilla troops, who were only awaiting the signal to swoop onto the prison camps to liberate all the prisoners, arm them, and give them a chance to fight for their lives.

What bitter enemies the Japs would have found us to be. We knew all their hiding places, how many troops were in the area and how to get at them. We would have gloried in the chance.

On 24 August, we were all awaiting the call to go to work when the Jap in charge informed us that there would be no work that day, and that in the afternoon we must be ready to move to Neike, further to the north, where another party of prisoners was stationed. This news caused quite a lot of speculation, as we knew our work was not completed. Some suggested making our break now, but instinct seemed to tell us not to. [It appears that Neike, which had railway sidings, was a convenient spot to concentrate POWs for transfer further south.]

Then something happened, which gave us food for more thought. A train came steaming down the line in broad daylight. This had not happened for months. Questioning looks passed from one to the other. When the train came to a halt right in front of our camp, two American bombers flew serenely overhead, taking no notice whatsoever of the train, as perfect a target as they could wish for. Thoughts turned to words: something big has happened! But what?

We were ordered to pack up and board the train. Everyone was strangely quiet; each occupied with his own thoughts. In the truck to which I was allotted with five other Australians were two wounded Japanese, with a nurse in attendance. Badly wounded and battle stained, with long hair and beards, they did not look much better than we did.

The nurse begged me, in Japanese, for a drink from my water bottle (a treasured possession) for the wounded men. I handed it to her and she asked, when returning it: 'Are you Australian?' When I answered in the affirmative, she went on to say, 'I thought so! I have asked Dutchmen for water, they say "no"; English also say "no". Thank you very much, Australia. I too am a Christian and I will not forget! That is why I am an army nurse and, if I found you wounded, I would treat you the same as a Japanese soldier.'

Images flashed through my mind of what other Japanese nurses had done, and I wondered. I thought I can but give her the benefit of the doubt. Trying to change the subject, I asked if she knew why we were travelling in the daytime and why the planes had not bombed the train? She answered, in some surprise, 'Do you not know the war is finished? Japan has been beaten, and you are free men again.'

Could I believe it? Why not! But to hear it from the lips of a Japanese woman, it did not seem real. Yet it must be right. What reason could she have for inventing a falsehood of that magnitude? Then it suddenly dawned on me that it was the glorious truth. Bubbling like an excited child I told my mates. As word spread from truck to truck, cheer upon cheer echoed through the hills. Men whose endurance had been tested to the limit embraced each other and cried like little children – and no one was ashamed of the tears. Why should we? Even the wounded Japanese smiled in sympathy, and the little Christian nurse broke down and cried with the rest.

What a happy crowd we were on that dirty old freight train. Dilapidated and battle-scarred, where shrapnel had torn great gaping holes in the wagons, to us it was the latest streamlined model carrying us to freedom – the first stage of our long journey home.

It was hard to realise that we were really free men again. As our train crawled along, over the line that had caused so much misery and sorrow, our thoughts turned towards home. Home, which had seemed so far away and remote, gradually began to take on a more tangible form, with memories of happy days and images of places and people we knew coming clearly into focus.

We were strangely silent. So silent in fact that the little Jap nurse, now chattering away and all smiles, as if she were pleased the war was over and our side had won, asked why

The rail line clinging to the cliffs at Wampo.

were we not happy, as before? At first I ignored her, but she was so persistent that, to quieten her, I tried to explain just how we felt.

Maybe home to the Asiatic does not mean the same as it does to us, or perhaps it was my limited knowledge of Japanese, because I failed to make her understand that each man was occupied with his own thoughts about what the future held and how his loved ones had fared in his absence; of what changes had taken place during his five years away, three and a half of them shut off from the world completely. It was little wonder we were silent.

The Japanese could never understand why, when we had loved our homes so much, we had so willingly left them. I finally gave up the attempt to explain all this and, going to the door of the truck, looked out upon the passing countryside. This time I could appreciate its grandeur. We were travelling along a mountain cutting and on the far side of the mighty basin was another mountain range, smoky blue in the distance.

Above us, on one side, was a mighty precipice towering away into the clouds, hanging like an immense curtain obscuring the peaks, the golden sunlit edges casting their reflection across the vast expanse of valley beneath. Ever changing shadows mottled the landscape: the jungle dark and mysterious against the brilliant green of the foliage reflected on the waters of a river, winding its way, snake-like, into the distance.

Flowers of every hue grew right up to the edge of the rail line, along with exotic orchids, creating a blaze of colour against the large clumps of bamboo that spread their leafy tangle across the line. How long, I wondered, before the jungle reclaims what we had toiled so hard to do.

How useless it all seemed.

As the train crawled towards civilization we saw signs of the devastation caused by our bombers, making the line impossible to use for war work. Almost every bridge had at one time or other suffered attack and giant craters showed where high explosive bombs had done their work. Twice we were held up while repairs were effected on the wooden viaducts to allow us to cross, which we did with considerable trepidation.

However, we made it without mishap and on 29 August reached the comparatively open country around our old Tamarkan camp. There was not a trace left of our compound – the entire area was bomb-pitted and blackened by fire and appeared to have been the target for a specially severe aerial blitz. The concrete and steel bridge was absolutely smashed. However, the wooden bridge, about 100 yards downstream, carried us safely across and we steamed on towards Kanchanaburi, just a few miles away.

Padi fields stretched for miles on either side of the line and the whole expanse, as far as the eye could see, was like a mighty bowling green. Chinese women, standing up to their waists in water planting rice, smiled and held their thumbs up as a sign of good luck. Water buffaloes, with only their heads and long curving horns visible, stared complacently at us from their wallows as we went by. Here and there native huts dotted the landscape, each with its quota of naked brown-skinned children, shouting and waving to us.

We at last came to within sight of our destination – Kanchanaburi, the old Siamese capital, where a camp had been prepared to welcome us back from the jungle. Cheer after cheer rent the air as we beheld a tattered and torn Union Jack, the world's greatest emblem, fluttering proudly from a flagpole. The meaning of the flag and all it stood for came to us in a rush of emotion. There it was – just an old piece of rag – bravely welcoming its lost children back into the haven of its protection. I defy any man to go through our experience and remain unaffected. For three and a half years we had waited for this day, and now, at long last, it was ours.

However, the knowledge that one of the trucks held the dead bodies of our two mates, who had died on the way, cast a gloom over our happiness. Bareheaded and silent, we stood while the remains of Bombardier Thomas Edols, 2/15 Field Regiment and Lance Bombardier Allan Porter, 4 Anti-tank, were carried to their last resting place.

Their sufferings were so great that even the knowledge that they were free at last was not enough to bring them back from the Valley of the Shadows.

Fred, master of the understatement, did not dwell on the appalling condition of those arriving at Kanchanaburi from up-country. However, John Coast, a British officer at Kanchanaburi, who had meticulously recorded his experiences throughout his imprisonment and endured hardship similar to that of Fred, was shocked, not only to hear the details of Durkin's death, but by the state of those who had survived.

We hurried out to the railway line and there we found difficulty in speaking and the Nips in charge of the party were within an ace of being killed on the spot. The sight of those trucks was unforgettable and unforgivable. Englishmen clad in sacking, gaunt, hollow-eyed, just bones, their skin flaking off in great dirty brown patches … One man, aged 45, had lost three toes up country. But that was little. Some of the jungle ulcers on other men were open pits, stretching from heel to toe and with ankles bared to the bone. There was one man who had a running ulcer on his back that made one of the amateur orderlies vomit as he helped to dress it.

Yet in spite of all their misery and pain and sickness, they were already saved in nearly every case; for we could see in their wide eyes that it was OVER, that all the bloodiness of work, beatings, pig-food and jungle existence was OVER, and that that had already lit the vital, spiritual spark in their poor bodies, and a terrific and desperate will to live had already been born in them again. Within half an hour they were all in hospital.

And then we really got cracking. Clean mats and sacking, spare blankets and clothing were collected and immediately issued, and their stinking, muddied old wet sacking, their only bedding, was thrown away. Doctors and orderlies were bandaging and dressing and examining; we were bathing, clothing, filling bottles with tea, distributing food, anything we could.

Rest, drugs, water, good food and careful attention did their work. I went back the same evening to see a man I had carried in, and after he had been bathed, combed, fed and given a clean vest I could hardly recognise him.

They had been working on the Thai-Burma border and up till several days after the war ended had been digging tank traps and artillery emplacements. The Nips in these camps had stolen the best of their rations, and they had lived on a wretched diet of insufficient rice, greens and a little of the dried 'stink fish'. They had Reveille at 5.30 am, were out at work by seven, and they were not back in camp until 9 pm. They left their camp in the dark and returned in the dark. They had no rest whatsoever. The mosquitoes and midges were a torment and everyone had fever. They lived at the scale of 100 men in a narrow hut 50 feet long, and they slept in three tiers, their bodies turned sideways as there was not room to lie on their backs. And on top of it all, it was the middle of the monsoon.

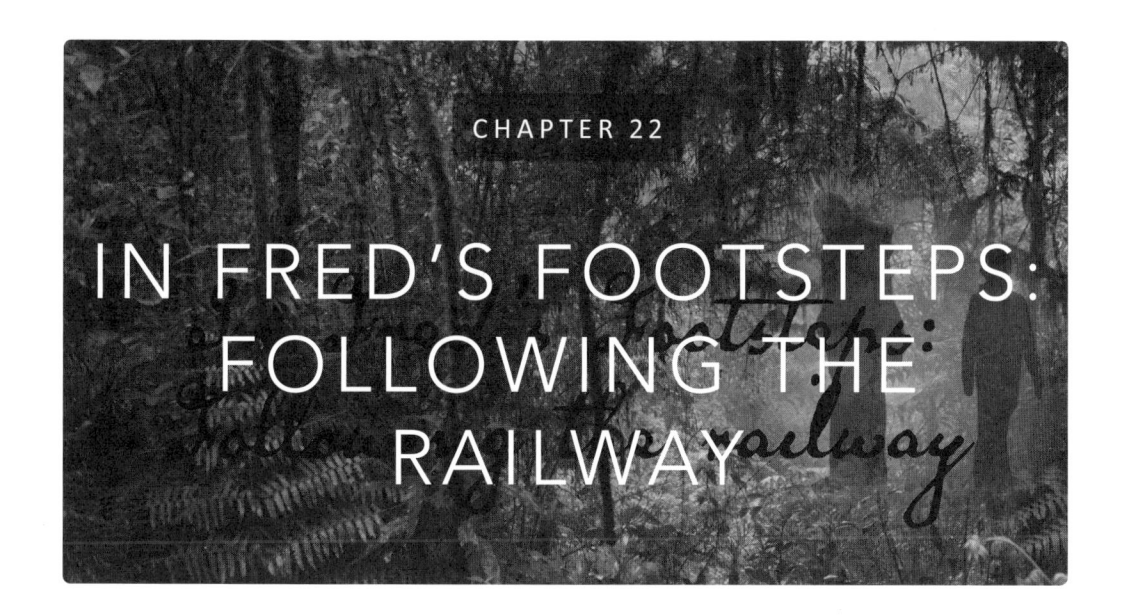

CHAPTER 22
IN FRED'S FOOTSTEPS: FOLLOWING THE RAILWAY

It was now time to follow Dad into captivity. Going to Burma (now known as Myanmar) was not an option, because of the political situation and civil unrest, so Paul and I flew to Bangkok, to trace Dad's movements from the hospital at Nakhon Pathom to the Three Pagodas Pass at the border.

I could not believe that, after sitting in a plane for a few hours, I was in Thailand in the 'Land of Smiles', a country that, for the last few years, had completely captivated my imagination. How strange things looked as we headed off on our journey: the odd shape of the trees outside the airport; sheets of cardboard leaning against a fence providing a home for the homeless; the incessant traffic, and what seemed like millions of people moving along the sidewalks in one big indistinguishable blob. As we made our way through the maze of Bangkok streets and freeways to head out into the countryside, my eyes were on sticks. It was like being on another planet.

Our first stop was Nakhon Pathom, right outside Pra Pathom, the enormous shining stupa that had guided the American planes on their way to bomb Bangkok. Dozens of worshippers were in attendance, carrying bowls of fruit and containers of rice to place below the various golden statues as offerings. The smell of heavy incense wafted through the air, which was filled with pieces of gold leaf that the faithful had failed to attach to the statues and which was now blowing about like exotic litter.

It was here, at the nearby hospital camp, where thousands of POWs were treated by the dedicated medical staff, that Dad received his life-saving blood transfusion from his mate, Chris Guerin. I thought of the wonderful work done by Coates and so many other doctors, including the well-known Edward 'Weary' Dunlop, Bruce Hunt, Lloyd Cahill and Major Walter Fisher, a rather taciturn man who had looked after Dad and was known as The Fuhrer.

Our next stop was Ban Pong, the staging point for prisoners arriving by train from Singapore. From here, the Australians in Dunlop D, F, H, K and L Forces had begun their nightmarish experiences on the Thai end of the railway. There was no trace of their camp, but St Joseph's Catholic Church, which would have been part of the local scene when the POWs were there, was still standing.

It was not far to Kanchanaburi and the Commonwealth War Graves Cemetery.

Kanchanaburi, pronounced 'Garn-cha-na-boori' and meaning town of gold, was confusingly called 'Kanburi' by the POWs, who were prone to bastardising or shortening Thai place names, sometimes to the point of being unrecognisable. Situated where the Khwae Noi and Khwae Yai Rivers now become the Mae Khlong, in 1943 Kanchanaburi had a population of around 5000, several hundred of whom were employed at the local paper factory. The unsealed main road, lined with two-storey wooden shophouses selling a variety of produce, passed through the town gate, a substantial square concrete portal, painted white.

The gate is still there, along with part of the old city walls, but the population of Kanchanaburi has swelled to about 30,000 souls and there is now a new main thoroughfare. About 1.5 kilometres from the old city gate and on the left-hand side of the new main street is the war cemetery, holding the remains of 6858 Allied POWs who died in Thailand – 1362 Australian, 3585 British, 1896 Dutch, 12 Indians, 2 New Zealanders and 1 Canadian. Another 1335 Australians are buried in Thanbyuzayat Cemetery. However, not all of them died in Burma. The bodies of all those who died in Thailand, north of Neike, are also there.

Passing through the sandstone gates at the entry to Kanchanaburi Cemetery, I was overcome by the sight of the thousands of graves, all carefully tended and set amid immaculate lawns and beautiful shrubs. As I strolled in silence along the rows of bronze headstones, keeping a lookout for the distinctive Rising Sun badge of the AIF, I was struck by the ages inscribed on them, many of them just boys, and struggled to comprehend just what the mothers endured when their sons were posted 'missing, believed to be prisoner of war'.

Immediately across the road from the cemetery is the Thai-Burma Railway Centre (the Thai taking priority as it is at the Thai end of the line), a privately run enterprise that serves two purposes. It has a small but very interesting interpretive centre and museum, with eight separate galleries, featuring items collected along the railway. Information boards tell the story of the thousands of POWs and civilians who toiled along its 415-kilometre length. Upstairs is a research area where visitors can obtain a great deal of information on Allied POWs, collated over decades. The centre also organises customised tours and pilgrimages with guides who have an in-depth knowledge of the POW story.

A short drive took us to the river, and the fabled 'Bridge on the River Kwai'. I caught a glimpse of it in the distance, and felt a thrill of excitement. THE bridge. However, I must admit that, when viewed up close, I was disappointed. I had imagined a huge structure – even from a distance it looked bigger than this. In place of the towering construction that I had pictured in my mind was a long, low, dark-grey steel bridge, perched high above the water.

Two square spans in the middle had replaced three of the arches damaged during the many Allied bombing raids from November 1944 to almost the end of the war. We walked across it, via narrow wooden planks set in the middle of the tracks, trying not to look down at the fast-flowing river beneath.

I had seen the movie, *Bridge on the River Kwai*, based on the novel of the same name by Pierre Boulle, and knew that the bridge depicted in it was nothing like the 'real' one. However, it was not only the bridge that was fictitious.

The award-winning movie, starring Alec Guinness as the slightly unhinged and totally fictitious Colonel Nicholson, who was nothing like the actual commander, Lieutenant Colonel Toosey, created such interest that tourists, believing the story to be true, began travelling to Thailand. To satisfy a growing demand to see the 'famous' bridge, in 1960 the Thai authorities changed the name of the river from Khwae Mae Khlong to Khwae Yai

Above: Kanchanaburi's old gate and wall.

Left: Kanchanaburi cemetery, where many of Fred's mates are buried.

Below: The fabled 'River Kwai' bridge.

(big), as there was already a Khwae Noi (little) River, which joined the Khwae Mae Khlong a short distance downstream. The river below the junction is now known as the Mae Klong. The decision to create a River Kwai at the site of the bridge to satisfy the tourists, who bring in hundreds of thousands of dollars each year, serves only to consolidate Boulle's story as fact.

Up a side street, about 200 metres from the bridge and behind a tall fence, I found the memorial that the Japanese had erected to honour all those who had died on the railway. A plaque, added post-war, read:

> This monument was erected by the then Japanese Army in February 1944, during World War II in memory of all the personnel of the Allied Forces together with our people, who died during the construction of the Thailand-Burma Railway. Once a year in March, voluntary members of the Japanese community in Thailand assemble here to hold a memorial ceremony for those who died.

The central obelisk is within four L-shaped walls, sited a few metres out from each corner. One, dedicated to prisoners of war, is inscribed *In memory of deceased prisoners of war 1944*, with a circle enclosing four floral emblems: wattle for the Australians, a tulip for the Dutch, a rose for the British and what looked like a hibiscus representing the Asian nations. A photo taken at the time of the dedication shows prisoners, Japanese and locals, in attendance. They all seem to be remarkably well dressed. Knowing the Japanese, the clothing was most likely supplied for the event, for propaganda purposes.

Also nearby is the JEATH (Japan, England, Australia, Thailand, Holland) Museum but, to reach the entrance, we had to run the gauntlet of dozens of stalls selling everything imaginable. Once inside, I noticed a large package on display with the name of my POW friend, Tom Morris, on the cover. He had sent some information to the museum staff and they had displayed it, along with the packaging! How typical of Tom to make sure the correct information on the railway was reaching the now inquisitive public.

A short journey by boat up the Khwae Noi and a short walk up a jungle-clad river bank brought us to Chungkai War Cemetery. Buried there are 1426 British and 313 Dutch, who died either in the nearby camp hospital or while working on the line. The labour force, tasked with excavating two large cuttings and constructing a small bridge linking the two, was housed in a large atap camp, alongside the railway tracks. A large number of Australians were treated at Chungkai, but none died there.

For the next stage of our journey, we made our way to Kanchanaburi Railway Station. The train was 45 minutes late and when it eventually arrived there was a mad rush for seats. The engine roared, the whistle blew and we were off in a cloud of diesel smoke and fumes. The seats were made of wood but, as we were travelling first class, railway staff had placed a cushion on each. A folding table, dragged from beneath our seat, was attached to the wall at one end with a drop-down leg to hold the other firmly in position. Although the temperature was approaching 40 degrees Celsius and the humidity was around 80 per cent, there was no air conditioning, but ceiling fans positioned at strategic points rotated the hot air, sending it in all directions.

After crossing the 'River Kwai', we passed through the Chungkai cuttings and into a kaleidoscope of fascinating scenery: thick jungle, rice paddies, fields planted with tapioca, corn, bananas and sugarcane. We crossed rivers and roads, travelled through numerous cuttings and over bridges, and rattled at speed across flat stretches. After about an hour, the train slowed.

Below us was the Khwae Noi River snaking off in the distance and immediately before us, and hugging the cliff face, was the huge curving spectacle of the Wampo Viaduct. How it was built, considering the conditions under which the POWs worked, is amazing. Perched high above the river on one side, with the vertical cliff face on the other, it is a masterpiece of engineering, built entirely of timber, all cut and dragged into position by the prisoners. At the end of the viaduct is the small station of Tham Krasae and a huge cavern that runs back into the side of the cliff. I was keen to see it as the POWs had told me the story of a Japanese guard who had disappeared in this very cave. There was no clue to his whereabouts until a huge python snake was discovered with a very large lump in its innards.

From Tham Krasae the train continued north to Nam Tok, known as Tarsao in wartime, travelling high above the river in many places. From the train window I spotted 'elephant hill', so named by the POWs because part of the mountain range resembled one. On arrival at Nam Tok, we left the train and travelled by road to Konyu Cutting, better known as Hellfire Pass.

It was so named because much of the work during the speedo period was carried out at night by the light of oil lamps and flickering bamboo brands which, when added to the spectral shadows of emaciated prisoners and the noise of rock drilling, created a surreal scene reminiscent of Dante's images of hell.

The prisoners in this sector worked on a stretch of railway that extended from Hellfire Pass to Compressor Cutting, and included the infamous Pack of Cards Bridge, constructed entirely from green timber, wooden wedges, bamboo and rattan vines. A whopping 400

Above: The Chungkai cutting.
Left: On the Wampo viaduct.

metres long and 27 metres high, it fell down three times during construction and was eventually replaced by an embankment.

POW and Asian work parties assigned to this area were housed in various compounds at Konyu and Hintok, including Hintok River Camp, comprising open-sided tents perched on a plateau high above the Khwae Noi. From these camps the POWs walked several kilometres to the various construction sites, along trails that were often steep and difficult. The workers excavating Compressor Cutting, in the mountain above their camp, were compelled to scramble up a steep cliff, coated in treacherous slimy mud during the monsoon season.

About 1500 Allied POWs and 2000 Asians started working on the Konyu-Hintok section of the railway in November 1942. In late April, Australian and British prisoners from D Force, recently arrived from Singapore, joined Dunlop Force, from Java, to labour on the two Konyu cuttings, linked together by a small viaduct over a stream. One cutting, just under 500 metres long and about eight metres deep, was cut into the face of the hillside. The other, usually referred to as 'Hellfire Pass', is a double-sided cutting through solid rock, about 75 metres long and more than 26 metres deep.

The limestone for both cuttings was removed by hand by a method known as 'hammer and tap'. Using a 25-centimetre-long drill, a small hole was made in the rock face, with one man holding the metal drill or 'tap' and another hitting the head of it with a four-kilogram hammer, before rotating it 90 degrees. The pulverised rock was removed from the hole with a piece of thick-gauge wire, flattened at one end to make a scoop. As the hole became deeper, longer drills were used, until it was one metre deep. Twice in each shift the holes were packed with dynamite and detonated. The resultant rubble was then removed by

A tented construction camp.

hand in baskets, or by the pole-and-rice-sack method, and tipped over the mountainside.

The daily quota of rock to be moved by each team was first set at 1.5 metres, then two but, when the strongest in the party were finished by 4 pm, it was increased to three. The excessive workload on the weaker men, lack of food, illnesses including cholera, and monsoonal rains diminished the workforce to such an extent that, by June 1943, the work had fallen far behind schedule. Wanting to free the bottleneck to allow the line laying teams to proceed, the Japanese brought in 600 Australian and British POWs from D and H forces, about 1000 Asian workers, known as romusha, plus Japanese jackhammer operators and an air compressor, which needed constant attention to keep it going. The POW labour force, including the hammer-and-tap men, worked up to 18 hours a day until the cutting was completed, six weeks later. The total time taken to excavate 'Hellfire Pass' was 12 weeks.

From January 1943 until October that year, when what was left of the labour force was moved to a new site, 7 Division's Edward 'Weary' Dunlop, CO of Dunlop Force, was the senior officer in the Konyu-Hintok area, including Hellfire Pass, a location with which his name is intrinsically linked. There is a longstanding claim, unsupported by any evidence, that 65 (or 68), POWs were beaten to death at Hellfire Pass in a 12-week period. If true, it would be a major war crime.

The story has its origins in a statement made post-war by Roaring Reg Newton, who spent just three weeks at Hellfire Pass with his D Force's U Battalion, from 29 June to 20 July. On the say so of Newton, a death toll, citing 68 deaths, first surfaced in 1958 as a footnote in Australia's Official History, *The Japanese Thrust*. Strangely, 68 is also the number of beatings to which Newton said he was subjected for intervening on behalf of his men. In 2/19 Battalion's unit history, *The Grim Glory*, which Newton compiled, the figure is 65 – 28 before he arrived and 37 while his men were working on the pass, a supposed death rate of 1.75 deaths from beatings per day.

The claim that so many were beaten to death has been repeated numerous times and, due to the Internet, has spread even further. Yet British accounts do not mention any of their prisoners dying from a beating during this period and not a single one of the affidavits, sworn by a large number of Australians, includes testimony that more than 60 POWs met their end in this way. Death records kept by Dunlop and Australian camp staff, along with the affidavits of the many POWs reporting atrocities at Hellfire Pass, show that, of the 197 Australians in Dunlop, D and H forces who died during the construction period, three deaths only were attributable to a beating.

The first victim was Gunner Geoffrey Singer, aged 26, who died at Konyu Camp on 20 June after being hit on the head with a drill. The second was Dunlop Force's Sergeant Stanley Hallam, of Tasmania.

Dunlop recorded that Hallam, who was very ill, collapsed from a high fever on the way to work on 22 June. Unable to carry on, he returned to Hintok Road Camp where he was diagnosed with enteritis and malaria. After lining up with the other men who could not work that day, he was 'mercilessly beaten by Nippon Engineer Sergeant Billie the Pig and his assistant, Mollie the Monk'. The latter, Sergeant Iwaya Taiko, whose Korean name was Kang Te Kong, had a mouthful of gold teeth and a very loud voice. He was an ironsmith by trade, which possibly accounted for his predilection to bash POWs with an iron bar. Hallam had been hit with one and 'returned to hospital deadly pale, face swollen, neck and chest contused, abrasions to the knees and legs and a sprained right ankle'. After

Ray Parkin's famous sketch, 'Two malarias and a cholera'.

suffering two periods of profound unconsciousness, he died on the morning of 26 June, four days later.

There was a third victim, unidentified, believed to be British, beaten at around the same time.

During the 12 weeks that the POWs were working at Hellfire Pass, 197 Australians died. A staggering 136 died from cholera, 71 of them in the H Force Camp, known as Malay Hamlet. Another 58 deaths were due to cholera at the Hintok camps, with 16 out of 16 succumbing at Hintok Road Camp. However, cholera accounted for just 7 of the 41 deaths at the D Force Konyu camps, where dysentery was rife.

It was while working at Hellfire Pass with Dunlop Force that Australian artist and sailor, Petty Officer Ray Parkin, ex-HMAS *Perth*, sketched two malaria victims supporting a cholera patient, which he aptly titled *Two Malarias and a Cholera*. It has become the quintessential image portraying, at one glance, the suffering endured by so many on the Burma-Thai Railway, and has been adopted as the logo of the Changi Museum in Singapore.

After the railway was demolished in 1947, Hellfire Pass, overgrown with bamboo and small saplings, remained 'lost' until rediscovered by Tom Morris in 1984. Due to his efforts, it was officially recognised as a memorial site in 1987, when Weary Dunlop unveiled a plaque there. A service conducted by the Australian government's Department of Veterans' Affairs is now held each ANZAC Day at a simple granite memorial, erected in the pass. Although Fred never worked at any of the sites near Hellfire Pass, its name is synonymous with the POW story and is, in its way, what Anzac Cove is to Gallipoli.

The 'lost' railway, near Hellfire Pass.

High above the pass is a museum erected by the Australian Government at the instigation of Tom Morris, who first advanced the idea in 1983. It was opened in 1998 as an education facility to help make visitors more aware about the history of the railway. It is one of the greatest disappointments of my life that I was not able to attend this event and share in Tom's triumph, although I was successful in nominating him for an Order of Australia, which he received in 2000. I had high hopes of attending, but Paul, our daughter and I had sustained serious injuries in a motor vehicle accident the previous year. We spent two weeks in hospital, mine in intensive care. On many occasions, struggling to survive, I drew strength from the memory of my father and his comrades who had fought their own battle for survival, 54 years previously. I was in a modern hospital with modern drugs and plenty of food, receiving attention from the most caring doctors and nursing staff. The only thing that the POWs and I had in common was the care we received. Their dedicated doctors and medical orderlies often had nothing to offer by way of medical assistance but their compassion and healing hands. When I was at my lowest point, I am sure that the strength to fight back came from forces more powerful than any medicine – strength that helped me recover, so that I could finish what I had set out to do.

My disappointment at not being able to join Tom at the museum opening was great but, as it also serves as a research centre, I was able to contribute by soliciting a large number of books from people from all around Australia to form a core library for visitors. Later, when the museum was remodelled, the library became redundant. The books are now with the Department of Veterans' Affairs in Canberra, for use by historians there.

After wandering through the various exhibits, we made our way down a set of steeply winding cement stairs to the railway trace, which led to the cutting on our right. Ballast still lay here and there and, before we knew it, we were in Hellfire Pass. No one said a word. As I looked at the towering precipice above, I marvelled at how underfed, overworked men, with only the most primitive of tools, could carve their way through the mountain.

Above: Di placing poppies on the Hellfire Pass Memorial.
Right: One of the railway skips.

Narrow channels created by the hammer-and-tap men were visible in the rock face, while underfoot, imbedded in the dirt, were bits of old sleepers that had stood the test of time. Looking out onto the vast valley below, I could see the Khawe Noi River, snaking its way around the base of the mountain range.

Along with the original plaque, dedicating the pass as a memorial site in 1987, is one honouring Weary Dunlop, who died in 1993. On ANZAC Day 1994, some of his ashes were scattered along a small section of line and sleepers laid on the railway trace. Other ashes were floated down the Khwae Noi River on a tiny, flower-bedecked raft. Not far from the plaques is a tree, growing straight and tall between the towering walls of the cutting, defiantly demonstrating that in that terrible place something could survive. More than just a tree, it is a symbol of hope and survival.

It is hard to put into words what it was like to be standing on that sacred ground, but I could now understand why men, like Dad, came home and didn't talk about their experiences. As Dad had not been at Hellfire Pass, I was only there out of academic interest, yet I find it hard to describe how it affected me, simply being where the POWs had been; where they had experienced starvation, illness, and mental and physical torture as they faced the seemingly impossible task of carving out this section of the line, virtually by hand.

A short detour, just north of the pass, took us into the Hintok River Camp area. Part way down the valley we stopped and followed an old railway embankment, constructed from thousands of rocks by British prisoners of war. It had survived the ravages of torrential rain in the monsoon seasons for decades, but I was shocked to discover that a large section had recently been torn apart. Discarded rocks had fallen into the valley below, while many more were stacked along the old railway trace. For me, it was desecration at its worst, tantamount to someone dismantling the pyramids. From the embankment, a newly made and well-worn path through the undergrowth led to the rear of the museum, where a garden wall had recently been constructed. How could this be? Was it possible that those responsible for the preservation and care of the railway and its history had actually destroyed part of it?

With my emotions running high, I took photographs as evidence and, on returning

Above: POWs carving out a mountainside by night (Murray Griffin). Below: Exploring the rail trace near Hintock.

home, arranged a meeting at the Office of Australian War Graves in Canberra. The person responsible for the museum in Thailand claimed that Burmese refugees digging for bamboo shoots had dislodged the rocks but, as no Burmese were known to be in that particular area, I rejected this 'explanation'. I was vindicated when, a few months later, guilt was admitted. I was assured he would never do it again. 'Too late', I cried. 'The damage has been done.'

Another detour took us to Hintok Road camp (also known as Hintok Mountain Camp) where many of the Dunlop Force prisoners and others walked to work each day, and to where Hintok Curved Trestle Bridge once stood. Over the years, photographs of this bridge have been repeatedly, and wrongly, identified as the 'Pack of Cards Bridge'. 'Pack of Cards Bridge' never stayed up long enough for a photo to be taken! In fact, the only image in existence is an aerial shot, taken by a reconnaissance plane at an opportune moment.

Back on the main road, we headed north into the mountains. On one of the hairpin bends were several small Thai spirit houses, indicating that many people had died in the area and, judging by the road, most likely from road accidents – a comforting thought. It is Thai tradition that, when someone dies, a spirit house is placed near the spot to allow the spirit to have somewhere to live. Offerings of food are made regularly, along with the burning of incense.

We passed through many areas where our POWs had worked, including the site of Kui Yae (Kuie) Station, near Dad's camp and where the Allies had bombed the train, killing many of the POWs on board. With the aid of a metal detector, we found a couple of old railway spikes, one of which I later gave to Dad's mate Jack O'Malley, who was also there to witness the carnage and clean up the mess.

We were now entering an area near Neike (also known as Ni Thea), where the tunnel parties had worked. I knew it was normally impossible to get there because, in the 1980s, the Vajiralongkorn (formerly Khao Laem) Dam had flooded the valley. However, due to drought, the water level had dropped considerably in recent months. The backwaters of the dam came into view, then a huge bridge that spanned the Ranti River. Crossing the bridge, we left the vehicle and looked across the lake.

Off to our right stood a bluff, the very spot where, according to the Railway Centre, Private Durkin had been killed. The water level of the dam was now very low, low enough for me to go and see where Dad had worked on the tunnels. The route I needed to take was boggy, and our guide advised me not to go any further, but I was on a mission. I took off, leaving Paul and the guide in my wake. Realising my determination, they had no option but to follow. Some areas were quite muddy, and there was a fair bit of water to avoid, but to me it was no challenge at all. I was about to see where Dad and his mates had dug the tunnels into the mountainside, and nothing, and I mean nothing, was going to stop me.

The route taken took us through a valley between two small rocky ranges, with waters of the dam hugging the cliffs on the opposite side but receding well away from the side where we were walking. As we trudged along, our guide pointed out the Neike Camp and Neike Station area, situated across the water. Here and there, he also drew my attention to man-made earthen walls along the edge of the water, just wide enough for a train track.

After slogging along for roughly two or more kilometres, we noticed what appeared to be a line of ballast emerging from the lake. According to our guide, this was possibly the railway trace, but we later learned it was actually a road. Following the ballast line, we reached an area littered with broken ceramic insulators. Knowing a telephone line had been erected along the railway, I scratched about and found one that was intact. Not only was it intact, but also attached to it was a large spike that screwed into a pole, or a well-positioned tree. I knew that Dad, being a PMG linesman before and after the war, would have been fascinated by my find.

The insulator.

A short distance further on, where the mountain range turned to our right, the guide pointed to an opening at the base of a hill. I was off like a shot. This is what I had come to see – where Dad and his tunnel party had worked. At last, I was about to stand on the very spot that Dad had written about all those years ago – or so I was led to believe. On reaching the opening, large rocks blocked my path and, as I stumbled across them in my haste, the guide explained that they were the result of people looking for gold and treasure, supposedly buried in the area by the Japanese during the war. Post-war, many treasure seekers had searched the length of the railway numerous times, but no trace of any loot was ever found. However, they had left evidence of their searches, and the guide said that this was one of them.

My heart was racing as I peered into what was a ground-level cave, about the size of a small bedroom and high enough for me to stand upright without any trouble. It was muddy underfoot and a musty smell hung in the air. To my right, standing on four legs, was a cage made of bamboo, indicating that someone had occupied the space in recent years and the cage had held some animal captive. The guide remarked that some monks had been living there when he visited the site many years ago. To the left of the cage, a small tunnel, barely big enough for someone to slide into, led into the depths of the mountain. I was highly tempted to explore further, but Paul warned me that something could be lurking in there, waiting for dinner to appear. Remembering the python in the cave at Wampo Viaduct, I restrained myself from going any further.

So I just stood, thinking about Dad, wondering if I were standing where he had once stood. I felt overwhelmed by a great sadness and tears flooded down my cheeks. However, once my emotions began to subside, doubts crept in. Something just didn't seem to add up. I recalled what Dad had noted: up a precipice, crude stairways, carrying huge logs up a mountain, tunnelling using explosives, pit props. There was no sign of any of this here and the cave at ground level seemed to be formed by nature, not a tunnel excavated by men. However, I was assured we were in the right place, so who was I to argue? Maybe I had to accept it, but would I? Could I?

By way of further 'proof', as we left the cave my attention was drawn to a gap in the hills where the rail line had run – a very good reason, I was told, to have heavy artillery in the cave, as a train carrying invasion troops could easily be stopped. The gap looked a bit far off to me, but we headed in that direction and, from a muddy ploughed field atop a hill, a most picturesque scene unfolded. Not far away, around a small bluff, was the 131 Kilo Camp, where Colonel Anderson and the No 1 Mobile Force rail-laying party had begun working in September 1943.

Heading back towards the area of the cave, I remained unconvinced. There just had to be more, I reasoned, but who was I, a female rapidly approaching 60, and blonde at that, to pursue this line of questioning any further, when experts told me otherwise?

The next place of interest was Shimo (Lower) Songkurai, a place synonymous with the terrible suffering of F Force. We drove down a muddy narrow road, grateful to be in a four-wheel drive vehicle, and stopped on the side of a hill – Cholera Hill. Although now denuded of jungle, I could identify the spot where POW George Aspinall took a photograph of three POWs with his secret camera.

The 2/19th's doctor, Lloyd Cahill, who had cared for the wounded during the retreat from Bakri, spent some time at this camp with F Force. In April 1943 he was one of 10 medical officers, plus a dentist, who left Changi by train for Thailand with 3400 British

Definitely not the caves!

and 3600 Australians. It took ten trains to move the 7000 men, with 30 crammed into each 6-metre x 2-metre enclosed steel wagon. The journey lasted four nights and five days, with spasmodic meal and toilet stops. Cahill carried with him an item of inestimable value – a copy of a book on tropical diseases.

Shortly after his arrival at Shimo Songkurai, following the arduous trek from Ban Pong and still toting his precious text book, there was an outbreak of cholera. As desperate situations call for desperate measures, to keep his dysentery and cholera patients hydrated, Cahill infused them through a hollow bamboo catheter, attached to a length of stethoscope tubing and an army water bottle filled with saline solution, made from boiled river water and rock salt stolen from the Japanese kitchen. Despite his efforts, and those of his fellow doctors at various camps, 59 per cent of the British died. The Australians lost 29 per cent of their men.

We walked up a slight rise to the top of Cholera Hill, so named because this was where those stricken with cholera were isolated from other prisoners in open-sided 'fly' tents, at the height of the monsoon. Frank Noakes, whose family we knew in Boorowa, was among those who died.

Looking back towards the main road, we could see a large flat expanse, freshly planted with tapioca, formerly the site of the main camp. The cemetery was not far away, the large hollows left by war graves recovery teams pinpointing the area where the bodies were exhumed post-war. The Thai farmers had not planted crops there but, in one hollow, where a huge clump of bamboo had taken hold, was a small bamboo cross, some dried gum leaves and several red poppies, signifying that those who died so far away from home were still remembered.

Leaving Shimo Songkurai behind, we continued on our way, passing Songkurai and Kami (Upper) Songkurai, where a good-sized wooden bridge was built over a tributary of the Khwae Noi, and then Changaraya, all camps where many members of F Force had also died. After winding through some more hills, the road flattened out, and there, in the centre of a large roundabout, were three little pagodas – Three Pagodas Pass. As with the 'bridge on the River Kwai', I had expected to see something much larger, but what they lacked in size was more than compensated by their raw beauty and sense of intrigue. Gleaming with a coat of fresh whitewash and bedecked in orange and yellow fabric, they stood amid a

Left: Cholera tents, Shimo Songkurai.

Below: POWs 'fit' for work, Shimo Songkurai.

Left: The Three Pagodas.

garden of yellow daisies, with the blue hue of the mountains of the Tenasserim Range, also known as Bilauktaung Mountains, making a stunning backdrop.

The Three Pagodas Pass is the oldest trade route in Asia. Used by Thai and Burmese armies, it was the invasion route favoured by Burmese soldiers during the Ayutthaya period, from 1350 to 1767. The three miniature pagodas, Darn Chedi Sam Ong, are memorials to that period and to the Karen, Mon and Burmese people who, centuries ago, settled their families along the border, inside the kingdom of Thailand. Traditionally, when the Burmese arrived at this spot, they threw a piece of rock to mark exactly where they entered Thailand. In time, the stones piled up to form simple stupas or cairns. The Mon community built what is there today as an historical landmark.

I was transfixed, but I knew from photographs that this was not how Dad saw them in December 1943, when he crossed the border into Thailand. At that time, they were a nondescript colour, isolated in the middle of the jungle, the only sign of civilisation some telegraph poles. As I stood in Thailand, with the soil of Burma almost in touching distance on the other side of the guarded border, the impact of why I was there hit me. I just hoped that, when Burma settled down, I would be able to visit the campsites where Dad had been.

For the time being, I had to be satisfied with seeing as many places as possible on the Thai side. Before leaving the Three Pagodas, we photographed a square concrete plinth, inscribed with a bronze relief map of the railway, sculptured by Australian Ross Bastiaan. A small plaque indicates that inside the plinth is a time capsule, left there by a group of Australians in 1995 to mark the 50th anniversary of the end of World War II. It contains messages of goodwill, books, documents, photographs and other material. The grand reopening date is Anzac Day 2045, but I doubt I'll be around to see it, as by then I will be 97 years old.

Heading south, past the dam and the cave, we stopped at our final destination – Kinsaiyok Jungle Camp at Kilo 244, where Allied prisoners, including a number of Australians from Dunlop Force, excavated a cutting. While Hellfire Pass may be deeper, the one here was longer. However, the most notable thing was a long embankment, 25 metres high in some places, at the end of which were the concrete footings of what was once a huge bridge. After decades of monsoonal rain, the embankment stands firm, a testament to those who built it. Luckily it is hidden far enough away, and in dense jungle, to avoid the fate of the other embankment at Hellfire Pass.

I returned home feeling very frustrated, even more so when, in response to my suggestion that, judging from photos of the landscape and Dad's description, the tunnels were north of the dam location and that they should search there, I received a message from the Railway Centre. It 'confirmed' that the cave I had visited was definitely made by the tunnel party and that treasure seekers had caused part of it to collapse. Annoyed that my suggestion, based on sound logic and Dad's notes, had been brushed aside, I contacted Lynette to seek a second opinion. After studying photographs of the cave and the area I thought it might be, and reading Dad's description, she agreed with me completely. The cave at the dam was not man-made and definitely not a tunnel.

If the tunnel party was not at the spot I had visited, where was it? Had I looked more carefully at Dad's notes, I would have discovered that he had later referred to a place he called 'Sun Kly' (Songkurai). However, a breakthrough came from a most unexpected quarter some months after I returned from Thailand.

The Time Capsule.

Lynette had been contacted by a member of the public, keen to nominate POWs killed while trying to escape, or executed as a result, for posthumous gallantry awards. However, while she agreed that Australian and British personnel who had escaped from German camps and made it back to the UK, especially airmen, were worthy recipients, she believed it inappropriate to confer gallantry awards on those who had tried to escape from the Japanese.

Unlike the situation in Europe, where local people were willing to assist escapees, and escape lines were set up with the help of the underground through Spain and Switzerland, most Japanese POW camps were deep in hostile territory, thousands of kilometres from Australia or any friendly country. In the camps, escape attempts were regarded not only as selfish but foolhardy in the extreme, as there was virtually no chance of success and, following an escape, life-endangering reprisals were taken against the camp population, whose already sick and starving prisoners were put on reduced rations, or none at all. Far from encouraging escapes, especially after it became clear that anyone who attempted to do so and was recaptured would be executed, senior officers forbade their men to escape.

Lynette's correspondent, however, would not be put off, and when he suggested the name of a POW, who had not been executed but had died of illness and neglect, she thought it was time to examine the matter a little more closely. She knew I would be interested, as I had firm ideas about the advisability of posthumous awards, so we decided to take a look at escape attempts in British North Borneo and on the Burma-Thai railway.

This led me to the Tavoy Eight, to Bell and Davis and Goulden and, some weeks later, to Durkin, whose name Dad had not mentioned, evidently in an effort to protect Durkin's family from distress. However, in war crimes' investigation files were statements by POWs, who not only knew Durkin's name, but exactly where the camp was and the work site where he had been found, which was nowhere near the dam. Their accounts of Durkin's death matched Dad's. As he and Dad were in the same camp, working on the tunnels, I knew that, at the time of Durkin's death, Dad and the tunnel party were based at Songkurai, 121 kilometres from Thanbyuzayat and 11 kilometres to the north of the dam. They had then walked further north to the various tunnel sites, including Changaraya, one kilometre from the border. The pieces of the jigsaw fitted!

In 2010, shortly after I had found this overwhelming evidence, I received a message from the Railway Centre. The expert there had done an about turn, and had searched for the tunnels north of the dam. Following a tip off from a farmer, he had located a small man-made tunnel near Songkurai camp. It was not one of the tunnels high on the hill – they have yet to be located and are closer to the work site at Changaraya, possibly over the border in Burma – but there was no doubt that the tunnel discovered at Songkurai had been made by Dad and the tunnel party. I have since learned of another, very similar tunnel and a cave near Kami Songkurai, discovered by a POW relative with the help of locals in 2005. The Songkurai tunnel's physical location tied in with my research and I was keen to get back to Thailand, but unfortunately various family issues decreed otherwise. Reluctantly, I put it on the back burner, waiting until Paul's retirement, still some years off.

Then, in 2017, Lynette was asked to accompany the family of the 2/19th's Dr Lloyd Cahill on a pilgrimage to Singapore, Malaya and Thailand the following February. As she had included Shimo Songkurai and the Cholera Camp on the itinerary, she suggested it would be an opportune time for her to take a look at the tunnel, at nearby Songkurai. As there was no likelihood of my going anytime soon, I agreed immediately. If I couldn't go, who better to look after my interests than my best friend?

On 21 February she sent me an email with a description and the images I had waited so long to see. The tunnel complex was directly opposite the campsite, on the far side of a steep hill, on the other side of the rail trace. The tunnel entrance, just large enough for two people, bored directly into the shale-and-clay earth of the hillside. The pit props had long gone, leaving only a groove to show where they had been, and the interior walls and roof were finished with small pick marks. One branch of the tunnel led to a dead end, a storage area most likely, while the other turned to the right to emerge on the railway side of the hillside, in what was evidently a machine-gun position, well concealed from the road: a perfect spot to set up an ambush. Troops advancing along the road or rail line from the border were hemmed in by the hill on one side and towering cliffs, immediately behind the camp area, on the other. Lynette also collected some rocks from the tunnel to bring home to me so I could have something tangible to keep as a reminder of this momentous day. As I was too overcome to respond at length, I sent a simple message that said it all.

You're walking in my Dad's footsteps – it feels weird. I wish he knew all this, but maybe he does.

This was the very last piece of my puzzle, the end of a journey that had taken me 25 years to complete. With the last link in the chain broken, I am finally freed from the shackles that anchored me to my father's past. I no longer feel guilty for not loving him enough, for not understanding. By walking in his footsteps, by treading that self-same path, by experiencing the horror of battle, the pain and suffering he went through and the deprivations he endured as a POW, I have now fully come to terms with his past, as well as my own, and have gained an insight into why he was what he was. At long last, my imprisonment is over. In spite of all his shortcomings, and the anguish he caused me, I can now find it in my heart to forgive him, unreservedly.

We have signed a truce.

Left: The tunnel, and final piece of the jigsaw.

Right: Lynette emerging from the tunnel at the machine gun position.

CHAPTER 23
HOMEWARD BOUND

It was necessary for me go to Tamuang (Tha Muang), about 14 kilometres east of Kanchanaburi for an operation to remove an abscess in my groin, the result of an infection I had contracted in the jungle, caused primarily by a kick from a Japanese boot. From Tamuang I and 15 other surgical cases travelled by ambulance back to Nakhon Pathom, where we met one of the world's loveliest women – Lady Mountbatten. With her was a staff of English society girls who had volunteered to go to Thailand to take care of the liberated prisoners of war.

Lady Edwina Mountbatten, wife of Admiral Lord Louis Mountbatten, Supreme Allied Commander South-East Asia command, and the first white woman the POWs had seen since their captivity, paid an impromptu visit to Fred and all those hospitalised at Nakhon Pathom on 10 September.

We also met General Slim, the senior officer in charge of the Burmese campaign. The senior Japanese officer at the prison camp at Nakhon Pathom, one of the fattest Japs I had ever seen, received Slim's personal attention. After about a week his surplus flesh was hardly noticeable.

From Nakhon Pathom we went to Bangkok for further medical treatment and all along the road saw defeated Japanese. In the hospital in Bangkok we were placed under the care of the Indian Army Medical Corps, with

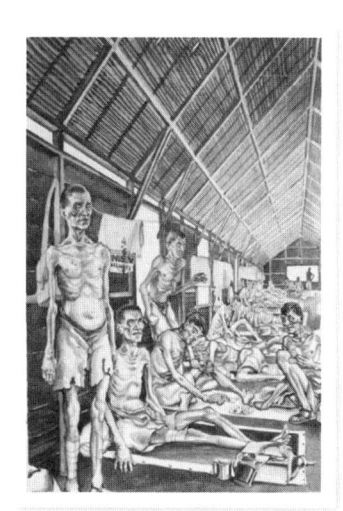

Above: Hospital ward (Murray Griffin).

Right: Emaciated survivors. Fred was in a similar condition.

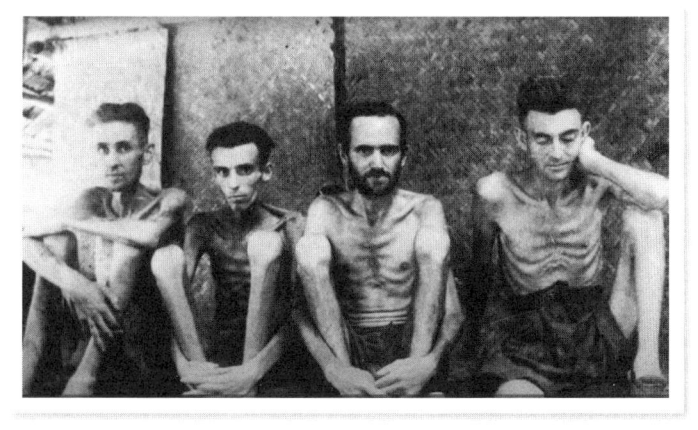

Lady Mountbatten meets some of the more able-bodied survivors.

specially trained nurses in attendance night and day. As medical supplies of the most modern type were available, we soon began to show improvement.

Sleeping on a bed, and between clean sheets, was the cause of much merriment. After years spent lying on bamboo platforms, no one seemed to be able to sleep that way. It was out of bed and onto the hard concrete floor, where sleep came immediately. The Indian nurses viewed this procedure with some anxiety, and on quite a number of occasions attempted to put their patients back into bed, only to find, when their backs were turned, that they had resumed their positions on the floor. Eventually the nurses called the doctor to see what was happening. He soon had the matter straightened out and we were allowed to sleep just where we wanted, much to the disgust of the nurses, who thought we were all 'damn fools'.

On reaching the convalescent stage I was moved to the hospital verandah. One morning a party of Japanese prisoners was brought in to clean up the grounds, which were badly neglected with grass about two feet high growing everywhere. Seeing us on the verandah, their Gurkha guards plied us with all sorts of questions. Were we prisoners? How had we been treated? And so on. One asked me: 'Are these Japs working hard enough?' What answer he expected from me it is hard to say but there was only one answer, and he would have got it from any of us. His reaction, however, was totally unexpected.

Calling the other guards, he issued some instructions. They went back to their posts with their faces wreathed in smiles. The reason why became apparent immediately, when the Japs began to hurry at their various jobs, almost falling over each other in their haste to get things done. Finally, on hands and knees, they reefed and tore at the grass, with the guards urging them on. It was a mad scene, but I had my first real laugh for some time.

In the midst of all this the Matron, a tall serious looking Englishwoman, arrived. She surveyed the spectacle, her face expressionless. Turning to me, she said, 'I suppose you're responsible for this?' I couldn't deny it. Then it seemed that all at once the humour of the situation struck her. She began to laugh. Tears ran down her cheeks and she finished up, as she afterwards said, by having a 'damn good old howl'.

The Gurkhas – small, dapper, efficient soldiers – seemed at all times to enjoy being in the company of the Australians and brought us little gifts each day. Neither could speak the other's language, but we understood each other amazingly well, for all that. Many of the soldiers were only boys, full of the joy of living.

As last I was classed as fit to travel and was transferred from hospital to the Chinese Chamber of Commerce, where those awaiting transport were stationed. We were granted leave to go into Bangkok, but riots had broken out between the Chinese and Thais. For three nights a miniature war went on in the main streets, until a curfew was imposed and Indian troops patrolled the city.

At last came the magic words: 'You are on draft to go to the aerodrome, where you will board the plane and proceed to Singapore to await transport to Australia'. So off to the aerodrome we went, 300 madly happy men. For me it was a real adventure, as it was my first aeroplane flight. As we neared the aerodrome we could see several transport planes, drawn up side by side. On our arrival they moved out onto the runway and in no time we were aboard. I secured a position at a window and had an excellent view.

Our start was delayed a little owing to a heavy rainstorm but at last we were on our way. What a thrill, as the plane took to the air, seemingly without any effort. Circling to gain altitude, we flew over Bangkok and, from a height of 2,000 feet, surveyed some of the places where we had been. How strange everything appeared from up above but unfortunately the storm returned, obscuring the view.

The plane climbed higher and higher, until we were above the clouds, flying at about 18,000 feet. My ears had a peculiar roaring sound in them one minute and the next I could hear nothing. The second pilot explained that the altitude was the cause. It was also piercingly cold.

Although actually flying at a speed of about 200 mph, we seemed to be just floating through space. Beneath us the clouds stretched endlessly in all directions, brilliantly white where the sun shone on them. They appeared for all the world like a great woollen fleece spread out over the whole universe. Then, through a break in the clouds, we saw the blue ocean beneath us. We were over the Gulf of Siam, heading for Singapore, a thousand miles away. The plane descended to about 5,000 feet and was flying through the clouds, with wisps of vapour at times floating past the windows when, with a bump and a jar that seemed to strain every part of the fuselage, we ran into an air pocket and fell what seemed like a thousand feet.

It was another three hours before we sighted land – a small island somewhere off the east coast of Malaya, just a black dot far below in an expanse of blue. Away in the distance was a vague outline that became more discernible with each second: the rugged coastline of Malaya and its jungle-clad hills. A narrow ribbon of road following the coastline was quite distinct, like a white chalk line on a blackboard. Viewed from this height, I could understand why artists raved about tropical splendour: the brilliant blue of the sea, edged with white where the waves broke onto a narrow strip of yellow sand, forming a vivid contrast with the green of the jungle.

Our return to Singapore from Bangkok was something like a homecoming, although our three-and-a-half-year absence had wrought few changes. The first recognisable landmarks were the Straits of Johor, then the Cathay Building, on top of which now flew a Union Jack. When last seen, the red ball of Japan had disgraced the flagstaff. Then the airport appeared beneath us, and the pilot executed a perfect landing, after just six hours in the air.

Drawn up on the airfield were many hundreds of Allied aircraft, large and small. What a difference planes like these would have made when we were struggling for our lives in the battle for Singapore. But that was all in the past. We now had the future to look forward to.

At the terminal were Australian troops who eyed us, and our nondescript clothes, as if we were strangers from another planet. However, when we spoke to them and they heard our accents, what a world of difference it made. In place of disapproval there was warm sympathy and an innate understanding that this was not the time to bombard us with questions.

Red Cross workers, the first Australian women we had encountered since our release, provided us with a dainty afternoon tea and gave us cigarettes and a shaving outfit, which we certainly needed. We were then taken to Changi. How different it was from when we had arrived.

Fred's destination was Changi Gaol, now part of a large new POW Camp. No Allied POWs were inside the prison walls until June 1944, following the transfer the previous month of civilian internees, locked up since February 1942, to General Percival's old HQ at Sime Road Camp. When they moved out, the Australians still in Selarang moved in, leaving the barracks free to accommodate Japanese air force personnel, transferred to Singapore following the completion of the nearby Changi airstrip.

By June 1944, many Allied POWs were returning from camps in Thailand and Burma, and the gaol, surrounded by barbed wire, served as a huge dormitory. It did not function as a prison in the normal sense as the massive entry gate was left open to allow access to the cells, each of which housed up to five prisoners. The overflow lived in tents and in long timber and atap huts, erected in the outer grounds.

As time wore on, the camp became very crowded. In an effort to reduce the crush at the main gate each morning, when POWs left their cells to join local work parties, the Allied administration suggested that perhaps an opening could be made at the opposite end of the gaol to reduce the congestion. They were astounded when the Japanese refused permission, on the grounds that the British would be very angry if they damaged the wall!

After inspecting the hospital 'facilities' and admiring the inventiveness of the prisoners in Thailand', Lady Mountbatten had also flown to Singapore where, on 12 September, Lord Louis formally accepted the Japanese surrender at the colonnaded city hall. The padang, immediately in front of the building, was packed with POWs well enough to make the trip from Changi to join in the celebrations.

Fred was there but number missed the big event, as they had been flown back home the previous day. The first aircraft, nine Catalina flying boats, left at dawn from Telok Ayer Basin with five officers and 130 other ranks on board, the most senior of whom was 2/15 Field Regiment's commanding officer, Colonel J M Wright. In an amazing twist of fate, 35 years later I would move into a house built on what was the orchard and tennis court of

Changi Gaol Camp, 1945 (Murray Griffin)

his large Sydney property. Back in Singapore

> the Chinese were cheering and waving and welcoming us back again, just as if we really belonged to them, but plainly showing they had not found the going any too easy under the Japanese rule. These were the same people who had braved death to bring us a drink of water when we had marched through their villages under Japanese guard, years before.
>
> To most people the Chinese are a very undemonstrative race. But, as we had lived with them and knew their ways, we could detect the very sincere pleasure in their welcome. They invaded our camp at Changi, all very curious and friendly and so willing to do little things to help us.
>
> There was plenty to do. There were clothes to wash and mend, tents and beds to make comfortable. One old chap, seeing me struggling to clean my face of six months' growth of beard, could not keep the smile from his face as he watched my efforts. When at last I succeeded he clapped his hands with glee, and then produced clippers and scissors to cut my hair. I felt like a new man – but I wondered why he had not produced the scissors before – it would have made my shaving effort so much easier.
>
> Just as he finished, a mate, who had gone to get a bottle of beer from the Red Cross, returned. He glanced at me and then asked if had I seen Fred anywhere. My roar of laughter soon made him realise that he was really talking to me. He had never seen me without a beard.
>
> On 28 September, the night before we were to sail, I did something that I had longed

Lord Louis Mountbatten at the surrender ceremony at the City Hall, 12 September 1945.

to do ever since my return to Singapore. Over the years I had often wondered what had become of the Chinese boy we rescued from Changi Beach, where he had been washed ashore after being shot by the Japanese.

Curiosity led me to the house where we had left him. Sure enough, the old Chinese woman answered our knock on the door. As I explained who we were, I could see the dawning of recognition in her eyes. From her signs, I realised that my loss of weight was responsible for her failure to recognise me. Calling in Chinese to someone inside, she bade us enter.

Into the room came a Chinese youth of about 15 years. When the old lady explained who I was, the boy's eyes lit up with joy. He said to me: 'It's really through you that I have become a Christian, so that I could pray to your God every day that you would be safe and return to your home'. In his quaint way he went on to say how wonderful it was that I had remembered him and returned to see him. I was deeply affected: a rough Australian soldier who had been prayed for by this lad for so many years! I must admit that somebody's prayers must have been answered, those of the Chinese boy included.

The next morning, decently clothed in new uniforms and looking far more respectable, we were taken to the wharf at Keppel Harbour to board the troop ship *Tamaroa*. As we lined up on the wharf waiting to embark, a number of men and women internees arrived, dressed in ragged bits of clothing. They were supposed to have been brought down early, taken on board ship and issued with clothing before we arrived. Seeing how embarrassed the women were, we immediately shed our shirts so that they could cover their nakedness. One Dutch woman later brought her husband and her two tiny children, who had been born in the prison camp, to thank us. She had heard, she said, that Australians were a crowd of ungentlemanly hoboes but, she remarked, nothing would make her forget how the detractors turned their backs and pretended to be interested in something else, while we came forward to offer our clothes.

How wonderful to be on board ship again, and going home to Australia, but not the way we had come. Instead, we steamed north up the Malacca Strait, following the same route we had taken on *Celebes Maru*, to the uppermost point of Sumatra, where we turned towards the south, and home. In the uneventful days that followed I amused myself by watching the flight of the flying fish, as they followed the bow wave. I was so glad to be able to see an unlimited expanse of ocean after the confinement of the jungle and really appreciated the fact that I was free.

On the twelfth day, just before nightfall, we saw a black line just above the horizon, the first glimpse of our homeland for over five years! All vantage points on the ship were crowded as we steamed slowly onward until, finally, we could see the twinkle of lights on Rottenest Island, near Fremantle. When the pilot boat arrived we thought we would go into port but, after taking the pilot and the mail onboard, the captain dropped anchor for the night, about a mile from shore. We watched the lights, so near but yet so far, until the bitter cold drove us down below to seek the warmth of our blankets.

Daylight found us up on deck to catch the first glimpse of Australia by daylight, afraid that somebody may have stolen it during the night. But there it was, with the first rays of the sun edging the surrounding hills with gold. Fremantle folk seemed to be early risers, with every chimney sending its lazy column of smoke skyward, where the morning breeze wafted it gently away. We were so busy looking that breakfast was completely forgotten!

The anchor was weighed and we were under way again. As the big ship slowly rounded the breakwater we saw the Fremantle wharves in the distance, already black with people. As we moved closer we could see them waving handkerchiefs and indeed, anything at all, to attract attention. A breathless silence pervaded as we neared the pier.

The silence was shattered by the ship's siren. It seemed to break the spell and cheer after cheer rolled out across the water, continuing until the ship slowly and gracefully came to rest along the wharf.

The immediate area was clear of people, as barriers had been erected, guarded by army pickets. Whether the crowd became unmanageable or the pickets did not care is hard to say, but the barriers were swept aside and the crowd poured onto the wharf.

Many of the lads on board were from Western Australia and there were touchingly heartfelt scenes as mothers and fathers, wives, sisters and brothers, spotted their lads waving to them from the ship. The people on the wharf seemed far more emotional than the boys on board, but I think even the hardest man that day swallowed a lump, and the outward show of nonchalance was only a cloak to hide our real feelings. At last the gangways were lowered and the Western Aussies were allowed to land. One bloke walked across the pier to a flower garden, scooped up a double handful of dirt, smell it, tasted it, then yelled, 'Come on boys, it's Aussie all right, but I had to be sure!'

We were the first shipload of POWs to land at this port and an onlooker would have thought we were all sons or brothers to every person in the city. Homes were thrown open and all public and private facilities seemed to be free, for no one would take a penny for any service or entry, once they spotted the 8 Divvy colour patch. Taxis vied with each other to take us places in nearby Perth. Beer ran freely and it is to the credit of the boys that only odd ones became the worse for it – and that was only to be expected.

Saying farewell to Fremantle next morning, we steamed off to the cheers of thousands of well wishers who thronged the wharf to wish us goodbye. Land again faded to an indistinguishable blur as we headed for Melbourne, our next port of call. Albatrosses appeared in great numbers, following the wake of the ship and looking for food scraps. These birds were a never-ending source of delight as I watched their dipping, circling flight. Then a whale appeared, spouting a stream of water skyward, while a school of dolphins gambolled in the bow wave. Every hour of daylight found me up on deck, looking for new sights to remember.

At last, on 16 October, we reached the entrance to Port Melbourne. Our arrival was a repetition of Fremantle, but on a more subdued note, as here we put ashore some of the worst stretcher cases, men who had suffered the most horrible of Japanese torture. After spending one night in Melbourne, we again set off for Sydney, and home.

We were never out of sight of land between Sydney and Melbourne and, just as day broke on the 20th, reached Sydney Heads. How we had longed for this moment. As the ship changed course to enter the harbour the thought in everyone's mind was 'this has been worth waiting for!'

We had scarcely cleared the heads when every siren within miles set up a wail, which continued unabated till we berthed at Darling Harbour. We could hardly wait for the gangways to be lowered. Good old Sydney, you were certainly worth fighting for!

Our trip through the city on Red Cross buses showed us Sydney's smiling face. In no other part of the world are the people so happy and carefree. At Ingleburn we were again reunited with our people. My wife, my only sister and my favourite cousin were there to meet me. How wonderful it was to see them once more and to know that nothing could part us again.

While Fred was away, Elsie had struggled to keep the family going on her own. The children missed their father and, on the day they knew the war was over, they not only had a day off school but collected every pot, pan and kettle they could find and beat them with sticks to make as much celebratory noise as possible. The youngest child, Nicky, joined in, but he had no memory, at all, of Fred.

I could not recall anything of my father before he went away to war and I was seven years old when he returned. The only details were gleaned from descriptions and stories told to me by my mother, who did a fantastic job raising four children, under very difficult circumstances, and on very little income.

While I was certainly proud of what my father was doing for his country, I often wondered why most of my friends had fathers at home and I did not. The knowledge that he was a prisoner of war meant little to me at my age and I could only wonder when I would get to know him and why such things were happening. Finally the war ended and I vividly recall the whole town being involved in noisy celebrations that went on for hours. My only regret at the time was that I wasn't allowed to join in some of the more rowdy demonstrations. 'When will Dad be home?' was my first question and to be honest I cannot recall what I was told. I do recall, however, receiving advice that my Father had been released and was to undergo an operation before being sent home. My Mother travelled to Sydney to meet the boat, and we waited in nervous expectation for their return.

On the fateful day my feelings were very mixed. I was looking forward to meeting my father, and for the first time, as far as I was concerned, but I was also very nervous and frightened. What would he be like and would he remember me?

As the train rolled into the station, packed with people, detonators set on the line made it a very noisy welcome. I can't recall if there were any other soldiers on the train but, as far as I was concerned, they were all there to meet my father and I certainly felt very proud.

Fred may have finally been home, but his reunion was to be of short duration as his ordeal was far from over. On 22 November, just over a month after setting foot on Australian soil, he was back in hospital, this time at the Army hospital at Ingleburn, suffering from retrobulbar neuritis. His loss of vision was undoubtedly caused by nutritional deficiency, not widely recognised in Australia at that time, hence his later battle for compensation that it was war related. After spending Christmas and New Year at Ingleburn, he was discharged on 4 January, only to be back again three days later suffering from hookworm, which had most likely entered his body through the soles of his bare feet. He was finally out of hospital on 6 March and was discharged from the army the following day, on compassionate grounds.

Fred was so pleased to be home at last that he named his house *Tamaroa*, after the ship that had delivered him safely back to his family. Having had very little contact over the last five years, it took him and Elsie many months to catch up on the things that had happened. Some, such as the death of Elsie's mother, were sad; others were highly amusing, at least to others.

Fred, shut off from the world for so long, often had no idea what people were talking about. It was as if they had been on another planet for almost four years, which in a way, they were. Not long after Fred returned home, someone remarked that his daughter Joan had a beautiful voice and sang 'like Vera Lynn', to which Fred replied, 'Who the hell is Vera Lynn?' He had no idea that she was known as the 'forces' sweetheart' or that her songs of hope had helped sustain the people of Britain in their darkest hours. It may have seemed funny to onlookers, but Fred and others like him found it very frustrating.

Like every other prisoner of war who returned to Australia, Fred had been told on his discharge to 'go home and forget about the war'. But how could he ever forget? The terrible experiences of his past three and a half years would remain with him forever. Far from forgetting, Fred joined the Ex-POW Association and took up a fight to obtain compensation for the many Australians who had suffered at the hands of the Japanese. By this time his articles about his own time as a POW had been published in *Burrowa News*, so local people were well versed in the horrors of the Burma-Thai railway, allowing him to lay the groundwork for his campaign.

He wrote numerous letters to the newspaper, and in May 1948 penned the following:

Sir,

As a representative of the AIF 8th Division and Ex-Prisoner of War and Relatives Association, I have been asked to solicit the support of the Boorowa RSL (this I have already gained) and of the general public, in bringing pressure to bear on the people who, as representatives of the Commonwealth Government, are hedging the question of seeking reparation from the Japanese for Ex-POWs or their relatives, who suffered at the hands of these brutes.

For such men as myself we ask nothing; we are happy in the knowledge that, compared with many of our comrades, we are well off. But every year, every week, every day, sees more and more of our men succumbing mentally and physically to the effects of the

Fred and Elsie, reunited at last.

three and a half years of starvation, torture, and horror through which we were forced to go, against every law which was ever formulated, international or even human.

It would be a miscarriage of justice if the dependent wives, children or aged parents of men who were murdered – as sure as night follows day – in those jungle prison camps, can get no compensation from the people responsible. These dependents have a moral right to have this compensation, which should come from the Japanese when the peace terms are finalised.

Let me quote one of many cases, which may make you realise just why Australians must ask for (and if necessary) fight for these reparations:

In Ballarat, in Victoria, there lives a man, now only twenty eight years of age who before the war was claimed by critics to be on the way to being one of Australia's greatest musicians. Music was his whole life. Even in the prison camps he was planning and shaping his career. And then, a Japanese doctor, knowing the man's genius, to punish him for some slight offence, worked his evil way on him amputating both his hands, grafting the stumps together – and in that condition this man arrived back in Australia as hideous testimony of the Jap's methods.

To be sure, he received a full military pension! But is that any compensation for the loss of his ability to do the only thing in life he really cared for?

He is only one of hundreds such cases. Not all the same but each in its way as tragic as his. A full military pension? So what? I know man who was never closer to a Jap than the Sydney Showground who receives the same benefit.

Is that any compensation to a mother whose son was slowly starved to death, or a wife whose mate met the same fate, or the children left fatherless for no other reason than to satisfy the sadistic appetites of the Japanese brutes.

The recent services held in remembrance of Anzac, at which the 'Last Post' and 'Reveille' were sounded, sent my thoughts racing back to the dark days of 1943, when these calls echoes through the Burmese jungle camps as many as twenty times a day, notifying the prisoners rotting away their lives that yet another of their number had ceased to suffer, many of them praying that they would be the next to follow.

These services stressed the phrase, 'Lest We Forget'! Can we ever forget? Yet it seems that many of our fellow Australians are only too happy to forget.

Promises were made by men in responsible positions that 'all' would be done to see that compensation was claimed and received. But recent events tend to show that these promises were only a hollow mockery, made at that time to keep us quiet till such time as 'we forgot' that they were made. It is for the purpose of reminding these people, by the weight of public opinion, that I ask your support – and the support of all fair minded Australians – to get for all these most deserving cases, the reparations they so richly deserve and by so doing make their burden a little easier to bear.

Yours sincerely,

Fred Howe

It took a while, but eventually reparations were made to the POWs. With the sale of Japanese assets, including the Burma-Thai Railway, sold by the British government to the Thailand government for £1,250,000, the first payment to POWs of £32 was made in 1952. Another payment of £54 was made in 1956/7 when the Japanese Government settled its obligation, under Article 16 of the Peace Treaty, by paying £4.5 million to the International Committee of the Red Cross for distribution. In 1963 a third payment of £16.10.0 was made from the balance of monies held from the sale of Japanese assets.

Fred, who died in 1975, lived long enough to receive his reparation money, but did not last the necessary 26 years until 2001, when the Australian Government decided to make a further payment of $25,000 to surviving POWs, in recognition of their suffering and hardships. Elsie, who had nursed Fred through his various bouts of illness throughout their marriage, had also died, so the $25,000 payable to her as a surviving spouse was also forfeited.

Fred's experiences as a prisoner of war had a profound effect on him for the rest of his life. While the bad far outweighed the good, he did admit that not all Japanese were fiends.

It would be telling an untruth to say that all the Japs were alike. There were some exceptionally good ones, but they were like a raindrop in the ocean.

AIF Joe, as we knew him, was good to Australians only. Dutch, English and American prisoners were as badly treated by Joe, as we were by some of the other guards. Australians could get away with anything with Joe, and woebetide any other Jap who touched one of us. Joe was a big powerful man and loved to fight.

Holy Joe was another. He professed to being a Christian and was certainly a big improvement on most. He had one vice – he loved to get drunk. We had been teaching him to speak English and to sing songs. One night, coming home from the village gloriously drunk, Joe abused the Jap on guard duty, was arrested and put in the guardhouse. For a time everything was quiet. Then the strains of 'There'll Always Be An

England' floated out from the guardhouse in Joe's unmistakable voice. Then we heard the sounds of a terrible struggle as the song was cut short and Joe found himself tied to a post, minus his pants and jacket. By morning he had sobered up and wondered what it was all about.

However, men like 'Dillinger', 'Boof Head', 'The Silver Bullet', 'Blood-pressure', 'Naito' and a host of others more than counteracted what good was done by the few. The years that have passed since our liberation have barely dulled the memory of some of their deeds.

Traumatic as his time in the jungle camps had been, Fred was a member of a remarkable group of men who had survived in the face of seemingly insurmountable odds; a band of brothers, united by suffering almost unimaginable. Like the men of his generation, he rarely betrayed his innermost feelings or displayed his emotions. However, in his final article, written for the Boorowa News, his message was one of reflection, for the generations to come and, given the hostilities in the region over the next 80 years, eerily prophetic.

> There is an unbreakable bond of fellowship that exists whenever one of us meets a fellow prisoner. We have been comrades in adversity, the like of which, unless experienced personally, is beyond most people's understanding. The ties that bind us together are so strong that any one of us would go far out of his way to help another who showed any signs of being in distress.
>
> And now we are back in the routine of civilian life, our own people, who know us so well, can see by our moods when our minds go back to days that have gone by. In these moments we are strangers to them, oblivious to our surroundings; young men prematurely aged, unable to recapture the joyousness of the youth that is every Australian's birthright.
>
> We who have lived in the occupied territories, experiencing at first hand the barbarism and suffering, shudder to think of how near Australia came to suffering the same fate. The atrocities in the Philippines and other countries, reported in the newspapers, show only too well what would have happened here to our own women and children had the Japanese overrun our country.
>
> But we trust and pray that the experience gained so dearly will be a lesson to future generations, so that they can face the problems of the world thoroughly prepared. It would be tragic indeed, should history should repeat itself and our sons have to face a similar experience, to know that the fault was ours, by not impressing on the nation the necessity of the need to be prepared, and not be caught unawares, as we were last time.
>
> Australian's isolation by distance has now ended and it is our duty to plan our defences in such a way that any enemy, who wishes to attack our shores, must run a gauntlet so great that the task will be an impossibility.
>
> Never again must any Asian nation be allowed to become a menace, as the Japanese were for the last decade.
>
> As yet Australia has never seen or felt the effects of a concentrated attack.
>
> Let us sincerely hope we never do.

CHAPTER 24

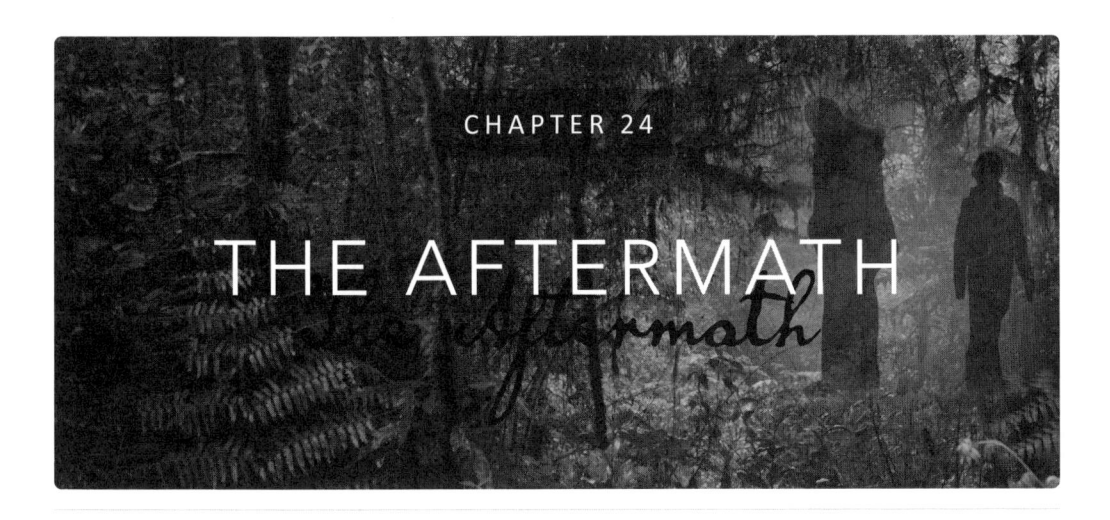

THE AFTERMATH

There were many people who crossed Fred's path in Malaya and Singapore, and in captivity. Some were memorable for all the right reasons, but many were not. Either way, all were disparate threads that became inextricably woven to create the rich tapestry that was Fred's life, as a soldier in battle and as a prisoner of war.

Following his escape from Singapore, Major General H. Gordon Bennett reached Australia. While he believed, because of first-hand knowledge gained while fighting the Japanese, that he had valuable information to impart, many very senior officers did not view his actions in a favourable light. During the interbellum years, the forthright and acerbic Bennett had trodden on too many toes by criticising the army and those running it.

On his arrival in Sydney on 1 March 1942, his enemies on the Staff Corps were ready, anxious to accuse him of abandoning his men. Backed by his loyal public, the Prime Minister and almost the entire cabinet, all of whom believed it was the General's duty to escape, Bennett weathered the storm. However, the Military Board, unwilling to let him escape scot-free, inflicted an exquisitely subtle form of punishment.

Promoted to Lieutenant General, the 'fighting general' was posted to a non-combatant role in Western Australia. He stuck it out until August 1944, when he resigned, the first general ever to resign his commission in wartime.

However, things were about to become a lot worse. In Malaya, Bennett had clashed on numerous occasions with his immediate superior, Lieutenant General Arthur Percival, who, on 8 March 1943, wrote a letter to the Military Board in Australia, explaining why it had been necessary to appoint Brigadier 'Boots' Callaghan to take command of 8 Division in captivity. At war's end he gave the letter to Callaghan. After being welcomed home by Bennett, Callaghan delivered it.

Percival accused Bennett, who believed he was a free agent following the ceasefire, of 'voluntarily and without permission relinquishing command of the AIF', a charge that was paraphrased by Bennett's long-time enemy and head of the AIF, General Thomas Blamey, into one of 'desertion' a crime that, in most military forces, invoked the death penalty.

Percival confirmed the allegations in another letter written on 4 September 1945, conveniently forgetting that his own Air and Naval chiefs, Air Vice Marshal Pulford and Admiral Spooner, as well as Brigadier Paris, had also escaped from Singapore. The screws tightened on Bennett, whose crime appeared to be that he had survived while the other three had perished.

Pursued by Blamey, Bennett was put through the military and public wringer. Percival, who started the ruckus, remained silent about Wavell's orders to escape, asserting only that Bennett had left Singapore without asking him. It is interesting that, considering the controversy that surrounded Bennett, Percival, the prime mover in his downfall, never made any reference to his escape in any despatches or in his book, published in 1949.

Two separate enquiries into Bennett's escape were held. The first was held in camera. The second was instituted to placate a public enraged by the army's treatment of Bennett. Both concluded, on what appear to be purely technical grounds, that Bennett was 'not justified in handing over his command or in leaving Singapore'. Strangely, neither panel recommended any censure.

However, in 1948, too late to save Bennett's reputation, an eminent military lawyer published a legal opinion on the legal aspects of the public enquiry, which shot the finding full of holes. But it made no difference to the hardline views of his detractors, led by General Blamey. The army hierarchy gave the fiery Bennett the cold shoulder for the rest of his life.

However, Bennett never lost the admiration of the general public or his troops, most of whom still treated him with affection akin to hero worship, never forgetting the way in which he had looked after their interests in Malaya. At war's end, they listened with askance to the allegations against him and, on their arrival home, draped bed sheets emblazoned with WE WANT BENNETT over the side of the ship as it sailed down Sydney Harbour to the wharf, where Bennett was waiting to greet them. For the second enquiry they formed an association and raised the money to pay for his defence.

On 15 February 1993, following allegations of cowardice against Bennett by a British journalist, members of 8 Division gathered, as they had done since 1946, at the Cenotaph in Sydney's Martin Place, to remember their mates. It was a tradition, supported by Bennett, that had followed on from vigils kept at the Cenotaph from 1943 to 1945, when POW families gathered to sustain and comfort each other, not knowing the fate of their men.

With the current allegations circling the globe, I chatted to as many diggers as I could find, to ascertain their feelings about Bennett and his escape. I had not managed to find anyone who would say anything adverse about him, when I approached a man standing to one side, wearing his medals and dressed in clothes, including a well-worn Akubra, that showed that he was clearly a 'bushie'. He was a former member of 2/19 Battalion, who had suffered terribly as a POW, and, if anyone had an axe to grind, it would have been him.

Referring to the fact that I had not been able to find anyone present that day who had a bad word to say about Bennett, I asked if this could possibly be due to his comrades looking at the past through rose-coloured glasses, or simply being unwilling to be disloyal to their commander.

Giving me a withering look, he drawled, 'Jeez love, do you think we would have followed bloody Bennett down bloody George Street every bloody Anzac Day, if we didn't think he was a bloody good general?'

Well, the simple answer is, they wouldn't!

Their loyalty to Bennett was so great that, when he died in 1962, the crowd at his funeral was the biggest ever seen in Sydney, with the forecourt of St Andrew's Cathedral and the adjoining Sydney Town Hall packed with mourners. As the cortege passed by, his men, proudly wearing their medals, formed a guard of honour that extended for a mile along George Street. Some historians may continue to view Bennett in a poor light, and arguments will doubtless continue over the rights and wrongs of his escape, but there are few generals who inspired such loyalty.

Left: Generals Percival and Bennett in Malaya, 1941.
Above: The hospital ship Manunda arriving in Sydney.

Three men of Bennett's 8 Division, Charles 'Chick' Warden, Russell Braddon and Roly Dean, all survived the war. Warden was sent with Reg Newton's D Force to the Burma-Thai railway, Dean went to Japan with C Force, while Braddon was assigned to H Force. Although a graduate with a Bachelor of Arts degree from the prestigious University of Sydney, on enlistment Braddon had eschewed a commission to remain in the ranks. The son of a Sydney barrister, he returned to university after the war to study law but, tormented by recurring dreams, attempted suicide and abandoned his studies. Instead, he sailed for England where he and fellow ex-POW Sydney Piddington developed a highly successful mind-reading act, which the pair had begun in Changi. A gifted raconteur with a cynical turn of phrase, in 1952 Braddon published an account of his wartime experiences in a book, *The Naked Island*, a title inspired by Churchill's statement that 'we everywhere were weak and naked'. The book, which was followed by others, became an international bestseller and, while not entirely accurate as it was written from memory, it gave great insight into life as a POW. However, as Braddon had heaped scorn on the quality of some of the division's officers, a number took great exception to his remarks, which, in most cases, appear to have been entirely justified.

Doctors Lloyd Cahill and Victor Brand also returned home. Cahill, after pedalling into Yong Peng on the borrowed bicycle, had collapsed. He was taken to 2/13 AGH at Katong where, in an unconscious state and having no identification or badges of rank, removed to avoid being a target for snipers, he was deemed to be a private and placed in the VD ward. When a nursing sister, going through his pockets, found a syringe, pandemonium ensued as it was assumed he was a drug addict. Fortunately, he came to, and was able to explain everything.

After heroically keeping his cholera victims alive at Shimo Songkurai, Cahill decided on returning home that he needed to do something different, something that did not involve illness or suffering. He furthered his medical skills to become an ophthalmologist, an eye specialist, and established a very successful practice in Macquarie Street, Sydney. He died in 2012, aged 97.

In April 1943, Brand was placed on the F Force draft to Thailand, where he contracted malaria on arrival and remained at Kanchanaburi for a month, before establishing a hospital at Tamaran Pat, near Kilo 237, for about 200 F Force stragglers. Using an axe head and parang, and a nearby stand of bamboo, they constructed a working camp isolated from the rest of F Force, so isolated that, at one stage, Brand walked 65 kilometres to Neike to prove to the Japanese that he really existed. He, too, kept his dysentery patients alive using makeshift saline drips. After the war he set up a private practice in Melbourne, which he combined with hospital work.

Captain Harold Wardale-Greenwood, the 'fighting padre', did not survive captivity. He was sent with B Force to Sandakan in British North Borneo in July 1942, where he proved that he could be just as heroic in captivity as he had been in battle. Continuing to demonstrate the same fearlessness and compassion that had so endeared him to the men of the 2/19th, he secretly took the place of ill men employed on airfield construction. When his subterfuge was detected, he was confined to a small cage for 36 hours and his ecclesiastical books were confiscated.

In May 1945 he was one of 536 POWs sent on a 260-kilometre 'death march' into Borneo's mountainous, jungle covered interior. Many died on the way but, after an arduous four-week trek, he reached the final destination, a small jungle camp hidden deep in a valley. Conditions were appalling. The Fighting Padre, who had comforted the despairing, the dying and the disconsolate for so long, endured terrible deprivations until 18 July, when he died of dysentery.

Sergeant Ron Croft, who miraculously escaped the conflagration at Parit Sulong, heeded Hackney's pleas to save himself. However, instead of attempting to make his way to Singapore, he joined a band of the Chinese guerrillas. He fought with them for some months before being killed in the latter half of 1942.

After young Reg Wharton also escaped what should have been certain death at Parit Sulong, he made his way to Singapore alone. He certainly had some spunk, despite his youth. After the surrender, he escaped and made his way to Malaya, where he was captured, for the third time, and sent to Pudu Gaol in Kuala Lumpur. It was here that he was reunited with Hackney, who told him he must never speak of the massacre with anyone. Even after the war, when Hackney provided the evidence to hang General Nishimura, he protected Wharton, allowing him to live a relatively normal life.

Hackney's life was far from normal. After the Australians in Pudu were transferred to Changi Camp in October 1942, his full account of the massacre was taken down by a young lawyer, Adrien Curlewis, later to become a judge, and buried in a shell casing at Changi Camp as an insurance policy, should Hackney not survive the war. However, like Wharton, Hackney was made of stern stuff. Drafted into F Force, he was sent to work on the railway in 1943. Although the conditions were horrendous, with a death rate of one in three, Hackney managed to survive and return home to *Wonalabee*, the family's beautiful grazing property at Burraga, near Bathurst. His outstanding courage was never recognised.

On his return home, he was reunited with his sweetheart, Helen St Vincent Welch, the daughter of a well-known Sydney medical specialist. They became engaged in January 1946, but the relationship was over by August, when Helen wrote to a Sydney tabloid newspaper stating that she was not his fiancée and had not dined out at the upmarket Princes Restaurant with him, as reported on 4 August.

On 12 May 1951, Hackney, aged 35, married Jill Brown and the couple had a daughter, Bettina, born seven months later. The marriage, which was troubled from the very beginning, ended in an acrimonious and very public divorce in May 1953.

In 1952 Hackney's father had died, leaving a considerable inheritance, and the property passed to him. Ben never remarried. He died on 5 May 1984 from emphysema, at the age of 68. Although he left $100,000 to his old battalion, the 2/29th, and large bequests to War Widows and Legacy – an organisation that cares for families of ex-servicemen – Hackney's death went almost unnoticed. Apart from a funeral announcement placed in the local paper by the undertaker, and one in Melbourne where many of his wartime comrades lived, there was nothing else in the press. He was buried without fanfare in the Bathurst Lawn Cemetery. There was no military funeral. There was not even a bugler to play the Last Post.

On the completion of the railway, Brigadier Arthur Varley, the A Force commander, returned to Singapore to await transfer to a camp in Formosa (now Taiwan), to join other very senior officers. On 6 September 1944, he boarded the transport ship, *Rakuyu Maru*, carrying 1318 Australians earmarked for labour camps in Japan. Another 2218 British were on board *Kachidoki Maru*. The vessels were part of a convoy ferrying Japanese wounded and supplies. Six days later, the American submarines USS *Sealion II* and USS *Pampanito* were patrolling in the South China Sea. Both prison ships, which were unmarked, were torpedoed. However, *Rakuyu Maru* remained afloat for 12 hours, allowing time for the POWs to escape from the slowly sinking vessel. The Japanese crew, which had lifeboats, was rescued soon after, but Allied prisoners, not shot by Japanese surface vessels, were left in the sea, clinging to debris and life rafts. Some were picked up by enemy ships and taken to Japan. American submarines rescued 150 others, including the 2/19th's Roy Cornford. However, 543 Australians were lost, including Varley, who was in command of a group of seven rafts, last seen heading north-west. What became of them is not known, but it is believed that they, too, were machine-gunned by Japanese surface vessels.

Colonel Charles Anderson, who had demonstrated brilliant leadership in battle and in captivity, returned home to his country property near Young. He had earned the undying respect of his men, whose only complaint was that 'there was only one of him', and Fred was one of the many who held great affection for their former commanding officer throughout their lives.

A dyed-in-the wool Labor Party supporter, Fred was a keen campaigner for the local Boorowa branch. So, much as he revered Anderson, when asked to campaign for him in the Federal election of 1949, Fred reminded the aspiring Country Party candidate that he was a Labor man, through and through. Undeterred, Anderson repeated his request. It is a measure of the loyalty he had engendered among his men that Fred, a staunch and committed left-winger all his life, resigned from the Labor Party and spearheaded the campaign. Charles Anderson was duly elected with a swing of 18.8 per cent. He served as Federal Member for Hume for the years 1949–1951 and from 1955–1961. After retiring from political life in 1961, he moved to Canberra, where he died on 11 November 1988, Remembrance Day, aged 91.

Dr Albert Coates, who had saved Fred's life and the lives of so many, returned from Thailand 32 kilos lighter. Settling back into family life, he returned to work almost immediately at Royal Melbourne Hospital, where he was an honorary surgeon for 27 years, continuing his distinguished medical career begun so many years before. A key witness at the Tokyo War Trials, Coates was awarded an OBE in 1947 by King George VI for his outstanding war work and, in 1951, went to the United States as an RSL delegate at the signing of the Peace Treaty with Japan. It became effective the following year.

Further honours followed in 1953 when Coates was made a Fellow of the Royal College of Surgeons, and again in 1955, when he received a knighthood from the Queen. The University of Melbourne, in its medical school's centenary year, conferred an Honorary Doctorate in Laws on Coates in 1962. As a lecturer in surgery, Bertie Coates passed his wealth of knowledge to hundreds of aspiring young doctors, and was twice elected president of the Victorian branch of the Australian Medical Association.

Along with war hero Vivian Bullwinkel and other AIF nurses who had survived captivity in Sumatra, Coates helped establish the Nurses' Memorial Centre in Melbourne and, as Chairman of the Board of Fairfield Infectious Diseases Hospital for many years, transformed it into a centre of excellence.

In 1977, at the age of 82, Sir Albert 'Bertie' Coates died at the Royal Melbourne, the hospital he had served so well. In a moving eulogy to his old friend, Weary Dunlop spoke for all those who owed their lives to this remarkable and very humble man.

> It is hard to imagine a man more fitted to be the image of a true Australian or a man more suitable as an Ambassador for our Nation. All in all I think we can say 'There was a man, we may not see his like again'.

Justice and the War Crimes Tribunal caught up with a number of the Japanese who had made life such a misery for Fred and his fellow prisoners of war. Lieutenant Colonel Nagatomo Yoshitada was one of 14 Japanese tried en masse in Singapore in August 1946. Twelve were found guilty as charged and, of these, eight were condemned to death. Nagatomo was hanged at Changi on 16 September 1947. The Boy Bastard, Arai Koei, and the camp commandant at Kilo 75 and 105 camps, Lieutenant Hoshi Aiki, were also condemned to death. They and four others were hanged at Changi Prison at 9.03 am on 25 February 1947.

Kitabata, The Screaming Corporal, and Wire Whiskers, Sergeant Major Ishida, who had brutally treated Fred's tunnel party and POWs at Hellfire Pass, were arrested and brought before a War Crimes Tribunal in Hong Kong in July 1948. Their sins were many and varied and the prosecutor had no trouble finding witnesses from Songkurai and other camps to testify against them. Kitabata, who declared he was never at Songkurai, was found guilty and sentenced to 20 years' imprisonment. Ishida, who had not only condoned but encouraged him, received 7 years.

The 20-year sentence handed down to The Screaming Corporal, to be served in Singapore's Outram Road Gaol, was of cold comfort to those who had suffered so hideously at Kitabata's hands. He was free by 7 November 1956, just eight years later, evidently on

Di Elliott, staunch friend and campaigner for POW veterans.

compassionate grounds. Had he not been given early release, he would have been freed in 1958, in any case. In 1952, when the peace treaty came into effect, all prisoners still in Allied hands, including Kitabata, were transferred to Sugamo Prison in Tokyo. As a result of pleas for mitigation, all were released by December 1958. Sugamo ceased to function as a gaol in 1962 and was demolished in 1971. The longest sentence served by any Japanese war criminal convicted at an Allied trial, including several, whose death sentences for appalling crimes had been commuted to life imprisonment in 1951 by Australian Prime Minister Robert Menzies, was less than 13 years.

Although already regarded internationally as an expert on the Burma-Thai Railway, Di Elliott continued her research work into prisoners of war, generously sharing her knowledge and passing the benefit of her decades of experience to visitors at the Australian War Memorial, where she worked as a volunteer to help others uncover the wartime past of their family members.

Having accompanied Di, literally, emotionally and figuratively, on the search for her father, I encouraged her to write down her own story. Eventually, in 2017, she made a start. However, distractions got in the way and it was a rather slow process. By the beginning of 2019, she had noted her personal thoughts and her physical journeys to Singapore, Malaya and Thailand, transcribed Fred's articles, all 27 of them, and compiled the story of his early life. While it was still very much a work-in-progress, she had made a start on putting the experiences her father described into historical context when she was diagnosed with glioblastoma. Inoperable and incurable brain cancer.

In the hope of prolonging her life long enough to collect her 20-year service badge from the War Memorial in December, and to celebrate her Golden Wedding Anniversary in January the following year, she opted to undergo treatment. By sheer determination she succeeded in reaching both milestones, but it soon became obvious that the tumours were spreading and that she did not have much time left. After asking me to conduct her funeral, she had one outstanding matter that needed to be resolved.

Aware that I had the historical knowledge, access to sufficient resources, insight into her feelings and the necessary writing skill to complete the job she had begun, she said 'Lynnie, you'll have to finish Dad's story for me'.

So I did.

Di died on 12 October 2020, just shy of her 72nd birthday.

This book is her legacy.

I also kept my promise to conduct Di's funeral, which was live-streamed, allowing her friends and fellow researchers around the world to join the many mourners at the actual service.

One of those watching in the UK was my friend and research colleague, Claire, who did not know Di and knew nothing about her, other than she was my closest friend and that I was conducting the service.

After the service, Claire, who has frequent psychic experiences for which there is no rational explanation, sent me an email.

> Di was there. Standing to the right of the coffin, in a red jacket.
> There is a message too, but I am afraid it is not for you.
> I don't know who it is for but, for what its worth, it's from someone named Fred.
> He says,
> **I am sorry.**

EPILOGUE

MYSTERIOUS LOVE AFFAIRS IN THE JUNGLE

The jungles of Burma and Thailand, occupied by the Japanese, do not come to mind readily as places where romance might flourish. However, according to Fred and another POW, Les Hall, who constructed the camp radio, two Australian POWs were involved in romantic liaisons with two beautiful young Chinese and Thai women.

The First Affair

Fred was especially keen to make people aware of the friendship extended to prisoners of war by the Chinese. He wrote of the kindness extended to him and others while in captivity and, in April 1946, also published a story about a POW, helped after his escape from the railway by a Chinese girl and her father.

Assuring his readers that the story was true, Fred called his informant Jim Egan. Whether this was because he didn't know the man's real name, or wanted to protect his identity, is not known. Details of where it all took place are also unknown, and some may be a little scrambled. However, the scene opens on the banks of a river, in an almost uninhabited area of Lower Burma.

> The mysterious silence of the jungle was unbroken save for the happy singing of Sun-La, a beautiful Chinese girl. Maybe 17 years of age, with soft skin and glossy black hair, she was busily washing the family linen at the edge of the river. For 10 of her 17 years, Sun-La had lived in this area, undisturbed by the outside world, her only companion her aged father.
>
> A ripple of air rustled the leaves of the bamboos overhead. Fitfully playing among the treetops, the breeze carried a new sound to the ears of Sun-La, something she had never heard before — the sound of discharging firearms. Gazing fearfully in the direction from which the sounds came, she could see figures moving in the long grass on the opposite shore.
>
> A movement in the river caught her attention. Shots rang out and spurts of water flew into the air. She realised that someone was trying to escape across the river, and was making directly for the spot where she stood. Further shots followed and it seemed

impossible that the person could escape being hit. However, on reaching the river's edge, a white man hauled himself out of the water and staggered to the top of the bank. As he sank to the ground, a bullet hit his leg.

Sun-La had not moved. Now, with a cry of sympathy, she dashed to the wounded man's side. What she intended to do she had no idea. Placing her hands beneath his armpits, she hauled and tugged, trying to make him understand the need for a hasty retreat. Finally, she had him on his feet. Limping painfully, he followed her along the jungle path as a new burst of firing from across the river indicated that they had been seen. Luckily no bullets found a target, and the jungle now hid them from view.

Sun-La had never seen a white man before, although she had heard her father tell stories of the race. What she could not understand was how and why the man came to be there. Her father, Ho-Kee, who had also heard the shooting, appeared on the pathway. That morning, he had heard that an Australian had escaped from a Japanese prison camp about 80 kilometres away, and that the Japanese had been looking for him for days. Together, they half-led and half-carried the semi-conscious man to their humble abode, where the man confirmed that he had escaped and, if recaptured, would be shot.

The two good Samaritans hid 'Jim Egan' in a large cave on the hillside, about 200 metres away, where he remained undetected when the Japanese crossed the river and searched the house. The fugitive, who ran a high fever and was semiconscious for quite some time, was cared for by Sun-La. However, worried about her safety, and that of her father, the time eventually came when he thought he should leave. Sun-La, who had fallen in love with her patient, begged to go with him. Although he too had grown very fond of her, he refused, because of the danger, but she followed him. In the weeks, possibly months, that followed, they had several near-brushes with the Japanese and food was often a problem, but Sun-La was able to obtain sufficient supplies for them both.

How far they travelled, how long the journey took and where they ended up is not clear, but one night, at around midnight, they were challenged in an unfamiliar language, possibly Gurkha. However, before they could respond in any way, there was a blinding flash and a terrific explosion. Egan passed out. When he came to, he heard the sound of rushing feet, and the screams of wounded and dying men filling the night. He was in a battle zone. The pair had been caught in the midst of a skirmish between British and Japanese forces.

Egan was unharmed but Sun-La was killed.

Somehow, at war's end, Egan met up with Fred. Just how, or where, Fred failed to divulge, and it appears that he was far more focused on promoting the story of the courage and kindness of the Chinese. However, he believed that Egan had returned to Australia and that, should he read the article, he would endorse Fred's sentiments about the bravery of the Chinese people.

This is a fascinating tale, which Fred believed was true. Assuming that it is, at least in part, who was Jim Egan, and how did Fred meet him? Fred left no clue as to Egan's true identity, and a check shows that no one by that name was a POW in Burma or Thailand or, indeed, anywhere. However, an investigation into the fate of every single Australian who worked on the railway reveals that all can be accounted for, alive or dead, apart from one.

He was a POW who, so the Japanese said, had escaped, and was never seen again:

Private Norman Harold Atkinson, of 2/2 Pioneer Battalion, who came from Victoria. He was a member of Williams Force working on the Burma end of the line near Kilo 55 when he vanished on 5 August 1943, aged 25.

Suffering from cerebral malaria, Atkinson was last seen by his fellow POWs walking along a river bank near the camp. The Japanese maintained he escaped. The POWs believed he fell into the river and drowned. However, there were no eyewitnesses and, whatever his fate, he has not reappeared, at least not as Norman Atkinson. If he later returned home, he did not contact the army or his grieving parents, who were members of a well-respected grazing family. He is still classified officially as 'missing believed dead'. Did he escape, as the Japanese maintained? Could Fred's Jim Egan be Norman Atkinson? Did he survive the cerebral malaria, under Sun-La's ministrations, only to suffer memory loss and brain impairment? If Egan is not Atkinson, who is he?

Intriguingly, Atkinson's name arose unexpectedly in February 1977, 44 years after he disappeared, when Australian authorities attempted to establish the identity of a man in Thailand. Dubbed 'Jim Friday' by the press, he made headlines when he claimed he was Australian, had been living for the past 35 years in a remote area of Thailand and the slums of Bangkok, and now wanted to return home.

He stated, variously, that he was 45, 52 and 56 years old; that his name was Thomas James Essex, the son of a British/Australian General, William Henry Essex, killed by the Japanese; that his father was a tin miner in Malaya and he was a corporal in the RAAF, serving in Hong Kong, Calcutta and Thailand. Elaborating, he said he had gone to live in Thailand with his father in 1938 and that, after he escaped from the Japanese, he had lived in the jungle for a number of years, sleeping in a tree, and had 'sometimes shot rabbits' with his revolver. He also claimed to have married a Thai woman in southern Thailand and had five children who, he believed, were still living there. He said his mother, now deceased, was Aboriginal, but he thought his sister Mary might be living in Darwin. His only consistent claim was that he was born in Australia and that his father was a general.

It transpired that Thomas Essex, who had an alias, Jim Kraidey, had been in and out of trouble with the Thai police for many years and, at the time of his appeal to be allowed to return home to Australia, was serving a 15-month gaol sentence for passing a forged banknote.

An immediate investigation was launched in Australia by police, the military and immigration officials, but no-one called Thomas James Essex had enlisted, let alone become a POW. In fact, only 31 people named Essex served in World War II and only one, who died in Sandakan, Borneo, became a prisoner of war. Nor could any General Essex, British or Australian, be found. A search of UK archives in 2021 for anyone in the military named Thomas James Essex, who could possibly fill the bill, proved negative, while further research showed no one by that name had enlisted in any of the volunteer forces in Malaya or Singapore.

Although he looked to be well into his 60s in 1977, there is no clue to Essex's real age. However, he could not possibly have been 45 in 1977, as that would make him only ten years old when he became a POW. If 52, he would not have been old enough to enlist and would only have been 17 at the time of Singapore's fall. It is far more likely that he was as old as he looked – a balding man with a weather-beaten face, who looked closer to 70 than 60.

On the face of it, it appeared that his story was a total fabrication from beginning to end. However, a newspaper article prompted a Mr John Knox to come forward with information from his 80-year-old mother, widow of a tin miner. She said that, in the 1920s, a tin miner named W Essex had worked in Thailand for the same firm as her husband. However, when the Japanese occupied Thailand, he had refused to be evacuated from the company's mining operations near Phuket. He failed to surface after the war and it was presumed he had been killed by the Japanese. Could he be William Essex, Thomas's alleged father?

The information was passed to the Department of Foreign Affairs, but did not advance the case. A search of files in 2021 relating to Australian internees executed by the Japanese in Thailand did not include anyone by that name. However, an ex-POW living in Brisbane, who had also read the newspaper story in 1977, recalled that Norman Atkinson had vanished in Burma and had never been found.

Essex resembled, somewhat, the photo in Atkinson's army file, but his eyes, according to Atkinson's enlistment details, were the wrong colour and he was not tall enough. However, as determining the colour of someone's eyes is subjective, mistakes have been made on enlistment forms and, with age, Essex could have 'shrunk'. As there was no further evidence produced to prove his identity and, as Essex did not put forward any name that could possibly be linked to an Australian, he was denied entry into his alleged country of birth.

A POW who disappeared; a POW, suffering from cerebral malaria, often a fatal disease which, if the patient survives, can result in memory loss and brain damage; a POW who became so ill that he ran a fever and was semi-conscious; a POW, whose identity Fred did not reveal, for whatever reason, and who said he escaped from a camp in Burma; a man about the same age as Atkinson would have been in 1977, claiming to be an Australian POW and wanting to go home.

Could Norman Atkinson have adopted the name, Thomas Essex / Jim Kraidey? Was he Fred's mysterious Jim Egan? Are Atkinson, Egan and Essex one and the same? Did Atkinson, suffering memory loss, but knowing that he had escaped from the Japanese and was Australian, call himself Essex and invent a plausible background, but, due to residual brain damage, kept changing the details? Or was he simply an out-and-out con artist?

The chances of ever finding out are remote. In 1997, Thomas James Essex died in Pattaya, a coastal area to the east of Bangkok known as 'sin city', famous for its sex shows and girlie bars and the haunt of criminals, petty and not so petty.

Perhaps DNA testing could one day solve the mystery of his real identity. His ashes are interred in the grounds of St Nikolaus, a Roman Catholic Church in Pattaya, where a plaque, bearing the name Thomas Jame [sic] Essex, and his year of death, was photographed by Bob, an American Vietnam veteran in his 80s, who has photographed thousands of POW graves in Kanchanaburi, Chungkai and Labuan Island, Borneo. While on one of his frequent visits to Thailand, where he is a lifetime member of a foreign veterans' association, Bob was directed to the plaque at the church.

Perhaps Essex, after failing to convince Thai and Australian authorities of his nationality and wartime service, was accepted by the local ex-service community who believed that he was, indeed, a World War II veteran.

The Second Affair

Another mysterious love affair allegedly took place in Thailand between a man named Howard Hunter and a beautiful Thai girl. It is not known if Hunter was his real name, if he adopted it as a cover-name, or if POW Les Hall, who wrote about him in his book, *The Blue Haze*, invented it to protect his identity. The latter seems unlikely, as Les spent many years trying to discover what happened to the man he knew as Howard Hunter.

Supposedly an English foundling who went to Australia and joined the army in the closing months of the war, Howard surfaced at Tamuang, the POW camp, 39 kilometres from Nong Pluduc.

He formed a romantic liaison with a 16-year-old Thai girl, whose name Les recorded as 'Mouneen', but whom Howard called Fon (pronounced Fawn), a pet name meaning 'rain' in Thai. The girl was the daughter of a riverboat trader who supplied the POWs with food, drugs, money, medicine and commodities, such as batteries, for their secret radios.

There was only one riverboat trader with access to the POWs – Kanchanaburi's mayor, the prominent businessman and trader Boonpong Sirivejjabhandu. Aged 38, he was also a key member of the local underground movement, based in Bangkok and known as V – V being the Roman numeral for 5, the number of founding members. Britain's covert unit, SOE's Force 136, and its American counterpart, Office of Strategic Services (OSS), supported the Free Thai underground movement.

As Thailand was under 'peaceful' occupation, the Japanese assumed that Boonpong was anti-British. In late 1942, following negotiations with the Japanese to buy land belonging to his mother for the POW cemetery at Chungkai, he managed to secure the contract to supply various POW camps, which he visited on his trading trips along the Khwae Noi River, as far as Tha Khanun near the 122-kilo mark, some 166 kilometres upstream from the 'River Kwai' bridge. Horrified by the way in which the prisoners were treated, he made it his business to do all he could to help relieve their situation.

Boonpong had a beautiful 16-year-old daughter, Panee (pronounced Poo-nee, a name that sounds very similar to that recorded by Les Hall). Panee and her mother, Surat, worked with Boonpong as he plied his trade up and down the river, feigning friendship with the Japanese by giving them food and sweets and distracting them so that Boonpong could make contact with the prisoners. At each camp they passed food, money and drugs to the POW workers unloading the canteen supplies, or smuggled in much-needed medicine after dark.

A substantial amount of money was provided to the prisoners by the underground organisation. It was obtained from expatriates living in Bangkok, who were guaranteed repayment in sterling after the war, allowing the purchase of much-needed drugs and other commodities. Some of the contraband was delivered from Bangkok, hidden in vegetable baskets. However, the real danger lay with smuggling it to the POWs. Time and again, Boonpong's family members risked their lives to supply what was needed to the work camps and base hospitals.

Colonel Toosey received regular supplies for the Tamarkan hospital and the trio smuggled a considerable amount of money, medicine and food up the river to Weary Dunlop, first at Hintok and then at Tarsao. In January 1944, Boonpong was supplying emetine and morphia to the hospital at Chungkai and smuggling in batteries to keep the radio going. At the large base camp at Tamuang, to which Les and many other Australians

Left: Boonpong Sirivejjabhandu.

Below: Boonpong, Japanese soldier and Panee, then aged about 13 (1942).

had been transferred, the family continued to obtain whatever drugs and supplies were needed and Surat also set up a stall where she sold clothing and other goods to the POWs.

At Tamuang, Howard was in frequent contact with Panee, obtaining various items for the camp. The warm friendship between the pair had not passed unnoticed by other POWs, who had noted the way the two acted when together, even openly holding hands. Consequently, Les and others believed Howard when he said that, one night, Panee's father had taken her to within a kilometre of the camp to deliver 50 eggs, a hand of bananas and iodoform powder for the MO Major Hobbs, and that he had gone under the wire to meet her. Running to an empty hut in the jungle, they had begun an affair and, according to Howard, she was now pregnant. The gestation period was calculated to be around three months. He said he wanted to marry her and that he would join her father in his business.

Les and Warrant Officer Max Nonmus, who were in charge of the camp's radio, along with Captain Gordon Cumming, a doctor with 2/10 Field Ambulance, were on the lookout for telltale signs of a pregnancy when the war suddenly ended. After a very public and affectionate meeting on the river bank at Tamuang with the supposed mother of his child, Howard took off, and was last seen heading downstream in the river boat, with Panee and a man, presumably her father, at the helm.

Di Elliott and I had tried for years to discover who Howard was, based on Les Hall's information. He was definitely not an Australian POW. There was only one person called Howard Hunter who enlisted in Australia in World War 2 – a sailor in the Royal Australian Navy, who died in 1941. No record has been found to date indicating that an Australian POW in Thailand at war's end deserted and did not return home. The only Australian POW unaccounted for is Norman Atkinson.

We formulated all kinds of theories, the most likely of which is that Howard was with Force 136 and had infiltrated the camp posing as an Australian POW. Howard told Les that a small British party had parachuted into the area about 5 kilometres away and was holed up at a secret camp in the jungle. Panee wanted him to go with her and join them, but he said he had refused, as he was afraid of repercussions in the camp if he went missing. The Japanese had already dug huge ditches, called bunds, right around the camp, which the POWs suspected might become their graves if things turned pear-shaped.

Howard Hunter was obviously a real person, but was the story of the love affair true? Was Panee really pregnant? Deciding to include the story in this book, I investigated further.

Panee, who died in 2015, was known as Panee Subhawat and had children of her own, with the same surname. She came from a very upright and highly respected family. While Panee often delivered contraband from her father to the POWs, acting as a go-between, it seems unlikely that Boonpong, given his status in the community, would have knowingly allowed his young daughter to meet a male foreigner, after dark and unchaperoned.

Was there a marriage and a baby? This too seems unlikely. In a small, closely knit Thai community, where gossip is practised to an art form, such a secret would be impossible to keep, and there is no evidence that either ever eventuated.

Which raises the question of Howard Hunter's motives, if he invented the story he told to Les Hall and others. I have not been able to ascertain what happened to Howard, or uncover any trace of him, but it is very possible that he was working for British intelligence, using a false name and the cover of an Australian POW. His claim that he was a foundling, born in Britain, could have been a means of explaining why he did not have an Australian accent. The story of the pregnancy and proposed marriage may simply have been a convenient way to allow Howard to avoid 'repatriation' to Australia. Whoever he was, he existed, was trusted by Les and others, and took risks to obtain supplies for the camp.

The chances of discovering his real identity, and therefore the truth, are virtually zero. There is no one by that name listed in SOE files. This is hardly surprising, as British agents did not operate under their own names.

The most plausible theory is that Howard was connected to the British Secret Service and Boonpong's underground movement, and, at war's end went back home, where he resumed his normal life. If Howard Hunter was an assumed name, like Thomas Essex, his real identity will probably never be known.

If Panee knew who Howard really was, she took that particular secret with her to the grave.

Nominal Rolls

2/19 Nominal Roll: 395 killed/died while serving in Malaya and Singapore

NX35841	ALCOCK	J	NX56143	BULLOCK	LAK
NX33129	ALLAN	DM	NX35393	BUNT	LF
NX73003	ALLEN	LJ	NX55329	BURDEN	ET
NX26733	ANDERSON	BR	NX44815	BURKE	WM
NX35899	ANDERSON	PH	NX44848	BUTLER	FA
NX58448	ATKINSON	TG	NX10764	BYRNE	PG
NX43392	AUSTIN	N	NX35771	BYRON	HW
NX55735	AUTON	JC	NX37007	CALLCOTT	AN
NX8228	BADDEN	JW	NX35523	CARNEGIE	IR
NX43964	BAILLIEU	G	NX57611	CARPENTER	NW
NX48761	BAKER	WF	NX35928	CASSELLS	VH
NX25180	BARBER	MP	NX35250	CHANDLER	GA
NX4389	BARCLAY	V	NX35815	CHESHIRE	JH
NX51170	BARKER	R	NX50943	CHRISTIAN	AC
QX22968	BARNES	ET	NX50159	CHRISTIE	AG
NX78183	BASSETT	R	NX59619	CHRISTIE (Brother of EL)	J
NX74048	BEACROFT	FL	NX54834	CLARK	JH
NX35342	BEDGGOOD	RM	NX35694	CLARK	LH
NX36049	BINSTED	MS	NX56219	CLARKE	JEL
NX48412	BLAKE	RJ	NX39765	CLARKSON	EH
NX49451	BLENCOWE	MG	NX36027	CLIFTON	AJ
NX35821	BLOOMFIELD (Brother of PE)	AE	NX35275	CLOUGH	EH
NX69361	BOLGER	KJ	NX35724	COLLINS	TC
NX48877	BOULTER	RG	NX10983	COLLINS	TC
NX35976	BOWDITCH	FE	NX72714	CORDWELL	AJ
NX31197	BRADBURY	EM	NX32892	CORNISH	A
NX34993	BRADLEY	BHJ	NX52468	COTTON (Brother of A)	R
NX35483	BRADSHAW	G	NX2696	COX (Brother of AJ)	HW
NX59399	BRADY	FB	QX21595	COZENS	ERC
NX59483	BRETT	F	NX33272	CRAIG	WNS
NX35868	BROMFIELD	GE	NX43781	CRAWFORD	RL
NX35904	BROWN (Father of EGM)	E	NX35885	CREIGHTON	J
NX27489	BROWN	JW	NX52579	CRITTENDEN	KA
NX55589	BROWN	SH	NX35386	CROUCH	GH
NX52467	BROWN	WC	NX10972	CROUCHER	HC
NX32856	BROWN	WS	NX35231	CURTIS	LW
NX905	BRUCE	JR	NX56212	DAVIES	JL
NX49374	BUCHANAN	CS	NX30110	DAVIS	S
NX25935	BUCKLEY	JS	NX54781	DAVIS	SR
NX35579	BUCKNELL (Brother of GV)	HG	NX29183	DEMPSEY	FH
NX40472	BUDERUS	AF	NX35266	DENGATE	AW

NX1077	DENNEEN	CG	NX51242	HALL	WH
NX48789	DONACHIE	H	NX31298	HAMMOND	WC
NX35392	DONLEY	E	NX48114	HANSON	A
NX7301	DONNELLY	JJ	NX35270	HARDING	LNM
NX35287	DOUGHTY	NM	NX49536	HARRIS	L
NX35910	DOWELL	P	NX56206	HERRING	RW
NX59215	DOWNS	RT	NX73508	HEWITT	LH
NX70233	DUNCAN	DIM	NX36007	HEWS	RK
NX4466	DUTTON (Brother of RA)	CW	NX35401	HILLAN	TB
NX49830	DUTTON (Brother of CW)	RA	NX36030	HOBDEN	AR
NX55759	EDMONDS	CT	NX31182	HOLCOMBE	R
NX35763	EMERSON	MH	NX35440	HOLMES	W
NX35458	EVANS	LE	NX31654	HOWARD	TAA
NX50982	EVANS	RS	NX31021	HOWE	G
NX49773	FAHEY	WJ	NX35079	HUGHES	L
NX27532	FAIRCLOTH	DH	NX28865	HUGHES	W
NX72769	FARRELL	J	NX5702	HULLAND	G
NX2131	FAULKNER	CK	NX12600	IBBOTT	AGC
NX49526	FAWCETT	SJ	NX4693	INGLIS	WW
NX52534	FELL	CA	NX56122	IRVIN	RL
NX35769	FERGUSON	WE	NX52498	IRWIN	LC
NX48183	FINDLAY	D	NX33064	ISOM	GHJ
NX35761	FINNIGAN	WJ	NX65527	IVERS (Brother of RB)	ER
NX60362	FITZGIBBON	JM	NX51889	IVERS (Brother of ER)	RB
NX48555	FLINT	GG	NX60056	JAMES	AA
NX4433	FLOWERS	EJ	NX35338	JAMIESON	RG
NX48208	FOLEY	KJ	NX60193	JENNINGS	AR
NX35806	FORREST	LW	NX49788	JEWELL	GA
NX54427	FRASER	RC	NX26995	JOHNSTON	H
NX48384	FULLER	RH	NX73006	JOHNSTON	JM
NX54782	GALLARD	CE	NX52480	JOHNSTONE	EA
VX61635	GARDNER	A	NX60185	JOHNSTONE	GS
NX53407	GAUGHAN	LH	NX35927	KAWELMACHER	JH
NX48111	GEORGE	S	NX35027	KEEGAN	RW
NX65743	GIBBS	EW	NX49969	KELLY	DH
NX65738	GIBSON	RH	QX24567	KELLY	JH
NX34935	GILL	GA	NX36148	KELLY	VM
NX72989	GILLOGLY	J	NX33508	KENNEDY	JW
NX52560	GLEN	WC	NX55401	KENT	CS
NX50099	GOODWIN	WH	NX60174	KENT	CV
NX53828	GORDON	MR	NX43435	KERRY	DW
NX58134	GOUGH	KD	NX50025	KIEM	JF
NX41822	GRACE	DLH	NX42562	KILMURRAY	PL
NX54322	GREENTREE	GE	NX58948	LAW	DC
NX44145	GRIEVE	KW	NX55098	LAYTON	OJ
NX4210	'HACKWORTHY/Burns, MH'	AJ	NX26748	LEE	AW
NX53964	HAFEY	GE	NX48445	LENNON	PC
NX60376	HALL	FT	NX51890	LEVICK	SM
NX58109	HALL	HM	NX55394	LOFTUS	JL
NX35156	HALL	P	NX35445	LOOBY	T

NOMINAL ROLLS

NX55570	LOTHIAN	GC	NX60364	MOONEY	CA
NX77858	LYNCH	AT	QX15738	MOORE	G
NX35917	MAGGS	DT	NX49870	MOORE	NT
NX36028	MAHON	KG	NX49175	MORGAN	JGT
NX58021	MAITLAND	FVG	NX30742	MORGAN	SFC
NX49598	MAITLAND	J	NX35611	MORRIS	LG
NX56205	MANWARING	LM	NX42492	MORRIS	RW
NX35731	MASKUS (Brother of JW)	JD	NX19535	MORRISON	FF
NX35717	MASKUS (Brother of JD)	JW	NX48945	MOWDER	FH
NX56220	MASTIN	VB	NX1084	MURRAY	LG
NX35398	MATHESON	WJ	NX34742	NEILD	FGE
NX35560	MATTHEWS	HB	NX35914	NESS (Brother of J)	D
NX52369	MAXWELL	C	NX35601	NESS (Brother of D)	J
NX35164	MAYES	JN	NX48472	NEWTON	LG
NX56157	McALEER	LH	NX36974	NICHOLLS	WB
NX39455	'McCAFFERY/ Harvey, CA /SC'	CA	NX73414	NICHOLS	MAM
NX40314	McCANNA	JP	NX35937	NIMMO	M
NX66837	McCARTHY	BF	NX52371	NORMAN	BO
NX34465	McCARTHY	E	NX56202	NORMAN	RE
NX6914	McCARTHY	WN	NX36940	NORTH	D
NX35964	McCLURE	H	NX66194	NORTH	HL
NX50142	McCOLL	N	NX49858	NOTT	R
VX51300	McCULLOCH	WA	NX48976	O'BRIEN	AF
NX49787	McDONNELL	K	NX40660	O'BRIEN	GJ
NX40577	McGEE	RW	NX60333	O'BRIEN	LA
NX35415	McGINLEY	BV	NX57593	O'DONNELL	MR
NX35608	McGLYNN (Brother of WA &WA	JP	NX44809	O'NEILL	WJP
NX73649	McGREGOR	AJ	NX52031	ORMAN	FJ
NX71609	McGUFFICKE	NM	NX35409	ORME	CH
NX35989	McINNES	J	NX4203	OSBORNE	HJ
NX35849	McKENZIE	D	NX34250	OTTLEY	D
NX54802	McKILLOP	WD	NX48360	PALMER	F
NX22886	McKINNON	A	NX35271	PARRAMORE	GB
NX48724	McLEAN	CT	NX45711	PARTRIDGE	WJ
NX32601	McMAHON	F	NGX141	PASCOE	RJ
NX65736	McMILLAN	KJN	NX55677	PEARCE	MS
NX35403	McNABB	GFT	NX36953	PENBERTHY	W
NX35873	McPHERSON	LD	NX72997	PERCEVAL (Brother of LG & RL)	DR
NX58964	MEADE	RF	NX36052	PETERS	J
NX52487	MEAKIN	RA	NX73665	PHILLIPS	WN
NX2746	MEETH	JA	NX35210	PHILPOTT	DT
NX53265	MELOUNEY	JAV	NX60272	PIGGOTT	JJ
NX52473	MERTEN	E	NX26364	POLLOCK	LE
NX35844	METCALFE	L	NX5711	POOLEY	E
NX33066	MIDDLETON	DLC	NX55117	PRICE	CT
NX30372	MILLER	A	NX73714	PRICE	JTA
NX2893	MILLER	AS	NX52546	PULLEY	KU
NX35712	MILLER	DJ	NX73717	PURCELL	RJ
NX4388	'MILLER/Ferguson, James'	J	NX35443	QUINLAN	JE
NX39413	MINERS	RL	NX73220	RAMAGE	WG

NX50092	REDDING	RG		NX57123	STOKES	ET
NX35684	REDMAN	S		NX56099	STONE	RC
NX49060	REDMOND	AR		NX73662	STUBBINGS	WA
NX31527	REEVES	LS		NX36937	SULLIVAN	S
NX43664	REILLY	EM		NX29352	SUMMERS	TG
NX55733	RESCORL	JC		NX60232	SWAN	H
NX45143	REYNOLDS	G		NX35591	TABER	RT
NX48609	RIGGS	AH		NX52263	TATE	DH
NX59618	RITCHIE	JM		NX2860	TAYLOR	D
NX35477	RIVETT	JA		NX35343	TAYLOR	EH
NX50087	ROACH	MT		NX51521	TAYLOR	RC
NX52565	ROBB (Brother of LW)	AS		NX35174	TAYLOR	WS
NX56119	ROBERTS	GA		NX43399	TEALE	J
NX35672	ROBERTS	TM		NX48595	TEMPLE	J
NX35171	ROBINSON			NX56102	THOMAS	P
NX35364	ROBSON	GH		NX36503	THOMSON	A
NX52538	ROGERS (Father of EC)	CL		NX6632	THOMSON	GA
NX48036	ROTCHFORD-WILLIAMS /Rotchford	RJ		NX49599	THOMSON	RK
NX35863	RULE	RA		NX53949	THORNLEY	EW
NX35857	RUSSELL	A		NX31586	TILLEY	GE
NX51910	RUSSELL	FWS		NX33005	TISDALE	RC
NX73716	RUSSELL	JR		NX50008	TODD	J
NX40432	SAUNDERS	KG		QX23204	TOMLINSON (Brother of AE)	MP
NX29299	SAWYER	GF		NX60274	TOZER	WH
NX41824	SEAGROTT	GB		NX29941	TREGONING	T
NX53180	SELLS	WG		NX36065	TRUSCOTT	LN
NX35947	SELLWOOD	VT		NX35522	TURNER	LM
NX35715	SEWELL	FJ		NX35356	TYSON	J
VX63411	SHALE	DJ		NX58490	TYSON	KE
NX25705	SHANNON	CP		NX7294	UPWARD	GE
NX57146	SHELDRICK	EL		NX35745	VAUGHAN	TL
NX60258	SHERIDAN	WH		NX34967	VINCENT	TG
NX33000	SHUTT	LL		NX53550	WAILES	AJ
NX32570	SIMMONS	CP		NX49633	WALKER	NC
NX42866	SMITH	AC		NX29859	WALSH	CR
NX20442	SMITH	AE		NX55958	WARBURTON	HE
NX6594	SMITH	CB		NX39931	WARNES	JR
NX35950	SMITH	J		NX35802	WASLEY	JW
NX19863	SMITH	JA		NX26753	WATKINS	J
NX2157	SMITH	TA		NGX155	WAUGH	DR
NX28616	SOHIER	EG		NX35456	WELLS	GC
VX51662	SPARKS	R		NX36044	WEYMOUTH	RH
NX52554	STAINES	HO		NX39531	WHITBY	R
NX35349	STANGER	JAS		NX35391	WHITE	GL
NX52460	STARR	E		NX48190	WHITTON	CE
NX52558	STEIN	BW		NX57118	WHYTE	AR
NX35607	STEVENSON	WA		NX35765	WILDER	LG
NX35158	STEWART (Brother of LN)	AD		NX35709	WILLIAMS	AA
NX35614	STEWART (Brother of AD)	LN		NX54364	WILLIAMS	HR
NX50359	STIBBARD	LKJ		NX26548	WILLIAMS	J

NOMINAL ROLLS

NX42493	WILLIAMS	JS		NX30277	WILTSHER	CC
NX35719	WILLIAMS	LT		NX36180	WINTER	WG
NX55090	WILSON	A		NX5668	WITHERS	ET
NX5670	WILSON	CV		NX41303	WOOD	LB
NX35972	WILSON	JE		NX57208	WOOLCOTT	LH
NX12522	WILSON	R		NX39169	WYMAN/Alberts V	V
NX35390	WILSON	SG				

2/19 Nominal Roll: 422 captured and killed or died while POW
*denotes those captured and killed

NX44688	ABBOTT	TL		NX35472	BOUSIE	G
NX73334	ADAMS	AH		NX39772	BOW	WN
NX49457	ADAMS	CW		NX43785	BOWMAN (Brother of J)	HR
NX49585	ADAMS	JD		NX49963	BOYD	JW
NX5676	ALLEN*	L		NX27788	BOYD (Brother of SGJ)	RT
NX5743	ALLEN	SS		NX35254	BOYLE	CR
NX48419	ALLIE	NR		NX56147	BRADY	WP
NX41469	ANDERSON	W		NX51241	BREAKSPEAR*	S
NX49143	ANDREW	A		NX71561	BRIGGS	HC
NX49646	ANNEAR	LJ		NX7072	BROOKER*	DC
NX40399	ANTHONEY	L		QX21870	BROWN	J
NX44381	ARCHARD	C		NX35336	BROWN*	LO
NX60270	ARMITT*	AE		NX36078	BROWN*	RC
NX49440	ATKINS	RJ		NX35234	BRYCE	W
NX59907	ATKINSON	RES		NX48677	BUCKLEY	JJ
NX58441	BADGERY	BC		NX35288	BURGUN	G
NX29073	BAGUST	R		QX15847	BURKE	JE
NX4392	BATEMAN	SH		NX52946	BURNS	AV
NX59687	BATHURST	RS		NX49672	BURROWS	CW
NX35236	BAXTER*	AC		NX56118	BURT*	KE
NX29291	BEATHE	HS		NX44870	BUTTSWORTH	HW
NX35563	BEDFORD	WLC		NX30859	BYCROFT	AB
NX55795	BEETSON	GJ		NX48361	BYRNE	B
NX39778	BELL	AM		NX32891	BYRNES*	RJ
NX35636	BELL	LT		NX52540	CAMERON	DT
NX35655	'BELLETTE/Burt, J P'	GB		NX30166	CAPON	WA
NX7061	BENNETT	WD		NX58159	CAREY	WG
NX35612	BERTRAM	RB		NX35932	CARN*	DJ
NX59898	BETTS	JM		NX47355	CARNLEY	JE
NX44154	BIGGS	F		NX35638	CARTER	TM
NX36222	BILL (BILLS) (Brother of CT)	L		NX35679	CAVENAGH	CR
NX49330	BILLS	T		NX69600	CHANT	JRA
NX44576	BLUNDEN	AJ		NX44384	CHRISTIE/Sherridan	CS
NX33171	BOLTON	ED		NX44634	CLARIDGE	HR
NX48846	BOLTON	LH		NX32502	CLARKE	LA
NX56154	BOOTH	CL		NX35915	COADY	KJ
NX52471	BORLASE	AWR		NX57575	COCKS	ANP
NX34111	BOSTOCK	WR		NX32301	CONNELL	JF
NX35235	BOURCHIER*	HL		NX42352	COOK	WS

NX51622	CORBETT	JWF		NX55861	EVANS*	CL
NX60171	CORCORAN	FL		NX35789	EVANS*	EJ
NX48471	CORE	SR		NX51274	EXTREM	TJ
NX52674	COSTELLO*	AG		NX34869	FALLAW*	C
NX35853	COTTAM	AE		NX50271	FERGUSON	KD
NX36763	COTTON* (Brother of R)	A		NX30059	FINIGAN*	R
NX35371	COUCH*	BR		NX33667	FITZGERALD	D
QX21876	COUSINS	SJ		NX49759	FITZGERALD	WJW
NX35598	COUZENS	F		NX43446	FITZPATRICK	DA
NX43552	CRAGO	G		NX19386	FLEMMING	AC
NX35512	CRAIG	DAL		NX52964	FLINT	AE
NX12601	CRAWFORD*	BDG		NX55738	FOGARTY	MJ
NX51989	CRAWFORD*	M		NX67705	FORRESTER	CH
NX33947	CRITTENDEN	HE		NX52751	FREEMAN*	LC
NX60312	CROMBIE	MM		NX35714	FULLER*	F
NX4208	CULBERT	PA		NX23144	FULLERTON	GA
NX41895	CULL	A		SX1794	FURNER	CP
NX35804	DAINES	H		NX60360	GALLAHER*	J
NX35961	DALE	R		NX49255	GALLARD	RF
NX35842	DALLAS	HF		NX58438	GARVIN	JT
NX58980	DANN	WMJ		NX52469	GAVEL	W
NX35628	DARE*	JN		NX67801	GEELAN	W
NX73453	DAVIDSON (Brother of NS)	FG		NX49469	GENTLE	TR
NX60348	DAVIS	ER		NX42478	GERAGHTY	RL
NX49304	DAVIS	RJ		NX5710	GIBSON	JB
NX35809	DAY*	CE		NX12538	GLASSON*	DJR
NX10913	DEACON	TP		NX10814	GOLDING	R
NX43486	DEAR	RJ		NX32109	GOOD	G
NX25349	DELANEY	RH		NX35794	GORHAM	HG
NX35820	DEVLIN	IA		NX55666	GOSS*	EF
NX70002	DICKMAN	FH		NX35646	GRAHAM	R
NGX70	DICKSON*	AG		NX22895	GRILLS	VE
NX50891	DIEWS	FT		NX35568	GROSVENOR*	H
NX58246	DILLEY	CD		NX73492	HALLAWAYS	D
NX2549	DODD	VA		NX33196	HAMILTON*	AMS
NX73684	DODDS	G		NX49269	HAMILTON	H
NX49746	DOYLE	AA		NX19506	HARDIE	MJ
NX35361	DOYLE	EA		NX53763	HARDING	FR
NX41437	DRABLOES (DRABLOS)	S		NX55430	HARDING	GN
NX25085	DUNBAR	D		NX35725	HARGRAVES	JV
NX13825	DUNHILL	EG		NX26890	HARPER	AJ
NX58890	DWYER	AS		QX22365	HARRIS	CH
NX48715	EASTON	H		NX35793	HARRIS*	MK
NX65393	EDMUNDS	T		NX35973	HARRIS	RH
NX35441	EDWARDES (EDWARDS)	HM		NX36101	HARRISON*	LJ
NX4344	EDWARDS	E		NX52527	HAYNES*	TE
NX35905	EDWARDS	JT		NX71574	HEALY	AT
NX36024	ELMY*	J		NX39936	HEDLEY	GW
NX2140	'ERWIN/ Irwin, RG'	LR		NX5671	HENWOOD	EJ
QX18446	ETHERIDGE	JO		NX60379	HEWSON	H

NOMINAL ROLLS

NX20271	HEYWOOD	JA	NX56221	LEONARD*	FJ
NX49021	HILL	JR	QX21993	LESLIE	C
NX49288	HINE	VM	NX50197	LEWIS	AL
NX27549	HOCKLEY	JE	NX51867	LOBB	FT
NX55163	HODGSON	LW	NX35700	LONGOBARDI	CJ
NX72964	HOLDAWAY	LJ	VX34801	LOVE	WH
NX35245	HOPKINS	AJ	QX22217	LOW	JH
NX25306	HORNE	N	QX22574	LUXTON (Brother of BC)	JM
NX49343	HORSEY	PR	NX25640	LYNCH*	J
NX34463	HOWARD*	J	QX23944	MABIN	DW
NX59839	HUBBARD	EAF	NX12599	MACDONALD*	HCH
NX44465	HUCKLE	RA	NX35726	MADDEN	W
NX49648	HUGHES	KG	NX71952	MAHONEY	JB
NX58270	HUMPHRIES	D	NX42217	MAKIM	GJ
NX54096	HUNTINGTON	JB	NX32285	MARCHBANK	WG
NX35228	HURST	RE	NX44954	MARSH	CK
NX5754	INGRAM	AE	NX53833	MARTIN	HA
NX39293	INGRAM	RE	NX41305	MARTIN	JT
NX65918	INGRAM-MOODY/Moody T*	T	NX51690	MASKELL	J
NX60355	INGS	EH	NX69998	MAVROTHALASITIS	G
NX73654	ISAACS	AE	NX50337	McCAULEY	JJG
NX60056	JAMES	AA	NX50961	McDONALD*	DA
NX73329	JAMES	GL	NX35609	McGLYNN (Brother of JP & WA)	WA
NX10826	JAMES	JR	NX65294	McGOWAN	AR
NX73023	JAMIESON	LA	NX35602	McGUIRE	AD
NX35623	JENKINS	R	NX35826	McILHAGGA	WJ
NX44582	JENKINS	RD	NX73001	McKENZIE	WJ
NX35926	JIGGINS*	FW	NX59906	McLACHLAN*	MB
NX34929	JOHNSON	RV	NX74021	McLAUGHLIN	RG
NX50852	JOHNSTON	AB	NX50085	McNAMARA	FA
NX21509	JOHNSTON	V	NX35438	McNEILL	GA
NX33265	JONES*	J	NX42402	MENZIES	HW
QX22064	JOYCE	HL	NX35260	MILES*	CC
NX50257	JUSTICE (Twin brother of MC)	AJ	NX56101	MILLARD	WG
NX58986	JUSTICE (Twin brother of AJ)	MC	NX55906	MILLER*	V
NX35550	KELLY	TJ	QX18477	MITCHELL	EW
NX52555	KENNEDY*	WP	NX35253	MITCHELL*	WJ
NX49191	KERR	JR	QX23316	MOESSINGER	L
NX73666	KIRKPATRICK	E	NX4334	MOFFATT	E
NX39588	KLINE	J	NX60225	MOORE	MF
QX9754	KNIGHT	JE	NX49559	MORAN	JP
NX53166	KNOX	CT	NX38423	MORGAN	E
NX35900	KNOX	JW	QX22250	MOSS	R
NX16994	LAIRD	JTM	NX35687	MOUAT*	LE
QX18430	LANGFORD	WF	NX35185	MUIR	RJ
NX60329	LAVERTY	A	NX37793	MULLENS	JR
NX52301	LAW	FT	NX35430	MULRAY	WP
NX36469	LEDWIDGE	FB	NX47341	MUNFORD	FA
NX36039	LEDWIDGE	SJ	NX56948	MURRAY*	M
NX54717	LEISHMAN	JR	NX33361	MURRAY	R

NX35279	MUSSETT	HV		NX50919	ROBERTSON*	K
NX56129	NEALE	DM		NX35896	ROBERTSON	RJ
NX49336	NICHOLLS	STA		NX43916	ROBINSON	AJ
NX35385	NOBLE*	WA		NX56657	ROEBUCK	JT
NX54952	NUGENT*	GE		NX51667	ROMEY	N
NX35584	OAG* (brother of WD)	AR		NX43021	ROUSE	JF
NX31462	OAG (brother of AR)	WD		NX49504	RUSSELL	AW
NX7991	O'CONNOR (Brother of RM)	AH		NX73960	RYAN	RL
NX7941	O'CONNOR (Brother of AH)	RM		NX52248	SANKEY	JG
NX43479	O'DONOHUE	EJ		NX7938	SARGEANT	WJ
NX55429	OLIVER*	RW		NX35447	SAYERS	LRT
NX72020	O'MARA	T		NX33377	SCULLY*	LV
NX43418	O'SHAUGHNESSY	TC		NX52285	SHAW	G
NX35508	OVERS	CH		NX48206	SHAW	R
NX47015	PALMER	EJ		NX26580	SHORT	MN
NX35246	PALMER*	JC		NX35491	SIMPSON	DG
NX36013	PARFREY	TH		NX23413	SIMS	FK
NX4668	PARKER	NL		NX27475	SINCLAIR	I
NX52135	PARKS	LR		NX39776	SINCLAIR	WC
NX49723	PATTERSON	C		NX49915	SLIP	EC
NX25894	PEARCE	JS		NX35791	SMITH*	AP
NX54537	PEPPER	GD		NX42439	'SMITH/Andrews,S'	EW
NX6578	PERRY	JC		NX26819	SMITH	GA
NX26342	PETTIT	JW		NX35596	SMITH*	GM
NX7129	PICKERING	JA		NX60198	SMITH	OES
NX30573	PITT	WJ		NX52476	SMITH	PJ
NX56047	PLATT	SH		NX23002	SMITH	WSC
NX44671	POWELL	CA		NX70191	SNELLING*	RRL
NX50396	POWER	CGR		NX51847	SOLOMON	JH
NX57672	PRESS	AD		NX42210	SOUTER	J
NX37189	PRYOR	DR		NX35656	SPENCER	HF
NX73463	PURCELL	JS		NX59479	SPURWAY	RS
NX32671	QUIGLY*	JB		NX40828	STACE	RA
NX35635	QUINLIVAN*	LJ		NX1080	STANTON	E
NX44574	QUINN	H		NX4521	STAPLETON	JD
NX35466	RAE	J		NX73332	STARR	JH
NX8768	RALPH	C		NX55682	STEDMAN	JN
NX55284	RAPHAEL	HN		NX56103	STEWART	FG
NX51511	REDFERN	E		NX25910	STITT	J
NX59145	REDGRAVE	EJW		NX39013	STOKER	RS
NX8319	REED	HE		NX58620	STOWE	WF
NX72761	REILLY	V		NX50941	SUGGATE	NF
NX59903	RIACH	GB		NX55069	SUISTED	FR
NX54950	RICKETTS	WG		NX60372	SYKES	CG
NX51339	RIVETT	GF		NX6953	SYMON*	JRA
NX52566	ROBB (Brother of AS)	LW		NX25902	SYMONS	AJ
NX23624	ROBERTS	F		NX73715	TAYLOR	AA
NX35661	ROBERTS	H		NX52482	TAYLOR	CR
NX6638	ROBERTS	HE		NX50899	TAYLOR	I
NX34912	ROBERTSON	AE		NX30243	TEMPLE	RJ

NX22997	THOMAS	GJ		NX49860	WALTON	RD
NX60211	THOMAS	RB		VX38675	WARDALE-GREENWOOD	H
NX35999	THOMAS*	TJ		NX51991	WARE	C
NX52646	THORPE	H		NX56139	WARK	TJ
NX58573	THURLOW*	R		NX35444	WATSON	VA
NX35175	TILDEN*	KL		NX54108	WELSH	WJ
NX32742	TOME	MJM		QX15701	WESTCOTT	HW
NX54801	TOMLINSON*	FM		NX10735	WESTON	FL
NX45897	TRACEY	CT		NX48755	WHALAN	R
NX35205	TRAVERS	K		NX43543	WHITEHEAD	W
NX35848	TURNER	EH		NX27755	WILDER	EW
NX33624	TURNER	EW		NX35496	WILSON	A
NX7937	TURNER	G		NX60208	WILSON	DA
NX51216	TURNER	TM		NX7123	WILSON	E
NX57645	TYSON	JS		QX22943	WILSON	H
NX35262	VERDON (Brother of TC)	PJ		QX23104	WILSON	SC
NX35203	VERDON* (Brother of PJ)	TC		QX15818	WINTERBOTTOM/Winters T	A
NX2749	WALKER*	EW		NX36294	WOOD	FA
NX35230	WALKER*	LR		NX51640	WOODCROFT	KR
NX52568	WALKER	M		NX35524	WORNER	HR
NX35346	WALKERDEN*	R		NX35877	WRIGHT	C
NX33806	WALLACE	HW		NX52261	WRIGHT	TJ

2/19 Nominal Roll: 1073 survived (including those who escaped when Singapore fell)

QX22218	ABELL	MR		NX72557	ASSER	FJ
NX49857	ABRAHAM	SJ		NX26762	ASSHETON	P
NX35315	ADAMS	T		NX70159	AUSTIN	RWL
NX53608	ADLER	J		NX33376	AVERY	GCT
NX33216	AHERN	KP		NX48301	AYLWIN/Lewis	DTK
NX39759	ALBRECHT	IE		NX51823	BADGER	CJ
NX53693	ALDHAM	J		NX49042	BADINIER	HJ
NX51733	ALLAN (born Jackson)	FL		NX73634	BAGNALL	NH
NX77652	ALLEN	C		NX57171	BAILEY	FJ
NX51772	ALLEN	NSB		NX73131	BAILEY	IE
NX53757	ALLERY	RF		NX35192	BAILEY	JM
NX71901	ANDERSON	AH		NX57400	BAILEY	L
NX12595	ANDERSON	CGW		NGX144	BAILEY	PF
NX44654	ANDERSON	HA		NX39196	BAILEY	WE
NX35358	ANDERSON	KA		NX48848	BAIN	RM
NX35431	ANSTEE	HJ		NX60278	BAIRD	WJ
NX35535	ANSTICE	LM		NX35808	BAIRD	WTR
NX50696	APPERLEY	WJJ		NX25903	BAKER	SG
NX35151	ARCHER	GS		NX73434	BALFOUR	L
NX54533	ARCHER	H		NX35548	BALL	SF
NX35374	ARMOUR	MJB		NX44462	BANKS	WG
QX21868	ARMSTRONG	TR		NX52472	BARDSLEY	R
NX56781	ARNEIL	JW		NX42479	'BARNIER (Barnier, W T)'	CM
NX48757	ARNETT	PA		NX35404	BARRATT	PR
NX41814	ARTHUR-SMITH	JA		NX57790	BARRON	WV

NX33737	BARRY	JH		NX51129	BOSCHETTI	RJ
NX2104	BARTLEY (Brother of S)	EJ		NX42191	BOTTERILL	K
NX2707	BARTLEY (Brother of E J)	S		NX35173	BOURKE	WP
NX56107	BARTLEY	WBG		NX52537	BOWHAY	SB
NX70749	BARTON	HN		NX60346	BOWMAN (Brother of HR)	J
NX55500	BARTON	HT		NX51985	BOWYER	AG
NX70190	BATHGATE	AF		NX53219	BOYD (Brother of RT)	SGJ
NX29866	BAXTER	RJ		NX12594	BRACHER	WP
NX34225	BAYLISS	CR		NX73648	BRADFORD	HJ
NX7068	BEASHEL	JP		NX47090	BRADLEY	E
NX626	BEASLEY	E		NX12551	BRAUND	FNB
NX55900	BEAUMONT	JR		NX1005	BREBNER	JW
NX41675	BEAVER	BA		NX52485	BRENNAN	MJ
NX49424	BEDFORD	CW		NX36061	BRIDEOAKE	AR
NX34413	BEGGS	LS		NX57296	BRIDGE	JW
NGX126	BELL	DJ		NX27258	BRIDGE	WCR
NX43513	BELL	JS		NX49427	BRIEN	CF
NX7091	BELL	LG		NX65739	BRIGHTFIELD	FF
NX52393	BELL	RJ		NX70592	BRINDLEY	JM
NX35457	BELL	RMA		NX10679	BRITTON	RS
NX36158	BENJAMIN	VAH		NX55569	BRODERICK	GE
NX54110	BENNETT	GR		NX2908	BRODERICK	GS
QX23248	BENNETT	J		NX35284	BROOK	AF
NX30369	BENNO	WTR		NX58088	BROOKS	MK
NX51756	BENNOCH	TR		NX35904	BROWN	E
NX49537	BERGAN	VFJ		NX60115	BROWN (Son of NX60119)	EGM
NX35532	BERKLEY	M		NX49804	BROWN	FH
NX31310	BERTHOLD	HCM		NX65745	BROWN	GW
NX35405	BERTHON	CF		NX55367	BROWN	HI
NX35850	BERTRAM	AC		NX65483	BROWN	LD
NX34902	BEVERLEY	FG		NX29898	BROWNLEE	J
NX71219	BIDDLE	J		NX45079	BUCHANAN	WR
NX35308	BILLETT	LC		NX35432	BUCK	GJ
NX33297	BILLS (Brother of L)	CT		NX51885	BUCKLEY	RT
NX48982	BISHOP	FE		NX31452	BUCKNELL (Brother of HG)	GV
NX65749	BLACK	CD		NX31853	BUCKNELL	WW
NX53384	BLACKMAN	E		NX10763	BURBURY	NG
NX41452	BLANCH	JW		NX14955	BURCHELL	HE
NX6932	BLAND	RV		NX36070	BURDEN	RF
NX72999	BLISS	R		NX48581	BURGESS	F
NX49190	BLOCKLEY	WA		NX35191	BURGUN	SS
NX52461	BLOOMFIELD (Brother of AE)	PE		NX60206	BURKE	PM
NX4405	BLUHDORN	BD		NX19873	BURNS	WJ
NX56187	BLUME	DM		NX34960	BURT	SF
NX57049	BLUNDELL (BLANDELL)	WA		NX35222	BUSH	CJ
NX73142	BOARDMAN	AH		NX35435	BUTT	AS
NX36994	BODEN	CD		NX35468	BUTT	CET
NX57518	BOND	CE		NX35419	BYE	AH
NX51304	BOND	DR		NX56316	BYRNE	JA
NX20633	BORLEY	SH		NX37313	BYRNE	KF

NX52405	BYRON	FP		NX49226	COCHRAN (Brother of LL)	PJ
NX35149	CAHILL	RL		QX22337	COLE	DK
NX49129	CAHILL	RW		NX35740	COLEMAN	TW
QX23311	CALLANAN	RJ		NX32561	COLLINS	F
NX35280	CAMERON	A		NX35720	COLLINS	FCN
NX52530	CAMERON	SE		NX49862	COLLINS	GEW
QX22507	CAMERON	WR		NX35528	COLLINS	J
NX35801	CAMPBELL	AJ		NX35743	COLLINS	JWF
NX49098	CAMPBELL	B		NX69296	COLLINS	TW
NX49044	CAMPBELL	CH		NX23837	COLLON	FD
NX35309	CAMPBELL	EE		NX35696	COLYER	JB
NX35935	CAMPBELL	ITC		NX56057	CONLAN	EM
NX44745	CAMPBELL	JE		NX43476	CONNELL	LJ
NX50128	CAMPBELL	RG		NX55841	CONSTANCE	R
NX51668	CANE	RA		NX48963	COOK	HJ
NX35494	CANNON	SB		NX44950	COOK	WT
NX49604	CANTWELL	B		NX48986	COOMBS	JF
NX56121	CARN	VS		NX35939	COOPER	GR
NX44645	CARR	CW		NX45053	COOPER	JA
NX36047	CARR	GJ		NX44713	COOPER	KS
NX44740	CARR	HJ		NX49889	COOPER	SJS
NX33595	CARR	J		NX57481	COOTE	FE
QX21873	CARSON	J		NX35893	CORBY	LJ
QX24444	CARSTENS	JTM		NX33597	CORDINGLEY	WS
NX51240	CARTER	P		NX44955	CORNFORD	RC
NX35722	CARTWRIGHT	W		NX53545	CORRY	JB
NX45655	CASHMAN	LJ		NX49415	COSTELLO	AJ
NX58784	CATTLEY	FJ		NX35503	COSTELLO	J
NX7052	CHALMERS	TH		NX52842	COTTER	CT
NX49461	CHAPMAN	AE		NX43468	COUGHLIN	RT
QX22345	CHAPMAN	HG		NX34932	COUSENS	CH
NX44931	CHATFIELD	JR		NX30276	COWD	AG
NX53588	CHEERS	LJ		NX2704	COX (Brother of HW)	AJ
NX35223	CHENEY	KC		NX36980	COX	CM
NX48158	CHERRY	EC		NX56123	COX	CMG
NX42895	CHESTERTON	JP		NX49691	COX	RG
NX55646	CHIDGEY	JP		NX35600	COX	STT
NGX140	CHRISTIE (Brother of J)	EL		NX43482	CRAGO	JB
NX45901	CLACK	EW		NX32511	CRAIG	L
NX32287	CLARK	AV		NX23190	CRAIG	LFD
NX48182	CLARK	F		NX35965	CRAIG	WA
NX2548	CLARK	RW		NX35616	CRAWFORD	H
NX35993	CLARKE	JW		NX73549	CRAWFORD	R
NX699	CLARKE	TW		NX56113	CREGAN	P
NX49246	CLARKE	WC		NX54319	CRIPPS	WG
NX49532	CLARKSON	HL		NX45122	CROCKETT	JA
QX24750	CLAY	EC		NX71795	CRONIN	AJ
NX56037	CLENDENNING	RA		NX35662	CROTON	RJ
NX2118	CLUTTERBUCK/Hartley	R		QX23105	CROWE	RM
NX42902	COCHRAN (Brother of PJ)	LL		NX52475	CROWLEY	JL

NX35380	CULLEN	FD		NX35883	DORE	EH
NX4517	CULLEN	JP		NX8365	DORNEY	CJ
NX48038	CUMMINS	FE		NX51080	DOUGLAS	KJ
NX36146	CUMMINS	KF		NX52477	DOUGLAS	NF
NX33041	CURLE	P		NX35204	DOWD	RK
NX25576	CURNOW	MWV		NX25424	DOWD	WJ
NX37529	CURRAN	MW		NX1186	DOYLE	WJ
NX50086	CURRIE	LL		NX73625	DREXEL	HH
NX42974	CUTLER	HJ		NX43419	DRUITT	EA
NX35161	DALY	WJ		NX35595	DRUMMOND	RRC
NX44639	DARCY	LA		NX73653	DUCK	PE
NX53597	DARGIN	F		NX4529	DUGGAN	H
NX35317	DARLING	RH		NX7053	DUNN	HG
NX24829	DAVEY	JP		NX27254	DUNSTONE	CR
NX35490	DAVIDSON	C		NX42896	DURMAN	JC
NX52464	DAVIDSON (Brother of FG)	NS		NX73333	DWARTE	DJ
NX30842	DAVIES	WE		NX29722	DYETT	W
NX35721	DAVIESS	FC		NX71836	DYSON	RJ
NX44834	DAWSON	AH		NX31944	EAGLESTON	EW
NX43441	DAY	HL		NX16282	EAGLETON	JR
NX56947	DAY	SG		NX40728	EASEY	WE
NX35448	DAY	WJ		NX36306	EDMONDS	R
NX32809	DE ABEL	J		NX55398	EDWARDS	AW
NX67344	DE GROEN	G		NX35590	EDWARDS	CA
NX35699	DE LOAS	JS		NX5729	ELLIOTT	CW
NX59496	DEAN	RM		NX37206	ELLIOTT	DK
NX6639	DEAS	RE		NX57069	ELLIS	AJG
NX73306	DEECE	GE		NX39832	ELPHICK	EG
NX73369	DEEVES	HG		QX22221	ELPHICK	WH
NX35157	DEMERY	RJ		NX60172	EVANS	CW
NX52470	DEMPSEY	FW		NX56797	EVANS	DB
NX35603	DENNIS	PG		NX54943	EVERSHAM	ECA
NX29335	DENNIS	RB		QX23847	EVERSON	EW
NX35998	DENT	R		NX41747	'FAHY aka Masters, Thomas/Larry'	RF
NX50513	DERRIMAN	AH		NX50125	FAICHNEY	EV
NX37051	DICK	P		NX27146	FAIR	HW
NX43442	DICKINSON	JP		NX35856	FANNING (Brother of JH &TR)	CJ
NX57036	DICKSON	KR		NX35860	FANNING (Brother of CJ &TR)	JH
NX40448	DIETRICH	CR		NX35865	FANNING (Brother of CJ &JH)	TR
NX49508	DILLON	JW		NX35756	FARLOW	CL
NX2158	DIMMOCK	R		NX31871	FARMER	JB
NX35232	DIXON	SJ		QX15946	FARR	AE
NX25874	DOIG	H		NX36050	FARRANDS	MR
NX56106	DONALDSON	GM		NX35902	FARRELL	AB
NX56216	DONALDSON	HJ		NX35527	FENNELL	JM
NX52557	DONNELLY	E		NX6963	FERGUSON	FW
NX49429	DONNELLY	JE		NX55452	FERGUSON	LV
NX35378	DOOLAN	FW		NX38559	FERRIS	LK
NX19468	DOOLIN	JTP		NX60375	FINN	TR
NX39735	DORAN	W		NX49312	FISHBURN	JH

NX44970	FITZPATRICK	FA		NX35193	GORDON	W
NX19508	FITZSIMMONS	HHE		NX35764	GORHAM	JP
NX35648	FITZSIMON	ML		NX66965	GOSLING	DA
NX35559	FIXTER	GL		NX36048	GOSLING	VG
NX35752	FLACK	NC		NX35547	GRAHAM	R
NX73601	FLAHERTY	J		NX36057	GRANGER	HG
NX65159	FLAWS	CS		NX69743	GRANT	RI
NX73643	FLEMING	DW		NX72010	GREATOREX	FT
NX71967	FLETCHER	WL		NX65750	GREEN	R
NX35206	FLORANCE	IH		QX23352	GREEN	RH
NX36504	FLOYD	AG		NX73681	GREEN	RH
NX13693	FLYNN	RJ		NX58630	GREENAN	J
NX35921	FOO	AF		NX49816	GREENE	FJ
NX42152	FOOT	HS		QX15856	GREENWAY	WJ
NX66678	FORBES (Brother of JWK)	GK		QX22338	GRIFFIN	KM
NX52562	FORBES (Brother of GK)	JWK		NX34188	GROW	VF
NX32845	FORD	FO		NX51735	GUERIN	C
NX25447	FORD	R		NX31402	HAGGART	NA
NX37205	FORWOOD	GW		NX73406	'HALL aka HALL, John'	HA
NX25334	FOSTER	RW		NX36074	HALLINAN	RV
NX78005	FOX	HW		NX51440	HALLORAN	A
NX48474	FRANCIS	CM		NX52571	HALLORAN	AJ
NX948	FRANCIS	NA		NX56177	HAMPSTEAD	DC
NX45016	FRASER	BH		NX22723	HANN	JC
NX43425	FREEMAN	AJ		NX35594	HANSON	GL
NX44636	FREEMAN	WL		NX56233	HARDEN	RV
NX35864	FUKS (aka Fookes)	JD		NX32431	HARGRAVES	GH
NX55292	FULTON	DI		NX2864	HARPER	WHH
NX36060	GALVIN	AM		NX35971	HARRINGTON	AV
NX49262	GARDINER	RE		NX4572	HARRINGTON	PE
NX35213	GARNER	JP		NX35952	HARRIS	AC
NX2910	GEDDES	JR		NX34662	HARRIS	FL
NX7336	GEORGE	FB		NX52548	HARRIS	K
NX49434	GEORGE	WF		NX49065	HARRISON	IW
NX56110	GERHARD	RF		NX35525	HARRISON	JW
NX35152	GIBBONS	H		NX26925	HARRISON	RG
NX27894	GIBBS	CCW		NX48940	HARRISON	VA
NX35376	GILCHRIST	PE		NX35587	HARVEY	AG
NX65334	GILLESPIE	JM		NX51647	HARVEY	C
NX36134	GLENN	DM		NX52529	HARVEY	C
NX68619	GLOVER	VG		NX49074	HARVEY	CF
NX41611	GLYTSOS /GLEESON)	E		NX73668	HARWOOD	EH
NX35574	GODFREY	DDH		QX20470	HASSETT	HR
NX35728	GODFREY	RA		NX38304	HAWKINS	A
NX23737	GODWIN	TN		NX43648	HAWTIN	SH
NX12534	GOLLAN	AB		NX35690	HAYES	AW
QX22600	GOLLER	FJ		NX67014	HAYNES	LK
NX60287	GOODFELLOW	I		NX25943	HAYWOOD	AC
NX22806	GORDON	AL		NX58938	HEAD	H
NX49906	GORDON	DL		NX35150	HEALEY	NH

NX50196	HEARN	MJ		NX34033	HUNT	CG
NX73552	HEDWELL	JW		NX20438	HUNT	EJB
NX32087	HENNESSY	MJ		NX50914	HUNT	PC
NX65522	HENRYS	IR		NX52483	HUNT	WG
NX52474	HEPPER	GH		NX1948	HUNT	WH
NX48180	HERRON	S		NX43466	HUNTER	LJ
NX49726	HEWISH	WJ		NX38802	HUSH	AE
NX36053	HEWITT	GR		NX57142	HUSH	CA
NX35497	HEYDON (Brother of JP)	JD		NX35702	HUTCHINS	AA
NX35499	HEYDON (Brother of JD)	JP		QX21882	HUTCHINS	CS
NX59745	HIBBERT	K		NX56542	HUTCHINSON	G
NX25216	HICKS	L		NX73738	INGLIS	R
NX42502	HIGGINS	B		NX77809	INGRAM	TJ
NX40496	HIGGINS	MA		NX23736	IRELAND	RC
NX35788	HILL	AG		NX49770	IRISH	HC
NX53773	HILL	JC		NX25802	IRVING	FA
NX76302	HINDER	DCC		NX35337	IRWIN	GL
NX31530	HINES	A		NX59783	ISLES	DW
NX26013	HINES	R		NX60181	JAMIESON	KA
NX73755	HINTON	CH		NX48039	JEFFERY	R
NGX152	HIRSCHEL	OJM		NX44914	JEFFRIES	KS
NX52580	HIRST	GB		NX32625	JOHNSON	RE
NX55749	HODSON	JF		NX55756	JOHNSON	TL
NX73491	HOLDER	GH		NX45090	JOLLY	A
NX49171	HOLLAND	P		NX51703	JONES	CEF
QX24166	HOLLINDALE	ED		NX44774	JONES	FW
NX56130	HOLM	AH		NX25904	JONES	JJ
NX54087	HOLMAN (Brother of RF)	JN		NX48092	JONES	RS
NX44861	HOLMAN (Brother of JN)	RF		NX49570	JORGENSEN	WV
NX33584	HOLMES	GMR		NX42969	KANE	TM
QX21759	HOLT	JF		NX40344	KARKOE	NF
NX60691	HOLZHAUSER	CVC		NX43412	KAUFMANN	CR
NX60231	HOPKINS	AG		NX44871	KAY	AW
NX60365	HORNE	RL		NX6967	KEAN	HJ
NX54097	HORSNELL	JH		NX48153	KELAHER	EJ
NX36981	HOSLER	R		NX32967	KELLY	GB
NX49767	HOTTES	MW		NX18995	KELLY	JF
NX56126	HOUNSELL	WJ		NX48954	KENNEDY	AR
NX35760	HOWARD	A		NX70897	KENSETT	CF
NX26768	HOWARD	JA		NX36182	KENYON	JA
NX35481	HOWE	F		NX56199	KIMBELL	MD
NX35597	HOWELL	CM		NX43370	KING	EJS
NX53839	HOWSE	PL		NX35685	KNIGHT	WG
NX36003	HUBBARD	HJ		NX14957	KOINA	AC
NX50763	HUBBARD	V		NX67286	KYLE	VL
NX73435	HUDSON	C		NX60296	LAKE	AF
NX35510	HUGH	A		NX32358	LANGHAM	SJ
NX56105	HUGHES	GK		NX36950	LANSER	T
NX26396	HUGHES	LG		NX43393	LARKIN	FX
NX35212	HULL	M		NX35159	LARKIN	JW

NX20162	'LAURIE (LAWRIE) /McBride, W'	GW		NX35285	MACMASTER	R
NX43249	LAWLER	AK		NX28343	MADDEN	TW
NX49667	LAWLER	WH		NX26254	MAGIN	JH
NX73726	LAWRENCE	ER		QX21691	MAJOR	WS
NX41461	LAWRENCE	W		NX25782	MALES (Brother of RJ)	LA
NX65740	Le DUC	AE		NX44885	MALES (Brother of LA)	RJ
NX44646	LEADBEATTER	R		NX35541	MANN	GR
NX36029	LEAKE	JDF		NX73308	MANSFIELD	AC
NX52564	LEAVER	MW		NX55915	MANT	GP
NX37148	LEDINGHAM	WJ		NX10767	MANWARING	A
NX35697	LEDWELL	L		NX35311	MANWARING	R
NX35394	LEDWIDGE	SJ		NX73281	MARINER	WH
NX37608	LEE	A		NX48394	MARTIN	DR
NX36020	LEE	EJ		NX32610	MARTIN	LC
NX35433	LEE	TJ		NX32788	MARTIN	PJ
NX52550	LEE	TS		NX33153	MARTIN	RH
NX49702	LEECH	GP		NX32563	MARTIN	WC
NX35746	LEES	LL		NX51211	MARTYN	M
NX51980	LEES	LR		NX51875	MASHMAN	A
NX35436	LEITCH	JF		NX73473	MASON	JC
NX36063	LESLIE	C		NX57299	MASTERTON	CM
NX50448	LEWIS	CW		NX39791	MATCHETT	AJ
NX36043	LEWIS	L		NX35169	MATHESON	TA
NX39408	LEWIS	RT		NX12610	MAXWELL	DS
NX51318	LING	AJ		NX68528	MAXWELL	GM
NX35710	LIPSCOMBE	AV		NX49431	MAY	F
NX35970	LITCHFIELD	EV		NX51422	McALISTER	SJ
NX48766	LIVESEY	KM		NX22573	McANNELLY	PF
NX60180	LOBLEY	RW		NX21275	McARTHY/(McCARTHY	SJE
NX59964	LOCOCK aka Murdoch	RA		NX35613	McCABE	ME
NX71896	LODDING	WG		NX52494	McCAFFREY	JF
NX60547	LONGMIRE	JH		NX35326	McCAW	EC
NX27450	LORD	CT		NX35913	McCAWLEY	CT
NX56120	LOUGHREY	WC		NX35889	McCOOK	DW
NX10329	LOW	JF		NX60200	McCOY	AH
NX48938	LOW	R		NX49170	McCURDY	RS
NX10682	LOWCOCK	WM		NX56393	McDONALD	RD
NX52032	LOWE	CC		NX69763	McELROY	RA
NX53593	LOWIEN	CE		QX23045	McFARLANE	FJ
NX60112	LOY	JJ		NX48423	McFARLANE	JB
QX22570	LUXTON (Brother of JM)	BC		NX35238	McGEACHIE	W
NX25652	LYNCH	J		NX35689	McGEADY Bbrother of LG)	AF
NX31812	LYNNE	HJ		NX35688	McGEADY Bbrother of AF)	LG
NX51782	LYONS	E		NX36042	McGLYNN (Brother of JP & WA)	WA
NX27855	LYONS	WJ		NX67699	McGOUGH	JK
NX31470	LYTTLE	C		NX33362	McGOWAN	H
QX23176	MACARTNEY	HK		NX35407	McGRATH (Brother of EW &TD)	AJ
NX73553	MACDONALD	NA		NX35742	McGRATH Bbrother of AJ & TD)	EW
NX81937	MACDOUGAL	MH		NX35758	McGRATH (Brother of AJ & EW)	TD
NX35352	MACKENZIE	H		NX58332	McGUFFIN	GS

NX56321	McKAY	DG	NX56666	MURRAY	LR
NX73659	McKEAN	R	NX25905	MURRAY	TE
NX35956	McKENNA	JStL	NX33988	MURRAY	VG
NX43501	McKENZIE	LK	NX59902	MYORS	RC
NX52382	McLAREN	CJ	NX53836	NEIL	JF
NX55100	McLEAN	HJ	NX49276	NEWMAN	N
NX55451	McLEOD	DL	NX34734	NEWTON	RWJ
QX22041	McLEOD	K	NX20436	NIBBS	JJ
QX18453	McLUCAS	MW	NX55551	NICHOLAOU/ NICHOLSON)	C
NX69953	McPHEE	J	NX35654	NICHOLS	A
NX55096	McRITCHIE	WR	NX48553	NICHOLS	J
NX56207	MEALE	FC	NX53710	NIXON	MG
NX35924	MENZ	J	NX33092	NOLAN	A
NX35217	MENZ	MT	NX67515	NORBERRY	JL
NX55943	MERCER	JT	NX49681	NORMAN	WD
NX58437	MERCHANT	J	NX43211	NORTHEY (WG)	WJ
NX51061	METHVEN	WA	NX55450	NUNAN	LV
NX55227	MIDDLETON	VCC	NX12525	OAKES	RF
NX48557	MILGATE	CW	NX56952	O'BREE	RR
NX35634	MILLARD	T	NX35898	O'BRIEN	PJ
QX23082	MILLER	CF	NX53405	O'BRIEN	T
NX35310	MILLER	JW	NX48624	O'CARROLL	S
NX57909	MINTO	WG	NX52231	O'CONNELL	DE
NX52528	MITCHELL	EC	NX35396	O'CONNOR (Brother of JF)	D
NX16787	MONK	RE	NX36010	O'CONNOR (Brother of D)	JF
NX52380	MONTGOMERY	TW	NX58091	O'CONNOR	JWG
NX42491	MOODY	MR	NX32689	O'CONNOR	L
NX35799	MOONA	PGJ	WX13420	ODERS	RA
NX72990	MOONEY	H	NX5657	O'KEEFE	S
NX77892	MOORE	R	NX48926	OLSEN	E
NX15582	MOORE	WE	NX51958	OLTMANNS	GF
NX26915	MORRIS	D	NX58635	ORR	GL
NX43483	MORRIS	RJ	NX35908	O'SHEA	P
NX30376	MORTON	H	NX49660	O'TOOLE	G
NX55623	MOSHER	RJ	NX37013	OWEN	B
NX35500	MOTT	EM	NX35300	OWEN	JH
NX50462	MOULT-SPIERS	R	NX43414	OXLEY	RF
NX50089	MOWBRAY	R	NX35784	PAGE	AC
NX49452	MUIR	RB	NX51012	PAPAGELOPOULOS aka ANGEL	L
NX35370	MULCAHY	DH	NX32598	PARKER	JG
QX24005	MULCAHY	JJ	NX48100	PARSONS	LJ
NX25901	MULCAHY	TJ	NX14554	PARSONS	WJ
NX31404	MULCAHY	WT	NX72239	PATIENCE	LA
NX55036	MULDOON	B	NX5700	PAWLEY	HH
NX38150	MULHEARN	T	NX56196	PAYNE	WG
NX35319	MULHOLLAND	RM	QX24259	PEARCE	GH
NX55011	MULVENA	GE	NX52459	PEARSON	AT
NX23085	MURPHY	JT	NX27767	PEEK	AJ
NX31888	MURRAY	J	NX35610	PEGG	JF
NX35861	MURRAY	JC	NX35870	PEISLEY	A

NX35795	PERCEVAL (Brother of DR & RL)	LG		NX5766	RICHARDSON	JL
NX30731	PERCEVAL (Brother of DR & LG)	RL		QX23179	RICHMOND	C
NX52352	PERFECT	JR		NX58133	RIDDELL	JR
NX53830	PETERSON	RJ		NX29315	RIDLEY	JW
QX22242	PETTERSSON	JB		NX48955	RILEY	E
NX35768	PETTET	KB		NX48081	RILEY	PT
NX35749	PETTIGREW	RB		NX35949	ROBBINS	AG
NX32638	PETTIT	JF		NX78365	ROBERTS	GG
NX56953	PHILIP	JG		NX55949	ROBERTS	L
NX52465	PHILLIPS	BT		NX42702	ROBERTSON	DH
QX15876	PHILLIPS	JC		NX4777	ROBERTSON	JN
NX34741	PICKUP	AC		NX55210	ROBERTSON	RM
NX48922	PIERCY	WJ		NX26932	ROBERTSON	W
NX57265	PIGGOTT	RP		NX27267	ROBINSON	EJ
NX55559	PINKARD	FC		NX44711	ROBINSON	GH
NX71440	PIRIE	RA		NX48456	ROBINSON	L
NX60199	PLUMMER	WL		NX49391	ROBINSON	RAH
NX39749	POLSTON	NA		NX48218	ROGERS	BC
NX43402	PORTER	JA		NX56228	ROGERS (Son of CL)	EC
QX15817	PORTER	TJ		NX49492	ROMA	LR
NX52525	POTTER	BG		NX49838	ROOKE	WE
NX35895	POTTER	LE		QX22593	ROONEY	A
NX56203	POWER	AL		NX54927	ROSE	JD
NX60388	POWER	FP		NX45126	ROSE	KR
NX48780	PRICE	P		NX59120	ROSEBERY	NJ
NX4672	PRICE	R		NX35553	ROSETTA (Brother of GA)	CB
NX49550	PRIDDIS	HJ		NX35619	ROSETTA (Brother of CB)	GA
NX37008	PRIMMER	A		QX23101	ROSS	RM
NX71917	PRYOR	RF		NX26761	ROSS	W
NX40503	PURCELL	GM		NX26757	ROW	RG
NX67851	PYKE	WE		NX36954	ROWE	JEG
NX44190	RANDALL	GG		NX10629	ROWETT	VR
NX35767	RATHMELL	K		NX35479	ROWLANDS	R
NX35651	REA	EOB		NX69721	RUDD	RA
NX52466	READ	HLC		NX60195	RUMPH	AE
NX49854	REAY	DW		NX68840	RUSSELL	CE
NX53832	REBERGER	N		QX18454	RUSSELL	CE
NX23961	REDFERN	RL		NX60130	RYAN	OJ
NX35787	REDGATE	DT		NX35934	RYAN	W
NX43452	REED	JMJ		NX60197	RYE	WE
NX78663	REED	R		NX35353	SAMS	HWL
NX5730	REES	WP		NX37617	SANDERS	EJ
NX32369	REID	AWJ		NX77960	SANDERSON	JP
NX56108	REID	CT		NX52532	SANDERSON	RE
NX6561	REID	M		QX24398	SANDERSON	WG
NX35851	REID	RA		QX21838	SANDFORD	NJ
NX49705	REILLY	J		NX49082	SAUNDERSON	WJ
NX35729	RENNIE	JD		NX54772	SAWERS	CRJ
NX48247	REYNOLDS	JJ		NX39734	SAWYER	FK
NX12527	REYNOLDS	PR		NX53045	SCHLYDER	R

NX73288	SCHNABEL	WG		NX35511	STEAR	NJ
NX56112	SCOBIE	WF		NX51914	STEEL	AE
NX29415	SCOTT	J		NX35592	STEPHEN	CH
NX29377	SCOTT	NO		NX55933	STEPHENS	FJ
NX29830	SCRIVEN	GW		NX20501	STEVENS	WJ
NX55153	SEDWELL	RW		QX22225	STEVENSON	MM
NX8372	SEYMOUR	AH		NX60241	STEWARD	GJ
NX40803	SEYMOUR	DA		NX55940	STEWART	JT
QX22576	'SHAHNOVSKY aka Dempsey, V'	V		NX50551	STEWART	RD
NX32559	SHANKLEY	RJ		NX52187	STONE	FF
NX55610	SHEARER	H		NX37479	STONE	KL
NX44567	SHEARIM	KS		NX78390	STOREY	ER
NX56104	SHEATHER	LR		NX49686	STREETER	JH
NX53930	SHELLEY	W		NX39770	STRINGER	HB
NX42015	SHELTON	MJ		NX52462	STRINGER	WW
NX44829	SHEPHERD	HG		NX49117	SULLIVAN	ES
NX44382	SHEPHERD	WG		NX26576	SURMAN	AG
NX24906	SHIELS	TW		NX20058	SWAIN	RS
NX39738	SHORNEY	W		NX41700	SWEENEY	EM
NX66013	SIMISTER	H		NX73321	SWEET	KO
NX48416	SIMMONDS	CH		NX49417	SYLVESTER	RJ
NX40429	SIMMONDS	TG		NX35509	TANNER	JH
NX35577	SINCLAIR	RS		NX10970	TAPRELL	RMJ
NX48834	SLATER	WG		NX41793	TARGETT	JL
NX35847	SMALL	AA		NX48265	TATE	CJ
NX54281	SMART	SHT		NX6571	TAYLOR	AH
NX40145	SMELLIE	JAM		NX27886	TAYLOR	GE
NX22743	SMITH	CR		QX21633	TAYLOR	LH
NX51721	SMITH	HE		NX73315	TAYLOR	RJ
NX54631	SMITH	HLP		NX43451	TEGGE	JL
NX51990	SMITH	JA		NX36181	TERRY	CG
NX43744	SMITH	JB		NX31781	THALLON	E
NX32726	SMITH	JO		NX1788	THATCHER	FW
NX6584	SMITH	MAG		NX48761	THIELE/Baker WF	EJ
NX35359	SMITH	P		NX52491	THOMAS	AO
NX35838	SMITH	TP		NX56131	THOMAS	FJ
QX22895	SMITH	W		NX8384	THOMAS	H
NX35599	SMITH	WH		NX35966	THOMAS	LD
VX24002	SMITHWICK	CL		NX5709	THOMAS	MH
NX56109	SNAPE	ML		NX70189	THOMAS	RE
QX21897	SOMERFIELD	HG		NX45058	THOMPSON	DJ
NX35345	SOMERVILLE	JH		NX56124	"THOMPSON aka Rasmussen, Dennis John 'Jack'"	JA
NX52549	SPARKE	KP		NX52561	THOMPSON	SW
NX44670	SPARKES	HL		NX32987	THOMPSON	W
NX29976	SPARKES	WF		NX26982	THOMPSON	WM
NX35887	SPRING	WW		NX54020	THOMSON	AGH
NX48939	ST LEON	S		NX52905	THOMSON	J
NX60214	STAFFORD	KLR		NX44865	THOROUGHGOOD/Greenslade	J
NX49737	STANTON	RD		NX60363	THROWER	MJL
NX45121	STANWELL	EG				

NOMINAL ROLLS

NX40751	THUELL	HC		NX35369	WALZ	RBF
NX42346	THWAITE	J		NX48400	WARD	HS
NX35744	TINDALL	HJ		NX35907	WARD	L
NX35400	TINDLE	RN		NX57871	WARD	SJ
NX60244	TOBIN	VJ		NX48900	WARD	WW
NX35418	TODD	K		NX4742	WARDEN	CA
NX52478	TOLEMAN	SJ		NX44404	WARDROP	RB
QX23203	TOMLINSON (brother of MP)	AE		NX56125	WARE	HH
NX7097	TOMS	M		VX34852	WARREN	E
NX35198	TONACIA	HJ		NX35487	WATERS	RJ
NX56158	TOOHEY	WB		NX7327	WATKINS	F
NX40272	TOPPS	GW		NX42085	WATKINS	RV
NX58729	TOWNSEND	RH		NX36534	WATSON	AW
NX26605	TRAVIS	B		NX4439	WATTERS	DW
QX23180	TRESEDER	AG		NX4438	WATTERS	MJ
NX35903	TREVASKIS	M		NX35513	WATTS	WG
NX35692	TRINDER	LC		NX52531	WEAVER	AB
NX55423	TUCKER	F		NX52199	WEBSTER	FP
NX49803	TUCKER	HTL		NX35747	WEEDEN	SA
NX35446	TUCKER	J		NX50822	WEGEMUND	G
NX43516	TUCKER-EVANS	NR		NX58094	WEILY	JG
QX13798	TULLY	JJ		NX55612	WELLINGTON	PR
NX35542	TUNNEY	KJ		NX48883	WELSH	FP
NX35194	TURNER	AA		NX34341	WELSH	JR
NX35475	TURNER	AR		NX6173	WERNER	WA
NX37050	TURNER	EG		NX48102	WEST	WH
NX52302	TURNER	JW		NX34771	WESTBROOK	KL
NX35701	TURNER	J		NX56659	WHETTON	SE
NX35347	TURNER	TWB		NX60366	WHIPP	AH
NX53759	TURRALL	KC		NX22888	WHIPP	GA
NX35162	TWAITS	CW		NX44989	WHITE	A
NX26993	TYDEMAN	R		NX34357	WHITE	L
NX32790	URQUHART	D		NX35567	WHITE	R
NX1000	URQUHART	WRB		NX32937	WHITE	T
NX49865	VARLEY	FHG		NX52490	WHITE	RJ
NX60090	VARLEY	JA		QX22687	WHITEHEAD	WA
NX1701	VARLEY	TH		NX35421	WHITING	EW
NX58017	VELLA	J		NX35423	WHITLEY	EA
NX28253	VINCENT	KS		QX22485	WHITMORE	T
NX35502	VINDEN	NS		NX52486	WHITTWER (WITTWER)	H
NX29412	WAKELY	FD		NX57298	WICKENS	RA
NX57191	WALDEN	TJJ		NX33301	WILDING	VB
NX27729	WALKER	CW		NX72756	WILKES	HR
NX12593	WALKER	GH		NX73629	WILKIE	JW
NX40434	WALLACE	DR		NX35474	WILKINSON	CH
NX34206	WALLACE	EC		NX39745	WILKINSON	R
NX56204	WALLACE	NA		NX50088	WILKINSON	RJ
NX54396	WALLER	J		NX73688	WILLARD	RJ
NX53540	WALSH	NK		NX22876	WILLIAMS	A
NX52003	WALSH	PF		NX49142	WILLIAMS	FA

377

NX55024	WILLIAMS	HC		NX57257	WILSON	JB
NX35890	WILLIAMS	JH		NX49120	WILSON	T
NX48539	WILLIAMS	JS		NX56218	WINBANK (Brother of VG)	JA
NX35566	WILLIAMS	KJ		NX52481	WINBANK (Brother of JA)	VG
NX5692	WILLIAMS	T		NX35754	WOOD	FM
NX57223	WILLIAMS	WG		NX35918	WOODLANDS	RJ
NX52497	WILLIAMS	WG		NX49832	WOODWARD	J
NX72988	WILLIAMS	WG		NX35753	WRIGHT	GHH
NX1793	WILLIAMSON	RH		NX52553	WRIGHT (Brother of WA)	JP
NX35919	WILLIAMSON	RJ		NX56193	WRIGHT (Brother of JP)	WA
NX56687	WILSON	EF		NX39835	YATES	TB
NX35671	WILSON	FJ		NX45391	YEATMAN	EA

2/19 Members of Ramsay Force who died and survived.

35 died before war's end

NX73334	ADAMS	AH		NX35508	OVERS	CH
NX49143	ANDREW	A		NX30573	PITT	WJ
NX29291	BEATHE	HS		NX51511	REDFERN	E
NX34111	BOSTOCK	WR		NX59145	REDGRAVE	EJW
NX35853	COTTAM	AE		NX8319	REED	HE
NX10913	DEACON	TP		NX54950	RICKETTS	WG
NX33667	FITZGERALD	D		NX51339	RIVETT	GF
NX2864	HARPER	WHH		NX51667	ROMEY	N
NX60379	HEWSON	H		NX73960	RYAN	RL
NX35623	JENKINS	R		NX27475	SINCLAIR	I
NX73666	KIRKPATRICK	E		NX39776	SINCLAIR	WC
QX9754	KNIGHT	JE		NX52476	SMITH	PJ
NX67286	KYLE	VL		NX55682	STEDMAN	JN
NX36039	LEDWIDGE	SJ		NX52482	TAYLOR	CR
QX22574	LUXTON	JM		NX32742	TOME	MJM
QX22570	LUXTON	BC		NX35205	TRAVERS	K
NX56101	MILLARD	WG		NX35262	VERDON	PJ
				NX56139	WARK	TJ

70 survived

NX31871	FARMER	JB		NX49074	HARVEY	CF
NX35527	FENNELL	JM		NX36053	HEWITT	GR
NX49312	FISHBURN	JH		NX54087	HOLMAN	JN
NX19508	FITZSIMMONS	HHE		QX21759	HOLT	JF
NX35206	FLORANCE	IH		NX35245	HOPKINS	AJ
NX36504	FLOYD	AG		NX35481	HOWE	F
NX52562	FORBES	JWK		NX38802	HUSH	AE
NX32845	FORD	FO		NX45090	JOLLY	A
NX36134	GLENN	DM		NX44871	KAY	AW
NX65750	GREEN	R		NX65740	Le DUC	AE
QX22338	GRIFFIN	KM		NX35394	LEDWIDGE	SJ
NX51735	GUERIN	C		NX35433	LEE	TJ
NX53763	HARDING	FR		NX36043	LEWIS	L

NX48938	LOW	R		NX48218	ROGERS	BC
NX10767	MANWARING	A		NX56228	ROGERS	EC
NX73659	McKEAN	R		NX26761	ROSS	W
NX55227	MIDDLETON	VCC		NX29415	SCOTT	J
NX35310	MILLER	JW		NX32726	SMITH	JO
NX42491	MOODY	MR		NX35359	SMITH	P
QX24005	MULCAHY	JJ		QX21897	SOMERFIELD	HG
NX59902	MYORS	RC		NX51914	STEEL	AE
NX35908	O'SHEA	P		NX52491	THOMAS	AO
WX13420	ODERS	RA		NX52561	THOMPSON	SW
NX35300	OWEN	JH		NX35744	TINDALL	HJ
NX56196	PAYNE	WG		NX56158	TOOHEY	WB
NX52465	PHILLIPS	BT		NX35903	TREVASKIS	M
NX43402	PORTER	JA		NX43516	TUCKER-EVANS	NR
NX49550	PRIDDIS	HJ		NX35194	TURNER	AA
NX49854	REAY	DW		NX40434	WALLACE	DR
NX23961	REDFERN	RL		NX48900	WARD	WW
NX35787	REDGATE	DT		NX72756	WILKES	HR
NX32369	REID	AWJ		NX72988	WILLIAMS	WG
NX43664	REILLY	EM		NX35754	WOOD	FM
NX48081	RILEY	PT		NX52553	WRIGHT	JP
NX55210	ROBERTSON	RM		NX58620	STOWE	WF

Members of the AIF in Fred Howe's tunnel party

WX12039	ADDISON	AR		VX36825	PORTER	A
NX33737	BARRY	JH		SX5198	RAINES	CR
?	BENNET	?		TX4877	RENNIE	IW
QX9944	BONNER	JJ		VX37916	REPACHOLI	NL
?	BURNETT	?		WX8952	RIEBE	RR
NX54347	CURYER	AW		NX66377	ROBERTS	J
NX51308	DUPREZ	HA		NX71946	ROBERTS	WO
VX19728	DURKIN	J		NX56228	ROGERS	EC
NX59088	EATHER	A		QX20846	SCHIPP	H
NX69934	GRUNDIE	A		?	SMITH	?
NX51735	GUERIN	C		SX6149	STANDFIELD	H
NX67852	HOGAN	HJ		QX9309	STEPHENSON	AN
QX15778	HOSIER	L		QX20815	STREET (AD)	H?
NX35481	HOWE	F		VX57495	TREWIN	GA
VX58629	KELLY	GA		NX68216	TURNER	GE
VX37274	McEWAN-COBDEN	WO		WX8585	VIDLER	CJ
?	MILLER	?		SX11466	WILLIAMS	PO
QX22007	MOSS	KW		WX8014	WILSON	RC
VX64060?	PATERSON	GC?		NX56971	YEO	WH
NX56887	PEARCE	NR				

Select Bibliography

The narratives of Fred Howe and Dianne Elliott have been adapted from their personal memoirs and private papers.

The background material, provided by the author, has been compiled from the following:

Printed Books

2/19 Battalion AIF Association, *The Grim Glory of the 2/19 Battalion AIF*, Sydney, 1975

2/29 AIF Battalion Association, (Christie R, ed), *A History of the 2/19 Battalion-8th Australian Division, AIF*, Sale (Victoria), 1983

Allen, Louis, *The Politics and Strategy of the Second World War, Singapore 1941–1942*, London, 1977

Barber, Noel, *Sinister Twilight*, Glasgow, 1968

Barker, A J, *Japanese Army Handbook 1939–1945*, New York, 1979

Bennett, Lieut-Gen H Gordon, *Why Singapore Fell*, Sydney, 1944

Blair, Joan and Clay, *Return from the River Kwai*, London, 1979

Braddon, Russell, *The Naked Island*, London, 1952

Chapman, F Spencer, *The Jungle is Neutral*, London, 1949

Chapman, Ivan, Tokyo *Calling The Charles Cousin Case*, Sydney, 1990

Churchill, Winston S, *The Second World War*, Vol 4, *The Hinge of Fate*; Vol 7, *The Onslaught of Japan*, London, 1951

Clarke, Hugh V, *A life for Every Sleeper*, North Sydney, 1986

Coates, Albert & Rosenthal, Newman, *The Albert Coates Story*, South Yarra (Melbourne), 1977

Coast, John, *Railroad of Death*, London, 1947

Daws, Gavin, *Prisoners of the Japanese*, New York, 1994

Day, David, *The Great Betrayal*, North Ryde (Sydney), 1988

Dunlop, E E, *The War Diaries of Weary Dunlop*, Ringwood (Melbourne), 1989

Falk, Stanley, *Seventy Days to Singapore*, London, 1979

Finkemeyer, Gunner, *It happened to Us, The Unique Experience of 20 members of the 4th Anti-Tank Regiment*, Melbourne, 1994

Frisch, Colin, *Heroes Denied The Malayan Harrier Conspiracy*, Wheelers Hill (Victoria),1990

Gherardin, Walter, *Against the Odds Albert Coates A Heroic Life*, Bakers Hill (Victoria), 2009

Hall, Leslie, *The Blue Haze*, Sydney, 1996

Hall, T, *The Fall of Singapore*, Sydney, 1965

Hamilton, Thomas, *Soldier Surgeon in Malaya*, Sydney 1957

Harrison, Kenneth, *The Brave Japanese*, Adelaide, 1966

Hastain, Ronald, *White Coolie*, London, 1947

Irwin, Mick, *Kicking with the Wind. The Wartime Experiences of Neil Collinson 4th Anti-tank Regiment*, Mildura (Victoria), 1984

Kirby, Major General S Woodburn, *Singapore: The Chain of Disaster*, New York, 1971

Kreefft, Otto, *Burma Railway A Visual Recollection*, Netherlands, 2004

Leason, James, *Singapore*, London, 1968

Lewis, Charles, *The Exceptional Melbourne Cup*, 2019 (privately published)

Legg, Frank, *The Gordon Bennett Story*, Sydney 1965

Lewis, T P M, *Changi the lost years, A Malayan Diary 1941–1946*, Kuala Lumpur, 1984

Lodge, AB, *The Rise and Fall of General Gordon Bennett*, North Sydney, 1986

Mackenzie, Compton, *Eastern Epic*, Vol I, London, 1951

Mant, Gilbert, *You'll be Sorry*, Sydney, 1944

McGregor, John, *Blood on the Rising Sun*, Perth (n.d)

Mills, Roy, *Doctor's Diary and Memoirs. Pond's Party F Force Thai-Burma Railway*, New Lambton (NSW), 1994

Nagase Yakashi & Watase Masaru (translators), *Crosses and Tigers*, Thailand, 1990

Nelson, David, *The Story of Changi Singapore*, West Perth, 1974

Nelson, Hank, *Prisoners of War, Australians Under Nippon*, Sydney, 1985

SELECT BIBLIOGRAPHY

Owen, Frank, *The Fall of Singapore*, London, 1960

Penfold, AW, Bayliss, WC, Crispin, KE, *Galleghan's Greyhounds, The story of the 2/30th Australian Infantry Battalion*, Sydney, 1979

Percival, Lieut-Gen A E, *The War In Malaya*, London 1949

Poole, Philippa, *Of Love and War, The letters and diaries of Captain Adrian Curlewis and his family, 1939–1945*, Sydney, 1982

Probert, Squadron Leader H A (compiler), *History of Changi*, Singapore, 1965

Queensland Ex-POW Association Reparation Committee, *Nippon Very Sorry – Many Men Must Die*, Bowen Hills (Brisbane), 1990

Rivett, Rohan D, *Behind Bamboo. An inside story of the Japanese Prison Camps*, Sydney, 1947

Russell, Lord, of Liverpool, *The Knights of Bushido*, London, 1958

Savage, Russell, *A Guest of the Emperor*, Moorooka (Queensland), 1995

Seki, Eiiji, *Mrs Ferguson's Tea Set, Japan and the Second World War; The global Consequences Following Germany's Sinking of the USS Automedon in 1940*, Folkestone (UK), 2007

Silver, Lynette Ramsay, *The Bridge at Parit Sulong, An Investigation of Mass Murder Malaya 1942*, Sydney, 2004

Silver, Lynette Ramsay, *The Heroes of Rimau*, Sydney, 1990

Simmons, Gary, *Tough & True A Story of the 2/29th through the eyes of a son*, East Doncaster (Victoria), 2008

Simson, Ivan, Singapore *Too Little Too Late*, London, 1971

Smith, Adele Shelton (ed), *The Boys Write Home*, Sydney, 1944

Smith, Neil C, *Tid Apa. The History of the 4th Anti-Tank Regiment*, Gardenvale (Victoria), 1992

Smyth, Sir John, VC, *Percival and the Tragedy of Singapore*, London, 1971

Summers, Julie, *The Colonel of Tamarkan. Philip Toosey and the Bridge on the River Kwai*, London, 2005

Swinson, Arthur, *Defeat in Malaya: the fall of Singapore*, London, 1979

Tsuji, Masanobu, *Singapore The Japanese Version*, Sydney, 1960

Uhr, Jaanet, *Against the Sun, The AIF in Malaya 1941–42*, St Leonards (Sydney), 1998

Walker, Allan S, *Clinical Problems of War. Australia in the War of 1939–1945*, Medical (Official History), Canberra, 1952

Walker, Allan S, *Middle East and Far East, Australia in the War of 1939–1945*, Medical (Official History), Canberra, 1953

Wall, Don, *Heroes at Sea*, Dee Why (Sydney), 1991

Warren, Alan, *Singapore Britain's Greatest Defeat*, South Yarra (Melbourne), 2002

Whitecross, Roy, *Slaves of the Son of Heaven*, Sydney, 1951

Whitelock, Cliff, *Gunners in the Jungle. A Story of the 2/15th Field Regiment*, Royal Australian Artillery, 8 Division Australian Imperial Force, Eastwood (Sydney), 1983

Wigmore, Lionel, *The Japanese Thrust, Australia in the War of 1939–1942*, Series One, Army, Volume IV, Canberra, 1958

Newspaper archives, journals, newsletters

Australian Women's Weekly: Barbed Wire and Bamboo, Journal of the ex-POW Association; *Boorowa News*; *Canberra Times*; *Catholic Weekly*, Sydney; *Daily Mirror*, Sydney; *Daily Telegraph*, Sydney; *Herald*, Melbourne; *Malay Mail*; *Malaya Tribune*; *Men of the AIF and AMF in Action*, Official War Photographs of the Department of Information; *Mercury* (Hobart); *Mufti*, The Journal of the Victorian RSL; Newsletters of the 1st Nineteenth and the 2nd Nineteenth Battalion Association; *Papua New Guinea Post-Courier*; *Photo Weekly* (Japanese publication); *Straits Times*, Singapore; *Sun*, Sydney; *Sunday Mail*, Adelaide; *Sydney Morning Herald*; *The Age*, Melbourne; *The Nineteenth*, Journal of 2/19 Battalion; *The Sporting Globe*; *Through*, 8 Division Signals; *Townsville Daily Bulletin*; *Vic Eddy*, The Official Journal of the 8th Division Signals Association

Official Despatches

Air Chief Marshal Sir Robert Brooke-Popham, Despatches to the British Chiefs of Staff, published in The London Gazette, 22 January 1948

Air Vice-Marshal Sir Paul Maltby, Despatches to the Secretary of State for Air, published in The London Gazette, 26 February 1948

Lieut-General A E Percival, Despatches to the Secretary of State for War, published in The London Gazette, Second supplement, 26 February 1948.

Documents in the Public Record

Australian War Memorial, Canberra:
AIF Casualties, AWM 171/11/2
Anderson, Charles, statements by, AWM 67 3/9 Part 1
Anderson, W, (2/29 Battalion), PR 88/51
Australian 8 Division, Casualties, Malaya, AWM 171/11/1
Burt, Stuart (IO 2/19 Battalion), Notes by, AWM 67 3/9 Part 2
Coates, AWM 54 481/8/13 Pt 1-6
Ellerman, Austin Yeats, Memoir, Malaya 1942, PR2080
Fisher, WE, AWM54 552/2/7
Hackney, Lieutenant Ben, Dark Evening, MSS0758
Hatton Alex, (real name A.H. Drummond) The Naked Truth, MSS 1530
Johnson, Pte J L, NX 55765, 2/19 Bt. Div. AIF, Just Me: The diary of, MSS2179
Kappe, G, Report by, AWM54 553/5/25
Maps, Military, of Muar, Batu Pahat, M'Okil, Parit Jawa
Montfort, A, (4 Anti-tank), PR 88/214
Oakes, Lieutenant-Colonel RF, AWM 73/65
Oakes, Roland Frank, typescript account of fighting in Malaya, Singapore and treatment as a POW, MSS0776
Operations of 8 Aust Div in Malaya, 1941–1942, AWM54 553/5/23
Spurgeon, Spud, PR 9/124
Unit Roll Books, 8 Division, AWM 127
War Crimes Trials, Sworn Affidavits : AWM54 1010/4/ 1, 10, 46, 63, 74, 84, 110, 120, 121, 122, 140, 141, 143, 148,157
War Diary, A Coy, 2/19 Battalion, AWM67 3/9 Part 2
War Diary, AIF HQ Malaya, AWM52 1/5/19
War Diary, HQ 22 Brigade, AWM52 8/2/22
War Diary, HQ 27 Brigade, AWM52 8/2/27
War Diary, 2/18 Battalion, AWM52 8/3/18
War Diary, 2/19 Battalion AWM52 8/3/19
War Diary, 2/29 Battalion, AWM52 8/3/29
War Diary, 2/30 Battalion, AWM52 8/3/30
War Diary, 2/15 Field Regiment, AWM52 4/2/15
War Diary, 34 Australian War Graves Unit, AWM52 21/2/26/1
War Diary, The Rose Force, AWM52 1/5/67

National Archives of Australia, ACT:
Boon Pong, Suggested reward for PW in Burma, MP742/1 66/1/1086
Graves Registration Sheets, A8231
Nishimura, ex-Lt-Gen, M1505/1 916 (Papers of Solicitor General)
Nishimura Takuma, Confirmation of Death Sentence, A4940 C431
Service Records, AIF, B883 (located by name)
Trial of Ishida Yoshio and Kitabata Shinichi, A471 81662
Trial of Itsui Hiroshi, A471 81847 Part A
Trial of Itsui Hiroshi and Tokoro Kenichi A471 81954
Trial of Hosumi Susumi, Okara Kisaburo, Otsuki Masao, A471/81246
Trial of Kimara Takeo, A471/81243
Trial of Nagatomo Yoshitada, A471 81655, parts 4,5,6,7,8
Trial of Nakanishi Jirohei, A471/81202
Trial of Nishimura Takuma and Nonaka Shoichi, A471/1 81942
War Crimes, Japanese, D 844 167/1/12 Part 1
War Crimes Questionnaire, Bashford, MP742/1 336/1/2018

National Archives of Australia, NSW
Braddon, Russell, affidavit, statement by SP459/1/0; SP573/1/457
Hackney, Lieutenant B, SP459/1 573/1/524
War Crimes, Massacre at Parit Sulong (Malaya), Lt. B C Hackney, SP459/1 573/1/234

National Archives of Australia, Victoria
Nishimura, Lt-Gen Takuma executed at Manus, MP 742 375/15 Item 88
Nishimura, Trial of Lt-Gen Takuma and others, MP742 336/1/2137
War crimes, Parit Sulong (Bakri) Massacre, MP742 3361/1962

National Archives, UK;
Trial of Usuki Kishio and nine others, WO235/918

SCMA (Army Records)
Routine Orders 2/19 Battalion, AIF

State Library of NSW
Tokyo War Crimes Trials (edited transcripts)

Internet Websites

Australian War Memorial, various digitised documents; Commonwealth War Graves Commission (CWGC) Honour Roll; Department of Veterans' Affairs (DVA) WW2 Nominal Roll; National Archives of Australia, various digitised documents

NOTE: For war crimes trials not under Australian jurisdiction see: https://www.singaporewarcrimestrials.com/case-summaries#all-cases

Private papers, reports, memoirs, letters etc in private collections

Anderson, Lieutenant-Colonel Charles, Private Papers
Brien, Private C E, diary, 2/19 Battalion
Brown, Ray, 2/30th Battalion. memoir
Bryant-Smith, Stan, various papers relating to 2/29 Battalion and Ogaki Unit (Japanese) at Muar
Curnow, MW, memoir
Dean, Roland M, memoir
Elliott, Dianne, personal memoirs and notes; report on death of George Gill from Dr Lloyd Cahill; 2/19 Nominal Roll, compiled from Routine Orders
Hackney, Ben (Iris Sheridan)
Howe, Frederick, diary and memoirs
Gerhadin, Dr Tony, article on Dr A E Coates
Kappe, Lt-Colonel Gus, Lecture at Changi, entitled The Malayan Campaign
Mettam, Bert, dairy
Morris, Tom, memoir
Mullins, Private Mervyn, reminiscences
Roxburgh, J D, 2/29 Battalion, diary
Silver, Lynette, report on Massacre Site at Parit Sulong
Warden, C A, 2/29 Battalion, memoir
White, Strachan McLaren, memoir

Personal Interviews by author with the following veterans:

Brand, Victor; Brown, Ray; Bryant-Smith, Stan; Cahill, Lloyd; Cornford, Roy; Edwards, Charles; Gardner, 'Titch'; Hunt, Bruce; Johnson, Lloyd; Kerr, James; Mettam, Bert; Sachs, Peter; Steele, Ray; Trevor, Terry; Varley, John; Whitecross, Roy; Young, William Keith

Audio

ABC Sound Archives, Interviews by Tim Bowden with ex-POWs

Documentaries

Horrors in the East, BBC; *Murder Under the Sun. Japanese War Crimes and Trials; The Fall of Singapore*, ABC; ABC 4 Corners, March 2002, and unedited footage (courtesy Ray Steele)

Photographic material

AWM Collection under headings of Bakri, Burma, Burma-Thai Railway, Changi, Muar, Parit Sulong, Singapore, Thailand; Department of Information, photographs taken in Bakri, Malaya, Singapore (Ramsay Collection); Edwards, Charles; Elliott Private Collection; Sheridan, Iris; Silver Private Collection

Index

Bold page numbers indicate supporting images.

Air raids, 33, 44, 49, 173, 263, 275, 294, 295–296, 303, 306
Alexandra Hospital, 191, 202, 202
Allied forces
  air raids, 263, 291, 293, 295–296, 302, 307, 316
  defence of Singapore, 190, 205–206
  at Parit Sulong, 130–131
  positions, 83 map
  surrender, 207
  and tanks, 43, 47, 72
  Thanbyuzayat, 246–247
  withdrawal from Malaya, 78, 92, 118–119, 131–135, 170, **171**
  see also Australian forces; British forces; Chinese forces; Indian forces
Anderson, Colonel Charles, **84**
  attending executions, 243
  communications, 82, 96, 98, 102, 108
  and Fred Howe, xiii, 37
  health, 180, 191
  memorial, **168**
  military tactics, 78, 94, 97, 99, 103–105
  post World War II, 349
  and Sergeant Ronald O'Donnell, 259–260
  support of troops, 116, 193
  Victoria Cross, 138, 192–193
  withdrawal from Malaya, 91–92, 118, 119, 120–121
Anderson Force, 116, 138, 139–140, 154, 233, 235, 242–243, 245–247
Anshinn (Gunso), Sergeant, 246–247, 249
Aspinall, George, 28, 229, 327

Atkinson, Private Norman, 354–355, 358
Atlantis, German raider, 31–32
Austin, Lieutenant Bunny, 107, 112
Australian Comforts Fund, 17, 19
Australian forces
  8th Division, xvi, 5–6, **6**, **27**
  anti-tankers, 32, 43, 58, 60, 69, 70, 72–74, 75, 85, 116, 130, 169, **184**, 214
  discipline, 217–218
  fall of Singapore, 211–212, 224
  General Base Depots, 45, 169, 183, 184, 192
  mascots, **8**, 20, 35, 77, 93–94
  military tactics, 42, 78
  Operation Rimau, 201
  positions, 71 map
  RAAF, 91, 113–114
  signallers, 42, 51, 57, 67, 77, 82, 84–86, 90, 96–97, 99, 105, 108, 114, 121, 126, 177, 180, 185–186, 188, 200, 202
  supplies, 51, 82, 92–93, 107–108, 114–115
  training, 6, 7, **30**, 31, 38, 39–40, 47, 217
  Unrecovered War Casualties Unit, 158
  withdrawal from Malaya, 116, 119
  see also Allied forces
Australian forces, 2/10th Australian General Hospital, 27, 33, 63
Australian forces, 2/15th Field Regiment, 57, 65, 175
Australian forces, 2/18th Battalion, 40, 174, 180–181, 183
Australian forces, 2/19th Battalion, 17, **26**, **30**, **183**
  98-mile peg, 96–97

  in the Bakri area, 76–79
  defence of Malaya, 52, 69
  defence of Singapore, 180–184
  friendly fire, 116
  Jemaluang-Mersing area, 40, 55
  at Kluang, 40
  Parit Sulong bridge, 105
  reinforcements, 169
  signallers, 11, 26, **27**, 42, 51, 57, 77, 82, 84–86, 96–97, 99, 105, 108, 121, 126, 180, 188
  at Tengah, **183**
  withdrawal from Malaya, 93
Australian forces, 2/20th Battalion, 40, 174, 181, 183
Australian forces, 2/29th Battalion
  98-mile peg, 96–97
  in the Bakri area, 75–79, 81
  defence of Muar, 69
  defence of Singapore, 174
  friendly fire, 72, 74
  Indian Brigade HQ, 70
  Parit Sulong bridge, 105
  signallers, 82
  withdrawal from Malaya, 85, 89 map, 90, 135
  Yong Peng, 135
Australian forces, 2/30th Battalion, 58, 128, 162, 174
Australian forces, 22nd Brigade, 6–7, 10–11, **13**, 40, 42, 45, 175–176, 184, 188–191
Australian forces, 23rd Brigade, 11–12, 37
Australian forces, 27th Brigade, 37, 40, 174–175, 175 map, 181, 184
Australian forces, 65th Battery, 65
Australian forces, Anderson Force, 116, 138, 139–140, 154, 233, 235, 242–243, 245–247

INDEX

Australian forces, X Battalion, 184–188, 201, 218, 223

Australian War Graves, 164, 229, 325

Australian War Memorial, 203, 222, 229, 252, 351

Bakri, 48 map, 60, 71 map, 72, 77, 87–89, 89 map, 91, 95, 95, 136 map, 145, 153–154

Bangkok, 234 map, 257, 291, 296, 301–302, 315, 333–336

Bashford, Padre Fred, 243–244

Batu Pahat, 39 map, 40, 78, 89 map, 136 map

Bell, Private Joseph (Ernest James), 237, 240, 331

Benedict, Sergeant John, 78, 145

Bennett, General Henry, **13**
  communications, 96, 108–110
  defence of Muar, 65, 69
  defence of Singapore, 175, 190–193
  leadership, 17, 19, 40
  on Percival, 36
  post World War II, 345–347, 347
  sails to Sumatra, 212
  on the surrender, 195–196
  withdrawal from Malaya, 120–121

Boonpong Sirivejjabhandu, 356, **357**, 358

Boxtel, Captain Van C J, 278, 280–281

Braddon, Gunner Russell, 96–97, 101, 110–111, 113–115, 134–135, 347

Brand, Captain Victor, 82–85, 89, 90, 92, 107, 114–119, 129 130, **156**, 347, 348

British forces
  18th Division, 173, 190
  Argyll regiment, 29, 43, 47, 55, 170
  friendly fire, 92
  Gurkha regiment, 47, 55, 132, 334–335
  Norfolk Regiment, 91–92
  RAF, 99, 113–114
  surrender, **195**
  Volunteer Air Force, 36
  withdrawal to Singapore, 170
  see also Allied forces

British High Command, 31, 173

British intelligence, 65, 69, 133, 302, 356, 358

Bukit Batok Memorial, **205**

Bukit Panjang, 175 map

Bullwinkel, Vivian, 229, 350

Burma, 233, 234 map, 244

Burma-Thailand Railway, 220, 234 map, 253–257, 256 map, **268**, **275**, 277, 284–287, **285**, 290, 299–300, **311**, 313–314, 316, 319, 320–322, **323**, **324**, 330, 350

Burns, Private Tom, 191, 212

Cahill, Captain Lloyd, 92, **93**, 97, 107, 114, 119, 126, **156**, 191, 225, 327–328, 331, 347

Callaghan, Major General Cecil 'Boots', 231, 345

Campbell, Private Alex 'Bluey', 249

Changi, 171 map, 210, 213, 214, 216, **217**, 218, 224, 225, **226**, 227–229, **228**, **230**, 231, **336**, **337**, 338, 347, 348, 350

Chinese forces, 47, 182
  see also Allied forces

Churchill, Sir Winston, 5, 36–37, 51, 188

Clarke, Hugh, xv, 286–287

Coates, Albert, 'Bernie' Lieutenant Colonel, 22, 233, **235**, 240, 254, 277–278, 279–281, **281**, 300, 349–350

Commonwealth War Graves Cemetery, 315–316

communications, 7, **51**, **52**, **53**, 57, 58, 67, 74, 81, 82, 85, 91, 96, 105, 108, 129, 177, 181

Cornford, Roydon 'Roy', 299–300, 349

Cousens, Charles 'Bill', Major, 8, **63**, 236, **239**

Cox, Corporal Stan, 186, **187**

Croft, Sergeant Ron, 145, 148, 150–151, 158

Cumming, Tom, 242–243

Curnow, Mick, 117, 122, 128

Danaher, Clifford, 242–243

Darlington, Jimmy, **12**

Davey, Private Frank, 237, 240

Dean, Roly, Signaller, 10, 99–100, 125–126, 347

Dobbie, William, Major General, 35–36, 42

Donnelly (Colonel Anderson's bodyguard), 96

Dunlop, Sir Edward 'Weary', 229, 321, 324, 350, 356

Duprez, Sergeant Major Hamilton, 304, 307

Durkin, John, 306–308

Edwards, Private Charles, **129**

Egan, Jim, 352–355

Elliott, Dianne, ix, **xiv**, xvii–xviii, **324**, 332, **350**, 358

Emerton, Flight Lieutenant, 45–46

Emmett, Aubrey, 242–243

Endau, 39 map, 40, 42, 43, 48 map, 56

Essex family, 354–355, 358

Fagan, Tom, 277, 287

Fisher, Major Walter, 302, 315

Fisher, Max, Gunner, 66, 67–68, 81

Flint, Alfie, **187**, 188

food and water supplies, 12, 16, 18, 20, 38, 67, 70, 77, 88, 96, 101, 108, 114–115, 128, 130, 133, 136, 142–143, 151, **198**, 206, 213–216, 219, 220, 221, 223, 233, 237–238, 240–243, 252, 257, 269–270, 273–275, 279, 289, 302, 306–310, 313, 337, 356

Forsman, Melfred Laverne 'Gus', 301–302

Fort Canning, 25, 205–206, **206**, 207–208, **207**

Gemas, 14, 39 map, 48 map, 58, **58**, 68, 69

385

Gibson, Sergeant Walter, 198
Gill, George, 105, 200
Glover, Alan, 242–243
Goulden, Private Bob, 244–245, 331
Green, Major Chris, 231, 244–245
Griffin, Murray, artworks, 59, 94, **103**, 104, 125, **183**, 209, **215**, **261**, **267**, **271**, **278**, **325**, **333**, 336
Grosvenor, Harry, 121, 162, 200
Guerin, Chris, 114, 121–122, 232, 236, 263, 272, 278, 280, 300, 302–303

Hackney, Lieutenant Ben, 81, 98, 108, 113, 119–120, **139**, 140–152, 158, 164–166, **168**, 348–349
Hall, Les, 352, 356–358
Hammond, Wally, 114, 121
Harding, Private George, 112, 154, 187
Hardy, (drummer), 170, 198
Hennessey, Captain, 243–244
Hoshi Aiki, Lieutenant, 270, 273, 277, 288, 350
Hosier, Private Les, 308–309
Howe, Dianne, ix, **xiv**, xvi, xvii–xviii, **324**, 332, **350**, 351
Howe, Elsie, x, xi, xiv, 2–4, **3**, 7–8, 13, **17**, 224, **256**, 257, 284, **284**, 340, **342**
Howe, Sergeant Frederick 'Fred', **xiii**
 and Anderson, xiii, 37, 112
 ANZAC Days, xii–xiii
 articles, letters and memoirs, ix, xiv–xv, 126–128, 282–283, 341–344, 351, 353–354
 Christmas Day, 258
 and Coates, 233
 defence of Singapore, 175–176, 180
 and Elsie, 2–4, **3**, 17, **342**
 employment, xii, xvii, 1–2, 4
 enlistment, 5
 Ex-POW Association, 341–344
 funeral and grave, ix, xiii
 health, xi, 21–22, 28, 280, 294, 300, 309, 341
 Imperial Service Medal, xii
 Japan surrenders, 310–311
 labour force, 219, 235, 236, 240, 259, 296
 military training, 6–7, 11, 20, 29
 moves between camps, 232, 241, 252–253, 289–290, 300, 302–303
 Parit Sulong, 162, 163
 Port Dickson, **21**
 post Japan's surrender, 333–334
 prisoner of war, xix
 promotion, 8, 40, 170
 punishments and torture, xix
 reaction to Singapore ceasefire, 211
 relationship with daughter Dianne, **xiv**, xvii–xviii, 331
 returns home, 335–340
 Seremban, Malaysia, 14–20
 Songkurai, 330–331
 sport, 2, **3**, 4
 in uniform, **viii**
 withdrawal from Malaya, 85, 93–94, 122 map
Howe family, xv–xvi, xvii–xviii, 1, **3**, 4, 340
Hughes, Colonel Kent, 188–189
Hunter, Howard, 356–358

Indian forces
 8th Brigade, 46
 11th Division, 55
 12th Brigade, 29
 45th Brigade, 65, 66, 78, 119, 169
 45th Division, 57
 and Australian 2/29th, 82–83
 discipline, 52, 78, 82, 84, 85–86, 89, 98, 220
 friendly fire, 68
 Headquarters, 70
 Indian Army Medical Corps, 333–334
 Indian National Army, 209
 Kota Bharu, 47, 48
Ison, Johnny, 113–114
Itsui Hiroshi, Captain, 238, 240, 243

Japan, x, 16, 42, 162, 177, 308, 336, **338**
Japanese forces
 advance on Malaya, 43–44, 45–47, 49–50, 52, 56
 advance to Singapore, 177, 179–180, 184, 192, 194
 control of Parit Sulong and Yong Peng area, 92
 divisions and regiments, 47–48, 65–68
 engineers, **265**
 fifth column, 31, 48, 177
 Gotanda Tank Company, 74
 Imperial Guard Division, 60, 65–68, 76, 106, 143, 153, 185, 216
 invade Malaya, **54**
 kempeitai (Military Police), 26, 216
 landings, 48 map
 military tactics, 22, 53, 83
 Miyazaki Butai Regiment, 26
 Nishimura's Imperial Guards Division, 216
 positions, 83 map
 propaganda, 281–283, **282**
 Singapore landings, 175 map
 tanks, 47, 52, 58, 66, 72–74, 104–105, 110–111, 116, 170
 war-time atrocities, xix, 62, 133–135, 145–148, 164, 191, 201, 212–213, 220, 238, 244–245, 269–270, 273–274, 297–298, 309–310
Japanese POW guards, 343, 350
Jemaluang-Mersing area, 40, 60–63
Johnson, Lloyd, 137–138
Johor, 36, 39 map, 40, 171 map, 175 map
Johor Bahru, 40, 48 map, 62, 171 map, **171**, 175 map, **178**, 197
Jones, Arthur, 242–243
Julius, Major William, 81, 94

Kitabata Shinichi, Lance Corporal 'The Screamer', 306–309, 350
Kluang, 39 map, 40, **41**, 48 map
Korean guards, 259–262, 269–272, 306–309, 350

INDEX

Kota Bharu, 46, 47, 48, 48 map, 49

Kuala Lumpur, 39 map, 40, 48 map, 55

Kuantan, 39 map, 43, 48 map, 49, 56

Lee, Corporal Max, 229

Levick, Private Stuart 'Ted', 102, 186–187

Lou, (WWI veteran), 99–100

Lovett, Captain Charles, 74, 246, 249, 251

Lynch, Val, 114, 116–118, 129–130

Macdonald, Captain Hamish, 80, 96

MacQueen, Private Wally, 249

Malacca (Meleka), **22**, 28, **28**, 39 map, 66

Malaya, 36–37, 39 map, 43, **54**, 60, 170

Malaya Command, 25, 29, 43, 45, 46, 47, 48, 50, 53, 190, 192, 194

Mant, Gilbert, 16

Maxwell, Brigadier Duncan, 6–7, **8**, 37–38, 185

McColl, Corporal Vincent, 248

McCure, Bill, 70, 73

McDonald, Lieutenant Ian, 262

media reports, 32, 33–35, 44, 46, 138, 173, 192, 282–283, 301

Mergui, 233, 234 map

Mersing, 39 map, 40, 42, 48 map, 56, **62**, **63**

Mettam, Bert, 130–132

Moore, Hugh, 110–111, 114–115, 134–135

Morgan, Hilton 'Tod', xvi, 11, 62, 201–202

Morris, John Gilbert 'Tom', xv, 322–324

Moss, Private Keith, 308–309

Mountbatten, Lady Edwina, 333, **334**, 336

Mountbatten, Lord Louis, **338**

Muar, 39 map, 48 map, 57, 60, 65, 66–67, **66**, 78, 89 map, 136 map, 138

Muir, Private Wilfred 'Wiff', 247, 251

Nagatomo Yoshitada, Colonel, 277, 287–288, 350

Naito, Lieutenant, 270, 305

Newton, Captain Reg, 42, 76, 79, 102, 135–137, 321

Nishimura Takuma, General, 66–67, **67**, 143, 157, 185, 348

Nong Pladuc, 255, 291, 293, 302

O'Donnell, Sergeant Ronald, 259–260

Olliff, Major, 85–86

O'Malley, Jack, 232, 326

Operation Matador, 46

Panee, 356, **357**, 358

Parit Sulong, 48 map, 89 map, **104**, 120 map, 136 map
  Australian forces, 116, 125
  bridge, 102, **104**, **118**, 119, **141**
  commemoration, 164–166, **165**
  defence of bridge, 92
  Hackney's hiding spot, **163**
  Japanese control, 60
  killing field, **146**
  PWD building, **141**, 143–145, **146**, 157, 162, 167, **168**
  search for remains, **159**
  Silver and Elliott visit, 156–166
  withdrawal to, 84, 89–90, 91

Parkin, Ray 'Two malarias and a cholera', 322

Perceval, Lance, 256–257

Percival, Lieutenant General Arthur, 35–36, 42, 52, 170, 173–174, 176, 179, 190, 191, 194–195, 198, 203, 205, 206, 345–346, **347**

Philips, Admiral Tom, 50–51

Port Dickson, **21**, 27, 39 map, 48 map, 56

Porter, Lance Bombardier Allan, 309, 313

prison camps
  air raids, 275, 293–294, 303
  allied air drops, 293
  Changi, 210, 218, 224, 230–231, 336, **337**, 347–348
  conditions, 218, 220, 221, **253**, **273**, **320**
  Hintok Road, 320–322, 325, 356
  hospitals and supplies, 210, **264**, **278**, 291, **333**, 356
  Kanchanaburi, 294, **317**, 355, 356
  Kilo 55, 256 map, 277, 279
  Kilo 75, 266, 270, 272
  Kilo 105, 256 map, 273, 276
  Kilo 244, 330
  Kui Kae, 297–298
  Kunhnitkway, 254, 256 map
  Neike, 310, 326
  Nong Pladuc, 293, 302
  propaganda, 282–283, 301
  Roberts Barracks, 220, **228**, 229
  Selarang Barracks, **226**
  Songkurai, 303–304, 305, 328, **329**
  Tamarkan, 291, 293–294, 301–302, 312, 356
  Thanbyuzayat, 246, 253–254, 256 map, 275, 316

prisoners of war, **333**
  American, 297–298
  ANZAC Days, 270
  debilitated and ill, xvi–xvii, 220, 232, 260–261, **264**, 272–280, 313, 322
  entertainment, 222, 246–252, **250**, **251**
  escapes, 212, 219, 230, 237, 242–246, 253, 259–263, 290, 307–308, 331, 345–349
  food and water supplies, 142–143, 213–216, 219, 221, 223, 233, 237–238, 240–242, 252, 257, 269–270, 273–275, 279, 289, 302, 306–310, 356
  A Force, 231–232, 245
  Imperial Japanese Army, 237
  inoculations, 272

387

labour force, 218–219, 221–222, 236–237, 240, 259, 260, 266, 267, 268, 272, 274–275, 279, 281, 305, 313–314, 320–321, 325, 329
moves between camps, 271, 272, 288, 289
punishments and torture, 261, 261, 269–270, 273–274, 276, 297–298
Ray Parkin' 'Two malarias and a cholera', 322
return home, 347
strike, 262, 269
supported by locals, 151, 214, 219–220, 238, 242–243, 337, 356
Pudu Gaol, 133, 135, 137–138, 152
Pulford, Air Vice-Marshall, 44, 190, 345

Quittendon, Warrant Officer Matthew, 242–243

Ramsay, Lieutenant Colonel George, 231–232, 237–238, 246, 247, 262–263, 277, 288
Reeve, Arthur, 242–243
Returned Services League (RSL), xii–xiii, 341, 349
River Kwai bridge, 317
Robertson, Colonel, 70, 74–76, 180, 182, 183
Rogers, Major, 301–302

Sanderson, Lieutenant, 108–109
Schuberth, Private Bill, 240–241
Sedili Besar River, 40, 41, 64
Segamat, 39 map, 40, 48 map, 69
Selarang Barracks, 214–216, 215, 221, 226
Seremban, 15, 17, 18, 20, 26, 26, 39 map
Shearer, Lieutenant James, 66, 67–68
Silver, Lynette, xvi, 160, 332
Silver, Lynette, *The Bridge at Parit Sulong*, 157–158
Silver, Neil, 160, 161

Simpang Kiri River, 69, 120 map, 125
Simson, Brigadier Ivan, 37, 42–43, 176
Singapore, 24, 39 map, 48 map, 171 map, 171, 178, 189
AIF, 14, 18–19
air-raids, 173
Allied troops, 170
assessment of vulnerability, 5, 36, 44
The Cathay Building, 191, 208–212, 208, 236
Changi Museum, 322
Commonwealth War Graves Cemetery, 199
defence of, 36–37, 42, 194
Di Elliott visit, 315–316
European residents, 49
fall of, 195–196, 204, 211–212
Japanese advancements, 177–179, 184, 192
Silver and Elliot visit, 199–200
Tanglin Barracks, 183, 212
Slim, Field Marshal, 303, 333
Slim River, 48 map, 55
Smith, Padre Henry, 243–244
Snelling, Captain Rewi 'Ray', 35, 51, 54–57, 84, 100, 119, 120, 140, 143–144, 146
Stewart, Brigadier Ian, 29, 170
Stewart, Jim 'Son', 21, 26
Sun-La, 352–353
Surat, 356–357

Tamarkan, 220, 257, 291, 292, 293–294, 295, 301–302, 312, 356
Tampoi, 169, 183
Tanglin Barracks, 183, 192, 193, 212, 223, 224
tanks
  Allied forces, 43, 47, 72
  Imperial Japanese Army, 55, 58, 66, 72–74, 104–105, 110–113, 116, 170
Taylor, Brigadier Harold, 13, 180
Tengah, 171 map, 175 map, 183
Thailand, 22, 46, 47, 234 map, 315

Thomas, Sir Shenton, 14, 49, 173–174, 180, 192
Three Pagodas, 303, 304, 328, 329, 330
Tibbits, Hugh, 98, 139–143
Tokoro Kinichi, Lieutenant, 237–238, 240–241
Tokugawa Yoshichika, 197
Toosey, Colonel, 290–291, 356

United States Forces, 47, 302, 356

Varley, Brigadier Arthur, 19, 231, 237, 243–244, 277, 349
Veterans' Affairs, Department of, 323
Vincent, Major Tom, 183, 199

War Crimes Tribunal, 350
Wardale-Greenwood, Harold, Padre, 82, 110, 120, 182–183, 183, 348
Warden, Charles 'Chick', 95–96, 103–106, 122 map, 126, 347
Warren, Bombardier Stanley, 227–228
Wavell, General Archibald, 43–44, 173, 188, 190–191, 194–195, 346
Wharton, Private Reg, 145, 147–148, 158, 348
Wilson, James, 242–243
Wood, Private Leonard, 112, 157
Wright, Colonel J M, 7, 336

Yamashita Tomoyuki, General, 47, 197, 206, 211, 218
Yong Peng, 48 map, 65, 83 map, 89 map, 108, 116, 123, 125, 126, 128–130, 135